enVisionmath®2.0

SCOTT FORESMAN • ADDISON WESLEY

Volume 1 Topics 1-7

Authors

Randall I. Charles
Professor Emeritus
Department of Mathematics
San Jose State University
San Jose, California

Jennifer Bay-Williams
Professor of Mathematics Education
College of Education and Human Development
University of Louisville
Louisville, Kentucky

Robert Q. Berry, III
Associate Professor of Mathematics Education
Department of Curriculum, Instruction and Special Education
University of Virginia
Charlottesville, Virginia

Janet H. Caldwell
Professor of Mathematics
Rowan University
Glassboro, New Jersey

Zachary Champagne
Assistant in Research
Florida Center for Research in Science, Technology, Engineering, and Mathematics (FCR-STEM)
Jacksonville, Florida

Juanita Copley
Professor Emerita, College of Education
University of Houston
Houston, Texas

Warren Crown
Professor Emeritus of Mathematics Education
Graduate School of Education
Rutgers University
New Brunswick, New Jersey

Francis (Skip) Fennell
L. Stanley Bowlsbey Professor of Education and Graduate and Professional Studies
McDaniel College
Westminster, Maryland

Karen Karp
Professor of Mathematics Education
Department of Early Childhood and Elementary Education
University of Louisville
Louisville, Kentucky

Stuart J. Murphy
Visual Learning Specialist
Boston, Massachusetts

Jane F. Schielack
Professor of Mathematics
Associate Dean for Assessment and Pre K-12 Education, College of Science
Texas A&M University
College Station, Texas

Jennifer M. Suh
Associate Professor for Mathematics Education
George Mason University
Fairfax, Virginia

Jonathan A. Wray
Mathematics Instructional Facilitator
Howard County Public Schools
Ellicott City, Maryland

PEARSON

Glenview, Illinois Boston, Massachusetts Chandler, Arizona Hoboken, New Jersey

Mathematicians

Roger Howe
Professor of Mathematics
Yale University
New Haven, Connecticut

Gary Lippman
Professor of Mathematics
and Computer Science
California State University,
East Bay
Hayward, California

ELL Consultants

Janice R. Corona
Independent Education
Consultant
Dallas, Texas

Jim Cummins
Professor
The University of Toronto
Toronto, Canada

Reviewers

Debbie Crisco
Math Coach
Beebe Public Schools
Beebe, Arkansas

Kathleen A. Cuff
Teacher
Kings Park Central School District
Kings Park, New York

Erika Doyle
Math and Science Coordinator
Richland School District
Richland, Washington

Susan Jarvis
Math and Science Curriculum
Coordinator
Ocean Springs Schools
Ocean Springs, Mississippi

ISBN-13: 978-0-328-88712-5
ISBN-10: 0-328-88712-9

PEARSON

8 18

Digital Resources

Go to PearsonRealize.com

MP

Math Practices Animations to play anytime

Solve

Solve & Share problems plus math tools

Learn

Visual Learning Animation Plus with animation, interaction, and math tools

Glossary

Animated Glossary in English and Spanish

Practice Buddy

Online Personalized Practice for each lesson

Tools

Math Tools to help you understand

Assessment

Quick Check for each lesson

Help

Another Look Homework Video for extra help

Games

Math Games to help you learn

eText

Student Edition online

ACTIVe-book

Student Edition online for showing your work

PEARSON realize™ Everything you need for math anytime, anywhere

Hi, we're here to help you. Let's have a great year!

Contents

KEY

- Operations and Algebra
- Numbers and Computation
- Measurement and Data
- Geometry

Digital Resources at PearsonRealize.com

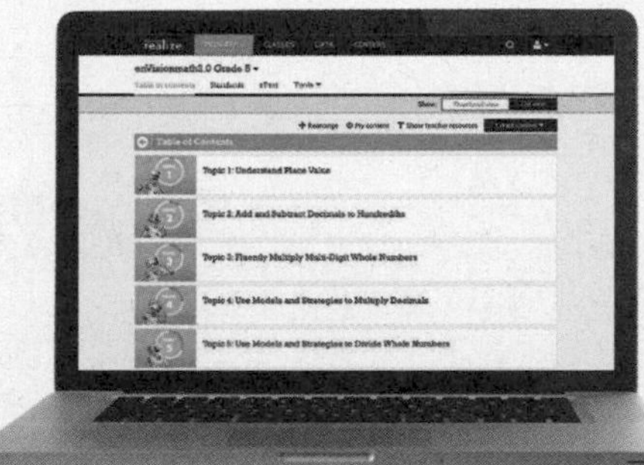

And remember your eText is available at PearsonRealize.com!

TOPICS

PearsonRealize.com

TOPIC 1 Understand Place Value

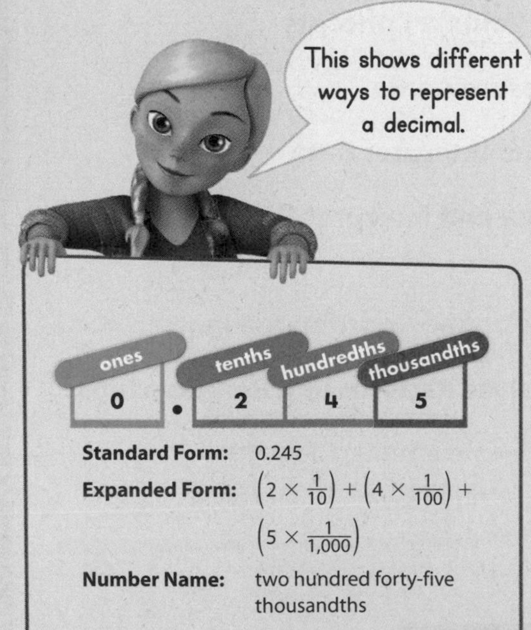

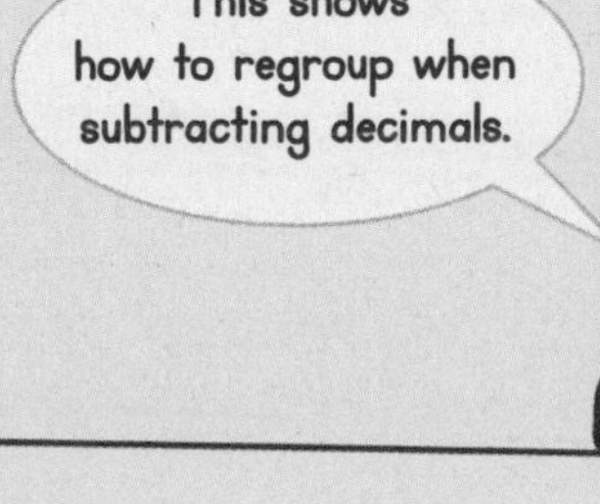

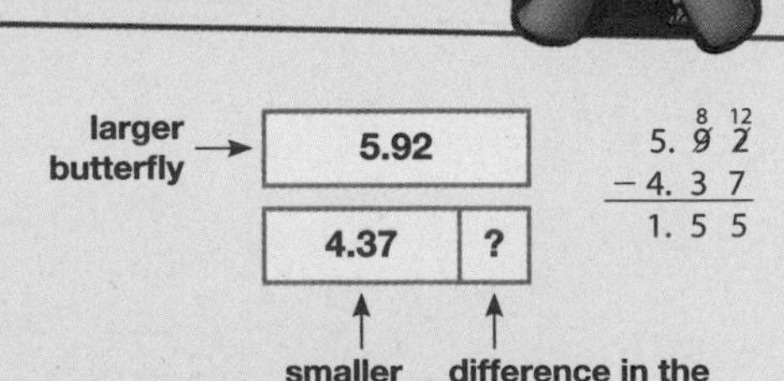

TOPIC 2 Add and Subtract Decimals to Hundredths

TOPIC 3 Fluently Multiply Multi-Digit Whole Numbers

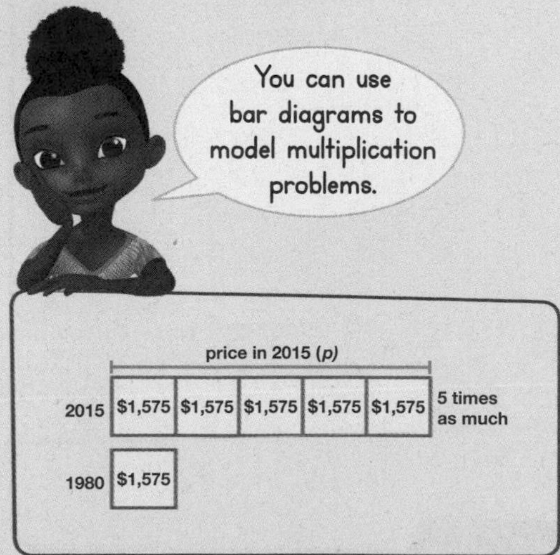

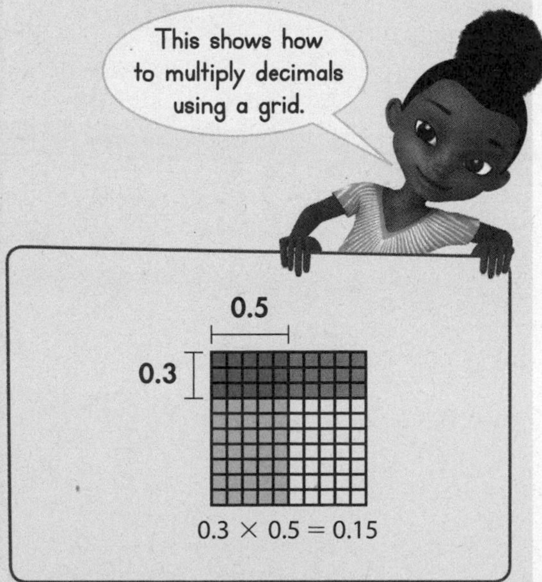

TOPIC 4 Use Models and Strategies to Multiply Decimals

TOPIC 5 Use Models and Strategies to Divide Whole Numbers

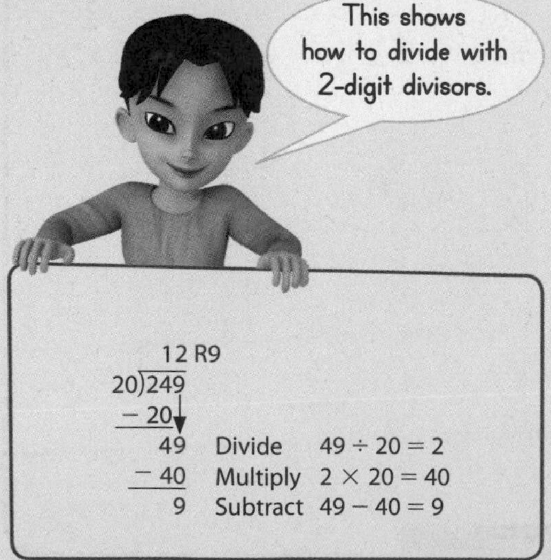

TOPIC 4 Use Models and Strategies to Multiply Decimals

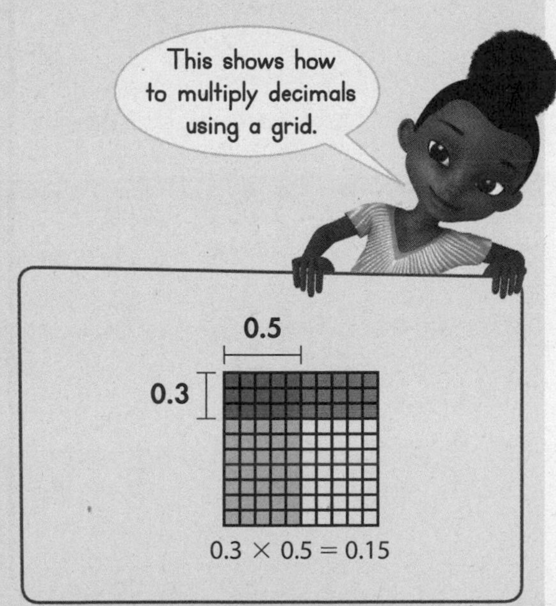

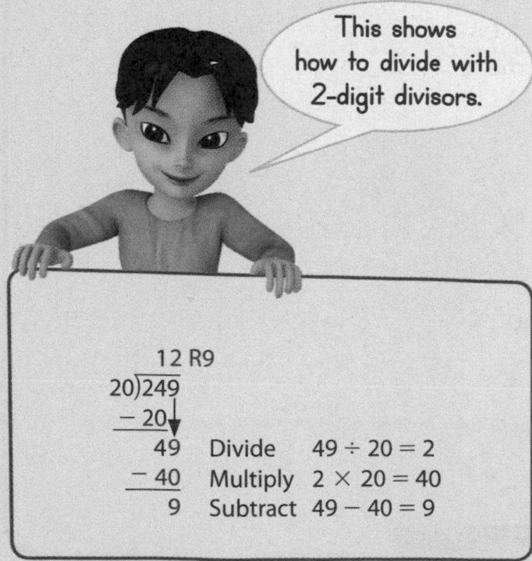

TOPIC 5 Use Models and Strategies to Divide Whole Numbers

TOPIC 6 Use Models and Strategies to Divide Decimals

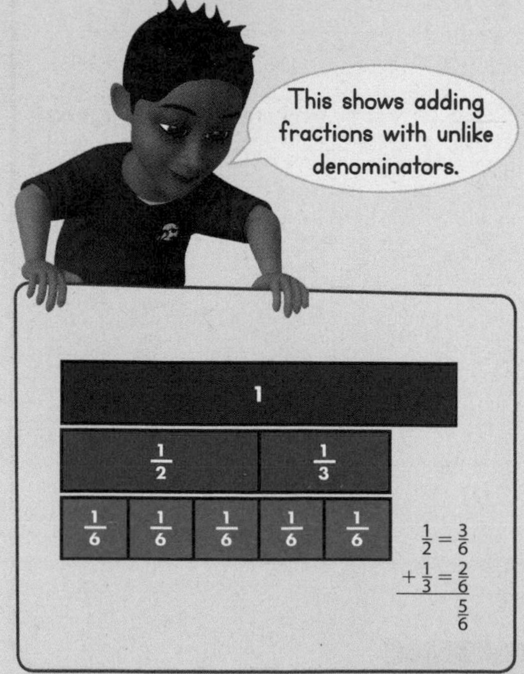

TOPIC 7 Use Equivalent Fractions to Add and Subtract Fractions

TOPIC 8 in volume 2
Apply Understanding of Multiplication to Multiply Fractions

TOPIC 9 in volume 2
Apply Understanding of Division to Divide Fractions

TOPIC 10 in volume 2
Understand Volume Concepts

TOPIC 11 in volume 2
Convert Measurements

TOPIC 12 in volume 2
Represent and Interpret Data

TOPIC 13 in volume 2
Algebra: Write and Interpret Numerical Expressions

TOPIC 16 in volume 2

Geometric Measurement: Classify Two-Dimensional Figures

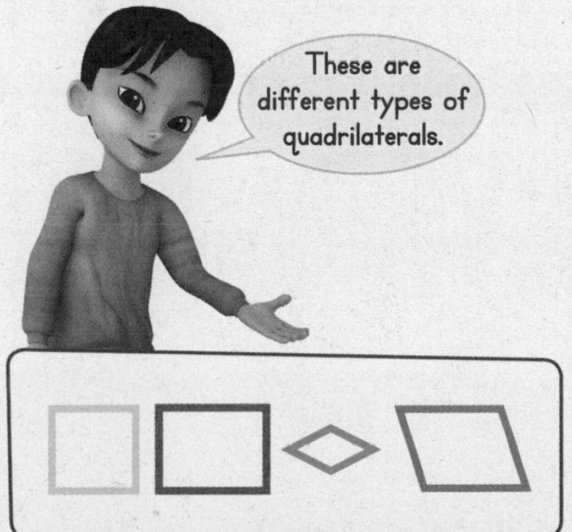

STEP UP to Grade 6 in volume 2

Problem Solving Handbook

Math practices are ways we think about and do math.

Math practices will help you solve problems.

Problem Solving Handbook

Math Practices

1 **Make sense of problems and persevere in solving them.**

2 **Reason abstractly and quantitatively.**

3 **Construct viable arguments and critique the reasoning of others.**

4 **Model with mathematics.**

5 **Use appropriate tools strategically.**

6 **Attend to precision.**

7 **Look for and make use of structure.**

8 **Look for and express regularity in repeated reasoning.**

There are good Thinking Habits for each of these math practices.

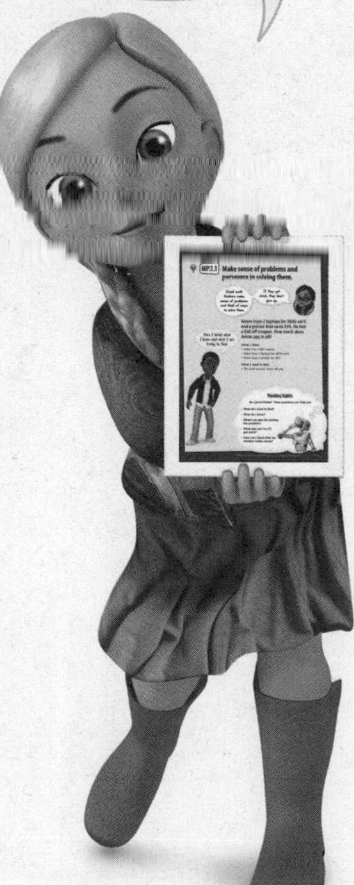

Make sense of problems and persevere in solving them.

Good math thinkers make sense of problems and think of ways to solve them.

If they get stuck, they don't give up.

Anton buys 2 laptops for $600 each and a printer that costs $99. He has a $50 off coupon. How much does Anton pay in all?

Here I listed what I know and what I am trying to find.

What I Know:

- Anton has a $50 coupon.
- Anton buys 2 laptops for $600 each.
- Anton buys a printer for $99.

What I need to find:

- The total amount Anton will pay.

Thinking Habits

Be a good thinker! These questions can help you.

- What do I need to find?
- What do I know?
- What's my plan for solving the problem?
- What else can I try if I get stuck?
- How can I check that my solution makes sense?

Reason abstractly and quantitatively.

Good math thinkers know how to think about words and numbers to solve problems.

I drew a bar diagram that shows how the numbers in the problem are related.

Derrick buys 6 games that cost a total of $150. How much does each game cost?

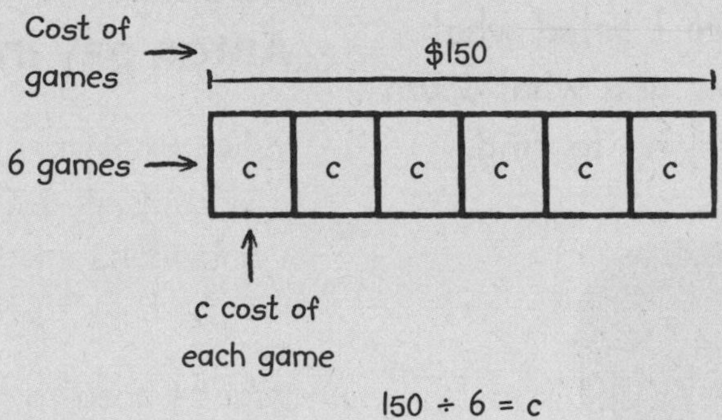

$150 \div 6 = c$

Thinking Habits

Be a good thinker! These questions can help you.

- What do the numbers and symbols in the problem mean?
- How are the numbers or quantities related?
- How can I represent a word problem using pictures, numbers, or equations?

Construct viable arguments and critique the reasoning of others.

Good math thinkers use math to explain why they are right. They can talk about the math that others do, too.

Molly says that every fraction whose denominator is twice as great as its numerator is equivalent to $\frac{1}{2}$. Do you agree? Explain.

I wrote a clear argument with words, numbers, and symbols.

Yes, Molly is correct. Every fraction that has a denominator that is twice as great as its numerator can be written as an equivalent fraction by dividing both the numerator and denominator by the same non-zero number.

$\frac{5}{10} = \frac{5 \div 5}{10 \div 5} = \frac{1}{2}$

Thinking Habits

Be a good thinker! These questions can help you.

- How can I use numbers, objects, drawings, or actions to justify my argument?
- Am I using numbers and symbols correctly?
- Is my explanation clear and complete?
- What questions can I ask to understand other people's thinking?
- Are there mistakes in other people's thinking?
- Can I improve other people's thinking?
- Can I use a counterexample in my argument?

Model with mathematic

Good math thinkers choose and apply math they know to show and solve problems from everyday life.

I can use what I know about division to solve this problem. I can draw a picture to help.

Jasmine has a strip of wood that i 75 centimeters long. She is going saw it into 5 equal pieces. How long wi each piece of wood be if the strip is cut in 5 equal pieces?

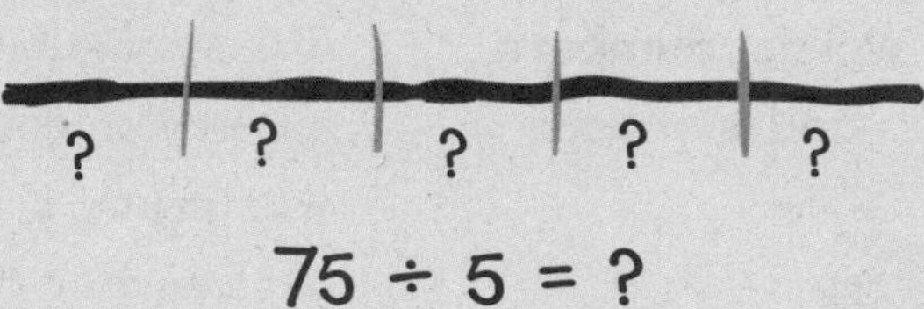

$75 \div 5 = ?$

Thinking Habits

Be a good thinker! These questions can help you.

- How can I use math I know to help solve this problem?
- How can I use pictures, objects, or an equation to represent the problem?
- How can I use numbers, words, and symbols to solve the problem?

Use appropriate tools strategically.

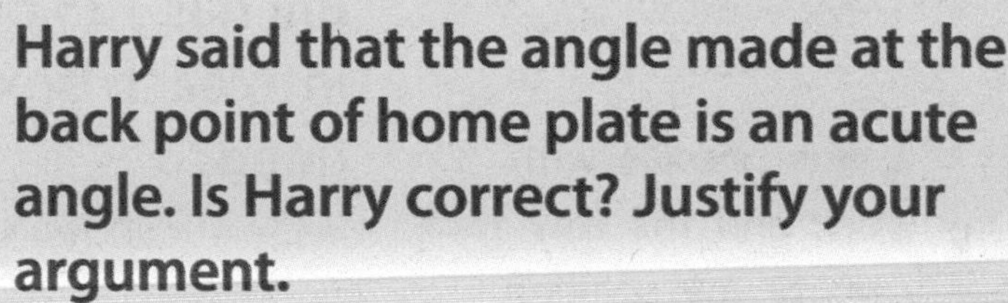

Harry said that the angle made at the back point of home plate is an acute angle. Is Harry correct? Justify your argument.

Harry is incorrect. The angle is a right angle because it has a measure of 90°.

Thinking Habits

Be a good thinker! These questions can help you.

- Which tools can I use?
- Why should I use this tool to help me solve the problem?
- Is there a different tool I could use?
- Am I using the tool appropriately?

6 Attend to precision.

Good math thinkers are careful about what they write and say, so their ideas about math are clear.

I was precise with my work and the way that I wrote my solution.

Bill has 125 oranges. He puts 6 oranges into each box. How many boxes does he need?

125 ÷ 6 = 20 R5

120 oranges will fit into 20 boxes.
So, Bill needs 21 boxes for 125 oranges.

Thinking Habits

Be a good thinker! These questions can help you.

- Am I using numbers, units, and symbols appropriately?
- Am I using the correct definitions?
- Am I calculating accurately?
- Is my answer clear?

Look for and make use of structure.

Good math thinkers look for patterns or relationships in math to help solve problems.

I broke numbers apart to multiply.

There are 5,280 feet in 1 mile. How many feet are in 3 miles?

5,280 feet = 1 mile

$$\begin{aligned} 3 \times 5{,}280 &= 3 \times (5{,}000 + 200 + 80) \\ &= (3 \times 5{,}000) + (3 \times 200) + (3 \times 80) \\ &= 15{,}000 + 600 + 240 \\ &= 15{,}840 \end{aligned}$$

There are 15,840 feet in 3 miles.

Thinking Habits

Be a good thinker! These questions can help you.

- What patterns can I see and describe?
- How can I use the patterns to solve the problem?
- Can I see expressions and objects in different ways?
- What equivalent expressions can I use?

Look for and express regularity in repeated reasoning.

Good math thinkers look for things that repeat, and they make generalizations.

I used reasoning to generalize about calculations.

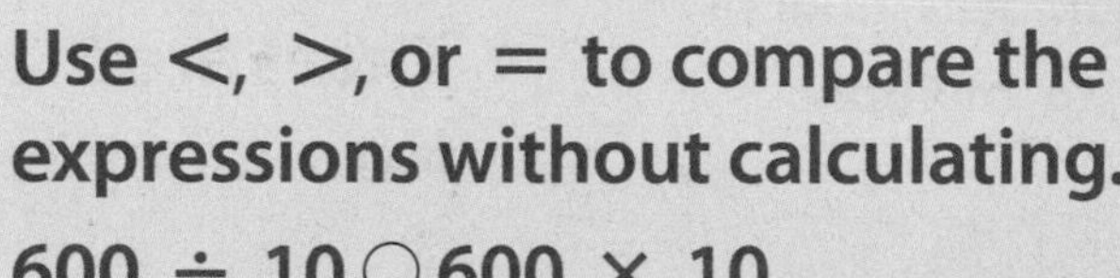

Use $<$, $>$, or $=$ to compare the expressions without calculating.

$600 \div 10 \bigcirc 600 \times 10$

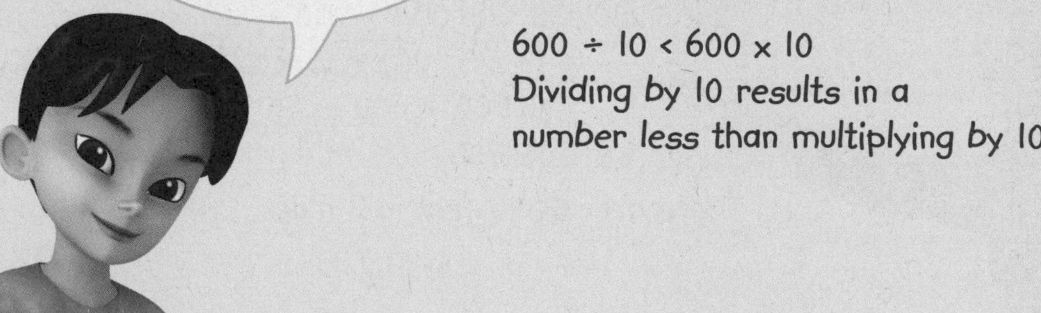

$600 \div 10 < 600 \times 10$

Dividing by 10 results in a number less than multiplying by 10.

Thinking Habits

Be a good thinker! These questions can help you.

- Are any calculations repeated?
- Can I generalize from examples?
- What shortcuts do I notice?

Problem Solving Handbook

Problem Solving Guide

These questions can help you solve problems.

Make Sense of the Problem

Reason Abstractly and Quantitatively

- What do I need to find?
- What given information can I use?
- How are the quantities related?

Think About Similar Problems

- Have I solved problems like this before?

Persevere in Solving the Problem

Model with Math

- How can I use the math I know?
- How can I represent the problem?
- Is there a pattern or structure I can use?

Use Appropriate Tools Strategically

- What math tools could I use?
- How can I use those tools strategically?

Check the Answer

Make Sense of the Answer

- Is my answer reasonable?

Check for Precision

- Did I check my work?
- Is my answer clear?
- Did I construct a viable argument?
- Did I generalize correctly?

Some Ways to Represent Problems

- Draw a Picture
- Make a Bar Diagram
- Make a Table or Graph
- Write an Equation

Some Math Tools

- Objects
- Grid Paper
- Rulers
- Technology
- Paper and Pencil

Problem Solving Handbook

Problem Solving Recording Sheet

This sheet helps you organize your work.

Name Carlos

Teaching Tool 1

Problem Solving Recording Sheet

Problem:
A store sold 20 sweatshirts. Of these, 8 were red. Twice as many were green as yellow. How many of each color sweatshirt did the store sell?

MAKE SENSE OF THE PROBLEM

Need to Find

How many sweatshirts were sold in each color?

Given

A total of 20 sweatshirts. 8 were red. Twice as many green sweatshirts as yellow.

PERSEVERE IN SOLVING THE PROBLEM

Some Ways to Represent Problems

- ☐ Draw a Picture
- ☐ Make a Bar Diagram
- ☑ Make a Table or Graph
- ☑ Write an Equation

Some Math Tools

- ☐ Objects
- ☐ Grid Paper
- ☐ Rulers
- ☐ Technology
- ☐ Paper and Pencil

Solution and Answer

20 - 8 = 12, so there are 12 green and yellow sweatshirts. If there are 2 green shirts, there will be 1 yellow shirt.

green	yellow	total
2	1	3
4	2	6
6	3	9
8	4	12

So, there are 8 green sweatshirts and 4 yellow sweatshirts.

CHECK THE ANSWER

I can add to check my work. 8 red, 8 green, and 4 yellow sweatshirts. 8 + 8 + 4 = 20. There are 20 sweatshirts in all.

T1

Problem Solving Handbook

Bar Diagrams

You can draw a **bar diagram** to show how the quantities in a problem are related. Then you can write an equation to solve the problem.

Add To

Draw this **bar diagram** for situations that involve *adding* to a quantity.

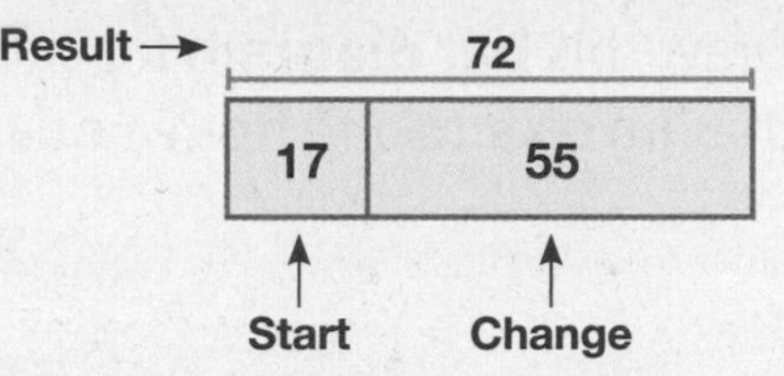

Result Unknown

Monica bought a new bicycle for \$279. She also bought a used bicycle for \$125. How much did she spend in all?

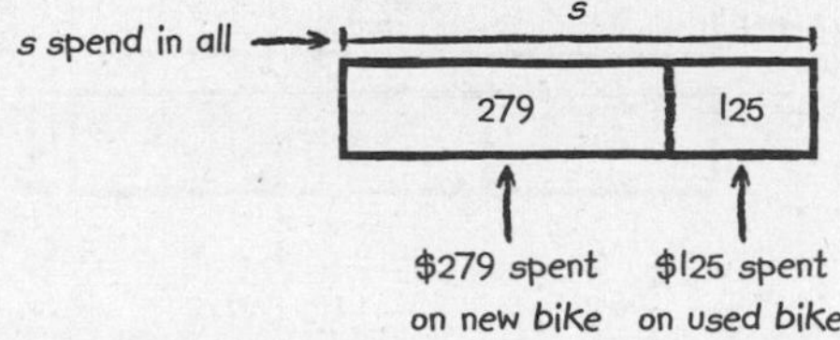

$279 + 125 = s$

Monica spent \$404 on the two bikes.

Start Unknown

Vanessa deposited \$750 in her bank account. After she made the deposit, she had \$2,200 in her account. How much did Vanessa start with in her account?

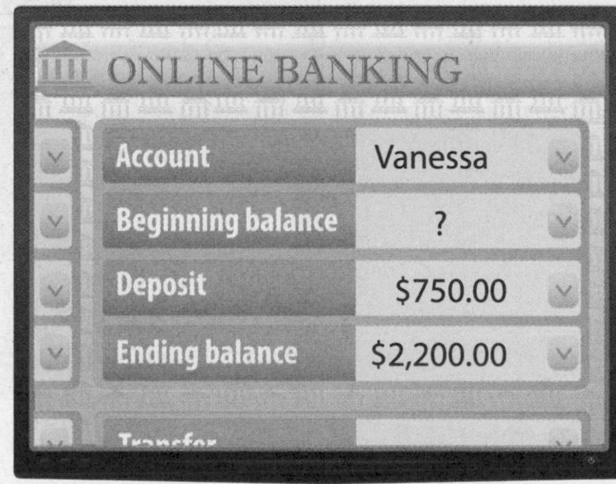

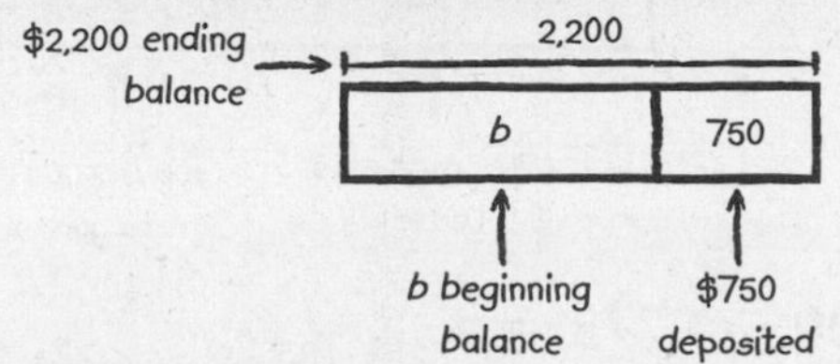

$b + 750 = 2{,}200$

Vanessa started with \$1,450.

Problem Solving Handbook

Bar Diagrams

You can use b diagrams to make se e of addition and subtrac on problems.

Take From

Draw this **bar diagram** for situations that involve *taking* from a quantity.

Start → 1,860

1,200	660

Change ↑ R ult ↑

Result Unknown

Nicolas has a goal of doing 2,600 push-ups this year. He has done 1,775 push-ups so far. How many more push-ups does he need to do to reach his goal?

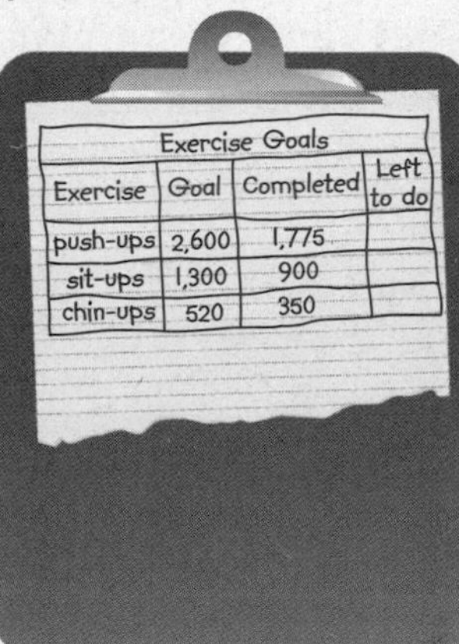

Exercise Goals

Exercise	Goal	Completed	Left to do
push-ups	2,600	1,775	
sit-ups	1,300	900	
chin-ups	520	350	

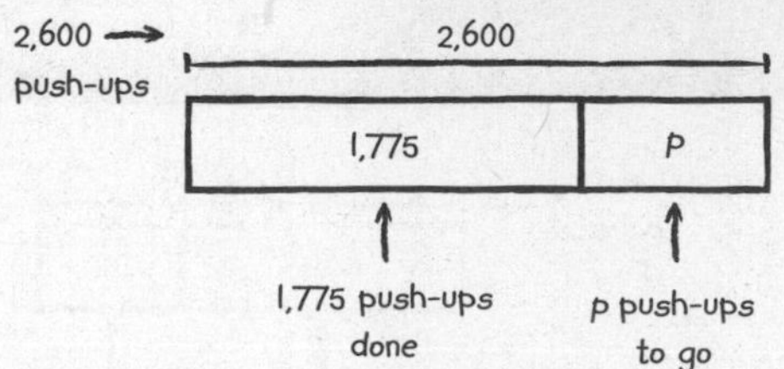

$2{,}600 - 1{,}775 = p$

Nicolas has 825 more push-ups to do to reach his goal.

Start Unknown

A store had a collection of DVDs. Th y sold 645 DVDs during a weekend sa How many DVDs did the store have before the sale?

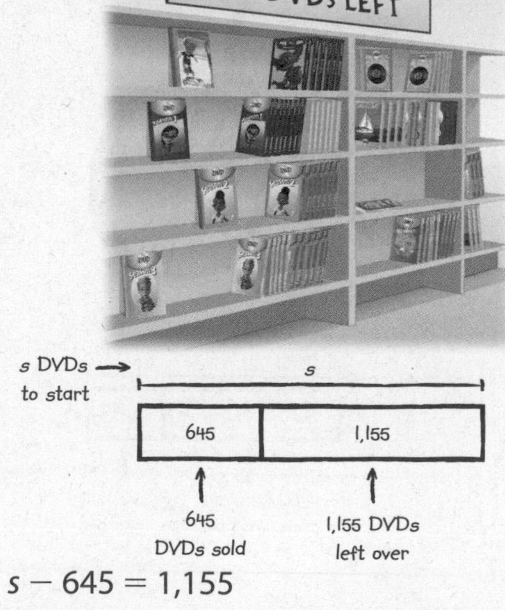

s DVDs to start → *s*

645	1,155

↑ 645 DVDs sold ↑ 1,155 DVDs left over

$s - 645 = 1{,}155$

The store had 1,800 DVDs before the sale.

The **bar diagrams** on this page can help you make sense of more addition and subtraction situations.

Put Together/Take Apart

Draw this **bar diagram** for situations that involve *putting together* or *taking apart* quantities.

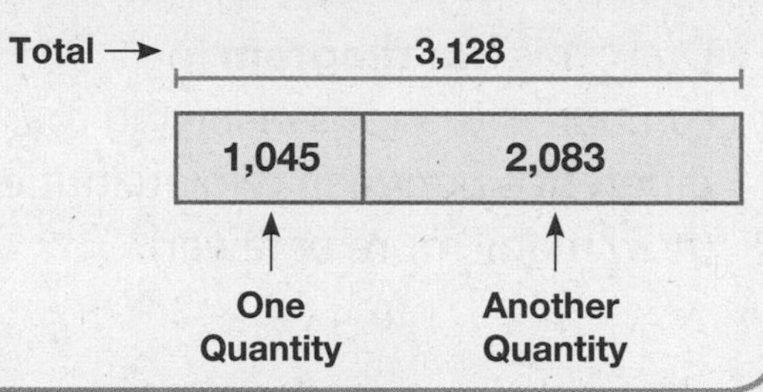

Whole Unknown

Rhode Island covers the least space of all states in the U.S. What is the total land and water area of Rhode Island?

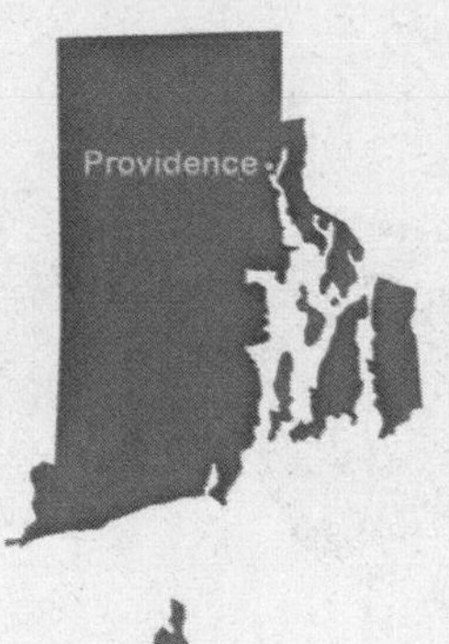

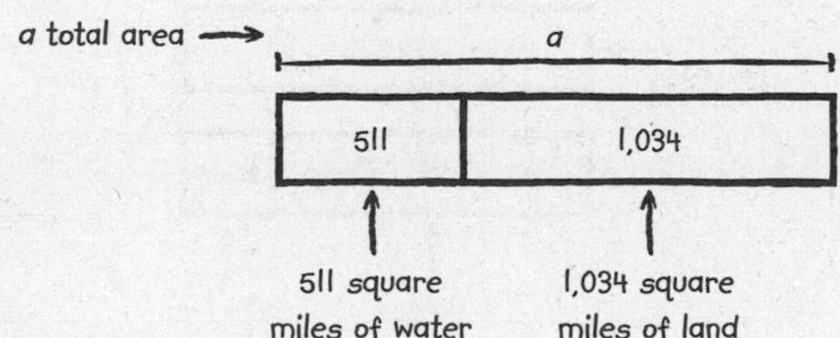

$511 + 1{,}034 = a$

The total land and water area of Rhode Island is 1,545 square miles.

Part Unknown

A farmer harvested 150 peppers on Saturday. He harvested more peppers on Sunday. He collected a total of 315 peppers over the two days. How many peppers did he harvest on Sunday?

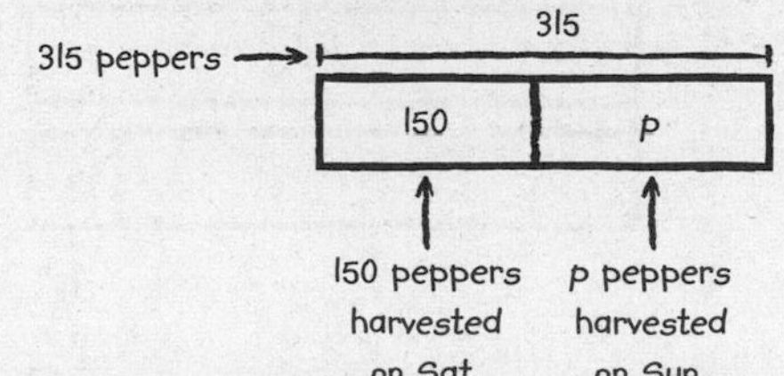

$150 + p = 315$ or $315 - 150 = p$

He harvested 165 peppers on Sunday.

Problem Solving Handbook

Bar Diagrams

Compare: Addition and Subtraction

Draw this **bar diagram** for *compare* situations involving the difference between two quantities (how many more or fewer).

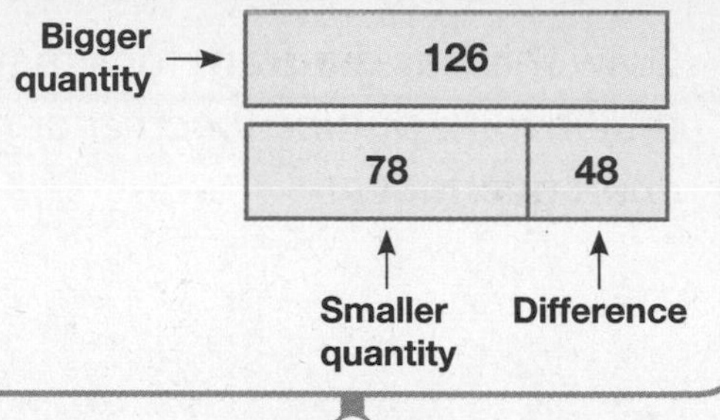

Difference Unknown

Last year, 1,796 people attended the county fair. This year 1,544 people attended. How many more people attended last year than this year?

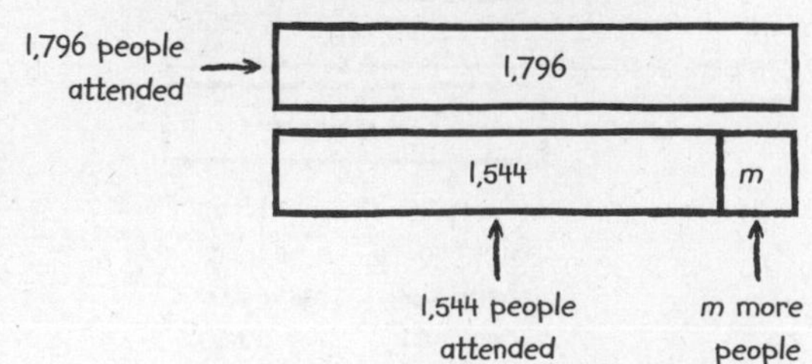

$1{,}796 - 1{,}544 = m$

Last year, 252 more people attended.

Smaller Unknown

Ann's school raised $2,375 for charity. Brian's school raised $275 less than Ann's school. How much did Brian's school raise?

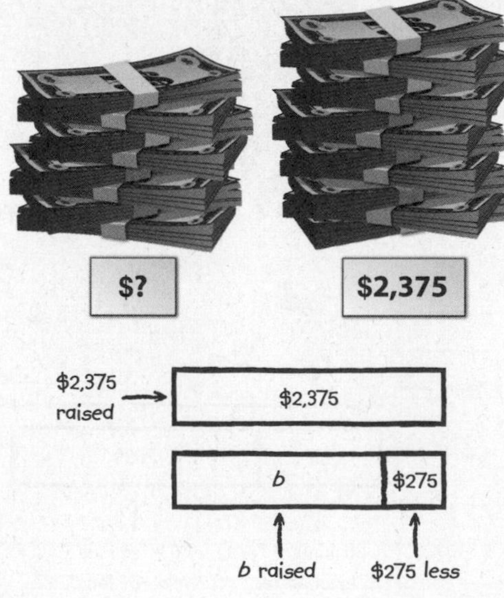

$2{,}375 - b = 275$ or $b + 275 = 2{,}375$

Brian's school raised $2,100.

The **bar diagrams** on this page can help you make sense of more addition and subtraction situations.

Put Together/Take Apart

Draw this **bar diagram** for situations that involve *putting together* or *taking apart* quantities.

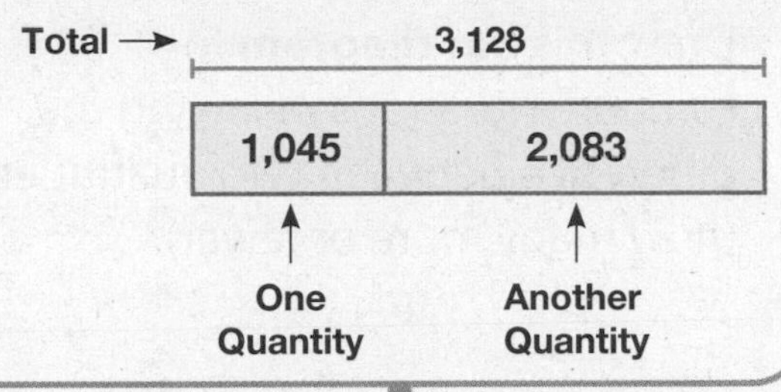

Whole Unknown

Rhode Island covers the least space of all states in the U.S. What is the total land and water area of Rhode Island?

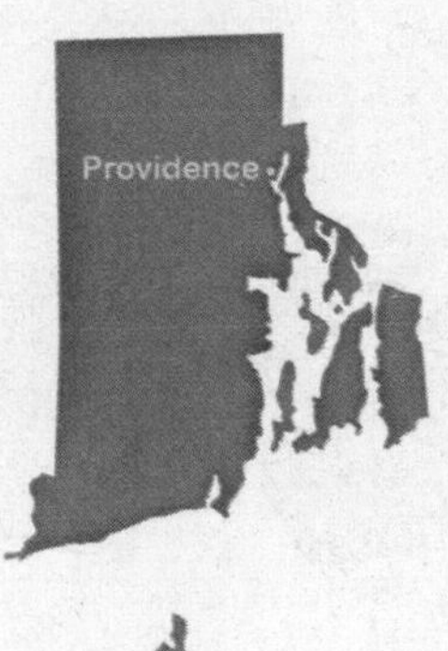

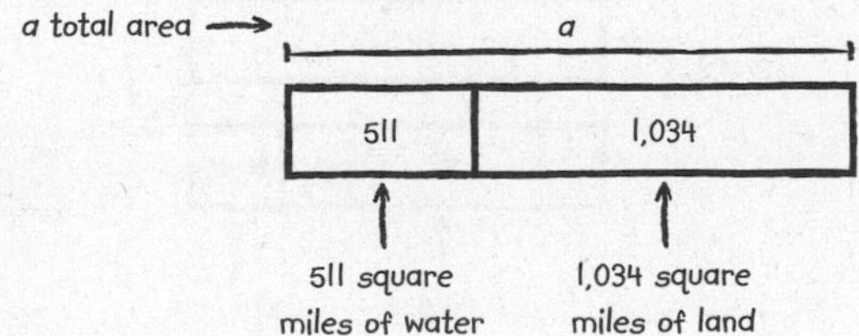

$511 + 1{,}034 = a$

The total land and water area of Rhode Island is 1,545 square miles.

Part Unknown

A farmer harvested 150 peppers on Saturday. He harvested more peppers on Sunday. He collected a total of 315 peppers over the two days. How many peppers did he harvest on Sunday?

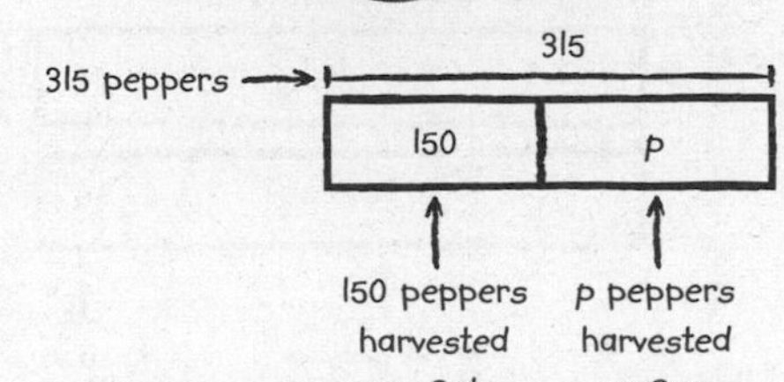

$150 + p = 315$ or $315 - 150 = p$

He harvested 165 peppers on Sunday.

Bar Diagrams

Compare: Addition and Subtraction

Draw this **bar diagram** for *compare* situations involving the difference between two quantities (how many more or fewer).

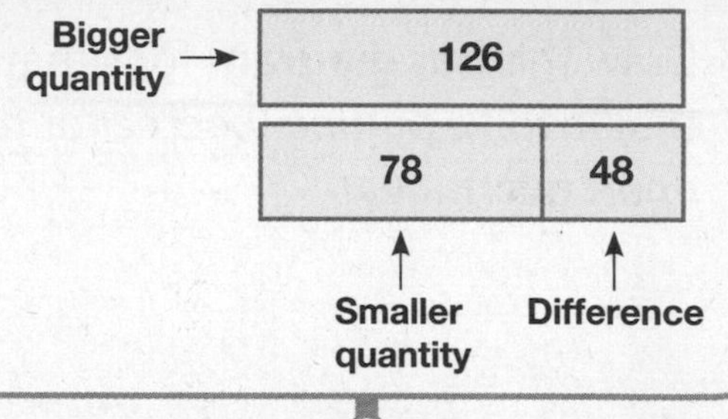

Difference Unknown

Last year, 1,796 people attended the county fair. This year 1,544 people attended. How many more people attended last year than this year?

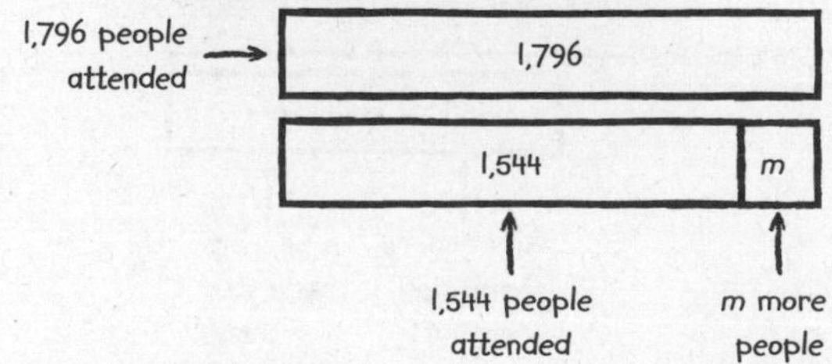

$1{,}796 - 1{,}544 = m$

Last year, 252 more people attended.

Smaller Unknown

Ann's school raised \$2,375 for charity. Brian's school raised \$275 less than Ann's school. How much did Brian's school raise?

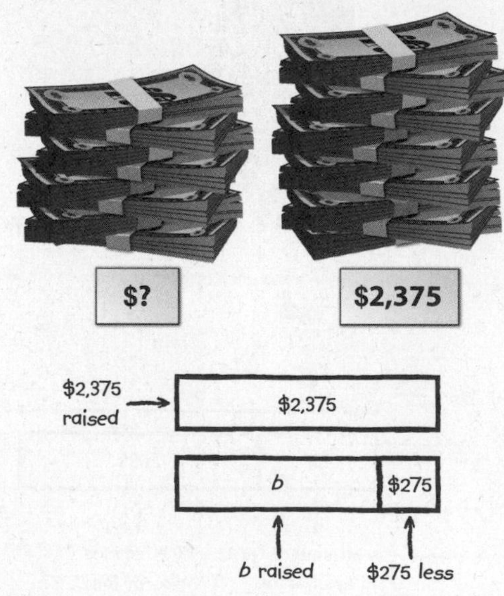

$2{,}375 - b = 275$ or $b + 275 = 2{,}375$

Brian's school raised \$2,100.

The **bar diagrams** on this page can help you solve problems involving multiplication and division.

Equal Groups: Multiplication and Division

Draw this **bar diagram** for situations that involve *equal groups.*

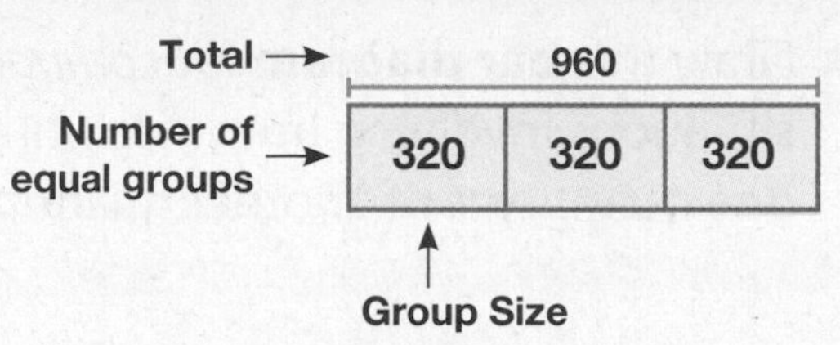

Number of Groups Unknown

Tom spent $135 on some new video games. Each game cost the same. How many video games did he buy?

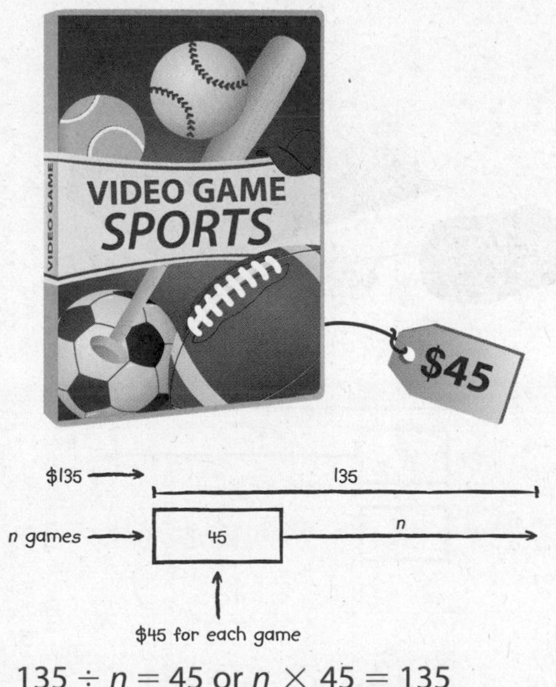

$135 \div n = 45$ or $n \times 45 = 135$

Tom bought 3 video games.

Group Size Unknown

Workers at an orchard harvested 480 apples. They separated the apples evenly into 4 bins. How many apples did they put in each bin?

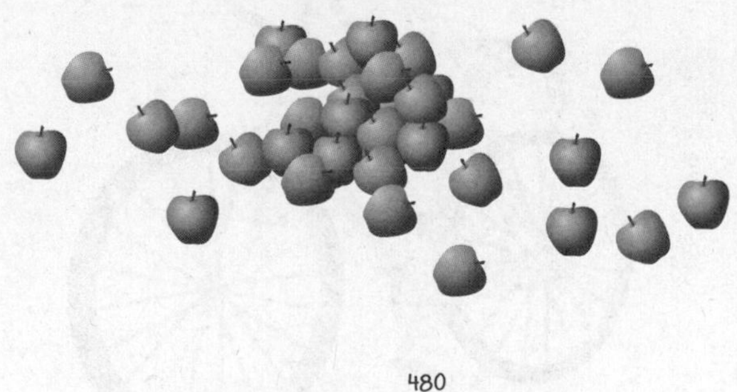

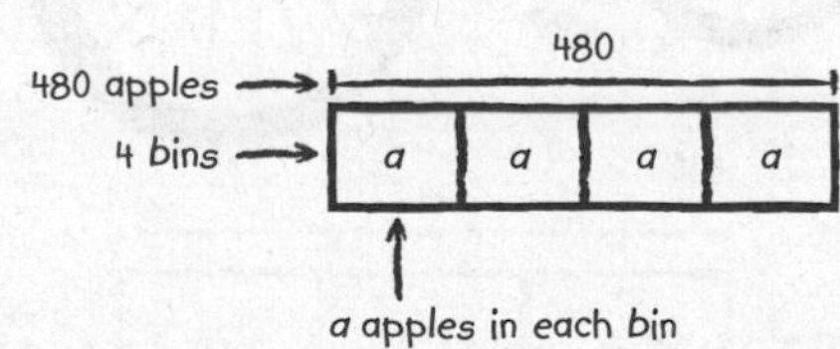

$4 \times a = 480$ or $480 \div 4 = a$

They put 120 apples in each bin.

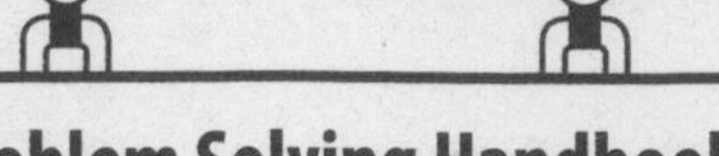

Problem Solving Handbook

Bar Diagrams

Compare: Multiplication and Division

Draw this **bar diagram** for *compare* situations involving how many times one quantity is of another quantity.

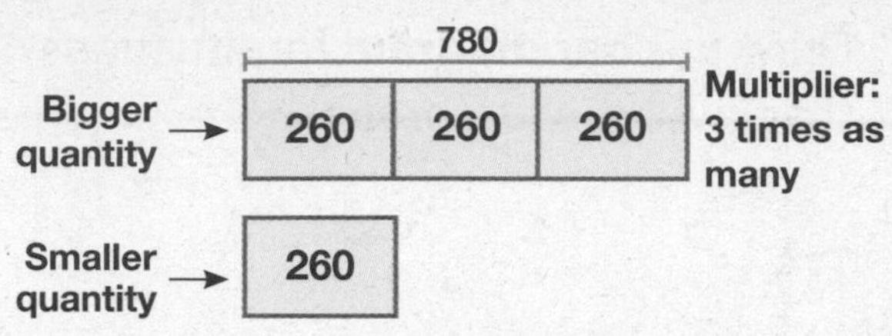

Bigger Unknown

Linda biked 175 miles last summer. Kendra biked 3 times as far as Linda. How many miles did Kendra bike?

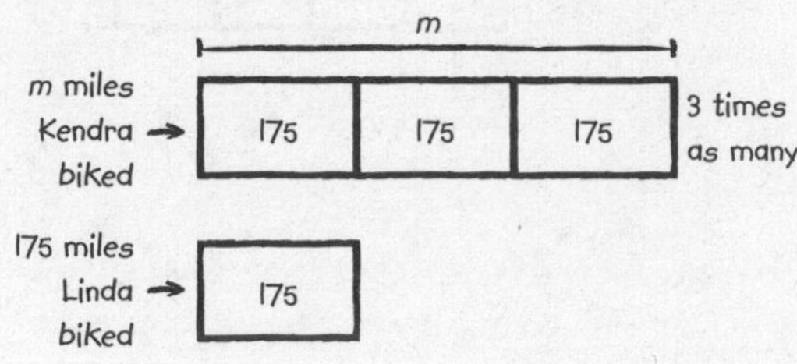

$3 \times 175 = m$

Kendra biked 525 miles.

Multiplier Unknown

Joe buys a new tent and sleeping bag. How many times as much as the sleeping bag does the tent cost?

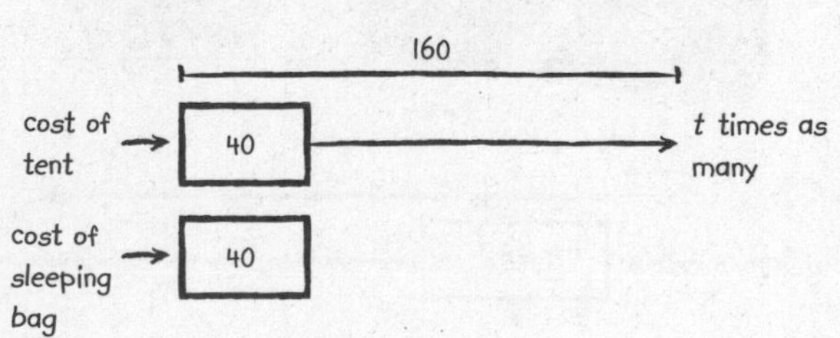

$160 \div 40 = t$ or $40 \times t = 160$

The tent costs 4 times as much as the sleeping bag.

TOPIC 1 Understand Place Value

Essential Question: How are whole numbers and decimals written, compared, and ordered?

Digital Resources

Solve · Learn · Glossary · Practice Buddy · Tools · Assessment · Help · Games

Math and Science Project: Pollinating Insects

Do Research Use the Internet or other sources to find out more about pollinating insects in the United States. What types of insects are they? How many are there of each type? How many crops and flowering plants depend on pollinating insects in order to produce the foods we eat?

Journal: Write a Report Include what you found. Also in your report:

- Choose two of the pollinating insects. Estimate how many crop plants each type of insect pollinates.
- Estimate how many of your favorite foods and beverages come from pollinated plants.
- Make up and solve ways to compare and order your data.

Name ______________________________

Review What You Know

Vocabulary

Choose the best term from the box. Write it on the blank.

- digits
- place value
- period
- whole numbers

1. ________ are the symbols used to show numbers.

2. A group of 3 digits in a number is a ________.

3. ____________ is the position of a digit in a number that is used to determine the value of the digit.

Comparing

Compare. Use <, >, or = for each ◯.

4. 869 ◯ 912
5. 9,033 ◯ 9,133
6. 1,338 ◯ 1,388
7. 417,986 ◯ 417,986
8. 0.25 ◯ 0.3
9. 0.5 ◯ 0.50

10. Kamal has 7,325 songs on his computer. Benito has 7,321 songs on his computer. Who has more songs?

Adding Whole Numbers

Find each sum.

11. 10,000 + 2,000 + 60 + 1
12. 20,000 + 5,000 + 400 + 3
13. 900,000 + 8,000 + 200 + 70 + 6
14. 7,000,000 + 50,000 + 900 + 4

Place Value

15. The largest playing card structure was made of 218,792 cards. What is the value of the digit 8 in 218,792?

Ⓐ 80 Ⓑ 800 Ⓒ 8,000 Ⓓ 80,000

16. **Construct Arguments** In the number 767, does the first 7 have the same value as the final 7? Why or why not?

A-Z Glossary

My Word Cards

Use the examples for each word on the front of the card to help complete the definitions on the back.

10^3

↑

exponent

$1{,}000 = 10 \times 10 \times 10 = 10^3$

10^3

↑

base

5,318

↑

The value of the 3 is 300.

$5 \times 10^3 + 3 \times 10^2 + 1 \times 10^1 + 8 \times 10^0$

or

$5 \times 1{,}000 + 3 \times 100 + 1 \times 10 + 8 \times 1$

0.629

↑

9 is in the thousandths place.

equivalent decimals

$0.7 = 0.70$

My Word Cards

Complete the definition. Extend learning by writing your own definitions.

The product that results from multiplying the same number over and over is a ____________ of that number.

The ________________ is the number that tells how many times a base number is used as a factor.

The place of a digit in a number tells you its ___________.

When a number is written using exponents, the __________ is the number that is used as a factor.

A ____________________ is one out of 1,000 equal parts of a whole.

_________________________ is a way to write a number that shows the sum of each digit multiplied by its place value.

Decimals that name the same part of a whole are called

_______________________________.

Name ____________________

Lesson 1-1
Patterns with Exponents and Powers of 10

I can ...
write numbers using exponents.

I can also choose and use a math tool to solve problems.

Solve & Share

A store sells AA batteries. There are 10 batteries in a package. How many batteries are in 10 packages? 100 packages? ***Solve these problems any way you choose.***

You can use appropriate tools. Place-value blocks can be used to help solve the problems. Show your work!

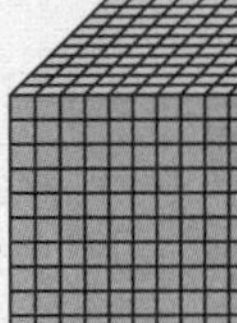

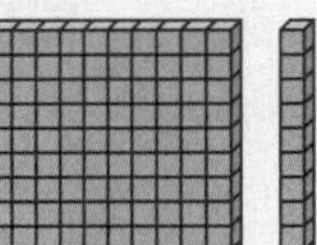

Look Back! Model with Math How many 10s are in 100? How many 10s are in 1,000? Write equations to show your work.

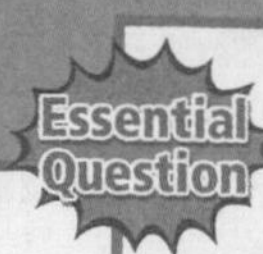

How Can You Explain Patterns in the Number of Zeros in a Product?

A

Tamara's new horse weighs about 1,000 pounds. How can you show 1,000 as a power of 10 using an exponent?

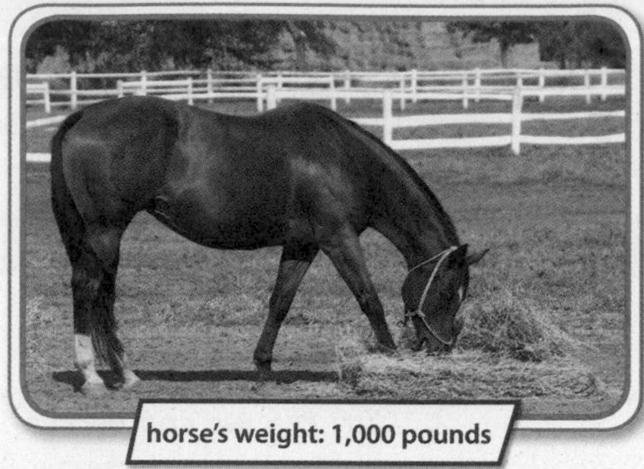

horse's weight: 1,000 pounds

B Write 1,000 as a product using 10 as a factor.

factors, exponent, base

$$1{,}000 = 10 \times 10 \times 10 = 10^3$$

The exponent, 3, shows that the base number, 10, is multiplied 3 times.

So, 1,000 is written as 10^3 using exponents.

C Tamara estimates that her horse will eat about 5,000 pounds of hay each year. How can you write 5,000 using exponents?

$5 \times 10^1 = 5 \times 10 = 50$

$5 \times 10^2 = 5 \times 10 \times 10 = 500$

$5 \times 10^3 = 5 \times 10 \times 10 \times 10 = 5{,}000$

The number of zeros in the product is the same as the exponent.

So, 5,000 is written as 5×10^3 using exponents.

Convince Me! Look for Relationships What pattern do you notice in the number of zeros in the products in Box C above?

Name ____________________

Guided Practice*

Do You Understand?

1. Reasoning Why are there three zeros in the product of 6×10^3?

2. Susan said that 10^5 is 50. What mistake did Susan make? What is the correct answer?

Do You Know How?

In **3** and **4**, complete the pattern.

3. $10^1 =$
$10^2 =$
$10^3 =$
$10^4 =$

4. $7 \times 10^1 =$
$7 \times 10^2 =$
$7 \times 10^3 =$
$7 \times 10^4 =$

Independent Practice

In **5–15**, find each product. Use patterns to help.

5. $3 \times 10^1 =$
$3 \times 10^2 =$
$3 \times 10^3 =$
$3 \times 10^4 =$

6. $2 \times 10 =$
$2 \times 100 =$
$2 \times 1{,}000 =$
$2 \times 10{,}000 =$

7. $9 \times 10^1 =$
$9 \times 10^2 =$
$9 \times 10^3 =$
$9 \times 10^4 =$

8. 8×10^4

9. $4 \times 1{,}000$

10. 5×10^2

11. $6 \times 10{,}000$

12. 4×10^1

13. 100×9

14. $10^3 \times 6$

15. 8×10^5

16. Write $10 \times 10 \times 10 \times 10 \times 10 \times 10$ with an exponent. Explain how you decided what exponent to write.

*For another example, see Set A on page 49.

Problem Solving

17. One box of printer paper has 3×10^2 sheets of paper. Another box has 10^3 sheets of paper. What is the total number of sheets in both boxes?

18. Make Sense and Persevere A post is put every 6 feet along a fence around a rectangular field that is 42 ft long and 36 ft wide. How many posts are needed?

19. Number Sense A company had 9×10^6 dollars in sales last year. Explain how to find the product 9×10^6.

20. An aquarium has the same shape as the solid figure shown below. What is the name of this solid figure?

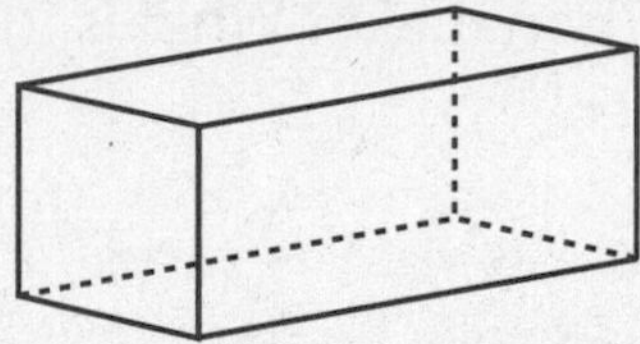

21. Model with Math Isaac takes 5 minutes to ride his bike down the hill to school and 10 minutes to ride up the hill from school. He attends school Monday through Friday. How many minutes does he spend biking to and from school in two weeks? Write an equation to model your work.

22. Higher Order Thinking Santiago hopes to buy a 4-horse trailer for about \$12,000. Describe all the numbers that when rounded to the nearest hundred are 12,000.

✓ Assessment

23. Choose all the equations that are true.

- ▢ $10 \times 10 \times 10 \times 10 = 40$
- ▢ $10 \times 10 \times 10 \times 10 = 10^4$
- ▢ $10 \times 10 \times 10 \times 10 = 1{,}000$
- ▢ $10 \times 10 \times 10 \times 10 = 10{,}000$
- ▢ $10 \times 10 \times 10 \times 10 = 4 \times 10^4$

24. Choose all the equations that are true.

- ▢ $6 \times 10^5 = 6 \times 100{,}000$
- ▢ $6 \times 10^5 = 6 \times 10{,}000$
- ▢ $6 \times 10^5 = 600{,}000$
- ▢ $6 \times 10^5 = 60{,}000$
- ▢ $6 \times 10^5 = 650{,}000$

Name ________________

Help | Practice Buddy | Tools | Games

Homework & Practice 1-1

Patterns with Exponents and Powers of 10

Another Look!

Patterns can help you multiply by powers of 10.

Find the product of 8×10^4.

Write the product in standard form.

The number of zeros in the product is the same as the exponent.

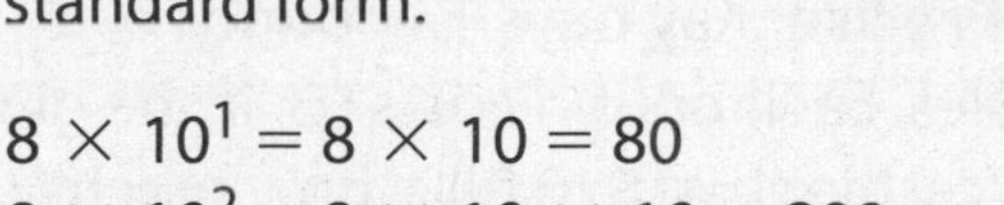

$8 \times 10^1 = 8 \times 10 = 80$
$8 \times 10^2 = 8 \times 10 \times 10 = 800$
$8 \times 10^3 = 8 \times 10 \times 10 \times 10 = 8,000$
$8 \times 10^4 = 8 \times 10 \times 10 \times 10 \times 10 = 80,000$

So, 8×10^4 written in standard form is 80,000.

1. Write $10 \times 10 \times 10 \times 10 \times 10 \times 10 \times 10$ with an exponent.

2. Write $6 \times 10 \times 10 \times 10 \times 10$ with an exponent.

3. How many zeros are in the standard form of 10^7? Write this number in standard form.

In **4–14**, find each product. Use patterns to help.

4. $4 \times 10^1 =$
$4 \times 10^2 =$
$4 \times 10^3 =$
$4 \times 10^4 =$

5. $7 \times 10 =$
$7 \times 100 =$
$7 \times 1,000 =$
$7 \times 10,000 =$

6. $5 \times 10^1 =$
$5 \times 10^2 =$
$5 \times 10^3 =$
$5 \times 10^4 =$

7. 3×10^1

8. 2×100

9. 3×10^4

10. $1,000 \times 9$

11. 6×10^2

12. 3×10^3

13. $10,000 \times 2$

14. 8×10^5

15. Explain how to find the number of zeros in the product for Exercise 14.

16. Maria saw 2×10^1 dogs in the park on Saturday. She saw twice as many dogs on Sunday as she saw on Saturday. How many dogs did she see over the two days?

17. **Number Sense** In which place is the digit in the number 5,341 that would be changed to form 5,841? How do the values of the two numbers compare?

18. **Math and Science** There are 2,000 pounds in a ton. How can you write 2,000 with an exponent?

Scientific notation is written as one digit times a power of ten.

19. **Be Precise** Kay buys 12 pounds of apples. Each pound costs $3. If she gives the cashier two $20 bills, how much change should she receive?

20. **Model with Math** James practiced piano for 48 minutes. Alisa practiced for 5 times as long as James. How many minutes did Alisa practice? How many minutes in all did James and Alisa practice? Write an equation to model your work.

	?					
Alisa →	48	48	48	48	48	5 times as long
James →	48					

21. **Higher Order Thinking** George said that 6×10^3 is 180. Do you agree or disagree? If you disagree, explain the mistake that he made and find the correct answer.

Assessment

22. Choose all the equations that are true.

- ☐ $10 \times 10 \times 10 \times 10 \times 10 = 100{,}000$
- ☐ $10 \times 10 \times 10 \times 10 \times 10 = 50$
- ☐ $10 \times 10 \times 10 \times 10 \times 10 = 50{,}000$
- ☐ $10 \times 10 \times 10 \times 10 \times 10 = 10^5$
- ☐ $10 \times 10 \times 10 \times 10 \times 10 = 500{,}000$

23. Choose all the equations that are true.

- ☐ $90{,}000 = 9 \times 1{,}000$
- ☐ $90{,}000 = 9 \times 10{,}000$
- ☐ $90{,}000 = 9 \times 10^4$
- ☐ $90{,}000 = 9 \times 10^5$
- ☐ $90{,}000 = 9 \times 10^6$

Name ______________________________ Solve

Lesson 1-2

Understand Whole-Number Place Value

I can ...
understand place-value relationships.

I can also look for patterns to solve problems.

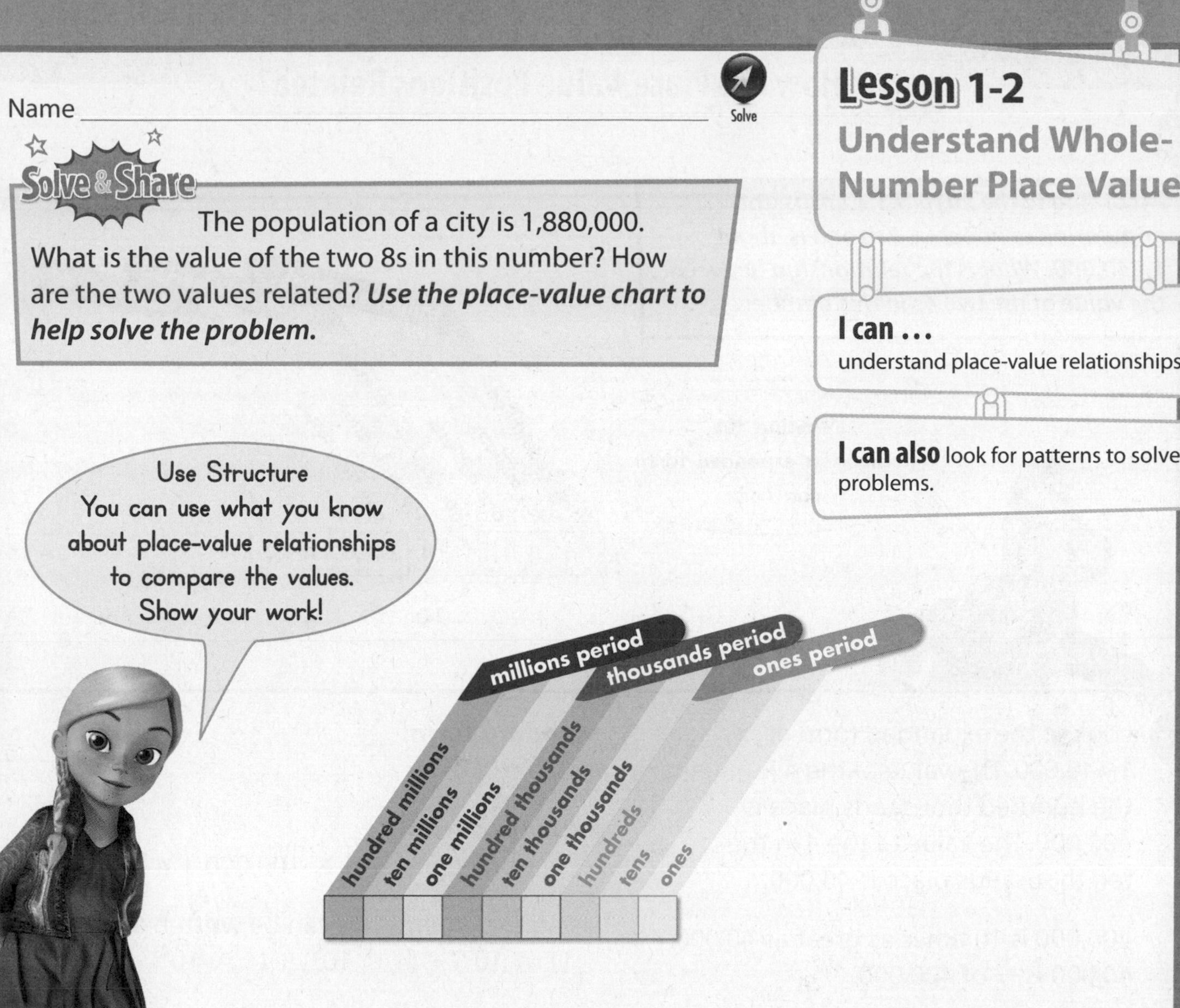

The population of a city is 1,880,000. What is the value of the two 8s in this number? How are the two values related? ***Use the place-value chart to help solve the problem.***

Look Back! Construct Arguments Is the relationship between the value of the two 8s in 1,088,000 the same as the relationship between the value of the two 8s in the problem above? Explain.

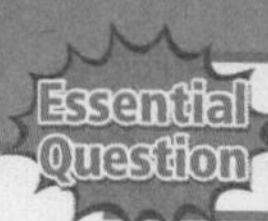

Essential Question

How Are Place-Value Positions Related?

A

According to the 2010 U.S. Census, the population of Phoenix, Arizona is about 1,440,000. What is the relationship between the value of the two 4s in this number?

Writing the number in expanded form can help.

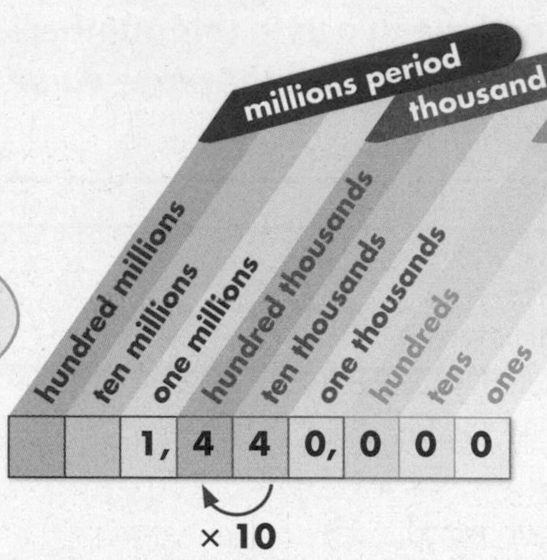

B Look at the expanded form of 1,440,000. The value of the 4 in the hundred thousands place is 400,000. The value of the 4 in the ten thousands place is 40,000.

400,000 is 10 times as great as 40,000. 40,000 is $\frac{1}{10}$ of 400,000.

Sometimes *word form* is used instead of *number name.*

Standard form:
1,440,000

Expanded form:
$1 \times 1{,}000{,}000 + 4 \times 100{,}000 + 4 \times 10{,}000$

Using exponents, this can be written as:
$(1 \times 10^6) + (4 \times 10^5) + (4 \times 10^4)$

Number name:
one million, four hundred forty thousand

Convince Me! **Reasoning** Is the value of the 1 in 1,440,000 10 times as great as the value of the 4 in the hundred thousands place? Explain.

Name ______________________________

Practice Buddy Tools Assessment

Another Example

When two digits next to each other in a number are the same, the digit on the left has 10 times the value of the digit to its right.

When two digits next to each other are the same, the digit on the right has $\frac{1}{10}$ the value of the digit to its left.

Guided Practice*

Do You Understand?

1. **Construct Arguments** In 9,290, is the value of the first 9 ten times as great as the value of the second 9? Explain.

Do You Know How?

2. Write 4,050 in expanded form.

In **3** and **4**, write the values of the given digits.

3. the 7s in 7,700
4. the 2s in 522

Independent Practice

In **5–7**, write each number in standard form.

5. 8,000,000 + 300 + 9
6. $(4 \times 10^4) + (6 \times 10^2)$
7. 10,000 + 20 + 3

In **8–10**, write each number in expanded form.

8. 5,360
9. 102,200
10. 85,000,011

In **11–13**, write the values of the given digits.

11. the 7s in 6,778
12. the 9s in 990,250
13. the 1s in 2,011,168

*For another example, see Set B on page 49.

Problem Solving

14. Write the number name and expanded form for the number of driver ants that could be in two colonies.

Up to 22,000,000 driver ants can live in a single colony.

15. **Math and Science** A queen ant can produce about nine million ants in her lifetime. Write this number in standard form.

16. **Critique Reasoning** Paul says that in the number 6,367, one 6 is 10 times as great as the other 6. Is he correct? Explain why or why not.

17. Jorge drew a square that had a side length of 8 inches. What is the perimeter of Jorge's square?

Remember, the *perimeter* of a shape is the distance around it.

18. **Higher Order Thinking** Dan wrote $(2 \times 10^6) + (3 \times 10^4) + (5 \times 10^3) + 4$ for the expanded form of two million, three hundred fifty thousand, four. What error did he make in the expanded form? What is the standard form of the number?

Assessment

19. Colleen says she is thinking of a 4-digit number in which all the digits are the same. The value of the digit in the hundreds place is 200.

Part A

What is the number? Explain.

Part B

Describe the relationship between the values of the digits in the number.

Name ______________________

Homework & Practice 1-2

Understand Whole-Number Place Value

Another Look!

A place-value chart can help you write larger numbers. What are the various ways to write 92,888,100?

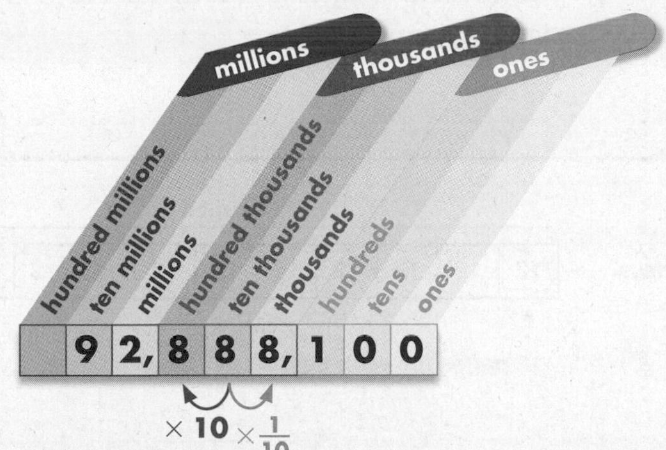

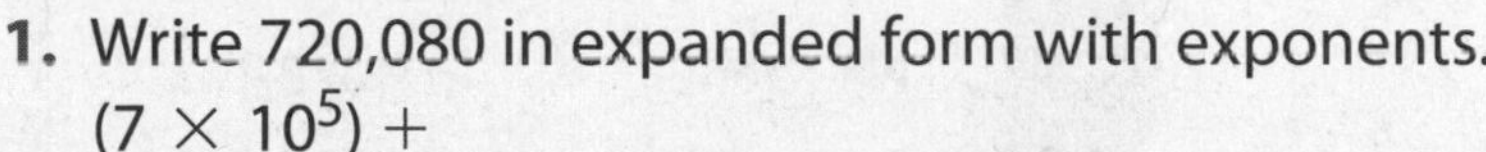

The value of the first 8 is $8 \times 100{,}000 = 800{,}000$, and the value of the second 8 is $8 \times 10{,}000 = 80{,}000$.

Expanded form: $(9 \times 10^7) + (2 \times 10^6) + (8 \times 10^5) + (8 \times 10^4) + (8 \times 10^3) + (1 \times 10^2)$

Standard form: 92,888,100

Number name: ninety-two million, eight hundred eighty-eight thousand, one hundred

1. Write 720,080 in expanded form with exponents.
   $(7 \times 10^5) +$

2. Write the number name for 43,080,700.

In **3–5**, write the values of the given digits.

3. the 2s in 42,256

4. the 9s in 9,905,482

5. the 4s in 305,444

6. Write 12,430,000 in expanded form.

7. Write 337,060 in expanded form using exponents.

8. Write the number name for 3,1<u>5</u>2,308.

   What is the value of the underlined digit?

9. Use Structure Sue and Jonah chose numbers for a place-value game. Sue chose the number one hundred fifty-two thousand. Jonah chose five million for his number. Who chose the greater number? Explain.

10. Higher Order Thinking One day, the state fair total attendance was 126,945. Round 126,945 to the nearest hundred thousand, nearest ten thousand, and nearest thousand. Which of these rounded amounts is closest to the actual attendance?

11. Model with Math Maricko and her family went on a 10-day vacation. She read 12 pages in her book each day. How many total pages did she read while on vacation?

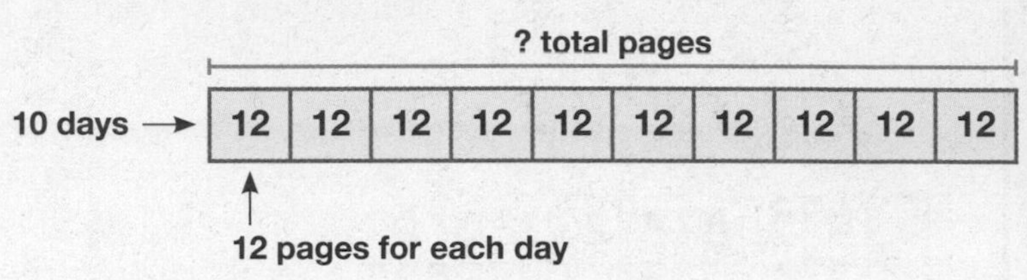

12. Construct Arguments Is the value of the first 5 in California's population 10 times as great as the value of the second 5? Explain.

13. Number Sense Write the population of Florida in expanded form using exponents.

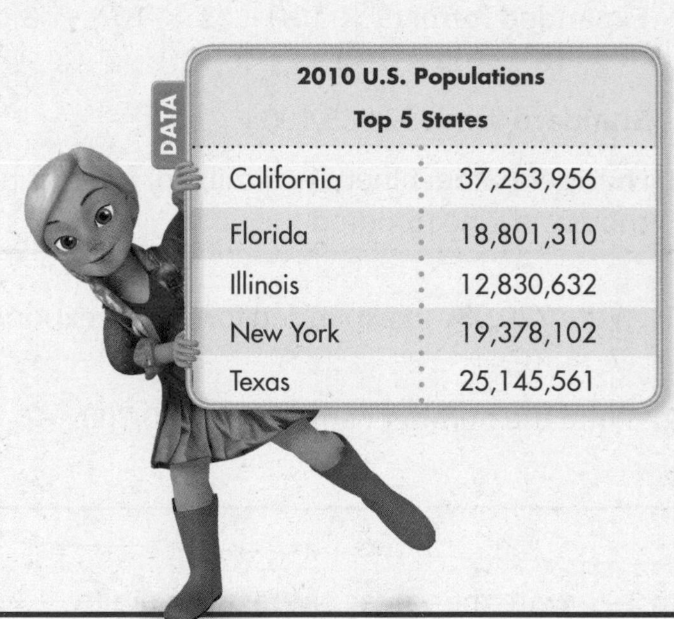

2010 U.S. Populations Top 5 States	
California	37,253,956
Florida	18,801,310
Illinois	12,830,632
New York	19,378,102
Texas	25,145,561

Assessment

14. Joseph says that in the number 9,999,999, all the digits have the same value.

Part A

Is Joseph correct? Explain.

Part B

Describe the relationship between the values of the digits in the number.

Name ______________________________________

Lesson 1-3
Decimals to Thousandths

I can …
read and write decimals to the thousandths.

I can also look for patterns to solve problems.

Solve & Share Jennie is training for a race. On Tuesday she finished her sprint 0.305 second faster than she did on Monday. How can you explain the meaning of 0.305? ***Solve this problem any way you choose.***

You can use structure. Use what you know about place value to help solve the problem. Show your work!

Look Back! Construct Arguments Gabriel says that there are 5 hundredths in 0.305. Do you agree or disagree? Explain.

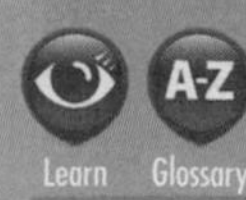

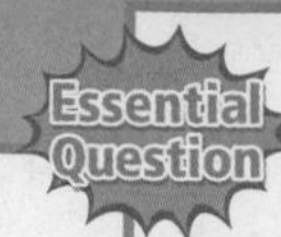

How Can You Read and Write Decimals to the Thousandths?

A

A box is filled with 1,000 cubes. Amy picks out 4 cubes. How can you represent 4 out of 1,000 cubes as a decimal?

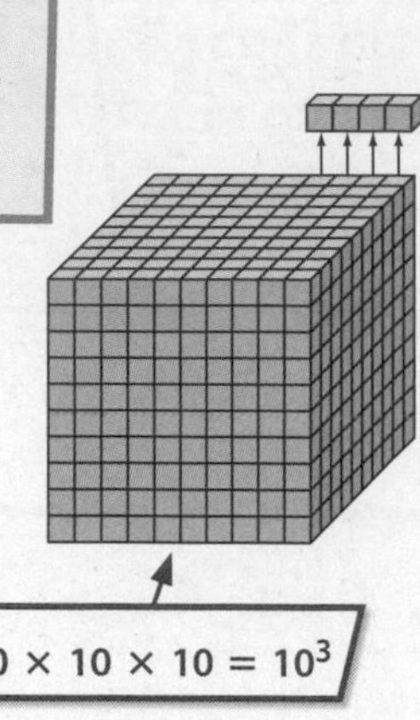

B

The number name for $\frac{4}{1,000}$ is four thousandths. A decimal place-value chart can help you determine the decimal. Notice that the thousandths place is three places to the right of the decimal point.

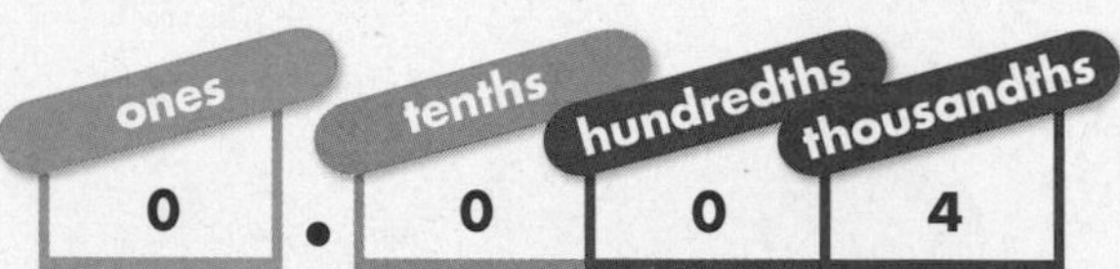

So, $\frac{4}{1,000}$ can be represented by the decimal 0.004.

C

How can $\frac{444}{1,000}$ be represented by a decimal?

$\frac{444}{1,000}$ is read as *four hundred forty-four thousandths* and represented by the decimal 0.444.

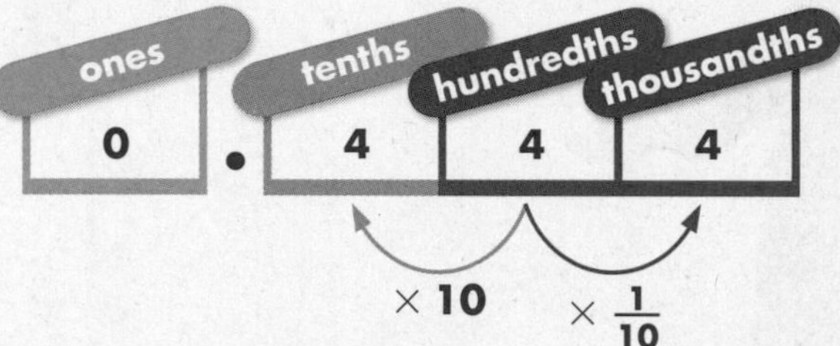

The value of the digit 4 in the hundredths place has 10 times the value of the digit 4 in the thousandths place and $\frac{1}{10}$ the value of the digit 4 in the tenths place.

Convince Me! **Reasoning** How is 0.004 the same as and different from 0.444?

Name ______________________________

Guided Practice*

Do You Understand?

1. **Be Precise** If four cubes are pulled from the box on the previous page, how would you write the fraction representing the cubes that are left? the decimal representing the cubes that are left?

2. **Reasoning** 0.3 is 10 times as great as what decimal? 0.003 is $\frac{1}{10}$ of what decimal?

Do You Know How?

In **3–6**, write each decimal as a fraction.

3. 0.001 =
4. 0.05 =
5. 0.512 =
6. 0.309 =

In **7–10**, write each fraction as a decimal.

7. $\frac{2}{1,000} =$
8. $\frac{34}{100} =$
9. $\frac{508}{1,000} =$
10. $\frac{99}{1,000} =$

Independent Practice

In **11–18**, write each decimal as a fraction.

11. 0.007
12. 0.08
13. 0.065
14. 0.9
15. 0.832
16. 0.203
17. 0.78
18. 0.999

In **19–26**, write each fraction as a decimal.

19. $\frac{434}{1,000}$
20. $\frac{3}{10}$
21. $\frac{873}{1,000}$
22. $\frac{17}{1,000}$
23. $\frac{309}{1,000}$
24. $\frac{5}{1,000}$
25. $\frac{6}{100}$
26. $\frac{999}{1,000}$

27. Look at the middle 9 in Exercise 18. How is its value related to the value of the 9 to its left? to the value of the 9 to its right?

*For another example, see Set C on page 49.

Problem Solving

28. Model with Math The Palmer's property tax bill for the year is \$3,513. In their first installment, they paid \$1,757. How much do they still owe on their bill? Write an equation to model your work.

29. Use Structure Write the fractions $\frac{22}{100}$ and $\frac{22}{1,000}$ as decimals. How are the values of the digit 2 related in each of the decimals?

30. Simon scored 4×10^2 points in a game. Joe scored 2×10^3 points in the same game. Whose score is higher? How much higher?

31. Higher Order Thinking Kelly said that $\frac{97}{1,000}$ can be written as 0.97. Is she correct? Explain.

32. Critique Reasoning Frank reasoned that in the number 0.555, the value of the 5 in the thousandths place is ten times as great as the 5 in the hundredths place. Is he correct? Explain.

33. Construct Arguments How many cubes are in the box? What fraction of the entire box do the 7 cubes represent? Explain your answer.

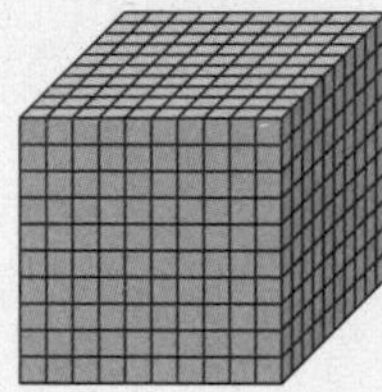

Assessment

34. 0.04 is 10 times as great as which decimal?

Ⓐ 0.4

Ⓑ 0.1

Ⓒ 0.004

Ⓓ 0.001

35. 0.009 is $\frac{1}{10}$ of which decimal?

Ⓐ 0.01

Ⓑ 0.09

Ⓒ 0.1

Ⓓ 0.9

Name ______________________

Help Practice Buddy Tools Games

Homework & Practice 1-3

Decimals to Thousandths

Another Look!

Patterns can help you read and write decimals.

Decimal	Fraction	Number Name
0.1	$\frac{1}{10}$	One tenth
0.01	$\frac{1}{100}$	One hundredth
0.001	$\frac{1}{1,000}$	One thousandth

0.01 is 10 times as great as 0.001.

0.01 is $\frac{1}{10}$ as great as 0.1.

0.1 is 10 times as great as 0.01.

The value of each place-value position is 10 times the value of the place to its right and $\frac{1}{10}$ the value of the place to its left.

1. 0.08 is 10 times as great as __________.

2. 0.002 is $\frac{1}{10}$ of __________.

3. 0.5 is 10 times as great as __________.

4. 0.07 is $\frac{1}{10}$ of __________.

In **5–12**, write each decimal as a fraction.

5. 0.009 **6.** 0.105 **7.** 0.2 **8.** 0.025

9. 0.563 **10.** 0.31 **11.** 0.6 **12.** 0.004

In **13–20**, write each fraction as a decimal.

13. $\frac{8}{1,000}$ **14.** $\frac{63}{100}$ **15.** $\frac{984}{1,000}$ **16.** $\frac{29}{1,000}$

17. $\frac{111}{1,000}$ **18.** $\frac{3}{10}$ **19.** $\frac{6}{1,000}$ **20.** $\frac{5}{1,000}$

21. Number Sense Tommy is beginning a science experiment in the lab. The instructions call for 0.322 kilogram of potassium. Write 0.322 as a fraction.

22. Mt. McKinley is the highest mountain peak in North America with an elevation of 20,320 feet. What is the value of the digit 3 in 20,320?

23. Construct Arguments Jorge said that 0.029 can be written as $\frac{29}{100}$. Is he correct? Explain.

24. Be Precise The area of the continent of North America is about 9,540,000 square miles. Write 9,540,000 in expanded form using exponents to show powers of 10.

25. Model with Math What part of the entire square is shaded? Write your answer as a fraction and as a decimal.

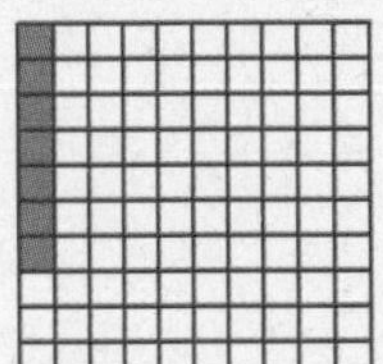

26. Higher Order Thinking Write the fractions $\frac{5}{10}$, $\frac{5}{100}$, and $\frac{5}{1,000}$ as decimals. How are the decimals related?

27. Vocabulary Complete the sentence using one of the words below.

power base exponent

The number 1,000,000 is a(n) ________ of 10.

28. Algebra In three months, Harold watched a total of 40 movies. If he watched 12 movies in June and 13 movies in July, how many movies did he watch in August? Write an equation using the variable *a* to model your work.

Assessment

29. 0.003 is $\frac{1}{10}$ of which decimal?

Ⓐ 0.3
Ⓑ 0.03
Ⓒ 0.33
Ⓓ 0.333

30. 0.8 is 10 times as great as which decimal?

Ⓐ 0.08
Ⓑ 0.88
Ⓒ 0.008
Ⓓ 0.888

Name ______________________________

Lesson 1-4
Understand Decimal Place Value

I can ...
read and write decimals in different ways.

I can also generalize from examples.

Solve & Share

A runner won a 100-meter race with a time of 9.85 seconds. How can you use place value to explain this time? Complete a place-value chart to show this time.

Look Back! Use Structure In the decimal 9.85, what is the value of the 8? the value of the 5?

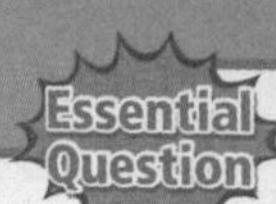

How Can You Represent Decimals?

A

Jo picked a seed from her flower. The seed has a mass of 0.245 gram. What are some different ways you can represent 0.245?

You can write the standard form, expanded form, and number name for a decimal just like you can for a whole number.

B

ones		tenths	hundredths	thousandths
0	.	2	4	5

Standard Form: 0.245

The 5 is in the thousandths place. Its value is 0.005.

Expanded Form:

$\left(2 \times \frac{1}{10}\right) + \left(4 \times \frac{1}{100}\right) + \left(5 \times \frac{1}{1,000}\right)$

Number Name: two hundred forty-five thousandths

A place-value chart can help you identify the tenths, hundredths, and thousandths place in a decimal.

Convince Me! **Reasoning** How many hundredths are in one tenth? How many thousandths are in one hundredth? Tell how you know.

Name ______________________

Practice Buddy Tools Assessment

Another Example

Equivalent decimals name the same amount.

What are two other decimals equivalent to 1.4?

One and four tenths is the same as one and forty hundredths.

$$1.4 = 1.40$$

One and four tenths is the same as one and four hundred thousandths.

$$1.4 = 1.400$$

So, $1.4 = 1.40 = 1.400$.

1 hundredth is equal to 10 thousandths.

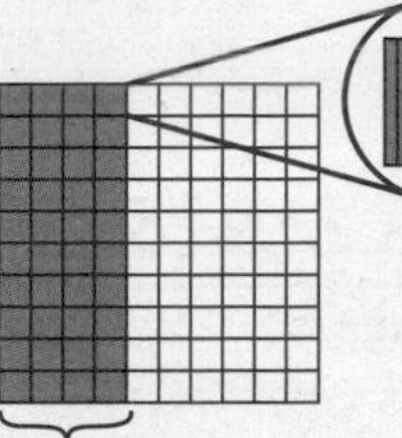

Guided Practice*

Do You Understand?

1. **Reasoning** The number 3.453 has two 3s. Why does each 3 have a different value?

Do You Know How?

In **2** and **3**, write each number in standard form.

2. $4 \times 100 + 7 \times 10 + 6 \times 1 + 6 \times \left(\frac{1}{10}\right) + 3 \times \left(\frac{1}{100}\right) + 7 \times \left(\frac{1}{1{,}000}\right)$

3. four and sixty-eight thousandths

Independent Practice

In **4–6**, write each number in standard form.

4. $(2 \times 1) + \left(6 \times \frac{1}{1{,}000}\right)$

5. $(3 \times 1) + \left(3 \times \frac{1}{10}\right) + \left(9 \times \frac{1}{1{,}000}\right)$

6. nine and twenty hundredths

In **7–10**, write two decimals that are equivalent to the given decimal.

7. 2.200

8. 8.1

9. 9.50

10. 4.200

*For another example, see Set C on page 49.

Problem Solving

11. Model with Math The annual fundraising goal of a charity is \$100,000. So far \$63,482 has been raised. How much more money is needed to reach the goal?

\$100,000

\$63,482	?

12. Santiago has a rope that measures 205.95 centimeters. Write this number in expanded form.

13. Reasoning How can you tell that 7.630 and 7.63 are equivalent decimals?

14. Make Sense and Persevere In Justin's school, 0.825 of the students participate in a sport. If there are one thousand students in Justin's school, how many participate in a sport?

15. Maria incorrectly placed the decimal point when she wrote 0.65 inch for the width of her tablet computer. What is the correct decimal number for the width?

16. Higher Order Thinking Three boys cut out hundredths decimal models. Derrick does not shade any of his models. Ari shades half of one model. Wesley shades two models and one tenth of another model. What decimal represents the amount each boy shades?

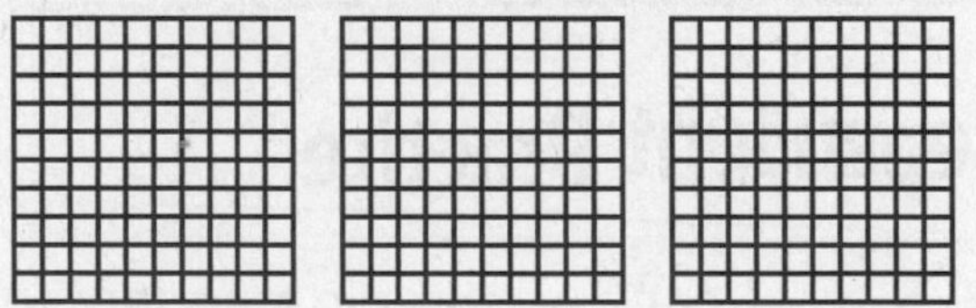

Assessment

17. Find two decimals that are equivalent to $(4 \times 10) + \left(7 \times \frac{1}{100}\right)$. Write the decimals in the box.

40.7 40.07 4.7 40.070 4.70 40.70

Name ______________________

Homework & Practice 1-4

Understand Decimal Place Value

Another Look!

One of the largest ostrich eggs laid weighed 5.476 pounds. What is the value of the digit 6 in 5.476?

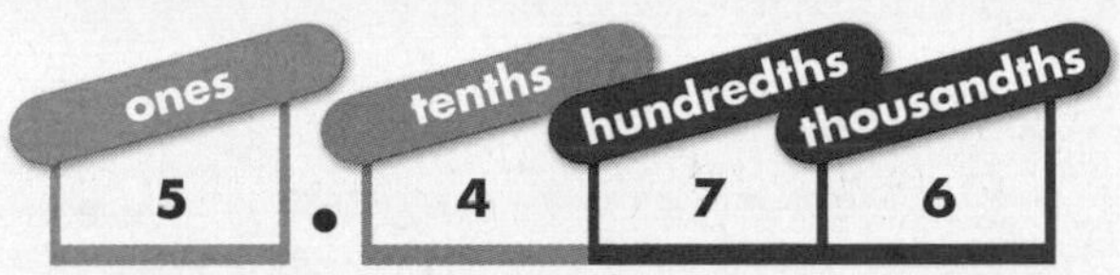

Standard Form: 5.476

Expanded Form: $(5 \times 1) + \left(4 \times \frac{1}{10}\right) + \left(7 \times \frac{1}{100}\right) + \left(6 \times \frac{1}{1{,}000}\right)$

Number Name: Five and four hundred seventy-six thousandths

The digit 6 is in the thousandths place, so the value is 0.006.

1. Complete the place-value chart for the following number. Write its number name and tell the value of the underlined digit.

6.3<u>2</u>4

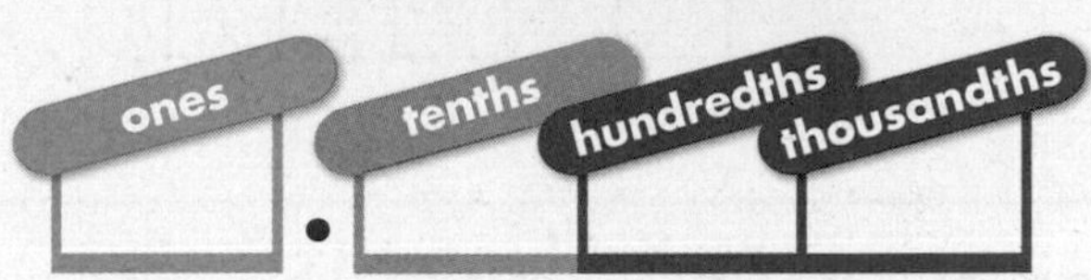

2. Write 863.141 in expanded form.

In **3–5**, write each number in standard form.

3. $(8 \times 1) + \left(5 \times \frac{1}{100}\right) + \left(9 \times \frac{1}{1{,}000}\right)$

4. $1 + 0.9 + 0.08 + 0.001$

5. Four hundred twenty-five and fifty-two hundredths

In **6–9**, write two decimals that are equivalent to the given decimal.

6. 5.300

7. 3.7

8. 0.9

9. 2.50

10. Model with Math Shade the models to show that 0.7 and 0.70 are equivalent.

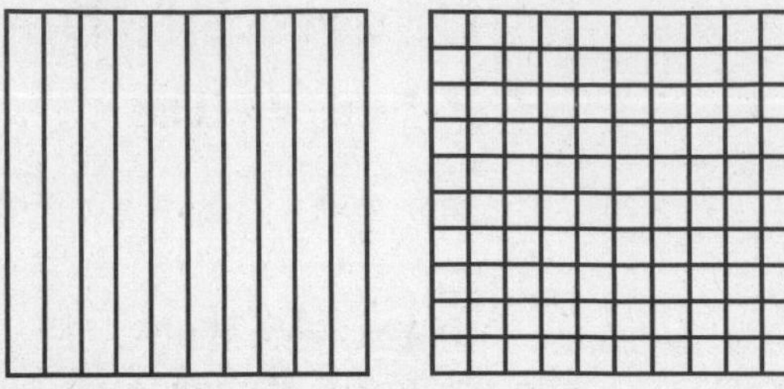

11. Marco has a piece of wood that measures $9 \times \frac{1}{10} + 6 \times \frac{1}{100} + 4 \times \frac{1}{1{,}000}$ meter. How can this measurement be written as a decimal?

12. There are 275 people in the movie theater. The same number of people are seated in each of the 5 different sections of the theater. How many people are seated in each section?

275 people

?	?	?	?	?

13. Construct Arguments Cheryl's softball batting average is 0.340, and Karin's is 0.304. Karin says they have the same average. What error did she make? Explain.

14. Number Sense Nico spent eight dollars and seventy-five cents on lunch. Which two items did Nico buy?

DATA

Lunch Menu

Item	Price
Hamburger	$4.20
Chef Salad	$4.50
Tuna Sandwich	$4.05
Pizza	$4.25

15. Higher Order Thinking Anthony drew a pentagon with each side measuring 6 inches. Carol drew a hexagon with each side measuring 5 inches. Which shape has a greater perimeter? Write an equation to help explain your answer.

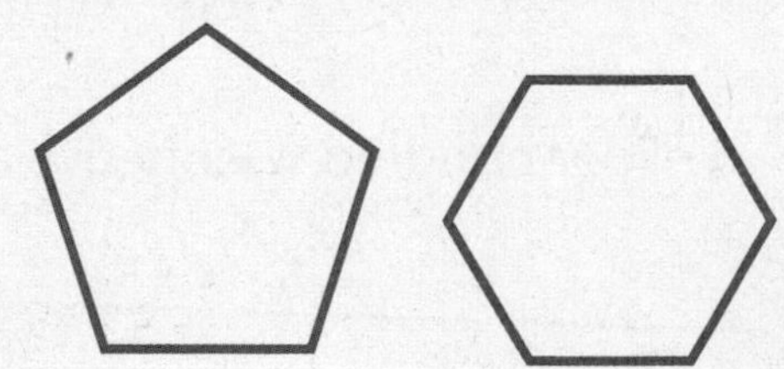

Assessment

16. Find two decimals that are equivalent to $(8 \times 100) + \left(3 \times \frac{1}{10}\right) + \left(6 \times \frac{1}{100}\right)$. Write the decimals in the box.

8.36 800.36 800.036 800.306 8.360 800.360

Name ____________________

Solve

Lesson 1-5
Compare Decimals

I can ...
compare decimals to the thousandths.

I can also look for patterns to solve problems.

Solve & Share

The lengths of three ants were measured in a laboratory. The lengths were 0.521 centimeter, 0.498 centimeter, and 0.550 centimeter. Which ant was the longest? Which ant was the shortest?

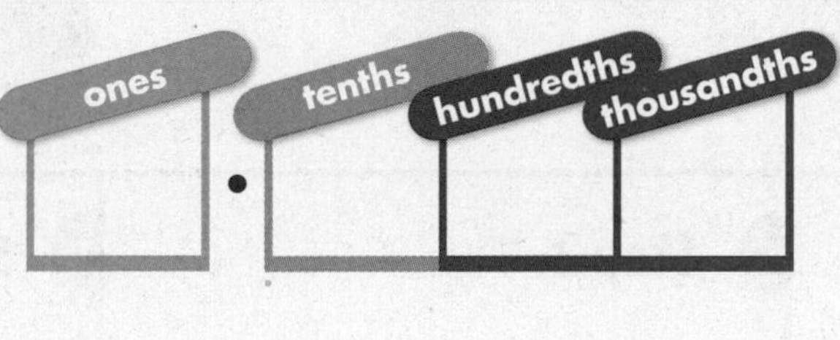

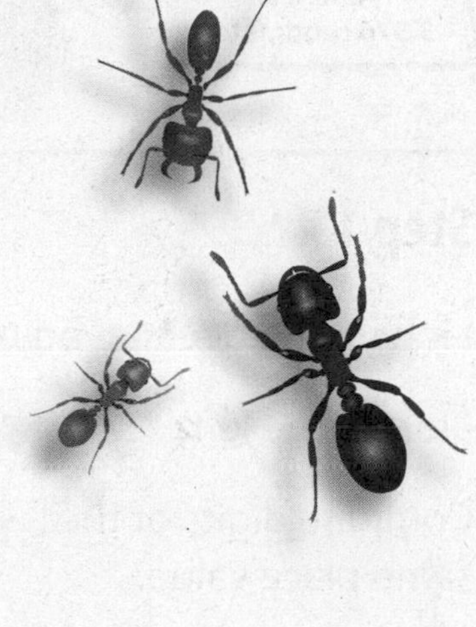

Look Back! Be Precise What are the lengths of the ants in order from least to greatest?

Essential Question: How Can You Compare Decimals?

A

Scientists collected and measured the lengths of different cockroach species. Which cockroach had the greater length, the American or the Oriental cockroach?

Comparing decimals is like comparing whole numbers!

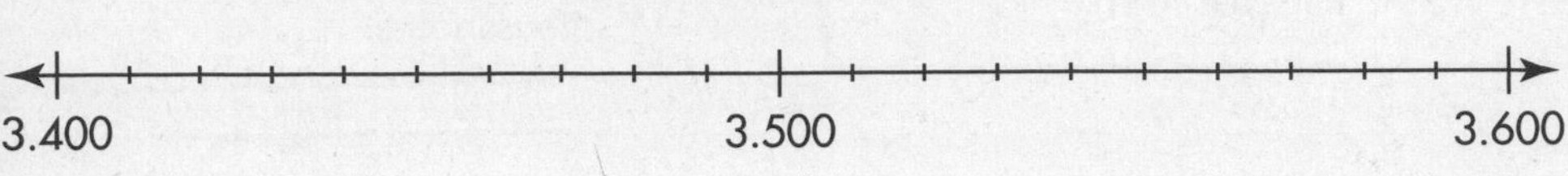

Australian
3.582 centimeters

Oriental
3.432 centimeters

B

Step 1

Line up the decimal points.

Start at the left.

Compare digits of the same place value.

3.576

3.432

C

Step 2

Find the first place where the digits are different.

3.576

3.432

D

Step 3

Compare.

$5 > 4$

$0.5 > 0.4$

So, $3.576 > 3.432$.

The American cockroach is longer than the Oriental cockroach.

Convince Me! **Critique Reasoning** Valerie said, "12.68 is greater than 12.8 because 68 is greater than 8." Is she correct? Explain.

Name ______________________

Practice Buddy   Tools   Assessment

Another Example

Order the cockroaches from least to greatest length.

Step 1

Write the numbers, lining up the decimal points. Start at the left. Compare digits of the same place value.

3.576
3.432
3.582

3.432 is the least.

Step 2

Write the remaining numbers, lining up the decimal points. Start at the left. Compare.

3.576
3.582

3.582 is greater than 3.576.

Step 3

Write the numbers from least to greatest.

3.432   3.576   3.582

From least to greatest lengths are the Oriental, the American, and the Australian.

Guided Practice*

Do You Understand?

1. **Critique Reasoning** Scientists measured a Madeira cockroach and found it to be 3.44 centimeters long. Toby says that the Madeira is shorter than the Oriental because 3.44 has fewer digits than 3.432. Is he correct? Explain.

Do You Know How?

In **2** and **3**, write $>$, $<$, or $=$ for each ◯.

2. 3.692 ◯ 3.697   **3.** 7.216 ◯ 7.203

In **4** and **5**, order the decimals from least to greatest.

4. 5.540, 5.631, 5.625

5. 0.675, 1.529, 1.35, 0.693

Independent Practice

In **6–8**, compare the two numbers. Write $>$, $<$, or $=$ for each ◯.

6. 0.890 ◯ 0.89   **7.** 5.733 ◯ 5.693   **8.** 9.707 ◯ 9.717

In **9** and **10**, order the decimals from greatest to least.

9. 878.403, 887.304, 887.043   **10.** 435.566, 436.565, 435.665

*For another example, see Set D on page 50.

Problem Solving

11. **Critique Reasoning** Explain why it is not reasonable to say that 4.23 is less than 4.135 because 4.23 has fewer digits after the decimal point than 4.135.

12. **Number Sense** Carlos wrote three numbers between 0.33 and 0.34. What numbers could Carlos have written?

13. **A-Z Vocabulary** Draw lines to match each decimal on the left to its **equivalent decimal** on the right.

0.75	0.750
1.50	0.075
1.05	1.500
0.075	1.050

14. Is 0.5 greater than or less than $\frac{6}{10}$? Draw a number line to show your answer.

15. **Higher Order Thinking** Ana's gymnastics scores were posted on the scoreboard in order from highest to lowest score. One digit in her floor score is not visible. List all the possible digits for the missing number.

16. Marcia's vault score is 15.050. How does it compare to Ana's vault score?

Ana's Scores

Vault	15.500
Floor	15._66
Uneven bars	15.133
Beam	14.200

✓ Assessment

17. A grain of fine sand can have a diameter of 0.125 millimeter. Which numbers are less than 0.125?

- ☐ 0.1
- ☐ 0.2
- ☐ 0.13
- ☐ 0.12
- ☐ 0.126

18. Cara weighed some apples at the grocery store. The apples weighed 4.16 pounds. Which numbers are greater than 4.16?

- ☐ 4.15
- ☐ 4.19
- ☐ 4.2
- ☐ 4.09
- ☐ 4.1

Name ______________________

Homework & Practice 1-5

Compare Decimals

Another Look!

Amanda completed a race in 8.016 minutes. Liz's time was 7.03 minutes, and Steve's time was 8.16 minutes. Order the times from least to greatest. Who won the race?

Write the numbers, lining up the decimal points. Start at the left. Compare digits of the same place value. 8.016 7.03 8.16 7.03 is the least.	Write the remaining numbers, lining up the decimal points. Start at the left. Compare. 8.016 8.16 8.16 is greater than 8.016.	 7.03, 8.016, 8.16

1. Order the speeds from least to greatest.

2. Driver D had a speed between Driver A and Driver C. Write a possible speed for Driver D.

DATA

Driver	Average Speed (mph)
Driver A	145.155
Driver B	145.827
Driver C	144.809

In **3–8**, write >, <, or = for each ◯.

3. 7.539 ◯ 7.344 **4.** 9.202 ◯ 9.209 **5.** 0.75 ◯ 0.750

6. 4.953 ◯ 4.951 **7.** 1.403 ◯ 1.4 **8.** 3.074 ◯ 3.740

In **9–12**, order from greatest to least.

9. 9.129, 9.37, 9.3, 9.219

10. 0.012, 0.100, 0.001, 0.101

11. 5.132, 5.123, 5.312, 5.231

12. 62.905, 62.833, 62.950, 62.383

13. Model with Math Write three different fractions that each match the shaded part of the drawing.

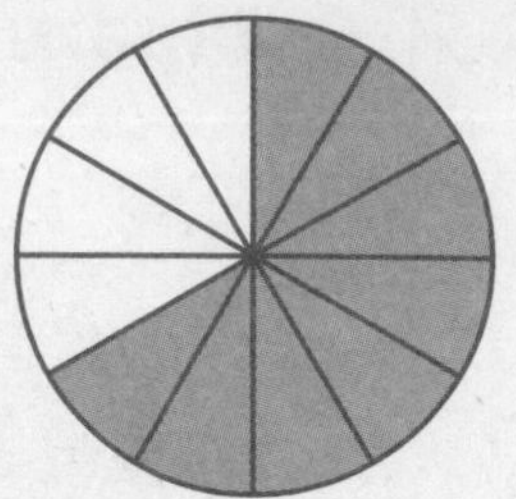

14. Model with Math The total cost to stay one night at Sleepy Head Motel is $119 without breakfast and $142 with breakfast included. What is the difference in the costs for a one-night stay with and without breakfast?

$142	
$119	?

15. Make Sense and Persevere Tanya bought the least expensive brand of dog food. Eddie bought the most expensive brand of dog food. Which brand did each person buy?

DATA

Dog Food Sale

Brand	Price per bag
A	$12.49
B	$11.55
C	$12.09
D	$11.59

16. Why can it help to line up the decimal points before comparing and ordering numbers with decimals?

17. Higher Order Thinking The heights of four boys measured 152.0 cm, 150.75 cm, 149.5 cm, and 149.25 cm. Bradley is the tallest, Calvin is taller than Josh, but shorter than Mark. Josh is the shortest. What is Mark's height?

Assessment

18. Jere is thinking of a number less than 28.431 and greater than 28.404. Which of the following could be Jere's number?

- ☐ 28.435
- ☐ 28.342
- ☐ 28.430
- ☐ 28.419
- ☐ 28.42

19. During this year's basketball season, Michael averaged 22.075 points per game. Which numbers are less than 22.075?

- ☐ 21.9
- ☐ 22.08
- ☐ 23.06
- ☐ 22.07
- ☐ 22.079

Name ______________________________

Solve

Lesson 1-6
Round Decimals

I can . . .
round decimals to different places.

I can also look for patterns to solve problems.

Solve & Share

In science class, Marci recorded numbers from an experiment as 12.87, 12.13, 12.5, and 12.08. Which numbers are closer to 12? Which are closer to 13? How can you tell?

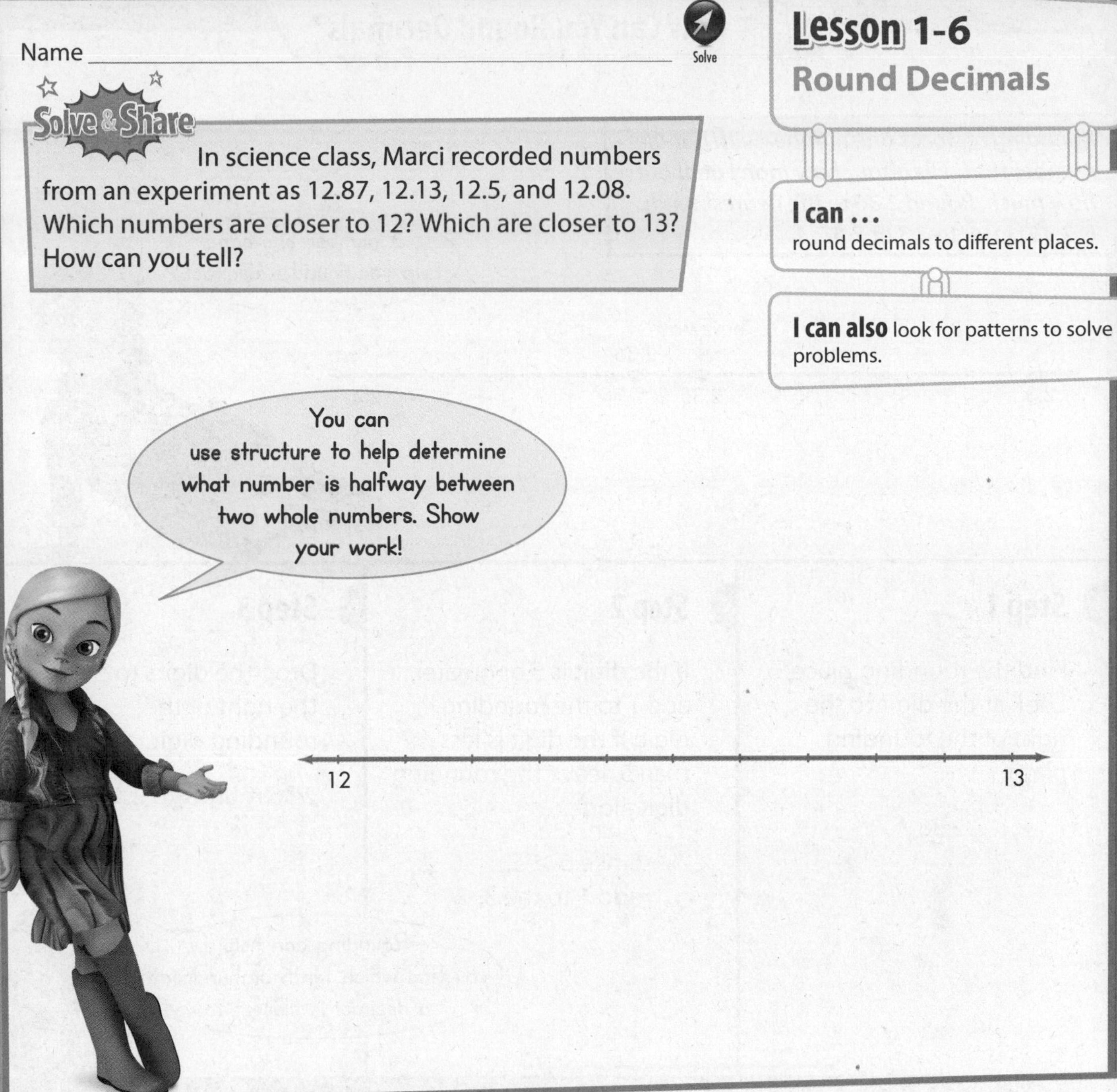

Look Back! Reasoning What is the halfway point between 12 and 13? Is that point closer to 12 or 13?

Learn Glossary

Essential Question How Can You Round Decimals?

A

Rounding replaces one number with another number that tells about how many or about how much. Round 2.36 to the nearest tenth. Is 2.36 closer to 2.3 or 2.4?

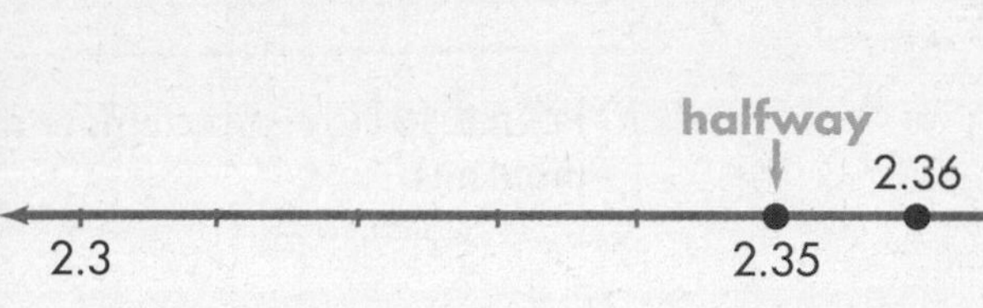

B

Step 1

Find the rounding place. Look at the digit to the right of the rounding place.

2.<u>3</u>6

C

Step 2

If the digit is 5 or greater, add 1 to the rounding digit. If the digit is less than 5, leave the rounding digit alone.

Since $6 > 5$,
add 1 to the 3.

D

Step 3

Drop the digits to the right of the rounding digit.

2.36 rounds to 2.4

Rounding can help you find which tenth or hundredth a decimal is closest to.

Convince Me! Critique Reasoning Carrie said, "448 rounds to 500 because 448 rounds to 450 and 450 rounds to 500." Is she correct? Explain. Use the number line in your explanation.

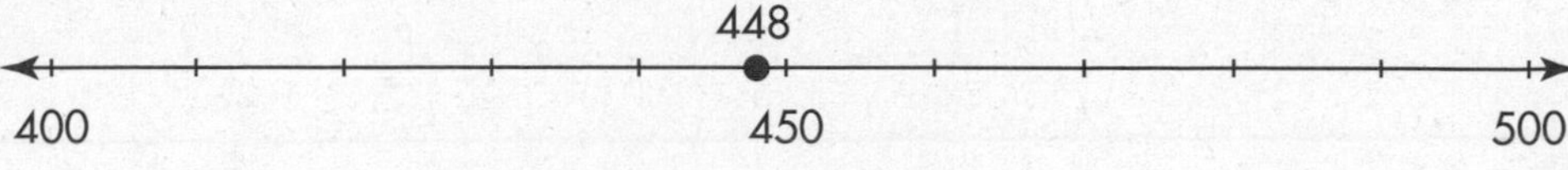

Name ______________________________

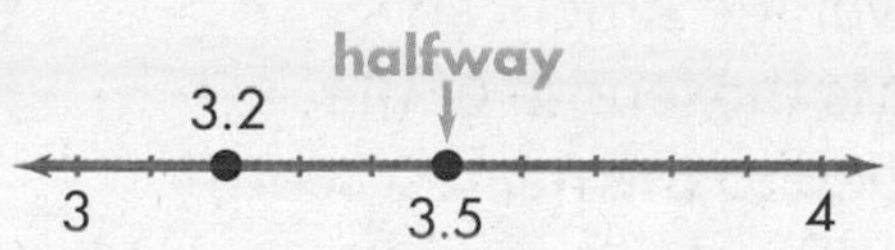

Another Example

Round 3.2 to the nearest whole number.

Is 3.2 closer to 3 or 4?

Step 1	Step 2	Step 3
Find the rounding place. Look at the digit to the right of the rounding place. $\underline{3}.2$	If the digit is 5 or greater, add 1 to the rounding digit. If the digit is less than 5, leave the rounding digit alone. Since $2 < 5$, leave 3 the same.	Drop the digits to the right of the decimal point. Drop the decimal point. 3.2 rounds to 3.

Guided Practice*

Do You Understand?

1. To round 74.58 to the nearest tenth, which digit do you look at? What is 74.58 rounded to the nearest tenth?

2. **Construct Arguments** A car-rental service charges customers for the number of miles they travel, rounded to the nearest whole mile. George travels 40.8 miles. For how many miles will he be charged? Explain.

Do You Know How?

In **3–10**, round each number to the place of the underlined digit.

3. $1\underline{6}.5$
4. $5\underline{6}.1$
5. $1.\underline{3}2$
6. $42.\underline{7}8$
7. $1.6\underline{5}2$
8. $582.\underline{0}4$
9. $80{,}547.6\underline{4}5$
10. $135{,}701.\underline{9}49$

Independent Practice

In **11–14**, round each decimal to the nearest whole number.

11. 4.5
12. 57.3
13. 34.731
14. 215.39

In **15–18**, round each number to the place of the underlined digit.

15. $7.\underline{1}58$
16. $0.7\underline{5}8$
17. $6.4\underline{3}82$
18. $84.\underline{7}32$

*For another example, see Set E on page 50.

Problem Solving

19. The picture at the right shows the length of an average American alligator. What is the length of the alligator rounded to the nearest tenth?

20. Reasoning Name two different numbers that round to 8.21 when rounded to the nearest hundredth.

21. Number Sense To the nearest hundred, what is the greatest whole number that rounds to 2,500? the least whole number?

22. Draw all of the lines of symmetry in the figure shown below.

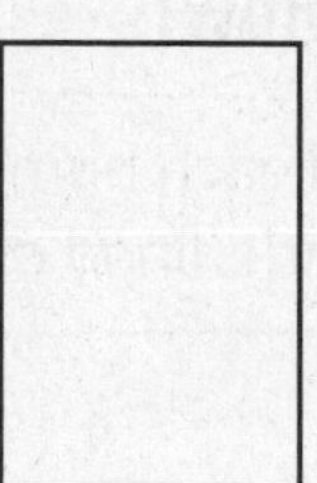

23. Higher Order Thinking Emma needs 2 pounds of ground meat to make a meatloaf. She has one package with 2.36 pounds of ground meat and another package with 2.09 pounds of ground meat. She uses rounding and finds that both packages are close to 2 pounds. Explain how Emma can choose the package closer to 2 pounds.

24. Make Sense and Persevere Robert slices a large loaf of bread to make 12 sandwiches. He makes 3 turkey sandwiches and 5 veggie sandwiches. The rest are ham sandwiches. What fraction of the sandwiches Robert makes are ham?

25. Algebra After buying school supplies, Ruby had $32 left over. She spent $4 on notebooks, $18 on a backpack, and $30 on a new calculator. How much money, *m*, did Ruby start with? Write an equation to show your work.

Assessment

26. Find two numbers that round to 35.4 when rounded to the nearest tenth. Write the numbers in the box.

35.45 34.42 35.391 35.345 35.44 35.041

Name ______________________________

Homework & Practice 1-6

Round Decimals

Another Look!

An African Watusi steer's horn measures 95.25 centimeters around. What is 95.25 rounded to the nearest tenth?

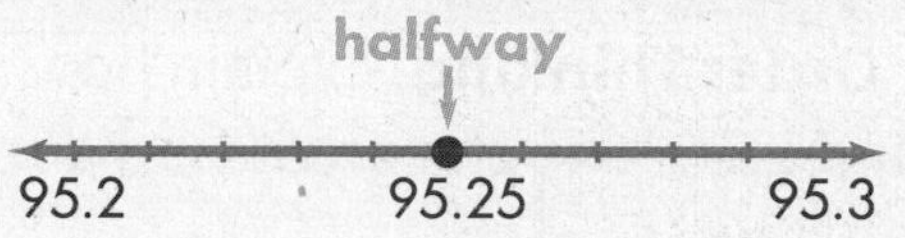

On a number line, 95.25 is halfway between 95.2 and 95.3.

Step 1

Find the rounding place. Look at the digit to the right of the rounding place.

95.$\underline{2}$5

Step 2

If the digit is 5 or greater, increase the rounding digit by 1. If the digit is less than 5, the rounding digit stays the same.

The digit to the right is 5, so increase the 2 in the tenths place to 3.

Step 3

Drop the digits to the right of the rounding digit.

95.25 rounded to the nearest tenth is 95.3.

1. Ian mailed a package that weighed 5.63 pounds. What is the first step in rounding this number to the nearest tenth? What is the next step? What is 5.63 rounded to the nearest tenth?

In **2–5**, round each decimal to the nearest whole number.

2. 6.7　　**3.** 12.1　　**4.** 30.92　　**5.** 1.086

In **6–13**, round each number to the place of the underlined digit.

6. 32.$\underline{6}$5　　**7.** 3.2$\underline{4}$6　　**8.** 41.$\underline{0}$73　　**9.** 0.4$\underline{2}$4

10. 6.$\underline{0}$99　　**11.** 6.$\underline{1}$3　　**12.** 18$\underline{3}$.92　　**13.** 905.2$\underline{5}$5

14. A-Z **Vocabulary** Complete the sentence using one of the words below.

power **base** **exponent**

In 10^6, the 10 is the ___________.

15. Be Precise If the area of a park is exactly halfway between 2.4 and 2.5 acres, what is the area of the park?

16. Does the blue line appear to be a line of symmetry? Explain.

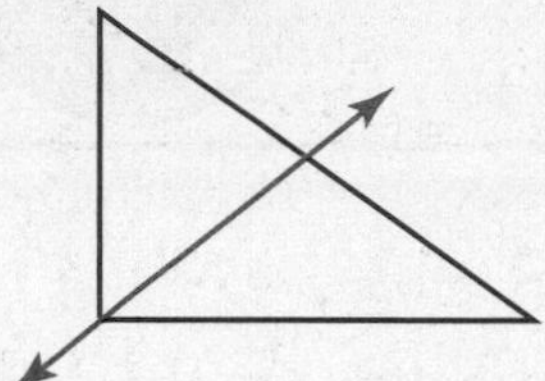

17. Higher Order Thinking Explain how you can round 25.691 to the greatest place.

18. Model with Math A professional baseball team won 84 games this season. The team won 14 more games than it lost. There were no ties. How many games did the team lose? How many did it play?

?	
84	?

19. Construct Arguments Rounded to the nearest dime, what is the greatest amount of money that rounds to $105.40? What is the least amount of money that rounds to $105.40? Explain your answers.

20. Math and Science The students in Mr. Bhatia's class measure the length of four bees. The students round the lengths to the nearest tenth. Whose bee has a length that rounds to 0.5 inch? 0.8 inch?

DATA

Student	Bee Lengths
Isabel	0.841 inch
Pablo	0.45 inch
Wendi	0.55 inch
Brett	0.738 inch

✓ Assessment

21. Find two numbers that round to 15.5 when rounded to the nearest tenth. Write the numbers in the box.

15.04 15.55 15.508 15.445 15.0 15.49

Name ______________________

Problem Solving

Lesson 1-7

Look for and Use Structure

I can ...
look for and use the structure of our decimal place value system to solve problems.

I can also use decimal place value to solve problems.

Solve & Share

Angie volunteers in the school library after school. The librarian gave her a stack of books and told her to use the number on each book to shelve it where it belongs.

How can Angie arrange the books in order from least to greatest to make shelving them easier?

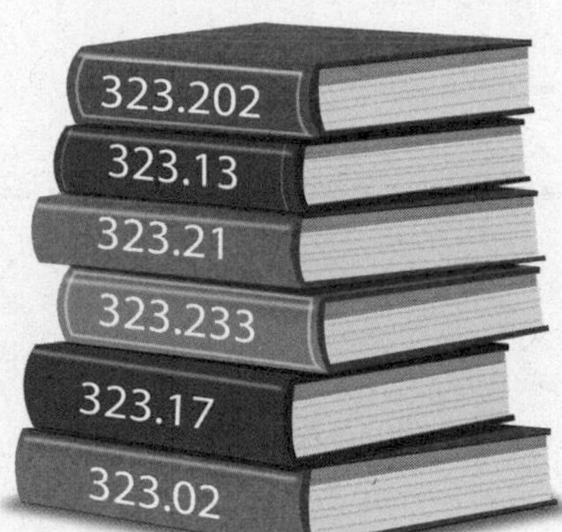

Thinking Habits

Be a good thinker!
These questions can help you.

- What patterns can I see and describe?
- How can I use the patterns to solve the problem?
- Can I see expressions and objects in different ways?
- What equivalent expressions can I use?

Look Back! **Use Structure** Explain why 323.202 is less than 323.21 even though 202 is greater than 21.

How Can You Use Structure to Solve Problems?

A

Analyze the chart. What do you notice that can help you complete the chart?

0.01	0.02	0.03					0.08		0.1
0.11				0.15	0.16			0.19	
0.21								0.29	
	0.32		0.34			0.37			

What do I need to do to solve this problem?

I can use the structure of the decimal place value system to complete the chart.

You can look for patterns to find the missing numbers.

B

How can I make use of structure to solve this problem?

I can

- find and describe patterns.
- use the patterns to see how the numbers are organized.
- analyze patterns to see the structure in the table.
- break the problem into simpler parts.

C

Solve

Here's my thinking...

As you move down the columns, tenths increase by 1 while the hundredths stay the same.

Moving from left to right in the rows, tenths stay the same, except for the last number, while the hundredths increase by 1.

Column 1

0.01
0.11
0.21
0.31

Row 1

0.01	0.02	0.03	0.04	0.05	0.06	0.07	0.08	0.09	0.1

Convince Me! **Use Structure** Write the missing numbers. Explain how you can use structure to find the last number in the bottom row.

0.01	0.02	0.03	0.04	0.05	0.06	0.07	0.08	0.09	0.1
0.11				0.15	0.16			0.19	
0.21								0.29	
0.31	0.32		0.34			0.37			

Name ______________________________

Practice Buddy Tools Assessment

Guided Practice*

Use Structure

Each of these grids is a part of a decimal number chart similar to the one on page 42.

1. Describe the pattern for moving from a pink square to a green square. Then write the missing numbers.

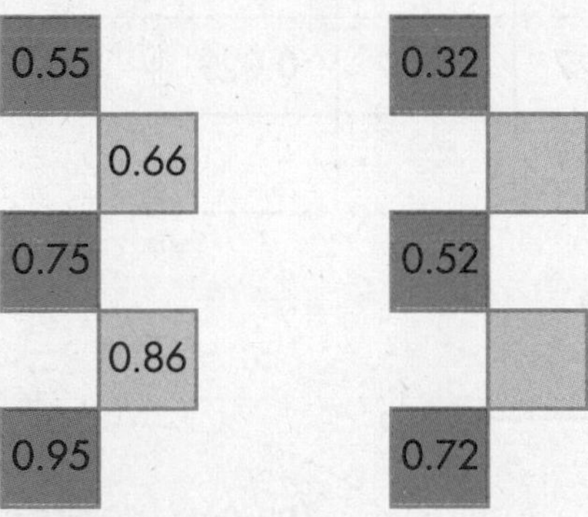

2. How can you use patterns to find the number that would be in the box below 0.52?

Independent Practice

Use Structure

Pamela is hiking. When she returns to camp, she passes the mile markers shown at the right.

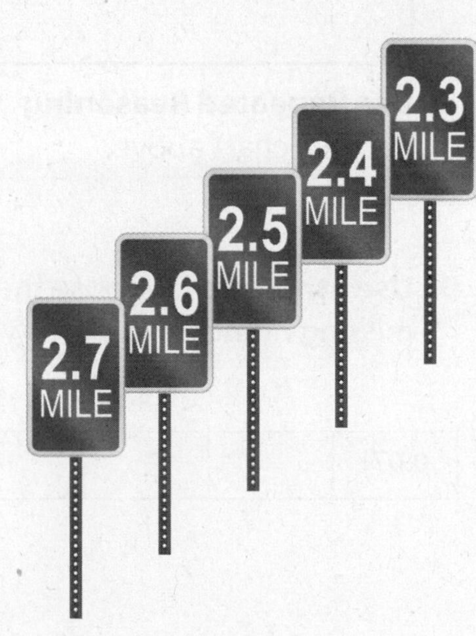

3. Explain how you can use structure to find the decimal numbers that will be shown on the next four mile markers.

4. Pamela stops at the 1.8 mile marker. Where will she be if she walks one tenth of a mile towards camp? one mile towards camp? Explain.

*For another example, see Set F on page 50.

Problem Solving

Performance Assessment

Thousandths Chart
The students in Ms. Lowell's class wrote a thousandths decimal chart on the board. Some of the numbers got erased.

0.001	0.002		0.004	0.005	0.006				0.01
0.011		0.013			0.016	0.017		0.019	0.02
	0.022					0.027		0.029	
0.031	0.032		0.034	0.035		0.037			

5. Use Structure Describe the pattern for moving across a row from left to right.

6. Be Precise How does the pattern change in the last square of each row?

7. Use Structure Describe the pattern for moving down a column.

8. Use Repeated Reasoning Write the missing numbers in the decimal chart above.

9. Use Structure Suppose the students add to the chart. Write the missing numbers in the row and the column below.

0.071						0.077			

0.056
0.086

Name ______________________________

Homework & Practice 1-7

Look for and Use Structure

Another Look!

This grid is a part of a decimal number chart similar to the one on page 42. Write the missing number in each of the colored squares.

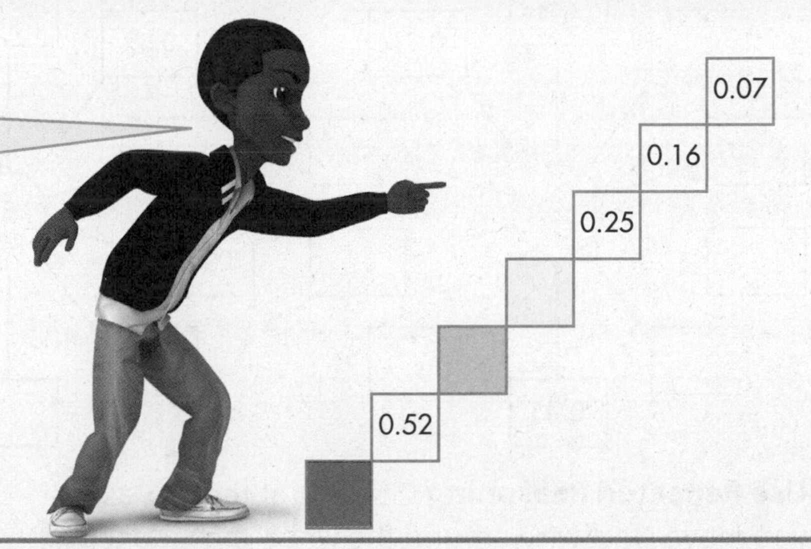

Tell how you can use structure.

Analyze the number pattern to find the structure of the grid.
Use the pattern to write the missing numbers.

Moving down and left, the tenths increase by 1, and the hundredths decrease by 1.
The number in the yellow box is 0.34.
The number in the green box is 0.43.
The number in the pink box is 0.61.

Use Structure

In **1–3**, each grid is a part of a decimal number chart similar to the one on page 42. Write the missing numbers.

1.

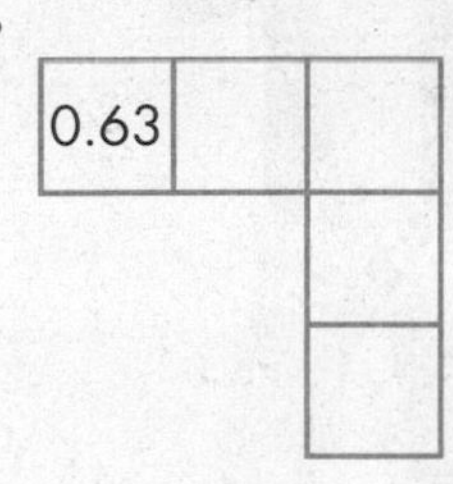

2.

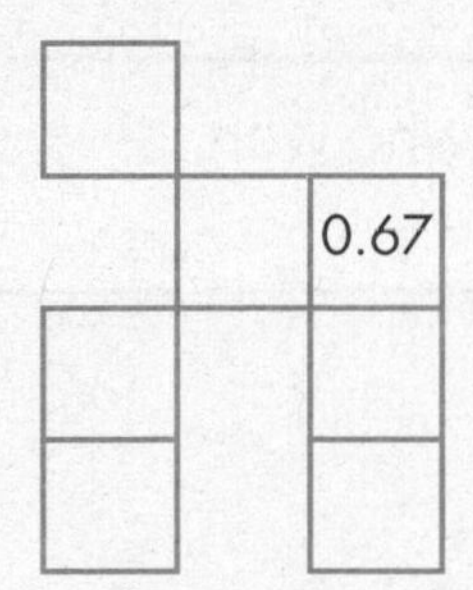

3.

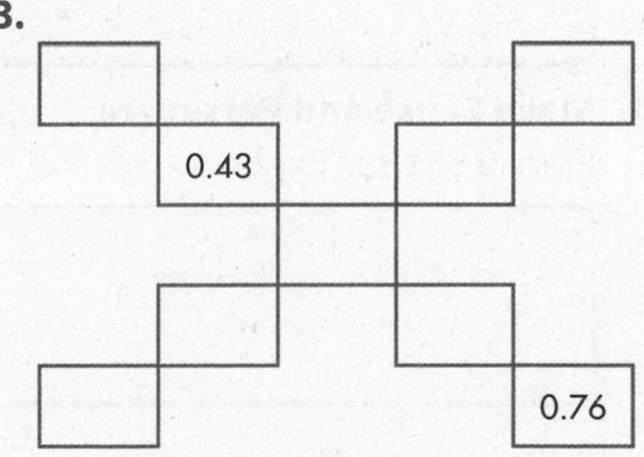

Performance Assessment

Decimal Wheels

Franco and Lisa are playing a game with decimal numbers. The first player to correctly write the missing numbers in each decimal wheel is the winner.

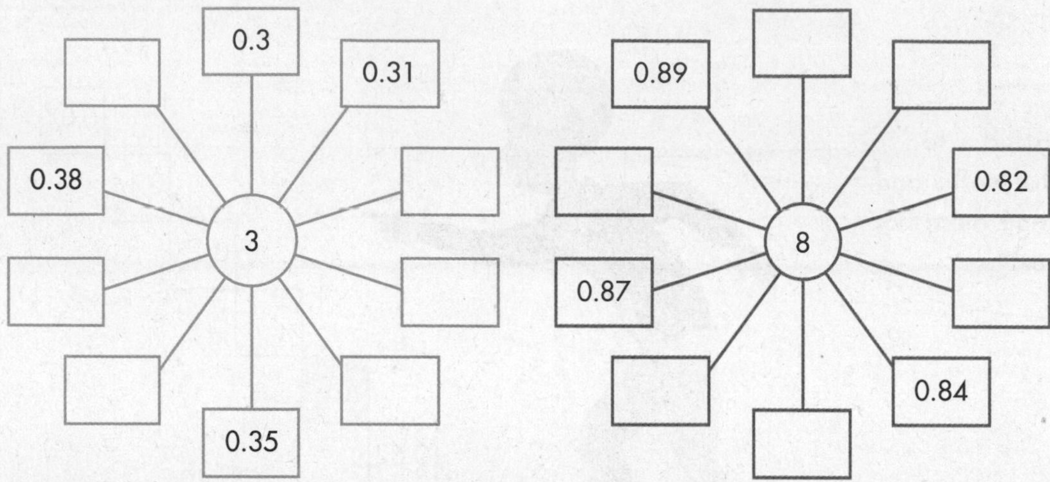

4. Use Repeated Reasoning Starting at the top, as you move clockwise around the wheel, how do the numbers change?

5. Be Precise Write the missing numbers in each decimal wheel.

6. Use Structure Suppose some of the boxes in a decimal wheel show these numbers: 0.62, 0.63, 0.67, and 0.69. Explain how to use structure to find the number that is written in the circle at the center of the decimal wheel.

7. Make Sense and Persevere Can you tell who won, Franco or Lisa? Explain.

Name ____________________

TOPIC 1 Fluency Practice Activity

Find a Match

Work with a partner. Point to a clue.

Read the clue.

Look below the clues to find a match. Write the clue letter in the box above the match.

Find a match for every clue.

I can ...
add and subtract multi-digit whole numbers.

Clues

A The sum is between 15,000 and 20,000.

B The difference is less than 10,000.

C The difference is between 41,000 and 42,000.

D The sum is exactly 52,397.

E The difference is between 82,000 and 84,000.

F The sum is greater than 79,000.

G The sum is exactly 52,407.

H The difference is exactly 42,024.

☐ 98,765 − 56,789	☐ 57,202 − 15,178	☐ 12,345 + 7,654	☐ 38,979 + 40,121
☐ 40,449 + 11,958	☐ 342,005 − 258,819	☐ 41,806 + 10,591	☐ 41,986 − 32,047

TOPIC 1

Vocabulary Review

Word List

- base
- equivalent decimals
- expanded form
- exponent
- power
- thousandths
- value

Understand Vocabulary

Choose the best term from the Word List. Write it on the blank.

1. Decimal numbers that name the same part of a whole or the same point on a number line are called __________________.

2. The __________________ of a digit in a number depends on its place in the number.

3. The product that results from multiplying the same number over and over is a(n) __________________ of that number.

4. A digit in the hundredths place has ten times the value of the same digit in the __________________ place.

5. In 10^5, the number 10 is the __________________.

Draw a line from each number in Column A to the same number in Column B.

	Column A	Column B
6.	$7 \times 1{,}000 + 9 \times 10 + 2 \times 1$	4,000
7.	10^4	7,092
8.	4×10^3	10,000
9.	3.08	3.080

Use Vocabulary in Writing

10. Explain why each 8 in the number 8.888 has a different value. Use one or more terms from the Word List in your explanation.

Name ___

TOPIC 1

Reteaching

Set A pages 5–10

How can you write 7,000 using exponents?

$7{,}000 = 7 \times 10 \times 10 \times 10 = 7 \times 10^3$

So, using exponents 7,000 is written as 7×10^3.

Remember the number of zeros in the product is the same as the exponent.

Find each product.

1. 9×10^1
2. $8 \times 1{,}000$
3. 5×10^2
4. 2×10^5

Set B pages 11–16

Write the number name and tell the value of the underlined digit for 93<u>0</u>,365.

Nine hundred thirty thousand, three hundred sixty-five

Since the 0 is in the thousands place, its value is 0 thousands, or 0.

Use digital tools to solve these and other problems.

Remember you can find the value of a digit by its place in a number.

Write the number name and tell the value of the underlined digit.

1. <u>9</u>,000,009
2. 4<u>8</u>5,002,000
3. 2<u>5</u>,678
4. <u>1</u>7,874,000

Set C pages 17–22, 23–28

A place-value chart can help you write the standard form, expanded form, and number name for a decimal.

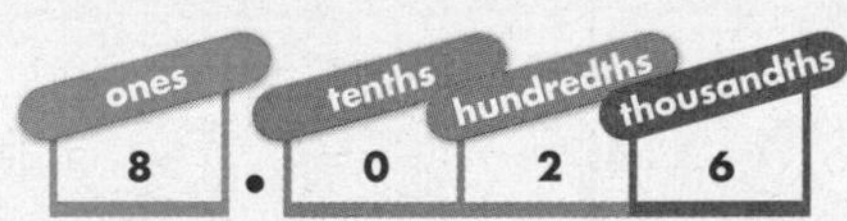

Standard form: 8.026

Expanded form: $8 + 2 \times \frac{1}{100} + 6 \times \frac{1}{1{,}000}$

Number name: Eight and twenty-six thousandths

Remember the word *and* is written for the decimal point.

1. How can you write 0.044 as a fraction? How are the values of the two 4s related in 0.044?

Write each number in standard form.

2. eight and fifty-nine hundredths
3. seven and three thousandths
4. $3 + 2 \times \frac{1}{10} + 4 \times \frac{1}{1{,}000}$

Set D pages 29–34

Compare. Write >, <, or =.

8.45 ◯ 8.47

Line up the decimal points. Start at the left to compare. Find the first place where the digits are different.

$8.4\underline{5}$
$8.4\underline{7}$ 0.05 < 0.07

So, 8.45 < 8.47.

Remember that equivalent decimals, such as 0.45 and 0.450, can help you compare numbers.

Compare. Write >, <, or =.

1. 0.584 ◯ 0.58

2. 9.327 ◯ 9.236

3. 5.2 ◯ 5.20

4. 5.643 ◯ 5.675

5. 0.07 ◯ 0.08

Set E pages 35–40

Round $12.0\underline{8}7$ to the place of the underlined digit.

$12.0\underline{8}7$ Look at the digit following the underlined digit. Look at 7.

Round to the next greater number of hundredths because 7 > 5.

12.087 rounded to the nearest hundredth is 12.09.

Remember that rounding a number means replacing it with a number that tells about how many or how much.

Round each number to the place of the underlined digit.

1. $10.\underline{2}45$ **2.** $\underline{7}3.4$

3. $0.1\underline{4}5$ **4.** $3.\underline{9}99$

5. $13.0\underline{2}3$ **6.** $45.\underline{3}98$

Set F pages 41–46

Think about these questions to help you **look for and use structure** to understand and explain patterns with decimal numbers.

Thinking Habits

- What patterns can I see and describe?
- How can I use the patterns to solve the problem?
- Can I see expressions and objects in different ways?
- What equivalent expressions can I use?

Remember to check that all of your answers follow a pattern.

Each grid is part of a decimal number chart. Write the missing numbers to complete the grids.

1.

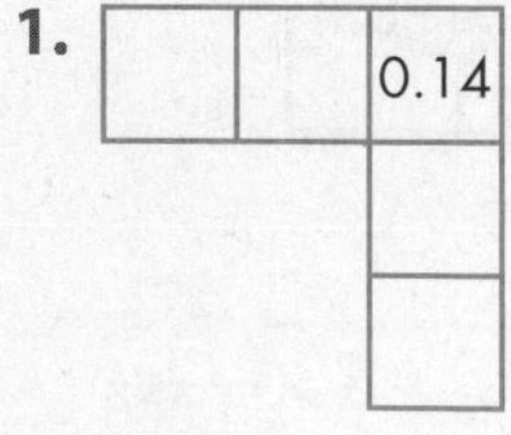

2.

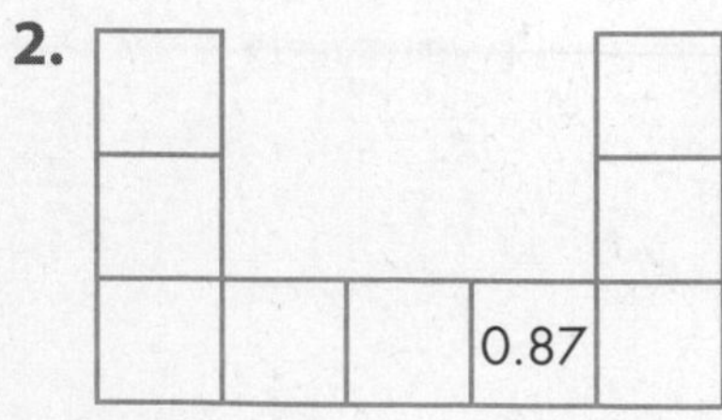

Name ______________________________

TOPIC 1

Assessment

1. Choose all the expressions that are equal to 6×10^3.

- ☐ 6×100
- ☐ $6 \times 1{,}000$
- ☐ $6 \times 10{,}000$
- ☐ $6 \times 10 \times 10 \times 10$
- ☐ $6 \times 10 \times 10 \times 10 \times 10$

2. A national park has eighty thousand, nine-hundred twenty-three and eighty-six hundredths acres of land. Which shows this in standard form?

- Ⓐ 80,923.086
- Ⓑ 80,923.68
- Ⓒ 80,923.806
- Ⓓ 80,923.86

3. For items **3a-3d**, choose Yes or No to tell if the digit in the hundreds place is $\frac{1}{10}$ the value of the digit in the thousands place.

3a. 8,556 ○ Yes ○ No

3b. 6,855 ○ Yes ○ No

3c. 5,568 ○ Yes ○ No

3d. 5,656 ○ Yes ○ No

4. Mrs. Martin has $7,000 in her savings account. Alonzo has $\frac{1}{10}$ as much money in his account as Mrs. Martin. How much money does Alonzo have in his account?

5. Choose all the comparisons that are true.

- ☐ $4.15 > 4.051$
- ☐ $1.054 > 1.45$
- ☐ $5.14 < 5.041$
- ☐ $5.104 < 5.41$
- ☐ $5.014 < 5.41$

6. Luke shaded 20 squares on his hundredths grid. Bekka shaded 30 squares on her hundredths grid.

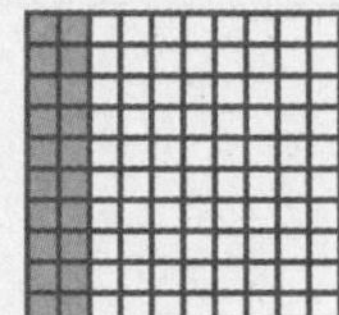

Part A

Write two decimals greater than Luke's decimal and less than Bekka's decimal.

Part B

Write two decimals equivalent to Luke's decimal.

7. Determine the pattern, then write the decimals to complete the decimal grid.

☐		☐
	0.34	
☐	☐	☐
	☐	
☐		0.65

8. The weight of Darrin's phone is 3.405 ounces. What is 3.405 written in expanded form?

Ⓐ $3 \times 1 + 4 \times \frac{1}{10} + 5 \times \frac{1}{1,000}$

Ⓑ $3 \times 10 + 4 \times \frac{1}{10} + 5 \times \frac{1}{1,000}$

Ⓒ $3 \times 10 + 4 \times \frac{1}{10} + 5 \times \frac{1}{100}$

Ⓓ $3 \times 1 + 4 \times \frac{1}{100} + 5 \times \frac{1}{1,000}$

9. Elaine has a piece of wire that is 2.16 meters long. Dikembe has a piece of wire that is 2.061 meters long. Whose piece of wire is longer? How can you tell?

10. In a basketball tournament, Dimitri averaged 12.375 rebounds per game. What is 12.375 written in expanded form? How is it written with number names?

11. The numbers below follow a pattern.

0.006 0.06 0.6 6 ____ ____

Part A

What are the next two numbers in the pattern?

Part B

What is the relationship between the terms in the pattern?

12. Kendra and her horse completed the barrel racing course in 15.839 seconds. What is this number rounded to the nearest tenth? Explain how you decided.

Name ______________________________

TOPIC 1

Performance Assessment

Fruits and Vegetables

Henry recorded how many pounds of fruits and vegetables his family bought during the past two months.

Fruit	Weight (lb)
apples	2.068
blueberries	1.07
lemons	1.031
oranges	3.502
peaches	2.608
pears	3.592

Vegetable	Weight (lb)
asparagus	2.317
beets	1.862
celery	1.402
corn	2.556
potatoes	3.441
red onions	1.861

1. Pick four fruits and list them in the table below.

Part A

Round each fruit's weight to the nearest 0.1 pound. Write the rounded weight in the next column.

Fruit	Rounded Weight (lb)	Fruit	Rounded Weight (lb)

Part B

Explain how you rounded the weights of the fruits.

2. Pick four vegetables and list them in the table below.

Part A

Round each vegetable's weight to the nearest 0.01 pound. Write the rounded weight in the next column.

Vegetable	Rounded Weight (lb)	Vegetable	Rounded Weight (lb)

Part B

Explain how you rounded the weights of the vegetables.

3. Use $<$, $>$, or $=$ to compare the weights of blueberries and lemons.

4. When rounded to the nearest hundredth, two items will round to the same decimal. What two items are they?

5. How does writing the weight for potatoes in expanded form show why the same digit can have different values?

6. What is the relationship between the values of the two 4s in the weight of the potatoes?

7. Write the number of pounds of celery Henry's family bought using number names and in expanded form.

8. The store where Henry's family shops sold 10^3 times as many pounds of corn as Henry's family bought.

Part A

How many pounds of corn did the store sell? Write your answer in standard form and with number names.

Part B

Explain how you found your answer.

Add and Subtract Decimals to Hundredths

Essential Questions: How can sums and differences of decimals be estimated? What are the standard procedures for adding and subtracting whole numbers and decimals? How can sums and differences be found mentally?

All living things are classified as producers, consumers, or decomposers.

Producers make food. Consumers use the food producers make or eat other organisms.

We are consumers! Here's a project on how much food consumers need.

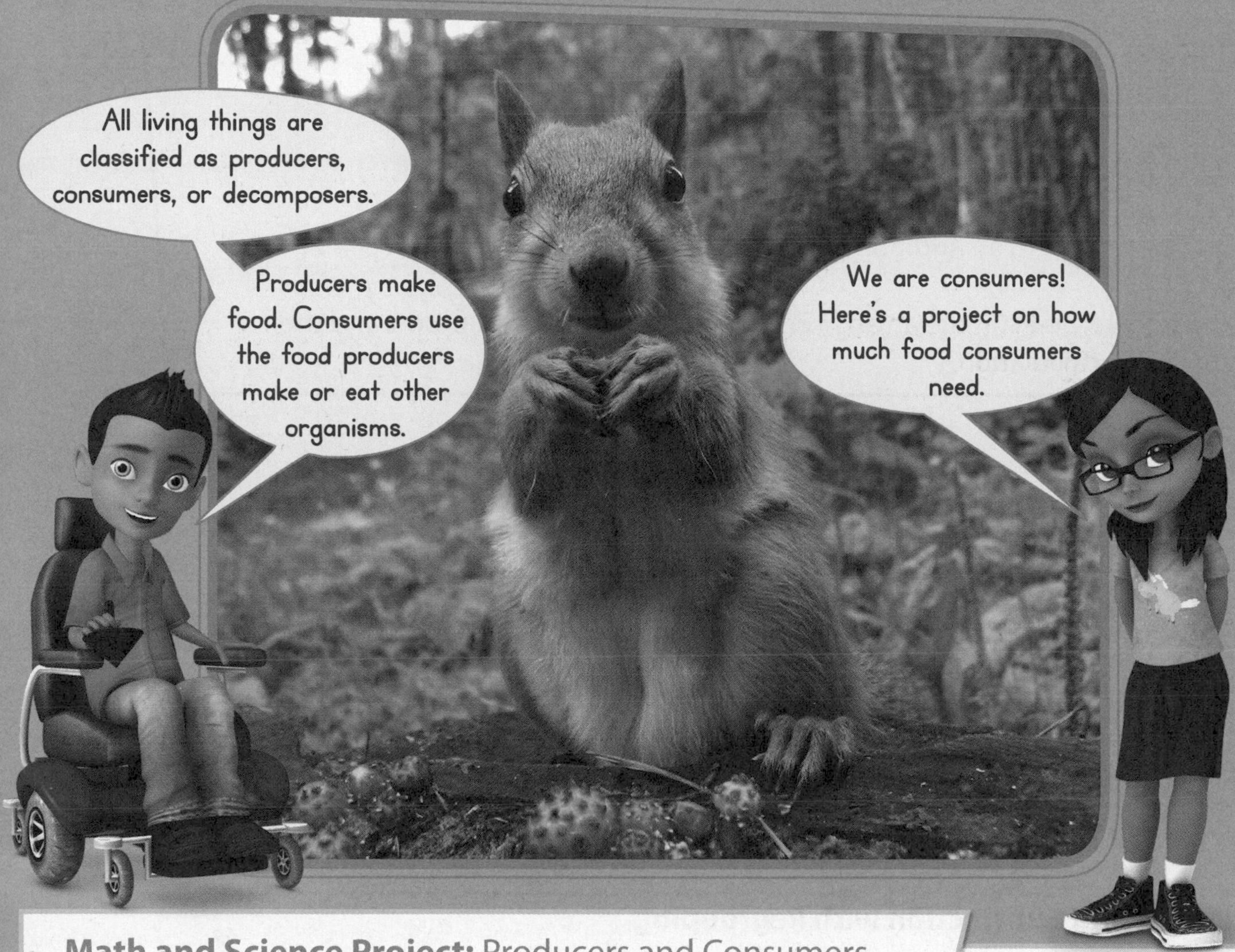

Math and Science Project: Producers and Consumers

Do Research Use the Internet or other sources to find information about producers and consumers.

Journal: Write a Report Include what you found. Also in your report:

- What do producers need to survive? What do consumers need to survive?
- Give at least three examples of both producers and consumers.
- Write and solve decimal addition and subtraction problems for the amounts of food the consumers need.

Name ________________________________

Review What You Know

Vocabulary

Choose the best term from the box.
Write it on the blank.

- addend
- difference
- equivalent
- inverse operations
- round
- sum

1. The __________ is the result of subtracting one number from another.

2. Two numbers or expressions that have the same value are __________.

3. The answer to an addition problem is the __________.

4. One way to estimate an answer is to __________ the numbers and then do the calculation.

Round Decimals

Round each number to the nearest tenth.

5. 74.362 **6.** 28.45 **7.** 13.09

Round each number to the nearest hundredth.

8. 43.017 **9.** 186.555 **10.** 222.222

Round each number to the underlined digit.

11. $8\underline{4}.59$ **12.** $2.9\underline{4}8$ **13.** $30.1\underline{2}5$

Addition and Subtraction with Regrouping

Find each sum or difference.

14. 9,536 + 495 **15.** 612 − 357 **16.** 5,052 − 761

17. Vivica sees that a printer costs $679 and a computer costs $1,358. What is the total cost of the printer and the computer?

18. The Pecos River is 926 miles long, and the Brazos River is 1,280 miles long. How many miles longer is the Brazos River than the Pecos River?

Ⓐ 2,206 miles Ⓑ 1,206 miles Ⓒ 364 miles Ⓓ 354 miles

My Word Cards

Use the examples for each word on the front of the card to help complete the definitions on the back.

A-Z Glossary

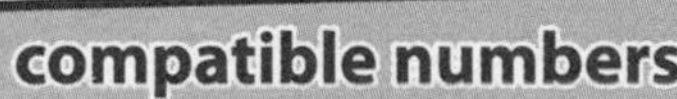

compatible numbers

Estimate 547 + 294 and 547 − 294.

547 is about 550; 294 is about 300.

547 + 294 is about 550 + 300 = 850.

547 − 294 is about 550 − 300 = 250.

compensation

Find 648 + 325.

↓ Add 2

650 + 325 = 975

↓ Subtract 2

So, 648 + 325 = 973.

Commutative Property of Addition

6,283 + 4,129 = 4,129 + 6,283

10,412 = 10,412

Associative Property of Addition

243 + (157 + 732) = (243 + 157) + 732

243 + 889 = 400 + 732

1,132 = 1,132

My Word Cards

Complete the definition. Extend learning by writing your own definitions.

_________________________ is adjusting one number to make a computation easier and balancing the adjustment by changing another number.

_________________________ are numbers that are easy to compute with mentally.

The _________________________ _________________________ states that addends can be regrouped and the sum remains the same.

The _________________________ _________________________ states that addends can be added in any order and the sum remains the same.

Name ____________________

Lesson 2-1
Mental Math

I can ...
use mental math to solve addition and subtraction problems.

I can also reason about math.

Solve & Share

Three pieces of software cost $20.75, $10.59, and $18.25. What is the total cost of the software? ***Use mental math to solve.***

You can use reasoning to help you. What do you know about adding three numbers that will make it easier to solve this problem?

Look Back! Construct Arguments Which two numbers above were easy to add in your head? Why?

Learn Glossary

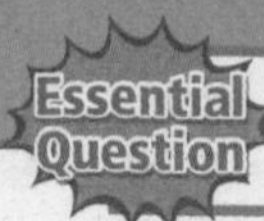

How Can You Use Mental Math to Add?

A

Properties of addition can help you find the total cost of these three items.

The Commutative Property and Associative Property make it easy to add $11.45 + $3.39 + $9.55.

Associative Property lets you change the grouping of addends.
($11.45 + $3.39) + $9.55 =
$11.45 + ($3.39 + $9.55)

Commutative Property lets you add two decimals in any order.
$11.45 + $3.39 = $3.39 + $11.45

$11.45

$3.39

$9.55

B

Use the Commutative Property to change the order.

$11.45 + ($3.39 + $9.55) =
$11.45 + ($9.55 + $3.39)

Use the Associative Property to change the grouping.

$11.45 + ($9.55 + $3.39) =
($11.45 + $9.55) + $3.39

C

Add $11.45 and $9.55 first because they are easy to compute mentally.

$11.45 + $9.55 = $21

$21 + $3.39 = $24.39

The three items cost a total of $24.39.

Compatible numbers are numbers that are easy to compute mentally.

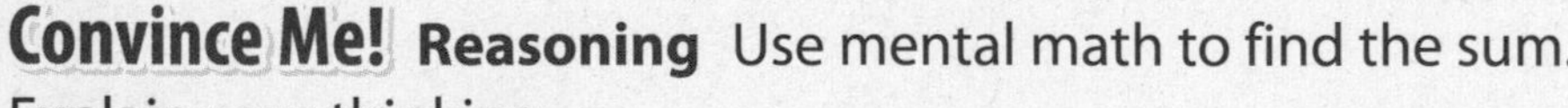

Convince Me! **Reasoning** Use mental math to find the sum. Explain your thinking.

Jim earns $22.50, $14.75, and $8.50 on three different days. How much did he earn in all?

Name ______________________

Practice Buddy Tools Assessment

Another Example

With compensation, adjust one or both numbers to make the calculation easier. Then adjust the difference or sum to get the final answer.

Use compensation to subtract.

Find 4.25 − 0.08 mentally.

4.25 − 0.10 = 4.15

0.02 too much was subtracted → Compensate, add back 0.02

4.25 − 0.08 = 4.17

Use compensation to add.

Find \$3.47 + \$4.35 mentally.

\$3.50 + \$4.35 = \$7.85

Add 0.03 → Compensate, take away 0.03

\$3.47 + \$4.35 = \$7.82

Guided Practice*

Do You Understand?

1. **Be Precise** In the addition example above, why is the answer \$0.03 less than \$7.85?

2. Which problem is easier to subtract, 15.50 − 8.75 or 15.75 − 9? Explain.

Do You Know How?

In **3–6**, use mental math to add or subtract.

3. 12 + 3.04 + 8.28

4. 6.97 + 4.15

5. 9.04 − 6.98

6. 4.02 + 0.19 + 16.48

Independent Practice

Leveled Practice In **7–12**, use properties and mental math to add or subtract.

7. 7.1 + 5.4 + 2.9 =
   ____ + 5.4 =
   ______

8. 373.4 − 152.9 =
   373.4 − ______ = 220.4
   ______ + 0.1 = ______

9. \$18.25 + \$7.99 + \$4.75

10. 1.05 + 3 + 4.28 + 0.95

11. 2,504 + 140 + 160

12. 35.7 − 14.8

*For another example, see Set A on page 103.

Problem Solving

13. **Model with Math** Joanne bought three books that cost \$3.95, \$4.99, and \$6.05. How much did she spend in all? Use compensation and mental math to find the sum.

? spent →

?		
\$3.95	\$4.99	\$6.05

14. **Construct Arguments** Use compensation to find each difference mentally. Explain how you found each difference.

A 67 − 29

B 456 − 198

15. **Number Sense** The table shows how many points Eduardo scored during each game. Use mental math to find how many points he scored in the first three games.

Game	Points
1	54
2	19
3	26
4	10

16. On three different days at her job, Sue earned \$27, \$33, and \$49. She needs to earn \$100 to buy a desk for her computer. If she buys the desk, how much money will she have left over?

17. A shelf can hold 50 DVDs. Jill has 27 DVDs. She plans to buy 5 new ones. Each DVD costs \$9. After she buys the new ones, how many more DVDs will the shelf hold?

18. **Reasoning** When finding the difference of two numbers mentally, can you use the Commutative Property? Explain.

19. **Higher Order Thinking** Daria bought a skein of alpaca yarn for \$47.50, a skein of angora yarn for \$32.14, a skein of wool yarn for \$16.50, and a pair of knitting needles for \$3.86. How much did she spend in all? Describe how you calculated your answer.

✓ Assessment

20. Mrs. Healer's class took a field trip to a park 12.3 miles away. Mr. Dean's class drove 4.9 miles to the public library. How much farther did Mrs. Healer's class travel than Mr. Dean's class? Explain how you used mental math to determine the difference.

Name ______________________

Homework & Practice 2-1

Mental Math

Another Look!

You can use properties of addition, compatible numbers, or compensation to help you find the answers.

Use properties of addition to find 5.7 + 6 + 4.3.	Use compensation to find 12.7 + 0.9.	Use compensation to find 18.3 − 6.9.
5.7 + 6 + 4.3 Use the Commutative Property. 5.7 + 4.3 + 6 Add. 10 + 6 = 16	12.7 + 0.9 Add 0.1 to 0.9. 12.7 + 1 = 13.7 Subtract 0.1. 12.7 + 0.9 = 13.6	18.3 − 6.9 Add 0.1 to 6.9. 18.3 − 7 = 11.3 0.1 too much was subtracted. Add 0.1. 18.3 − 6.9 = 11.4

Leveled Practice In **1–15**, use properties and mental math to solve.

1. 275 + 180 + 120 =
275 + ______ =
______

2. 19.5 + 24 + 7.5 =
19.5 + ______ + 24 =
______ + 24 = ______

3. 87.2 − 25.9 =
87.2 − ______ = 61.2
______ + 0.1 = ______

4. 8.4 + 6.21 + 2.6

5. 7.35 + 1.47 + 9.65

6. 12.32 − 8

7. 75.25 − 11.92

8. 34.76 + 170 + 16.24

9. 54.3 − 19.74

10. 192.63 − 7.95

11. 201.96 + 38.7 + 0.84

12. 100.6 + 296.5

13. 421.2 − 305.8

14. 1,050 + 815 + 250

15. \$5.40 + \$8.70 + \$6.30

16. Model with Math James is buying school supplies. He buys a notebook for \$2.45, a package of mechanical pencils for \$3.79, and an eraser for \$1.55. Use mental math to find how much he spent in all.

? spent → ?

\$2.45	\$3.79	\$1.55

17. Generalize How is using mental math to add with decimals like using mental math to add whole numbers? How is it different?

18. Isabel made the following graph to show the daily share price for Company XYZ. What was the change in the price from Monday to Friday?

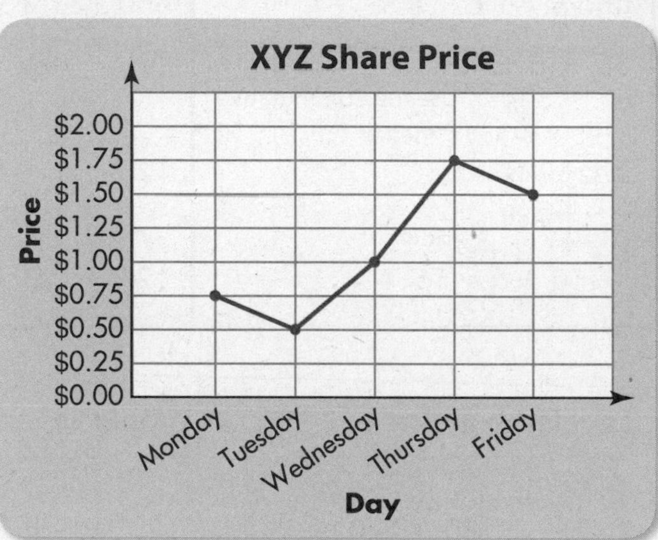

19. Higher Order Thinking Julia went to the supermarket and bought a dozen eggs, two pounds of bananas, and a jar of tomato sauce. A store coupon for \$0.70 off any purchase does not appear on the receipt. If Julia used the coupon, how much did she spend in all?

eggs 1 dozen	\$2.51
bananas 2 lb @ \$0.99/lb	\$1.98
tomato sauce	\$1.49

✓ Assessment

20. In a week Karry ran 9.3 miles and Tricia ran 4.4 miles. Use mental math to find how much farther Karry ran than Tricia. Explain how you determined the difference.

Name ___________________________

Lesson 2-2
Estimate Sums and Differences

I can ...
estimate sums and differences of decimals.

I can also reason about math.

Solve & Share

An amusement park has two roller coasters. One is 628 feet long, and the other is 485 feet long. If you ride both roller coasters, about how many feet will you travel in all? ***Use estimation to solve.***

You can use reasoning to decide what you are asked to find. Is the problem looking for an exact answer? How can you tell?

Look Back! Model with Math About how much longer is the one coaster than the other? Show your work.

Learn Glossary

Essential Question

How Can You Estimate Sums?

A

Students are collecting dog food to give to an animal shelter. Estimate how many pounds were collected in Weeks 3 and 4.

DATA

Week	Pounds of dog food
1	172.3
2	298
3	237.5
4	345.1
5	338

B

One Way

Round each addend to the nearest hundred.

$$\begin{array}{r} 237.5 \\ +\ 345.1 \\ \hline \end{array} \longrightarrow \begin{array}{r} 200 \\ +\ 300 \\ \hline 500 \end{array}$$

237.5 + 345.1 is about 500.

The students collected about 500 pounds of dog food in Weeks 3 and 4.

C

Another Way

Substitute compatible numbers.

$$\begin{array}{r} 237.5 \\ +\ 345.1 \\ \hline \end{array} \longrightarrow \begin{array}{r} 250 \\ +\ 350 \\ \hline 600 \end{array}$$

Compatible numbers are easy to add!

237.5 + 345.1 is about 600.

The students collected about 600 pounds of dog food in Weeks 3 and 4.

Convince Me! **Critique Reasoning** Tomás said, "We did great in Week 4! We collected just about twice as many pounds as in Week 1!"

Use estimation to decide if he is right. Explain your thinking.

Name ____________________

Another Example

You can estimate differences.

Estimate 22.8 − 13.9.

One Way

Round each number to the nearest whole number.

$$\begin{array}{r} 22.8 \\ -\ 13.9 \\ \hline \end{array} \longrightarrow \begin{array}{r} 23 \\ -\ 14 \\ \hline 9 \end{array}$$

22.8 − 13.9 is about 9.

Another Way

Substitute compatible numbers.

$$\begin{array}{r} 22.8 \\ -\ 13.9 \\ \hline \end{array} \longrightarrow \begin{array}{r} 25 \\ -\ 15 \\ \hline 10 \end{array}$$

22.8 − 13.9 is about 10.

Guided Practice*

Do You Understand?

1. **Construct Arguments** In the example above, which estimate is closer to the actual difference? How can you tell without subtracting?

2. In the example on page 66, the students collected more pounds of dog food in Week 4 than in Week 3. Estimate about how many more.

Do You Know How?

In **3–10**, estimate the sums and differences.

3. 49 + 22.88

4. 86.9 − 18

5. 179 + 277.1

6. 23.2 − 9.71

7. 23.8 − 4.7

8. 87.2 + 3.9

9. 38.9 − 21.4

10. 576 + 94.6

Independent Practice

In **11–18**, estimate each sum or difference.

11. 79.1 + 32.4

12. 788.9 − 572

13. 837 + 488.12

14. 418.5 − 23.7

15. 2.9 + 3.9

16. \$12.99 − \$3.95

17. 8.1 + 3.7 + 7.9

18. 3.8 + 4.1 + 3.3

For another example, see Set B on page 103.

Problem Solving

19. **Construct Arguments** The cost of one DVD is $16.98, and the cost of another DVD is $9.29. Ed estimated the cost of the two DVDs to be about $27. Is his estimate higher or lower than the actual cost? Explain.

20. **Higher Order Thinking** A teacher is organizing a field trip. Each bus can seat up to 46 people. Is it better to estimate a greater or lesser number than the actual number of people going on the field trip? Why?

21. The size and shape of Golden Gate Park are often compared to the size and shape of Central Park. About how many more acres does Golden Gate Park cover than Central Park?

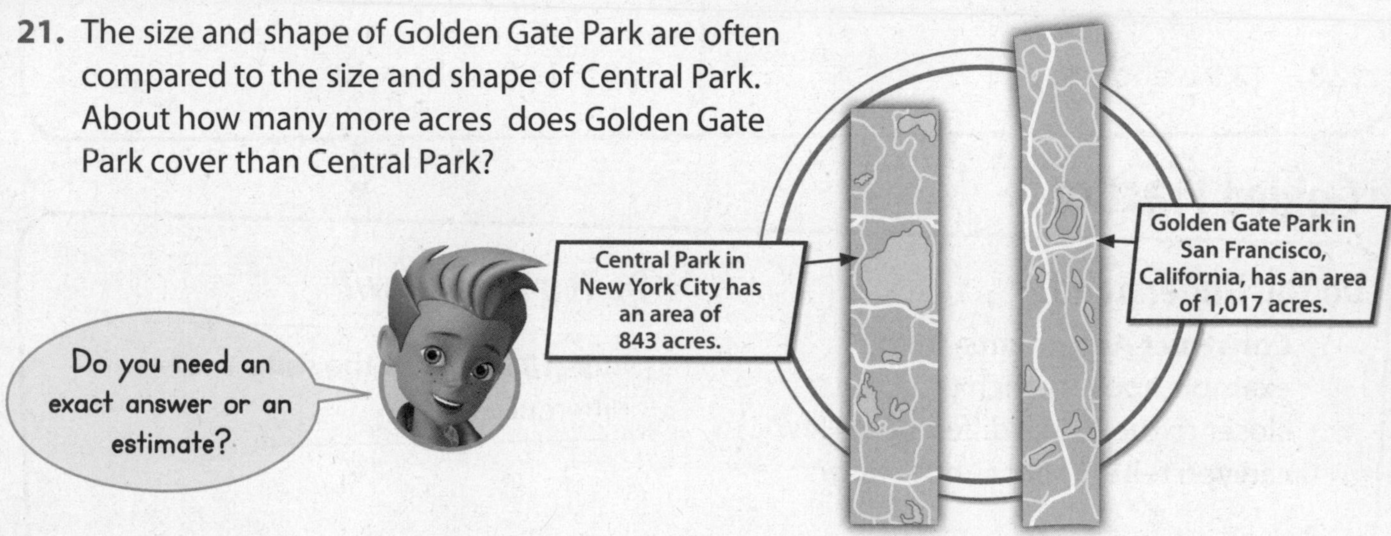

Assessment

22. Three rock samples have masses of 74.05 grams, 9.72 grams, and 45.49 grams. A scientist estimates the total mass of the samples by rounding each mass to the nearest whole number. Which lists the numbers will he add?

   Ⓐ 75, 10, and 46
   Ⓑ 74.1, 9.7, and 45.5
   Ⓒ 74, 10, and 45
   Ⓓ 75, 10, and 50

23. Umberto buys a game for $7.89 and some batteries for $5.49. He pays with a $20 bill. Which is the best estimate of how much change he should get?

   Ⓐ $5.00
   Ⓑ $7.00
   Ⓒ $13
   Ⓓ $17.00

Name ______________________________

Homework & Practice 2-2

Estimate Sums and Differences

Another Look!

DATA

Mr. Graham's Mileage Log

Day	Cities	Mileage
Monday	Mansley to Mt. Hazel	243.5
Tuesday	Mt. Hazel to Perkins	303
Wednesday	Perkins to Alberton	279.1
Thursday	Alberton to Fort Maynard	277.4

Round each number to the nearest hundred.

$$\begin{array}{rcr} 243.5 & \rightarrow & 200 \\ 303 & \rightarrow & 300 \\ 279.1 & \rightarrow & 300 \\ +\ 277.4 & \rightarrow & +\ 300 \\ \hline & & 1{,}100 \end{array}$$

Mr. Graham drove about 1,100 miles.

Estimate the difference to the nearest ten.

$$\begin{array}{rcr} 279.1 & \rightarrow & 280 \\ -\ 243.5 & \rightarrow & -\ 240 \\ \hline & & 40 \end{array}$$

Mr. Graham drove about 40 more miles on Wednesday than on Monday.

1. Marisol rode her bicycle each day for five days. Estimate how far she biked in all. Round each number to the nearest whole number.

12 + ____ + 18 + ____ + ____ = ____

She biked about ____ miles.

DATA

Marisol's Bike Rides

Day	Mileage
Monday	12.3
Tuesday	14.1
Wednesday	17.7
Thursday	11.8
Friday	15.2

2. About how much farther did she bike on Wednesday than on Thursday?

18 − ____ = ____

She biked about ____ more miles on Wednesday.

Estimate each sum or difference.

3. 19.7 − 6.9 **4.** 59 + 43.6 **5.** 5.82 + 1.69 + 2.3 **6.** 87.99 − 52.46

7. **Math and Science** About how many more inches of rain did Asheville get than Wichita? About how many more days did it rain in Asheville than Wichita?

DATA

Average Yearly Precipitation of U.S. Cities

City	Inches	Days
Asheville, North Carolina	47.71	124
Wichita, Kansas	28.61	85

8. **Reasoning** Four friends made a bar graph to show how many baseball cards they collected over the summer.

About how many cards did they collect in all?

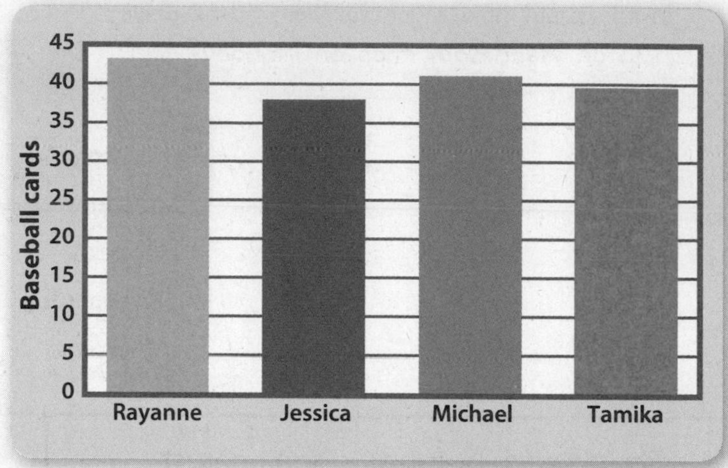

9. **Construct Arguments** Estimate the total weight of two boxes that weigh 9.4 pounds and 62.6 pounds using rounding and compatible numbers. Which estimate is closer to the actual total weight? Why?

10. **Higher Order Thinking** A gardener is estimating the amount of mulch needed for two garden beds. There is no room to store extra mulch. Is it better to estimate a greater or lesser amount than the mulch he needs? Why?

 **Assessment**

11. Martha bought an apple for $0.89 and a drink for $1.95. Which is the best estimate of how much money she spent?

Ⓐ $2.00

Ⓑ $3.00

Ⓒ $4.00

Ⓓ $5.00

12. Rachel bought a book for $5.49 and a game for $10.98. She paid with a $20 bill. Which is the best estimate of the amount of change she should receive?

Ⓐ $4

Ⓑ $6

Ⓒ $14

Ⓓ $16

Name ______________________________________

Lesson 2-3

Use Models to Add and Subtract Decimals

I can ...
model sums and differences of decimals.

I can also choose and use a math tool to solve problems.

Solve & Share Gloria rode her bicycle 0.75 mile in the morning and 1.10 miles in the afternoon. How many miles did Gloria ride in all? ***Solve this problem any way you choose.***

You can use appropriate tools, such as decimal grids, to help determine how many miles Gloria rode.

Look Back! Make Sense and Persevere How can you check that your answer is correct?

Learn Glossary

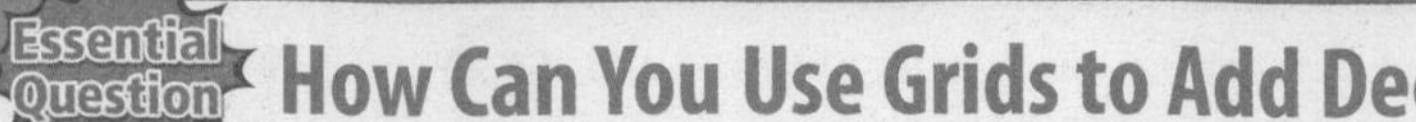

Essential Question: How Can You Use Grids to Add Decimals?

A

Use the table at the right to find the total monthly cost of using the dishwasher and the DVD player.

DATA

Device	Monthly Cost
DVD player	\$0.40
Microwave oven	\$3.57
Ceiling light	\$0.89
Dishwasher	\$0.85

B Use hundredths grids to add \$0.85 + \$0.40.

It costs \$0.85 to use the dishwasher per month.

 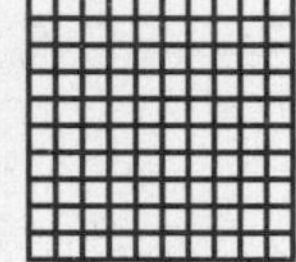

Shade 85 squares to show \$0.85.

C It costs \$0.40 to use the DVD player per month.

Use a different color and shade 40 more squares to show \$0.40. Count all of the shaded squares to find the sum.

\$0.85 + \$0.40 = \$1.25

The monthly cost of using the dishwasher and DVD player is \$1.25.

Convince Me! **Critique Reasoning** For the example above, Jesse said, "The total monthly cost of using the ceiling light and the dishwasher was \$0.74." Is Jesse correct? Explain.

Name ______________________

Another Example

You can subtract decimals with grids.

Use hundredths grids to find 1.57 − 0.89.

Step 1

Shade 1 grid and 57 squares to show 1.57.

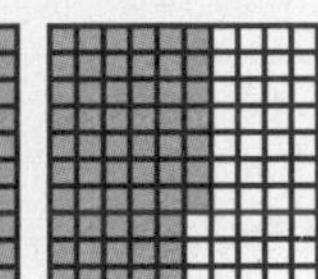

Step 2

Cross out 8 columns and 9 squares of the shaded grid. The difference is the squares that are shaded but not crossed out.

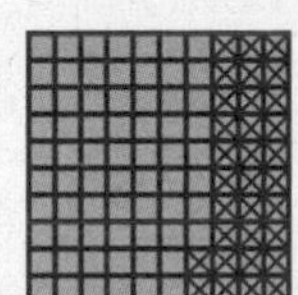
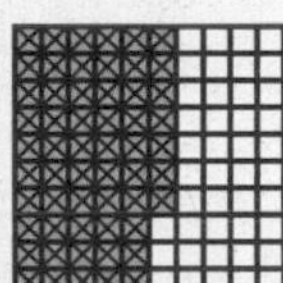

1.57 − 0.89 = 0.68

Guided Practice*

Do You Understand?

1. **Model with Math** Explain how to use grids to find the difference between the monthly cost of using the DVD player and the dishwasher. Then find the difference.

Do You Know How?

In **2–7**, use hundredths grids to add or subtract.

2. 1.22 + 0.34
3. 0.63 + 0.41
4. 2.73 − 0.94
5. \$1.38 − \$0.73
6. 0.47 − 0.21
7. 2.02 + 0.8

Independent Practice

In **8–11**, add or subtract. Use hundredths grids to help.

8. 0.1 + 0.73

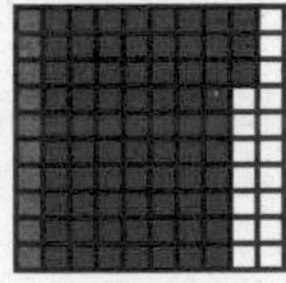

9. \$1.33 − \$0.35

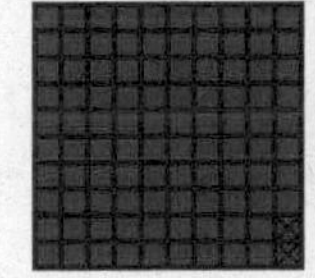
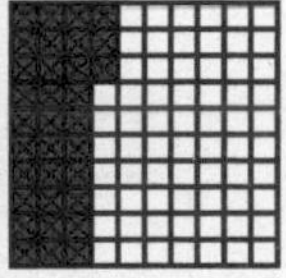

10. \$0.37 + \$0.47

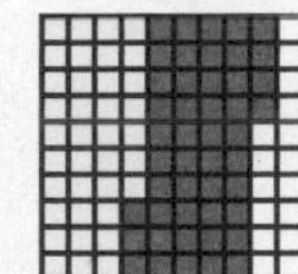

11. 1.11 + 0.89

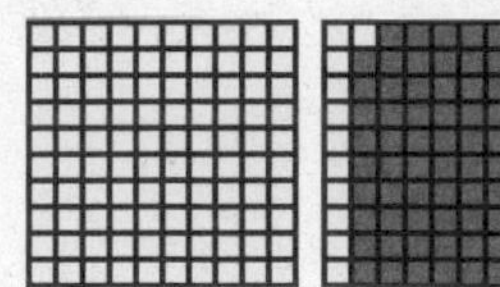

*For another example, see Set C on page 103.

Problem Solving

12. **Construct Arguments** How is adding 4.56 + 2.31 similar to adding \$2.31 + \$4.56?

13. **Model with Math** Write an expression that is represented by the model below.

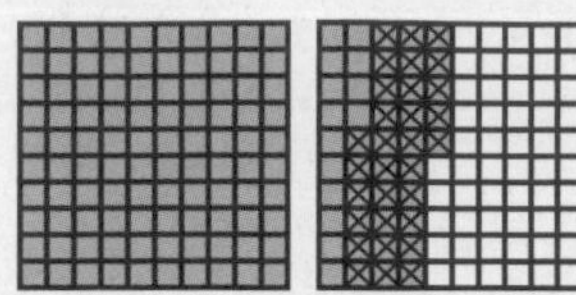

14. Is the sum of 0.46 + 0.25 less than or greater than one? Explain.

15. **Number Sense** Estimate to decide if the sum of 314 + 175 is more or less than 600.

16. **Higher Order Thinking** Do you think the difference of 1.4 − 0.95 is less than one or greater than one? Explain.

17. **A-Z Vocabulary** Estimate 53.8 − 27.6. Circle the **compatible numbers** to substitute.

54 − 28 53 − 28 55 − 27 55 − 25

18. **Algebra** Write an expression that can be used to find the perimeter of the pool shown to the right. Remember, perimeter is the distance around a figure.

Length = 50 meters

Width = 25 meters

Assessment

19. Each shaded area in the grids below represents a decimal.

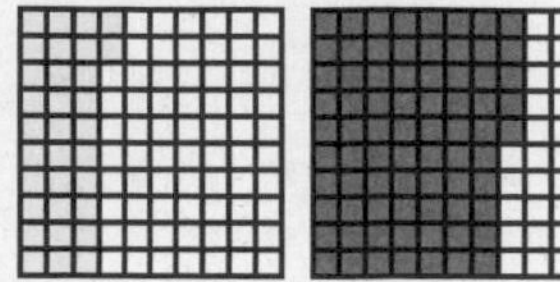

Part A

What is the sum of the decimals?

Part B

Explain how you found your answer.

Name ______________________

Homework & Practice 2-3

Use Models to Add and Subtract Decimals

Another Look!

Find 0.22 + 0.17.

Step 1

Shade 22 squares to show 0.22.

Step 2

Use a different color to shade 17 squares to show 0.17.

Step 3

Count all the squares that are shaded. Write the decimal for the shaded squares: 0.39.

So, 0.22 + 0.17 = 0.39.

Find 0.61 − 0.42.

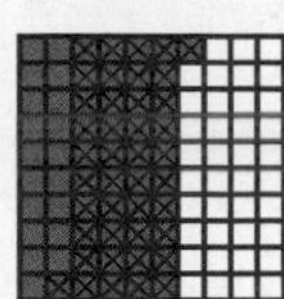

Step 1

Shade 61 squares to show 0.61.

Step 2

Cross out 42 squares to show subtracting 0.42.

Step 3

Count the squares that are shaded but not crossed out. Write the decimal: 0.19.

So, 0.61 − 0.42 = 0.19.

Count all the shaded squares to find the sum and cross out shaded squares to find the difference.

In **1** and **2**, use hundredths grids to add or subtract.

1. 0.27 + 0.19 = ____

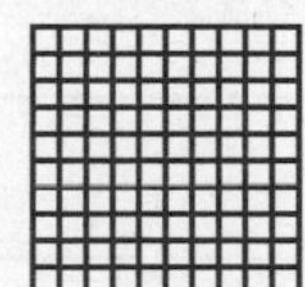

2. 0.39 − 0.14 = ____

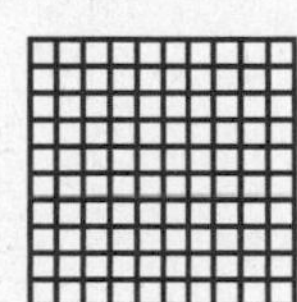

3. 0.68 − 0.24 = ____

4. 0.88 + 0.25 = ____

5. 2.88 − 0.59 = ____

6. 1.24 + 0.44 = ____

7. 0.96 + 1.05 = ____

8. 0.52 − 0.19 = ____

9. Write the number sentence that is shown by the hundredths grids to the right.

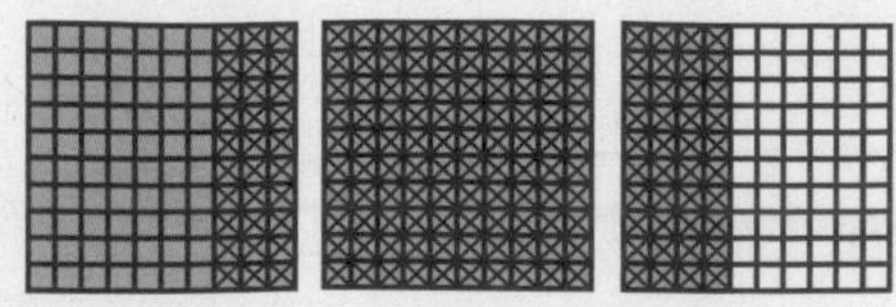

10. **Construct Arguments** Is the difference of 1.48 − 0.25 less than or greater than one? Explain.

11. **Higher Order Thinking** A bottle of perfume holds 0.55 ounce. A bottle of cologne holds 0.2 ounce. How many more ounces does the bottle of perfume hold?

12. **Model with Mathematics** As part of his workout, Jamal does 2 sets of 25 push-ups. If he does this 10 times each month, how many push-ups does he do each month? Write an equation to show your work.

13. The smallest video camera in the world is 0.99 millimeter in diameter. Is the diameter of the video camera less than or great than 0.1 millimeter?

14. A restaurant bought 48.5 pounds of apples from a local orchard. The next month, the restaurant bought another 65.3 pounds of apples and 24.5 pounds of pears. How many pounds of fruit did the restaurant buy?

15. **Model with Mathematics** Write an expression that is represented by the model below.

Assessment

16. Each shaded area in the grids below represents a decimal.

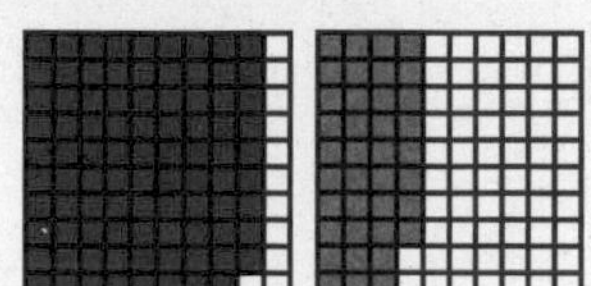

Part A

What is the sum of the decimals?

Part B

Explain how you found your answer.

Name ______________________________________

Lesson 2-4
Add Decimals

I can ...
add decimals using the standard algorithm.

I can also generalize from examples.

Solve & Share

Mr. Davidson has two sacks of potatoes. The first sack weighs 11.39 pounds. The second sack weighs 14.27 pounds. How many pounds of potatoes does Mr. Davidson have in all? ***Solve this problem any way you choose.***

You can generalize what you know about whole number addition to decimal addition.

Look Back! Generalize How is adding decimals like adding whole numbers?

Learn Glossary

Essential Question: How Can You Add Decimals?

A

A swim team participated in a relay race. The swimmers' times for each leg of the race were recorded in a table. What was the combined time for Caleb and Bradley's legs of the relay race?

DATA

Swimmers in Relay	Time in Seconds
Caleb	21.49
Bradley	21.59
Vick	20.35
Matthew	19.03

B

Step 1

Write the numbers, lining up the decimal points.

$$\begin{array}{r} 21.49 \\ +\ 21.59 \\ \hline \end{array}$$

Adding decimals is just like adding whole numbers!

C

Step 2

Add the hundredths.

Regroup if necessary.

$$\begin{array}{r} \overset{1}{} \\ 21.49 \\ +\ 21.59 \\ \hline 8 \end{array}$$

D

Step 3

Add the tenths, ones, and tens. Align the decimal point in the sum with the decimal point in the addends. Compare the sum to your estimate.

$$\begin{array}{r} 1\ 1\ \ \ \\ 21.49 \\ +\ 21.59 \\ \hline 43.08 \end{array}$$

The combined time for Caleb and Bradley was 43.08 seconds. The sum is close to the estimate.

Convince Me! Critique Reasoning André said the last two legs of the race took 3,938 seconds. What mistake did he make?

Name ____________________

Practice Buddy Tools Assessment

Another Example

Carson ran 7.81 miles last week. He ran 14 miles this week. How many miles did he run in the two weeks?

Step 1

Write the numbers, lining up the decimal points.

Annex two zeros so that both addends have the same number of decimal places.

$$\begin{array}{r} 14.00 \\ +\ 7.81 \\ \hline \end{array}$$

Step 2

Add the hundredths.

Regroup if necessary.

$$\begin{array}{r} 14.00 \\ +\ 7.81 \\ \hline 1 \end{array}$$

Step 3

Add the tenths, ones, and tens. Align the decimal point in the sum with the decimal point in the addends.

$$\begin{array}{r} \overset{1}{1}4.00 \\ +\ 7.81 \\ \hline 21.81 \end{array}$$

Carson ran 21.81 miles in all.

Guided Practice*

Do You Understand?

1. In the example on page 78, what was the combined time for the middle two legs of the relay race?

Do You Know How?

In **2–5**, find each sum.

2. $\begin{array}{r} 0.82 \\ +\ 4.21 \\ \hline \end{array}$

3. $\begin{array}{r} 9.1 \\ +\ 7.21 \\ \hline \end{array}$

4. 0.26 + 8.3

5. 4.98 + 3.02

Independent Practice

You can estimate first to be sure your answers are reasonable.

Leveled Practice In **6–12**, find each sum.

6. $\begin{array}{r} 1.03 \\ +\ 0.36 \\ \hline \square.3\square \end{array}$

7. $\begin{array}{r} 6.9 \\ +\ 2.8 \\ \hline \square.7 \end{array}$

8. $\begin{array}{r} 45.08 \\ +\ 2.01 \\ \hline \square7.\square9 \end{array}$

9. $\begin{array}{r} 2.00 \\ +\ 0.78 \\ \hline \end{array}$

10. \$271.90 + \$34.22

11. 7.2 + 3.96 + 8.8

12. 16.62 + 4 + 2.38

*For another example, see Set D on page 104.

Problem Solving

13. Model with Math A farmer sold 53.2 pounds of carrots and 29.4 pounds of asparagus to a restaurant. How many pounds of these two vegetables did the restaurant buy?

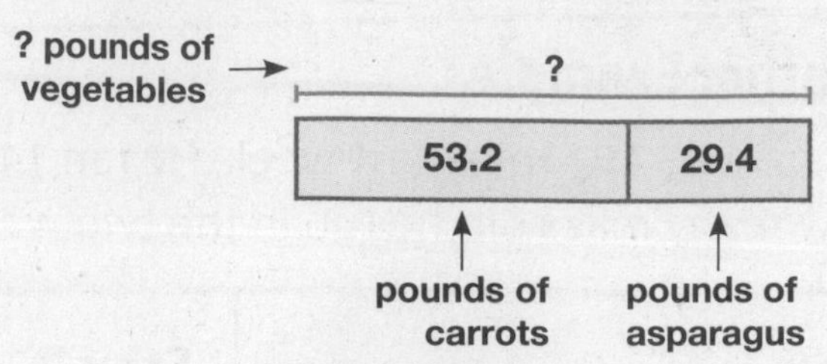

For **14** and **15**, use the table.

14. Math and Science Which two cities have the greatest combined rainfall for a typical year?

15. Number Sense Which location had less than 45 inches of rain but more than 40 inches of rain?

DATA

Location	Rainfall Amount in a Typical Year (in inches)
Macon, GA	45
Boise, ID	12.19
Caribou, ME	37.44
Springfield, MO	44.97

16. Higher Order Thinking Tim earned $16 babysitting and $17.50 mowing a lawn. He paid $8.50 for a movie and bought a small popcorn for $1.95. Write an expression to show how much money he has left.

17. Critique Reasoning Juan adds 3.8 + 4.6 and gets a sum of 84. Is his answer correct? Tell how you know.

Assessment

18. Choose all expressions that are equal to 12.9.

- ☐ 0.02 + 12 + 0.88
- ☐ 0.06 + 12.03
- ☐ 11.9 + 1
- ☐ 6.2 + 3.4 + 2.3
- ☐ 3.01 + 2.01 + 7.7

19. Choose all expressions that are equal to 16.02.

- ☐ 16 + 0.02
- ☐ 3.42 + 8 + 4.6
- ☐ 16.01 + 1
- ☐ 12.06 + 3.14
- ☐ 7.36 + 8.66

Name ______________________

Help Practice Buddy Tools Games

Homework & Practice 2-4
Add Decimals

Another Look!

A scientist used 0.62 milliliter of solution for an experiment and 0.56 milliliter of solution for a different experiment. How much solution did he use for the two experiments?

You can estimate first to be sure that your answer is reasonable.

Write the numbers, lining up the decimal points. Include the zeros to show place value.

$$\begin{array}{r} 0.62 \\ +\,0.56 \\ \hline \end{array}$$

Add the hundredths and the tenths.

Remember to write the decimal point in your answer.

$$\begin{array}{r} \overset{1}{0}.62 \\ +\,0.56 \\ \hline 1.18 \end{array}$$

The scientist used 1.18 milliliters of solution.

Leveled Practice In **1–11**, find the sum.

1. Find 55.25 + 2.98 + 16.3.

$$\begin{array}{r} 55.25 \\ 2.98 \\ +\,16.3 \\ \hline 7\square.\square 3 \end{array}$$

2.
$$\begin{array}{r} 37.2 \\ 103. \\ +\quad 8.52 \\ \hline \end{array}$$

3.
$$\begin{array}{r} 2.97 \\ +\,0.35 \\ \hline \end{array}$$

4.
$$\begin{array}{r} 5.62 \\ +\,7.99 \\ \hline \end{array}$$

5.
$$\begin{array}{r} 23.59 \\ +\,6.56 \\ \hline \end{array}$$

6. 13 + 7.69

7. 41.5 + 12.61

8. 39.48 + 26.7

9. 67.55 + 0.83

10. 88.8 + 4.27 + 78.95

11. 2.94 + 45 + 58.06

For **12** and **13**, use the table.

12. How much combined snowfall was there in Milwaukee and Oklahoma City?

13. What is the combined snowfall total for all three cities?

DATA

City	Snowfall (inches) in 2000
Milwaukee, WI	87.8
Baltimore, MD	27.2
Oklahoma City, OK	17.3

In science class, students weighed different amounts of clay. Carmen weighed 4.361 ounces, Kim weighed 2.704 ounces, Simon weighed 5.295 ounces, and Angelica weighed 8.537 ounces.

14. How many ounces of clay did Carmen and Angelica have in all?

15. How many ounces of clay did Kim and Simon have in all?

16. Model with Math Three bags of beads have masses of 10.3 grams, 5.23 grams, and 3.74 grams. Complete the bar diagram to find the total mass of all the beads.

? grams of beads →

?

bag 1 bag 2 bag 3

17. Reasoning Reilly adds 45.3 and 3.21. Should his sum be greater than or less than 48? Tell how you know.

18. Higher Order Thinking Patrick has a 600-meter skein of yarn. He used 248.9 meters of yarn to make a hat. Does he have enough yarn left to make a scarf that uses 354.03 meters of yarn? Explain.

✓ Assessment

19. Choose all expressions that are equal to 15.02.

- ☐ 12.96 + 2.06
- ☐ 0.56 + 14.64
- ☐ 2.62 + 12.4
- ☐ 1.22 + 1.8 + 12
- ☐ 1 + 0.5 + 13.8

20. Choose all expressions that are equal to 13.99.

- ☐ 13 + 0.9
- ☐ 6.25 + 3.9 + 3.84
- ☐ 4.635 + 9.355
- ☐ 8 + 5.99
- ☐ 10 + 3.09

Name ______________________________

Lesson 2-5
Subtract Decimals

I can …
subtract decimals using the standard algorithm.

I can also generalize from examples.

Solve & Share Ms. Garcia is an electrician and has a length of wire that is 32.7 meters long. She has another length of wire that is 15.33 meters long. How much longer is one wire than the other? ***Solve this problem any way you choose.***

You can generalize what you know about whole number subtraction to subtract decimals.

Look Back! **Use Structure** How can you use addition to check the problem about Ms. Garcia's wires?

Learn Glossary

Essential Question How Can You Subtract Decimals?

A

What is the difference in the wingspans of the two butterflies?

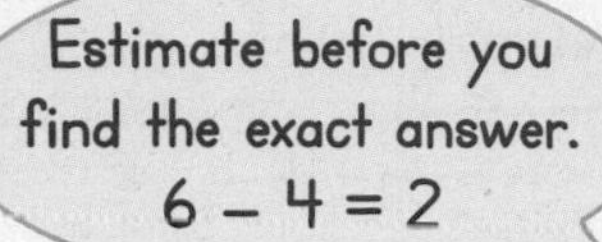

5.92 cm

4.37 cm

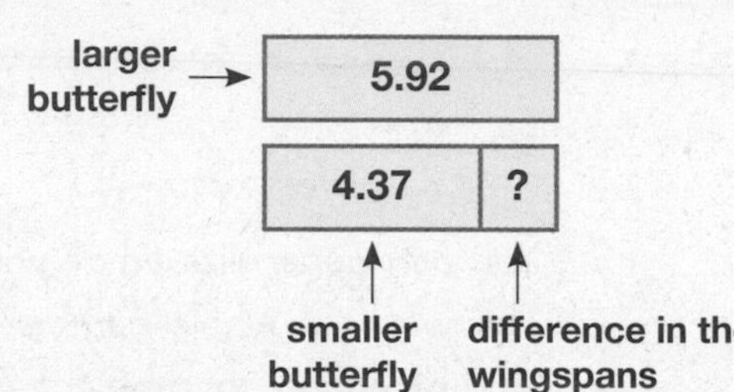

B

Step 1

Write the numbers, lining up the decimal points.

$$\begin{array}{r} 5.92 \\ -\,4.37 \\ \hline \end{array}$$

C

Step 2

Subtract the hundredths. Regroup if needed.

$$\begin{array}{r} 5.\overset{8}{\cancel{9}}\overset{12}{\cancel{2}} \\ -\,4.3\,7 \\ \hline 5 \end{array}$$

You can use subtraction to compare numbers!

D

Step 3

Subtract the tenths and ones. Bring down the decimal point.

$$\begin{array}{r} 5.\overset{8}{\cancel{9}}\overset{12}{\cancel{2}} \\ -\,4.3\,7 \\ \hline 1.5\,5 \end{array}$$

The difference in the wingspans is 1.55 centimeters.

The estimate was 2, so the difference is reasonable.

Convince Me! **Model with Math** An average adult's upper leg measures 19.88 inches, and the lower leg measures 16.94 inches. How much longer is the upper leg than the lower leg? Use a bar diagram to help.

upper leg	19.88 in.	
lower leg	?	16.94 in.

Name ______________________

Guided Practice*

Do You Understand?

1. **Number Sense** Explain why 1.55 centimeters is a reasonable answer for the difference in the wingspans of the two butterflies.

2. Maria rewrote 45.59 − 7.9 as 45.59 − 7.90. Is the value of 7.9 changed by annexing a zero after 7.9? Why or why not?

Do You Know How?

In **3–10**, subtract the decimals.

3. $\begin{array}{r} 16.82 \\ -\ 5.21 \\ \hline \end{array}$

4. $\begin{array}{r} 7.21 \\ -\ 6.1 \\ \hline \end{array}$

5. $\begin{array}{r} 23.06 \\ -\ 8.24 \\ \hline \end{array}$

6. $\begin{array}{r} \$4.08 \\ -\ \$2.12 \\ \hline \end{array}$

7. 56.8 − 2.76

8. $43.80 − $16.00

9. 22.4 − 10.7

10. $36.40 − $21.16

Independent Practice

Leveled Practice In **11–26**, subtract to find the difference.

11. $\begin{array}{r} 7.8 \\ -\ 4.9 \\ \hline \square.9 \end{array}$

12. $\begin{array}{r} \$20.60 \\ \$14.35 \\ \hline \$\ \square.2\square \end{array}$

13. $\begin{array}{r} 43.90 \\ -\ 7.52 \\ \hline 3\square.\square8 \end{array}$

14. $\begin{array}{r} 65.9\square \\ -\ 28.38 \\ \hline 3\square.5\square \end{array}$

15. 15.03 − 4.12

16. 13.9 − 3.8

17. 65.18 − 12.05

18. $52.02 − $0.83

19. 7.09 − 3.65

20. 34.49 − 12.61

21. 85.22 − 43.5

22. $10.05 − $4.50

23. 5.27 − 3.4

24. 23.6 − 8.27

25. 8.04 − 0.3

26. $21.37 − $10.95

*For another example, see Set D on page 104.

Problem Solving

27. **Algebra** The Pyramid of Khafre measured 143.5 meters high. The Pyramid of Menkaure measured 65.5 meters high. Write and solve an equation to find d, the difference in the heights of these two pyramids.

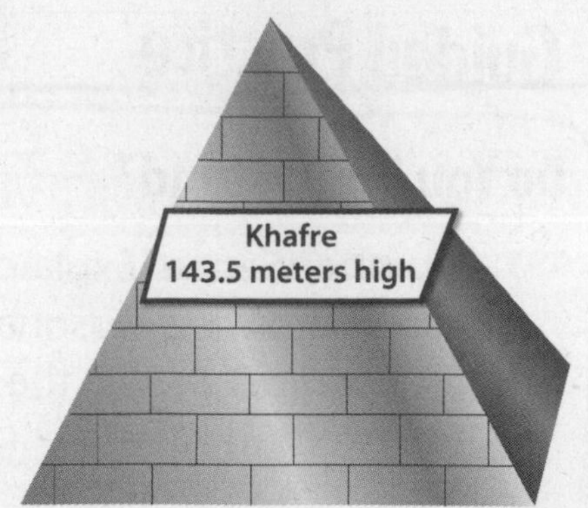

28. **Higher Order Thinking** Jonah bought a 1.5-liter bottle of seltzer. He used 0.8 liter of seltzer in some punch. Which is greater, the amount he used or the amount he has left? Explain how you decided.

29. **Critique Reasoning** Sue subtracted 2.9 from 20.9 and got 1.8. Explain why this is not reasonable.

30. **Make Sense and Persevere** Abe had $156.43 in his bank account at the beginning of the month. He made the two withdrawals shown in his check register. How much money does he have left in his bank account? He must have at least $100 in his account by the end of the month or he will be charged a fee. How much money does he need to deposit to avoid being charged a fee?

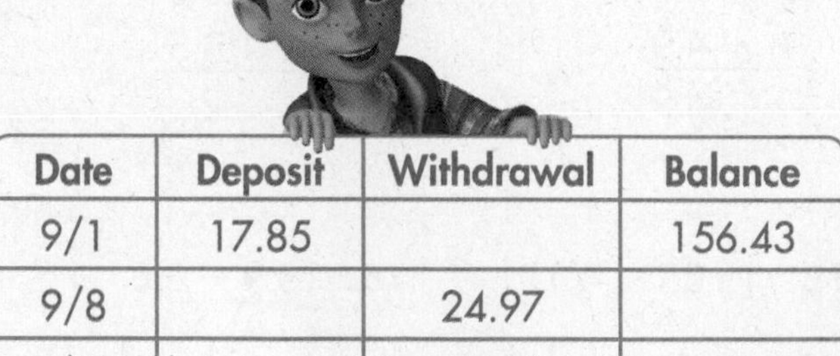

Date	Deposit	Withdrawal	Balance
9/1	17.85		156.43
9/8		24.97	
9/10		39.41	

Assessment

31. Which two subtraction problems have a difference of 1.65? Write those subtraction problems in the box.

Difference = 1.65

27.30 − 16.65 11.23 − 9.58
40.4 − 23.9 12.68 − 2.03 21.74 − 20.09

Name ______________________

Help | Practice Buddy | Tools | Games

Homework & Practice 2-5
Subtract Decimals

Another Look!

Mr. Montoya bought 3.5 pounds of ground beef. He used 2.38 pounds to make hamburgers. How much ground beef does he have left?

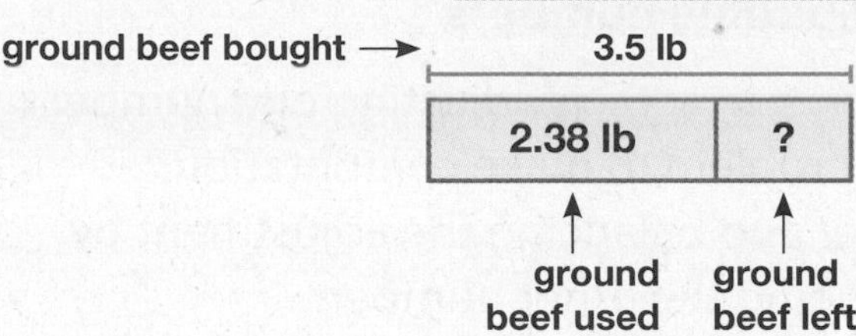

Write the numbers, lining up the decimal points. Include the zero to show place value.

$$\begin{array}{r} 3.50 \\ -\ 2.38 \\ \hline \end{array}$$

Subtract the hundredths. Regroup if necessary.

$$\begin{array}{r} {}^{4\,10} \\ 3.\not{5}\not{0} \\ -\ 2.38 \\ \hline 2 \end{array}$$

Subtract the tenths and the ones.

$$\begin{array}{r} {}^{4\,10} \\ 3.\not{5}\not{0} \\ -\ 2.38 \\ \hline 1.12 \end{array}$$

So, Mr. Montoya has 1.12 pounds of ground beef left.

1. Anya bought 1.4 pounds of peaches. She used 0.37 pound in a fruit salad. How much is left? Use the bar diagram to help you.

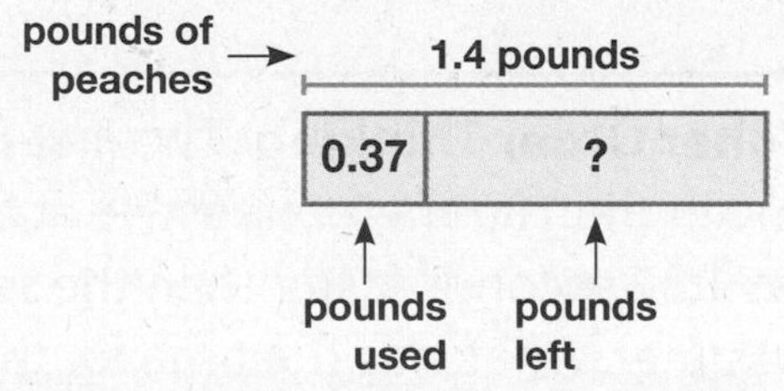

Leveled Practice In **2–7**, find the difference.

2. $\begin{array}{r} 82.7\square \\ -\ 5.59 \\ \hline \end{array}$

3. $\begin{array}{r} 43.3\square \\ -\ 12.82 \\ \hline \end{array}$

4. $\begin{array}{r} 7.28 \\ -\ 4.9\square \\ \hline \end{array}$

5. $\begin{array}{r} \$72.35 \\ -\ 6.19 \\ \hline \end{array}$

6. $\begin{array}{r} 1.24 \\ -\ 0.92 \\ \hline \end{array}$

7. $\begin{array}{r} 6.04 \\ -\ 3.48 \\ \hline \end{array}$

8. **Vocabulary** Complete the sentence using one of the terms below.

Commutative property
Compensation
Compatible numbers

__________ is adjusting one number in a problem to make computations easier and balancing the adjustment by changing the other number.

9. **Generalize** Describe the steps you would use to subtract 7.6 from 20.39.

In **10** and **11**, use the table.

10. **Math and Science** How much greater was Miami's annual rainfall than Albany's?

11. The annual rainfall in Albany is 0.33 inch less than the annual rainfall in Nashville. How much less rainfall did Nashville get than Miami? Show your work.

Annual Precipitation

City	Rainfall (inches)
Miami	61.05
Albany	46.92

12. **Model with Math** Lila would like to take a ceramics class. The class costs \$120. She has saved \$80 so far. Use the bar diagram to write and solve an equation to find the amount that Lila still needs.

\$120	
\$80	*d*

13. **Higher Order Thinking** The first-place swimmer's time in the 100-meter freestyle at a local swim meet was 1.32 seconds faster than the second-place swimmer. What was the time for the first-place swimmer? What was the difference in time between the second- and third-place swimmers?

100-m Freestyle

Finish	Time (seconds)
First	?
Second	9.33
Third	13.65

Assessment

14. Which two subtraction problems have a difference of 10.2? Write those subtraction problems in the box.

Difference = 10.2
12.05 − 2.03   16.29 − 6.09   36.1 − 25.9 22.09 − 21.07   10.82 − 9.8

Name ______________________________

Solve

Lesson 2-6
Add and Subtract Decimals

I can ...
add and subtract decimals.

I can also model with math to solve problems.

Solve & Share

Julie and Paulo are building a tree house. Julie has a wood board that is 1.15 meters long and Paulo has a board that is 0.7 meter long. What is the total length of the two boards? ***Solve this problem any way you choose.***

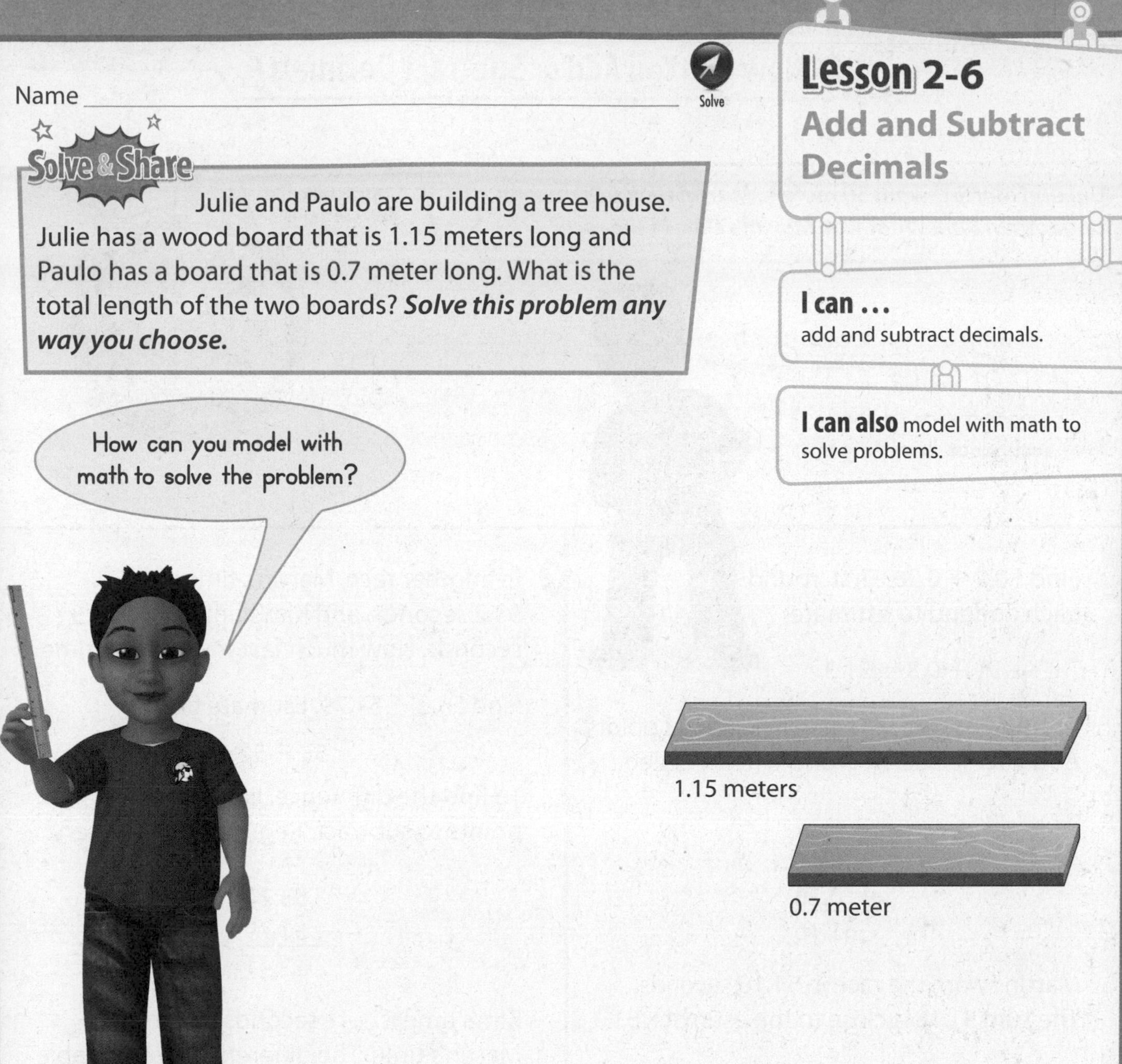

Look Back! **Model with Math** How much longer is one board than the other? Use a bar diagram to find your answer.

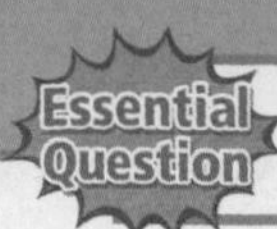

How Can You Add or Subtract Decimals?

A

Kim and Martin swam 50 meters. Martin took 0.26 second longer than Kim. What was Martin's time in the race?

If needed, annex a zero so that each place has a digit.

B

Find 50.9 + 0.26. First, round each addend to estimate.

$$51 + 0.3 = 51.3$$

To find the sum, line up the decimal points. Add each place. Regroup when needed.

$$\begin{array}{r} \overset{1}{5}0.90 \\ +\ \ 0.26 \\ \hline 51.16 \end{array}$$

Martin swam the race in 51.16 seconds. The sum 51.16 is close to the estimate, 51.3.

C

In another race, Martin's time was 53.2 seconds, and Kim's time was 51.79 seconds. How much faster was Kim's time?

Find 53.2 − 51.79. Estimate first.

$$53 - 52 = 1$$

To find the difference, line up the decimal points to subtract. Regroup as necessary.

$$\begin{array}{r} 5\overset{2}{\cancel{3}}.\overset{11}{\cancel{2}}\overset{10}{\cancel{0}} \\ -\ 51.79 \\ \hline 1.41 \end{array}$$

Kim's time is 1.41 seconds faster than Martin's time. The difference is reasonable and close to the estimate.

Convince Me! **Make Sense and Persevere** In a race the next day, Kim's time was 51.7 seconds. Martin's time was 0.79 second slower than Kim's time. Estimate Martin's time and then find his exact time.

Name ______________________

Practice Buddy | Tools | Assessment

Guided Practice*

Do You Understand?

1. **Generalize** How are adding and subtracting decimals similar to and different from adding and subtracting whole numbers?

2. **Construct Arguments** Describe how you know whether to add or subtract to solve a decimal problem.

Do You Know How?

In **3–10**, find each sum or difference.

3. 5.9 + 2.7

4. 4.01 − 2.95

5. 2.57 + 7.7

6. 1.5 − 1.05

7. 10 + 3.28

8. 15 − 6.01

9. 3.45 − 1.6

10. 9.12 + 2.06

Independent Practice

Leveled Practice In **11–24**, find each sum or difference.

11. 2.17 − 0.8☐ = 1.☐

12. 4.3☐ + 4.16 = 8.☐6

13. 7.62 − 3.86 = ☐6

14. 4.81 + 2.☐7 = ☐.9☐

15. 5.87 − 0.48

16. 5.78 + 16.59

17. 9.5 − 9.45

18. 14 + 9.8

19. 46.91 − 28.7

20. 5.61 + 2.4

21. 27 + 0.18

22. 0.46 − 0.33

23. 8.92 + 56 + 3.08

24. 219.51 + 127.2 + 2.49

Remember to line up the decimal points.

*For another example, see Set D on page 104.

Problem Solving

25. Construct Arguments Mr. Smith gave a cashier a \$50 bill for a purchase of \$38.70. The cashier gave him a \$10 bill, two \$1 bills, and three dimes back. Did Mr. Smith get the correct change? Why or why not?

26. Critique Reasoning Minh wrote the following number sentence: $2.6 + 0.33 = 5.9$. Use estimation to show that Minh's answer is incorrect.

27. Look for Relationships Becky is counting backward from 18.5. Identify the pattern she is using and complete the sequence of numbers.

18.5, 17.25, 16, ______, ______

28. The price of one share of a company at the end of the day Monday was \$126.38. The price of a share decreased \$7.95 the next day. What was the price of the share at the end of the day Tuesday?

29. Higher Order Thinking A visitor to the Grand Canyon hiked the South Kaibab Trail and the River Trail on one day. The next day, she hiked the Bright Angel Trail. How far did she hike the first day? How much farther did she hike the first day than the second day? How much longer was her total route than if she had hiked the North Kaibab Trail?

DATA

Trails in Grand Canyon National Park

Trail	Length (kilometers)
South Kaibab	10.1
River	2.7
Bright Angel	12.6
North Kaibab	22.9

Assessment

30. Choose all expressions that are equal to 3.89.

- ☐ $16.09 - 12.2$
- ☐ $48.5 - 9.6$
- ☐ $4.01 - 0.12$
- ☐ $128 - 124.11$
- ☐ $6 - 3.89$

31. Choose all of the addition problems in which you annex zeros to align place values in the addends.

- ☐ $4 + 1.23 + 45.62$
- ☐ $0.09 + 12$
- ☐ $0.11 + 12.11$
- ☐ $19.9 + 0.6$
- ☐ $8.3 + 2 + 6.01$

Name ______________________

Help | Practice Buddy | Tools | Games

Homework & Practice 2-6
Add and Subtract Decimals

Another Look!

Find 1.93 + 41.6.

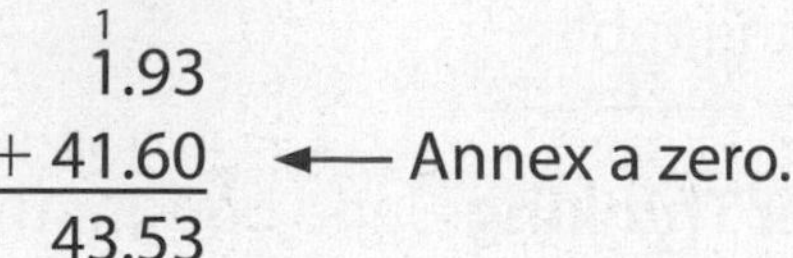

Write the numbers, lining up the decimal points. Annex zeros so all numbers have the same number of decimal places.

$$\begin{array}{r} \overset{1}{1}.93 \\ +\ 41.60 \\ \hline 43.53 \end{array}$$ ← Annex a zero.

Add the numbers. Regroup if necessary. Write the decimal point in your answer.

43.53 is close to 44, so the answer is reasonable.

Find 18.5 − 7.82.

Write the numbers, lining up the decimal points. Annex zeros so all numbers have the same number of decimal places.

$$\begin{array}{r} 1\overset{7}{\cancel{8}}.\overset{14}{\cancel{5}}\overset{10}{\cancel{0}} \\ -\ 7.82 \\ \hline 10.68 \end{array}$$ ← Annex a zero.

Subtract. Regroup if necessary. Write the decimal point in your answer.

10.68 is close to 10.5, so the answer is reasonable.

Leveled Practice 1–12, find the sum or difference.

1. $\begin{array}{r} 17.2\square \\ +\ 6.08 \\ \hline \end{array}$

2. $\begin{array}{r} 14.25 \\ -\ 5.14 \\ \hline \end{array}$

3. $\begin{array}{r} 45.6 \\ +\ 26.3 \\ \hline \end{array}$

4. 24.84 − 22.7

5. 13.64 − 8.3

6. 0.21 + 15.9

7. 3.65 − 1.41

8. 18.06 + 9.79 + 12

9. 8 − 6.38

10. 55.5 − 4.56

11. 8.32 + 95 + 12.68

12. 57.3 − 42.81

13. Critique Reasoning Jaime wrote 4.4 − 0.33 = 1.1. Is his answer reasonable? Why or why not?

14. Critique Reasoning Trey wrote 9.09 − 0.1 = 9.08. Is his answer correct? Why or why not?

For **15–17**, use the table.

15. Higher Order Thinking Jane bought three sheets of poster board and a pack of markers. Denise bought two packs of construction paper and a tube of glue. Who spent more? How much more?

Craft Supplies	
Poster board	$1.29/sheet
Markers	$4.50/pack
Tape	$1.99/roll
Glue	$2.39/tube
Construction paper	$3.79/pack

16. If Jane buys two more sheets of poster board, how much does she spend all together?

17. Reasoning Julene has $25 to make posters. She buys two packs of markers, one pack of construction paper, two tubes of glue, and a roll of tape. How many sheets of poster board can she buy with the money she has left? Explain your answer.

18. Look for Relationships Mrs. Ibara wrote three decimal numbers on the board followed by two blank spaces. Complete the sequence of numbers.

4.15, 6.3, 8.45, ________, ________

Assessment

19. Choose all expressions that are equal to 0.8.

- [ ] 15.3 − 14.5
- [ ] 12.96 − 12.88
- [ ] 128.2 − 120.2
- [ ] 1.77 − 0.08
- [ ] 1.79 − 0.99

20. Choose all of the addition problems in which you annex zeros to align place values in the addends.

- [ ] 0.54 + 12.1
- [ ] 2.55 + 145.05
- [ ] 25.59 + 1.2
- [ ] 23.04 + 124.1 + 34.06
- [ ] 1.51 + 3.07 + 4.18

Name ______________________

Solve

Problem Solving

Lesson 2-7

Model with Math

Solve & Share

At a baseball game, Sheena bought a sandwich for $6.95 and two pretzels for $2.75 each. She paid with a $20 bill. How much change did she receive? ***Solve this problem any way you chose. Use bar diagrams to help.***

I can . . .
use the math I know to solve problems.

I can also solve multi-step problems.

Thinking Habits

Be a good thinker!
These questions can help you.

- How can I use math I know to help solve the problem?
- How can I use pictures, objects, or an equation to represent the problem?
- How can I use numbers, words, and symbols to solve the problem?

Look Back! Model with Math What other way can you represent this problem situation?

How Can You Represent a Problem with Bar Diagrams?

A

Monica wants to buy all of the art supplies shown on this sign. She has a coupon for $5.50 off the cost of her purchases. What will Monica's total cost be after the discount?

What do I need to do to solve the problem?

I need to find Monica's cost for the art supplies.

B **How can I model with math?**

I can

- use the math I know to help solve the problem.
- find and answer any hidden questions.
- use bar diagrams and equations to represent and solve this problem.

C

I will use bar diagrams to represent this situation.

? total cost			
$59.95	$24.95	$9.75	$13.50

$\$59.95 + \$24.95 + \$9.75 + \$13.50 = \$108.15$

The total cost before the discount is $108.15.

$108.15 total before discount	
$5.50	? total after discount

$\$108.15 - \$5.50 = \$102.65$

Monica's cost after the discount is $102.65.

Convince Me! Model with Math How could you decide if your answer makes sense?

Name

Guided Practice*

Model with Math

Nate has $30.50. He wants to buy his dog a sweater that costs $15, a toy that costs $3.79, and a leash that costs $14.79. How much more money does he need?

1. What do you need to find before you can solve the problem?

2. Draw bar diagrams to represent the problem and then solve the problem. Show the equations you used to solve the problem.

Independent Practice

Model with Math

Luz Maria has $15. She buys a ticket to a movie and a smoothie. How much money does she have left?

Ticket	$9.50
Popcorn	$4.50
Smoothie	$2.85

3. What do you need to find before you can solve the problem?

4. Draw two bar diagrams to represent the problem.

5. What is the solution to the problem? Show the equations you used to solve the problem.

*For another example, see Set E on page 104.

Problem Solving

Performance Assessment

School Trip
Audrey is saving for a school trip. She needs $180 for the bus tickets, $215 for the hotel, and $80 for meals. The table shows how much money she and her sister, Kelsey, have saved over a 4-month period. How much more money does Audrey need for the trip?

DATA

Monthly Savings		
Month	**Audrey's Savings**	**Kelsey's Savings**
September	$68	$28
October	$31.50	$42.50
November	$158	$90.25
December	$74.75	$89

6. **Make Sense and Persevere** What are you trying to find?

7. **Construct Arguments** Should you multiply Audrey's savings for September by 4 since there are 4 months? Explain.

8. **Model with Math** Draw bar diagrams to represent the total cost of Audrey's trip and the total she has saved. Then find the total cost and total savings.

9. **Model with Math** Write and solve an equation to determine how much more money Audrey needs for the trip.

Name ______________________________

Homework & Practice 2-7
Model with Math

Another Look!

For her birthday, Lucy received $20 from her aunt, $15 from her grandmother, and $32 from her cousins. She bought an e-book for $10.85. How much birthday money does Lucy have left?

Show how you can model this problem.

I can use bar diagrams and equations to represent and solve this problem.

How much money did Lucy receive?

? total money received

$20	$15	$32

$20 + $15 + $32 = $67 received

How much money does Lucy have left?

$67 total received

$10.85	? money left

$67.00 − $10.85 = $56.15. Lucy has $56.15 left.

Model with Math
Jeffrey earned $65 doing yard work. He bought a pair of jeans for $31.25 and a sweatshirt for $16.50. He set aside the money left from his shopping trip to buy a gift for his cousin. How much money did he set aside for the gift?

1. What do you need to find before you can solve the problem?

2. Draw bar diagrams to represent the problem.

Remember, a bar diagram clearly shows how the quantities in the problem are related.

3. Write equations to represent the problem. Then solve the problem.

Performance Assessment

Snowfall
The total snowfall for last year was 36.4 inches. The graph shows snowfalls for 3 months last year and for the same 3 months this year. Find how much greater this year's 3-month snowfall was than last year's.

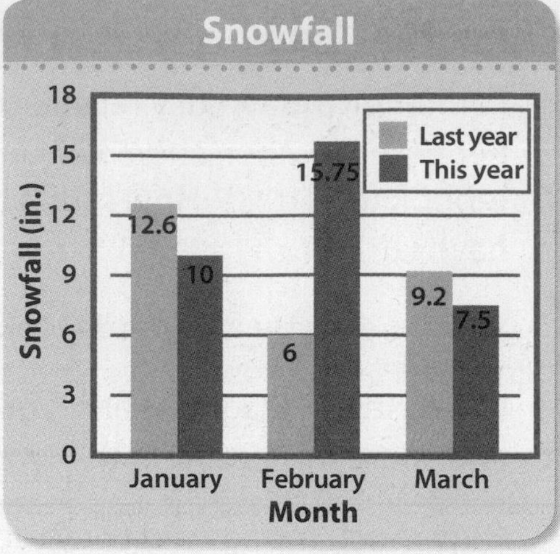

4. Make Sense and Persevere Do you need all of the information given to solve the problem? Explain.

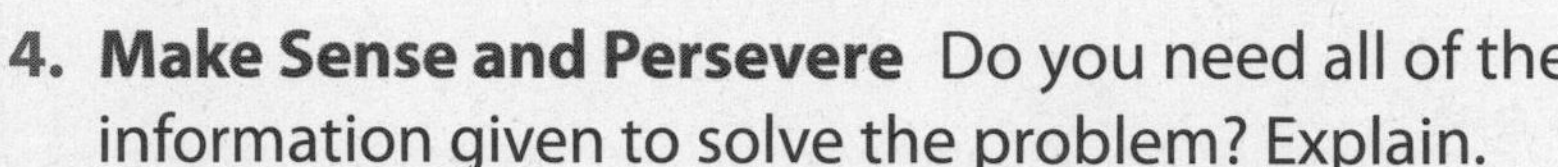

5. Model with Math Draw bar diagrams to represent last year's total 3-month snowfall and this year's total 3-month snowfall. Then find the total 3-month snowfalls for each year.

6. Model with Math Write and solve an equation to find how much greater this year's 3-month snowfall was than last year's.

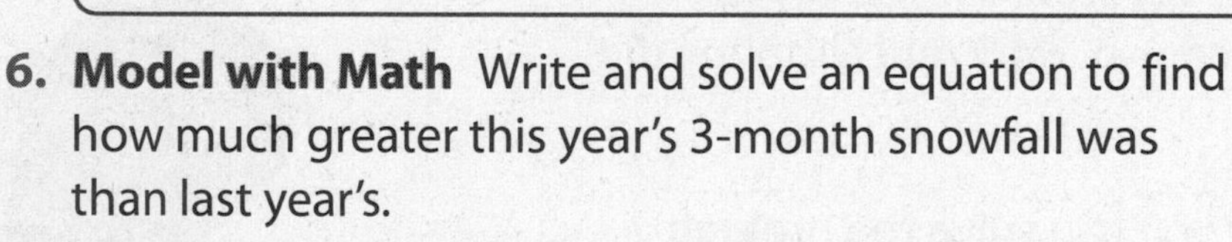

7. Reasoning Describe a way to determine how much more snow needs to fall so this year's total is 37.4 inches. Then find the answer.

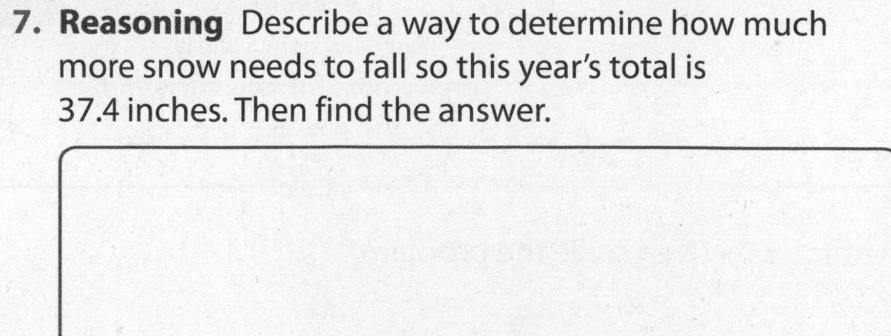

Name ____________________

Fluency Practice Activity

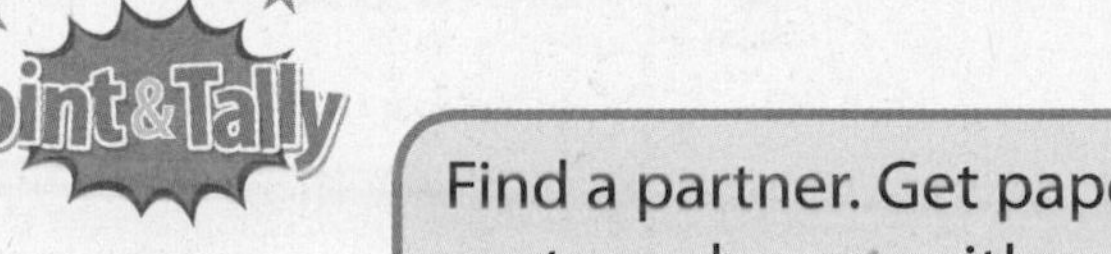

Find a partner. Get paper and a pencil. Each partner chooses either light blue or dark blue.

Partner 1 and Partner 2 each point to a black number at the same time. Each partner subtracts the lesser number from the greater number.

If the answer is on your color, you get a tally mark. Work until one partner has twelve tally marks.

I can ...
subtract multi-digit whole numbers.

Partner 1
500
750
961
1,945
5,520

383	1,705	721	1,517
260	733	5,280	1,891
1,928	907	483	322
696	5,503	5,092	72
5,153	446	944	594
133	533	5,466	1,578

Partner 2
17
54
240
367
428

Tally Marks for Partner 1	Tally Marks for Partner 2

TOPIC 2

Vocabulary Review

Word List

- Associative Property of Addition
- Commutative Property of Addition
- compatible numbers
- compensation
- equivalent decimals
- inverse operations

Understand Vocabulary

Choose the best term from the Word List. Write it on the blank.

1. When you adjust one number and change another number in the problem to make a computation easier, you use ______________.

2. You can replace the values in a problem with ______________ so that it's easier to use mental math to complete the computation.

3. To align decimal points in a decimal addition problem, annex zeros to write ______________ so that all addends have the same number of decimal places.

4. Because of the ______________, I know that $477.75 + (76.89 + 196.25) = (76.89 + 196.25) + 477.75$ without adding.

5. Cross out the numbers below that are NOT equivalent to 500.0.

500.00 5×10 5×10^2 50.05 500.500

6. Cross out the numbers below that are NOT equivalent to $53.2 + 16.8$.

7×10^1 0.070 7.0 $7 \times \frac{1}{10}$ $(7 \times 10) + (0 \times 1)$

Circle the problem that uses compensation.

7. $32.7 + 15.6 = 32.6 + 15.7$ $45.7 + 26.2 = 45.7 + 26.3 - 0.1$

8. $14.24 - 11.8 = 14.24 - 12 + 0.2$ $168.3 - 53.8 = 168.3 - 53.4 - 0.4$

Use Vocabulary in Writing

9. Explain how the Commutative Property of Addition, the Associative Property of Addition and mental math can help you find $75.2 + (57.376 + 24.8)$. What is the sum?

Name ______________________________

Reteaching

Set A pages 59–64

Add 15.3 + 1.1 + 1.7 using mental math.

15.3 and 1.7 are compatible numbers because they are easy to calculate mentally.

The Commutative Property of Addition allows us to add in any order.

$15.3 + 1.1 + 1.7 = 15.3 + 1.7 + 1.1$
$= 17.0 + 1.1$
$= 18.1$

Remember that you can use compatible numbers or compensation to find sums and differences.

Use mental math to add or subtract.

1. 8.6 + 23.4 + 1.4

2. 27 − 9.9

3. 13.5 + 5.7 + 36.5

4. 205.4 − 99.7

Set B pages 65–70

Estimate 22.4 − 16.2.

22.4	⟶	20	Use compatible
− 16.2	⟶	− 15	numbers.
		5	

22.4 − 16.2 is about 5.

Remember that compatible numbers can give a different estimate than rounding.

Estimate each sum or difference.

1. 358 + 293

2. 15.01 − 4.4

3. 80.01 + 2.89

4. 25,003 − 12,900

Set C pages 71–76

Use hundredths grids to subtract 1.86 − 0.95.

Shade one whole grid and 86 squares to show 1.86.

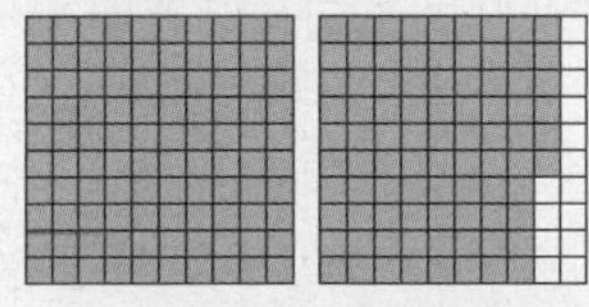

To subtract 0.95, cross out 95 of the shaded squares on the grids.

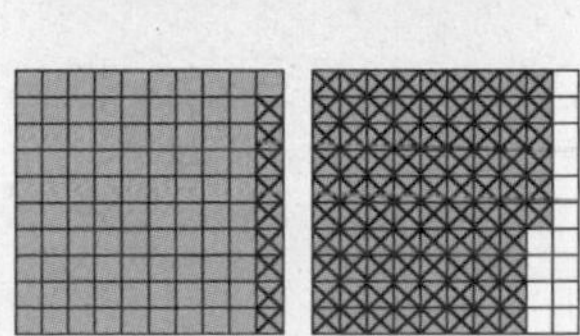

Count the squares that are shaded but not crossed out.

1.86 − 0.95 = 0.91

Remember that to add decimals, shade the first addend in one color. Then continue by shading the second addend with another color.

1. 0.02 + 0.89

2. 0.67 − 0.31

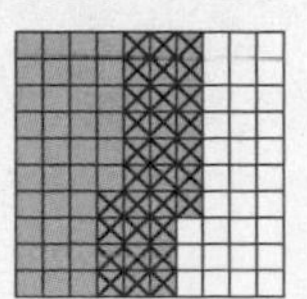

3. 0.34 + 0.34

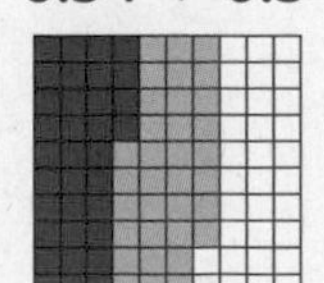

4. 0.81 − 0.78

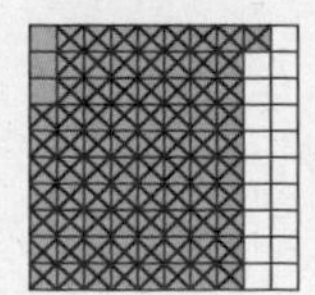

Set D pages 77–82, 83–88, 89–94

Lucy bought 3.12 pounds of pears and 9 pounds of apples. Find how many more pounds of apples than pears Lucy bought.

Write the numbers. Add a decimal point to the whole number. Annex zeros. Line up the decimal points.

$$\begin{array}{r} 9.00 \\ -\ 3.12 \\ \hline \end{array}$$

Subtract the hundredths, tenths, and ones.

$$\begin{array}{r} \overset{8}{\not{9}}.\overset{\overset{9}{\not{10}}}{\not{0}}\overset{10}{\not{0}} \\ -\ 3.12 \\ \hline 5.88 \end{array}$$

Remember to annex zeros so that each place has a digit and all of the decimal points line up.

1. 7.06 + 0.85
2. 24.07 − 5.316
3. 51.92 − 28.003
4. 8.71 − 0.4
5. 98 + 3.79
6. Talia measured two strings. The green string was 2.37 cm long. The blue string was 4 cm long. How many centimeters longer was the blue string than the green string?

Set E pages 95–100

Think about these questions to help you **model with math.**

Thinking Habits

- How can I use math I know to help solve the problem?
- How can I use pictures, objects, or an equation to represent the problem?
- How can I use numbers, words, and symbols to solve the problem?

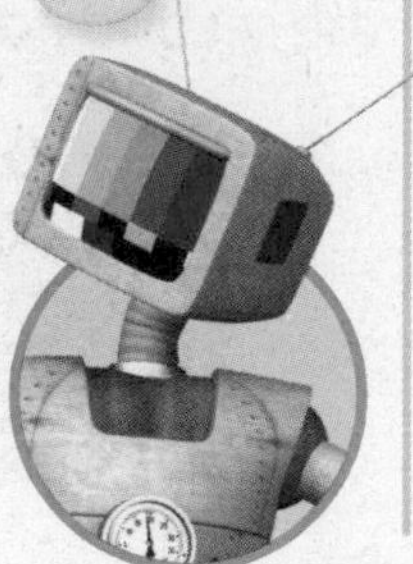

Remember a good model clearly shows how the quantities in the problem are related.

Alberto ran 15.6 km on Monday, 12.8 km on Tuesday, and 6.5 km on Wednesday. Dennis ran 11.25 km on Monday, 14.6 km on Tuesday, and 8 km on Wednesday. Who ran farther? How much farther?

1. What do you need to find before you can solve the problem?

2. Write equations to model this problem. Then solve the problem.

Name ___________________________

1. A dollhouse has 15.15 square feet downstairs and 6.25 square feet upstairs. Which of the following is the best estimate of the total area in the dollhouse?

Ⓐ 9 square feet

Ⓑ 21 square feet

Ⓒ 78 square feet

Ⓓ 90 square feet

2. Use mental math to find the sum of $12.15, $16.85, and $1.74.

Ⓐ $29.00

Ⓑ $30.74

Ⓒ $30.85

Ⓓ $32.74

3. Choose all the expressions that are equal to 2.65 + 3.78.

☐ 2.56 + 3.87

☐ 3.78 + 2.65

☐ 10 − 3.67

☐ 9.51 − 3.08

☐ 8.21 − 2.78

4. For questions 4a-4d, choose Yes or No to tell if the number 7.15 will make each equation true.

4a. 4.95 + ☐ = 12.1 ○ Yes ○ No

4b. 10.82 − ☐ = 3.77 ○ Yes ○ No

4c. 8.47 + ☐ = 15.52 ○ Yes ○ No

4d. 9.14 − ☐ = 1.99 ○ Yes ○ No

5. Lawrence spent $1.89 on a bottle of paint and $0.45 on a brush.

Part A

What was the total amount he spent? Use the model to help you.

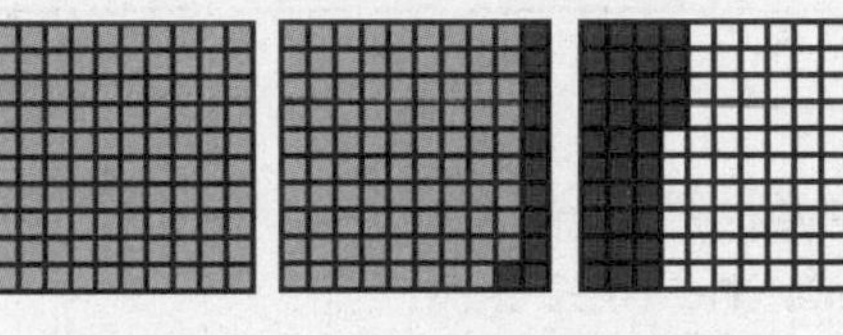

Part B

Explain how the model helps you find the sum.

6. Draw lines to match each expression on the left to the equivalent decimal on the right.

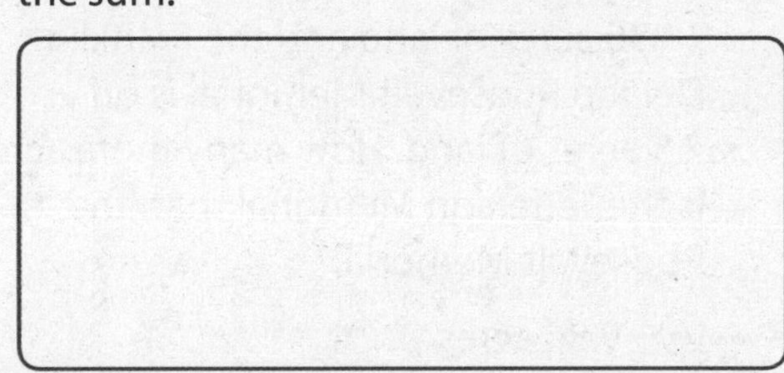

7. Ed is training for a race. He ran 12.56 miles on one day and 12.98 miles the next day.

Part A

What is his combined distance for the first two days?

Part B

How much farther did he run the second day than the first day?

8. The Thomas Jefferson Memorial is on 18.36 acres of land and the Franklin Delano Roosevelt Memorial is on 7.5 acres of land. How many more acres is the Jefferson Memorial than the Roosevelt Memorial?

Ⓐ 9.86 acres

Ⓑ 10.86 acres

Ⓒ 11.31 acres

Ⓓ 17.61 acres

9. A box weighs 23.7 pounds. Another box weighs 6.91 pounds. What is the combined weight of the two boxes? Draw and label a bar diagram to model the problem.

10. Kassandra has a rectangular patio in her backyard. The patio is 12.74 meters long and 5.45 meters wide.

5.45 m

12.74 m

Part A

Round the length and width to the nearest whole number. Then estimate the perimeter of Kassandra's patio. Write an equation to model your work.

Part B

Round the length and width to the nearest tenth. Then estimate the perimeter of Kassandra's patio. Write an equation to model your work.

Part C

Find the exact perimeter. Which estimate is closer? Explain why you think that estimate is closer.

Name ____________________

Video Games

Four students are playing the same video game. Their scores for the first three levels are added together to see if the student has enough points to move on to Round 2.

1. The students' scores are shown in the table below.

Round 1				
Level	**Kim**	**Sally**	**Tina**	**Zoey**
1	7.18	5.49	8.02	8.64
2	6.55	6.18	7.94	8.32
3	6.45	5.72	8.38	8.13
Total Points				

Part A

A student must have at least 18 points to advance to Round 2. Use estimation to decide if any of the students did not get 18 points.

Part B

Use estimation to decide which student had the greatest number of points. Explain your reasoning.

2. Complete the table to find the total number of points for each student.

3. How many more points did Zoey score than Sally? Write an equation to model your work.

4. Use the total points scored for each student.

Part A

About how many points did the four students score in Round 1? Estimate by rounding each point total to the nearest whole number.

Part B

Complete the bar diagram to show the exact total number of points the students scored.

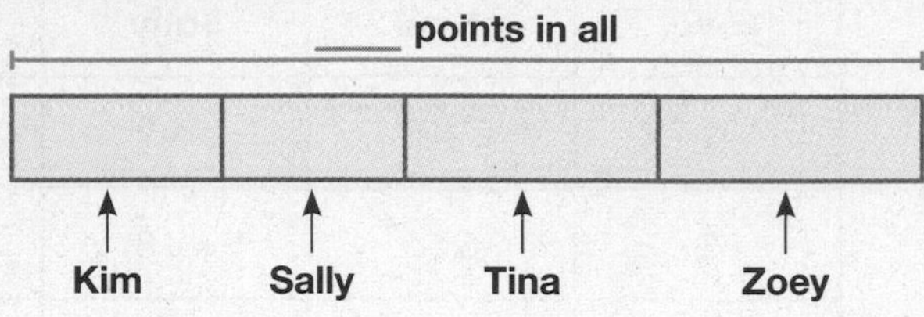

5. In Round 2, Zoey had a total of 23.43 points. She got a score of 7.96 in Level 2 and a score of 8.03 in Level 3.

Part A

What score did she receive in Level 1?

Part B

Explain how you found your answer.

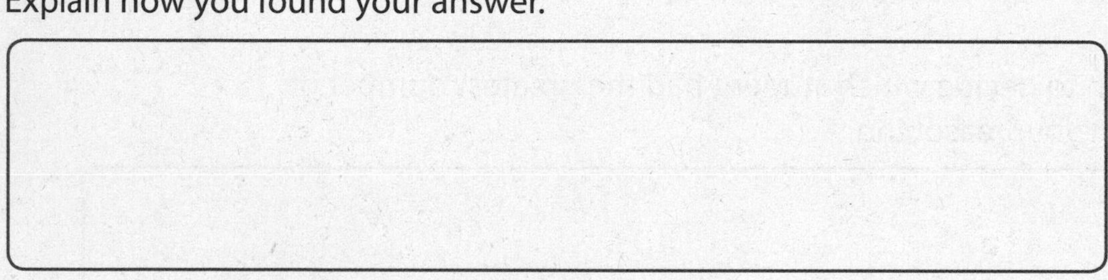

6. Kim recorded her scores for Round 2. To estimate her total, she rounds to the nearest whole number and says, "$7 + 9 + 7 = 23$, so my total is at least 23 points." Do you agree? Explain your reasoning.

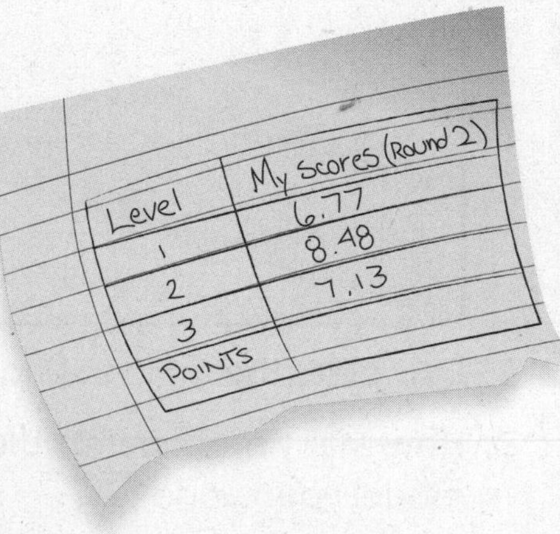

Level	My Scores (Round 2)
1	6.77
2	8.48
3	7.13
POINTS	

Fluently Multiply Multi-Digit Whole Numbers

Essential Question: What are the standard procedures for estimating and finding products of multi-digit numbers?

Natural resources like water and coal come from Earth.

Water is a renewable resource because it can be used over and over again.

I'll get a giant straw! Here's a project on water usage and multiplication.

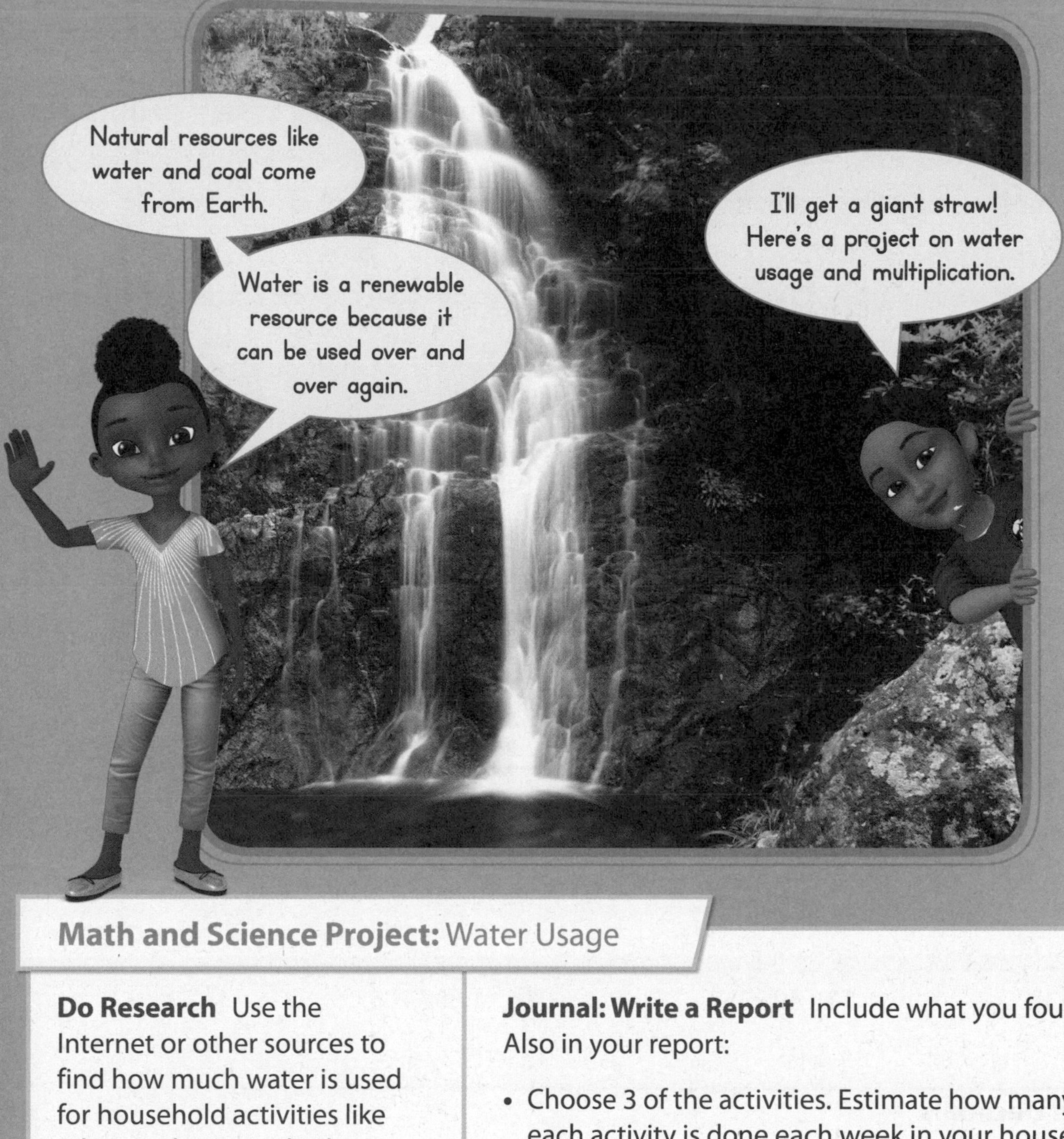

Math and Science Project: Water Usage

Do Research Use the Internet or other sources to find how much water is used for household activities like taking a shower or bath, using a dishwasher, hand washing dishes, and using a washing machine.

Journal: Write a Report Include what you found. Also in your report:

- Choose 3 of the activities. Estimate how many times each activity is done each week in your household.
- Estimate the weekly water usage for each activity. Organize your results in a table.
- Make up and solve multiplication problems based on your data.

Name ______________________________

Review What You Know

A-Z Vocabulary

Choose the best term from the box. Write it on the blank.

- equation
- exponent
- factor
- multiple
- power
- product

1. The answer to a multiplication problem is the __________.
2. A number sentence that shows two expressions with the same value is a(n) __________.
3. A(n) __________ tells the number of times the base is used as a(n) __________.
4. 50 is a(n) __________ of 10 because $5 \times 10 = 50$.

Operations

Find each sum or difference.

5. $9{,}007 + 3{,}128$
6. $7{,}904 - 3{,}199$
7. $27{,}924 - 13{,}868$
8. $9.27 + 3.128$
9. $119.04 - 86.5$
10. $165.2 - 133.18$

Round Whole Numbers and Decimals

Round each number to the place of the underlined digit.

11. $1\underline{4}.3$
12. $3\underline{8}5.7$
13. $0.\underline{5}45$
14. $49\underline{6}.533$
15. $49\underline{6}.353$
16. $1{,}857.2\underline{0}5$

Compare Decimals

17. Write the numbers in order from least to greatest. 8.062 8.26 8.026 8.6
18. Write the numbers in order from greatest to least. 0.115 0.15 0.005 0.5

My Word Cards

Use the examples for each word on the front of the card to help complete the definitions on the back.

A-Z Glossary

underestimate

70×30 is an underestimate for 72×34 because $70 < 72$ and $30 < 34$.

overestimate

50×20 is an overestimate for 45×19 because $50 > 45$ and $20 > 19$.

partial products

$$\begin{array}{r} 57 \\ \times\ 14 \\ \hline 228 \\ +\ 570 \\ \hline 798 \end{array}$$

228 and 570 ← partial products

variable

$25 + n = 37$

n ↑ variable

My Word Cards

Complete the definition. Extend learning by writing your own definitions.

The result of using greater numbers to estimate a sum or product is called an

________________________.

The result of using lesser numbers to estimate a sum or product is called an

________________________.

A letter, such as *n*, that represents a number in an expression or an equation is called a ________________.

________________________ are products found by breaking one of two factors into ones, tens, hundreds, and so on, and then multiplying each of these by the other factor.

Name ______________________________

Lesson 3-1
Multiply Greater Numbers by Powers of 10

I can ...
use mental math to multiply a whole number by a power of 10.

I can also choose and use a math tool to solve problems.

Solve & Share

At Izzy's Party Store, party invitations come in packages of 8. How many invitations are in 10 packages? 100 packages? 1,000 packages?

You can use appropriate tools. Place-value blocks are useful for picturing problems that involve powers of 10.

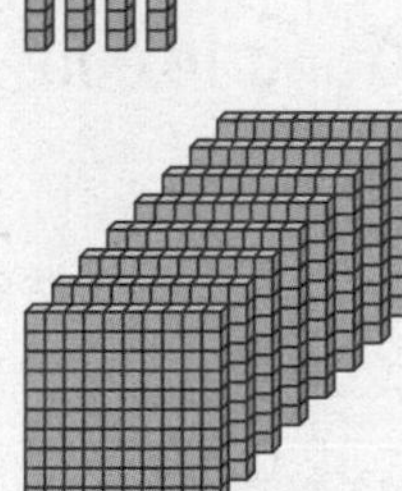

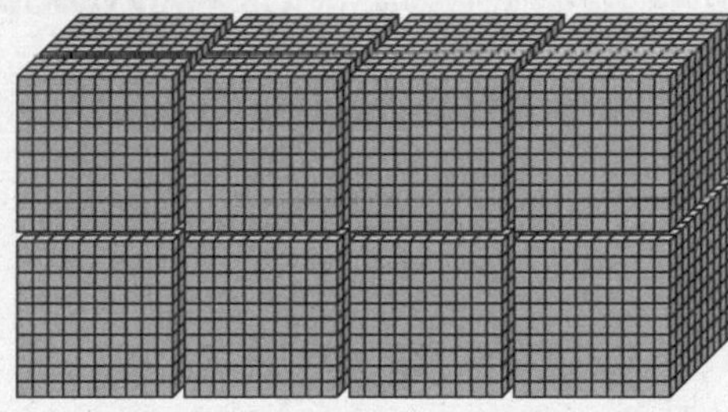

Look Back! Use Structure Thank-you cards come in packages of 12. How would this place-value model be different from the one above?

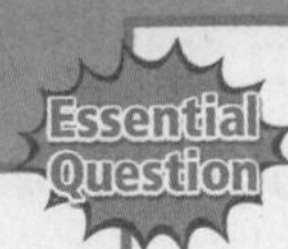

Essential Question

How Can You Use Patterns and Mental Math to Multiply a Whole Number by a Power of 10?

A

Arnold read a newspaper article about how much garbage each person produces each week. How many pounds of garbage are produced each week by 10,000 people?

PEOPLE MAKE LOTS OF GARBAGE

In Benders County, each person produces 32 pounds of garbage per week. This is more than people produced

Patterns will help show how to use mental math to multiply by powers of ten.

Find $32 \times 10{,}000$. Use place-value relationships and look for patterns.

B

One Way

Multiply 32 by 1; 10; 100; 1,000 and 10,000.

$32 \times 1 = 32$ ones $= 32$
$32 \times 10 = 32$ tens $= 320$
$32 \times 100 = 32$ hundreds $= 3{,}200$
$32 \times 1{,}000 = 32$ thousands $= 32{,}000$
$32 \times 10{,}000 = 32$ ten thousands $= 320{,}000$

So, 320,000 pounds of garbage are produced.

Shortcut rule:
Count the number of zeros in the power of 10. Annex that number of zeros to the other factor to find the product.

C

Another Way

Write each power of 10 using exponents.

$32 \times 1 = 32 \times 10^0 = 32$
$32 \times 10 = 32 \times 10^1 = 320$
$32 \times 100 = 32 \times 10^2 = 3{,}200$
$32 \times 1{,}000 = 32 \times 10^3 = 32{,}000$
$32 \times 10{,}000 = 32 \times 10^4 = 320{,}000$

So, 320,000 pounds of garbage are produced.

Shortcut rule:
Look at the exponent for the power of 10. Annex that number of zeros to the other factor to find the product.

Convince Me! **Critique Reasoning** Nellie says that the product of $60 \times 1{,}000$ is 60,000 because you annex three more zeroes to 60. Kara says the answer is 6,000 because the answer should have only three zeros. Who is right? How do you know?

Name ______________________

Practice Buddy Tools Assessment

Guided Practice*

Do You Understand?

1. How many zeros will there be in the product of 39 × 1,000? How many zeros will there be in the product of 50 × 1,000?

2. Explain how to find the product of 90×10^4.

Do You Know How?

In **3** and **4**, write the products.

3. 60 × 1
60 × 10
60 × 100
60 × 1,000
60 × 10,000

4. 13×10^0
13×10^1
13×10^2
13×10^3
13×10^4

Independent Practice

Leveled Practice In **5–24**, find each product.

5. 89 × 1
89 × 10
89 × 100
89 × 1,000
89 × 10,000

6. 30 × 1
30 × 10
30 × 100
30 × 1,000
30 × 10,000

7. 41×10^0
41×10^1
41×10^2
41×10^3
41×10^4

8. 90×10^0
90×10^1
90×10^2
90×10^3
90×10^4

9. 4×10^3

10. 85 × 100

11. 16×10^2

12. $10^3 \times 38$

13. 52×10^5

14. 4×10^4

15. 29 × 10,000

16. 10 × 6,837

17. 1,000 × 10

18. $10^1 \times 615$

19. 250×10^0

20. 382 × 10,000

21. 1,000 × 57

22. 80×10^3

23. $10^3 \times 374$

24. 194 × 100

For another example, see Set A on page 157.

Problem Solving

25. **Use Structure** At a football championship game, the home team gave a football to each of the first 100 fans who arrived at the stadium. Each football cost the team $28. How much did the team pay for the footballs it gave away?

26. **Construct Arguments** Which expression is greater, 93×10^3 or 11×10^4? How do you know?

27. A truck is carrying 10^2 bushels of onions, 10^1 bushels of peaches, and 10^3 bushels of corn. What is the total weight of the crops?

DATA

Crop	Weight per bushel (pounds)
Apples	48
Onions	57
Peaches	50
Ears of corn	70

28. **Make Sense and Persevere** Norman bought a 16-pound bag of charcoal for $7.89 and a 10.4-pound bag of charcoal for $5.69. What was the total weight of the two bags of charcoal?

29. **Higher Order Thinking** There are 2,000 pounds in 1 ton. In the United States, the weight limit for a truck and its cargo is 40 tons. How many pounds is that? How did you find the answer?

Assessment

30. Choose all equations that are true.

- ☐ $48 \times 1{,}000 = 4{,}800$
- ☐ $48 \times 10^2 = 4{,}800$
- ☐ $48 \times 10^4 = 480{,}000$
- ☐ $48 \times 10^3 = 4{,}800$
- ☐ $48 \times 10^3 = 48{,}000$

31. Choose all equations that are true.

- ☐ $20 \times 100 = 2{,}000$
- ☐ $20 \times 10^3 = 20{,}000$
- ☐ $20 \times 1{,}000 = 2{,}000$
- ☐ $20 \times 10 = 2{,}000$
- ☐ $20 \times 10^5 = 2{,}000{,}000$

Name ______________________

Homework & Practice 3-1

Multiply Greater Numbers by Powers of 10

Another Look!

Patterns can help you multiply by powers of 10.

$53 \times 1 = 53$
$53 \times 10 = 530$
$53 \times 100 = 5{,}300$
$53 \times 1{,}000 = 53{,}000$
$53 \times 10{,}000 = 530{,}000$

$70 \times 10^0 = 70$
$70 \times 10^1 = 700$
$70 \times 10^2 = 7{,}000$
$70 \times 10^3 = 70{,}000$
$70 \times 10^4 = 700{,}000$

Look at the number of zeros or the exponent for the power of 10. Annex that number of zeros to the other factor.

1. To find $61 \times 1{,}000$, annex _____ zeros to _____ to form the product _______.

2. To find 20×10^4, annex _____ zeros to _____ to form the product _______.

In **3–6**, use patterns to find each product.

3. 75×1
75×10
75×100
$75 \times 1{,}000$
$75 \times 10{,}000$

4. 50×1
50×10
50×100
$50 \times 1{,}000$
$50 \times 10{,}000$

5. 60×10^0
60×10^1
60×10^2
60×10^3
60×10^4

6. 18×10^0
18×10^1
18×10^2
18×10^3
18×10^4

In **7–18**, find each product.

7. 84×100

8. 90×10

9. 54×10^2

10. $10^3 \times 12$

11. 72×10^5

12. $278 \times 1{,}000$

13. 36×10^4

14. $10^2 \times 539$

15. 4×10^1

16. $3{,}510 \times 10^0$

17. 100×17

18. 102×10^4

19. Construct Arguments Ms. O'Malley's cousin lives 1,650 miles away. Ms. O'Malley won a gift card for 100 gallons of gas. If her car can travel 35 miles on each gallon, can she drive roundtrip to see her cousin on the free gas? Explain how you know.

20. Each beehive on Larson's Honey Farm usually produces 85 pounds of honey per year. About how many pounds of honey will 10^3 hives produce in a year?

21. Make Sense and Persevere A hotel chain is ordering new furnishings. What is the total cost of 1,000 sheet sets, 1,000 pillows, and 100 desk chairs?

DATA

Item	Price
Towel sets	$18
Sheet sets	$24
Pillows	$7
Desk chair	$114

22. Be Precise Which number is greater: 87 or 13.688? How do you know?

23. Higher Order Thinking The weight of an elephant is 10^3 times the weight of a cat. If the elephant weighs 14,000 pounds, how many pounds does the cat weigh? How did you find the answer?

Assessment

24. Choose all equations that are true.

- ☐ $14 \times 1{,}000 = 1{,}400$
- ☐ $95 \times 10 = 950$
- ☐ $30 \times 100 = 300$
- ☐ $6 \times 10{,}000 = 60{,}000$
- ☐ $50 \times 100 = 50{,}000$

25. Choose all equations that are true.

- ☐ $72 \times 10^2 = 7{,}200$
- ☐ $40 \times 10^3 = 40{,}000$
- ☐ $164 \times 10 = 16{,}400$
- ☐ $55 \times 10^2 = 55{,}000$
- ☐ $97 \times 10^4 = 970{,}000$

Name ______________________________

Lesson 3-2
Estimate Products

I can ...
estimate products using mental math.

I can also reason about math.

Solve & Share

A school club wants to buy shirts for each of its 38 members. Each shirt costs $23. About how much money will all the shirts cost? ***Solve this problem any way you choose.***

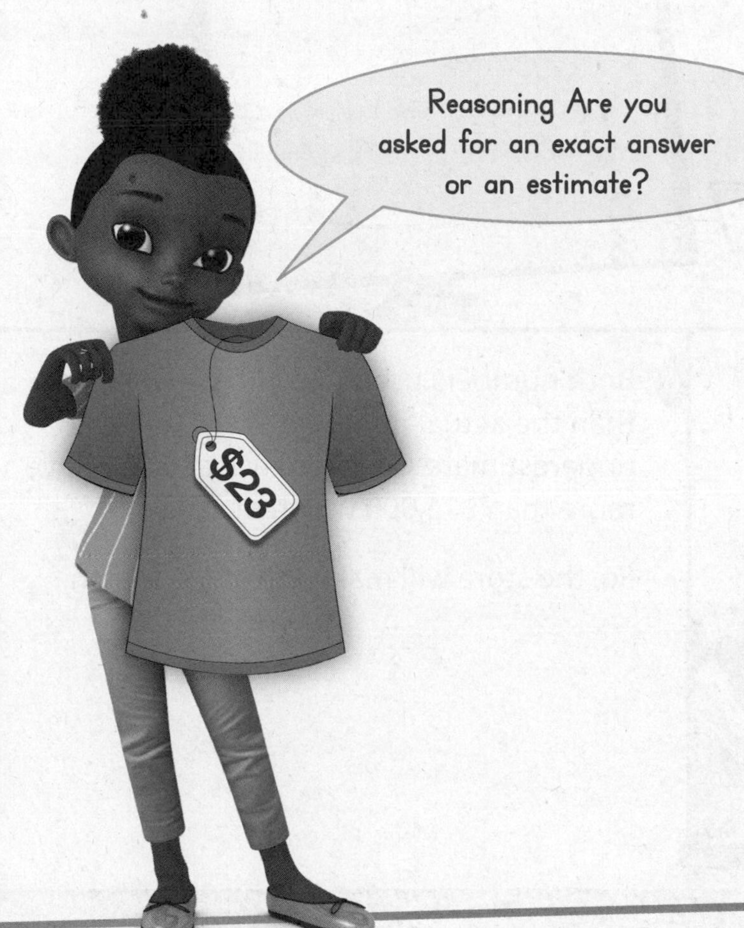

Look Back! Construct Arguments How can you use number sense to tell that the exact answer has to be greater than $600? Explain how you know.

Essential Question: How Can You Estimate Products?

A

A store needs at least $15,000 in sales per month to make a profit. If the store is open every day in March and sales average $525 per day, will the store make a profit in March?

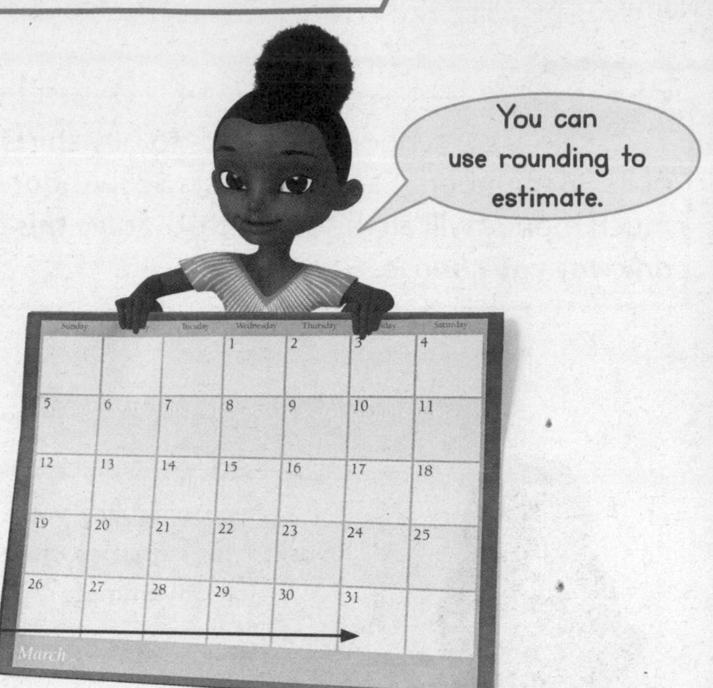

Is the sales total for March at least $15,000?

B

Use Rounding to Estimate

$525 rounds to $500.

31 rounds to 30.

Find 30×500.

$30 \times 500 = 15{,}000$

You know that $3 \times 5 = 15$.

C

Both numbers used to estimate were less than the actual numbers, so 15,000 is an underestimate. The store will actually have more than $15,000 worth of sales.

So, the store will make a profit in March.

Convince Me! **Critique Reasoning** A different store needs to make at least $20,000 to make a profit in March. They average $685 a day for the month. James used rounding and estimation to say, "$685 is almost $700. $700 × 30 days is $21,000. I think it is going to be a close call!" What do you think?

Name ______________________________

Practice Buddy · Tools · Assessment

Another Example

Estimate 24 × 398.

25 and 4 are compatible numbers because their product is easy to compute mentally.

25 × 4 = 100

25 × 40 = 1,000

25 × 400 = 10,000

So, 10,000 is a good estimate for 24 × 398.

You can also use compatible numbers to estimate.

Both numbers used to estimate were greater than the actual numbers.

So, 10,000 is an overestimate.

Guided Practice*

Do You Understand?

1. **Number Sense** Each egg carton holds one dozen eggs. Michael's chicken farm fills 121 egg cartons. He thinks that there were over 1,500 eggs. Is he correct? Use an estimate to find out.

Do You Know How?

In **2–5**, estimate. Then, tell if your estimate is an overestimate or underestimate.

2. 29 × 688
3. 210 × 733
4. 43 × 108
5. 380 × 690

Independent Practice

Leveled Practice In **6–17**, estimate each product.

6. 180 × 586
7. 300 × 118
8. 19 × 513
9. 38 × 249
10. 11 × 803
11. 44 × 212
12. 790 × 397
13. 42 × 598
14. 25 × 191
15. 408 × 676
16. 290 × 12
17. 854 × 733

*For another example, see Set B on page 157.

Problem Solving

18. **Reasoning** Estimate 530 × 375. Is the estimated product closer to 150,000 or 200,000? Explain.

19. **Vocabulary** Is 500 an underestimate or overestimate for the product of 12 and 53?

20. **Construct Arguments** Samuel needs to estimate the product of 23 × 395. Explain two different methods Samuel can use to estimate.

21. Rebekah said that 10^3 is 30 because $10 + 10 + 10 = 30$. Do you agree? Explain.

22. **Higher Order Thinking** Abby counts 12 large boxes and 18 small boxes of pencils in the supply cabinet. Each large box contains 144 pencils. Each small box contains 24 pencils. Estimate the total number of pencils. Is your estimate an overestimate or an underestimate? Explain why it might be better to have an underestimate rather than an overestimate.

23. **Critique Reasoning** Susan used rounding to estimate 24 × 413 and found 20 × 400. Jeremy used compatible numbers and found 25 × 400. Whose method gives an estimate closer to the actual product? Explain.

Assessment

24. Lance has 102 packages of sports cards. Each package has 28 cards. Use rounding to estimate. About how many cards does Lance have?

Ⓐ 2,000
Ⓑ 2,500
Ⓒ 3,000
Ⓓ 3,500

25. Which does NOT show a reasonable estimate of 24 × 338?

Ⓐ 6,000
Ⓑ 7,000
Ⓒ 7,500
Ⓓ 10,000

Name ______________________

Homework & Practice 3-2

Estimate Products

Another Look!

DATA

Supplies	
Electronic thermometers	$19 each
Pulse monitors	$189 each
Pillows	$17 each
Telephones	$19 each

Use rounding to estimate.

Estimate 14 × 189.

You can round 14 to 10 and 189 to 200.

10 × 200 = 2,000

Use compatible numbers to estimate.

Estimate 14 × 189.

Replace 14 with 15 and 189 with 200.

15 × 200 = 3,000

The 14 pulse monitors will cost between $2,000 and $3,000.

1. About how much would it cost to buy 18 MP3 players? About how much would it cost to buy 18 CD/MP3 players?

DATA

Electronics Prices	
CD player	$74.00
MP3 player	$99.00
CD/MP3 player	$199.00
AM/FM radio	$29.00

In **2–15**, estimate each product.

2. 184 × 210
Round 184 to ______.
Round 210 to ______.
Multiply ______ × ______ = ______.

3. 77 × 412
Round 77 to ______.
Round 412 to ______.
Multiply ______ × ______ = ______.

4. 87 × 403

5. 19 × 718

6. 888 × 300

7. 352 × 20

8. 520 × 797

9. 189 × 46

10. 560 × 396

11. 498 × 47

12. 492 × 22

13. 928 × 89

14. 308 × 18

15. 936 × 410

16. **Reasoning** Laura's family is going on a vacation. They will drive 4,180 miles over the next two weeks. About how many miles will they drive on average each week?

17. **Make Sense and Persevere** A bus service drives passengers between Milwaukee and Chicago every day. They travel from city to city 8 times each day. The distance between the two cities is 89 miles. In February, there are 28 days. The company's budget allows for 28,000 total miles for February. Do you think the budget is reasonable? Explain.

18. **Higher Order Thinking** Explain whether rounding or compatible numbers gives a closer estimate for the product below.

$48 \times 123 = 5{,}904$

19. A case of 24 pairs of the same kind of sports shoes costs a little more than $800. Explain whether $28 per pair with tax included is a good estimate of the price.

20. The number of Adult tickets is the same as the number of Child (age 5–12) tickets. A total of 38 tickets was purchased. What is the total cost of the tickets? Explain.

DATA

Ticket	Price (in $)
Adult	23
Child, age 5–12	17
Under 5	8

Assessment

21. Which does **NOT** show a reasonable estimate of 360×439?

Ⓐ 100,000
Ⓑ 140,000
Ⓒ 160,000
Ⓓ 180,000

22. A club orders 124 T-shirts at a cost of $18 each. Which is the best estimate of the total cost of the order?

Ⓐ $1,000
Ⓑ $2,000
Ⓒ $3,000
Ⓓ $4,000

Name ____________________

Lesson 3-3
Multiply 3-Digit by 2-Digit Numbers

I can …
multiply 3-digit by 2-digit numbers.

I can also make sense of problems.

Solve & Share

A local charity collected 163 cans of food every day for 14 days. How many cans did they collect in the first 10 days? How many did they collect in the remaining 4 days? How many cans did they collect in all? ***Solve this problem any way you choose!***

You can make sense and persevere in solving this problem. You know how to multiply by 10 and by a single-digit number.

Look Back! Reasoning How can you check that your answer is reasonable?

Essential Question

How Do You Multiply 3-Digit Numbers by 2-Digit Numbers?

A

Last month a bakery sold 389 boxes of bagels. How many bagels did the store sell last month?

B

Step 1

Multiply by the ones, and regroup if necessary.

$$\begin{array}{r} \scriptstyle 1\,1 \\ 389 \\ \times \quad 12 \\ \hline 778 \end{array}$$

2 × 9 ones = 18 ones or 1 ten and 8 ones
2 × 8 tens = 16 tens
16 tens + 1 ten = 17 tens
17 tens = 1 hundred 7 tens

2 × 3 hundreds = 6 hundreds
6 hundreds + 1 hundred = 7 hundreds

C

Step 2

Multiply by the tens, and regroup if necessary.

$$\begin{array}{r} 389 \\ \times 12 \\ \hline 778 \\ +\ 3890 \\ \hline \end{array}$$

10 × 9 ones = 90 ones

10 × 8 tens = 80 tens, or 8 hundreds

10 × 3 hundreds = 30 hundreds, or 3 thousands

D

Step 3

Add the partial products.

$$\begin{array}{r} 389 \\ \times \quad 12 \\ \hline 778 \\ +\ 3890 \\ \hline 4{,}668 \end{array}$$

The store sold 4,668 bagels last month.

Convince Me! Construct Arguments Is 300 × 10 a good estimate for the number of bagels sold at the bakery? Explain.

Name ______________________________

Guided Practice*

Do You Understand?

1. Use Structure A theater can seat 540 people at one time. How many tickets are sold if the theater sells out every seat for one 30-day month?

2. Number Sense Is 500 × 30 a good estimate for the number of tickets sold at the theater in one month?

Do You Know How?

In **3–6**, find each product. Estimate to check that your answer is reasonable.

3. $\begin{array}{r} 236 \\ \times\ 46 \\ \hline \end{array}$

4. $\begin{array}{r} 61 \\ \times\ 25 \\ \hline \end{array}$

5. $\begin{array}{r} 951 \\ \times\ 62 \\ \hline \end{array}$

6. $\begin{array}{r} 185 \\ \times\ 5 \\ \hline \end{array}$

Independent Practice

Leveled Practice In **7–22**, find each product. Estimate to check that your answer is reasonable.

7. $\begin{array}{r} 51 \\ \times\ 10 \\ \hline \end{array}$

8. $\begin{array}{r} 892 \\ \times\ 18 \\ \hline \end{array}$

9. $\begin{array}{r} 946 \\ \times\ 33 \\ \hline \end{array}$

10. $\begin{array}{r} 735 \\ \times\ 41 \\ \hline \end{array}$

11. 25 × 100

12. 81 × 11

13. 106 × 7

14. 90 × 59

15. 18 × 360

16. 75 × 222

17. 481 × 35

18. 659 × 17

19. 340 × 89

20. 439 × 22

21. 273 × 9

22. 64 × 475

*For another example, see Set C on page 157.

Problem Solving

23. Math and Science How many times does a rabbit's heart beat in 1 hour?

24. Make Sense and Persevere In 1 hour, how many more times does a rabbit's heart beat than a dog's heart? Write an equation to show your work.

DATA

Animal	Heart Rate (beats per minute)
Dog	100
Gerbil	360
Rabbit	212

25. Construct Arguments Is 3,198 a reasonable product for 727×44? Why or why not?

26. Higher Order Thinking A garden store sells plants in flats. There are 6 plants in each tray. Each flat has 6 trays. The garden store sold 18 flats on Saturday and 21 flats on Sunday. How many plants did the garden store sell in all?

27. Tricia is building a rectangular patio. The patio will be 108 bricks wide and 19 bricks long. She has 2,000 bricks. Does she have enough bricks to build the patio? Explain. Show your work in the box.

Name ___________________

Homework & Practice 3-3

Multiply 3-Digit by 2-Digit Numbers

Another Look!

Last year, 23 students in fifth grade were assigned a kindergarten student as a reading buddy. Each student read for 1 hour during each reading session and for a total of 128 sessions. How many hours in all did the fifth-grade students read?

Estimate: 130 times 20 is 2,600

Step 1

Multiply by the ones. Regroup as needed.

$$\begin{array}{r} \overset{2}{1}28 \\ \times \quad 3 \\ \hline 384 \end{array}$$

Step 2

Multiply by the tens. Regroup as needed.

$$\begin{array}{r} \overset{1}{1}28 \\ \times \quad 20 \\ \hline 2,560 \end{array}$$

Step 3

Add the partial products.

$$\begin{array}{r} 128 \\ \times \quad 23 \\ \hline \overset{1}{3}84 \\ +\,2,560 \\ \hline 2,944 \end{array}$$

The fifth-grade students read for 2,944 hours in all. The answer is reasonable because it is close to the estimate.

In **1–10**, find each product. Estimate to check that your answer is reasonable.

1. 282 × 19

← Multiply by the ones.
+ ← Multiply by the tens.
← Add the partial products.

2. 538 × 46

← Multiply by the ones.
+ ← Multiply by the tens.
← Add the partial products.

3. 395 × 76

4. 83 × 57

5. 628 × 33

6. 154 × 35

7. 682 × 25

8. 324 × 71

9. 158 × 6

10. 16 × 29

11. Critique Reasoning Is 2,750 a reasonable answer for 917 × 33? Explain.

12. A-Z **Vocabulary** What two partial products would you add to find 513 × 46?

13. How many kilometers could the red car travel in 12 hours? Write an equation to show your work.

14. Higher Order Thinking In 12 hours, how many more kilometers could the yellow car go than the red car? Show your work.

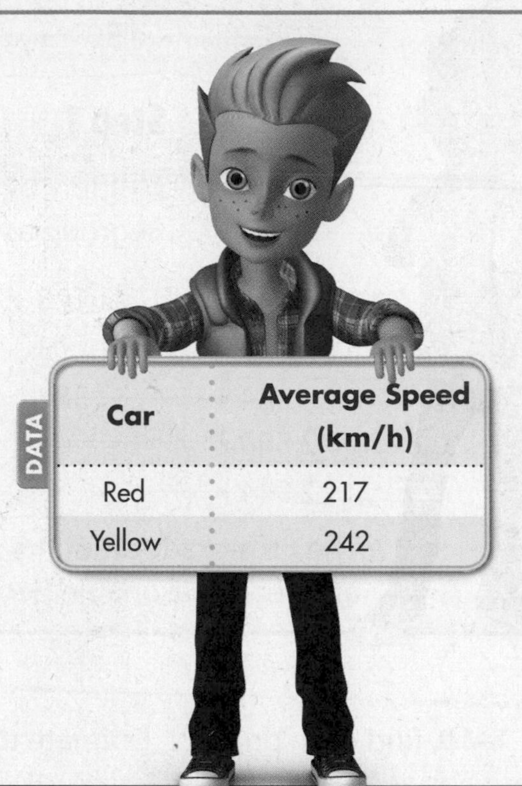

DATA

Car	Average Speed (km/h)
Red	217
Yellow	242

Assessment

15. Katie is building a rectangular wall. The wall will be 332 bricks wide and 39 bricks tall. She has 15,000 bricks. Does she have enough bricks to build the wall? Explain. Show your work in the box.

Name ____________________

Lesson 3-4
Multiply Whole Numbers with Zeros

I can ...
multiply numbers that have a zero in them.

I can also look for patterns to solve problems.

Solve & Share

A school district is replacing all of the desks in its classrooms. There are 103 classrooms and each classroom needs 24 new desks. How many desks will the school district need to buy?

Use Structure Use what you know about multiplying 3-digit and 2-digit numbers. Show your work!

Look Back! Reasoning What is a good estimate for the problem above? Explain.

Learn Glossary

Essential Question How Can You Multiply with Zeros?

A

An antique steam train makes one sight-seeing tour each day. If every seat is filled for each trip, how many passengers can it carry for 31 tours?

You can use multiplication to find the total number of passengers.

B

Step 1

Find 31 × 208.

Estimate:

30 × 200 = 6,000

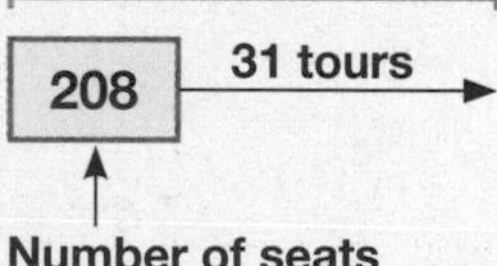

C

Step 2

Multiply the ones.

Regroup if necessary.

Remember that multiplying with a zero gives a product of zero.

$$\begin{array}{r} 208 \\ \times \quad 31 \\ \hline 208 \end{array}$$

D

Step 3

Multiply the tens.

Regroup if necessary.

$$\begin{array}{r} \overset{2}{2}08 \\ \times \quad 31 \\ \hline 208 \\ +\ 6240 \\ \hline 6,448 \end{array}$$

Add the Partial Products.

The train can carry 6,448 passengers.

Convince Me! Model with Math Suppose the train fills an average of 102 seats for each tour. What is a reasonable estimate for the number of passengers that the train can carry in 28 tours? Write an equation to show your work.

Name ____________________

Guided Practice*

Do You Understand?

1. In an auditorium, there are 104 rows with 24 seats in each row. How many seats are available?

2. **Reasoning** Why is it important to "estimate to check for reasonableness"?

Do You Know How?

In **3–6**, multiply to find the product. Estimate to check for reasonableness.

3. $\begin{array}{r} 205 \\ \times\ 23 \\ \hline \end{array}$

4. $\begin{array}{r} 108 \\ \times\ 34 \\ \hline \end{array}$

5. $\begin{array}{r} 410 \\ \times\ 44 \\ \hline \end{array}$

6. $\begin{array}{r} 302 \\ \times\ 30 \\ \hline \end{array}$

Independent Practice

Leveled Practice In **7–18**, find each product. Estimate to check for reasonableness.

7. $\begin{array}{r} 302 \\ \times\ 17 \\ \hline \end{array}$

8. $\begin{array}{r} 608 \\ \times\ 23 \\ \hline \end{array}$

9. $\begin{array}{r} 109 \\ \times\ 47 \\ \hline \end{array}$

10. $\begin{array}{r} 510 \\ \times\ 72 \\ \hline \end{array}$

11. $\begin{array}{r} 902 \\ \times\ 35 \\ \hline \end{array}$

12. $\begin{array}{r} 207 \\ \times\ 61 \\ \hline \end{array}$

13. $\begin{array}{r} 108 \\ \times\ 58 \\ \hline \end{array}$

14. $\begin{array}{r} 505 \\ \times\ 77 \\ \hline \end{array}$

15. $\begin{array}{r} 407 \\ \times\ 39 \\ \hline \end{array}$

16. $\begin{array}{r} 280 \\ \times\ 66 \\ \hline \end{array}$

17. $\begin{array}{r} 105 \\ \times\ 24 \\ \hline \end{array}$

18. $\begin{array}{r} 360 \\ \times\ 48 \\ \hline \end{array}$

For another example, see Set C on page 157.

Problem Solving

19. Make Sense and Persevere There are 27 students in Mr. Mello's class. Find the total number of pages the students read by the end of November.

20. Each student read 41 pages in December. How many total pages did the students read by the end of December?

DATA

History Book Progress

Month	Chapter	Pages
September	1	35
October	2	38
November	3	35

21. Critique Reasoning Meredith says that 15.17 is greater than 15.8 because 17 is greater than 8. Do you agree? Explain your reasoning.

22. Use Structure Trudy wants to multiply 66×606. She says that all she has to do is find 6×606 and then double that number. Explain why Trudy's method will not give the correct answer. Then show how to find the correct product.

23. Higher Order Thinking Maria needs a trombone for only 12 months. Renting the trombone costs $34 per month. She can buy the trombone for $495. Should she buy or rent the trombone? Explain. How much does she pay?

24. Reasoning Another music store rents trombones for $30 per month plus a yearly fee of $48. Which deal is better? Should Maria change her rental plan?

Assessment

25. What are two partial products you would add to find 41×709? Write those partial products in the box.

41×709

709 710 719 2,836 3,545 28,360 28,760

Name ____________________

Homework & Practice 3-4

Multiply Whole Numbers with Zeros

Another Look!

Find the product of 304 × 23.

$$\begin{array}{r} \overset{1}{3}04 \\ \times \quad 23 \\ \hline 912 \\ + \; 6080 \\ \hline 6,992 \end{array}$$

Step 1: First, multiply 304 by 3 ones.

Step 2: Then, multiply 304 by 2 tens.

Step 3: Finally, add the partial products.

1. Use the place-value chart at the right to multiply 36 × 405. Record each partial product in the correct place in the chart.

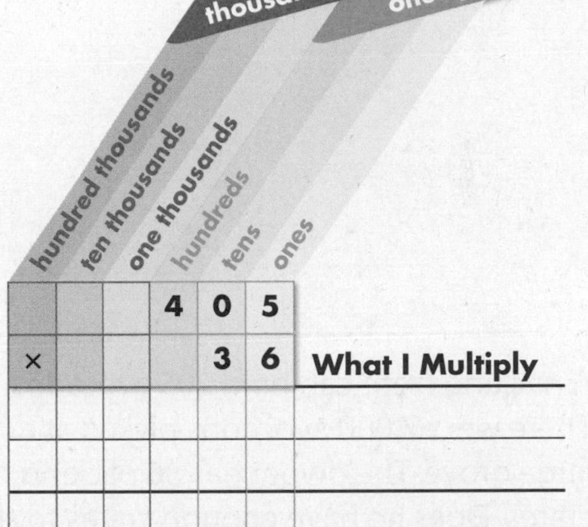

In **2–9**, find each product. Estimate to check for reasonableness.

2. 203 × 12

3. 306 × 21

4. 109 × 73

5. 601 × 45

6. 708 × 34

7. 520 × 63

8. 405 × 70

9. 802 × 94

10. **Reasoning** The Memorial Middle School Band has 108 members. They want to buy jackets with the name of the band on the back. What is the difference in the total price of the screen-print and the embroidered jackets?

DATA

Jackets	Price (in $)
Screen print name	35
Embroidered name	48

11. **Critique Reasoning** Wildlife protection groups build bat houses to help save bats. One bat house holds about 300 bats. Larry says that 12 bat houses can hold about 4,500 bats. Do you agree? Explain.

12. **Higher Order Thinking** Replace the *a*, *b*, *c*, and *d* with the digits 2, 4, 6, 8 to form the greatest product. Each digit can only be used once. Explain your substitutions.

$$\begin{array}{r} a\,0\,b \\ \times \quad c\,d \\ \hline \end{array}$$

13. A packing crate can hold 205 avocados. There were 7,000 avocados picked at a large grove. The owner has 36 packing crates. Does he have enough crates to ship out the avocados? Explain.

14. **Construct Arguments** Sarah found that the product of 49 and 805 is 3,165. How would finding an estimate help her know that the answer is NOT reasonable?

Assessment

15. What are two partial products you could add to find 990 × 37? Write those partial products in the box.

990 × 37

297 2,970 6,930 69,300
693 6,330 29,700

Name ______________________

Lesson 3-5
Multiply Multi-Digit Numbers

I can ...
find the product of multi-digit factors.

I can also reason about math.

Solve & Share

Write and solve a real-world problem with a question that can be answered by the equation.

$$36 \times 208 = n$$

You can use reasoning to connect mathematics to everyday life. Think about the situations multiplication describes.

Look Back! Construct Arguments Write a real-world problem for the equation $208 \times 36 = n$. Tell how your two problems are the same and how they are different.

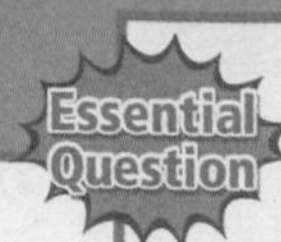

How Can You Use Multiplication to Solve Problems?

A

How much does the Carson family pay each year for their cell phones?

A bar diagram can be used to show joining equal groups.

I can use the Commutative, Associative, and Distributive Properties to make the computations easier.

B

Step 1

Draw a bar diagram that represents the problem.

n

271	271	271	271	271	271	271	271	271	271	271	271

Then write an equation.

$12 \times 271 = n$

C

Step 2

Multiply to solve.

$$\begin{array}{r} \overset{1}{2}71 \\ \times \quad 12 \\ \hline 542 \\ +\,2710 \\ \hline 3{,}252 \end{array}$$

The Carson family pays $3,252 a year for their cell phones.

Convince Me! **Reasoning** Is $3,252 a year a reasonable answer? Explain.

Name ____________________

Guided Practice*

Do You Understand?

1. Carlos saves 18 cents every day of the year. If there are 365 days this year, how many cents will he have saved by the end of the year? Write an equation that represents the problem. Then solve the equation.

2. **Model with Math** Lila drives 129 kilometers round trip to work. How many kilometers does she drive in 31 days? Write an equation that represents the problem. Then solve the equation.

Do You Know How?

In **3–6**, estimate each product. Then complete each calculation. Check that your answer is reasonable.

3. 134×11

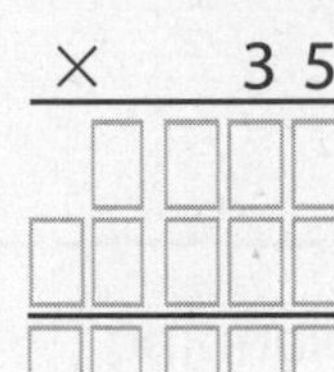

4. 208×26

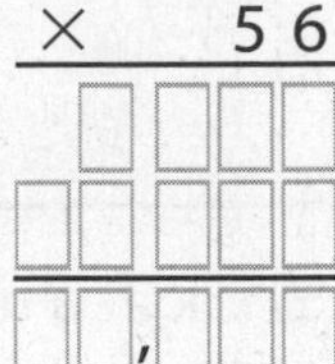

5. 428×35

6. 275×56

Independent Practice

Leveled Practice In **7–22**, estimate and then compute each product. Check that your answer is reasonable.

7. 531×47

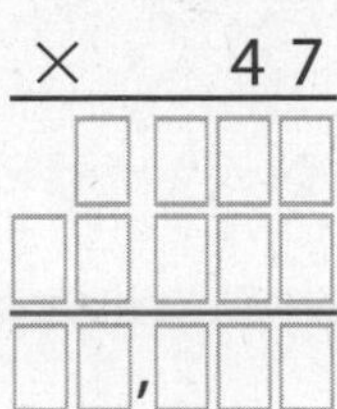

8. 759×68

9. 367×92

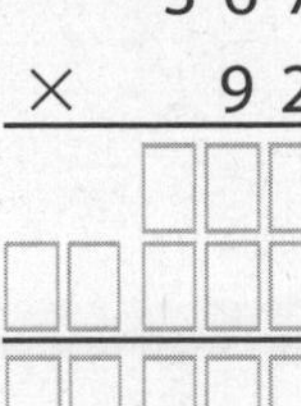

10. 817×45

11. $1{,}206 \times 77$

12. 543×18

13. 908×62

14. 750×81

15. $6{,}755 \times 9$

16. 869×46

17. 922×81

18. 783×14

19. 684×15

20. 650×22

21. $2{,}525 \times 37$

22. 615×41

*For another example, see Set C on page 157.

Problem Solving

For **23** and **24**, use the table.

23. Model with Math Jason frequently travels for work. This year he plans to make 15 trips to Chicago. What is the total cost for the airfare? Write an equation that represents the problem. Then solve the equation.

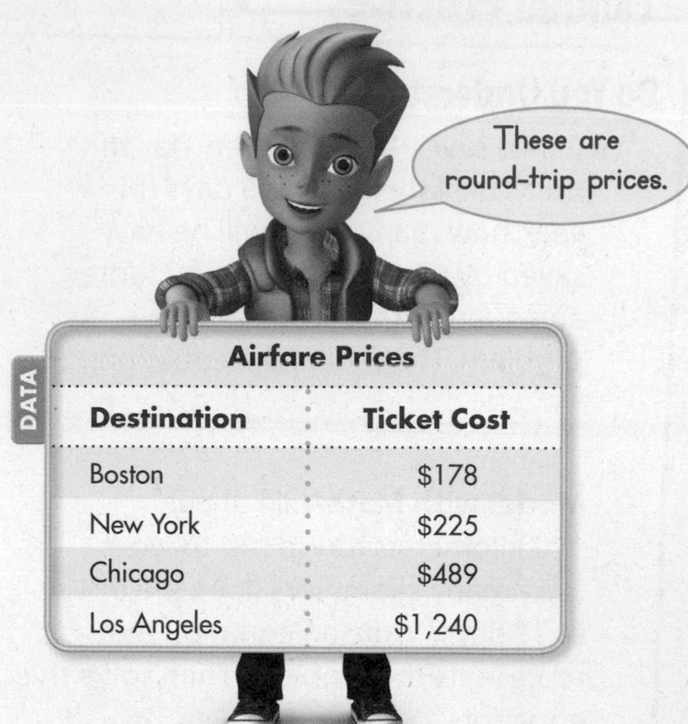

Airfare Prices

Destination	Ticket Cost
Boston	$178
New York	$225
Chicago	$489
Los Angeles	$1,240

24. Reasoning Which would cost more: 15 trips to Boston or 11 trips to New York? Explain.

25. A cook at a restaurant is planning her food order. She expects to use 115 pounds of potatoes each day for 12 days. How many pounds of potatoes will she order?

? number of pounds

115	115	115	115	115	115	115	115	115	115	115	115

12 days

26. Higher Order Thinking Carolyn bought a gallon of paint that covers 250 square feet. She wants to paint a wall that is 16 feet wide and 12 feet high. Explain whether or not she will need more than one gallon of paint.

Assessment

27. Jack estimates the product 257 × 29 is less than 6,000. Marta disagrees. She estimates the product is more than 7,000. Whose estimate is better? Explain your thinking.

28. When you multiply a 3-digit number by a 2-digit number, what is the greatest number of digits the product can have? Explain.

Name ____________________

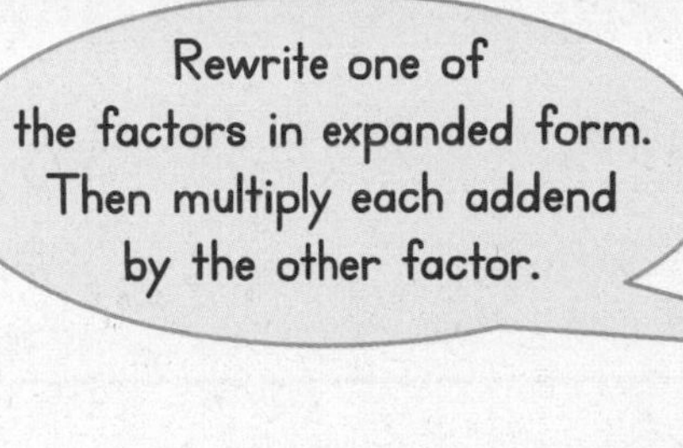

Homework & Practice 3-5

Multiply Multi-Digit Numbers

Another Look!

A sports store sells skateboards for $112. Last month the store sold 45 skateboards. How much money did the store make from selling them?

Use mental math to multiply.

112 = 100 + 10 + 2

2 × 45 = 90

10 × 45 = 450

100 × 45 = 4,500

90 + 450 + 4,500 = 5,040

The store made $5,040 from selling skateboards.

1. Find 1,206 × 5 using expanded form.

1,206 = 1,000 + 200 + 0 + ______

1,000 × 5 = ______

200 × 5 = ______

______ × 5 = ______

5,000 + ______ + 30 = ______

So, 1,206 × 5 = ______.

2. Find 240 × 15 using partial products.

240 × 5 = ______

240 × ______ = 2,400

1,200 + ______ = ______

So, 240 × 15 = ______.

For **3–10**, find each product.

3. 423 × 18

4. 914 × 12

5. 125 × 15

6. 425 × 82

7. 185 × 24

8. 1,288 × 33

9. 6,301 × 47

10. 3,440 × 75

11. **Vocabulary** Circle all the **partial products** below.

$$\begin{array}{r} 452 \\ \times \quad 12 \\ \hline 904 \\ +\,4{,}520 \\ \hline 5{,}424 \end{array}$$

12. **Reasoning** Tomika plans to run 84 miles in 4 weeks. If she continues the pattern, how many miles will she run in 1 year? Explain.

1 year = 52 weeks

13. Pete owns several pizza restaurants. He sells cheese pizzas for $12 each. How much money was made in January at the Westland location?

DATA

Cheese Pizza Sales for January

Location	Number Sold
Downtown	1,356
Center City	998
Westland	1,824

14. How many more pizzas did the Downtown location sell than the Center City location? Write an equation to show your work.

15. **Make Sense and Persevere** How many more pizzas does the Westland location need to sell to equal the total number of pizzas sold by the Downtown and Center City locations? Explain your work.

16. **Higher Order Thinking** A farmer grows 128 red tomato plants and 102 yellow tomato plants. Each plant produces about 32 tomatoes. The farmer plans to sell each tomato for $2. Explain how to find a reasonable estimate for the total amount of money the farmer will earn if she sells all of the tomatoes.

Assessment

17. Jane multiplied 825 × 22 and got 3,300. Flynn multiplied the same numbers and got 18,150. Which student is correct? What mistake did the other student make?

18. Lisa estimates the product 351 × 34 is more than 10,000. Gene disagrees. He estimates the product is less than 10,000. Whose estimate is better? Explain your thinking.

Name ____________________

Solve & Share

Kevin's family took 239 photos on their summer vacation. Marco and his family took 12 times as many photos on their vacation. How many photos did Marco's family take? ***Solve this problem any way you choose.***

Lesson 3-6
Solve Word Problems Using Multiplication

I can ...
solve word problems involving multiplication.

I can also model with math to solve problems.

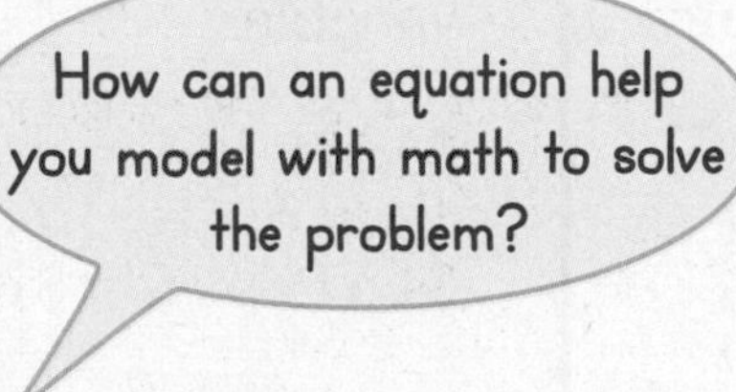

Look Back! Construct Arguments How can you use estimation to tell if your answer is reasonable? Explain.

Essential Question

How Can You Use a Bar Diagram to Solve a Multiplication Problem?

A

In 1980, a painting sold for $1,575. In 2015, the same painting sold for 5 times as much. What was the price of the painting in 2015?

You can draw a bar diagram and use a variable to find the new price of the painting.

B *What am I asked to find?*

The price of the painting in 2015.

Let p = the price of the painting in 2015.

Draw a bar diagram to represent the problem.

price in 2015 (p)

2015	$1,575	$1,575	$1,575	$1,575	$1,575	5 times as much
1980	$1,575					

C Write and solve an equation using the variable.

$\$1{,}575 \times 5 = p$

$\$1{,}575 \times 5 = \$7{,}875.$

So, $p = \$7{,}875$.

In 2015, the painting sold for $7,875.

You can use repeated addition or division to check your answer!

Convince Me! **Construct Arguments** How can you use estimation to justify that the answer $7,875 is reasonable?

Name ______________________

Practice Buddy Tools Assessment

Guided Practice*

Do You Understand?

1. **Model with Math** Write a real-world problem that uses multiplication. Then draw a bar diagram and write an equation to solve your problem.

Do You Know How?

In **2**, write and solve an equation.

2. Sharon's Stationery Store has 1,219 boxes of cards. May's Market has 3 times as many boxes of cards. How many boxes of cards does May's Market have?

b boxes of cards

May's	1,219	1,219	1,219	3 times as many
Sharon's	1,219			

Independent Practice

In **3–5**, draw a bar-diagram to model the situation. Then write and solve an equation.

3. There are 14 theaters at the mall. Each theater has 175 seats. How many seats are there in all?

? seats → ?

14 theaters →	175	175	175	175	175	175	175	175	175	175	175	175	175	175

175 seats for each theater

4. Brad lives 12 times as far away from the ocean as Jennie. If Jennie lives 48 miles from the ocean, how many miles from the ocean does Brad live?

5. A hardware store ordered 13 packs of nails from a supplier. Each pack contains 155 nails. How many nails did the store order?

*For another example, see Set D on page 158.

Problem Solving

6. **Algebra** Sandi's school has 1,030 students. Karla's school has 3 times as many students as Sandi's school. Write an equation to find *s*, the number of students in Karla's school. Then solve your equation.

	s			
Karla's school	1,030	1,030	1,030	3 times as many
Sandi's school	1,030			

7. **Math and Science** Jupiter is about 5 times the distance Earth is from the Sun. Earth is about 93,000,000 miles from the Sun. About how far is Jupiter from the Sun?

Look for a relationship to help you solve this problem.

8. **Higher Order Thinking** William travels only on Saturdays and Sundays and has flown 1,020 miles this month. Jason travels every weekday and has flown 1,200 miles this month. If each man travels about the same number of miles each day, who travels more miles per day for this month? Explain.

9. **Reasoning** Hwong can fit 12 packets of coffee in a small box and 50 packets of coffee in a large box. He has 10 small boxes of coffee and would like to reorganize the packets into large boxes. How many large boxes could he fill? Explain.

Assessment

10. Choose all the expressions that are equal to $25 \times 4{,}060$.

- ☐ $4{,}060 \times 25$
- ☐ $20 \times 5 \times 4{,}060$
- ☐ $25 \times (4{,}000 + 60)$
- ☐ $25 \times (406 \times 10^2)$
- ☐ $(20 + 5) \times 4{,}060$

11. Choose all the expressions that are equal to $38 \times 8{,}500$.

- ☐ $(85 \times 10^3) \times 38$
- ☐ $(30 + 8) \times (850 \times 10)$
- ☐ $30 \times 8 \times 8{,}500$
- ☐ $8{,}500 \times 38$
- ☐ $(30 + 8) \times 8{,}500$

Name ______________________

Help | Practice Buddy | Tools | Games

Homework & Practice 3-6

Solve Word Problems Using Multiplication

Another Look!

Hailey's family is saving money for a vacation. If they save $525 each month for 12 months, how much will they save?

Draw a bar diagram.

s total amount saved

$525	$525	$525	$525	$525	$525	$525	$525	$525	$525	$525	$525

Write and solve an equation.

$12 \times 525 = s$

$s = 6{,}300$

Hailey's family will save $6,300 over the 12 months.

The variable *s* represents the total amount saved. You can draw a bar diagram and write an equation to model the problem.

In **1–5**, draw a bar diagram and write an equation. Solve.

1. A stadium has 7,525 seats. What is the total attendance for 5 games if each game is sold out? Complete the bar diagram to help you.

n total number of people

2. An aquarium has display tanks that each contain 175 fish. How many fish are on display in 6 tanks?

? fish → ?

6 tanks →

175	175	175	175	175	175

3. Each elephant at the zoo eats 125 pounds of food per day. How many pounds of food will 18 elephants eat?

4. Joy travels a lot for her job. She flies 2,840 miles each week for 4 weeks. How many miles in all does she fly?

5. Jerry weighs 105 pounds. If a male brown bear weighs 11 times as much, what is the brown bear's weight?

6. Meg measured the length of some pieces of wire. What is the difference in length between the longest and shortest piece of wire?

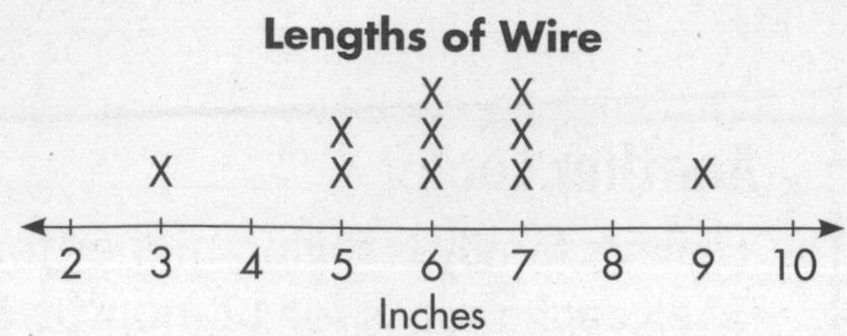

7. What is the combined length of all the pieces Meg measured? Write an equation using a variable to show your work.

8. **Higher Order Thinking** Daniel has 102 stamps. Manuel has twice as many stamps as Daniel. Kendra has twice as many stamps as Manuel. How many stamps do they have in all?

9. **Make Sense and Persevere** Caroline has enough pumpkin seeds to cover an area of 350 square feet. Her garden measures 18 feet by 22 feet. Does she have enough pumpkin seeds to fill the whole garden? Explain.

10. **Be Precise** The table shows the number of miles 3 runners ran last week. Order the numbers from least to greatest. Which runner ran the farthest? How do you know?

DATA

Name	Miles
Darla	15.2
Casey	15.25
Juan	15.03

Assessment

11. Choose all the expressions that are equal to 4,300 × 17.

- ☐ $(43 \times 10^2) \times 17$
- ☐ $17 \times 4{,}300$
- ☐ $(43 \times 10) \times (10 + 7)$
- ☐ $10 \times 7 \times 4{,}300$
- ☐ $4{,}300 \times (10 + 7)$

12. Choose all the expressions that are equal to 66 × 7,250.

- ☐ $(725 \times 10^2) \times 66$
- ☐ $(725 \times 10) \times 60 \times 6$
- ☐ $7{,}250 \times (60 + 6)$
- ☐ $7{,}250 \times 66$
- ☐ $66 \times (7{,}000 + 200)$

Name ______________________________

Solve & Share

A group of 44 students is planning a train trip to Washington, D.C. They held many fundraisers and raised $10,880. Nathan said, "We should have enough money to pay for the train tickets. There are about 50 students going on the trip and one round trip ticket costs about $200. That makes the total cost of the tickets less than $10,000."

Does Nathan's reasoning make sense?

Train Travel	
April 14 Clorisville to Washington, D.C.	$92
April 18 Washington, D.C., to Clorisville	$92
Total Ticket Price	**$184**

Problem Solving

Lesson 3-7

Critique Reasoning

I can ...
critique the reasoning of others by using what I know about estimating products.

I can also estimate products.

Thinking Habits

Be a good thinker!
These questions can help you.

- What questions can I ask to understand people's thinking?
- Are there mistakes in other people's thinking?
- Can I improve other people's thinking?

Look Back! Critique Reasoning What argument would I make to support Nathan's estimate?

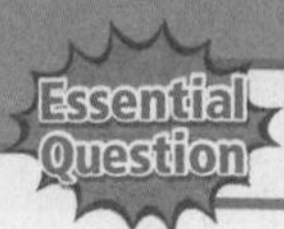

How Can You Critique Reasoning of Others?

A

Ms. Lynch needs to ship 89 boxes. 47 boxes weigh 150 pounds each. Each of the other boxes weighs 210 pounds.

Mia says that all 89 boxes can fit into one container. She reasons that 47 × 150 is less than 7,500 and 42 × 210 is a little more than 8,000, so the sum of their weights should be less than 15,400.

What is Mia's reasoning to support her estimate?

Mia estimates the total weight of the lighter boxes and the total weight of the heavier boxes, then adds the two estimates.

B

How can I critique the reasoning of others?

I can

- ask questions for clarification.
- decide if the strategy used makes sense.
- look for flaws in estimates or calculations.

C

Here's my thinking...

Mia's reasoning has flaws. She estimated that 42 × 210 is a little more than 8,000, but a better estimate is 9,000.

She underestimated the products so her conclusion is not valid.

The weight of the heavier boxes is 8,820 pounds. The weight of the lighter boxes is 7,050 pounds.

The total weight is 15,870 pounds. The sum is greater than 15,400. Mia's reasoning does not make sense.

Convince Me! Critique Reasoning Raul states that one way to get the cargo under the weight limit is to remove two of the heavier boxes and one of the lighter boxes. How can you decide if Raul's reasoning makes sense?

Name ___

Guided Practice*

Critique Reasoning

A stadium has 58 sections of seats. There are 288 seats in each section. Mary estimated the total number of seats by multiplying 60×300. She concluded that the stadium has fewer than 18,000 seats.

1. What is Mary's argument? How does she support it?

2. Describe at least one thing you would do to critique Mary's reasoning.

3. Does Mary's conclusion make sense? Explain.

Independent Practice

Critique Reasoning

An office manager has $10,000 to spend on new equipment. He planned to purchase 300 lamps for $72 each. He completed the calculations at the right and concluded that there would be plenty of money left to buy additional equipment.

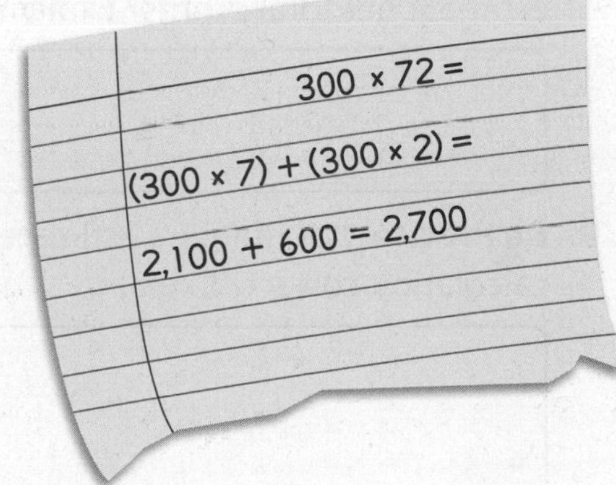

4. What does the office manager do to support his thinking?

5. Describe how you could decide if the office manager's calculation is reasonable.

When you critique reasoning, you need to explain if the method used by another makes sense.

6. Does the office manager's conclusion make sense? Explain.

*For another example, see Set E on page 158.

Problem Solving

Performance Assessment

Buying a Piano

Over the summer Kathleen sold 1,092 jars of jam at outdoor markets. She made a $12 profit on each one. She wants to use the profits to buy the Ivory-5K piano. She said, "Since 1,000 × 12 = 12,000, and 1,092 is greater than 1,000, I know my profits add up to more than $12,000. So, I can buy the piano."

Piano Model	Price with tax
Harmony-2L	$8,675
Ivory-5K	$11,500
Goldtone-TX	$14,250

7. **Make Sense and Persevere** Does it make sense for Kathleen to find an overestimate or an underestimate to decide if she has earned enough money? Why?

8. **Reasoning** Should Kathleen use multiplication to estimate her total profits? Explain your reasoning.

9. **Be Precise** Is Kathleen's estimate appropriate? Is her calculation correct? Explain.

10. **Critique Reasoning** Explain whether Kathleen's conclusion is logical. How did you decide? If it is not logical, what can you do to improve her reasoning?

Name ___________________________

Homework & Practice 3-7
Critique Reasoning

Another Look!

Mr. Jansen needs to order picture frames for his paintings. He has $4,000 to buy 98 frames priced at $42 each. Mr. Jansen says he has enough money because $100 \times \$40 = \$4{,}000$.

Tell how you can critique Mr. Jansen's reasoning.

- I can decide if his strategy makes sense to me.
- I can look for flaws in his estimates.

Critique Mr. Jansen's reasoning.

His reasoning does not make sense. He should find an overestimate or an exact amount to be sure he has enough money. An overestimate would be $100 \times \$42 = \$4{,}200$, and the exact amount is $98 \times \$42 = \$4{,}116$.

He does not have enough money.

When you critique reasoning, you explain why someone's thinking is correct or incorrect.

Critique Reasoning
Jason has 75 feet of wallpaper border. He wants to put up a wallpaper border around his rectangular bedroom that measures 12 feet by 14 feet. He multiplies $12 \times 14 = 168$ to get an exact answer of how much border he needs. He concludes that he does not have enough border for the whole job.

1. Tell how you can critique Jason's reasoning.

2. Critique Jason's reasoning.

3. Jason uses an overestimate to decide how many rolls of wallpaper he needs for another room. Explain why his reasoning to use an overestimate does or does not make sense.

Performance Assessment

A Spool of Wire

Todd has a new spool of wire like the one pictured. He needs 48 pieces of wire, each 22 feet long. He estimates that he needs $50 \times 20 = 1{,}000$ feet, and he concludes that 1 spool with 1,000 feet will be enough.

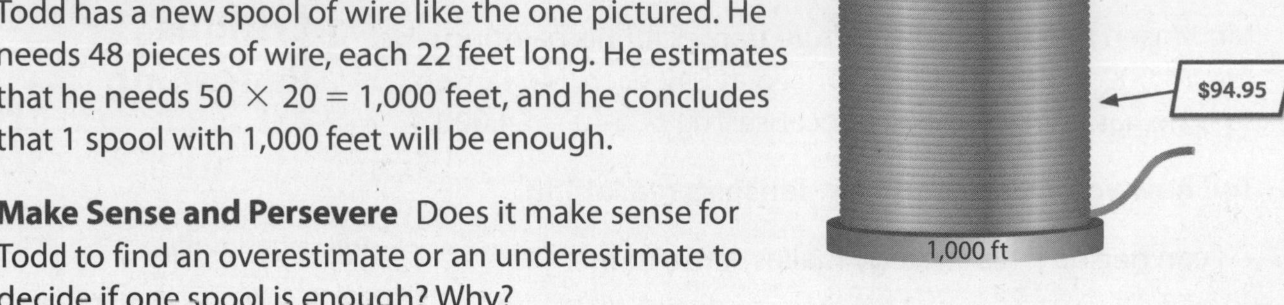

4. **Make Sense and Persevere** Does it make sense for Todd to find an overestimate or an underestimate to decide if one spool is enough? Why?

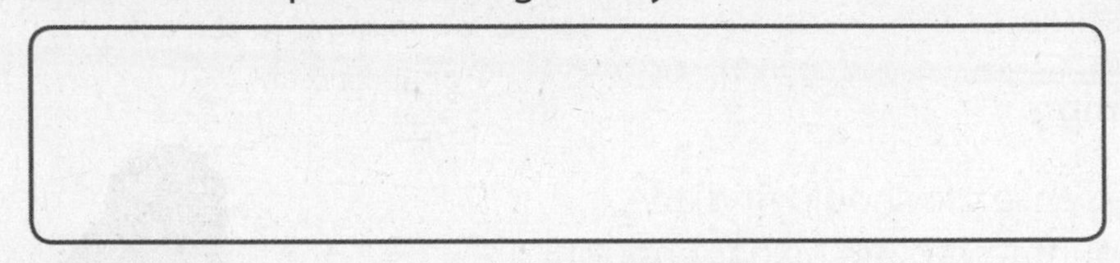

5. **Reasoning** Should Todd use multiplication to estimate the total amount of wire he needs? Explain your reasoning.

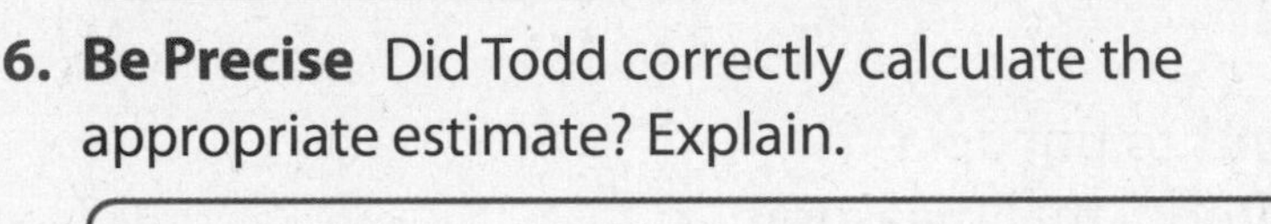

6. **Be Precise** Did Todd correctly calculate the appropriate estimate? Explain.

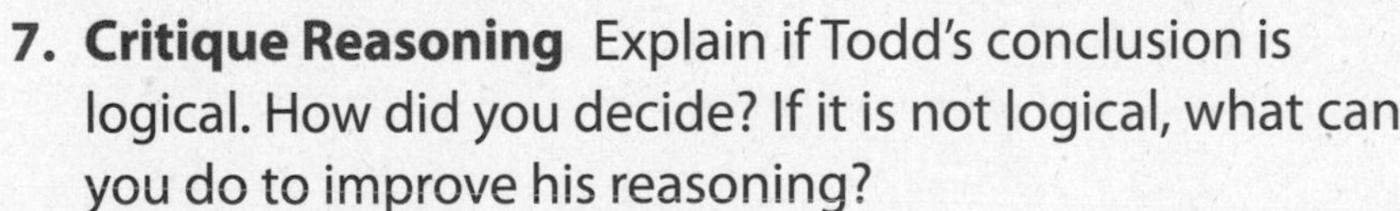

7. **Critique Reasoning** Explain if Todd's conclusion is logical. How did you decide? If it is not logical, what can you do to improve his reasoning?

Name ___________________________

Fluency Practice Activity

Solve each problem. Then follow multiples of 10 to shade a path from **START** to **FINISH**. You can only move up, down, right, or left.

I can ...

multiply multi-digit numbers fluently.

Start

53 × 20	70 × 89	84 × 40	35 × 63	241 × 62
19 × 83	55 × 17	30 × 80	77 × 24	57 × 32
60 × 90	10 × 57	80 × 14	526 × 47	64 × 32
50 × 30	73 × 73	45 × 35	47 × 85	17 × 13
70 × 12	15 × 90	20 × 14	70 × 17	100 × 100

Finish

Word List

- expression
- multiple
- overestimate
- partial products
- power
- underestimate
- variable

For each of these terms, give an example and a non-example.

	Example	Non-example
1. Power of 10	________	________
2. Multiple of 10^2	________	________
3. An expression with a variable	________	________
4. An underestimate of 532×11	________	________

Write *always*, *sometimes*, or *never*.

5. The sum of partial products is equal to the final product.

6. A multiple of a number is a power of the number.

7. An underestimate results from rounding each factor to a greater number.

8. A power of a number is a multiple of the number.

Write T for *true* or F for *false*.

9. The partial products for 34×321 are 9,630 and 1,284.

10. The partial products for 49×601 are 5,409 and 2,404.

11. $642 \times 12 = 642$ tens $+$ 1,284 ones

12. $41 \times 10^6 = 41{,}000{,}000$

13. $80 \times 10^3 = 8{,}000$

14. Suppose both factors in a multiplication problem are multiples of 10. Explain why the number of zeros in the product may be different than the total number of zeros in the factors. Include an example.

Name ______________________________

TOPIC 3

Reteaching

Set A pages 113–118

Find 65×10^3.

Step 1

Look at the exponent for the power of 10. 10^3

Step 2

Annex that number of zeros to the other factor to find the product. 65,000

Remember to look at the number of zeros or the exponent for the power of 10.

1. 12×10^4
2. 100×815
3. $10^2 \times 39$
4. $6{,}471 \times 10^1$
5. 3×10^5
6. $20 \times 1{,}000$

Set B pages 119–124

Estimate 37×88.

Step 1

Round both factors. 37 is about 40 and 88 is about 90.

Step 2

Use mental math and multiply the rounded factors. $40 \times 90 = 3{,}600$

Remember to either round the factors or use compatible numbers.

Estimate each product.

1. 7×396
2. 17×63
3. 91×51
4. 70×523
5. 256×16
6. 45×806
7. 27×89
8. 8×415

Set C pages 125–130, 131–136, 137–142

Find 53×406.
Estimate: $50 \times 400 = 20{,}000$

Multiply the ones. Multiply the tens. Then add the partial products.

$$\begin{array}{r} \scriptstyle 3 \\ \scriptstyle 1 \\ 406 \\ \times \quad 53 \\ \hline 1218 \\ +\ 20300 \\ \hline 21{,}518 \end{array} \quad \begin{array}{l} \\ \\ \\ \\ \leftarrow 3 \times 406 \\ \leftarrow 50 \times 406 \\ \\ \end{array}$$

Remember to regroup if necessary. Estimate to check that your answer is reasonable.

Find each product.

1. 54×9
2. 76×59
3. 47×302
4. 32×871
5. $\begin{array}{r} 604 \\ \times \ 55 \\ \hline \end{array}$
6. $\begin{array}{r} 7{,}133 \\ \times \quad 4 \\ \hline \end{array}$

Set D pages 143–148

Draw a picture and write an equation. Solve.

The length of James's pool is 16 feet. The length of the pool at Wing Park is 4 times as long. How long is the pool at Wing Park?

Let $\ell =$ the length of Wing Park pool.

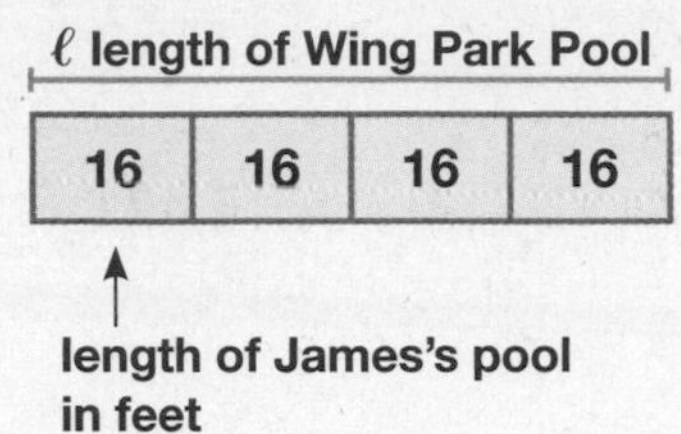

$16 \times 4 = \ell$
$\ell = 64$

The length of Wing Park pool is 64 feet.

Remember that pictures and equations can help you model and solve problems.

Write an equation with a variable to model each Exercise. Draw a picture to help you, if needed.

1. Alexandria has a collection of 34 dolls. A toy store has 15 times as many dolls as Alexandria. How many dolls are in the store?

2. A store received a shipment of 37 TVs valued at $625 each. What is the total value of the shipment?

3. Jessica saved $1,250 last year. Courtney saved 7 times as much as Jessica saved. How much money did Courtney save last year?

Set E pages 149–154

Think about these questions to help you **critique the reasoning of others.**

Thinking Habits

- What questions can I ask to understand other people's thinking?
- Are there mistakes in other people's thinking?
- Can I improve other people's thinking?

Remember you need to carefully consider all parts of an argument.

Sarah teaches craft classes. She has 214 bags of beads. Each bag has enough beads for 22 bracelets. She estimates that since $200 \times 20 = 4{,}000$, there are enough beads for at least 4,000 bracelets.

1. Tell how you can critique Sarah's reasoning.

2. Does Sarah's argument make sense? Explain.

Name ______________________________

TOPIC 3

Assessment

1. Dr. Peterson works about 178 hours each month. Which of the following is the best estimate of the number of hours she works in a year?

Ⓐ 200×20

Ⓑ 180×10

Ⓒ 100×12

Ⓓ 100×10

2. A banana contains 105 calories. Last week, Brendan and Lea ate a total of 14 bananas. How many calories does this represent?

3. At a warehouse, 127 delivery trucks were loaded with 48 packages on each truck.

Part A

Estimate the total number of packages on the trucks. Write an equation to model your work.

Part B

Did you calculate an overestimate or an underestimate? Explain how you know.

4. Choose all of the expressions that are equal to 5,600.

☐ 56×10^2

☐ 56×10^3

☐ 56×10^4

☐ 100×56

☐ $1{,}000 \times 56$

5. The latest mystery novel costs $24. The table shows the sales of this novel by a bookstore.

DATA

Day	Books Sold
Thursday	98
Friday	103
Saturday	157
Sunday	116

Part A

What was the dollar amount of sales of the mystery novel on Saturday? Write an equation to model your work.

Part B

What was the dollar amount of sales of the mystery novel on Friday? Write an equation to model your work.

6. There are 45 cans of mixed nuts. If each can has 338 nuts, what is the total number of nuts, n, in all of the cans? Write and solve an equation for n.

7. There are 36 large fish tanks at the zoo. Each tank holds 205 gallons of water. How many gallons of water would it take to fill all of the tanks?

8. Kai ordered 1,012 baseball cards. Sharon ordered 5 times as many cards as Kai. Write and solve an equation to find b, the number of baseball cards Sharon ordered.

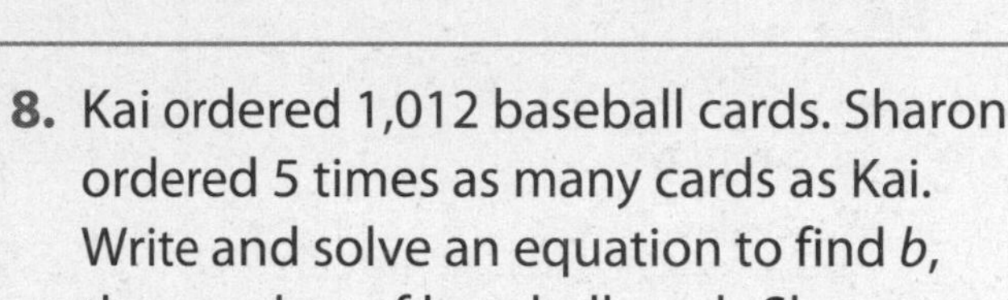

9. Ted's sales goal for this month is \$6,000. Ted sells 289 tickets for \$16 each. He says, "Since $300 \times \$20 = \$6,000$, I made my sales goal." Do you agree with Ted? Explain.

10. Draw lines to match each number on the left to its equivalent expression on the right.

1,200	12×10^0
120	12×100
12	12×10^3
12,000	12×10^1

11. For questions 11a–11d, choose Yes or No to tell if the number 10^2 will make each equation true.

11a. $39 \times \square = 390$ ○ Yes ○ No

11b. $4 \times \square = 400$ ○ Yes ○ No

11c. $20 \times \square = 200$ ○ Yes ○ No

11d. $517 \times \square = 51,700$ ○ Yes ○ No

12. Rosanne has 142 songs on her MP3 player. Teresa has 11 times as many songs as Rosanne. How many songs does Teresa have?

Name ____________________

TOPIC 3

Performance Assessment

Baseball Apparel

Coach Sandberg wants to buy items for the baseball league. The league already has caps with the league logo on them, but the coach would like to offer the option of purchasing a T-shirt, sweatshirt, sweatpants, or jacket with the logo. Use the information in the table to answer the questions.

Jackie's Sports Store

Item	Item Price
jacket	$53
sweatshirt	$32
T-shirt	$14
sweatpants	$24

1. The players asked their families and friends if they want to buy T-shirts with the league logo. If 254 people want T-shirts, what would be the total cost? Write an equation to model your work.

2. Coach Sandberg wants to order 127 sweatshirts.

Part A

Will the total cost of the sweatshirts be greater than or less than $3,000? Use estimation to decide. Explain your reasoning.

Part B

What is the total cost of 127 sweatshirts?

3. Which would cost more, 32 T-shirts or 14 sweatshirts? How can you tell without multiplying?

4. There are 18×10^1 players in the league.

Part A

The league raised $1,560 through fundraisers. Trenton estimates the cost of buying jackets for each player in the league. He concludes that the league has raised enough money. Do you agree with Trenton? Explain.

180 rounds to 200.
53 rounds to 50.
200 × $50 = $1,000

Part B

How much would it cost to order sweatpants for each player? Write and solve an equation with a variable to show your work.

5. Which costs more: 136 sweatpants or 103 sweatshirts? How much more?

6. Coach Sandberg wants to order 115 jackets and 27 caps for $12 each.

Part A

Estimate the total cost for his order. Show your work.

Part B

What is his total cost? Compare your answer to your estimate.

Use Models and Strategies to Multiply Decimals

Essential Question: What are the standard procedures for estimating and finding products involving decimals?

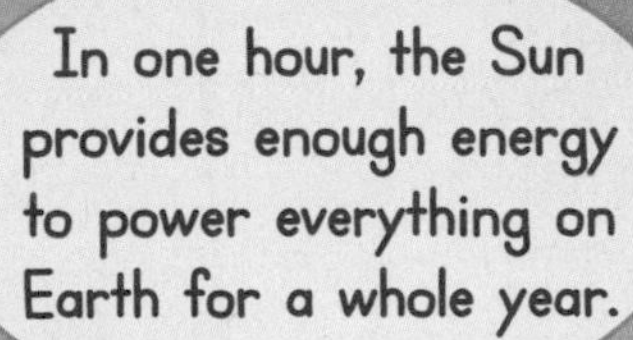

We can use solar energy for heat and electricity without polluting the air.

Let's see if we can use the Sun to charge my music player. Here's a project about solar energy.

Math and Science Project: Solar Energy

Do Research Use the Internet or other sources to learn about solar energy. Find at least five ways that we use the Sun's energy today.

Journal: Write a Report Include what you found. Also in your report:

- Describe at least one way that you could use solar energy. Could it save you money?
- Estimate how much your family pays for energy costs such as lights, gasoline, heating, and cooling.
- Make up and solve problems by multiplying whole numbers and decimals.

Name ____________________

Review What You Know

Vocabulary

Choose the best term from the box.
Write it on the blank.

- exponent
- hundredths
- overestimate
- partial products
- power
- round
- tenths
- thousandths
- underestimate

1. One way to estimate a number is to __________ the number.

2. Using 50 for the number of weeks in a year is a(n) ____________ .

3. In the number 3.072, the digit 7 is in the __________ place and the digit 2 is in the __________ place.

4. 10,000 is a(n) __________ of 10 because $10 \times 10 \times 10 \times 10 = 10{,}000$.

Whole Number Multiplication

Find each product.

5. 64×100

6. $7{,}823 \times 10^3$

7. $10 \times 1{,}405$

8. 53×413

9. 906×57

10. $1{,}037 \times 80$

Round Decimals

Round each number to the nearest tenth.

11. 842.121

12. 10,386.145

13. 585.055

Properties of Multiplication

Use the Commutative and Associative Properties of Multiplication to complete each multiplication.

14. $96 \times 42 = 4{,}032$ so $42 \times 96 =$ __________

15. $4 \times (58 \times 25) = 4 \times (25 \times$ ____$) = ($____ $\times$ ____$) \times 58 =$ ________

16. $(293 \times 50) \times 20 = 293 \times (50 \times$ ____$) =$ ________

Name ___________________________________ Solve

Lesson 4-1
Multiply Decimals by Powers of 10

I can ...
find the product of a decimal number and a power of 10.

I can also look for patterns to solve problems.

Solve & Share

Javier is helping his parents put up posters in their movie theater. Each poster has a thickness of 0.012 inch. How thick is a stack of 10 posters? 100 posters? 1,000 posters?

How can you use the structure of our number system and mental math to help you?

Look Back! **Use Structure** How does your answer for 1,000 posters compare to 0.012?

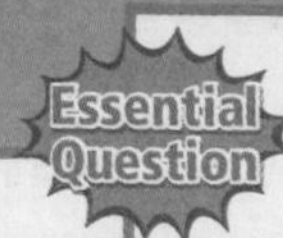

What Patterns Can Help You Multiply Decimals by Powers of 10?

A

A baker has a 10-lb bag of pecans and a 100-lb bag of flour. How many cups of each ingredient does the baker have?

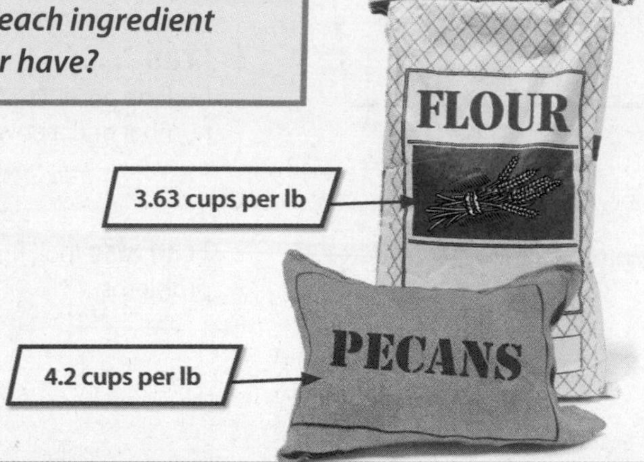

Multiplying decimals is like multiplying whole numbers.

You can use multiplication to join equal groups.

B Use patterns to find the products.

Multiply by		Examples
Standard Form	Exponential Form	
10	10^1	$3.63 \times 10^1 = 36.3$
100	10^2	$3.63 \times 10^2 = 363$
1,000	10^3	$3.63 \times 10^3 = 3{,}630$

So, $3.63 \times 10^2 = 363$ and $4.2 \times 10^1 = 42$. The baker has 363 cups of flour and 42 cups of pecans.

C Continue the pattern to find the number of cups for 100 lb, 1,000 lb, or 10,000 lb of pecans.

$4.2 \times 10^2 = 420$

$4.2 \times 10^3 = 4{,}200$

$4.2 \times 10^4 = 42{,}000$

So, 100 lb of pecans has 420 cups, 1,000 lb of pecans has 4,200 cups, and 10,000 lb of pecans has 42,000 cups.

Convince Me! **Use Structure** Complete the chart. What patterns do you see in the placement of the decimal point?

	$\times 10^1$	$\times 10^2$	$\times 10^3$
1.275			
26.014			
0.4			

Name ______________________________

Practice Buddy   Tools   Assessment

Another Example

You can use patterns to multiply by decimals.

Multiply 3.63 by 1, 0.1, and 0.01.

$3.63 \times 1 = 3.63$

$3.63 \times 0.1 = 0.363$

$3.63 \times 0.01 = 0.0363$

Guided Practice*

Do You Understand?

1. Tell how you can use mental math to find 45.8×10^3 and 45.8×0.01.

Do You Know How?

In **2–5**, find each product.

2. 0.009×10
3. 3.1×10^3
4. 0.062×10^2
5. 1.24×0.01

Independent Practice

Place-value patterns can help you solve these problems.

Leveled Practice In **6** and **7**, find each product.

6. $42.3 \times 1 =$ ________
   $42.3 \times 0.1 =$ ________
   $42.3 \times 0.01 =$ ________

7. $0.086 \times 10^1 =$ ________
   $0.086 \times 10^2 =$ ________
   $0.086 \times 10^3 =$ ________

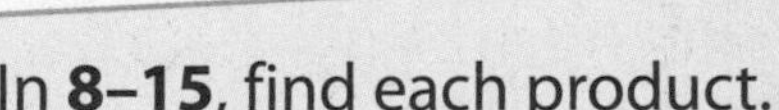

In **8–15**, find each product.

8. 63.7×0.01
9. 563.7×10^2
10. 0.365×10^4
11. 5.02×0.1
12. 94.6×10^3
13. 0.9463×10^2
14. 0.678×0.1
15. 681.7×0.01

*For another example, see Set A on page 227.

Problem Solving

In **16–18, use structure** and the table to find the answers.

16. Monroe uses a microscope to observe specimens in science class. The microscope enlarges objects to 100 times their actual size. Find the size of each specimen as seen in the microscope.

17. Monroe's teacher wants each student to draw a sketch of the longest specimen. Which specimen is the longest?

18. Seen through the microscope, a specimen is 0.75 cm long. What is its actual length?

Specimen	Actual Length (cm)	Size Seen in the Microscope (cm)
A	0.008	
B	0.011	
C	0.0025	
D	0.004	

19. Use Structure Jon's binoculars enlarge objects to 10 times their actual size. If the length of an ant is 0.43 inches, what is the length as seen up close through his binoculars?

20. Higher Order Thinking Jefferson drew a line 9.5 inches long. Brittany drew a line 10 times as long. What is the difference in length between the two lines?

21. Reasoning José ran 2.6 miles. Pavel ran 2.60 miles. Who ran farther? Explain your reasoning.

Assessment

22. Choose all equations that are true.

- ☐ $4.82 \times 1{,}000 = 482{,}000$
- ☐ $4.82 \times 10^2 = 482$
- ☐ $0.482 \times 10^1 = 48.2$
- ☐ $0.482 \times 10^3 = 482$
- ☐ $0.0482 \times 10^4 = 4{,}820$

23. Choose all equations that are true.

- ☐ $37 \times 0.01 = 0.37$
- ☐ $0.37 \times 0.1 = 0.037$
- ☐ $370 \times 0.1 = 3.7$
- ☐ $0.37 \times 0.01 = 0.037$
- ☐ $3.7 \times 0.01 = 0.037$

Name ______________________

Help | Practice Buddy | Tools | Games

Homework & Practice 4-1

Multiply Decimals by Powers of 10

Another Look!

A builder is installing tiles at a restaurant. The area of each tile is 0.25 square meter. What is the area of 1,000 tiles?

$0.25 \times 10 = 0.25 \times 10^1 = 2.5$
$0.25 \times 100 = 0.25 \times 10^2 = 25$
$0.25 \times 1{,}000 = 0.25 \times 10^3 = 250$

So, the area of 1,000 tiles is 250 square meters.

In **1** and **2**, use patterns to find the products.

1. $0.057 \times 10 =$ ______
$0.057 \times 100 =$ ______
$0.057 \times 1{,}000 =$ ______

2. $214.8 \times 1 =$ ______
$214.8 \times 0.1 =$ ______
$214.8 \times 0.01 =$ ______
$214.8 \times 0.001 =$ ______

In **3–16**, find each product. Use place-value patterns to help you.

3. 0.62×10

4. 0.0063×100

5. 7.25×0.1

6. 19.212×10^2

7. 17.6×0.01

8. 6.1×0.01

9. 37.96×0.01

10. $0.024 \times 1{,}000$

11. 0.418×0.1

12. 92.3×10^4

13. 5.001×10^1

14. 1.675×1

15. 14.8×0.01

16. 843.5×10^2

17. Use Structure Jennifer planted a tree that was 0.17 of a meter tall. After 10 years, the tree was 100 times as tall as when she planted it. What is the height of the tree after 10 years?

18. Critique Reasoning Marco and Suzi each multiplied 0.721×10^2. Marco got 7.21 for his product. Suzi got 72.1 for her product. Which student multiplied correctly? How do you know?

19. Use Structure The table shows the distance a small motor scooter can travel using one gallon of gasoline. Complete the table to find the number of miles the scooter can travel for other amounts of gasoline.

Gallons	Miles
0.1	
1	118
10	

What pattern do you see in the table?

20. Reasoning Give an example of two numbers that both have six digits, but the greater number is determined by the hundreds place.

21. Higher Order Thinking A store has a contest to guess the mass of 10,000 peanuts. If a peanut has a mass of about 0.45 gram, what would be a reasonable guess for the mass of 10,000 peanuts?

Assessment

22. Choose all equations that are **NOT** true.

- ☐ $360 \times 10^3 = 36{,}000$
- ☐ $0.36 \times 100 = 3{,}600$
- ☐ $360 \times 10^0 = 360$
- ☐ $0.036 \times 1{,}000 = 36$
- ☐ $3.6 \times 10^1 = 36$

23. Choose all equations that are **NOT** true.

- ☐ $0.42 \times 0.1 = 0.042$
- ☐ $42 \times 0.01 = 0.42$
- ☐ $420 \times 0.1 = 4.2$
- ☐ $0.42 \times 0.01 = 0.042$
- ☐ $4.2 \times 0.01 = 0.0042$

Name ____________________

Lesson 4-2
Estimate the Product of a Decimal and a Whole Number

I can …
use rounding and compatible numbers to estimate the product of a decimal and a whole number.

I can also generalize from examples.

Solve & Share

Renee needs 32 strands of twine for an art project. Each strand must be 1.25 centimeters long. About how many centimeters of twine does she need? ***Solve this problem any way you choose!***

Generalize
How can you relate what you know about estimating with whole numbers to estimating with decimals? Show your work!

Look Back! Reasoning Is your estimate an overestimate or an underestimate? How can you tell?

Learn Glossary

What Are Some Ways to Estimate Products with Decimals?

A

A wedding planner needs to buy 16 pounds of sliced cheddar cheese. About how much will the cheese cost?

B

One Way

Round each number to the nearest dollar and nearest ten.

$$\$2.15 \times 16 \rightarrow \$2 \times 20$$

$\$2 \times 20 = \$40$

The cheese will cost about $40.

C

Another Way

Use compatible numbers that you can multiply mentally.

$$\$2.15 \times 16 \rightarrow \$2 \times 15$$

$\$2 \times 15 = \$30$

The cheese will cost about $30.

Convince Me! **Reasoning** About how much money would 18 pounds of cheese cost if the price is $3.95 per pound? Use two different ways to estimate the product. Are your estimates overestimates or underestimates? Explain.

Name ______________________________

Another Example

Manuel walks a total of 0.75 mile to and from school each day. If there have been 105 school days so far this year, about how many miles has he walked in all?

Round to the nearest whole number.

105 × 0.75

↓ ↓

105 × 1 = 105

Use compatible numbers.

105 × 0.75

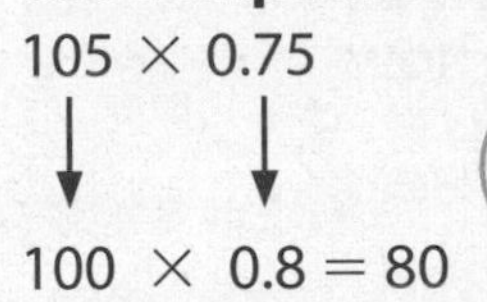

100 × 0.8 = 80

Both methods provide reasonable estimates of how far Manuel has walked.

Guided Practice*

Do You Understand?

1. **Number Sense** There are about 20 school days in a month. About how many miles does Manuel walk each month? Write an equation to show your work.

2. **Reasoning** Without multiplying, which estimate in the Another Example do you think is closer to the exact answer? Explain your reasoning.

Do You Know How?

In **3–8**, estimate each product using rounding or compatible numbers.

3. 0.87 × 112 **4.** 104 × 0.33

5. 9.02 × 80 **6.** 0.54 × 24

7. 33.05 × 200 **8.** 0.79 × 51

Independent Practice

In **9–16**, estimate each product.

9. 0.12 × 105 **10.** 45.3 × 4 **11.** 99.2 × 82 **12.** 37 × 0.93

13. 1.67 × 4 **14.** 3.2 × 184 **15.** 12 × 0.37 **16.** 0.904 × 75

*For another example, see Set A on page 227.

Problem Solving

17. About how much money does Stan need to buy 5 T-shirts and 10 buttons?

18. Joseph buys a pair of shorts for \$17.95 and 4 T-shirts. About how much money does he spend?

DATA

Souvenir	Cost
Button	\$1.95
T-Shirt	\$12.50

19. Marcy picked 18.8 pounds of peaches at the pick-your-own orchard. Each pound costs \$1.28. About how much did Marcy pay for the peaches? Write an equation to model your work.

20. Be Precise Joshua had \$20. He spent \$4.58 on Friday, \$7.43 on Saturday, and \$3.50 on Sunday. How much money does he have left? Show how you found the answer.

21. Higher Order Thinking Ms. Webster works 4 days a week at her office and 1 day a week at home. The route to Ms. Webster's office is 23.7 miles. The route home is 21.8 miles. About how many miles does she drive for work each week? Explain how you found your answer.

Assessment

22. Rounding to the nearest tenth, which of the following give an **underestimate**?

- ☐ 39.45×1.7
- ☐ 27.54×0.74
- ☐ 9.91×8.74
- ☐ 78.95×1.26
- ☐ 18.19×2.28

23. Rounding to the nearest whole number, which of the following give an **overestimate**?

- ☐ 11.6×9.5
- ☐ 4.49×8.3
- ☐ 12.9×0.9
- ☐ 0.62×1.5
- ☐ 8.46×7.38

Name ______________________

Help Practice Buddy Tools Games

Homework & Practice 4-2

Estimate the Product of a Decimal and a Whole Number

Another Look!

Zane needs to buy 27 party favors for the family reunion. The favors cost \$2.98 each. About how much will the party favors cost in all?

Is an overestimate or an underestimate better when estimating how much something will cost?

Here are two ways you can estimate.

Round both numbers.

\$2.98 × 27

↓ ↓

\$3 × 30 = \$90

The favors will cost about \$90.

Replace the factors with compatible numbers and multiply mentally.

\$2.98 × 27

↓ ↓

\$3 × 25 = \$75

The favors will cost about \$75.

Since 27 is between 25 and 30, the total cost will be between \$75 and \$90.

1. Round to the greatest place to estimate 23 × 1.75.

   23 × 1.75

   ↓ ↓

   ____ ____

   So, 23 × 1.75 is about ____

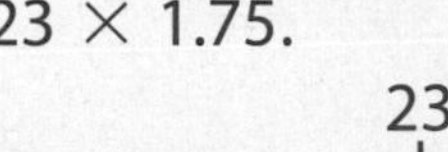

2. Use compatible numbers to estimate 12 × 0.49.

   12 × 0.49

   ↓ ↓

   ____ ____

   So, 12 × 0.49 is about ____

In **3–14**, estimate each product.

3. 19.3 × 6 **4.** 345 × 5.79 **5.** 9.66 × 0.46 **6.** 8.02 × 70

7. 1.56 × 48 **8.** 45.1 × 5 **9.** 0.13 × 11 **10.** 99.7 × 92

11. 147 × 10.4 **12.** 23.7 × 4.76 **13.** 3 × 0.85 **14.** 0.35 × 9

15. Can Mrs. Davis and her two sisters get their hair colored for less than $100 if they include a $10 tip? Explain.

16. If Mrs. Davis and her sisters also get haircuts, about how much will they pay in all?

DATA

Treatment	Cost
Shampoo	$7.95
Haircut	$14.95
Coloring	$28.95

17. Reasoning Mrs. Smith bought her three children new raincoats. Each raincoat cost $25.99. About how much did Mrs. Smith spend on the 3 raincoats? Is your estimate an overestimate or underestimate? Write an equation to show your work.

18. Higher Order Thinking Some Native American tribes made jewelry with Dentalia shells. Each Dentalia shell is about 1.5 inches long. About how much longer would a necklace made with 24 shells be than a necklace made with 18 shells? Use compatible numbers.

19. Algebra A youth hockey league is selling boxes of popcorn to raise money for new uniforms. Sidney sold 9 boxes for a total of $72 in sales. Use the bar diagram and write an equation to find the value of *c*, the cost of each box Sidney sold.

$72

c	*c*	*c*	*c*	*c*	*c*	*c*	*c*	*c*

✓ Assessment

20. Rounding to the nearest tenth, which of the following give an **overestimate**?

- ☐ 37.63×0.54
- ☐ 54.49×0.45
- ☐ 1.19×1.45
- ☐ 0.81×8.01
- ☐ 27.83×13.64

21. Rounding to the nearest whole number, which of the following give an **underestimate**?

- ☐ 2.7×13.5
- ☐ 4.51×8.7
- ☐ 9.19×8.48
- ☐ 7.49×11.4
- ☐ 3.6×6.5

Name ______________________________

Lesson 4-3

Use Models to Multiply a Decimal and a Whole Number

I can ...
use models to represent multiplying a decimal and a whole number.

I can also model with math to solve problems.

Solve & Share

Mara has 4 garden plots. Each is 0.7 acre in area. What is the total area of the garden plots? Use objects or the grids below to show your work.

Model with math
How can you represent multiplying a decimal and a whole number?

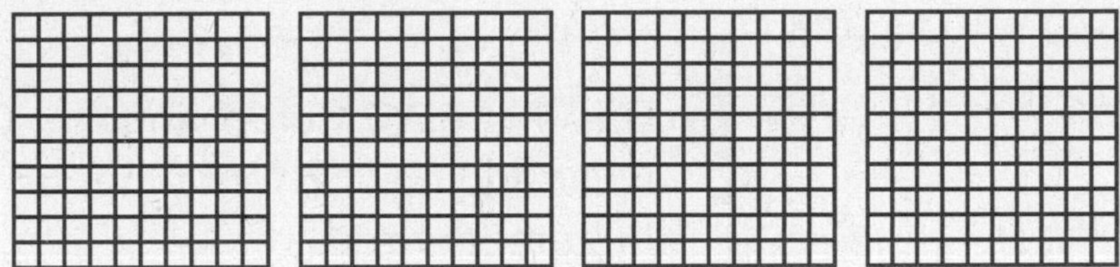

Look Back! Critique Reasoning Ed says a decimal grid shows 10 tenths. Monica says a decimal grid shows 100 hundredths. Who is correct? Explain.

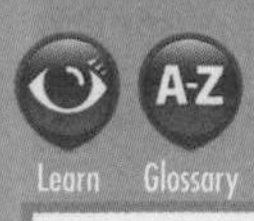

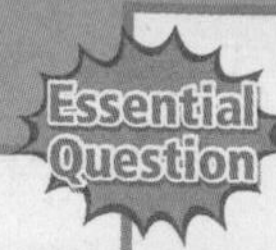

How Can You Model Multiplying a Decimal by a Whole Number?

A

Bari displayed four paintings side-by-side in one row. Each painting has the same width. What is the total width of the 4 paintings?

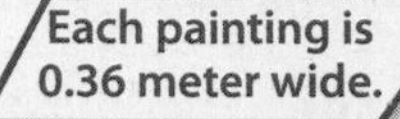

B Estimate first:

Rounding to the nearest tenth, 0.36 rounds to 0.4.

$4 \times 0.4 = 1.6$, so the answer should be close to this.

C Find 4×0.36. Multiplying 4×0.36 is like adding 0.36 four times on a hundredths grid.

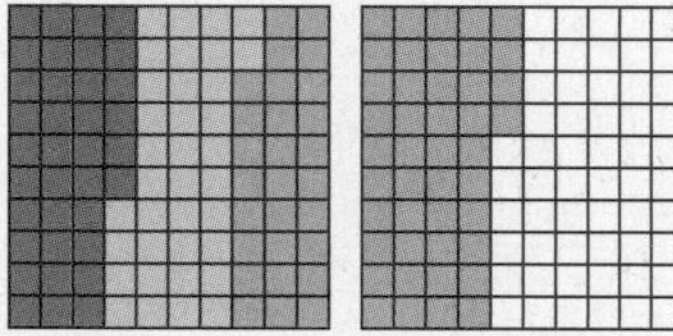

The product is the total area shaded.

There are 144 squares shaded, so $4 \times 0.36 = 1.44$.

The total width is 1.44 meters.

Convince Me! Model with Math Bari also has 5 drawings that are each 0.27 meter wide. If they are set side-by-side in one row, what would the total width be? Fill in the grids to model the problem. Then find the product using an equation and compare the answers.

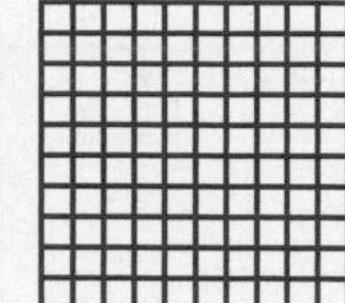

Name ______________________________

Practice Buddy Tools Assessment

Guided Practice*

Do You Understand?

1. How does a grid help you find the product of a decimal and a whole number?

Do You Know How?

In **2–5**, find the product. You may use grids to help.

2. 0.8 × 4

3. 0.7 × 21

4. 0.5 × 6

5. 0.6 × 5

Independent Practice

In **6** and **7**, find the product. Use the decimal grids to help.

6. 0.55 × 3 = ____

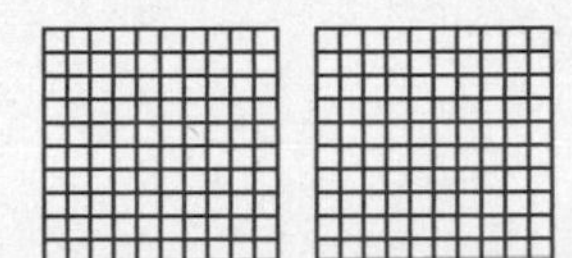

7. 0.45 × 2 = ____

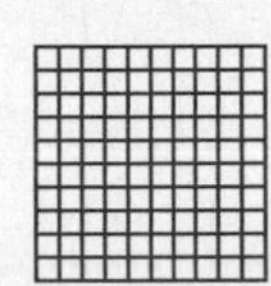

In **8–23**, find the product. You may use grids or arrays to help.

8. 5 × 0.5

9. 4 × 0.27

10. 6 × 0.13

11. 0.78 × 5

12. 10 × 0.32

13. 6 × 2.03

14. 1.35 × 5

15. 100 × 0.12

16. 4 × 0.15

17. 3 × 2.5

18. 0.9 × 7

19. 0.35 × 3

20. 0.25 × 5

21. 2.5 × 5

22. 2.04 × 2

23. 3 × 4.8

*For another example, see Set B on page 227.

Problem Solving

24. Model with Math A city is building 3 parks in a new subdivision. Each park will be 1.25 acres. How many total acres will the 3 parks be? Use the models to help.

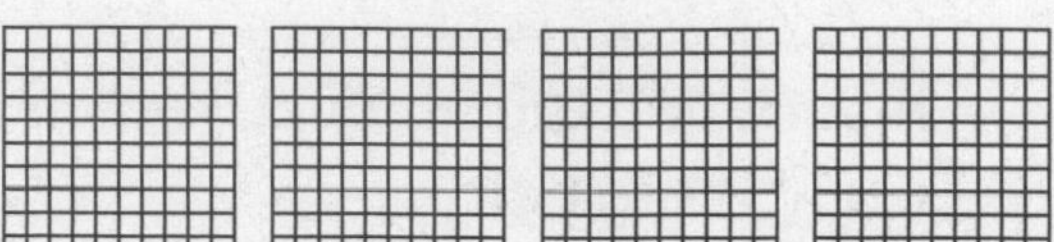

25. Higher Order Thinking The city acquired more land next to the subdivision. If it decides to make each park 12.5 acres, how many additional acres would the parks occupy?

26. Model with Math Write a multiplication number sentence that matches the shading on the grid.

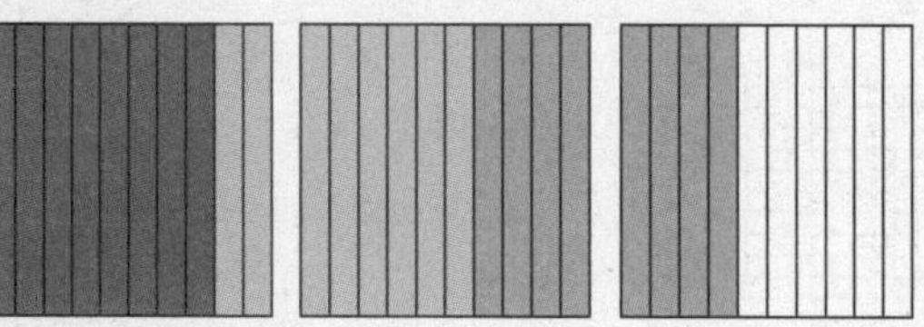

27. Critique Reasoning Jen multiplied 9 by 0.989 and got an answer of 89.01. How can you use estimation to show that Jen's answer is wrong? What mistake do you think she made?

Assessment

28. Anita needs 5 pounds of bananas to make banana bread for a bake sale. Each pound of bananas costs $0.50.

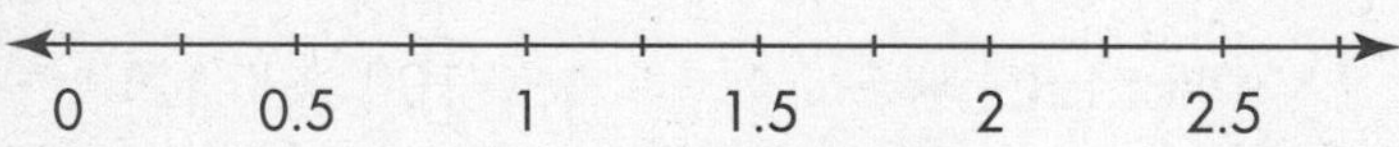

Part A

How can Anita use the number line to find the total cost of the bananas? What is the total cost?

Part B

How can Anita use place-value patterns to check her answer?

Name ______________________

Homework & Practice 4-3

Use Models to Multiply a Decimal and a Whole Number

Another Look!

A nature preserve has two hiking trails. Trail 1 is 1.3 miles long. Trail 2 is twice as long as Trail 1. How long is Trail 2?

Use a decimal grid as a model to find the product.

Shade 1.3 two times.

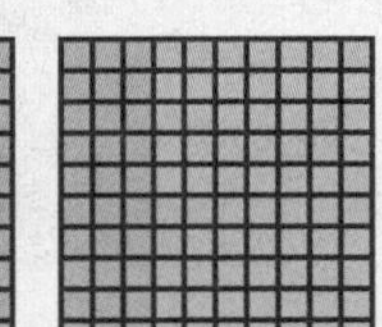

Count the shaded squares in the hundredths grids to find the product. There are 2 whole grids and 6 columns, or tenths, shaded.

So, $1.3 \times 2 = 2.6$. Trail 2 is 2.6 miles long.

You can use place value-patterns to check your work. Compare your answer to 2×13 and look for a pattern!

In **1** and **2**, shade the grids to model each product. Then write the product.

1. $0.45 \times 3 =$

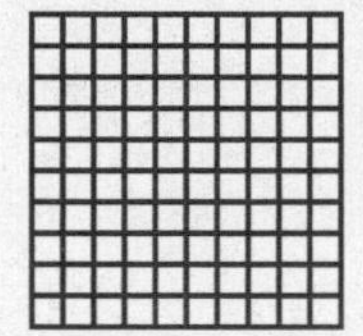
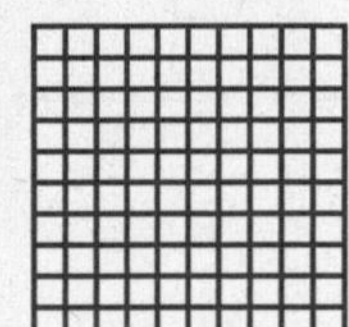

2. $0.08 \times 6 =$

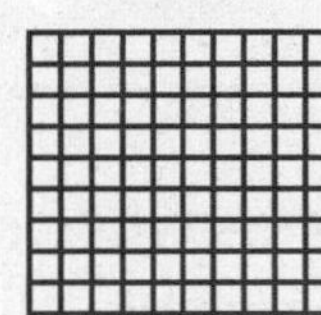

In **3–10**, find the product. Use models to help, if needed.

3. 12×0.08

4. 1.75×4

5. 0.85×3

6. 6×0.12

7. 3×0.33

8. 0.45×10^2

9. 3×2.89

10. 7.6×2

11. Ryan measures the perimeter of his square painting so he can make a wood frame. Find the perimeter of the painting in centimeters. Remember, the formula for perimeter is $P = 4 \times s$.

30.5 centimeters

12. Model with Math Write a multiplication number sentence that matches the shading on the grid.

Remember, each small square is 1 hundredth.

13. Model with Math Anth[illegible]y bikes a 16.2-mile long trail. If he bik[illegible] it 4 times, how far will he have traveled? [illegible]aw a bar diagram to help you.

14. Math and Science If 7 giant solar power plants generate 1.3 gigawatts (GW) of energy to power 900,000 homes, how many gigawatts can 21 giant solar plants generate?

15. Higher Order Thinking If $0.36 \times 4 = 1.44$, h[illegible]w would your product be different if the factors were 0.3[illegible] and 0.4?

Assessment

16. Doug's family buys 7 postcards while on vacation. Each postcard costs $0.25 including tax.

0 0.25 0.5 0.75 1 1.25 1.5 1.75 2 2.25 2.5

Part A

How can Doug use the number line to find the total cost of the postcards? What is the total cost?

Part B

How can Doug use place-value patterns to check his answer?

Name ____________________

Lesson 4-4
Multiply a Decimal by a Whole Number

I can …
multiply a decimal by a whole number.

I can also generalize from examples.

Solve & Share

A car travels 1.15 kilometers in 1 minute. If it travels at a constant speed, how far will it travel in 3 minutes? in 5 minutes? ***Solve this problem any way you choose!***

Look Back! Reasoning How can addition be used to answer the questions above?

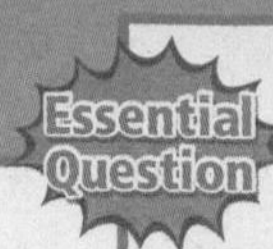

How Do You Multiply a Decimal by a Whole Number?

A

The ticket price to a minor league baseball game increased by 0.17 times last year's ticket price. If last year's price was \$26, how much is the increase?

You can multiply 0.17 × 26 by thinking about 17 × 26 and place-value patterns.

B Multiply as you would with whole numbers.

$$\begin{array}{r} \overset{1}{\overset{4}{1}}7 \\ \times\ 26 \\ \hline 102 \\ +\ 340 \\ \hline 442 \end{array}$$

C Use place-value patterns to help you place the decimal point.

Since 1.7 is $\frac{1}{10}$ of 17, 26 × 1.7 is $\frac{1}{10}$ of 442.

$26 \times 17 = 442$

$26 \times 1.7 = 44.2$

Since 0.17 is $\frac{1}{100}$ of 17, 26 × 0.17 is $\frac{1}{100}$ of 442.

$26 \times 0.17 = 4.42$

The factors have a total of 2 decimal places, so the product has 2 decimal places.

The increase is \$4.42.

Convince Me! **Generalize** Here are two similar problems:

33	0.33
× 19	× 19
297	297
+ 330	+ 330
627	627

Place the decimal point correctly in each answer. Explain your thinking.

Name ______________________

Practice Buddy | Tools | Assessment

Guided Practice*

Do You Understand?

1. What is the difference between multiplying a whole number by a decimal and multiplying two whole numbers?

2. Use the admission information on the previous page. How much will admission cost to a minor league game this year? Explain how you found your answer.

Do You Know How?

For **3–8**, find each product.

3. $\begin{array}{r} 9.8 \\ \times\ 2 \\ \hline \end{array}$

4. $\begin{array}{r} 0.67 \\ \times\ 8 \\ \hline \end{array}$

5. 34 × 5.3

6. 4.6 × 21

7. 0.6 × 15

8. 55 × 1.1

Independent Practice

For **9–20**, find each product.

Use what you know about whole-number multiplication to help you!

9. $\begin{array}{r} 34.6 \\ \times\ 9 \\ \hline \end{array}$

10. $\begin{array}{r} 64.2 \\ \times\ 20 \\ \hline \end{array}$

11. $\begin{array}{r} 40 \\ \times\ 0.22 \\ \hline \end{array}$

12. $\begin{array}{r} 57 \\ \times\ 2.3 \\ \hline \end{array}$

13. 5.8 × 11

14. 56 × 0.4

15. 170 × 0.003

16. 0.3 × 99

17. 26 × 1.61

18. 50 × 0.914

19. 10.76 × 100

20. 2.54 × 12

**For another example, see Set B on page 227.*

Problem Solving

21. Math and Science To meet peak energy demand, an electric power cooperative buys back electricity generated locally. They pay \$0.07 per solar-powered kWh (kilowatt-hour). How much money does a school make when it sells back 956 kWh to the cooperative?

Round and estimate to check for reasonableness.

22. The airline that Vince is using has a baggage weight limit of 41 pounds. He has two green bags, each weighing 18.4 pounds, and one blue bag weighing 3.7 pounds. Are his bags within the weight limit? Explain.

23. Be Precise Michael keeps track of how much time he uses his family's computer each week for 10 weeks. He created the frequency table with the data he collected. How many hours did Michael spend on the computer?

DATA

Number of Hours	Frequency
$3\frac{1}{2}$	2
4	4
$4\frac{1}{2}$	3
5	1

24. Reasoning Sara is multiplying two factors, one with one decimal place and one with two decimal places. She says the product could have two decimal places. Is she correct? Explain your reasoning.

25. Higher Order Thinking Heather clears a rectangular region in her yard for a garden. If the length is a one-digit whole number and the width is 5.5 meters, what is the least possible area? What is the greatest possible area? Explain how you found your answers.

Assessment

26. Which of the following equations is **NOT** true?

Ⓐ $75 \times 3 = 225$

Ⓑ $75 \times 0.3 = 22.5$

Ⓒ $7.5 \times 3 = 2.25$

Ⓓ $75 \times 0.03 = 2.25$

27. Which of the following equations is **NOT** true?

Ⓐ $50 \times 12 = 600$

Ⓑ $50 \times 0.12 = 6$

Ⓒ $0.5 \times 12 = 60$

Ⓓ $50 \times 1.2 = 60$

Name ______________________

Help | Practice Buddy | Tools | Games

Homework & Practice 4-4
Multiply a Decimal by a Whole Number

Another Look!

Travis can read a book chapter in 2.3 hours. The book has 18 chapters. How long will it take Travis to read the book?

Multiply as with whole numbers.

$$\begin{array}{r} \overset{2}{2}3 \\ \times\ 18 \\ \hline 184 \\ +\ 230 \\ \hline 414 \end{array}$$

So, $23 \times 18 = 414$. Now think about the number of decimal places to find 2.3×18.

Since there is a total of 1 decimal place in the factors, there is 1 decimal place in the product.

41.4

It will take Travis 41.4 hours.

In **1** and **2**, use place-value patterns to find the products.

1. $46 \times 3 = 138$

$4.6 \times 3 =$ ______

$0.46 \times 3 =$ ______

2. $17 \times 15 = 255$

$17 \times 1.5 =$ ______

$17 \times 0.15 =$ ______

In **3–14**, find each product.

3. $\begin{array}{r} 27.4 \\ \times\ \ 7 \\ \hline \end{array}$

4. $\begin{array}{r} 336 \\ \times\ 0.4 \\ \hline \end{array}$

5. $\begin{array}{r} 88 \\ \times\ 1.8 \\ \hline \end{array}$

6. $\begin{array}{r} 4.02 \\ \times\ \ 9 \\ \hline \end{array}$

7. 1.7×12

8. 105×0.4

9. 1.4×32

10. 0.89×21

11. 4.4×18

12. 0.3×279

13. 95×5.7

14. 46×0.46

15. If each month in Reno had the same average rainfall as in August, what would the total amount of rainfall be after 12 months?

DATA

Desert Rainfall in August

Desert	Average Rainfall (mm)
Mojave	0.1
Reno	0.19
Sahara	0.17

16. List the deserts in order from greatest amount of rainfall in August to least amount of rainfall in August.

17. **Number Sense** Write two numbers that are greater than 32.46 and less than 32.56. Then find the difference of your two numbers.

18. Each juice bottle contains 8.6 fluid ounces. How many fluid ounces of juice are in a carton with 12 bottles?

19. **Be Precise** A 100-watt solar power panel usually costs \$146. They are on sale for 0.75 of the regular price. Multiply 146 by 0.75 to find the sale price.

20. **Higher Order Thinking** A family has a huge array of solar panels to make electricity. If each month they sell back 420 kWh for \$0.07 per kWh, how much money could they make in a year?

21. **Use Appropriate Tools** Carla had a piece of rope that was $14\frac{7}{8}$ in. long. She used some of the rope for a crafts project. Now there is $14\frac{3}{8}$ in. left. How much rope did she use? Use the number line to help.

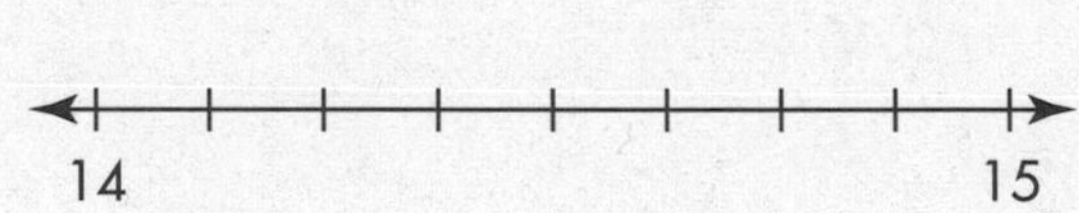

Assessment

22. Which of the following equations is **NOT** true?

Ⓐ $225 \times 4 = 9{,}000$

Ⓑ $225 \times 0.04 = 9$

Ⓒ $22.5 \times 4 = 90$

Ⓓ $225 \times 0.4 = 90$

23. Which of the following equations is **NOT** true?

Ⓐ $80 \times 15 = 1{,}200$

Ⓑ $0.8 \times 15 = 12$

Ⓒ $80 \times 0.15 = 1.2$

Ⓓ $80 \times 1.5 = 120$

Name ____________________

Lesson 4-5

Use Models to Multiply a Decimal and a Decimal

I can ...
use grids to multiply decimals.

I can also choose and use a math tool to solve problems.

Solve & Share

A rectangle has an area of 0.24 square meter. What is one possibility for the length and width of the rectangle? Tell why. ***Solve this problem any way you choose. You may use a hundredths grid if you like.***

Use Appropriate Tools
You can draw a picture on a hundredths grid to help you find the answer. *Show your work in the space below!*

0.1

Look Back! **Generalize** Is there another pair of dimensions that would work? Explain how you know.

Essential Question

How Can You Model Decimal Multiplication?

A

A carpenter cut two shelves with the dimensions given below. Show how to use a model to find the area of each shelf.

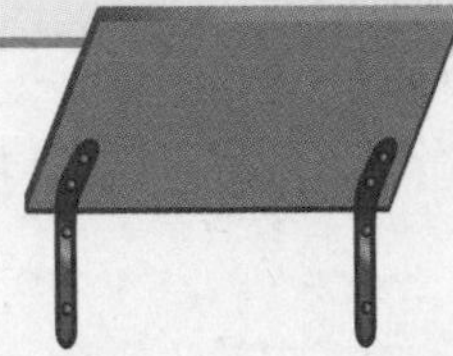

0.3 meter by 0.5 meter

0.5 meter by 1.5 meters

B For the shorter shelf, shade the first 5 columns and the first 3 rows of the hundredths grid.

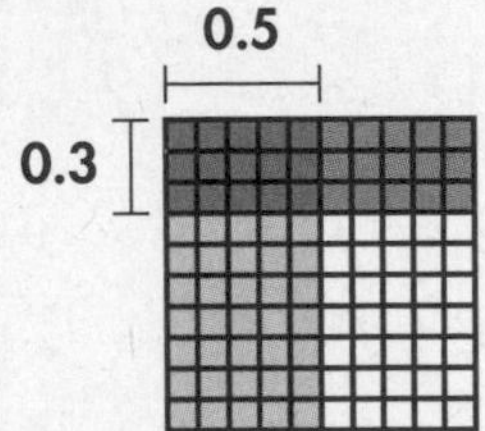

The area of the shelf is the brown area where the shading overlaps. You can write this area as a product of decimals.

$0.3 \times 0.5 = 0.15$

The area of the shorter shelf is 0.15 square meter.

C For the longer shelf, use two hundredths grids side by side. Shade 15 columns and 5 rows.

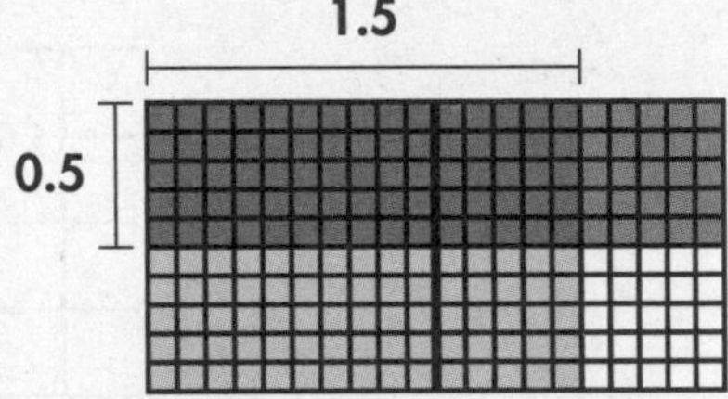

The area of the shelf is the brown area where the shading overlaps.

$0.5 \times 1.5 = 0.75$

The area of the longer shelf is 0.75 square meter.

Convince Me! **Model with Math** Use the hundredths grid to model 0.7×0.6. Explain how to find the product.

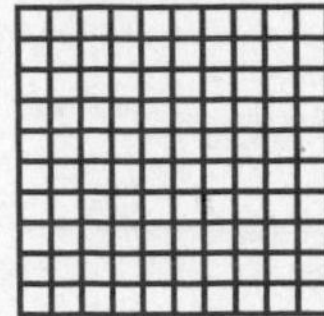

Name ____________________

Practice Buddy Tools Assessment

Guided Practice*

Do You Understand?

1. Model with Math Each square shown has a side length of one-tenth unit. Write a multiplication equation to match the model.

2. Construct Arguments Explain why 2.7 is not a reasonable answer for 0.3 × 0.9. What is the correct answer?

Do You Know How?

In **3** and **4**, shade the hundredths grids to find the product.

3. 0.7 × 0.8

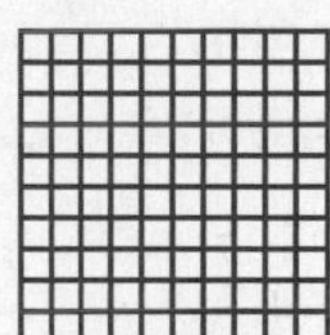

4. 0.1 × 2.1

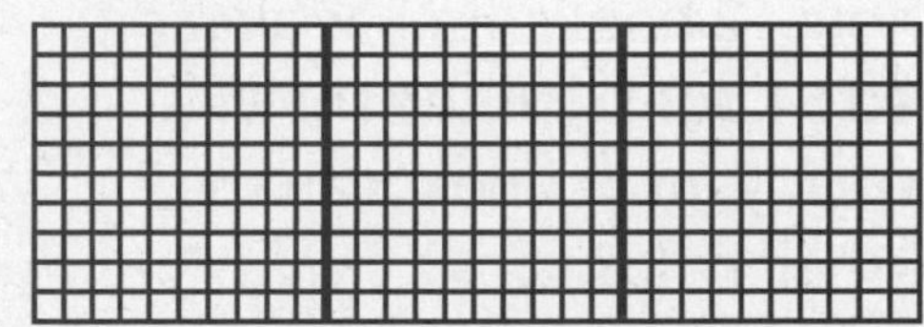

Independent Practice

In **5–8**, shade the hundredths grids to find the product.

5. 0.4 × 0.5

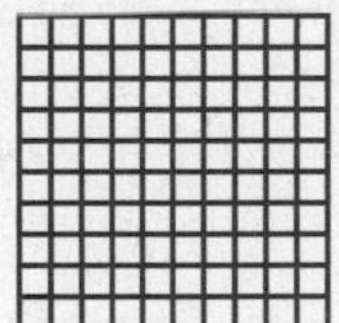

6. 0.3 × 0.7

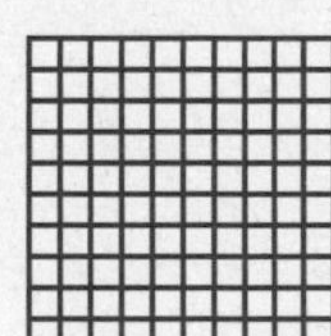

7. 0.5 × 1.7

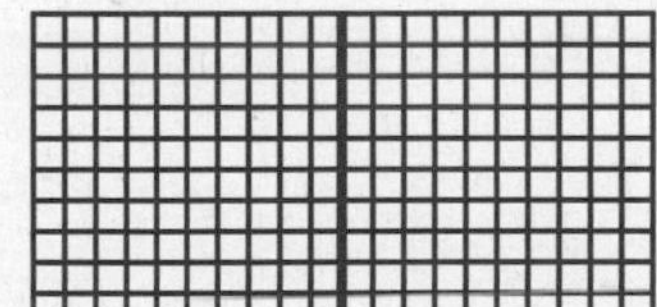

8. 0.6 × 1.2

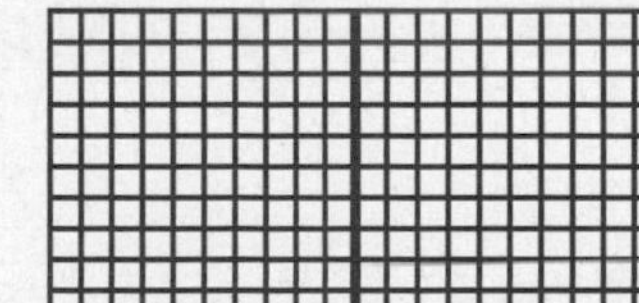

In **9–16**, find the product. You may use grids to help.

9. 0.2 × 0.8 **10.** 2.4 × 0.7 **11.** 3.9 × 0.4 **12.** 0.5 × 0.7

13. 0.9 × 0.1 **14.** 0.2 × 1.5 **15.** 0.6 × 0.6 **16.** 2.8 × 0.3

*For another example, see Set C on page 228.

Problem Solving

17. **Model with Math** Write a multiplication equation to represent this decimal model.

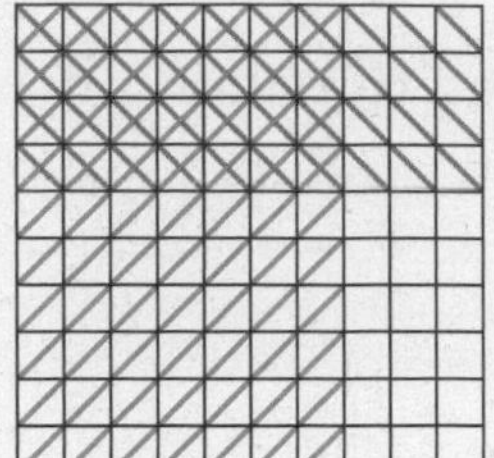

18. **Higher Order Thinking** Tony's calculator correctly shows $3.4 \times 0.5 = 1.7$. Explain why the number of decimal places in the product is not the same as the number of decimal places in the two factors.

19. Jack's bookshelf has 6 shelves. Each shelf can hold 12 books. He has already placed 54 books on the shelves. How many more books can the bookshelf hold?

20. **Number Sense** Write a number that has a 6 in the thousandths place, a 5 in the hundredths place, and a 0 in the tenths place. Then write a number less than your number and a number greater than your number.

21. **Generalize** If you multiply two decimals less than 1, can you predict whether the product will be less than or greater than either of the factors? Explain.

22. **Critique Reasoning** Judy claims that she can find 0.5×2.4 by dividing 2.4 into two equal parts. Is she correct? Draw a decimal model to explain your answer.

Assessment

23. Find two numbers that you can multiply to get a product of 0.54. Write the numbers in the box.

Product = 0.54							
6	0.7	0.9	0.8	7	8	0.6	9

Name ____________________

Help Practice Buddy Tools Games

Homework & Practice 4-5

Use Models to Multiply a Decimal and a Decimal

Another Look!

Find 0.7×0.9. Use an area model to find the product.

Use each factor as a side of a rectangle on a hundredths grid.

0.9

0.7

Shade the area of the 0.7 by 0.9 rectangle. Count the squares in the shaded area to find the product.

The shaded area contains 63 hundredths squares, so $0.7 \times 0.9 = 0.63$.

Multiply the two dimensions of the rectangular area to find its area.

In **1–3**, shade the hundredths grids to find the product.

1. 0.8×0.8

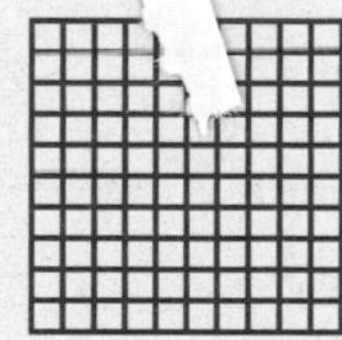

2. 0.5×0.6

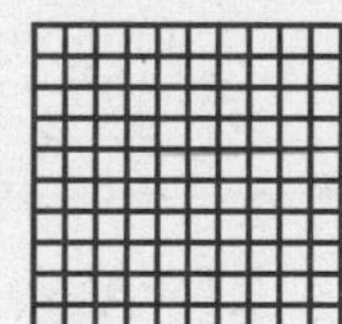

3. 0.7×1.6

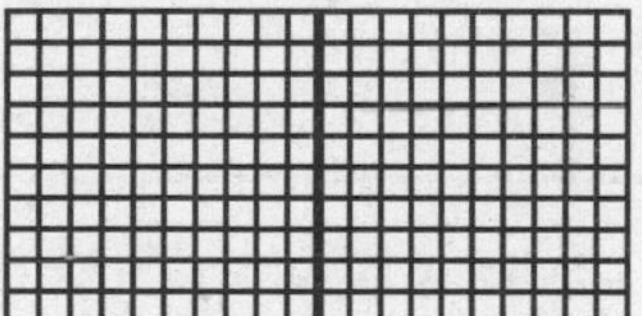

In **4–15**, find the product. You may use grids to help.

4. 1.9×0.4

5. 0.2×0.9

6. 2.8×0.6

7. 0.3×3.4

8. 5.6×0.8

9. 0.8×0.1

10. 0.9×4.1

11. 3.7×0.2

12. 4.4×0.7

13. 0.9×0.5

14. 0.2×6.8

15. 9.1×0.3

16. **Model with Math** Phil uses the model below to help him multiply decimals. Write a multiplication equation to represent the decimal model.

17. **Number Sense** Write a problem that requires multiplying two decimals to find the answer. The product must have two decimal places.

18. **Vocabulary** Describe the difference between an **underestimate** and an **overestimate**.

19. Raul can hit a golf ball 26.4 yards. A.J. can hit a golf ball 10 times as far. How far can A.J. hit the ball?

20. **Be Precise** Marco wants to set up 12 small wind turbines with 3 blades each. If 4 wind turbine blades cost $79.64, how much will all the blades cost? Show your work.

21. **Higher Order Thinking** Explain why multiplying 37.4×0.1 gives a product that is less than 37.4.

22. Leslie is buying cans of diced tomatoes that weigh 14.5 ounces each. If she buys 8 cans, how many total ounces does she buy?

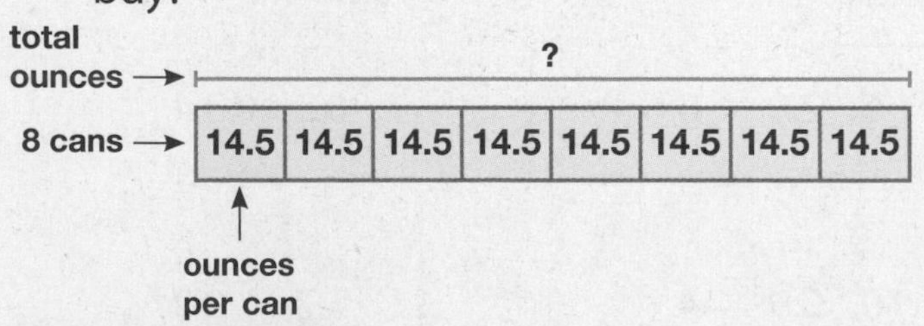

23. **Algebra** Jorge reads 15 pages each day for 7 days. Write and solve an algebraic equation to find p, the total number of pages he reads.

Assessment

24. Find two numbers that you can multiply to get a product of 0.4. Write the numbers in the box.

Product = 0.4						
0.9	0.5	8	0.1	0.8	9	5

Name ______________________________

Lesson 4-6
Multiply Decimals Using Partial Products

I can ...
multiply two decimals using partial products.

I can also choose and use a math tool to solve problems.

Solve & Share

Julie has 0.5 of her backyard set up for growing vegetables. Of the vegetable area, 0.4 has bell peppers in it. What part of the backyard contains bell peppers?

You can use appropriate tools, such as a grid, to model decimal multiplication.

Look Back! Reasoning What do you notice about the factors and their product in the above problem?

Learn Glossary

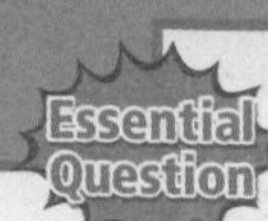

How Can You Multiply Decimals Using Partial Products?

A

June walked 1.7 miles in 1 hour. If she walks at the same rate, how far will she walk in 1.5 hours?

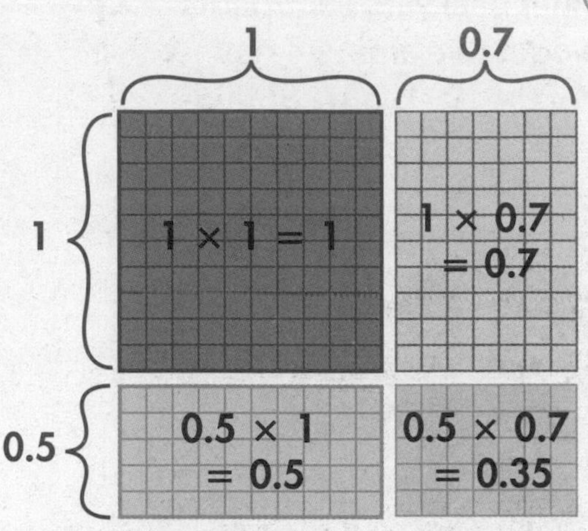

You can use properties or a model to represent the multiplication.

B Step 1

Estimate.

1.7 × 1.5
↓ ↓
$2 \times 2 = 4$

Since 2 is greater than 1.7 and 1.5, 4 is an overestimate.

C Step 2

Find the partial products.

$1.0 \times 1.0 = 1.0$
$1.0 \times 0.7 = 0.7$
$0.5 \times 1.0 = 0.5$
$0.5 \times 0.7 = 0.35$

Then add the partial products.

D Step 3

$$\begin{array}{r} \overset{1}{1}.0 \\ 0.7 \\ 0.5 \\ +\ 0.35 \\ \hline 2.55 \end{array}$$

Since 2.55 is close to your estimate of 4, the answer is reasonable.

In 1.5 hours, June will walk 2.55 miles.

Convince Me! **Make Sense and Persevere** In the example above, how many miles will June walk in 2.8 hours? Estimate first, then compare your answer to the estimate.

Name

Guided Practice*

Do You Understand?

1. **Reasoning** How is multiplying two decimals different from multiplying one decimal by a whole number? Explain your reasoning.

2. Carter is filling 6.5-ounce bottles with salsa that he made for gifts. He was able to fill 7.5 bottles. How many ounces of salsa did he make?

Do You Know How?

In **3–6**, estimate first. Then find each product. Check that your answer is reasonable.

3. 9.3×4.1

4. 3.2×0.6

5. 0.7×1.9

6. 12.6×0.2

Independent Practice

7. Find 7.5×1.8 using partial products.

Estimate: 7.5×1.8

$\square \times \square = \square$

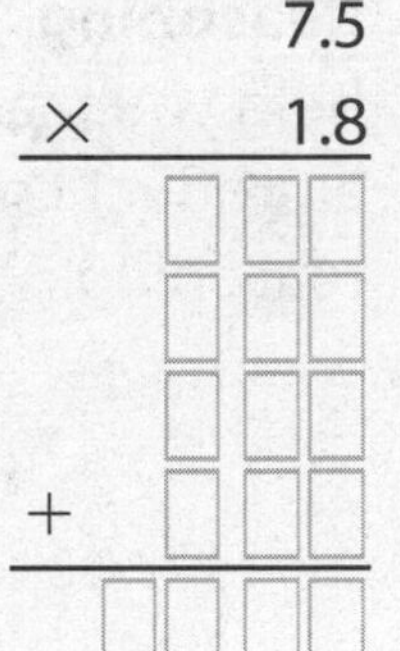

In **8–19**, estimate first. Then find each product. Check that your answer is reasonable.

8. 5.2×4.6

9. 19.1×8.5

10. 0.5×4.5

11. 8.6×0.8

12. 5.5×0.6

13. 3.5×0.4

14. 6.8×7.2

15. 8.3×6.4

16. 9.1×11.6

17. 18.1×3.7

18. 0.6×1.5

19. 2.8×3.7

*For another example, see Set C on page 228.

Problem Solving

20. Math and Science The gravity of Venus is 0.35 times that of Jupiter. What is the gravity of Venus in relation to Earth's gravity?

DATA

Relative (to Earth) Surface Gravity

Planet	Gravity
Mercury	0.39
Neptune	1.22
Jupiter	2.6

21. About how many times as great is Jupiter's relative surface gravity as Neptune's relative surface gravity?

22. Model with Math One quart of water weighs about 2.1 pounds. There are 4 quarts in a gallon. How much does a gallon of water weigh?

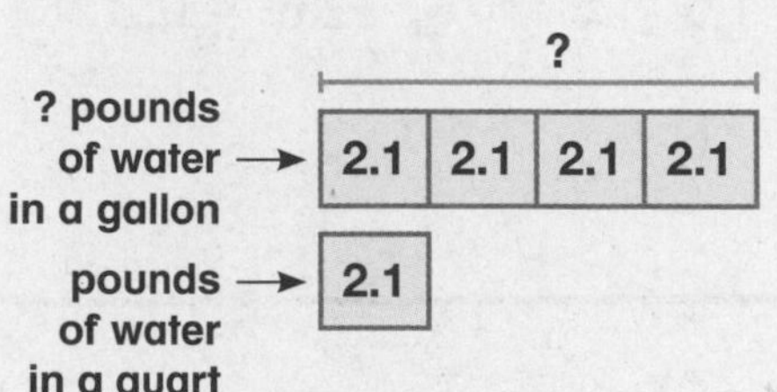

23. Isaac bought three packages of nuts. He bought one package of peanuts that weighed 3.07 pounds. He also bought two packages of pecans that weighed 1.46 pounds and 1.5 pounds. Did the peanuts or the pecans weigh more? How much more?

24. Reasoning How does estimation help you place the decimal point in a product correctly? Explain your reasoning.

25. Higher Order Thinking The area of Dimitri's table top is a whole number of square feet. Could the length and width be decimal numbers each with one decimal place? Explain your answer.

Assessment

26. Joy drinks 4.5 bottles of water per day. Each bottle contains 16.5 fluid ounces. How many fluid ounces of water does she drink per day?

Ⓐ 20.10 fluid ounces

Ⓑ 64.00 fluid ounces

Ⓒ 74.25 fluid ounces

Ⓓ 82.50 fluid ounces

27. One square mile equals 2.6 square kilometers. How many square kilometers are in 14.4 square miles?

Ⓐ 11.52 square kilometers

Ⓑ 17.00 square kilometers

Ⓒ 37.44 square kilometers

Ⓓ 86.40 square kilometers

Name ______________________________

Help | Practice Buddy | Tools | Games

Homework & Practice 4-6

Multiply Decimals Using Partial Products

Another Look!

If a semi-truck travels 9.5 miles on 1 gallon of fuel, how many miles will the truck travel on 5.6 gallons of fuel?

Step 1

First, estimate your product so you can check for reasonableness.

9.5×5.6

$\downarrow \quad \downarrow$

$10 \times 6 = 60$

Step 2

Find the partial products. Then add.

$$\begin{array}{rr} & 9.5 \\ & \times\ 5.6 \\ \hline 0.6 \times 0.5 = & 0.30 \\ 0.6 \times 9 = & 5.4 \\ 5 \times 0.5 = & 2.5 \\ 5 \times 9 = & 45 \\ \hline & 53.2 \end{array}$$

The truck will travel 53.2 miles on 5.6 gallons of fuel.
Since 53.2 is close to the estimate 60, the answer is reasonable.

1. If a truck travels 8.6 miles on 1 gallon of fuel, how many miles will the truck travel on 9.2 gallons of fuel? Estimate. Then find the product. Is your answer is reasonable? Explain.

Estimate:
8.6 × 9.2

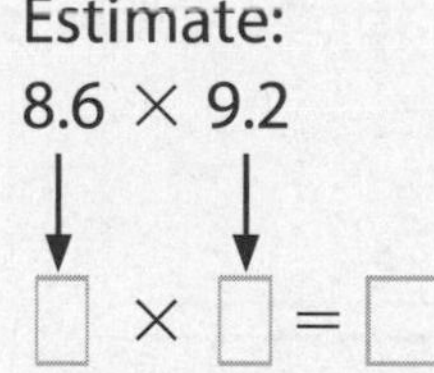

$$\begin{array}{r} 8.6 \\ \times\ 9.2 \\ \hline \end{array}$$

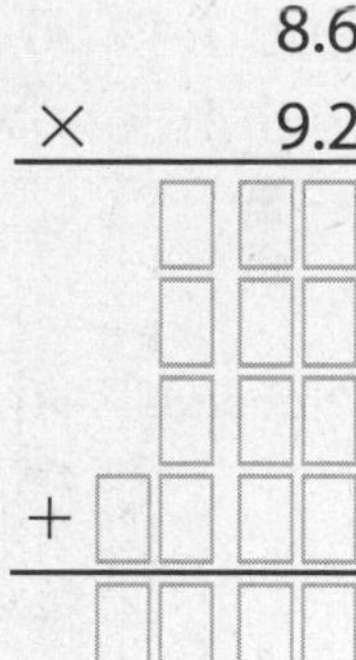

In **2–13**, estimate first. Then find each product. Check that your answer is reasonable.

2. $\begin{array}{r} 0.2 \\ \times\ 4.6 \\ \hline \end{array}$

3. $\begin{array}{r} 3.9 \\ \times\ 7.1 \\ \hline \end{array}$

4. $\begin{array}{r} 5.4 \\ \times\ 0.1 \\ \hline \end{array}$

5. $\begin{array}{r} 15.3 \\ \times\ 6.4 \\ \hline \end{array}$

6. 9.3 × 5.8

7. 23.7 × 4.4

8. 0.8 × 0.5

9. 13.2 × 0.3

10. 7.9 × 6.8

11. 1.6 × 26.1

12. 0.9 × 0.6

13. 0.5 × 96.4

14. Find the approximate length of each highway in kilometers.

One mile is about 1.6 kilometers.

DATA

Highway	Length (miles)
A	11.9
B	46.2
C	121

15. Higher Order Thinking Why does multiplying numbers by 10 move the decimal point to the right, but multiplying by 0.10 moves the decimal point to the left?

16. Make Sense and Persevere A pick-your-own pecan farm charges $1.35 per pound of pecans plus $0.40 per pound to crack the pecans. Amelia picks 20 pounds of pecans. The farm cracks 5 pounds for her. How much does Amelia pay all together?

17. Model with Math Adrian bought fruit to make a salad for a picnic. He bought 0.89 pound of grapes, 2.45 pounds of oranges, and 1.49 pounds of apples. What is the weight of the fruit?

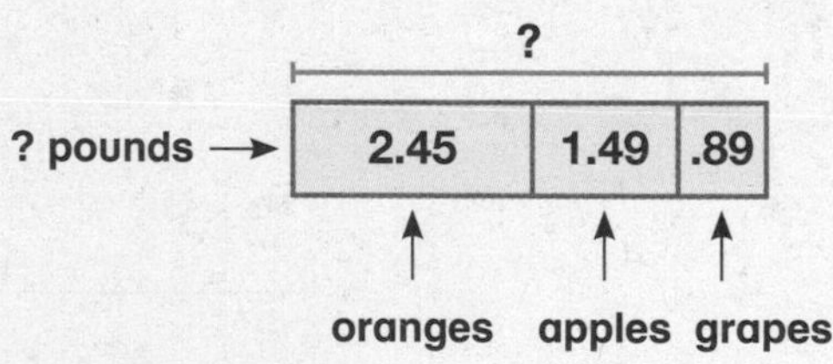

18. In exercise 17, suppose grapes cost $2.35 per pound, oranges cost $0.99 per pound, and apples cost $1.65 per pound. Rounding to the nearest whole number, about how much did Adrian pay for all the fruit?

Assessment

19. Karly used 3.5 cans of tomato sauce to make lasagna. Each can contains 10.5 ounces. How many ounces of tomato sauce is in the lasagna?

Ⓐ 24.00

Ⓑ 36.75

Ⓒ 52.50

Ⓓ 63.00

20. A bag of grass seed weighs 5.8 pounds. How many pounds would 2.5 bags weigh?

Ⓐ 14.5 pounds

Ⓑ 13.8 pounds

Ⓒ 8.3 pounds

Ⓓ 3.3 pounds

Name ____________________

Solve

Lesson 4-7
Use Properties to Multiply Decimals

I can . . .
use properties to multiply decimals.

I can also reason about math.

Solve & Share The weight of small bag of raisins is 0.3 times the weight of a large bag. The large bag weighs 0.8 pound. What is the weight of the small bag? ***Solve this problem any way you choose.***

You can use reasoning to estimate whether the answer is greater than or less than 0.5 pound.

Look Back! Look for Relationships How is solving this problem like finding the product of 3 and 8? How is it different?

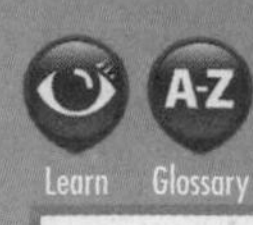

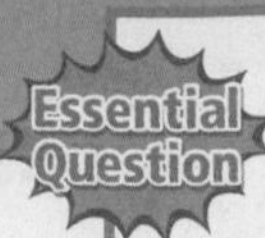

How Can You Use Properties to Multiply Decimals?

A

The length of a Bearded Dragon Lizard is 0.6 times the length of a basilisk lizard. What is the length of the Bearded Dragon?

B

Step 1

Use fractions to rewrite the multiplication expression.

$0.6 \times 0.9 =$

$\frac{6}{10} \times \frac{9}{10} =$

$\left(6 \times \frac{1}{10}\right) \times \left(9 \times \frac{1}{10}\right)$

C

Step 2

Use the Associative and Commutative Properties to rearrange the factors.

$\left(6 \times \frac{1}{10}\right) \times \left(9 \times \frac{1}{10}\right) =$

$(6 \times 9) \times \left(\frac{1}{10} \times \frac{1}{10}\right)$

D

Step 3

Multiply the whole numbers. Multiply the fractions. Write the product as a decimal.

$(6 \times 9) \times \left(\frac{1}{10} \times \frac{1}{10}\right) =$

$54 \times \frac{1}{100} =$

$\frac{54}{100} = 0.54$

One tenth of one tenth is one hundredth.

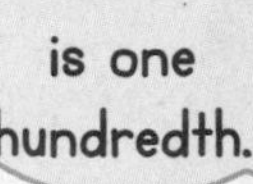

The bearded dragon is 0.54 meter long.

Convince Me! **Use Structure** Tyler explained how he multiplies 0.7 × 0.2. "I multiply 7 × 2 = 14. I know that a tenth times a tenth is a hundredth, so I use hundredths to write the product. The product is 0.14." Use properties to show that Tyler is correct.

Name ______________________________

Practice Buddy Tools Assessment

Another Example

A slice of bread has 1.25 grams of fat. How many grams of fat are in 1.5 slices?

$$1.25 \times 1.5 = \frac{125}{100} \times \frac{15}{10}$$
$$= \left(125 \times \frac{1}{100}\right) \times \left(15 \times \frac{1}{10}\right)$$
$$= (125 \times 15) \times \left(\frac{1}{100} \times \frac{1}{10}\right)$$
$$= 1{,}875 \times \frac{1}{1{,}000}$$
$$= \frac{1875}{1{,}000} = 1.875$$

There are 1.875 grams of fat in 1.5 slices of bread.

Guided Practice*

Do You Understand?

1. Mason is multiplying $(3 \times 5) \times \left(\frac{1}{10} \times \frac{1}{10}\right)$. What decimal multiplication problem is he solving?

2. Complete Mason's work to find the product. Write it as a decimal.

Do You Know How?

In **3–6**, use properties to find each product. Write the product as a decimal.

3. 0.3×0.7

4. 0.63×2.8

5. 2.6×1.4

6. 4.5×0.08

Independent Practice

In **7–15**, write each product as a decimal.

7. 0.6×0.2

8. 0.33×0.8

9. 1.7×0.22

10. 1.8×0.9

11. 0.03×1.6

12. 4.2×4.2

13. 11.1×0.8

14. 1.16×0.4

15. 1.6×0.01

*For another example, see Set D on page 228.

Problem Solving

16. Use Structure The total rainfall in March was 3.6 inches. In April, the total rainfall was 1.4 times as much. What was the total rainfall in April?

17. A newly hatched alligator is 0.5 foot long. An adult alligator is 16.4 times as long. How many feet longer is the adult alligator than the newborn alligator?

18. Make Sense and Persevere The Nature Club held a grasshopper jumping contest. The distance Bugmaster jumped is 1.2 times the distance Green Lightning jumped. The distance Top Hopper jumped is 1.5 times the distance Bugmaster jumped. Complete the table to show the distances Bugmaster and Top Hopper jumped.

Grasshopper	Distance
Green Lightning	1.4 feet
Bugmaster	
Top Hopper	

19. Amanda bought a 6-cup bag of shredded cheese for \$6.89. She used .25 cups to make lasagna and 1.25 cups to make pizza. How much cheese is left?

Is there any information that you don't need to solve this problem?

20. Higher Order Thinking Jodi drew the Eiffel Tower 6.5 inches tall. She thought it was too tall, so she multiplied its height by 0.8. The second drawing was too short, so she multiplied its height by 1.2. Predict whether her last drawing was shorter, the same as, or taller than her first drawing. Check your prediction by finding the height of the last drawing.

Assessment

21. Which expression is equivalent to 0.4×0.3?

Ⓐ $\left(4 \times \frac{1}{100}\right) \times \left(3 \times \frac{1}{100}\right)$

Ⓑ $(4 \times 10) \times (3 \times 10)$

Ⓒ $\left(4 \times \frac{1}{10}\right) \times \left(3 \times \frac{1}{10}\right)$

Ⓓ $\left(4 \times \frac{1}{10}\right) \times \left(3 \times \frac{1}{100}\right)$

22. Which expression is equivalent to 0.71×2.8?

Ⓐ $(71 \times 28) \times \left(\frac{1}{100} \times \frac{1}{10}\right)$

Ⓑ $(71 \times 28) \times \left(\frac{1}{10} \times \frac{1}{10}\right)$

Ⓒ $(0.71 \times 2.8) \times \left(\frac{1}{100} \times \frac{1}{10}\right)$

Ⓓ $(71 \times 28) \times (100 \times 10)$

Name ____________________

Help | Practice Buddy | Tools | Games

Homework & Practice 4-7

Use Properties to Multiply Decimals

Another Look!

Marco hiked 2.5 miles in an hour. If he continues at the same speed, how far will he hike in 3.25 hours?

$$2.5 \times 3.25 = \frac{25}{10} \times \frac{325}{100}$$
$$= (25 \times 325) \times \left(\frac{1}{10} \times \frac{1}{100}\right)$$
$$= 8{,}125 \times \frac{1}{1{,}000}$$
$$= \frac{8125}{1{,}000} = 8.125$$

Remember, one tenth times one hundredth equals one thousandth.

Marco will hike 8.125 miles in 3.25 hours.

1. To find 0.6 × 0.35, multiply the whole numbers ______ and ______ by the fractions ______ and ______. The product, written as a decimal, is ______.

Find each product.
In **2–16**, write each product as a decimal.

2. 0.2 × 0.9

3. 0.58 × 0.3

4. 2.5 × 0.77

5. 3.1 × 0.4

6. 0.07 × 1.2

7. 14.3 × 0.8

8. 0.1 × 2.85

9. 1.18 × 0.6

10. 9.2 × 0.01

11. 0.45 × 5.5

12. 3.9 × 3.9

13. 0.16 × 0.5

14. 0.55 × 6.9

15. 0.1 × 7.25

16. 0.13 × 0.5

17. Use Structure Helen uses 0.12 kilogram of nuts in each batch of granola that she makes. If she makes 2.5 batches, how many kilograms of nuts will she use?

18. The weight of an empty pickup truck is 2.1 times the weight of an empty car. If the empty car weighs 1.8 tons, how many tons does the pickup weigh carrying a 0.5-ton load?

19. Make Sense and Persevere Mr. Chaplin measured his sons' rectangular bedrooms for new carpeting. Whose bedroom has the greatest area?

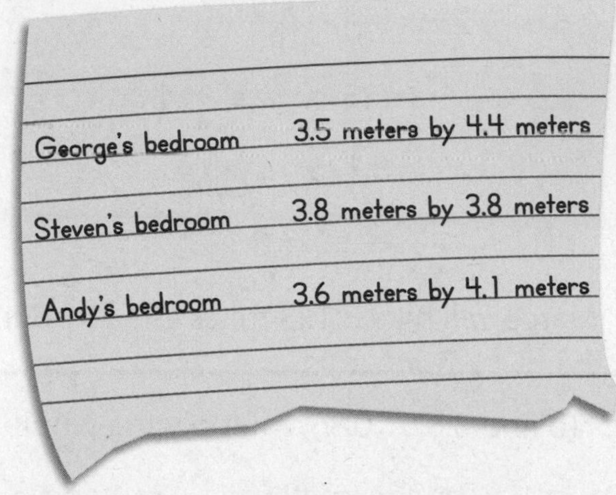

20. Higher Order Thinking Hank has a board 1.75 meters long. He used 0.8 meter to build the walls of a birdhouse. He used 0.4 of what is left for the floor. He needs 0.6 meter for the roof. Does he have enough wood for the roof? Explain.

21. Be Precise The times for five sprinters in a 50-meter dash were 6.72 seconds, 6.4 seconds, 6.08 seconds, 7.03 seconds, and 6.75 seconds. Write these times from fastest to slowest.

Assessment

22. Which expression is equivalent to 1.18×0.6?

Ⓐ $\left(1.18 \times \frac{1}{100}\right) \times \left(0.6 \times \frac{1}{10}\right)$

Ⓑ $\left(118 \times \frac{1}{100}\right) \times \left(6 \times \frac{1}{10}\right)$

Ⓒ $(118 \times 100) \times (6 \times 10)$

Ⓓ $\left(118 \times \frac{1}{10}\right) \times \left(6 \times \frac{1}{10}\right)$

23. Which expression is equivalent to 0.4×8.7?

Ⓐ $(4 \times 87) \times \left(\frac{1}{100} \times \frac{1}{10}\right)$

Ⓑ $(4 \times 87) \times (100 \times 10)$

Ⓒ $(4 \times 87) \times \left(\frac{1}{100} \times \frac{1}{100}\right)$

Ⓓ $(4 \times 87) \times \left(\frac{1}{10} \times \frac{1}{10}\right)$

Name ______________________________

Lesson 4-8
Use Number Sense to Multiply Decimals

I can …
use number sense to place the decimal point in a product.

I can also reason about math.

Solve & Share Three students in Ms. Cho's class wrote the following problems on the board. The correct digits in the products are given, but the decimal point isn't placed yet. Where should the decimal point go in each product?

1. $7.85 \times 16 = 1256$

2. $0.98 \times 0.5 = 49$

3. $1.06 \times 1.5 = 159$

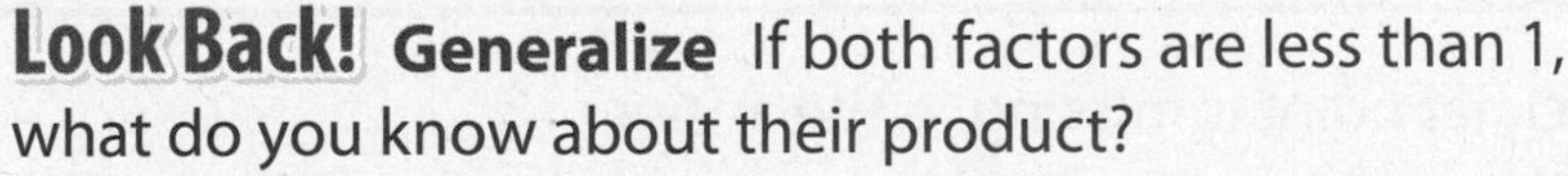

Look Back! Generalize If both factors are less than 1, what do you know about their product?

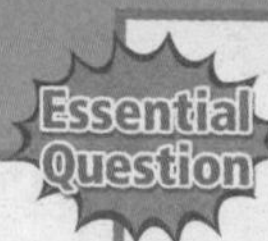

How Can You Use Number Sense to Multiply Decimals?

A

You have learned how to estimate when multiplying with decimals. You can also use number sense to reason about the relative size of factors and the product.

$49.20 \times 0.55 = 2706$

B Think about the relative size of the factors.

Multiplying a number by a decimal less than 1 gives a product less than the other factor.

Since 0.55 is less than 1, the product is less than 49.2.

Since 0.55 is about one half, the product is about half of 49.2, or about half of 50. So, the decimal point should be between the 7 and 0.

$49.2 \times 0.55 = 27.06$

C Use number sense to reason about the product.

How can you place the decimal point in the product of the equation below?

6.2×5.1 is 3162.

Notice that the smallest unit in both factors is a tenth (0.1). Since the product of 0.1 and 0.1 is 0.01, the product of 6.2 and 5.1 will have two decimal places.

So, $6.2 \times 5.1 = 31.62$.

This makes sense because 6 times 5 equals 30.

Convince Me! Reasoning The decimal point is missing in the answer for each of these problems. Use number sense to decide where the decimal point should be placed. Explain your thinking.

$54.7 \times 0.53 = 28991$

$54.7 \times 5.3 = 28991$

Name ____

Practice Buddy Tools Assessment

Guided Practice*

Do You Understand?

1. Describe the unknown factor.

_______ × 5.1 is about 300.

2. Number Sense Janelle wrote 23.4 for the product of 7.8 × 0.3. Use number sense to decide if Janelle placed the decimal point in the correct place in the product. If it is incorrect, give the correct product.

Do You Know How?

Use number sense to decide where the decimal point belongs in the product. Tell the place.

3. 5 × 3.4 = 17

4. 3.1 × 6.2 = 1922

5. 0.6 × 0.4 = 24

Independent Practice

In **6–9**, the product is shown without the decimal point. Use number sense to place the decimal point correctly.

6. 5.01 × 3 = 1503

7. 6.22 × 3 = 1866

8. 0.9 × 0.9 = 81

9. 1.8 × 1.9 = 342

In **10–15**, tell whether or not the decimal point has been placed correctly in the product. If not, rewrite the product with the decimal point correctly placed.

10. 12 × 4.8 = 57.6

11. 5.2 × 6.4 = 3.328

12. 6.99 × 21 = 14.679

13. 0.05 × 12.4 = 6.2

14. 18 × 3.38 = 60.84

15. 9.01 × 91 = 81.991

Use number sense or estimation to help you!

*For another example, see Set E on page 229.

Problem Solving

16. **Reasoning** A pig farmer needs 60 square feet to house a sow. Is the pen pictured to the right large enough? Explain your reasoning.

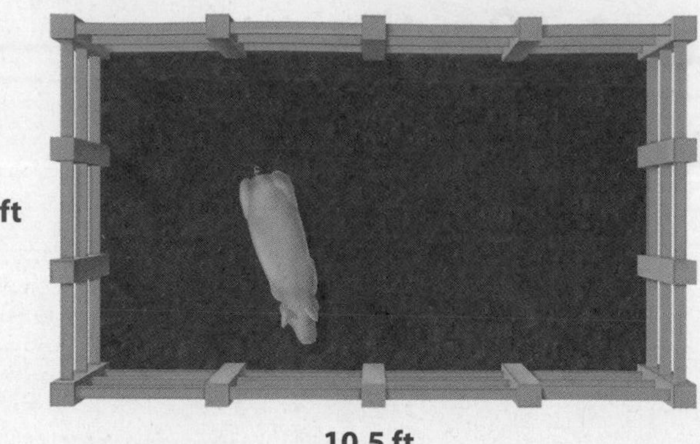

17. **Critique Reasoning** Quincey says that 3 is a good estimate for 3.4×0.09. Is he correct? Why?

18. Ron bought 2 DVDs for $12.95 each. He spent $25 on magazines. Did he spend more on DVDs or magazines? How much more? Write equations to show your work.

19. You can convert gallons to liters by using a factor of 3.79. That is, 1 gallon is about 3.79 liters. About how many liters are in 37 gallons? Is your answer an underestimate or overestimate? Explain.

20. **Higher Order Thinking** Find two factors that would give a product of 0.22.

Assessment

21. Which of the following is the missing factor?

$\_\_\_\_ \times 2.3 = 34.73$

Ⓐ 0.151
Ⓑ 1.51
Ⓒ 15.1
Ⓓ 151

22. Which two factors would give a product of 7.5?

Ⓐ 0.3 and 0.25
Ⓑ 0.3 and 2.5
Ⓒ 3 and 0.25
Ⓓ 3 and 2.5

Name ____________________

Help | Practice Buddy | Tools | Games

Homework & Practice 4-8

Use Number Sense to Multiply Decimals

Another Look!

Amelia can walk 3.6 miles in one hour. How far can she walk in 2.1 hours?

$3.6 \times 2.1 = 756$

Use number sense to place the decimal in the product.

75.6 and 756 are not reasonable answers.

Estimate: $3 \times 2 = 6$ and $4 \times 2 = 8$.

So the answer is between 6 and 8.

Amelia will walk 7.56 miles in 2.1 hours.

In **1–4**, the product is shown without the decimal point. Use number sense to place the decimal point appropriately.

1. $6 \times 5.01 = 3006$

2. $12.8 \times 3.2 = 4096$

3. $4.06 \times 20.1 = 81606$

4. $24 \times 6.3 = 1512$

In **5–10**, tell whether or not the decimal point has been placed correctly in the product. If not, rewrite the product with the decimal point correctly placed.

5. $0.6 \times 0.7 = 0.042$

6. $1.1 \times 13.8 = 1.518$

7. $8.06 \times 3 = 241.8$

8. $19 \times 8.3 = 157.7$

9. $2.8 \times 345.1 = 966.28$

10. $56.2 \times 7.9 = 4{,}439.8$

11. Jordan enters 3.4×6.8 into his calculator. He writes the digits 2312 from the display and forgets the decimal point. Where should Jordan write the decimal point? Explain.

12. Mrs. Cooper has $20. Can she buy a museum ticket for her 10-year-old daughter, a ticket for herself, and a book that costs $3.99? Explain.

DATA

Science Museum

Ticket	Price
Child	$5.75
Adult	$11.25

13. Estimate the product of 3.9 and 4.6 using mental math. Explain the method you used.

14. **Reasoning** Will the actual product of 7.69×5 be greater than or less than its estimate of 8×5? Explain your reasoning.

15. One serving of yogurt has 95 calories. What is a reasonable estimate for the number of calories in 2.5 servings of yogurt?

16. **Higher Order Thinking** Bruce jogs from his house to the library and back again to tutor students. The distance from his house to the library is 0.28 mile. If Bruce tutored at the library 328 days last year, about how many miles did he jog?

17. **Make Sense and Persevere** Alicia drew a pentagon with equal side lengths and equal angles. Then she added red lines of symmetry to her drawing. How many lines did she draw? Use the picture to show how you know.

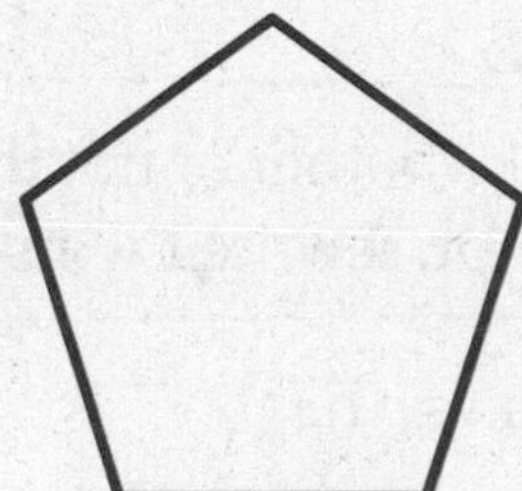

Assessment

18. Which of the following is the missing factor?

$\_\_\_\_ \times 0.7 = 0.287$

Ⓐ 0.041

Ⓑ 0.41

Ⓒ 4.1

Ⓓ 41

19. Which two factors would give a product of 8.34?

Ⓐ 0.06 and 1.39

Ⓑ 0.06 and 13.9

Ⓒ 0.6 and 1.39

Ⓓ 0.6 and 13.9

Name ____

Lesson 4-9
Multiply Decimals

I can . . .
multiply decimals using the standard algorithm.

I can also look for patterns to solve problems.

Solve & Share

Kala's teacher asked the students to write one digit on each blank and find the products. How would you complete the expressions? What are the products? ***Solve these problems any way you choose!***

a. 0.____ × 0.____

b. 0.____ × ____

c. 0.____ × 0.0____

d. ____.____ × 0.____ ____

Look for relationships between the number of decimal places in the factors and the number of decimal places in the product.

Look Back! Generalize How many decimal places will there be in the product of 3.5 and 0.21? Explain.

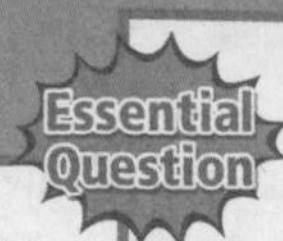

How Can You Use the Standard Algorithm to Multiply Decimals?

A

Melissa is making fruit punch. She wants to make 2.5 batches using the recipe shown.

How much cranberry juice should Melissa use?

Aunt Sandy's Fruit Punch
0.5 liter sparkling water
1.5 liters cranberry juice
1 liter orange juice
6 tablespoons sugar

You can use the standard multiplication algorithm to multiply 1.5 × 2.5.

B

Step 1

Estimate the product.

Use compatible numbers that you can multiply mentally.

1.5 × 2.5
↓
2 × 2.5 = 5 liters

C

Step 2

Multiply as you would with whole numbers.

$$\begin{array}{r} 25 \\ \times\ 15 \\ \hline 125 \\ 250 \\ \hline 375 \end{array}$$

Since 2 is greater than 1.5, 5 is an overestimate.

D

Step 3

Add the number of decimal places in each factor to find the number of decimal places in the product.

Since there is a total of 2 decimal places in the factors, there will be 2 decimal places in the product.

Melissa needs to use 3.75 liters of cranberry juice.

3.75 liters is a little less than the estimate of 5 liters, so the answer is reasonable.

Convince Me! Look for Relationships How many tablespoons of sugar does Melissa need? Explain how you found the answer.

Name ____

Another Example

Find 0.5 × 0.03.

Multiply as you would with whole numbers.

$$\begin{array}{r} 5 \\ \times\ 3 \\ \hline 15 \end{array}$$

Locate the decimal point in the product.

$$\begin{array}{rl} 0.5 & \text{1 decimal place} \\ \times\ 0.03 & \text{2 decimal places} \\ \hline 0.015 & \text{3 decimal places} \end{array}$$

Since the product 15 does not have enough digits to show 3 decimal places, annex zeros to the left of the product.

Remember, a tenth times a hundredth equals a thousandth.

Use number sense or estimation to check your answer.

Since 0.5 < 1, the product must be less than the other factor, 0.03. 0.015 < 0.03, so the answer is reasonable.

Guided Practice*

Do You Understand?

1. Sasha wants to multiply 0.5 × 0.8. How many decimal places will the product have? Explain.

2. If 112 × 38 = 4,256, what is the product of 1.12 × 3.8?

Do You Know How?

In **3–6**, find each product. Use number sense or estimation to check your answer.

3. $\begin{array}{r} 12.5 \\ \times\ 0.09 \\ \hline \end{array}$

4. $\begin{array}{r} 9.1 \\ \times\ 6.8 \\ \hline \end{array}$

5. 0.8 × 5.4

6. 0.4 × 0.07

Independent Practice

In **7–14**, find each product. Use number sense or estimation to check your answer.

7. 0.4 × 1.3

8. 0.63 × 5.5

9. 6.5 × 4.4

10. 10.3 × 0.3

11. 2.9 × 2.9

12. 27 × 4.9

13. 0.8 × 0.09

14. 5.6 × 100

*For another example, see Set F on page 229.

Problem Solving

15. **Be Precise** Preston bought a drum set priced at \$187.90. The sales tax was found by multiplying the price of the drum set by 0.08. What was the total cost of the drum set with sales tax? Round to the nearest cent.

16. Ms. White drives 8 miles each way, to and from her office. If she does this 5 days each week for 10 weeks, how many total miles will she drive?

17. **Make Sense and Persevere** Jordan bought 3.8 pounds of turkey, 2.2 pounds of cheese, and 3.6 pounds of egg salad for a party. What was the total cost before sales tax? Round your answer to the nearest cent.

18. **Higher Order Thinking** How many decimal places do you think are in the product of $3.2 \times 0.77 \times 1.6$? Explain. Then multiply to check.

Assessment

19. Ella measured some of the distances on a map of her county. On the map, each inch represents 4.5 miles.

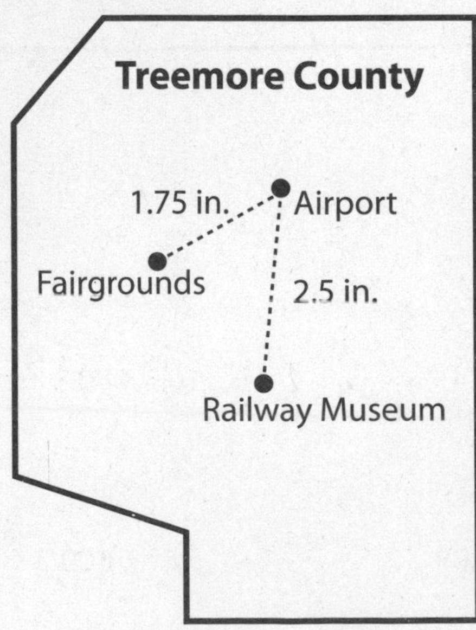

Part A

What is the actual distance between the airport and the railway museum?

Part B

What is the actual distance between the airport and the fairgrounds?

Name ____________________

Homework & Practice 4-9
Multiply Decimals

Another Look!

Javier has two pet birds. One weighs 1.25 times as much as the other. The smaller bird weighs 0.7 pound. How much does the larger bird weigh?

Step 1

Estimate the product.

1.25 × 0.7
↓ ↓
1 × 1 = 1 pound

Step 2

Multiply as you would with whole numbers.

$$\begin{array}{r} 125 \\ \times\ 7 \\ \hline 875 \end{array}$$

Step 3

Add the number of decimal places in the factors to find the number of decimal places in the product.

1.25	2 decimal places
× 0.7	1 decimal place
0.875	3 decimal places

The larger bird weighs 0.875 pound.

0.875 pound is close to the estimate of 1 pound, so the answer is reasonable.

You can also use number sense to check that you have put the decimal point in the correct place.

1. To find 1.56 × 2.7, multiply ____ × ____. Then place the decimal point in the product to show ____ decimal places.

In **2–13**, find each product. Use number sense to check your answer.

2. 9.7 × 0.4

3. 2.2 × 0.73

4. 8.1 × 8.1

5. 0.5 × 3.04

6. 0.75 × 3.2

7. 5.2 × 88

8. 0.4 × 0.7

9. 1,000 × 0.94

10. 2.5 × 64

11. 1.17 × 5.7

12. 0.16 × 0.3

13. 0.33 × 9.2

14. Be Precise Anna's family had a party in a restaurant. Their food bill was $214.58. The tip for the servers was found by multiplying the food bill by 0.18. What was the cost of the food bill and tip before sales tax? Round to the nearest cent.

15. Make Sense and Persevere One serving of scrambled eggs contains 7.8 grams of fat. Mr. Jensen is trying to eat no more than 60 grams of fat per day. If he eats 1.5 servings of scrambled eggs for breakfast, how many more grams of fat can he eat that day?

16. Make Sense and Persevere Meghan's vegetable garden is pictured below. What is its area?

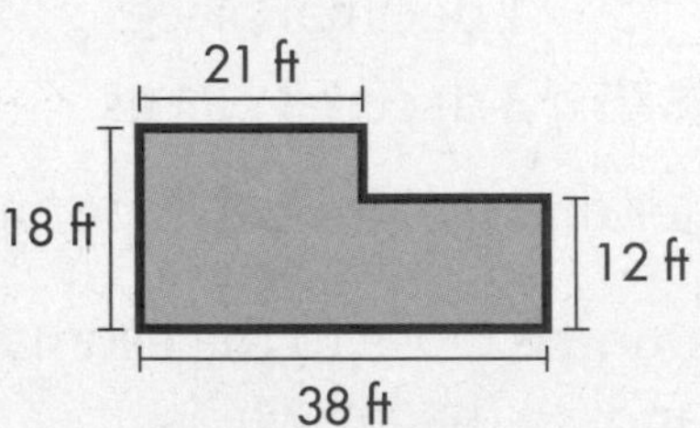

17. Construct Arguments Without multiplying or estimating, explain how you can tell which product is greater, 4.5×7.32 or 0.45×732.

18. Higher Order Thinking Use the fact that $147 \times 16 = 2{,}352$ to write two different multiplication problems that have a product of 2.352.

Assessment

19. 14-karat gold is a mixture of pure gold and other metals. One ounce of 14-karat gold contains 0.58 ounce of pure gold.

Part A

If a 14-karat gold necklace weighs 1.8 ounces, how many ounces of pure gold does it contain?

Part B

If a 14-karat ring weighs 0.5 ounce, how many ounces of pure gold does it contain?

Name ______________________

Problem Solving

Lesson 4-10

Model with Math

I can . . .
apply the math I know to solve problems.

I can also solve multi-step problems.

Solve & Share

Susan is making sandwiches for a picnic. She needs 1.2 pounds of ham, 1.5 pounds of bologna, and 2 pounds of cheese. How much will she spend in all? ***Solve this problem any way you choose. Use models to help.***

	price per pound
Ham	$3.40
Bologna	$2.90
Cheese	$4.99

Thinking Habits

Be a good thinker!
These questions can help you.

- How can I use math I know to help solve this problem?
- How can I use pictures, objects, or an equation to represent the problem?
- How can I use numbers, words, and symbols to solve the problem?

Look Back! Model with Math What math did you use to solve this problem?

Learn Glossary

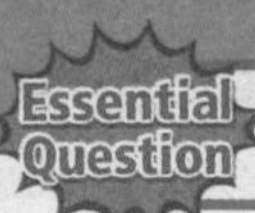

How Can You Model a Problem with an Equation?

A

Alex is buying vegetables for dinner. He buys 6 ears of corn, 1.4 pounds of green beans, and 2.5 pounds of potatoes. How much money does he spend?

Green Beans	\$1.80/lb
Potatoes	\$0.70/lb
Corn	\$0.35/ear

What do I need to do to solve the problem?

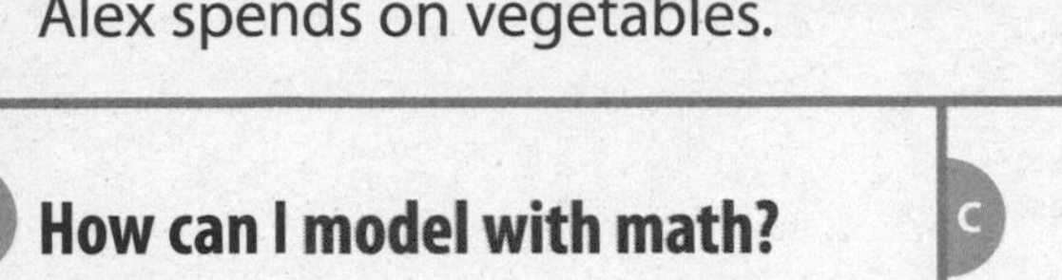

I need to find how much money Alex spends on vegetables.

B

How can I model with math?

I can

- use previously learned concepts and skills.
- decide what steps need to be completed to find the final answer.
- use an equation to represent and solve this problem.

C

I will use an equation to represent this situation.

Let t be the total cost.

$t = (6 \times \$0.35) + (1.4 \times \$1.80) + (2.5 \times \$0.70)$

Multiply with money as you would multiply with decimals.

Corn	Green beans	Potatoes
$\begin{array}{r} \overset{2}{0}.\overset{3}{3}5 \\ \times \quad 6 \\ \hline 2.10 \end{array}$	$\begin{array}{r} \overset{3}{1}.80 \\ \times \; 1.4 \\ \hline 720 \\ +\,1800 \\ \hline 2.520 \end{array}$	$\begin{array}{r} \overset{1}{\overset{3}{0}}.70 \\ \times \; 2.5 \\ \hline 350 \\ +\,1400 \\ \hline 1.750 \end{array}$

Now add the subtotals.

$\$2.10 + \$2.52 + \$1.75 = \$6.37$

So, Alex spends \$6.37 on vegetables.

Convince Me! Model with Math Beth buys 3.2 pounds of potatoes and gives the clerk a \$5 bill. Write an equation that shows how much change she will get back. Explain how your equation represents this problem.

Name ____________________

Practice Buddy Tools Assessment

Guided Practice*

Model with Math

Jackie downloaded 14 songs priced at $0.99 each and 1 song for $1.29. She had a coupon for $2.50. What was the total amount Jackie paid?

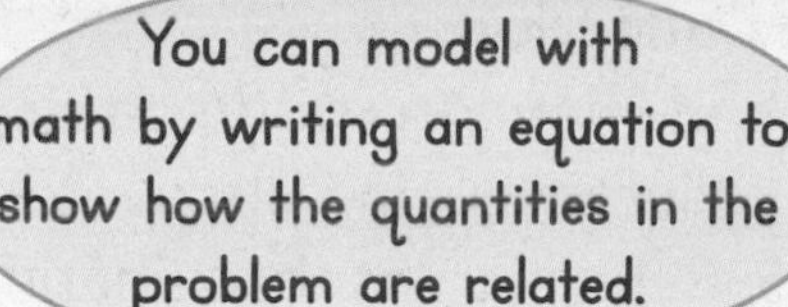

1. What do you need to find first?

2. Write an equation to represent the problem.

3. What is the solution to the problem?

Independent Practice

Model with Math

George bought 2.5 pounds of each type of fruit shown on the sign. What was the total cost of the fruit he bought?

Apples	$1.30/lb
Grapes	$1.65/lb
Bananas	$0.49/lb

4. What do you need to find?

5. Write an equation to represent the problem.

6. What is the solution to the problem?

*For another example, see Set G on page 230.

Problem Solving

Performance Assessment

Coin Collection

Tina and Shannon counted the coins in their coin collections. Tina discovered that she had 538 more coins than Shannon. Whose collection is worth more? How much more?

Type of Coin	Number Saved	
	Tina	Shannon
(penny)	917	488
(nickel)	100	23
(dime)	45	10
(quarter)	19	22

7. **Make Sense and Persevere** Do you need all of the information given to solve the problem? Explain.

8. **Reasoning** How is finding the total value of the coins in Tina's collection similar to finding the total value of coins in Shannon's collection?

9. **Model with Math** Write and solve an equation to represent the total value of the coins in Tina's collection. Then write and solve an equation to represent the total value of the coins in Shannon's collection.

10. **Be Precise** Whose collection is worth more? How much more? Show your work.

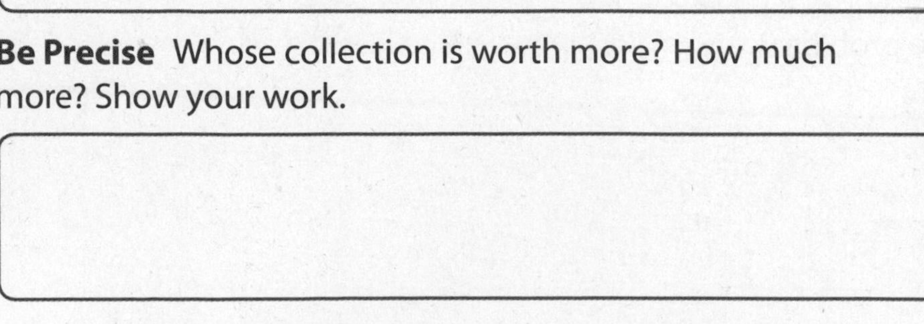

Name ________________________________

Homework & Practice 4-10
Model with Math

Another Look!

The Franklin School library is made up of two rectangular regions, the Reading Room and the Computer Lab. What is the total area of the library?

Franklin School Library	
Section	**Dimensions**
Reading room	24 meters by 19.6 meters
Computer lab	9.2 meters by 8.5 meters

Write an equation to represent this situation. Let A represent the total area.
$A = (24 \times 19.6) + (9.2 \times 8.5)$

Multiply to find the area of each room.

$$\begin{array}{r} \overset{1\,1}{\overset{3\,2}{1}}9.6 \\ \times \quad 24 \\ \hline 784 \\ 3920 \\ \hline 470.4 \end{array} \qquad \begin{array}{r} \overset{1}{\overset{1}{9}}.2 \\ \times \quad 8.5 \\ \hline 460 \\ 7360 \\ \hline 78.20 \end{array}$$

Add to find the total area.

$$\begin{array}{r} \overset{1}{4}70.4 \\ +\ 78.2 \\ \hline 548.6 \end{array}$$

The total area is 548.6 square meters.

You can use equations to apply the math you know to solve a problem.

Model with Math

Mrs. Gordon measured three rectangular rooms she wants to tile. What is the total area of the rooms?

Family room	24.5 ft by 16 ft
Kitchen	15 ft by 12.75 ft
Laundry room	10.5 ft by 10.5 ft

1. Describe the steps you would take to solve the problem.

2. Write an equation to represent the problem.

3. What is the solution to the problem?

Performance Assessment

Trail Mix Sales

The table shows the number of bags of trail mix sold last month at Patsy's Pantry and Mo's Munch-and-Crunch. Each small bag of trail mix sells for \$5.87 at Patsy's Pantry and \$4.59 at Mo's Munch-and-Crunch. Which store earned more money from the sales of small bags of trail mix? How much more?

DATA

Trail Mix Bag	Number of Bags Sold	
	Patsy's Pantry	Mo's Munch and Crunch
Small (1.5 lb)	31	40
Medium (3 lb)	14	68
Large (4.5 lb)	53	35

4. **Make Sense and Persevere** What are you asked to find?

5. **Model with Math** Write and solve an equation to represent the total amount earned from the sale of small bags at Patsy's. Then write and solve an equation to represent the total amount earned from the sales of small bags at Mo's.

6. **Be Precise** Which store earned more money from the sales of small bags of trail mix? How much more? Show your work.

7. **Reasoning** At both Patsy's and Mo's, each medium bag of trail mix sells for \$8.49. Explain how to find which store earned more money from the sales of medium bags without doing the calculation.

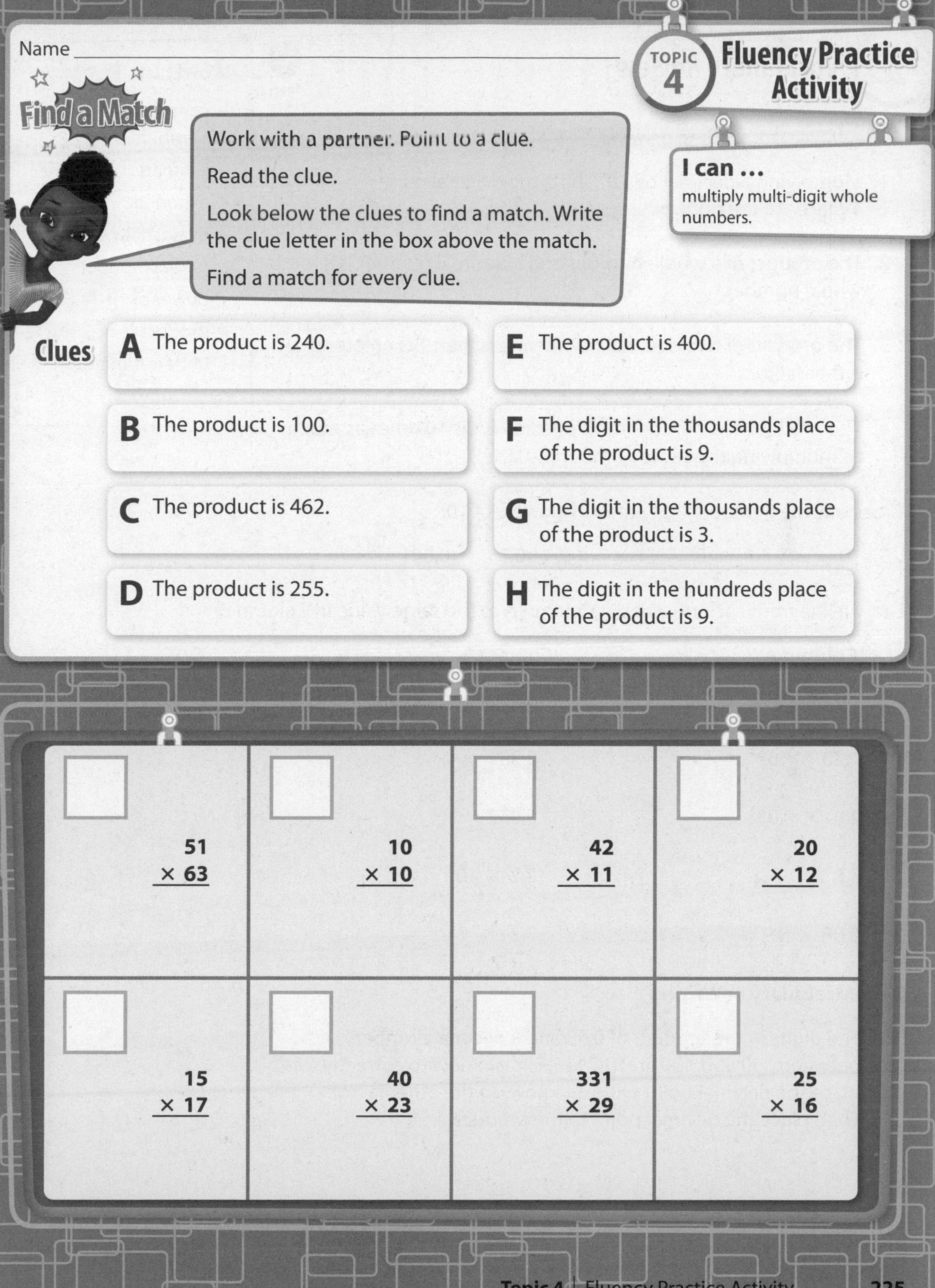

Name ______________________________

TOPIC 4

Fluency Practice Activity

Find a Match

Work with a partner. Point to a clue.

Read the clue.

Look below the clues to find a match. Write the clue letter in the box above the match.

Find a match for every clue.

I can ...
multiply multi-digit whole numbers.

Clues

A The product is 240.

B The product is 100.

C The product is 462.

D The product is 255.

E The product is 400.

F The digit in the thousands place of the product is 9.

G The digit in the thousands place of the product is 3.

H The digit in the hundreds place of the product is 9.

☐ $\begin{array}{r} 51 \\ \times\ 63 \\ \hline \end{array}$	☐ $\begin{array}{r} 10 \\ \times\ 10 \\ \hline \end{array}$	☐ $\begin{array}{r} 42 \\ \times\ 11 \\ \hline \end{array}$	☐ $\begin{array}{r} 20 \\ \times\ 12 \\ \hline \end{array}$
☐ $\begin{array}{r} 15 \\ \times\ 17 \\ \hline \end{array}$	☐ $\begin{array}{r} 40 \\ \times\ 23 \\ \hline \end{array}$	☐ $\begin{array}{r} 331 \\ \times\ 29 \\ \hline \end{array}$	☐ $\begin{array}{r} 25 \\ \times\ 16 \\ \hline \end{array}$

Vocabulary Review

Word List

- compatible numbers
- estimate
- exponent
- overestimate
- partial products
- power of 10
- product
- underestimate

Write *always, sometimes,* or *never.*

1. Multiplying a decimal by 10^4 shifts the decimal point 4 places to the right.

2. The product of a whole number and a decimal number is a whole number.

3. The product of two decimal numbers less than 1 is greater than either factor.

4. The product of a number multiplied by 0.1 is 10 times as much as multiplying the same number by 0.01.

Cross out the numbers that are **NOT** powers of 10.

5. 10^6 $\quad 40 \times 10^3$ $\quad 1 \times \frac{1}{1{,}000}$ $\quad$ 0.55 $\quad$ 0.001

Draw a line from each number in Column A to the same value in Column B.

Column A	Column B
6. $7.2 \times 1{,}000$	3,800
7. 0.38×10^4	0.38
8. 240×0.03	0.072
9. 3.8×0.1	7.2×10^3
10. 0.08×0.9	7.2

Use Vocabulary in Writing

11. The digits in the product of 0.48 and a decimal number between 350 and 400 are 182136. Explain how to correctly place the decimal point without knowing the other factor. Then place the decimal point in the product.

Name ____________________

TOPIC 4

Reteaching

Set A pages 165–170, 171–176

Use the patterns in this table to find 8.56×10 and 0.36×100.

Multiply by	Move the decimal point to the right
10	1 place
100	2 places
1,000	3 places

$8.56 \times 10 = 85.6 = 85.6$

$0.36 \times 100 = 36.0 = 36$

Remember you can use rounding or compatible numbers to estimate.

Find each product.

1. 10×4.5 **2.** $10^3 \times 3.67$

3. 100×4.5 **4.** 0.008×10^2

Estimate each product.

5. 0.38×99 **6.** 8×56.7

7. 11×4.89 **8.** 24×3.9

Set B pages 177–182, 183–188

Find 12×0.15.

Step 1

Multiply as you would with whole numbers.

$$\begin{array}{r} 12 \\ \times\ 0.15 \\ \hline 60 \\ +\ 120 \\ \hline 180 \end{array}$$

Step 2

Count the decimal places in both factors. Then, place the decimal point in the product the same number of places from the right.

$$\begin{array}{rl} 12 & \\ \times\ 0.15 & \text{2 places} \\ \hline 60 & \\ +\ 120 & \\ \hline 1.80 & \end{array}$$

So, $12 \times 0.15 = 1.8$.

Remember to count the decimal places in both factors before you place the decimal point in the product.

Find each product. Use grids or arrays as necessary.

1. 50×3.67 **2.** 5.86×5

3. 14×9.67 **4.** 8×56.7

5. 11×0.06 **6.** 2.03×6

7. 25×1.63 **8.** 5.62×75

Set C pages 189–194, 195–200

Find 8.2×3.7.

Find the partial products and add.

$$\begin{array}{rl} 8.2 & \\ \times\ 3.7 & \\ \hline 0.14 & = 0.7 \times 0.2 \\ 5.6 & = 0.7 \times 8 \\ 0.6 & = 3 \times 0.2 \\ +\ 24 & = 3 \times 8 \\ \hline 30.34 & \end{array}$$

So, $8.2 \times 3.7 = 30.34$.

Remember that area models and arrays can help you find the product.

Find each product.

1. 1.3×0.4
2. 5.8×5.2
3. 8.3×10.7
4. 3.4×0.7
5. 2.4×3.6
6. 9.7×11.2
7. 1.5×0.6
8. 67.5×9.2

Set D pages 201–206

Use properties to find 0.8×0.4.

Rewrite each decimal as a fraction. Then rewrite again using unit fractions. Next use the Associative and Commutative Properties to rearrange the fractions.

$$\begin{aligned} 0.8 \times 0.4 &= \frac{8}{10} \times \frac{4}{10} \\ &= \left(8 \times \frac{1}{10}\right) \times \left(4 \times \frac{1}{10}\right) \\ &= (8 \times 4) \times \left(\frac{1}{10} \times \frac{1}{10}\right) \\ &= 32 \times \frac{1}{100} \\ &= 32 \times 0.01 \\ &= 0.32 \end{aligned}$$

So, $0.8 \times 0.4 = 0.32$.

Remember if two factors less than one are multiplied, their product is less than either factor.

Use properties to find each product. Write the product as a decimal.

1. 0.6×0.3
2. 2.5×0.7
3. 0.04×1.9
4. 0.23×0.8
5. 0.1×8.2
6. 5.7×3.6
7. 4.2×6.5
8. 9.11×0.3

Name ________________________________

TOPIC 4

Reteaching
Continued

Set E pages 207–212

The decimal is missing in the product below. Use number sense to place the decimal point correctly.

43.5 × 1.7 = 7395

Since 1.7 is greater than 1, the product will be greater than 43.5. Since 1.7 is about 2, the decimal point should be between the 3 and the 9.

$$\begin{array}{r} 43.5 \\ \times \quad 1.7 \\ \hline 73.95 \end{array}$$

So, 43.5 × 1.7 = 73.95.

Remember that it may be helpful to compare each factor to 1 in order to determine the relative size of the product.

The decimal point is missing in each product. Use number sense to place the decimal point correctly.

1. 4 × 0.21 = 84
2. 4.5 × 6.2 = 279
3. 7 × 21.6 = 1512
4. 6.4 × 3.2 = 2048
5. 31.5 × 0.01 = 315
6. 1.4 × 52.3 = 7322
7. 0.12 × 0.9 = 108
8. 12.5 × 163.2 = 2040

Set F pages 213–218

Find 52.5 × 1.9.

Estimate: 50 × 2 = 100.

52.5	←	1 decimal place
× 1.9	←	+ 1 decimal place
4725		
5250		
99.75	←	2 decimal places

The answer is reasonable because 99.75 is close to 100.

Remember to count the number of decimal places in both factors in order to place the decimal correctly in the product.

Find each product.

1. 0.9 × 0.11
2. 2.4 × 3.67
3. 8.3 × 10.4
4. 0.25 × 0.3
5. 23.3 × 6.5
6. 0.7 × 31.4
7. 11.2 × 9.7
8. 1.4 × 9.67

Set G pages 219–224

Think about these questions to help you **model with math**.

Thinking Habits

- How can I use math I know to help solve this problem?
- How can I use pictures, objects, or an equation to represent the problem?
- How can I use numbers, words, and symbols to solve the problem?

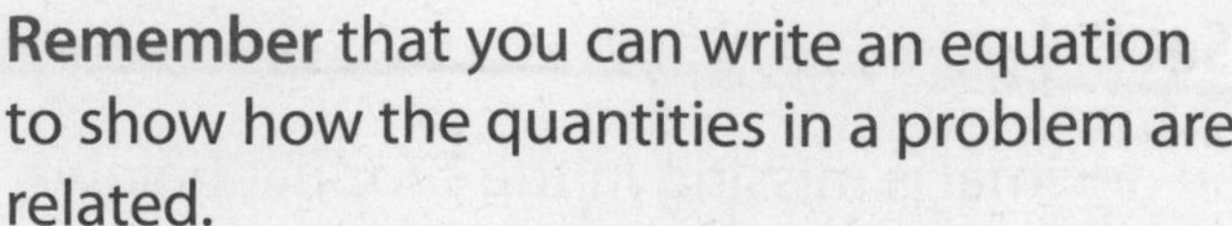

Remember that you can write an equation to show how the quantities in a problem are related.

Mr. Jennings made the stained glass window below with the dimensions shown. What is the total area of the window?

1.8 ft by 1.25 ft
1.5 ft by 0.75 ft
1.5 ft by 0.5 ft

1. What do you need to find first?

2. Write an equation to model the problem. Then solve the problem.

Patti went to the bakery. She bought a loaf of bread for \$3.49, 6 muffins that cost \$1.25 each, and a bottle of juice for \$1.79. She gave the cashier a \$20 bill.

3. What do you need to find first?

4. How much change should Patti receive? Write equations to show your work.

Name ______________________________

TOPIC 4

Assessment

1. Credit cards are 0.76 mm thick. How thick is a stack of 10^3 credit cards piled one on top of the other?

Ⓐ 760 mm

Ⓑ 76 mm

Ⓒ 0.076 mm

Ⓓ 0.00076 mm

2. Leo has 59 bricks each measuring 0.19 m long. He lines up the bricks to make a row.

Part A

Estimate the length of Leo's row of bricks. Write an equation to model your work.

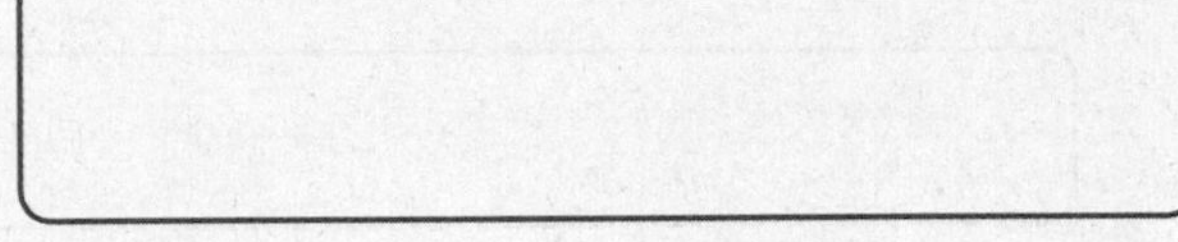

Part B

Find the actual length of the row of bricks.

3. Susan colored in the decimal grid shown below. Which expression shows the area of the grid Susan colored?

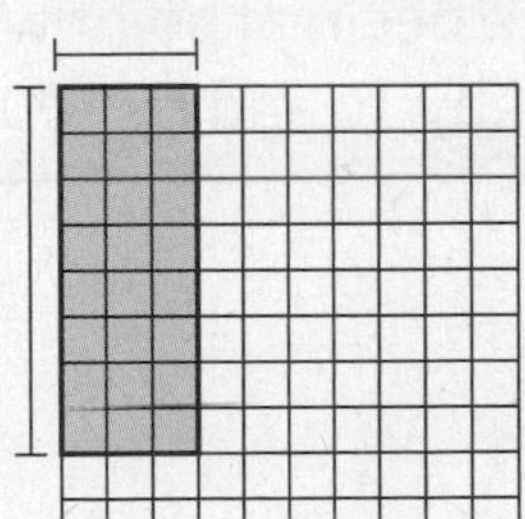

Ⓐ 0.08×0.03

Ⓑ 0.8×0.3

Ⓒ 0.7×0.2

Ⓓ 0.4×0.6

4. Draw lines to match each expression on the left with the correct product on the right.

5×0.08	4
0.5×0.08	40
50×0.8	0.4
5×0.8	0.04

5. Michelle bought 4.6 meters of fabric. Each meter of fabric cost \$3.50.

Part A

What are the partial products of 4.6×3.5? Write equations to model your work.

Part B

How much did Michelle spend on the fabric?

6. Choose all the expressions that are equal to 0.75×0.5.

☐ $\frac{5}{10} \times \frac{75}{10}$

☐ $\frac{5}{100} \times \frac{75}{100}$

☐ $\frac{75}{100} \times \frac{5}{10}$

☐ $\frac{5}{10} \times \frac{75}{100}$

☐ $\frac{50}{100} \times \frac{75}{100}$

7. For questions 7a-7d, choose Yes or No to tell if the number 10^2 will make each equation true.

7a. $0.031 \times \square = 31$ ○ Yes ○ No

7b. $0.501 \times \square = 501$ ○ Yes ○ No

7c. $4.08 \times \square = 408$ ○ Yes ○ No

7d. $0.97 \times \square = 97$ ○ Yes ○ No

---

8. Nadia drew a square in her notebook. Each side measured 2.5 centimeters.

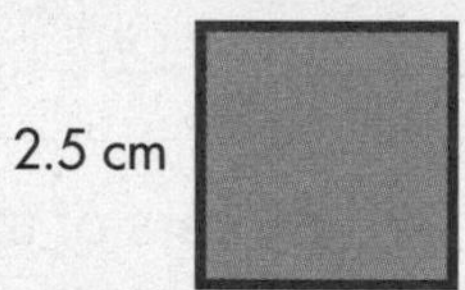

Part A

What is the perimeter of Nadia's square? Write an equation to model your work.

Part B

What is the area of Nadia's square? Write an equation to model your work.

---

9. Draw lines to match each expression on the left with the correct product on the right.

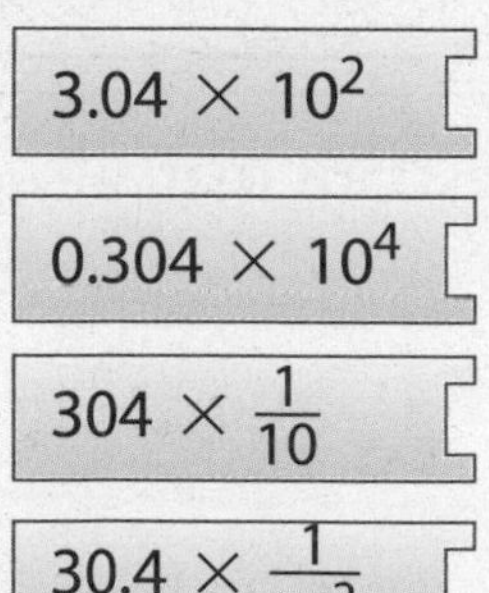

0.304

30.4

304

3,040

10. Choose all the expressions that are equal to 0.09×0.4.

- ☐ $\frac{9}{100} \times \frac{4}{10}$
- ☐ $\frac{4}{100} \times \frac{9}{100}$
- ☐ $\frac{9}{10} \times \frac{4}{10}$
- ☐ $\frac{4}{10} \times \frac{9}{100}$
- ☐ $\frac{40}{100} \times \frac{9}{100}$

---

11. Natalie likes to mail lots of postcards when she goes on vacation. In 2014, the cost of a postcard stamp was \$0.34.

Part A

Natalie buys 10 postcard stamps. What is the total cost of the stamps?

Part B

Natalie and her friends decide to buy 100 postcard stamps. What will be the total cost of the stamps?

Part C

What pattern do you notice in the placement of the decimal point when multiplying 0.34 by 10 and by 100?

Name ______________________________

TOPIC 4 Assessment Continued

12. For questions 12a-12d, choose Yes or No to tell if the decimal 0.65 will make each equation true.

12a. $10^2 \times \square = 65$ ○ Yes ○ No

12b. $10^4 \times \square = 650$ ○ Yes ○ No

12c. $10^1 \times \square = 6.5$ ○ Yes ○ No

12d. $10^3 \times \square = 65$ ○ Yes ○ No

13. Alyssa is painting 3 of the walls in her art studio blue. Each of the walls is 8.3 feet tall and 7.5 feet wide.

Part A

Round the length and width to the nearest whole number. Then estimate the area that Alyssa will paint. Write equations to model your work.

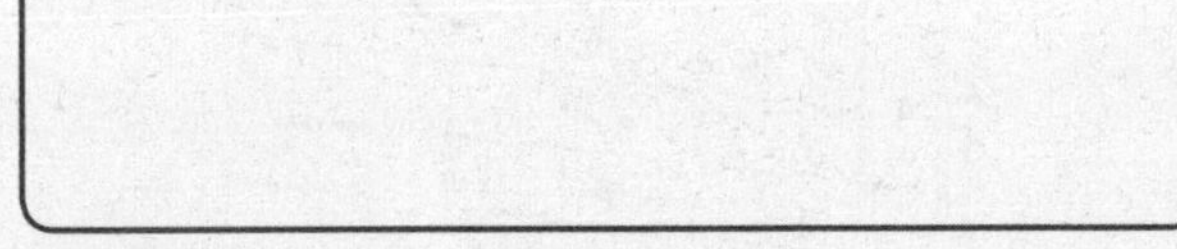

Part B

Find the exact area. Write equations to model your work.

Part C

Compare your estimate to the exact answer. Why is your answer reasonable?

14. Derrick runs 2.25 miles each day. How many total miles will he have run after 10 days?

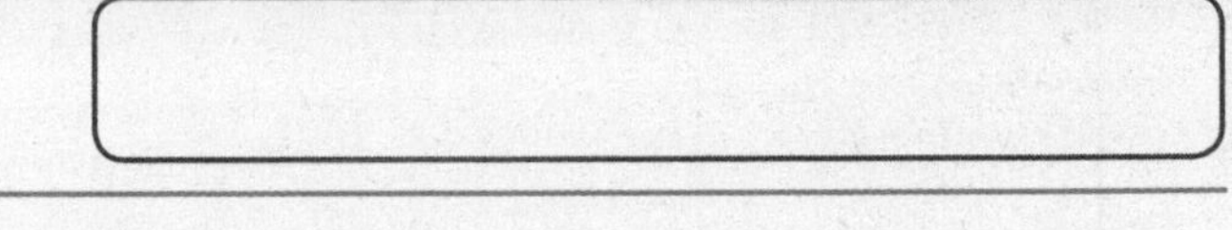

15. One glass of lemonade has 115 calories. How many calories are in 3.5 glasses of lemonade? Write an equation to model your work.

16. A farmer plants 0.4 of a field with wheat. The field is 2.3 acres.

Part A

Shade the grids to model the multiplication.

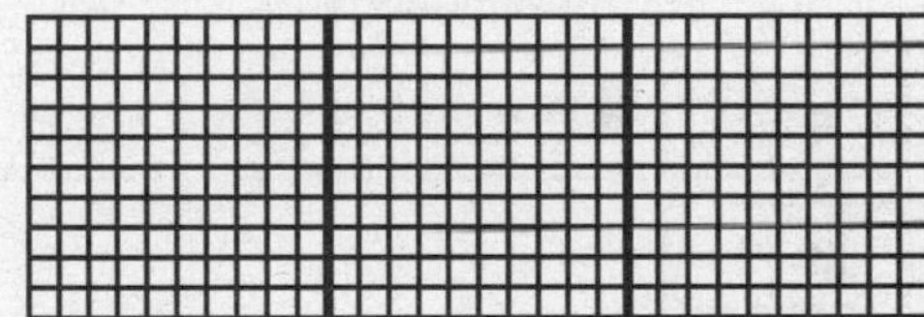

Part B

How many acres are planted with wheat? Write an equation to model your work.

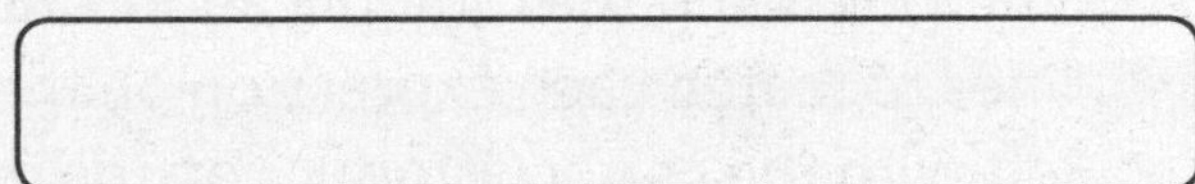

Part C

How does the model help you find the product?

17. Bradley walks 0.65 mile each Friday to his friend's house. He takes a different route home that is 1.2 miles. How many miles will Bradley walk to his friend's house and back in a year? Show your work. Reminder: there are 52 weeks in a year.

18. The area of one fabric square is 4.85 square inches. What is the area of a quilt made with 10^2 fabric squares?

19. Jen bought 3.72 pounds of apples at a farmer's market. Andrea bought 4 times as much as Jen. How many pounds of apples did Andrea buy? Use the bar diagram to help you.

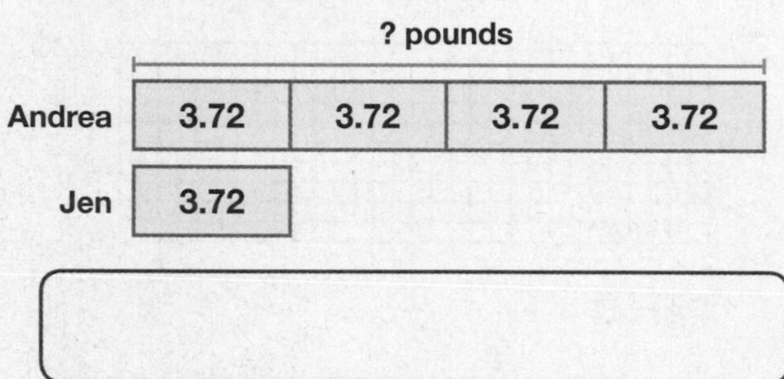

20. Without doing the multiplication, draw lines to match each expression on the left with the correct product on the right. Use number sense to help you.

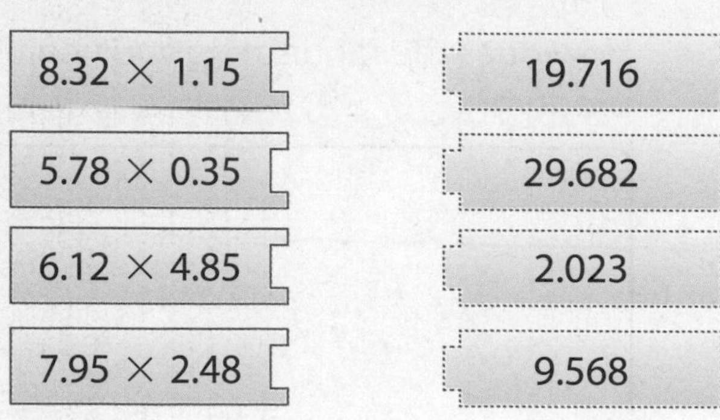

21. Leticia and Jamal go to a bakery.

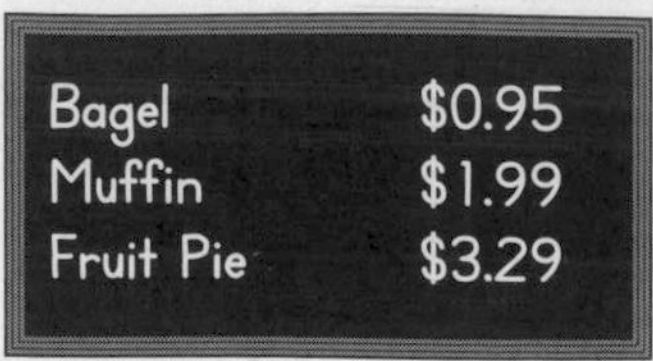

Part A

Jamal wants to buy 6 muffins. How much will this cost? Write an equation to model your work.

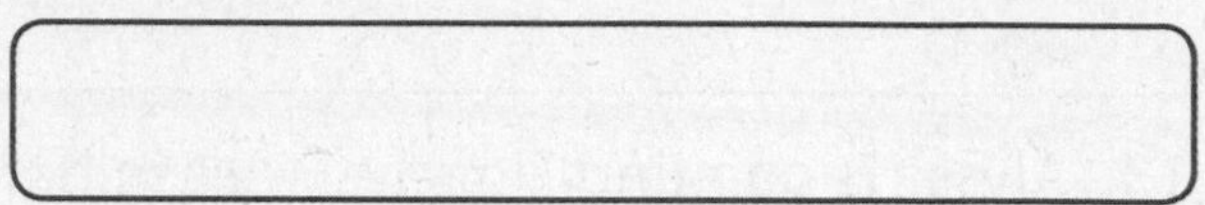

Part B

Leticia wants to buy 12 bagels. She uses partial products to find her total. She says "$16.80 is close to my estimate of $12 \times \$1 = \$12$, so this total is reasonable." Do you agree with her? Explain your reasoning.

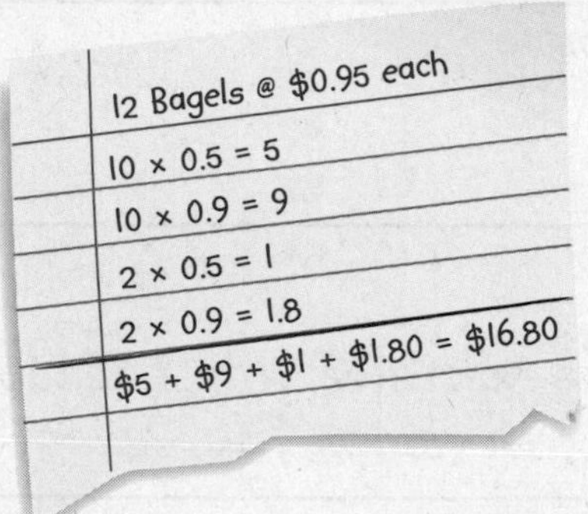

Name ______________________________

TOPIC 4

Performance Assessment

An *exchange rate* is how much of one country's currency (money) you would get for another country's currency. The table below shows the recent exchange rate between the U.S. dollar and the currency of some other countries.

For example, if you had $2 (U.S.) dollars, you could exchange that for 26.48 Mexican pesos:

$2 \times 13.24 = 26.48$.

U.S. $1.00 =
6.29 Venezuelan bolívares
6.45 Swedish Krona
61.92 Indian rupees
101.82 Japanese yen
86.4 Kenyan shillings
13.24 Mexican pesos

1. Jade has $10, Julio has $100, and Anna has $1,000. How many Japanese yen would each person get in exchange for their dollars?

2. Ivana has $5.50. Luc has 1.4 times as much money as Ivana.

Part A

How many Indian rupees would Ivana get?

Part B

How many dollars does Luc have? How many rupees can he exchange for that? Round your answer to the nearest hundredth.

3. Use estimation to solve. Marcus has $250. About how many Venezuelan bolívares could he obtain? Is your estimate an overestimate or an underestimate? Explain.

4. Jorge is traveling to Kenya to photograph wildlife. How many Kenyan shillings will he receive for $500? His friends give him a $50 gift certificate right before he leaves. How many Kenyan shillings can he exchange for that amount?

5. Kofi is taking a trip to Mexico to see Mayan and Aztec pyramids. He wants to exchange $300 before arriving there. How many Mexican pesos can he receive? Write and solve an equation to show your work.

6. Mary is planning a vacation to Europe. The exchange rate between the U.S. dollar and the Euro is 0.73.

Part A

Shade the grid to model how many Euros Mary will get for $3 U.S. dollars.

Part B

How many Euros can Mary get for $3? Write an equation to show your work.

Part C

How does the model help you find the product?

Use Models and Strategies to Divide Whole Numbers

Essential Question: What is the standard procedure for division and why does it work?

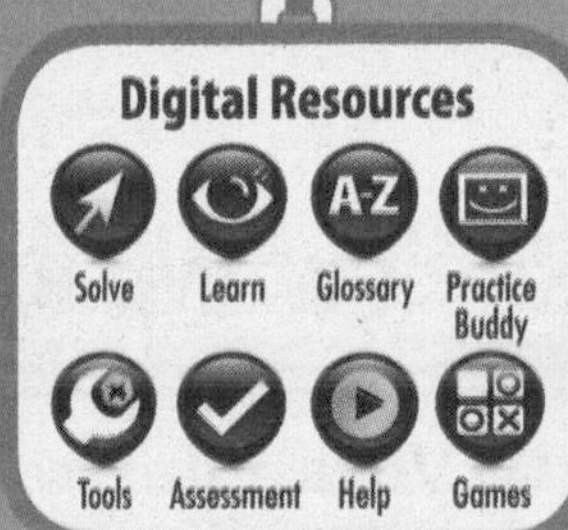

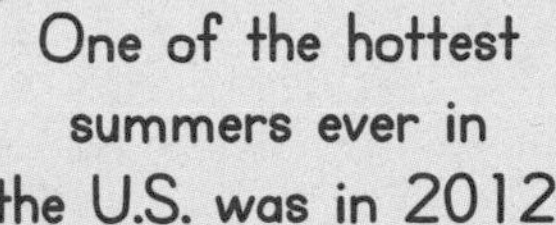

More iced tea, anybody? Here's a project on finding the average temperature using division.

Math and Science Project: Average Temperature

Do Research Use a weather site from the Internet or another source of daily weather reports to find the average daily temperature for your city or town for every day of one month. The average daily temperature is the average temperature for a whole 24-hour period.

Journal: Write a Report Include what you found about daily temperatures. Also in your report:

- Find the average daily high temperature for the month. Which day had the greatest high temperature?
- Find the average daily low temperature for the month. Which day had the least low temperature?
- Make up and solve division problems based on your data.

Name ______________________________

Review What You Know

Vocabulary

Choose the best term from the box.
Write it on the blank.

- dividend
- quotient
- divisor
- remainder

1. In the equation $80 \div 10 = 8$, the number 80 is the __________.

2. The number used to divide another number is the __________.

3. The result of dividing two numbers is the __________.

Multiplication and Division

Multiply or divide.

4. $630 \div 9$
5. $480 \div 6$
6. $755 \div 5$
7. $657 \div 9$
8. 57×13
9. 71×109

10. For the state fair next month, 132 people volunteered to plan the fair's activities. The volunteers formed 12 equal groups. How many volunteers were in each group?

11. A town is holding a competition for various athletic games. Each community has 14 players. There are 112 communities competing in the games. How many players are competing?

Ⓐ 1,676 Ⓑ 1,568 Ⓒ 126 Ⓓ 98

Estimate

12. A county has a goal to build 12,000 bus stop shelters in 48 months. If the county builds 215 bus shelters each month, will it reach its goal? Explain one way to estimate the answer.

Name ____________________

Lesson 5-1
Use Patterns and Mental Math to Divide

I can ...
use patterns to find quotients.

I can also look for patterns to solve problems.

Solve & Share A bakery sells muffins to local grocery stores in boxes that hold 20 muffins each. How many boxes are used if 60 muffins are sold? 600 muffins? 6,000 muffins? ***Solve this problem any way you choose.***

Find the answer for 60 muffins. Then you can look for relationships to help find the answers for 600 and 6,000 muffins. *Show your work!*

Number of Muffins Sold	Number of Muffins per Box	Number of Boxes
60	20	
600	20	
6,000	20	

Look Back! Generalize How can you use multiplication to help you divide 6,000 by 20?

How Can Patterns Help You Divide Multiples of 10?

A

A jet carries 18,000 passengers in 90 trips. The plane is full for each trip. How many passengers does the plane hold?

Find 18,000 ÷ 90, the number of passengers on each trip.

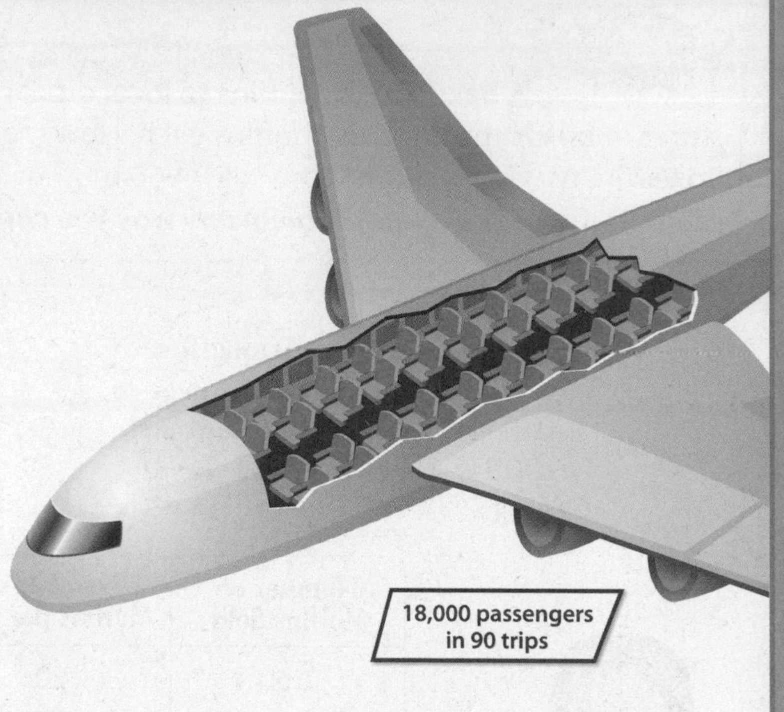

B

Think of a basic fact to help you.
$18 \div 9 = 2$

Think about multiples of 10:

$180 \div 90 = 18 \text{ tens} \div 9 \text{ tens} = 2$

$1,800 \div 90 = 180 \text{ tens} \div 9 \text{ tens} = 20$

$18,000 \div 90 = 1,800 \text{ tens} \div 9 \text{ tens} = 200$

C

The pattern shows that
$18,000 \div 90 = 200$.

So, the jet can hold 200 passengers during each trip.

$200 \times 90 = 18,000$

Convince Me! Look for Patterns If the jet above carried 10,000 people in 50 trips, how many people did it carry each trip? The jet carried the same number of people each trip.

What basic fact helped you find the answer?

Name ______________________

Practice Buddy | Tools | Assessment

Guided Practice*

Do You Understand?

1. Generalize Why is 210 ÷ 30 the same as 21 tens ÷ 3 tens?

2. A jet carried 12,000 people in 40 trips. If the jet was full each trip, how many people did it carry for each trip?

Use a basic fact to help you.

Do You Know How?

In **3–9**, find each quotient. Use mental math.

3. 210 ÷ 30 = 21 tens ÷ 3 tens = ____

4. 480 ÷ 60 = 48 tens ÷ 6 tens = ____

5. 15,000 ÷ 30 = 1,500 tens ÷ 3 tens = ____

6. 8,100 ÷ 90 = ____ **7.** 2,800 ÷ 70 = ____

8. 30,000 ÷ 50 = ____ **9.** 1,800 ÷ 60 = ____

Independent Practice

Leveled Practice In **10–25**, use mental math to find the missing numbers.

10. 560 ÷ 70 = 56 tens ÷ 7 tens = ____

11. 360 ÷ 60 = 36 tens ÷ 6 tens = ____

12. 6,000 ÷ 50 = 600 tens ÷ 5 tens = ____

13. 24,000 ÷ 60 = 2,400 tens ÷ 6 tens = ____

14. 2,000 ÷ 20 = ____

15. 6,300 ÷ 90 = ____

16. ____ ÷ 10 = 24

17. 21,000 ÷ ____ = 700

18. 2,500 ÷ 50 = ____

19. 72,000 ÷ ____ = 800

20. 56,000 ÷ ____ = 800

21. ____ ÷ 10 = 100

22. 45,000 ÷ 90 = ____

23. 42,000 ÷ 70 = ____

24. 64,000 ÷ ____ = 800

25. 32,000 ÷ ____ = 400

*For another example, see Set A on page 289.

Problem Solving

26. The table shows the number of passengers who flew on airplane flights in or out of one airport. Each flight had the same number of passengers. How many passengers were on each flight?

DATA	
Total passengers	27,000
Number of flights	90
Crew members	900

27. **Algebra** A truck delivers 478 dozen eggs to stores in one day. Write and solve an equation to find *n*, the number of eggs the truck delivers in one day.

28. Paula wants to divide 480 tomatoes equally among 80 baskets. How many tomatoes will Paula put in each basket?

29. **Be Precise** Ernesto measured the width of each of the three coins shown below.

0.7 inch

0.84 inch

0.74 inch

What is the difference in width between the widest coin and the least wide coin?

30. **Higher Order Thinking** A baker uses 30 grams of sea salt for each batch of bread. Sea salt comes in an 18-kilogram package or an 800-gram package. Which size package should the baker buy so that no sea salt is left after all of the batches are made? Explain.

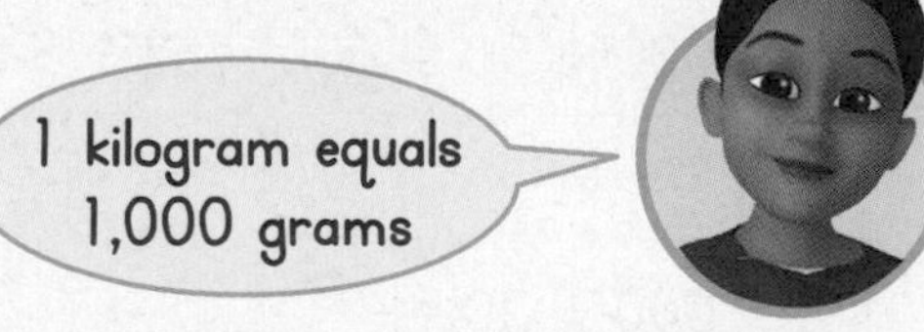

Assessment

31. Which is 2,400 divided by 80?

Ⓐ 3
Ⓑ 4
Ⓒ 30
Ⓓ 40

32. Which expression has a quotient of 70?

Ⓐ 420 ÷ 60
Ⓑ 4,200 ÷ 6
Ⓒ 4,200 ÷ 60
Ⓓ 4,200 ÷ 600

Name ____________________

Help | Practice Buddy | Tools | Games

Homework & Practice 5-1

Use Patterns and Mental Math to Divide

Another Look!

A school spends $12,000 on 20 new computers. Each computer costs the same amount. How much does each computer cost?

Find a basic fact and then use patterns.

A basic fact that can be used for $12{,}000 \div 20$ is $12 \div 2 = 6$.

$120 \div 20 = 6$
$1{,}200 \div 20 = 60$
$12{,}000 \div 20 = 600$

Multiply to check: $600 \times 20 = 12{,}000$

Each computer costs $600.

Use place-value patterns to help find the quotient.

Leveled Practice In **1–16**, use a basic fact and a pattern to help solve.

1. $720 \div 90 = 72$ tens $\div$ 9 tens = ____

2. $4{,}800 \div 60 = 480$ tens $\div$ 6 tens = ____

3. $1{,}200 \div 30 =$ ____ tens $\div$ ____ tens = ____

4. $25{,}000 \div 50 =$ ____ tens $\div$ ____ tens = ____

5. $320 \div 40$

6. $9{,}000 \div 30$

7. $1{,}800 \div 90$

8. $2{,}000 \div 40$

9. $24{,}000 \div 80$

10. $32{,}000 \div 40$

11. $3{,}600 \div 90$

12. $40{,}000 \div 50$

13. $42{,}000 \div 60$

14. $5{,}400 \div 60$

15. $49{,}000 \div 70$

16. $56{,}000 \div 80$

17. Use Structure A carton of staples has 50 packages. The carton contains 25,000 staples in all. Each package has an equal number of staples. How many staples are in each package? Explain how to use a basic fact to find the answer.

18. Reasoning A club collected $3,472 to buy computers. If each computer costs $680, estimate the number of computers that the club can buy. Explain.

19. Higher Order Thinking A railroad car container can hold 42,000 pounds. Mr. Evans wants to ship 90 ovens and some freezers in the same container. If each freezer weighs 600 pounds, how many freezers could be shipped in the container? Explain.

20. Critique Reasoning There are 50 communities in Kalb County. Each community has about the same number of people. Marty estimates there are about 300 people living in each community. Is his estimate reasonable? Justify your answer.

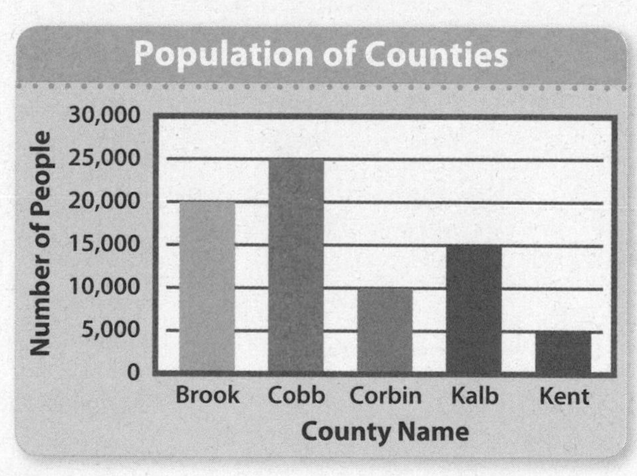

Assessment

21. Which is 2,000 divided by 50?

Ⓐ 4
Ⓑ 40
Ⓒ 400
Ⓓ 4,000

22. Which expression has a quotient of 400?

Ⓐ 800 ÷ 20
Ⓑ 8,000 ÷ 2
Ⓒ 8,000 ÷ 20
Ⓓ 80,000 ÷ 20

Name ______________________________

Lesson 5-2
Estimate Quotients with 2-Digit Divisors

I can . . .
estimate quotients.

I can also reason about math.

Solve & Share

Kyle's school needs to buy posters for a fundraiser. The school has a budget of $147. Each poster costs $13. About how many posters can his school buy? ***Solve this problem any way you choose.***

You can use reasoning to find compatible numbers to estimate quotients. *Show your work!*

Look Back! Make Sense and Persevere What numbers are close to 147 and 13 that would be easy to divide using mental math?

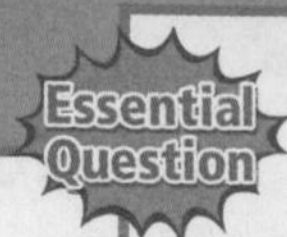

How Can You Use Compatible Numbers to Estimate Quotients?

A

Betty earned $159 by selling 75 bracelets. Each bracelet was the same price. About how much did each bracelet cost?

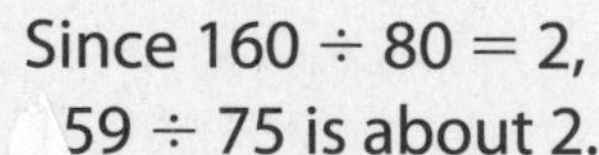

B The question asks, "About how much?" So, an estimate is enough.

Use compatible numbers to estimate 159 ÷ 75.

160 and 80 are close to 159 and 75, and 80 divides 160 evenly.

So, 160 and 80 are compatible numbers.

16 can be divided evenly by 8.

C Since 160 ÷ 80 = 2, 159 ÷ 75 is about 2.

Betty charged *about* $2 for each bracelet.

Use multiplication to check for reasonableness:

2 × 80 = 160.

Convince Me! **Make Sense and Persevere** Suppose Betty earned $230 selling the 75 bracelets. Estimate the cost of each bracelet. What compatible numbers did you use?

Name ______________________________

Practice Buddy | Tools | Assessment

Guided Practice*

Do You Understand?

1. **Critique Reasoning** Betty has 425 more bracelets to sell. She wants to store these in bags that hold 20 bracelets each. She estimates she will need about 25 bags. Do you agree? Why or why not?

Do You Know How?

In **2–7**, estimate using compatible numbers.

2. 287 ÷ 42

3. 320 ÷ 11

4. 208 ÷ 72

5. 554 ÷ 62

6. 815 ÷ 23

7. 2,491 ÷ 48

Independent Practice

Leveled Practice In **8–10**, fill in the blanks to find each estimate.

8. 412 ÷ 84
400 ÷ ☐ = ☐

9. 288 ÷ 37
280 ÷ ☐ = ☐

10. 2,964 ÷ 73
2,800 ÷ ☐ = ☐

In **11–22**, estimate using compatible numbers.

11. 228 ÷ 19

12. 1,784 ÷ 64

13. 7,260 ÷ 83

14. 2,280 ÷ 12

15. 485 ÷ 92

16. 540 ÷ 61

17. 1,710 ÷ 32

18. 2,740 ÷ 67

19. 4,322 ÷ 81

20. 5,700 ÷ 58

21. 7,810 ÷ 44

22. 6,395 ÷ 84

*For another example, see Set B on page 289.

Problem Solving

23. **Model with Math** The sign shows the price of baseball caps for different pack sizes. Coach Lewis will buy the medium-size pack of caps. About how much will each cap cost? Write an equation to model your work.

Packs of Baseball Caps

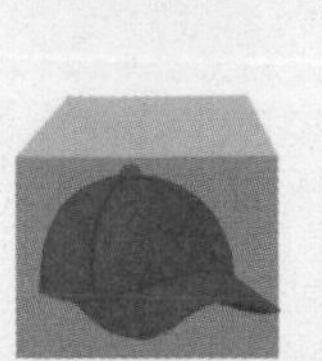
20 Small Caps
$180.00

32 Medium Caps
$270.00

50 Large Caps
$360.00

24. **Make Sense and Persevere** There are 91 days until the craft sale. Autumn needs to make 817 rings before the sale. She wants to make about the same number of rings each day. About how many rings should she make each day? Explain how Autumn can use compatible numbers to estimate.

25. **Higher Order Thinking** A company purchased 3,128 bottles of water. Each department needs 55 bottles. Which compatible numbers provide a better estimate for the number of departments that can get the bottles needed — 3,000 ÷ 60 or 3,000 ÷ 50? Explain. Then make the estimate.

26. **Model with Math** Rita had $20. Then she saved $5.85 each week for 8 weeks. How much money does she have now? Use the bar diagram to solve the problem. Show your work.

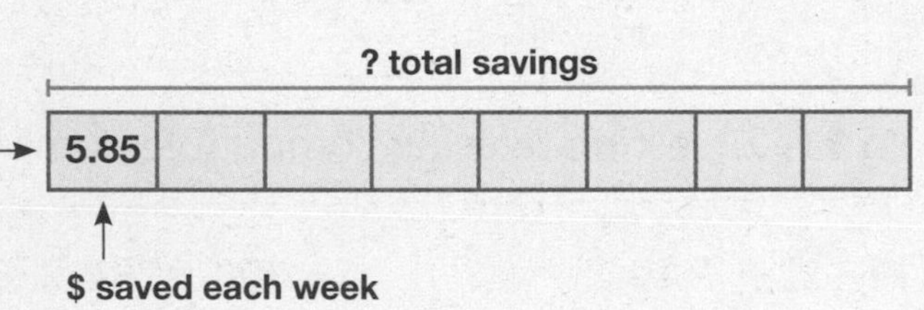

Assessment

27. Lea bought 225 flowers and 12 vases. She put about the same number of flowers in each vase. Which is the best estimate for the number of flowers in each vase?

Ⓐ 40 flowers
Ⓑ 30 flowers
Ⓒ 20 flowers
Ⓓ 10 flowers

28. A school has 617 students. Each class has between 28 and 32 students. Which is the best estimate of the number of classes in the school?

Ⓐ 14 classes
Ⓑ 20 classes
Ⓒ 30 classes
Ⓓ 60 classes

Name ______________________

Help Practice Buddy Tools Games

Homework & Practice 5-2

Estimate Quotients with 2-Digit Divisors

Another Look!

Frog Trail is 1,976 meters long. Shondra walks 43 meters of the trail each minute. About how many minutes will it take Shondra to walk the trail?

Find compatible numbers. Think of a basic fact. Then use place-value patterns.

1,976 ÷ 43
↓ ↓
2,000 ÷ 40 = 50

2,000 ÷ 40 = 50, so
1,976 ÷ 43 is about 50.

It would take Shondra about 50 minutes.

You can use a basic fact and place-value patterns.

Leveled Practice In **1–3**, fill in the blanks to find the estimates.

1. 1,769 ÷ 23
1,800 ÷ ☐ = ☐

2. 516 ÷ 48
500 ÷ ☐ = ☐

3. 891 ÷ 32
☐ ÷ ☐ = ☐

In **4–15**, estimate using compatible numbers.

4. 231 ÷ 34

5. 705 ÷ 11

6. 8,968 ÷ 22

7. 5,624 ÷ 72

8. 1,043 ÷ 23

9. 986 ÷ 12

10. 642 ÷ 94

11. 4,870 ÷ 58

12. 5,721 ÷ 79

13. 148 ÷ 51

14. 9,073 ÷ 11

15. 3,514 ÷ 58

16. Critique Reasoning Meredith says "Since 1 times 1 equals 1, then 0.1 times 0.1 equals 0.1." Do you agree? Explain your reasoning.

17. Math and Science A gray whale traveled 152 kilometers in one day. The whale swam between 7 and 8 kilometers each hour. About how many hours did it take the whale to swim the distance? Show two different ways that you can use compatible numbers to find an answer. Then solve.

18. Construct Arguments Meg wants to find about how many phones the company activated in one minute. Explain why Meg can use 15,000 ÷ 50 to find the answer.

DATA

Clear Connect Company
phones activated: 14,270 in 50 minutes
calls made: 59,835
text messages sent: 2,063

19. Higher Order Thinking Ester's choir wants to learn a new song for the school concert in 7 weeks. The song has 3,016 lines. The choir learns an equal number of lines each day. About how many lines do they need to learn each day to learn the song in time for the concert? Explain.

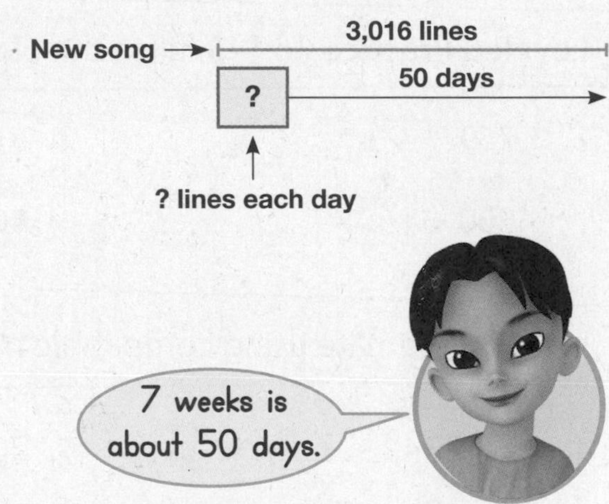

Assessment

20. Mr. Crane's farm is 593 acres. He divides the farm into 32 equal parts. Which is the best estimate of the number of acres in each part?

Ⓐ 10 acres

Ⓑ 20 acres

Ⓒ 100 acres

Ⓓ 200 acres

21. A scientist counted 3,921 total eggs in 49 sea turtle nests. Each nest had about the same number of eggs. Which is the best estimate of the number of eggs she counted in each nest?

Ⓐ 800 eggs

Ⓑ 100 eggs

Ⓒ 80 eggs

Ⓓ 10 eggs

Name ____________________

Solve

Lesson 5-3
Use Models to Divide with 2-Digit Divisors

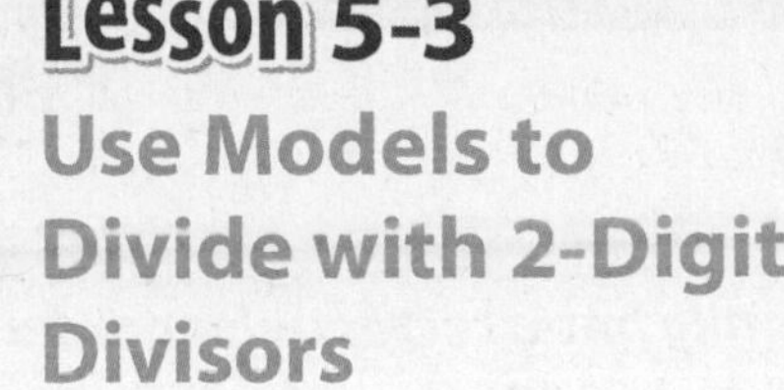

I can ...
use models to help find quotients.

I can also choose and use a math tool to solve problems.

Solve & Share A parking lot has 270 parking spaces. Each row has 18 parking spaces. How many rows are in this parking lot? ***Solve this problem any way you choose.***

Look Back! Make Sense and Persevere How can you use estimation to check that your answer to the problem above is reasonable?

How Can You Use Area Models to Find Quotients?

A

Emily has a rectangular garden with an area of 360 square feet. The length of her garden measures 20 feet. How many feet wide is her garden?

You can have w stand for the unknown side.

Think: $20 \times w = 360$ or $360 \div 20 = w$.

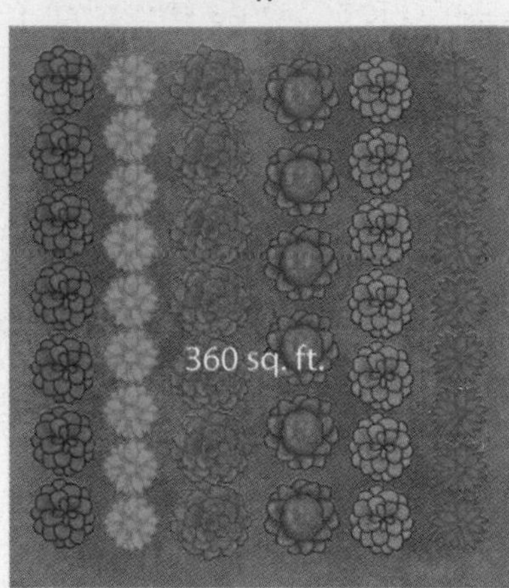

B **Find the unknown side length.**

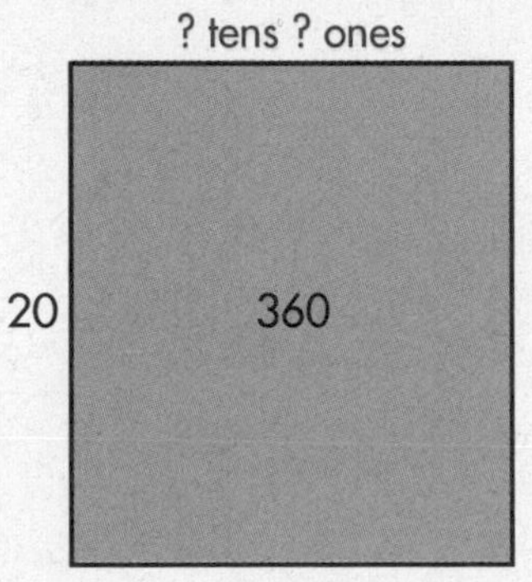

C **Find the number of tens.**

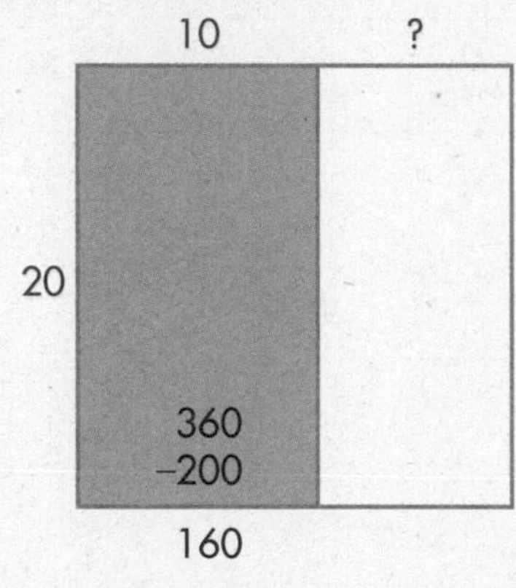

D **Find the number of ones.**

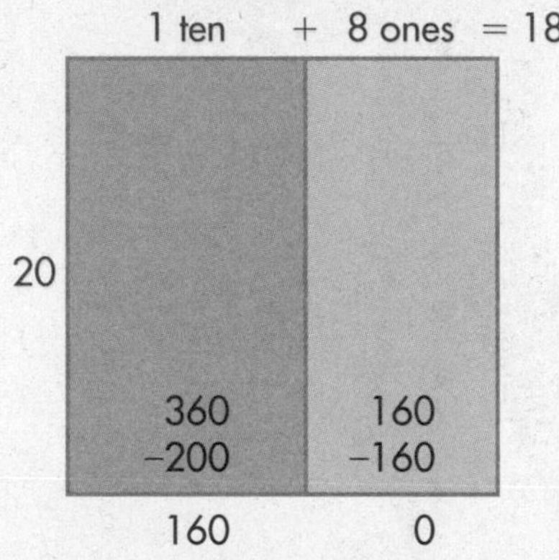

1 ten + 8 ones = 18.
So, the garden is 18 feet wide.

Convince Me! **Make Sense and Persevere** Use the model to find the quotient $408 \div 12$. Hint: Find the value of x and solve.

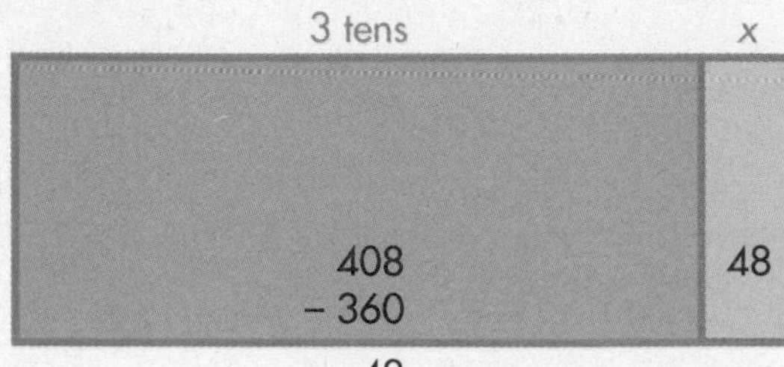

Name ___________________________

Lesson 5-3
Use Models to Divide with 2-Digit Divisors

I can ...
use models to help find quotients.

I can also choose and use a math tool to solve problems.

Solve & Share

A parking lot has 270 parking spaces. Each row has 18 parking spaces. How many rows are in this parking lot? ***Solve this problem any way you choose.***

Look Back! Make Sense and Persevere How can you use estimation to check that your answer to the problem above is reasonable?

How Can You Use Area Models to Find Quotients?

A

Emily has a rectangular garden with an area of 360 square feet. The length of her garden measures 20 feet. How many feet wide is her garden?

You can have w stand for the unknown side.

Think: $20 \times w = 360$ or $360 \div 20 = w$.

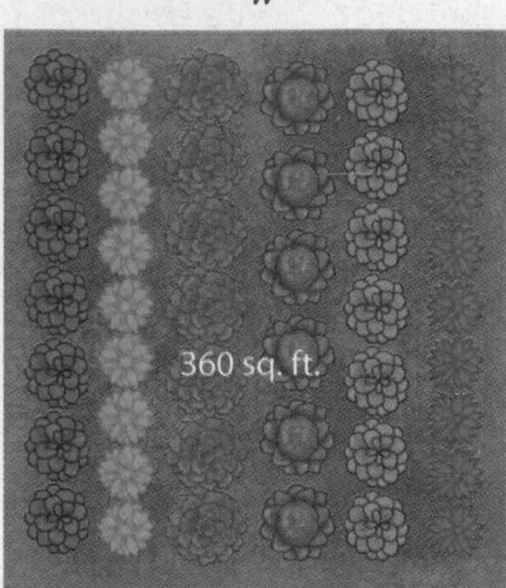

B **Find the unknown side length.**

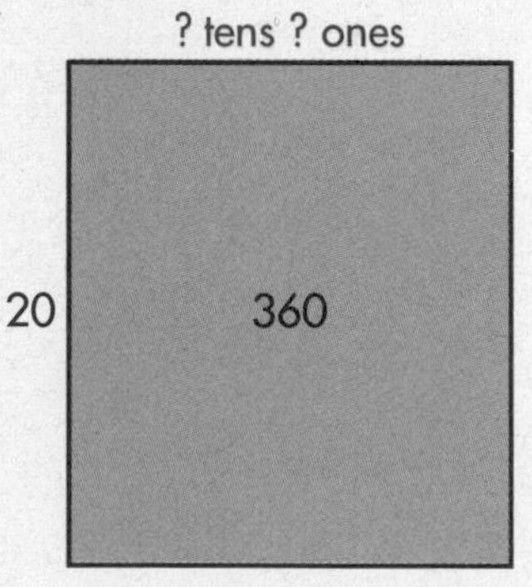

C **Find the number of tens.**

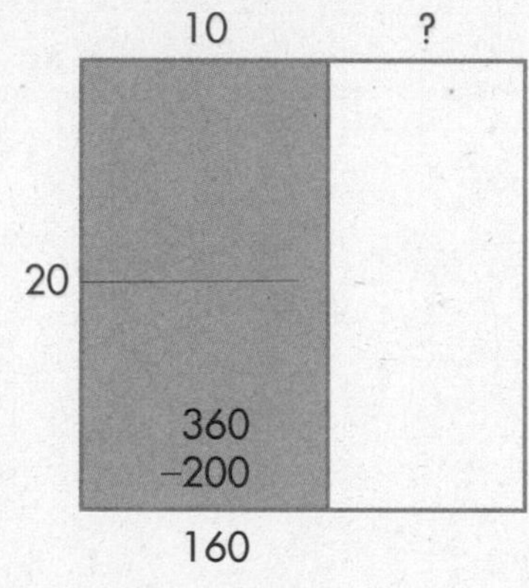

D **Find the number of ones.**

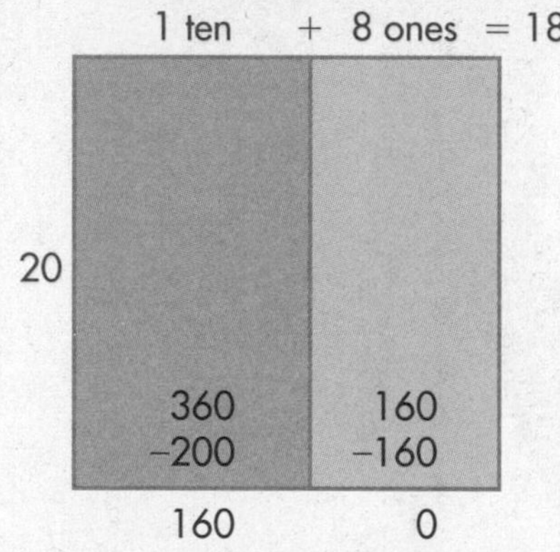

1 ten + 8 ones = 18.
So, the garden is 18 feet wide.

Convince Me! **Make Sense and Persevere** Use the model to find the quotient $408 \div 12$. Hint: Find the value of x and solve.

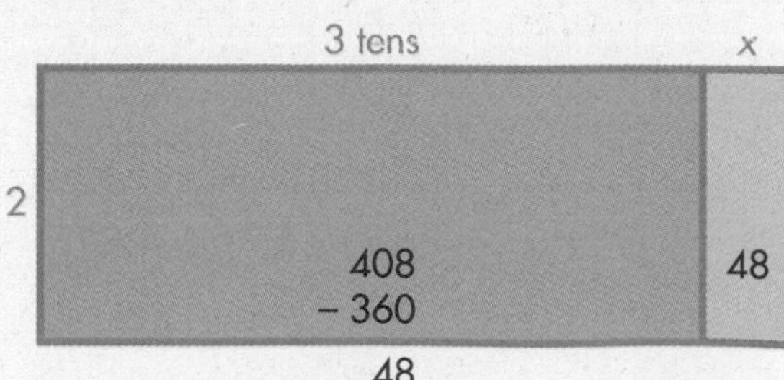

Name ____________________

Practice Buddy | Tools | Assessment

Guided Practice*

Do You Understand?

1. Write the missing numbers to find 154 ÷ 11.

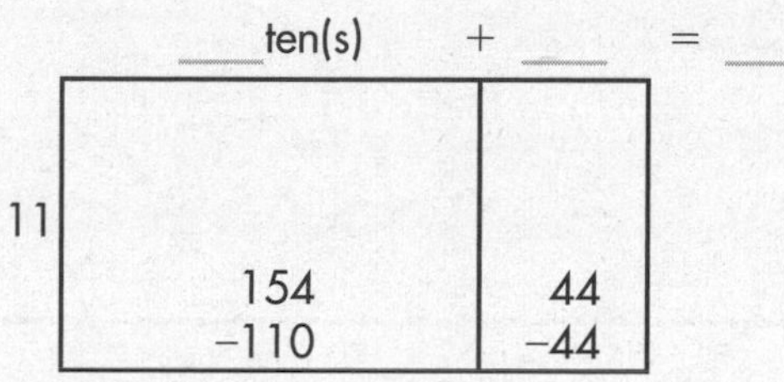

So, 154 ÷ 11 = ___

2. Make Sense and Persevere Write a multiplication equation and a division equation that represent the model shown below. Then solve.

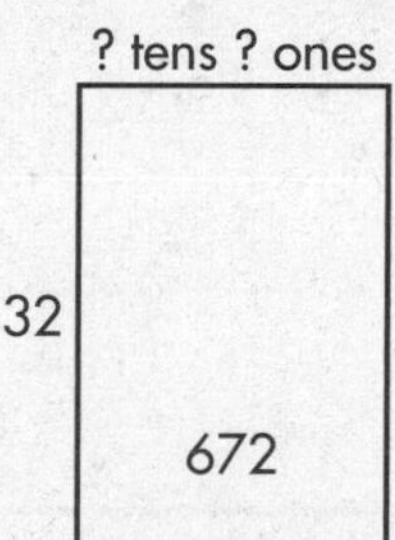

Do You Know How?

3. Use the model to find 156 ÷ 12.

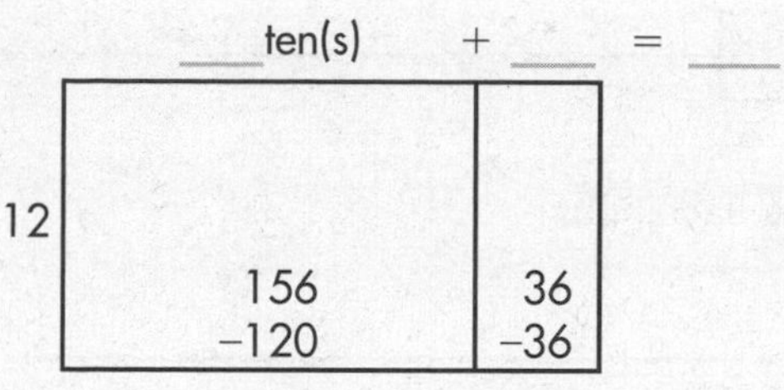

So, 156 ÷ 12 = ___

In **4** and **5**, use grid paper or draw a picture to find each quotient.

4. 682 ÷ 22

5. 143 ÷ 11

Start by estimating how many tens will be in the quotient.

Independent Practice

Leveled Practice In **6–12**, use grid paper or draw a picture to find each quotient.

6. Use the model to find 182 ÷ 13.

So, 182 ÷ 13 = ___.

___ ten(s) ___ = ___

13 | 182 |
− ___ | − ___
52 | 0

7. 342 ÷ 38

8. 720 ÷ 16

9. 608 ÷ 19

10. 752 ÷ 47

11. 375 ÷ 25

12. 576 ÷ 24

*For another example, see Set C on page 289.

Problem Solving

13. **Model with Math** Angelo is training for a long-distance bicycle ride. He travels 15 miles each hour. How many hours will it take him to ride 210 miles?

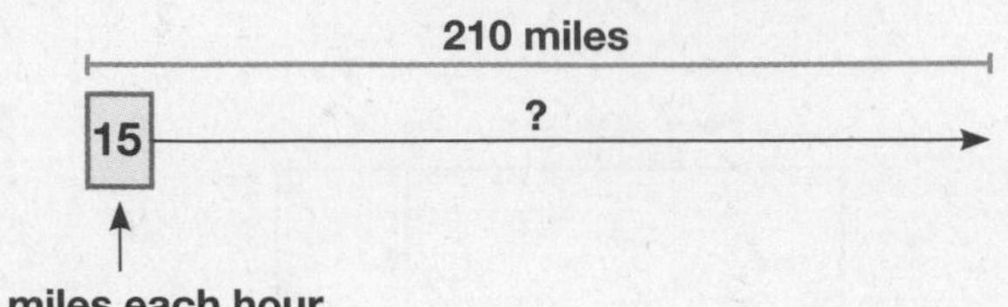

14. **Higher Order Thinking** A rectangular doormat is 21 inches long and has an area of 714 square inches. Find its width. Will the doormat fit in an entryway that is 36 inches wide? Show your work.

15. **Be Precise** Use the map. How much longer is the distance from the library to the park to the train station than the distance from the library straight to the train station?

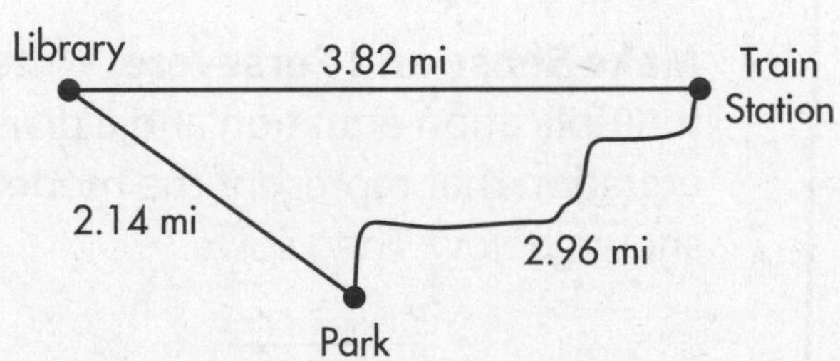

16. **Algebra** If you walk from the train station to the library, then to the park, and then back to the train station, how many miles would you walk in all? Write an equation to model your work.

17. **Make Sense and Persevere** Explain how you can use the picture to show that $391 \div 23 = 17$.

	1 ten	7 ones
23	391 −230	161 −161

Assessment

18. There are 16 rows of chairs in the auditorium. Each row has the same number of chairs. There are 512 chairs in all. How many chairs are in each row?

Ⓐ 22 chairs
Ⓑ 30 chairs
Ⓒ 32 chairs
Ⓓ 33 chairs

19. A patio has an area of 286 square feet. If the length of the patio is 22 feet, what is the width?

Ⓐ 10 feet
Ⓑ 13 feet
Ⓒ 14 feet
Ⓓ 144 feet

Name ____________________

Help Practice Buddy Tools Games

Homework & Practice 5-3

Use Models to Divide with 2-Digit Divisors

Another Look!

Hal's store just got a shipment of 195 cans of soup. Hal wants to divide the cans equally on 13 shelves. How many cans should he put on each shelf?

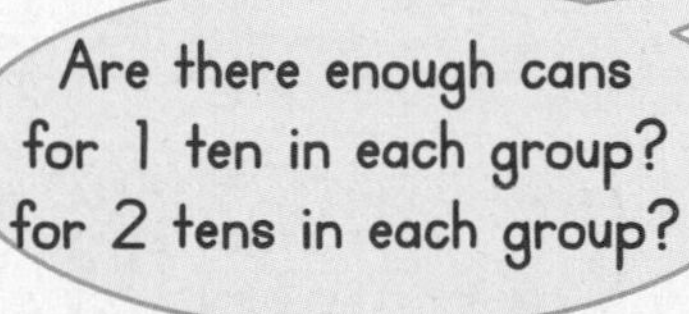

Step 1

Divide the tens. Record.

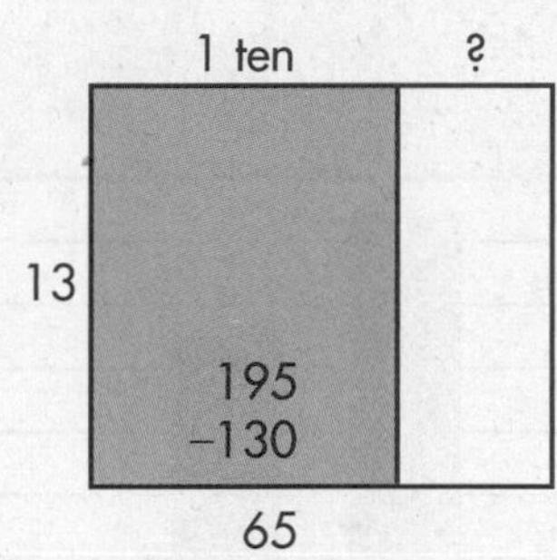

Step 2

Divide the ones. Record.

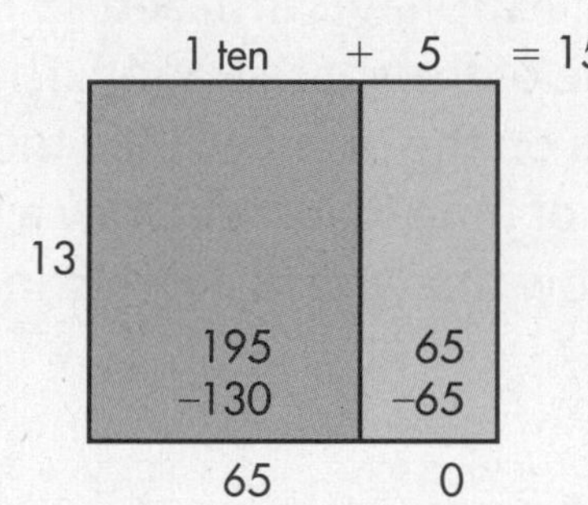

He should put 15 cans on each shelf.

In **1** and **2**, use the model to find each quotient.

1. $12\overline{)168}$

___ + ___ = ___

12 | 168 −120 | 48 −48

___ ___

2. $16\overline{)208}$

___ + ___ = ___

16 | 208 − 160 | 48 −48

___ ___

In **3–8**, use grid paper or draw a picture to find each quotient.

3. 420 ÷ 14

4. 385 ÷ 11

5. 744 ÷ 24

6. 675 ÷ 27

7. 558 ÷ 18

8. 228 ÷ 19

9. Reasoning Anna has 10^2 quarters. Jazmin has 10^2 dimes. Who has more money, Anna or Jazmin? How much more? Explain your reasoning.

10. Make Sense and Persevere A 208-yard-long road is divided into 16 parts of equal length. Mr. Ward paints a 4-yard-long strip in each part. How long is the unpainted strip of each part of the road?

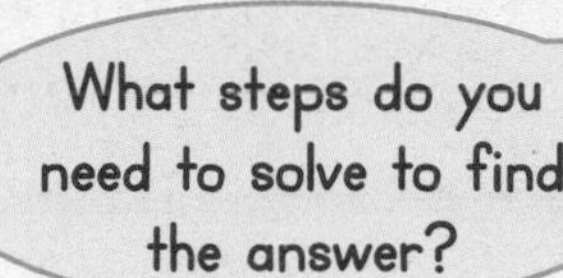

11. Use the bar graph. Astronauts installed 15 new tiles on the outside of the space station. They spent 390 minutes on the task. Each tile took the same amount of time to install. Draw a bar in the graph to show the time needed to install a tile. Explain.

12. How much longer does an astronaut take to install a light than to install a cable?

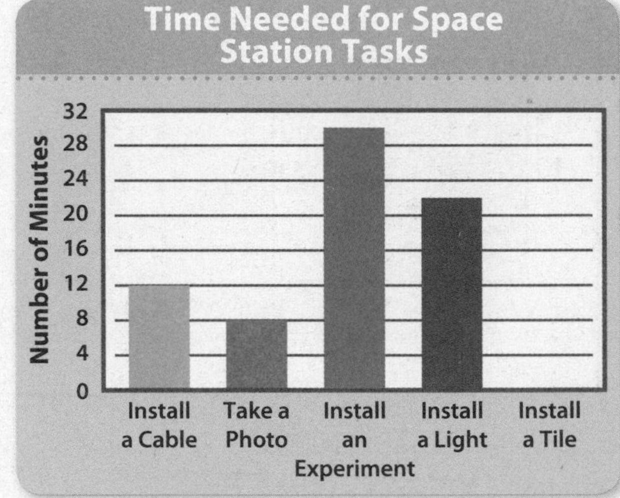

13. Higher Order Thinking A rectangular poster has an area of 504 square centimeters. The width of the poster is 14 centimeters. How long is the poster? Write equations to show your work.

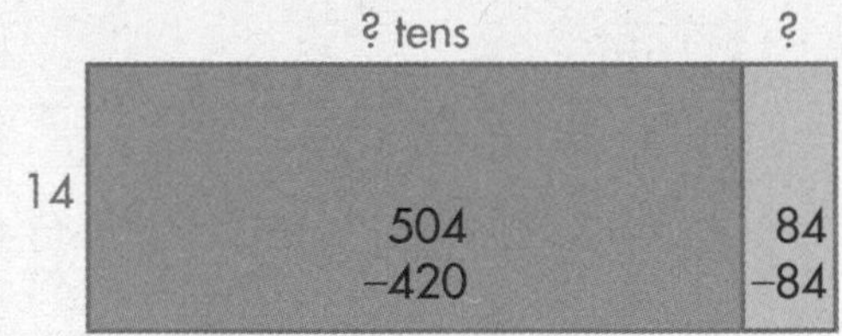

Assessment

14. Which is 540 divided by 30?

Ⓐ 17
Ⓑ 18
Ⓒ 170
Ⓓ 180

15. Which is 391 divided by 17?

Ⓐ 23
Ⓑ 24
Ⓒ 230
Ⓓ 240

Name ____________________

Lesson 5-4
Use Partial Quotients to Divide

I can ...
find quotients of whole numbers.

I can also reason about math.

Solve & Share

A hotel sets up tables for a conference for 156 people. If each table seats 12 people, how many tables will be needed? ***Solve this problem any way you choose.***

You can use estimation and reasoning to help solve this problem. Think about how many groups of 12 you can take away from 156. *Show your work!*

Look Back! Generalize How can you check that the answer to a division problem is correct?

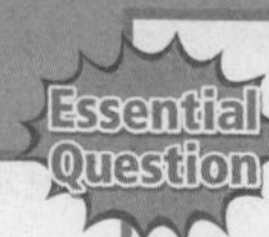

How Can You Use Partial Quotients to Solve Division Problems?

A

A theater has 375 seats arranged in rows with 15 seats in each row. How many rows are in this theater? Let r equal the number of rows.
Think: 15 × *r* = 375 or 375 ÷ 15 = *r*.

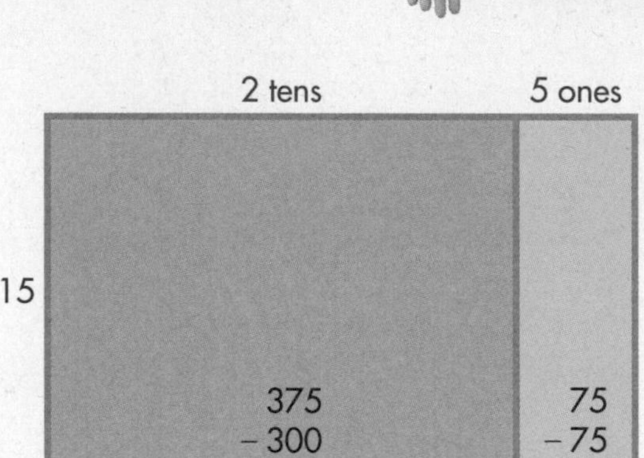

B

	2 tens	5 ones
15	375 − 300	75 − 75
	75	0

```
       5
      20
  15)375   Estimate: How many 15s in 375? Try 20.
   − 300   Multiply 20 by 15 and subtract.
      75   Estimate: How many 15s in 75? Try 5.
    − 75   Multiply 5 by 15 and subtract.
       0   Stop when the difference is 0.
```

Add the partial quotients: 20 + 5 = 25.

375 ÷ 15 = 25

So, there are 25 rows in the theater.

Convince Me! **Critique Reasoning** Dinah's solution to the problem above is shown at the right. Is her solution correct? Explain.

```
       5
      10
      10
  15)375
    −150
     225
    −150
      75
     −75
       0
```

Name ______________________________

Practice Buddy   Tools   Assessment

Guided Practice*

Do You Understand?

1. Show one way of using partial quotients to find 231 ÷ 11.

2. How can you use estimation to check that your answer to Problem 1 is reasonable?

Do You Know How?

In **3–6**, use partial quotients to divide. Show your work.

3. $15\overline{)210}$

4. $13\overline{)286}$

5. $25\overline{)575}$

6. $32\overline{)960}$

Independent Practice*

Leveled Practice In **7–16**, use partial quotients to divide. Show your work.

7. $19\overline{)247}$
−190 Multiply ___ by 19.
57
−57 Multiply ___ by 19.
0

Add the partial quotients:
___ + ___ = ___

8. $14\overline{)630}$
−560 Multiply ___ by 14.
70
−70 Multiply ___ by 14.
0

Add the partial quotients:
___ + ___ = ___

9. $11\overline{)132}$

10. $21\overline{)840}$

11. $16\overline{)304}$

12. $32\overline{)480}$

13. $23\overline{)713}$

14. $30\overline{)660}$

15. $43\overline{)731}$

16. $16\overline{)608}$

*For another example, see Set D on page 290.

Problem Solving

17. A 969-acre wildlife preserve has 19 cheetahs. About how many acres does each cheetah have to itself, if each cheetah roams the same number of acres?

18. **Be Precise** A factory produces 272 chairs in an 8-hour shift. If the factory produces the same number of chairs each hour, how many chairs does it produce in 30 minutes?

19. A cafeteria can seat 5×10^2 students. Each table has 2×10^1 seats. How many tables are in the cafeteria?

20. **Model with Math** Peter is driving 992 miles from Chicago to Dallas. His sister Anna is driving 1,068 miles from Phoenix to Dallas. Write and solve an equation to find how much farther Anna drives than Peter drives.

21. **Make Sense and Persevere** Write a multiplication equation and a division equation that represent the model shown below.

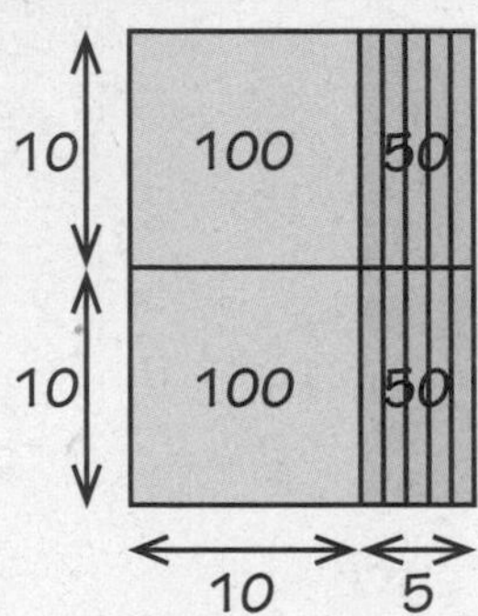

22. **Higher Order Thinking** How can you use partial quotients to find $325 \div 13$? Explain.

Assessment

23. Which expressions are equivalent to 35?

- ☐ $1,400 \div 4$
- ☐ $420 \div 12$
- ☐ $875 \div 25$
- ☐ $7,700 \div 22$
- ☐ $14,000 \div 40$

24. Which expressions are equivalent to 22?

- ☐ $704 \div 32$
- ☐ $1,078 \div 49$
- ☐ $1,890 \div 30$
- ☐ $1,430 \div 65$
- ☐ $4,500 \div 50$

Name ______________________

Help Practice Buddy Tools Games

Homework & Practice 5-4

Use Partial Quotients to Divide

Another Look!

A baker made 312 bagels in one day. If he puts 12 bagels in each package, how many packages did he make that day?

```
     6
    20
12)312   Try 20.
  −240   Multiply 20 by 12 and subtract.
    72   Try 6.
  − 72   Multiply 6 by 12 and subtract.
     0   Stop when the difference is 0.
```

Add the partial quotients: $20 + 6 = 26$.

So, the baker made 26 packages of bagels.

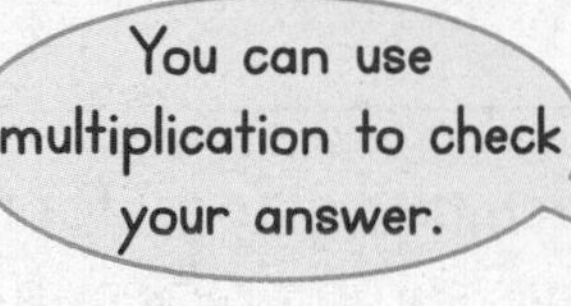

Leveled Practice 1–13, use partial quotients to divide. Show your work.

1. 21)7 1 4 Try ___.
   − ☐☐☐ Multiply ___ by 21 and subtract.
   ☐☐ Try ___.
   − ☐☐ Multiply ___ by 21 and subtract.
   0

   So, $714 \div 21 =$ ___

2. 41)533

3. 15)330

4. 39)780

5. 50)700

6. 11)792

7. 24)648

8. 33)396

9. 17)765

10. 23)920

11. 30)810

12. 16)464

13. 53)954

14. Use the table. What is the total amount of electricity a computer, a television, and a heater use in 1 hour? Show your work.

15. Number Sense How many hours does it take for a light bulb to use as much electricity as a heater uses in 1 hour?

DATA

Electricity Used	
Appliance	**Kilowatts Per Hour**
Computer	0.09
Heater	1.5
Light bulb	0.1
Television	0.3

16. The cost of each plane ticket for the Baltazar family's summer vacation is \$329. If there are 7 family members, what is the total cost of the plane tickets?

17. Reasoning Shannon biked in an endurance cycling race. She traveled 2,912 miles and biked about 95 miles each day. About how many days did it take her to complete the race?

18. Algebra Twelve buses bring a total of 420 people to The Alhambra in Granada, Spain. Each bus carries the same number of people. How many people are on each bus? Write and solve an equation to find *p*, the number of people on each bus.

19. Higher Order Thinking How can you use partial quotients to find 684 ÷ 57? Explain.

Assessment

20. Which expressions are equivalent to 28?

- ☐ 980 ÷ 35
- ☐ 480 ÷ 16
- ☐ 1,400 ÷ 50
- ☐ 625 ÷ 25
- ☐ 1,680 ÷ 60

21. Which expressions are equivalent to 53?

- ☐ 1,680 ÷ 40
- ☐ 2,385 ÷ 45
- ☐ 1,612 ÷ 62
- ☐ 3,127 ÷ 59
- ☐ 3,763 ÷ 71

Name ______________________________

Lesson 5-5
Divide by Multiples of 10

I can ...
find the quotient when the divisor is a multiple of 10.

I can also generalize from examples.

Solve & Share Cameron's soccer team has $168 to buy uniforms that cost $20 each. How many uniforms can his team buy? Will there be any money left over? ***Solve this problem any way you choose.***

Look Back! Reasoning How much more money is needed to buy an additional uniform?

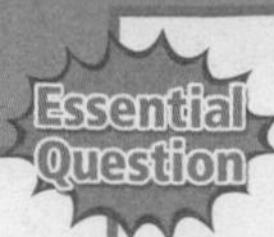

What Are the Steps in Dividing by a Multiple of Ten?

A

This year, a group of 249 students is taking a field trip. One bus is needed for every 20 students. How many buses are needed?

B

Step 1

Find 249 ÷ 20.

Estimate: 240 ÷ 20 = 12

$$\begin{array}{r} 1 \\ 20\overline{)249} \\ -\,20 \\ \hline 4 \end{array}$$

Divide	24 ÷ 20
Multiply	1 × 20
Subtract	24 − 20
Compare	4 < 20

C

Step 2

Bring down the ones. Divide the ones.

$$\begin{array}{r} 12 \text{ R}9 \\ 20\overline{)249} \\ -\,20\downarrow \\ \hline 49 \\ -\,40 \\ \hline 9 \end{array}$$

Divide	49 ÷ 20
Multiply	2 × 20
Subtract	49 − 40
Compare	9 < 20

Since there is a remainder, one more bus is needed. A total of 13 buses is needed.

The answer is reasonable because 13 is close to the estimate.

Convince Me! **Construct Arguments** For the example above, show how you can check that the quotient is correct. Explain your answer.

Name ______________________

Practice Buddy · Tools · Assessment

Guided Practice*

Do You Understand?

1. In the example at the top of page 264, if only 137 students were going on the trip, how many buses would be needed?

2. Reasoning In the example at the top of page 264, why is 12 buses a reasonable estimate?

Do You Know How?

In **3** and **4**, divide. Write the missing numbers.

3.

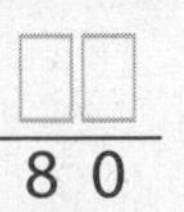

```
    □□
20)2 8 0
  −□□
    8□
  − 8 0
      0
```

4.

```
      □ R 46
80)7 6 6
  −□□□
     □□
```

Independent Practice

Leveled Practice In **5–13**, divide. Write the missing numbers.

5.

```
     □5
20)3 0 0
  −2□
   □0□
  −1□□
      □
```

6.

```
      □ R □
60)5 9 3
  −□□□
     □□
```

7.

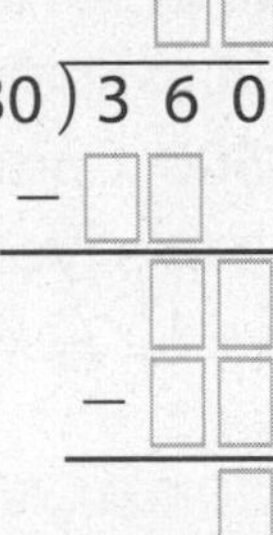

```
     □□
30)3 6 0
  −□□
    □□
  −□□
      □
```

8. 40)453

9. 50)250

10. 70)867

11. 60)720

12. 80)492

13. 40)375

*For another example, see Set E on page 290.

Problem Solving

14. Reasoning Rita's family is moving from Grand Junction to Dallas. The moving van averages 60 miles each hour. About how many hours does the van take to reach Dallas? Explain your work.

DATA

Dallas, TX, to Grand Junction, CO	980 miles
Nashville, TN, to Norfolk, VA	670 miles
Charleston, SC, to Atlanta, GA	290 miles
Denver, CO, to Minneapolis, MN	920 miles
Little Rock, AR, to Chicago, IL	660 miles

15. Due to construction delays on the trip from Little Rock to Chicago, a van driver averaged 50 miles each hour. About how long did that trip take?

16. Higher Order Thinking A scientist needs 70 milliliters of distilled water for each of 15 experiments. She has a bottle that contains 975 milliliters of distilled water. Is there enough water in the bottle for all 15 experiments? Explain.

17. Model with Math The Port Lavaca fishing pier is 3,200 feet long. There is one person fishing for every ten feet of length. Write and solve an equation to find how many people are fishing from the pier.

18. Make Sense and Persevere
Todd made a table to show different plans he can use to save $500. Complete the table. Which plan can Todd use to save $500 in less than 16 weeks and have $20 extra? Explain how you found your answer.

Plans for Saving $500

Plan	Amount to Save Each Week	Number of Weeks Needed to Make Goal
A	$20	25
B	$30	
C	$40	
D	$50	

Assessment

19. Find an expression that gives a quotient of 9 R15. Write the expression in the box.

Quotient: 9 R15		
335 ÷ 40	360 ÷ 40	365 ÷ 40
375 ÷ 40	409 ÷ 40	415 ÷ 40

Name ______________________

Homework & Practice 5-5

Divide by Multiples of 10

Another Look!

Bo has 623 bottle caps to divide equally among 40 friends. How many caps will each friend get? Will there be any caps left?

Step 1	**Step 2**	**Step 3**	**Step 4**
Divide the tens.	Subtract the tens. Bring down the ones.	Divide the ones.	Subtract the ones. Write the remainder.
$40\overline{)623}$ quotient 1 ← 62 tens ÷ 40; 40 ↑ 40×1 ten = 40 tens	$40\overline{)623}$ quotient 1; − 40 ↓; 223	$40\overline{)623}$ quotient 15; − 40; 223 ← 223 ones ÷ 40; 200 ↑ 40×5 ones = 200 ones	$40\overline{)623}$ quotient 15 R 23; − 40; 223; − 200; 23. Each friend will get 15 caps and 23 caps will be left.

Leveled Practice In **1–8**, find the quotient.

1. 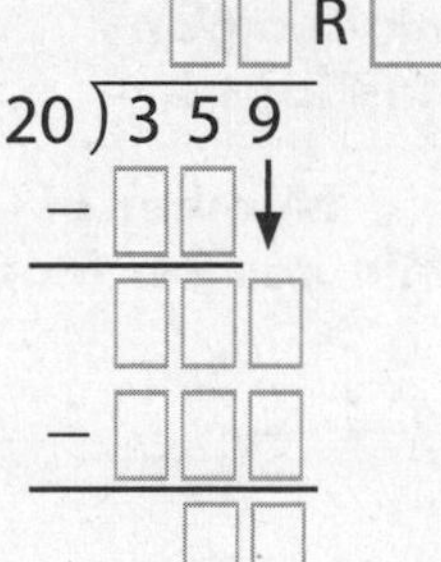

2. 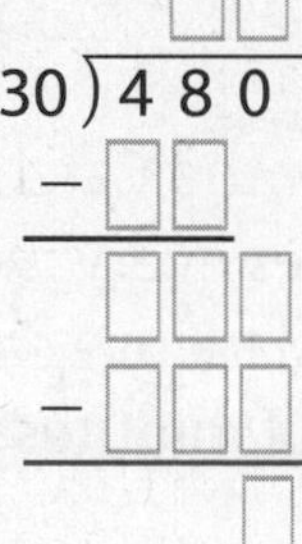

Remember to compare the remainder to the divisor.

3. $40\overline{)746}$ 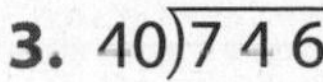

4. $50\overline{)800}$

5. $70\overline{)632}$

6. $60\overline{)779}$

7. $40\overline{)920}$

8. $30\overline{)332}$

9. Use Structure Why can the calculations in red be thought of as simpler problems? Describe the simpler problems.

```
      1 2 R 13
80 ) 9 7 3   ←— 97 tens ÷ 80 groups
   − 8 0     ←— 80 × 1 ten
     1 7 3   ←— 173 ones ÷ 80 groups
   − 1 6 0   ←— 80 × 2 ones
       1 3
```

10. Construct Arguments A county has 90 schools. The county received 992 new computers. Are there enough computers so that each school can get 11 new computers? Explain.

11. Twin Oaks Soccer Field is a rectangle. The longer side of the field is 108 yards long. What is the perimeter of the field?

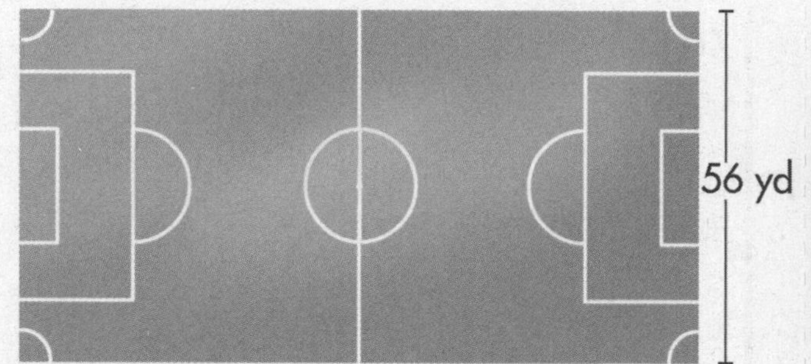

12. Higher Order Thinking Liza makes 20 minutes of phone calls each day. Which plan will give Liza enough minutes for June, with between 30 and 50 minutes left? Show your work.

13. Mark and his brother signed up for the Catch Up phone plan. They share the minutes every month equally. How many minutes can Mark use each day without going over his share of minutes?

DATA

Speed Link Company Phone Plans

Plan Name	Number of Minutes Per Month
Connect	550
Chat	625
Share	650
Catch Up	700

Assessment

14. Find an expression that gives a quotient of 16. Write the expression in the box.

Quotient: 16		
600 ÷ 40	620 ÷ 40	640 ÷ 40
644 ÷ 40	660 ÷ 40	680 ÷ 40

Name ______________________

Homework & Practice 5-5

Divide by Multiples of 10

Another Look!

Bo has 623 bottle caps to divide equally among 40 friends. How many caps will each friend get? Will there be any caps left?

Step 1	**Step 2**	**Step 3**	**Step 4**
Divide the tens.	Subtract the tens. Bring down the ones.	Divide the ones.	Subtract the ones. Write the remainder.
$40\overline{)623}$ quotient 1; 62 tens ÷ 40; 40×1 ten = 40 tens	$40\overline{)623}$ quotient 1; -40; 223	$40\overline{)623}$ quotient 15; -40; 223 ← 223 ones ÷ 40; 200; 40×5 ones = 200 ones	$40\overline{)623}$ quotient 15 R 23; -40; 223; -200; 23. Each friend will get 15 caps and 23 caps will be left.

Leveled Practice In **1–8**, find the quotient.

1. $20\overline{)359}$

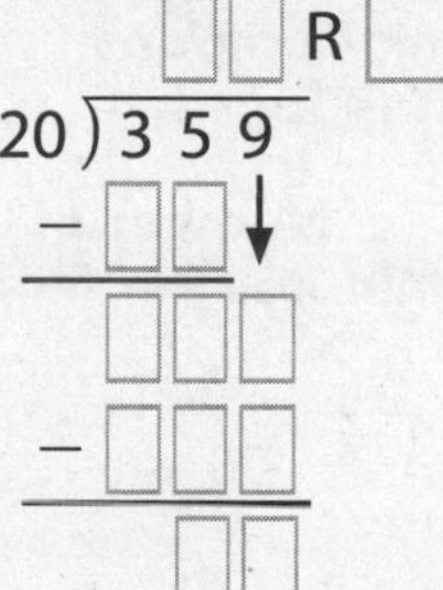

2. $30\overline{)480}$

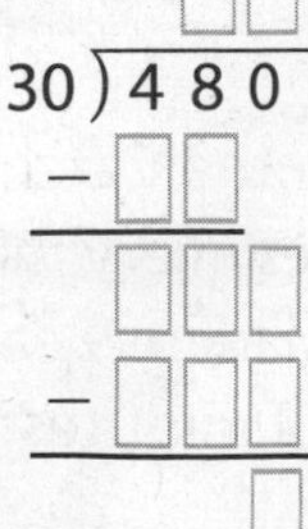

Remember to compare the remainder to the divisor.

3. $40\overline{)746}$

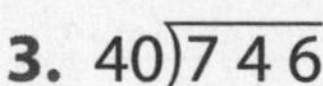

4. $50\overline{)800}$

5. $70\overline{)632}$

6. $60\overline{)779}$

7. $40\overline{)920}$

8. $30\overline{)332}$

9. Use Structure Why can the calculations in red be thought of as simpler problems? Describe the simpler problems.

```
     1 2 R13
80 ) 9 7 3    ←— 97 tens ÷ 80 groups
   − 8 0      ←— 80 × 1 ten
     1 7 3    ←— 173 ones ÷ 80 groups
   − 1 6 0    ←— 80 × 2 ones
       1 3
```

10. Construct Arguments A county has 90 schools. The county received 992 new computers. Are there enough computers so that each school can get 11 new computers? Explain.

11. Twin Oaks Soccer Field is a rectangle. The longer side of the field is 108 yards long. What is the perimeter of the field?

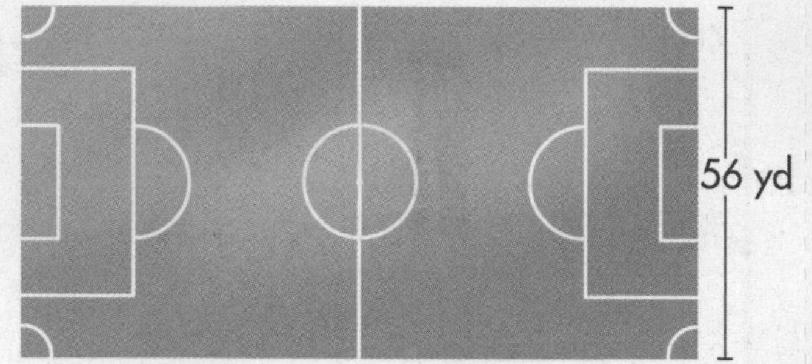

12. Higher Order Thinking Liza makes 20 minutes of phone calls each day. Which plan will give Liza enough minutes for June, with between 30 and 50 minutes left? Show your work.

13. Mark and his brother signed up for the Catch Up phone plan. They share the minutes every month equally. How many minutes can Mark use each day without going over his share of minutes?

DATA

Speed Link Company Phone Plans

Plan Name	Number of Minutes Per Month
Connect	550
Chat	625
Share	650
Catch Up	700

✔ Assessment

14. Find an expression that gives a quotient of 16. Write the expression in the box.

Quotient: 16		
600 ÷ 40	620 ÷ 40	640 ÷ 40
644 ÷ 40	660 ÷ 40	680 ÷ 40

Name ______________________

Lesson 5-6

Use Estimation to Place the First Digit of the Quotient

I can ...
decide where to place the first digit of the quotient when I divide whole numbers.

I can also look for patterns to solve problems.

Solve & Share Marty's teacher asked the students to predict how many digits are in the quotient of a division problem. All of the quotients are whole numbers. Draw lines to the buckets to show how the students should sort the cards. **Do not solve the problems.** Use reasoning, number sense, and estimation to make your decisions.

Look Back! Use Structure Will the quotient 7,825 ÷ 25 be greater than 100 or less than 100? How do you know?

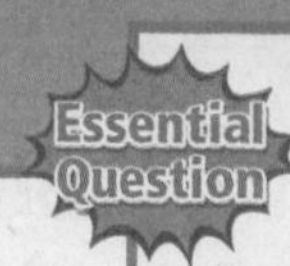

How Can You Decide Where to Place the First Digit of a Quotient?

A

Jake works at a flower shop. The shop just received a delivery of 2,535 roses. Jake divides 2,535 by 12 to find the number of bouquets he can make. Where should he place the first digit of the quotient?

You can use structure to decide where to place the first digit of the quotient. Think about the relationship between multiplication and division.

Rose Bouquet
1 dozen roses

B Multiply by powers of 10 to estimate.

$12 \times 10 = 120$

$12 \times 100 = 1{,}200$

← 2,535

$12 \times 1{,}000 = 12{,}000$

Since 2,535 is between 1,200 and 12,000, the quotient is between 100 and 1,000.

C The quotient is in the hundreds, so Jake should place the first digit in the hundreds place.

$12\overline{)2{,}535}$

Use compatible numbers to check. Since $24 \div 12 = 2$, you know that $2{,}400 \div 12 = 200$. So, $2{,}535 \div 12$ will be about 200. The quotient will have 3 digits.

Convince Me! **Reasoning** Can Jake make at least 100 bouquets? Can Jake make at least 1,000 bouquets? Explain.

Name ______

Practice Buddy Tools Assessment

Another Example

Where should you place the first digit of the quotient 4,108 ÷ 80?

Since 4,108 is between 800 and 8,000, the quotient is between 10 and 100.

$80 \times 10 = 800$

⟵ 4,108

$80 \times 100 = 8,000$

$80 \times 1,000 = 80,000$

The quotient is in the tens, so place the first digit in the tens place.

Guided Practice*

Do You Understand?

1. In which place should you write the first digit of the quotient 3,710 ÷ 18? Complete the following to help you decide.
   $18 \times 10 =$
   $18 \times 100 =$
   $18 \times 1,000 =$

Do You Know How?

In **2–5**, without completing the division problem, tell in which place to write the first digit of the quotient.

2. 4,632 ÷ 15

3. 3,332 ÷ 30

4. 25)1,013

5. 40)916

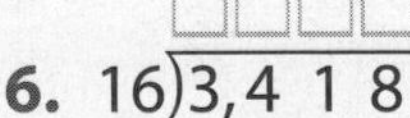

Independent Practice

In **6–8**, without completing the division, shade a box to show the placement of the first digit of the quotient.

6. 16)3,4 1 8

7. 50)1,5 7 7

8. 24)8,0 4 5

In **9–14**, without completing the division, tell in which place to write the first digit of the quotient.

9. 7,905 ÷ 35

10. 5,500 ÷ 90

11. 2,838 ÷ 11

12. 46)875

13. 28)1,240

14. 18)6,020

**For another example, see Set F on page 291.*

Problem Solving

15. **Number Sense** The booster club picked 1,370 apples. They plan to sell bags of apples with 15 apples in each bag. Can they make at least 100 bags? How do you know?

16. **Make Sense and Persevere** Mason teaches ice skating. He earns $24.50 per lesson. How much does he earn in 5 days if he gives 6 lessons per day?

17. **Reasoning** A delivery to the flower shop is recorded at the right. The shop makes centerpiece arrangements using 36 flowers that are all the same type. Will they be able to make at least 10 arrangements using each type of flower? At least 100 arrangements? Explain.

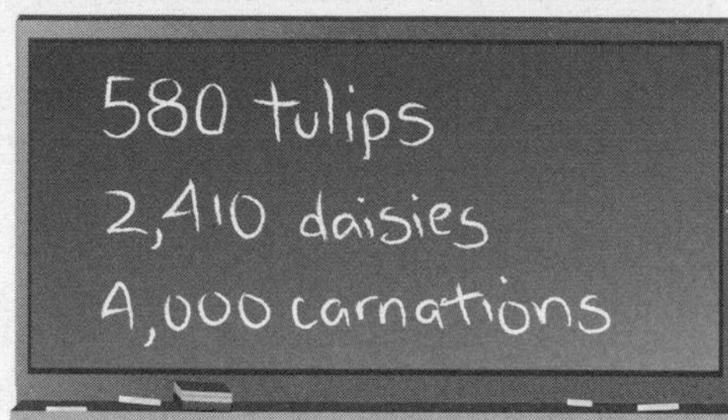

18. **Construct Arguments** Amelia and Ben have two different answers for 1,955 ÷ 85. Without dividing, how can you tell who might be correct?

Amelia: 1,955 ÷ 85 = 23
Ben: 1,955 ÷ 85 = 203

19. **Higher Order Thinking** Tell where you should place the first digit of the quotient 4,839 ÷ 15. Then determine the first digit and explain how you decided.

Assessment

20. In which place should you write the first digit of the quotient 5,075 ÷ 38? How can you determine that without using division?

Name ____________________

Help · Practice Buddy · Tools · Games

Homework & Practice 5-6

Use Estimation to Place the First Digit of the Quotient

Another Look!

In which place should you write the first digit of the quotient 5,890 ÷ 65?

$65 \times 10 = 650$

⟵ 5,890

$65 \times 100 = 6{,}500$

$65 \times 1{,}000 = 65{,}000$

Since 5,890 is between 650 and 6,500, the quotient is between 10 and 100.

The quotient is in the tens, so write the first digit in the tens place.

1. Since 43 × 10 = ________, 43 × 100 = ________, and 43 × 1,000 = ________, the first digit of the quotient of 5,813 ÷ 43 is in the __________ place.

In **2–4**, without completing the division, shade a box to show the placement of the first digit of the quotient.

2. 11)2,0 1 4   **3.** 34)7,0 0 6   **4.** 70)5,5 9 1

In **5–13**, without completing the division, tell in which place to write the first digit of the quotient.

5. 1,620 ÷ 18   **6.** 4,400 ÷ 30   **7.** 8,899 ÷ 61

8. 40)8,175   **9.** 28)770   **10.** 14)1,726

11. 75)688   **12.** 29)5,123   **13.** 17)1,699

14. Number Sense Will the quotient 7,818 ÷ 25 be greater than 100 or less than 100? How do you know?

15. Reasoning Choose the best estimate for 2,819 ÷ 13 from the following:

100 200 500

How did you decide?

16. Makes Sense and Persevere Jordan bought 1.8 pounds of ham, 2.15 pounds of onions, and 8 cans of soup. What was the total cost before sales tax? Round your answer to the nearest cent.

Ham $3.95 per pound	Onions $0.89 per pound	Soup $1.05 per can

17. The sales tax for the food Jordan bought is $0.87. He has a coupon for $1.75 off any purchase. Use your answer for Exercise 16 to find the final amount Jordan needs to pay.

18. Construct Arguments Does each quotient have the same number of digits? Explain how you can tell without dividing.

3,444 ÷ 42
4,368 ÷ 42

19. Higher Order Thinking There are 347 students going on a field trip. Each bus holds 44 students. If each bus costs $95, Is the total cost of the buses more than $1,000? How can you decide without using division?

Assessment

20. In which place should you write the first digit of the quotient of 3,381 ÷ 47? How can you determine that without using division?

Name ____________________

Solve

Lesson 5-7
Divide by 2-Digit Divisors

I can ...
use estimation to decide if a quotient is reasonable when dividing by 2-digit divisors.

I can also make sense of problems.

Solve & Share A bakery needs to make a batch of 198 bagels. Each baking sheet holds the same number of bagels. How many baking sheets are needed? Solve this problem any way you choose.

You can make sense and persevere by using rounding or compatible numbers. *Show your work!*

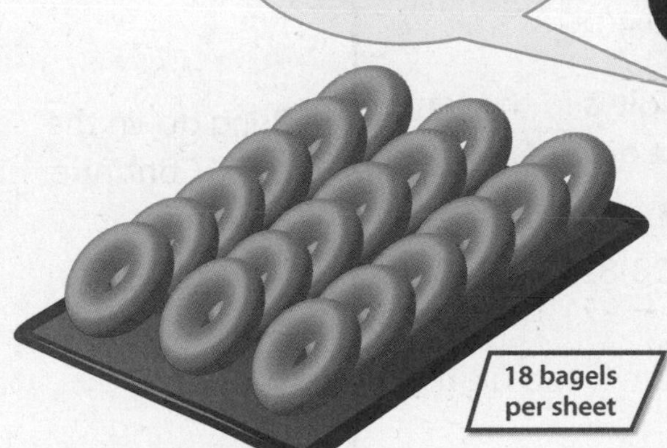

Look Back! Reasoning How did your estimate help you find the quotient?

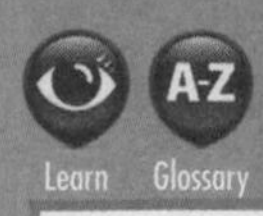

How Can You Use Estimation to Decide if Your Quotient Is Reasonable?

A

Orchard workers have grapefruit seedlings to plant in 23 equal rows. How many seedlings will be in each row?

You can use compatible numbers to estimate 828 ÷ 23.

B

Step 1

828 is about 800.
23 is about 20.

$800 \div 20 = 40$

The first digit is in the tens place. Start dividing tens.

$$\begin{array}{r} 4 \\ 23\overline{)828} \\ -92 \end{array}$$

The estimate is too high.

C

Step 2

Try 3.

$$\begin{array}{r} 3 \\ 23\overline{)828} \\ -69 \\ \hline 13 \end{array}$$

Bring down the ones. Continue dividing.

$$\begin{array}{r} 36 \\ 23\overline{)828} \\ -69 \\ \hline 138 \\ -138 \\ \hline 0 \end{array}$$

D

Step 3

Compare your answer to the estimate.

There will be 36 grapefruit seedlings in each row.

36 is close to 40. So the answer is reasonable.

Convince Me! **Reasoning** In Step 1 above, how do you know the estimate is too high? Explain.

Name ______________________

Guided Practice*

Do You Understand?

1. Can the remainder be greater than the divisor? Why or why not?

2. How can you use estimation to check if a quotient is reasonable?

Do You Know How?

3. Estimate 452 ÷ 21.

4. Complete.

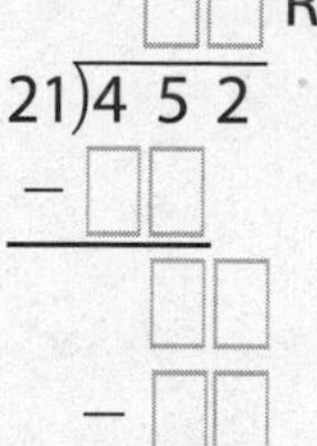

21)452

Remember to check that your answer is reasonable.

Independent Practice

Leveled Practice For **5–7**, fill in the boxes.

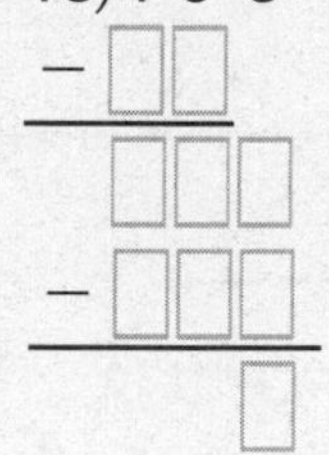

5. 18)468

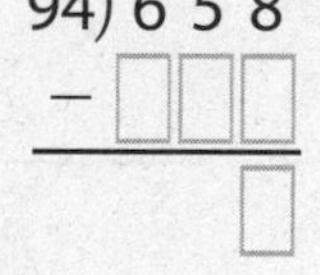

6. 94)658

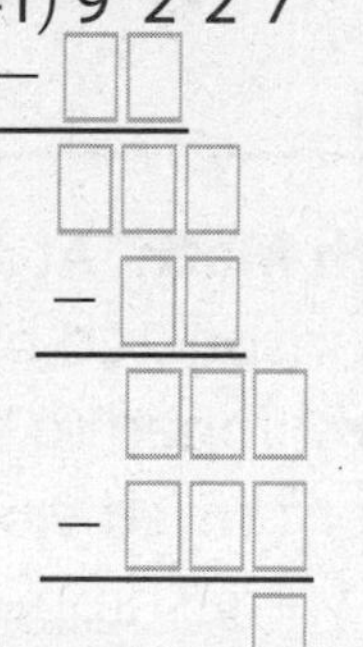

7. 41)9227

In **8–15**, estimate and then find the quotient. Use your estimate to check for reasonableness.

8. 54)378

9. 83)664

10. 761 ÷ 5

11. 510 ÷ 30

12. 7,704 ÷ 24

13. 7,830 ÷ 33

14. 3,136 ÷ 64

15. 6,253 ÷ 71

*For another example, see Set G on page 291.

Problem Solving

For **16–18**, use the table at right.

16. Make Sense and Persevere Bob's Citrus and Nursery sells citrus gift cartons. They have 5,643 oranges to pack into gift cartons. How many cartons can they fill?

Bob's Citrus Gift Cartons

Citrus Fruit	Number per Carton
Grapefruits	18
Oranges	24
Tangelos	12

17. Of the 4,325 grapefruits harvested so far, Bob's has sold 1,250 of them at a farmer's market. How many gift cartons can Bob's fill with the remaining grapefruits? How many grapefruits will be left?

18. Bob's sells tangelo gift cartons each December. Last year, they shipped a total of 3,300 tangelos. If each carton sells for $28, how much money did Bob's earn from the tangelo gift cartons sold?

19. Higher Order Thinking A period of 20 years is called a *score*. The Statue of Liberty was dedicated in 1886. About how many scores ago was that?

20. Model with Math At an automobile plant, each car is inspected by 34 different workers before it is shipped to a dealer. One day, workers performed 9,690 inspections. How many cars were shipped? Explain.

9,690

?

Assessment

21. For which division problems is 46 the quotient? Write those division problems in the box.

Quotient = 46
10)4,600   21)966   53)2,385   43)946   46)2,116

Name ____________________

Homework & Practice 5-7

Divide by 2-Digit Divisors

Another Look!

At the driving range, golfers can rent buckets of 32 golf balls. The range has a supply of 2,650 golf balls. How many buckets are needed for the balls?

Use compatible numbers to estimate 2,650 ÷ 32. You can use 2,700 ÷ 30 = 90.

Use the estimate to place the first digit in the quotient.

$$\begin{array}{r} 9 \\ 32\overline{)2{,}650} \\ -\,2\,88 \end{array}$$

← The estimate is too high because 288 > 265.

Try 8.

$$\begin{array}{r} 8 \\ 32\overline{)2{,}650} \\ -\,2\,56 \end{array}$$

Complete the division.

$$\begin{array}{r} 82 \text{ R}26 \\ 32\overline{)2{,}650} \\ -\,2\,56 \\ \hline 90 \\ -\,64 \\ \hline 26 \end{array}$$

They can fill 82 buckets with golf balls. They need 1 more bucket for the 26 balls that are left. So the range needs 83 buckets.

83 is close to 90, so the answer is reasonable.

Leveled Practice In **1–4**, fill in the boxes.

1. $42\overline{)926}$ = 2☐ R☐

2. $38\overline{)1{,}558}$ = ☐☐

3. $77\overline{)693}$ = ☐

4. $21\overline{)2{,}567}$ = ☐☐☐ R☐

In **5–16**, estimate and then find the quotient. Use your estimate to check reasonableness.

5. 462 ÷ 77

6. $44\overline{)817}$

7. $21\overline{)777}$

8. $35\overline{)280}$

9. 2,465 ÷ 29

10. 203 ÷ 29

11. 8,114 ÷ 46

12. $13\overline{)1{,}748}$

13. 6,264 ÷ 87

14. 5,578 ÷ 68

15. 9,855 ÷ 45

16. 7,308 ÷ 12

17. Make Sense and Persevere A farmer has 4,700 carrots to put in bunches of 15 carrots. He plans to sell the carrots for $5 per bunch at his farm stand. About how many bunches will the farmer make?

18. Higher Order Thinking You are dividing 3,972 by 41. Explain why the first digit in the quotient should be placed over the tens place of the dividend.

19. Vocabulary Write a division story problem with 53 as the divisor and 2,491 as the dividend. Solve.

20. Reasoning How can estimating the quotient help you check that your answer to a division problem is reasonable?

21. Number Sense Maya has 462 pennies. Use mental math to find how many pennies are left if she puts them in stacks of 50 pennies. Explain your reasoning.

22. Model with Math A caravan crossed 1,378 miles of desert in 85 days. It traveled 22 miles on the first day and 28 miles on the second day. If the caravan traveled the same number of miles on each of the remaining days, how many miles did it travel on each of those days? Complete the bar diagram to show how you found the answer.

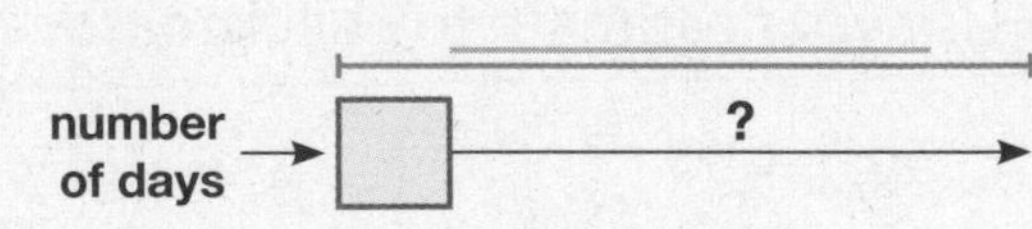

Assessment

23. For which division problems is 54 the quotient? Write those division problems in the box.

Quotient = 54
$45\overline{)2,430}$ $12\overline{)660}$ $81\overline{)3,645}$ $11\overline{)594}$ $19\overline{)950}$

Name ______________________________

Solve

Solve & Share

There are 120 students in a school's marching band. They march in an array with the same number of students in each row. What are the dimensions of the different arrays that the band can form?

Problem Solving

Lesson 5-8

Make Sense and Persevere

I can . . .
make sense of problems and keep working if I get stuck.

I can also solve multi-step problems.

Thinking Habits

Be a good thinker! These questions can help you.

- What do I need to find?
- What do I know?
- What's my plan for solving this problem?
- What else can I try if I get stuck?
- How can I check that my solution makes sense?

Look Back! Use Structure How can finding the arrays for 12 band members help you solve the above problem?

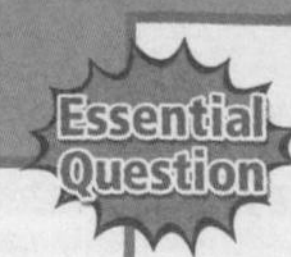

Essential Question

How Can You Make Sense of Problems and Persevere in Solving Them?

A

For 3 months, a fifth-grade class raised money for charities. If the class divides the money equally among 30 different organizations, how much will each organization receive?

DATA

Funds Raised	
September	$435
October	$450
November	$615

You can make sense of the problem by answering these questions. How much money was raised in all? How much should each organization get?

B

How can I make sense of and solve the problem?

I can

- identify the quantities given.
- understand how the quantities are related.
- choose and implement an appropriate strategy.
- check to be sure my work and answer make sense.

C

Here's my thinking...

First, I can write an equation to find the total amount raised:

$435 + $450 + $615 = $1,500.

Next, I can write a division equation to model equal sharing:

$1,500 ÷ 30 =

I can use mental math to find the quotient:

150 tens ÷ 3 tens = 50

So, each organization will receive $50.

Convince Me! **Critique Reasoning** Julio says that you can solve this problem by dividing each month's total by 30 and then adding the three quotients together. Do you agree? Do you think his approach is easier or harder? Justify your answer.

Stuck? Try solving a simpler problem.

Name ______________________________

Guided Practice*

Make Sense and Persevere

Dana starts with 875 stamps in her stamp collection. Her grandparents give her 332 stamps. Then she buys 72 more. How many pages in her scrapbook can she fill?

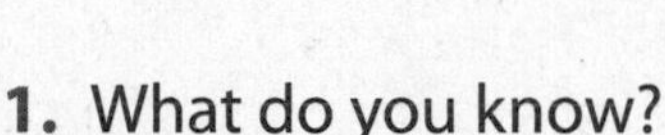

1. What do you know?

2. What are you trying to find?

3. How are the quantities related? What is the answer to the problem? Write equations to model your work.

Independent Practice

Make Sense and Persevere

Tanya is saving for a vacation. She wants to have at least $75 for each of the 12 days of her trip. If she saves $85 each month for 10 months, will she save enough money?

4. Use the strategy of mental math to find the total amount she will save. Then write a division equation to see if she will save enough.

5. Jorge says he can solve this problem a different way. He says that he can compare 85×10 and 75×12. Do you agree? Explain your thinking.

*For another example, see Set H on page 292.

Problem Solving

Performance Assessment

Pumpkin Patch Farms
The table shows the number of seeds the owners of Pumpkin Patch Farms received from different seed suppliers. Each of the pumpkins they harvest usually weighs between 10 and 12 pounds. There are 60 rows, and the farmers will plant the same number of seeds in each row. How many seeds will they plant in each row?

DATA

Seed Supplier	Number of Seeds
Sid's Seeds	1,220
Vicki's Seed Supply	750
Seeds and More	1,450

6. **Make Sense and Persevere** What do you know? What are you trying to find?

7. **Reasoning** How are the quantities in the problem related? What steps are needed to solve the problem?

8. **Model with Math** Write equations with variables to represent the steps needed to solve the problem.

9. **Be Precise** Solve the equations and answer the question.

10. **Reasoning** What strategy can you use to check that your answer makes sense?

Think about the problem-solving strategies to help you!

Name ______________________________

Homework & Practice 5-8

Make Sense and Persevere

Another Look!

Dex works at a dog adoption shelter. He has 4 large boxes of dog treats with 34 treats in each box and 3 small boxes with 28 treats in each box. How many bags of 20 treats can Dex make from all the treats?

You can use bar diagrams to model the steps you need to solve.

What Do You Know? There are 4 large boxes with 34 treats each and 3 small boxes with 28 treats each.

What Are You Trying to Find? The number of bags of 20 treats that Dex can make.

Use bar diagrams and equations to find the number of treats in the large and small boxes.

ℓ total treats in large boxes

34	34	34	34

$4 \times 34 = \ell, \ell = 136$ treats

s total treats in small boxes

28	28	28

$3 \times 28 = s,\ s = 84$ treats

Add to find the number of treats in all. $136 + 84 = 220$

Divide to find the number of bags Dex can make with 220 treats. $220 \div 20 = b, b = 11$

Dex can make 11 bags of treats.

In **1** and **2**, solve the multi-step problems.

1. A tropical storm has been moving at 15 miles per hour for the past two days. Bess recorded that the storm moved 135 miles yesterday and 75 miles today. For how many hours has Bess been keeping track of the storm? Draw a bar diagram and write equations to help you solve.

2. A parking garage has 6 levels. Each level has 15 rows. Each row has the same number of parking spaces. There are 2,250 parking spaces in all. How many parking spaces are in each row? Write an equation or equations to show your work.

Performance Assessment

Fruit Punch

Ana's fifth-grade class is making a large batch of punch for the all-day science fair. There are 25 students in Ana's class. The ingredients they mixed together to make the punch are listed on the recipe card. The class is going to pour 12-ounce servings. How many full servings can they make?

Fruit Punch Recipe

Ingredient	Number of Ounces
Grape Juice	240
Apple Juice	480
Orange Juice	640
Ginger Ale	150

3. **Make Sense and Persevere** What do you know? What are you trying to find?

4. **Reasoning** How are the quantities in the problem related? What steps are needed to solve the problem?

5. **Model with Math** Write equations with variables to represent the steps needed to solve the problem.

Think about the steps needed to solve the problem!

6. **Be Precise** Solve the equations and answer the problem.

7. **Critique Reasoning** Alejandro says that the division has remainder 10, so one more serving can be poured. Do you agree? Explain.

Name ___________________________

TOPIC 5

Fluency Practice Activity

Work with a partner. Get paper and a pencil. Each partner chooses light blue or dark blue.

At the same time, Partner 1 and Partner 2 each point to one of their black numbers. Both partners find the product of the two numbers.

The partner who chose the color where the product appears gets a tally mark. Work until one partner has seven tally marks.

I can ...
multiply multi-digit whole numbers.

Partner 1

52
68
97
451
213

884	5,238	3,672	5,964
24,354	11,502	7,668	2,808
1,649	1,156	2,448	20,746
12,628	2,716	1,456	4,462
1,872	2,392	7,667	9,798
16,236	3,128	3,621	1,904

Partner 2

17
54
46
36
28

Tally Marks for Partner 1

Tally Marks for Partner 2

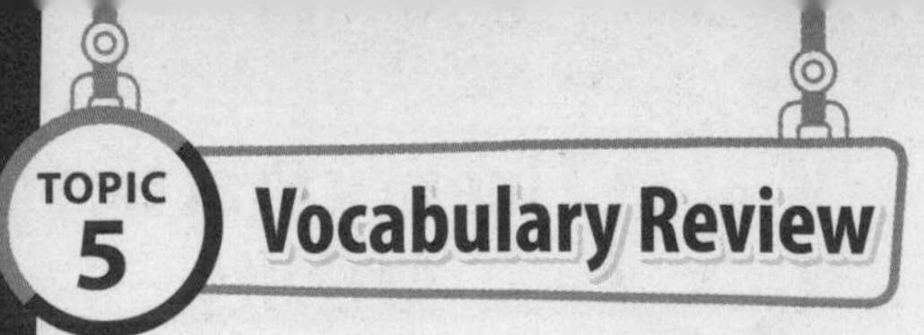

Word List

- compatible numbers
- dividend
- divisor
- estimate
- multiple
- product
- quotient
- remainder

Understand Vocabulary

Choose the best term from the Word List. Write it on the blank.

1. One way to estimate the answer to a division problem is to replace the divisor and dividend with ______________.

2. The part that is left when you divide into equal groups is called the ______________.

3. To decide where to place the first digit of a quotient, ______________ the number of digits in the answer.

4. The answer to a division problem is the ______________.

For each of these terms, give an example and a non-example.

	Example	Non-example
5. Multiple of 10	______	______
6. Product of 10	______	______
7. Quotient of 10	______	______

Use Vocabulary in Writing

8. Write a division problem with a 3-digit dividend, a divisor of 20, and remainder of 10. Use at least three of the terms in the Word List to explain how you chose the numbers for your example.

Name ____________________

TOPIC 5

Reteaching

Set A pages 239–244

Find 32,000 ÷ 80 using mental math.

Use basic facts and place-value patterns to help.

32 ÷ 8 = 4
320 ÷ 80 = 4
3,200 ÷ 80 = 40
32,000 ÷ 80 = 400

Remember to look for a basic division fact in the numbers. Check your answer by multiplying.

Find each quotient. Use mental math.

1. 360 ÷ 40
2. 270 ÷ 90
3. 2,100 ÷ 30
4. 4,800 ÷ 80
5. 72,000 ÷ 80
6. 81,000 ÷ 90

Set B pages 245–250

Estimate 364 ÷ 57.

Use compatible numbers and patterns to divide.

364 ÷ 57
↓ ↓
360 ÷ 60 = 6

So, 364 ÷ 57 is about 6.

Remember that compatible numbers are numbers that are easy to compute mentally.

Estimate using compatible numbers.

1. 168 ÷ 45
2. 525 ÷ 96
3. 379 ÷ 63
4. 234 ÷ 72
5. $613 ÷ 93
6. $748 ÷ 92

Set C pages 251–256

Find 195 ÷ 13.

Draw a model to help you find the number of tens and ones in the quotient.

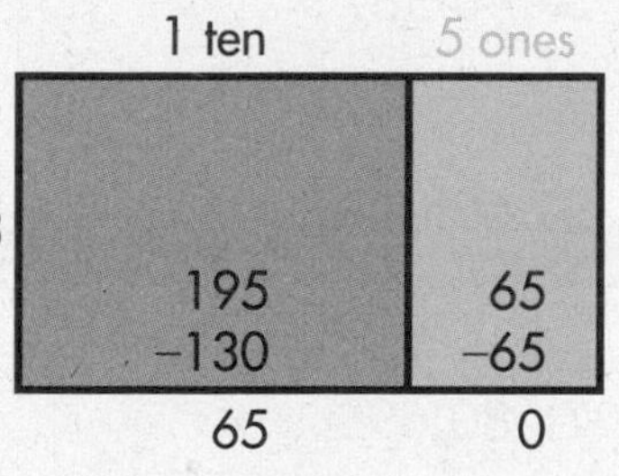

1 ten + 5 ones = 15.

So, 195 ÷ 13 = 15.

Remember find the number of tens first, then find the number of ones.

Use a model to find each quotient.

1. 180 ÷ 15
2. 154 ÷ 14
3. 351 ÷ 27
4. 192 ÷ 16
5. 143 ÷ 11
6. 217 ÷ 31
7. 130 ÷ 26
8. 270 ÷ 18

Set D pages 257–262

Find 336 ÷ 21 using partial quotients.

```
     6
    10
21)336   Estimate: How many 21s in 336? Try 10.
  -210   Multiply 10 by 21 and subtract.
   126   Estimate: How many 21s in 126? Try 6.
  -126   Multiply 6 by 21 and subtract.
     0
```

Add the partial quotients: $10 + 6 = 16$.

So, $336 \div 21 = 16$.

Remember to add the partial quotients to find the actual quotient.

Use partial quotients to divide.

1. 30)570
2. 17)714
3. 24)984
4. 40)920
5. 13)858
6. 29)986
7. 35)980
8. 73)803

Set E pages 263–268

Find 461 ÷ 50.

Estimate to decide where to place the first digit in the quotient.

Use compatible numbers. $450 \div 50 = 9$

So, write 9 in the ones place of the quotient. Multiply and subtract. Compare the remainder to the divisor.

```
    9 R11
 50)461
  - 450    Multiply 9 × 50 = 450
     11
```

So, 461 ÷ 50 = 9 R11. The quotient is close to the estimate, so the answer is reasonable.

Remember that you can check your answer by multiplying the quotient by the divisor, and then adding any remainder.

1. 20)420
2. 30)540
3. 40)387
4. 50)653
5. 60)840
6. 70)910
7. 80)698
8. 90)849
9. Ivan uses 30 craft sticks to make each toy cabin. He has a box of 342 craft sticks. How many toy cabins can Ivan make? How many sticks will be left?

Name ____

Set F pages 269–274

Tell in which place to write the first digit of the quotient 3,657 ÷ 23.

Multiply 23 by powers of 10 to estimate.

$23 \times 10 = 230$
$23 \times 100 = 2{,}300$
$23 \times 1{,}000 = 23{,}000$

Since 3,657 is between 2,300 and 23,000, the quotient is between 100 and 1,000.

So, the quotient is in the hundreds. Write the first digit of the quotient in the hundreds place.

Remember you can multiply the divisor by powers of 10 to estimate the quotient.

Without completing the division problem, tell which place to write the first digit of the quotient.

1. $14\overline{)966}$ **2.** $53\overline{)6{,}519}$

3. $91\overline{)728}$ **4.** $72\overline{)2{,}376}$

5. $26\overline{)8{,}164}$ **6.** $68\overline{)612}$

7. $40\overline{)5{,}520}$ **8.** $39\overline{)3{,}861}$

Set G pages 275–280

Find 789 ÷ 19.

Estimate first: 800 ÷ 20 = 40.

So, the first digit of the quotient is in the tens place.

Divide the tens. Multiply, subtract, and compare.

Bring down the ones. Divide the ones. Multiply, subtract, and compare. Compare the quotient with your estimate.

$$\begin{array}{r} 41 \text{ R}10 \\ 19\overline{)789} \\ -76 \\ \hline 29 \\ -19 \\ \hline 10 \end{array}$$

Remember that you can check your answer by multiplying the quotient by the divisor, and then adding any remainder.

1. $16\overline{)224}$ **2.** $38\overline{)792}$

3. $42\overline{)504}$ **4.** $47\overline{)5{,}170}$

5. $58\overline{)7{,}211}$ **6.** $12\overline{)3{,}549}$

7. $25\overline{)1{,}352}$ **8.** $33\overline{)1{,}500}$

9. $42\overline{)5{,}825}$ **10.** $28\overline{)2{,}941}$

Set H pages 281–286

Think about these questions to help you **make sense and persevere** in solving problems.

Thinking Habits

- What do I know?
- What do I need to find?
- What's my plan for solving the problem?
- What else can I try if I get stuck?
- How can I check that my solution makes sense?

Selena is planning to visit her aunt in 5 weeks. She has saved $365 but thinks the trip will cost $500. She plans to save the same amount each week so she has $500 for the trip. How much does she need to save each week?

I can write an equation to find how much more money Selena needs:

$500 - 365 = 135$

Then divide the amount she needs by 5 weeks: $135 \div 5 = 27$

Selena needs to save $27 each week.

My answer is reasonable because $365 + 27 + 27 + 27 + 27 + 27 = 500$.

Remember to think about what steps are needed to solve each problem.

Solve. Show your work.

1. The football coach spent a total of $890 including $50 in tax for 35 shirts for the team. Each shirt cost the same amount. What was the price of one shirt before tax was added?

2. A gymnast practices 6 days each week. She practices the same number of hours each day. If she practices a total of 120 hours in a 4-week period, how many hours each day does she practice?

3. Nathan works the same number of hours each day, 5 days each week. He earns $12 per hour. Last week he earned $420. How many hours did he work each day last week? Write equations to model your work.

4. A high-rise apartment building has 15 floors with 26 apartments on each floor. There are 3 kinds of apartments in the building: 1-, 2-, and 3-bedroom. The building has the same number of each kind of apartment. How many of each kind of apartment are in the building? Show your work.

Name ____________________

1. For questions 1a–1d, choose Yes or No to tell if the number 60 will make each equation true.

1a. 420 ÷ ☐ = 70 ○ Yes ○ No

1b. 1,800 ÷ ☐ = 300 ○ Yes ○ No

1c. 5,400 ÷ ☐ = 90 ○ Yes ○ No

1d. 24,000 ÷ ☐ = 400 ○ Yes ○ No

2. Which of the following is the best estimate of 487 ÷ 67?

Ⓐ 80

Ⓑ 70

Ⓒ 10

Ⓓ 7

3. The carnival committee has purchased 985 small prizes. The prizes are to be divided equally among the 20 game booths.

Part A

In what place will the first digit of the quotient be?

☐

Part B

How many prizes will each booth have?

☐

Part C

How many prizes will be left?

4. A rectangular living room has an area of 425 square feet. The width of the room is 17 feet.

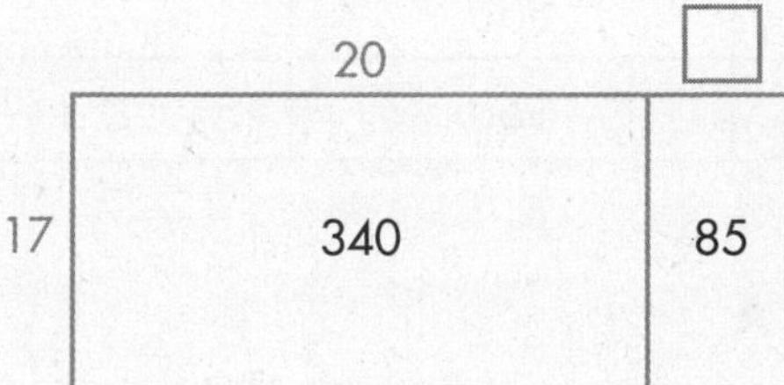

Write a number in the box to show the missing dimension.

What is the length of the room?

___ feet

5. Choose all the expressions that are equal to 27,000 ÷ 30.

☐ 270 ÷ 30

☐ 270 tens ÷ 3 tens

☐ 2,700 tens ÷ 3 tens

☐ 2,700 ÷ 3

☐ 2,700 tens ÷ 30 tens

6. Five Star Farm purchased 2,400 apple trees. If 80 trees can be planted on each acre of land, how many acres will be needed to plant all the trees?

☐

7. Use the table.

Althea's Plans for Saving $384		
Plan	Amount to Save Each Week	Number of Weeks Needed
A	$20	20
B	$30	
C	$50	8

Part A

Using Plan B, how many weeks will it take Althea to reach her savings goal? Write the missing number in the table.

Part B

Show how you found your answer to Part A.

8. Draw lines to match each expression on the left to its quotient on the right.

420 ÷ 6	700
420 ÷ 60	7
4,200 ÷ 6	60
4,200 ÷ 70	70

9. Mrs. Reiss has 264 crayons for her art class of 22 students. How many crayons will each student get if the crayons are divided equally? Use the model.

10. Dan divides $16\overline{)608}$. In which place should he write the first digit of the quotient?

11. Kari wants to find 3,277 ÷ 29.

Part A

In which place should she write the first digit of the quotient?

Part B

Tell how you decided where to write the first digit of the quotient.

Name ____

12. The cost to rent a lodge for a family reunion is $975. If 65 people attend and pay the same price, how much does each person pay?

Ⓐ $16

Ⓑ $15

Ⓒ $14

Ⓓ $13

13. Shady Rivers summer camp has 188 campers this week. If there are 22 campers to each cabin, what is the fewest number of cabins needed?

Ⓐ 7 cabins

Ⓑ 8 cabins

Ⓒ 9 cabins

Ⓓ 10 cabins

14. The area of a rectangular banquet hall is 7,400 square feet. The length of one side of the hall is 82 feet. Explain how you can use compatible numbers to estimate the width of the hall.

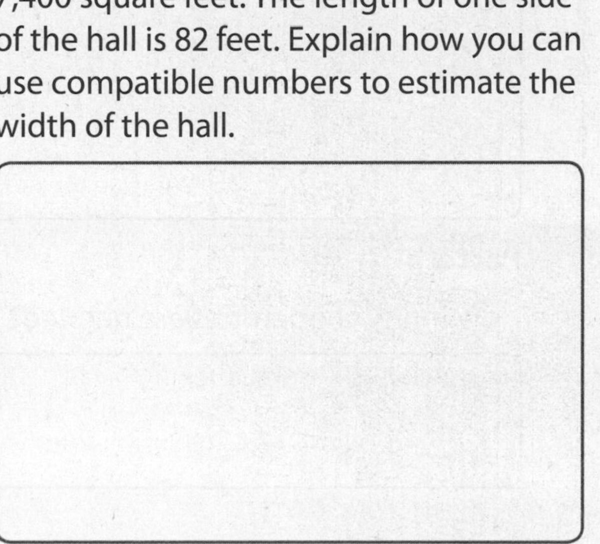

15. The cost of renting a bus is $1,344. Tony wants to find how much each person will pay if 32 people ride the bus and share the cost equally. Fill in the partial quotients that are missing from Tony's work below.

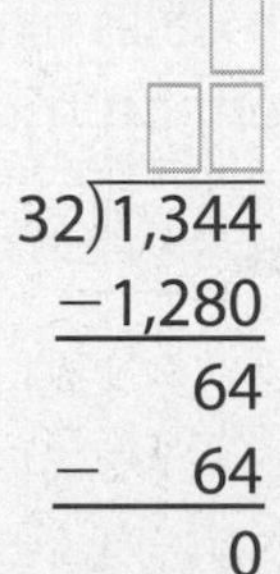

$$
\begin{array}{r}
32\overline{)1{,}344} \\
-1{,}280 \\
\hline
64 \\
-\quad 64 \\
\hline
0
\end{array}
$$

16. Jessie made 312 mini energy bars. She puts 24 bars in each bag. She plans to sell each bag for $6.

Part A

Write two equations with variables that Jessie can use to find the amount of money she will earn if she sells all of the bags.

Part B

How much will she earn if she sells all of the bags?

17. For questions 17a–d, choose Yes or No to tell if the number 40 will make each equation true.

17a. 280 ÷ ☐ = 7 ○ Yes ○ No

17b. 800 ÷ ☐ = 20 ○ Yes ○ No

17c. 4,000 ÷ ☐ = 10 ○ Yes ○ No

17d. 32,000 ÷ ☐ = 800 ○ Yes ○ No

18. Draw lines to match each expression on the left to its quotient on the right.

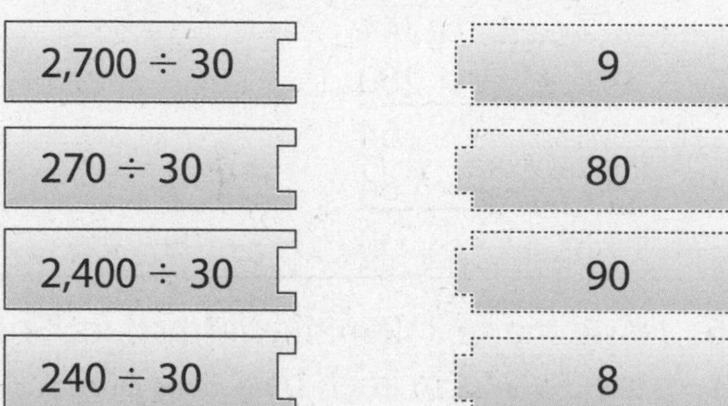

19. Charles burns 4,350 calories hiking 15 miles of the Appalachian Trail. He burns the same number of calories each mile. How many calories does he burn each mile?

20. Mary needs to find 432 ÷ 48. In which place should she write the first digit of the quotient?

21. Which partial quotients could be added to find 465 ÷ 15?

Ⓐ 20 and 1

Ⓑ 30 and 1

Ⓒ 30 and 9

Ⓓ 30 and 10

22. The table shows the number of students going on a field trip. One chaperone is needed for every 12 students.

DATA

Grade	Number of Students
Fifth Grade	310
Sixth Grade	305
Seventh Grade	225

Part A

Write two equations with variables that you can use to find the number of chaperones needed.

Part B

How many chaperones are needed?

Name ____

School Supplies

A store had a sale on school supplies in August. The store manager recorded how many of several types of items were sold. Each of the same type of item cost the same amount. Use the information in the table to answer the questions.

School Supply	Backpacks	Paper	Notebooks	Pens	Pencils
Number Sold	60	616	432	568	784

1. Backpack sales totaled $1,200. How much did each backpack cost? Write an equation to model your work.

2. The store sold 71 packages of pens. Use compatible numbers to estimate how many pens were in each package. Show your work.

3. There were 16 pencils in each box. Olivia wants to find how many boxes of pencils were sold.

Part A

When Olivia divides 784 by 16, in which place should she write the first digit of the quotient? Tell how you know without dividing.

Part B

How many boxes of pencils were sold?

4. The store manager has ordered the calculators shown, but the shipment has been delayed.

$19 for each calculator

Part A

If all the calculators ordered are sold, the total sales would be $2,014. Was the number of calculators ordered less than or greater than 100? How do you know without dividing?

Part B

How many calculators were ordered? Write an equation to model your work.

5. The manager wants to order 408 more notebooks. The notebooks are shipped in packages of 12. He used partial quotients to find the number of packages to order. His work is shown at the right. Is his solution correct? Explain.

$$\begin{array}{r} 40 \\ 30 \\ 12\overline{)408} \\ -360 \\ \hline 48 \\ -48 \\ \hline 0 \end{array}$$

6. An additional 40 packages of paper were ordered at a total cost of $520. How much did each package of paper cost? Write an equation to model your work.

Use Models and Strategies to Divide Decimals

Essential Question: What are the standard procedures for estimating and finding quotients involving decimals?

Math and Science Project: States of Water

Do Research Use the Internet or other sources to learn about the states of water. Find at least 5 examples of water in nature as a solid, as a liquid, and as a gas. At what temperature does liquid water change to ice? At what temperature does liquid water change to water vapor?

Journal: Write a Report Include what you found. Also in your report:

- Explain how liquid water changes to ice and to water vapor.
- At 23°F, 1 inch of rain equals 10 inches of snow. Convert 2 inches of rainfall to snowfall.
- Make up and solve division problems that involve decimals.

Name ______________________

Review What You Know

Vocabulary

Choose the best term from the box. Write it on the blank.

- decimal
- divisor
- dividend
- quotient

1. __________ is the name for the answer to a division problem.

2. A number that is being divided by another number is called the __________.

Whole Number Operations

Find each value.

3. 9,007 − 3,128 **4.** 725,864 + 39,798 **5.** 35 × 17

6. 181 × 42 **7.** 768 ÷ 6 **8.** 506 ÷ 22

9. 6,357 ÷ 60 **10.** 3,320 ÷ 89 **11.** 88,888 ÷ 20

Rounding Decimals

Round each number to the place of the underlined digit.

12. $0.\underline{3}4$ **13.** $9\underline{6}.5$ **14.** $81.\underline{2}7$ **15.** $\underline{2}05.3$

Decimals

16. An insect measured 1.25 cm long. Which number is less than 1.25?

Ⓐ 1.35 Ⓑ 1.3 Ⓒ 1.26 Ⓓ 1.2

17. Explain What decimal does this model represent? Explain.

Decimal Operations

Find each value.

18. 23.7 − 11.82 **19.** 66.8 + 3.64 **20.** 9 × 1.4 **21.** 3.2 × 7.6

Name ______________________________

Lesson 6-1
Patterns for Dividing with Decimals

I can ...
use patterns to solve decimal division problems.

I can also look for patterns to solve problems.

Solve & Share An object is 279.4 centimeters wide. If you divide the object into 10 equal parts, how wide will each part be? ***Solve this problem any way you choose.***

How can you use structure and the relationship between multiplication and division to help you?

Look Back! Reasoning What do you notice about the width of the object and the width of each part?

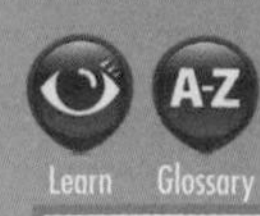

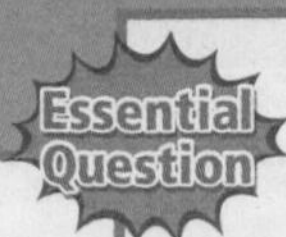

How Can You Divide Decimals by Powers of 10?

A

Shondra wants to cut a cloth into 10 strips. All the strips should be exactly the same size. How long will each strip be?

Remember that $10 = 10^1$ and $100 = 10^2$.

B Find $89.5 \div 10$.

A number divided by 10 is less than the number. Moving the decimal point to the left decreases the number's value.

Place value is based on 10, so dividing by 10 has the same result as moving the decimal point one place to the left.

C Notice the patterns in the table.

Divisor		
Standard Form	Exponential Form	Examples
1	10^0	$89.5 \div 1 = 89.5$
10	10^1	$89.5 \div 10 = 8.95$
100	10^2	$89.5 \div 100 = 0.895$
1,000	10^3	$89.5 \div 1,000 = 0.0895$

$89.5 \div 10^1 = 8.95$

Each cloth strip will be 8.95 centimeters long.

Convince Me! **Use Structure** Suppose you have a rope that is 293.5 cm long. If you cut the rope into 10^1 equal pieces, how long would each piece be? If you cut the rope into 10^2 pieces, how long would each piece be? How are the quotients you found related?

Name ____

Practice Buddy   Tools   Assessment

Guided Practice*

Do You Understand?

1. **Use Structure** Suppose Shondra wanted to cut the cloth into 10^2 strips. How wide would each strip be?

2. **Construct Arguments** Krista divides a number by 10. Then she divides the same number by 50. Which quotient is greater? How can you tell?

Do You Know How?

In **3–10**, use mental math to find each quotient.

3. $370.2 \div 10^2$

4. $126.4 \div 10^1$

5. $7.25 \div 10$

6. $72.5 \div 10^3$

7. $281.4 \div 10^0$

8. $2{,}810 \div 10^4$

9. $3{,}642.4 \div 10^2$

10. $364.24 \div 10^1$

Independent Practice

Leveled Practice In **11–25**, find each quotient. Use mental math.

11. $4{,}600 \div 10$
$460 \div 10$
$46 \div 10$
$4.6 \div 10$

12. $134.4 \div 10^3$
$134.4 \div 10^2$
$134.4 \div 10^1$
$134.4 \div 10^0$

13. $98.6 \div 1$
$98.6 \div 100$
$98.6 \div 10$
$98.6 \div 1{,}000$

14. $136.5 \div 10$

15. $753 \div 100$

16. $890.1 \div 10^0$

17. $3.71 \div 10^2$

18. $8{,}100 \div 10^4$

19. $864 \div 10^3$

20. $0.52 \div 10^1$

21. $15.7 \div 1{,}000$

22. $7{,}700 \div 10^2$

23. $770 \div 10^2$

24. $77 \div 10^1$

25. $7.7 \div 10^1$

*For another example, see Set A on page 357.

Problem Solving

For **26–28**, use the table that shows the winning times at the Pacific Middle School swim meet.

DATA

50-yard freestyle	22.17 seconds
100-yard backstroke	53.83 seconds
100-yard butterfly	58.49 seconds

26. What was the difference between the winning butterfly time and the winning backstroke time?

27. The winning time for the 100-yard freestyle was twice the time for the 50-yard freestyle. What was the winning time for the 100-yard freestyle?

28. What was the difference between the winning 100-yard freestyle time and the winning butterfly time?

29. Reasoning A pickup truck carrying 10^3 identical bricks weighs 6,755 pounds. If the empty truck weighs 6,240 pounds, what is the weight of each brick? Explain how to solve the problem.

30. Higher Order Thinking Katie noticed a pattern in the answers for each of the expressions below. What do you notice?

14.6×0.1 $\quad$ $14.6 \div 10$

146×0.01 $\quad$ $146 \div 100$

146×0.001 $\quad$ $146 \div 1{,}000$

Assessment

31. Choose the equations in which $n = 1{,}000$ makes the equation true.

- ☐ $2.5 \div n = 0.025$
- ☐ $947.5 \div n = 0.9475$
- ☐ $8{,}350 \div n = 8.35$
- ☐ $16.4 \div n = 0.0164$
- ☐ $0.57 \div n = 0.0057$

32. Choose the equations in which $d = 10^2$ makes the equation true.

- ☐ $386.2 \div d = 3.862$
- ☐ $4{,}963.6 \div d = 4.9636$
- ☐ $0.6 \div d = 0.006$
- ☐ $5.8 \div d = 0.58$
- ☐ $15.3 \div d = 0.153$

Name ______________________

Homework & Practice 6-1

Patterns for Dividing with Decimals

Another Look!

To divide by 10, or 10^1, move the decimal point 1 place to the left.

To divide by 100, or 10^2, move the decimal point 2 places to the left.

$275 \div 100 = \mathbf{2.75} = 2.75$

Sanjai uses 2.75 pounds of clay for each bowl.

Leveled Practice In **1–18**, use mental math and patterns to complete each problem.

1. $2{,}500 \div 10 =$ _____
$250 \div$ _____ $= 25$
_____ $\div 10 = 2.5$
$2.5 \div 10 =$ _____

2. $20 \div$ _____ $= 2$
$20 \div 10^2 =$ _____
$20 \div 10^3 =$ _____
$20 \div 10^4 =$ _____

3. _____ $\div 10 = \$675$
$\$675 \div$ _____ $= \$67.50$
$\$6{,}750 \div 10^2 =$ _____
$\$6{,}750 \div 10^3 =$ _____

4. $9{,}600 \div 10^1 =$ _____
$960 \div 10^1 =$ _____
$96 \div 10^1 =$ _____
$9.6 \div 10^1 =$ _____

5. $\$800 \div$ _____ $= \$80$
_____ $\div 10 = \$8$
$\$8 \div 10 =$ _____
$\$0.80 \div 10 =$ _____

6. $1{,}200 \div 10^3 =$ _____
$120 \div$ _____ $= 12$
_____ $\div 10^1 = 1.2$
$1.2 \div 10^2 =$ _____

7. $4 \div 100$

8. $15 \div 10^0$

9. $450 \div 10$

10. $60 \div 100$

11. $55 \div 10$

12. $30.9 \div 100$

13. $8{,}020 \div 10^2$

14. $150 \div 10^3$

15. $16 \div 10^3$

16. $1.8 \div 10^1$

17. $720 \div 100$

18. $3{,}500 \div 10^4$

19. The city has a section of land that is 3,694.7 feet long. The city wants to partition this length to form 10 equal-sized garden plots. How long will each garden plot be?

20. Higher Order Thinking A stack of 10^2 pennies is 6.1 inches tall. A stack of 10^2 dimes is 5.3 inches tall. How much taller is a stack of 10 pennies than a stack of 10 dimes?

21. For a party, 10 friends are buying 100 cups, 100 plates, a punchbowl, and 200 balloons. If the friends share the cost equally, how much should each friend contribute?

DATA

Party Supplies	
100 balloons	$7.80
100 plates	$4.75
100 cups	$5.45
100 napkins	$2.09
10 invitations	$1.60
plastic punchbowl	$11.50

22. Critique Reasoning Lance says that $2{,}376 \div 10^2$ is the same as $2{,}376 \times 0.1$. Is he correct? Why or why not?

23. Reasoning On a large map, the distance from Austin, Texas, to Milwaukee, Wisconsin, is 13.7 inches. The actual distance is about 1,000 miles. What is the distance on the same map from Indianapolis, Indiana, to Louisville, Kentucky, if the actual distance is about 100 miles? Round your answer to the nearest tenth.

Assessment

24. Choose the equations in which $n = 100$ will make the equation true.

- ☐ $12.4 \div n = 0.124$
- ☐ $3.8 \div n = 0.038$
- ☐ $52{,}350 \div n = 52.35$
- ☐ $850.4 \div n = 85.04$
- ☐ $0.41 \div n = 0.0041$

25. Choose the equations in which $d = 10^3$ will make the equation true.

- ☐ $37{,}162 \div d = 3.7162$
- ☐ $1{,}041.6 \div d = 1{,}041.6$
- ☐ $2.7 \div d = 0.0027$
- ☐ $168.2 \div d = 1.682$
- ☐ $80.7 \div d = 0.0807$

Name ____________________________________

Lesson 6-2
Estimate Decimal Quotients

I can …
estimate quotients in problems involving decimals.

I can also reason about math.

Solve & Share

A 135.8-foot piece of construction material needs to be cut into pieces that are each 16 feet long. About how many pieces can be cut? ***Solve this problem any way you choose.***

135.8 is about __________.

16 is about __________.

Look Back! Reasoning Can you find a different way to estimate the answer for the problem above? Explain.

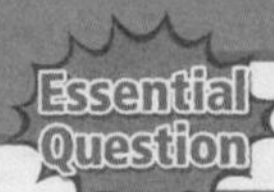

Essential Question How Can You Use Estimation to Find Quotients?

A

Diego purchased a video gaming system for $473.89 (including tax). About how much are his monthly payments if he wants to pay this off in one year?

B

One Way

Estimate $473.89 ÷ 12. Use rounding.

Round to the nearest ten:
473.89 rounds to 470;
12 rounds to 10.

$473.89 ÷ 12 is about
$470 ÷ 10 = $47.

Each monthly payment will be about $47.

C

Another Way

Estimate $473.89 ÷ 12.
Use compatible numbers.

Look for compatible numbers.

$473.89 ÷ 12 is close to
$480 ÷ 12 = $40.

Each monthly payment will be about $40.

Convince Me! **Construct Arguments** In the example above, which estimate is closer to the exact answer? Tell how you decided.

Name ________________

Practice Buddy Tools Assessment

Guided Practice*

Do You Understand?

1. **Number Sense** Leo is estimating 53.1 ÷ 8.4. Do you think he should use 53 ÷ 8 or 54 ÷ 9 to estimate? Why?

2. **Construct Arguments** Is each quotient greater than or less than 1? How do you know?

   A 0.2 ÷ 4

   B 1.35 ÷ 0.6

Do You Know How?

In **3–8**, estimate each quotient. Use rounding or compatible numbers.

3. 42 ÷ 6.8 **4.** 102 ÷ 9.6

5. 48.9 ÷ 4 **6.** 72.59 ÷ 7

7. 15.4 ÷ 1.9 **8.** 44.07 ÷ 6.3

Independent Practice

Leveled Practice In **9** and **10**, complete the work to estimate each quotient.

9. Estimate 64.5 ÷ 12.3 using rounding.

65 ÷ 10 = ____

10. Estimate 64.5 ÷ 12.3 using compatible numbers.

60 ÷ 12 = ____

In **11–19**, estimate each quotient.

11. 7 ÷ 0.85 **12.** 9.6 ÷ 0.91 **13.** 17.7 ÷ 3.2

14. 91.02 ÷ 4.9 **15.** 45.64 ÷ 6.87 **16.** 821.22 ÷ 79.4

17. 22.5 ÷ 3 **18.** 15.66 ÷ 9.3 **19.** 156.3 ÷ 14.5

*For another example, see Set B on page 357.

Problem Solving

20. Luci's mother gave her $7.50 to buy 8 spiral notebooks. With tax, the cost of each notebook is $1.05. Does Luci have enough money? Use compatible numbers and estimation to help you decide.

21. Critique Reasoning Kerri said that the quotient of 4.2 ÷ 5 is about 8 tenths. She reasoned that 4.2 ÷ 5 is close to 40 tenths ÷ 5. Do you agree with Kerri's reasoning? Explain.

22. Higher Order Thinking Write a decimal division problem that has an estimated quotient of 4. Explain how to get that estimate.

23. Reasoning Lei's car averages 14.5 miles per gallon while Roman's car averages 28.5 miles per gallon. Use estimation to find how many times as many miles per gallon Roman's car gets compared to Lei's car.

In **24–26**, use the table.

DATA

Sample	Mass	Temperature
1	0.98 g	37.57°C
2	0.58 g	57.37°C
3	0.058 g	75.50°C
4	0.098 g	73.57°C

24. Math and Science Which sample from the experiment had the least mass? Which had the lowest temperature?

25. Sample 3 was used in another experiment. A temperature of 82.14°C was recorded. How many degrees did the temperature change?

26. What is the difference in mass between Sample 1 and Sample 2?

✓ Assessment

27. Mauricio scored a total of 34.42 points in five gymnastic events. Which number sentence shows the best way to estimate Mauricio's score for each event?

Ⓐ 35 ÷ 5 = 7

Ⓑ 35 ÷ 7 = 5

Ⓒ 30 ÷ 10 = 3

Ⓓ 40 ÷ 10 = 4

28. Terry paid $117.50 for 18 identical flash drives. Which is the best estimate for the cost of each flash drive?

Ⓐ $6

Ⓑ $10

Ⓒ $12

Ⓓ $60

Name ______________________

Help | Practice Buddy | Tools | Games

Homework & Practice 6-2

Estimate Decimal Quotients

Another Look!

To estimate with decimal division, you can use rounding or compatible numbers.

Estimate 28.4 ÷ 9.5.

One Way

Use rounding. Round to the nearest whole number.

28.4 ÷ 9.5 — Write the original problem.

↓ ↓

28 ÷ 10 = 2.8 — Round 28.4 to 28. Round 9.5 to 10.

Another Way

Use compatible numbers.

28.4 ÷ 9.5 — Write the original problem.

↓ ↓

27 ÷ 9 = 3 — Use compatible numbers.

Leveled Practice In **1** and **2**, complete the work to estimate each quotient.

1. Estimate 52.3 ÷ 11.4 using rounding.

52.3 ÷ 11.4

↓ ↓

52 ÷ 10 = ______

2. Estimate 52.3 ÷ 11.4 using compatible numbers.

52.3 ÷ 11.4

↓ ↓

55 ÷ 11 = ______

In **3–11**, estimate each quotient.

3. 25.1 ÷ 8

4. 59.67 ÷ 11.1

5. 82.77 ÷ 7.5

6. 496.3 ÷ 98

7. 1.76 ÷ 0.91

8. 13.07 ÷ 7.41

9. 41.3 ÷ 6.76

10. 81.4 ÷ 10.03

11. 384.4 ÷ 88.1

12. Ms. Barton and three neighbors purchased a snowblower to share. The snowblower cost $439.20. Describe how you can estimate each person's share of the cost.

13. **Reasoning** Is 100 a reasonable estimate for $915.25 \div 88.22$? Explain.

14. **Make Sense and Persevere** Hodi is building a birdhouse. Each of the four walls of the birdhouse needs to be 5.5 inches long. Hodi has a piece of board that is 24.5 inches long. Is the board long enough to be cut into the four walls of the birdhouse? Estimate using compatible numbers.

15. On Monday, 3.11 inches of rain fell and on Tuesday, 0.81 inch of rain fell. On Wednesday, twice as much rain fell as on Tuesday. How much rain fell during the 3-day period?

16. **Number Sense** A veterinarian weighs three cats. The American Shorthair weighs 13.65 pounds. The Persian weighs 13.07 pounds, and the Maine Coon weighs 13.6 pounds. List the cats in order from least to greatest weight.

17. **Higher Order Thinking** Use estimation to decide which is the better value: 12 pairs of socks for $35.75 or 8 pairs of socks for $31.15. Explain your answer.

✔ Assessment

18. Elena wants to estimate $197.6 \div 5.48$. Which number sentence shows the best way to estimate this quotient?

Ⓐ $100 \div 5 = 20$

Ⓑ $100 \div 10 = 10$

Ⓒ $200 \div 5 = 40$

Ⓓ $200 \div 10 = 20$

19. Connor cuts a board with a length of 78.5 centimeters into four equal pieces. Which is the best estimate for the length of each piece?

Ⓐ 2 cm

Ⓑ 5 cm

Ⓒ 20 cm

Ⓓ 25 cm

Name ____________________

Lesson 6-3

Use Models to Divide by a 1-Digit Whole Number

Solve & Share

Chris paid $3.60 for 3 colored pens. Each pen costs the same amount. How much did each pen cost? ***Solve this problem any way you choose.***

I can ...
use models to help find quotients in problems involving decimals.

I can also choose and use a math tool to solve problems.

You can use appropriate tools such as place-value blocks to help you divide. *Show your work!*

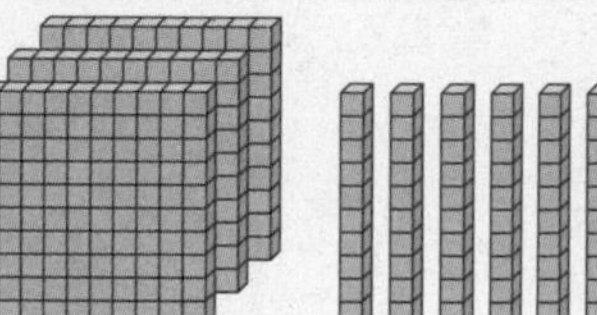

Look Back! Reasoning Without dividing, how do you know that the answer to the problem above must be greater than 1?

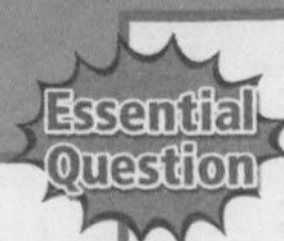

How Can You Use Models to Find a Decimal Quotient?

A

Three friends received $2.58 for aluminum cans they recycled. They decided to share the money equally. How much will each friend get?

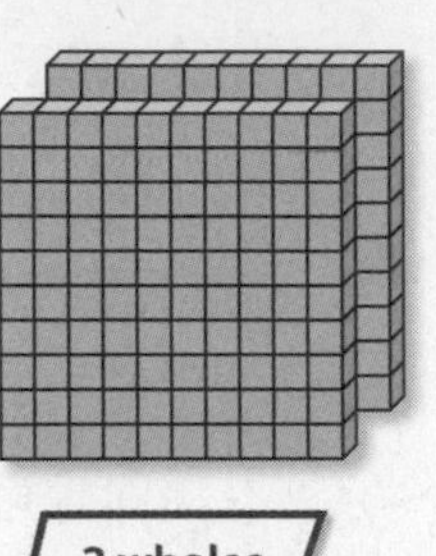
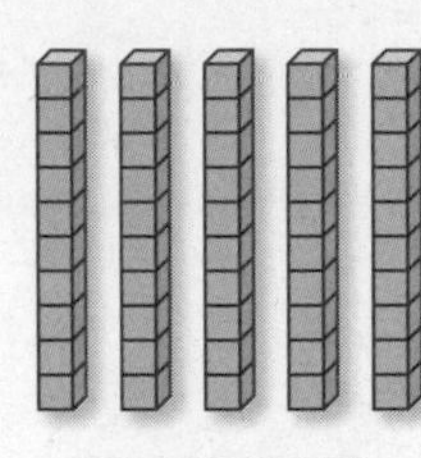

2 wholes

5 tenths

8 hundredths

B What You Think

Find $2.58 \div 3$. Estimate using compatible numbers.

$3 \div 3 = 1$, so $2.58 \div 3 < 1$.

Divide the models into 24 tenths and 18 hundredths to share equally.

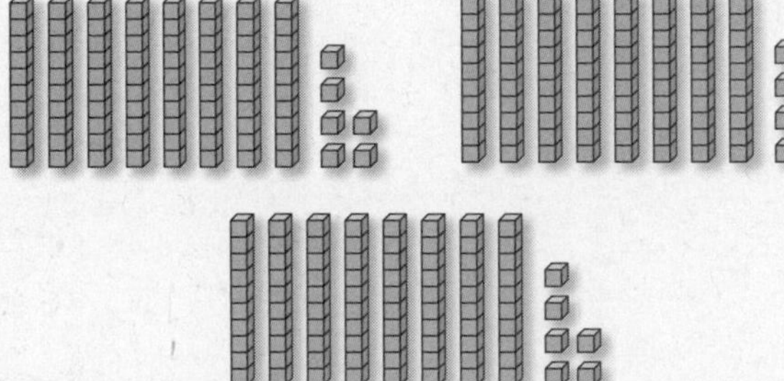

C What You Write

$$\begin{array}{r} 0.86 \\ 3\overline{)2.58} \\ -\,24 \\ \hline 18 \\ -\,18 \\ \hline 0 \end{array}$$

Place the decimal point in the quotient above the decimal point in the dividend. Divide as usual.

Each of the three friends will get $0.86.

Convince Me! **Reasoning** The next week 4 friends got $8.24 for the cans they collected. How much money will each friend make? Estimate using compatible numbers and then calculate.

Name ____________________

Guided Practice*

Do You Understand?

1. Construct Arguments Should you start dividing the ones first or the tenths first to find 9.36 ÷ 4? Explain.

2. Generalize How is dividing a decimal by a whole number similar to dividing a whole number by a whole number? Explain.

Do You Know How?

3. Use models to help you divide 2.16 ÷ 4. Complete the division calculation.

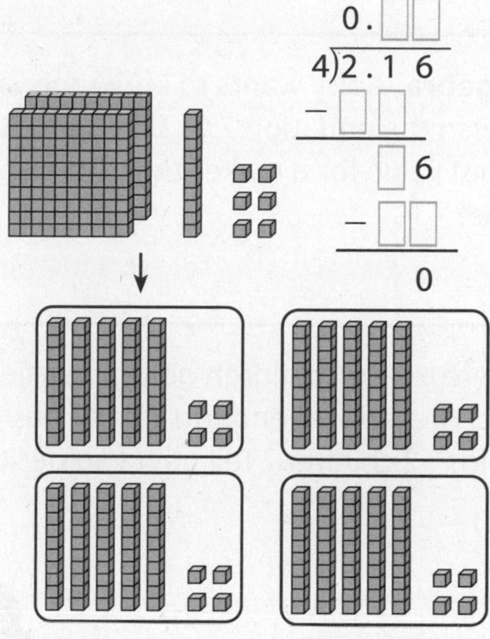

$$\begin{array}{r} 0.\square\square \\ 4\overline{)2.16} \\ -\square\square \\ \hline \square 6 \\ -\square\square \\ \hline 0 \end{array}$$

Independent Practice

Leveled Practice In **4–11**, divide. Use models to help.

4. $\begin{array}{r} 0.4\square \\ 3\overline{)1.35} \\ -\square\square \\ \hline \square 5 \\ -\square\square \\ \hline \square \end{array}$

5. $\begin{array}{r} 0.\square\square \\ 6\overline{)2.76} \\ -\square\square \\ \hline \square 6 \\ -\square\square \\ \hline \square \end{array}$

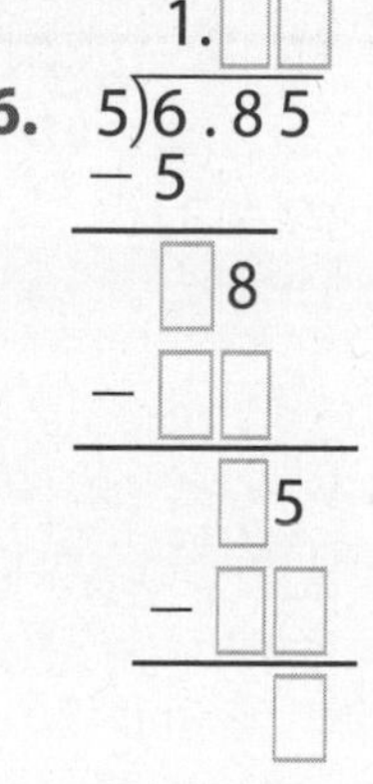

6. $\begin{array}{r} 1.\square\square \\ 5\overline{)6.85} \\ -5 \\ \hline \square 8 \\ -\square\square \\ \hline \square 5 \\ -\square\square \\ \hline \square \end{array}$

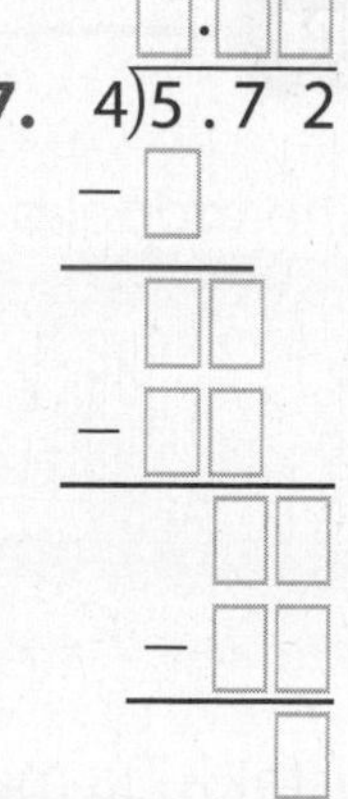

7. $\begin{array}{r} \square.\square\square \\ 4\overline{)5.72} \\ -\square \\ \hline \square\square \\ -\square\square \\ \hline \square\square \\ -\square\square \\ \hline \square \end{array}$

8. 2.38 ÷ 7

9. 4.71 ÷ 3

10. 1.76 ÷ 8

11. 5.36 ÷ 2

*For another example, see Set C on page 358.

Problem Solving

12. **Model with Math** Alan is modeling $2.65 \div 5$. How should he exchange the place-value blocks so he can make 5 equal shares?

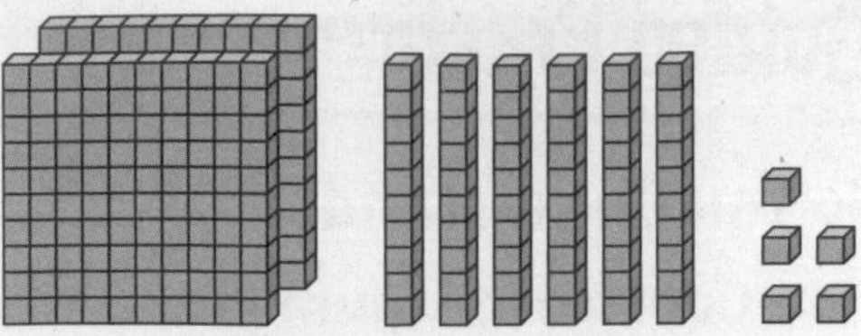

13. **Algebra** Abby wants to know the value of n in the equation $7.913 \times n = 791.3$. What value for n makes the equation true?

14. **Construct Arguments** To find $5.16 \div 6$, should you divide the ones first or the tenths first? Why?

15. There are 264 children going on a field trip. Are 5 buses enough if each bus holds 52 children? Tell how you decided.

16. **Higher Order Thinking** Ginny earned \$49.50 for 6 hours of gardening and \$38.60 for 4 hours of babysitting. For which job did she earn more money per hour? How much more per hour did she earn? Explain how you found the answers.

Assessment

17. Tia drew the model below for $1.35 \div 3$.

 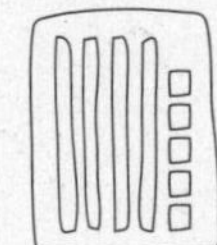 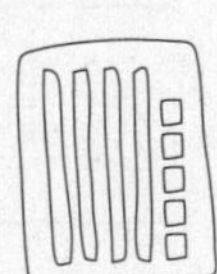 

Part A

Explain the mistake Tia made.

Part B

Draw the correct model and find the quotient.

Name ______________________

Help | Practice Buddy | Tools | Games

Homework & Practice 6-3

Use Models to Divide by a 1-Digit Whole Number

Another Look!

Draw a model to help you find $3.25 \div 5$.

3 wholes, 2 tenths, and 5 hundredths

↓

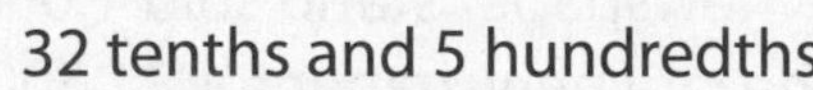

32 tenths and 5 hundredths

↓

30 tenths and 25 hundredths

Think about how you can exchange place-value blocks to make 5 equal shares.

What You Show

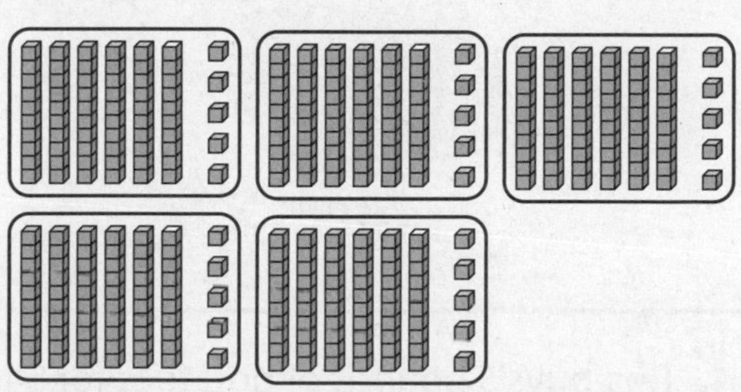

What You Write

$$\begin{array}{r} 0.65 \\ 5\overline{)3.25} \\ -\,30 \\ \hline 25 \\ -\,25 \\ \hline 0 \end{array}$$

Think: Each equal share has 6 tenths and 5 hundredths.

Leveled Practice In **1–8**, divide. Use models to help.

1.
$$\begin{array}{r} 0.\square\square \\ 4\overline{)3.48} \\ -\,\square\square \\ \hline 2\square \\ -\,\square\square \\ \hline 0 \end{array}$$

2.
$$\begin{array}{r} 0.\square\square \\ 5\overline{)4.25} \\ -\,\square\square \\ \hline \square 5 \\ -\,\square\square \\ \hline \square \end{array}$$

3.
$$\begin{array}{r} \square.2\square \\ 6\overline{)7.44} \\ -\,6 \\ \hline \square\square \\ -\,12 \\ \hline \square\square \\ -\,\square\square \\ \hline \square \end{array}$$

4.
$$\begin{array}{r} 1.\square\square \\ 8\overline{)9.68} \\ -\,\square \\ \hline 1\square \\ -\,\square\square \\ \hline \square\square \\ -\,\square\square \\ \hline \square \end{array}$$

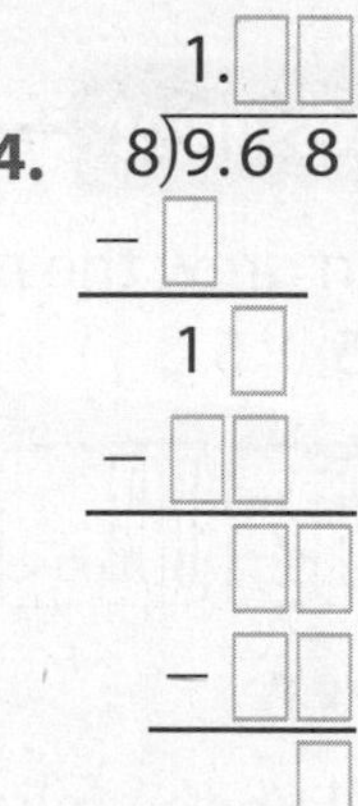

5. $3\overline{)2.91}$

6. $4\overline{)6.52}$

7. $7.02 \div 6$

8. $4.75 \div 5$

9. Model with Math Janice is dividing 1.92 ÷ 6. Why does she exchange the place-value blocks shown for 18 tenths and 12 ones?

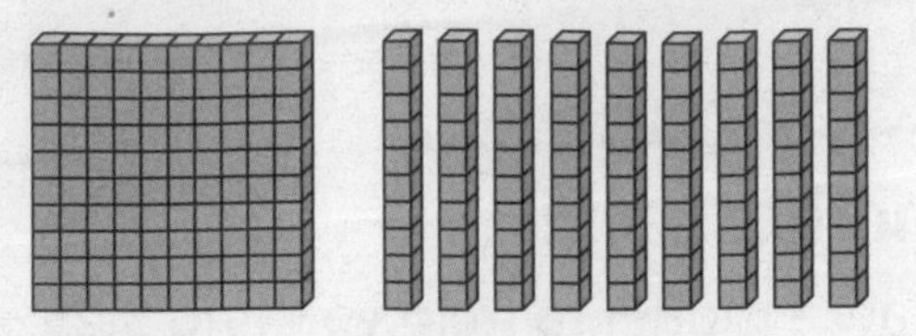

10. Keith has 7.8 ounces of tuna salad. If he makes 3 sandwiches with an equal amount of tuna on each, how much tuna does he put on each one?

11. Algebra A newspaper stand sold 1,000 copies of the city newspaper for $1,600. Write and solve an equation to find the price of one copy.

12. Higher Order Thinking Inez bought a package of wrapping paper and 4 bows. If she wrapped 4 identical gifts with the paper and bows, how much did it cost to wrap each gift?

13. Number Sense Without dividing, how can you decide whether the quotient 7.16 ÷ 4 will be less than or greater than 2?

14. Tina buys 5 pounds of potatoes for $4.35 and 3 pounds of carrots for $3.57. How much does one pound of potatoes cost?

Assessment

15. Glen drew the model shown below for 1.95 ÷ 5.

Part A

Explain the mistake Glen made.

Part B

Draw the correct model and find the quotient.

Name ____________________

Lesson 6-4
Divide by a 1-Digit Whole Number

I can ...
divide decimals by a whole number.

I can also generalize from examples.

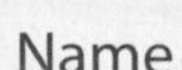

Solve & Share

A concrete mason separated 107.25 pounds of sand evenly into 3 containers. How much sand did he put into each container? ***Solve this problem any way you choose.***

Generalize How can you connect what you know about dividing whole numbers to dividing a decimal by a whole number? *Show your work!*

Look Back! Reasoning How can you estimate the answer to the problem above?

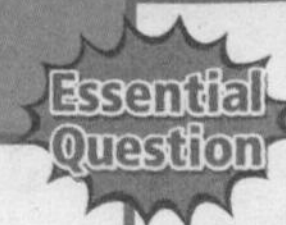

How Can You Divide a Decimal by a Whole Number?

A

While on a backpacking trip, Bradley hiked 23.6 miles in 8 hours. If he hiked the same number of miles each hour, how many miles did he hike each hour?

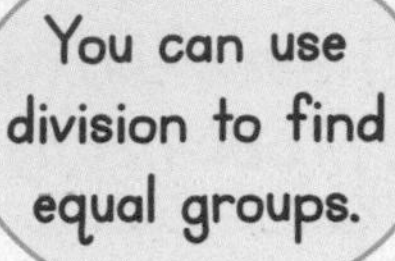

23.6 miles

m	m	m	m	m	m	m	m

$23.6 \div 8 = m$

B

Step 1

Estimate.

Since $24 \div 8 = 3$, start dividing in the ones place.

$$\begin{array}{r} 2 \\ 8\overline{)23.6} \\ -\,16 \\ \hline 7 \end{array}$$

Compare: $7 < 8$

C

Step 2

Divide the tenths.

$$\begin{array}{r} 2.9 \\ 8\overline{)23.6} \\ -\,16\downarrow \\ \hline 76 \\ -\,72 \\ \hline 4 \end{array}$$

Place the decimal point.

Bring down.

Compare: $4 < 8$

D

Step 3

Divide the hundredths.

$$\begin{array}{r} 2.95 \\ 8\overline{)23.60} \\ -\,16\downarrow \\ \hline 76 \\ -\,72\downarrow \\ \hline 40 \\ -\,40 \\ \hline 0 \end{array}$$

Annex a zero.

Bring down.

Bradley hiked 2.95 miles each hour.

Convince Me! Reasoning Write a problem that could be represented by the expression $5.68 \div 8$. Then explain how to use compatible numbers to estimate the solution.

Name ________________________________

Practice Buddy Tools Assessment

Guided Practice*

Do You Understand?

1. When you divide a decimal by a whole number, where do you place the decimal point in the quotient?

2. Reasoning In the example on the previous page, why is a zero annexed in the dividend?

Do You Know How?

In **3** and **4**, complete each division.

3. $6\overline{)43.8}$, quotient 7.□; −4□; 1□; −18; □

4. $4\overline{)37.□□}$, quotient 9.2□; −□6; 1□; −8; □□; −□□; 0

Independent Practice

Leveled Practice In **5–16**, find each quotient.

5. $6\overline{)4.56}$, quotient 0.□□; −□□; □6; −□□; □

6. $5\overline{)32.□}$, quotient □.□; −□□; 20; −□□; □

7. $7\overline{)20.3}$, quotient □.□; −□□; □□; −□□; □

8. $4\overline{)33.8□}$, quotient □.□□; −□□; □□; −□□; □□; −□□; □

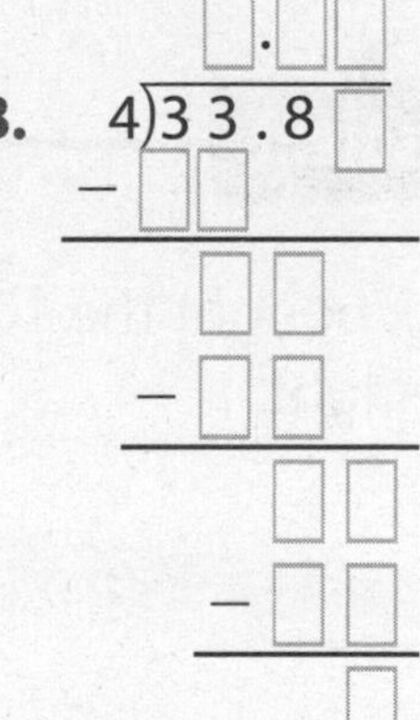

9. 19 ÷ 5 **10.** 7.83 ÷ 3 **11.** 48.62 ÷ 2 **12.** 62 ÷ 8

13. 35.5 ÷ 5 **14.** 100 ÷ 8 **15.** 1.44 ÷ 9 **16.** $7.20 ÷ 6

*For another example, see Set C on page 358.

Problem Solving

17. Model with Math A 32-ounce tub of yogurt contains 5 servings. Write and solve an equation to find how many ounces of yogurt are in 1 serving.

18. Number Sense Write three decimals that each round to 2.7 when rounded to the nearest tenth.

19. Construct Arguments Which package of cheese has heavier slices? How do you know?

20. Higher Order Thinking Harriet calculated $27 \div 4 = 6.75$. How can she find $270 \div 4$ without dividing?

21. Manny has $75. He wants to buy a tree for $24. Will he have enough money left to buy 4 bushes that each cost $12.25? Show how you found your answer.

Assessment

22. Patrick bought the 10 stamps shown at the right.

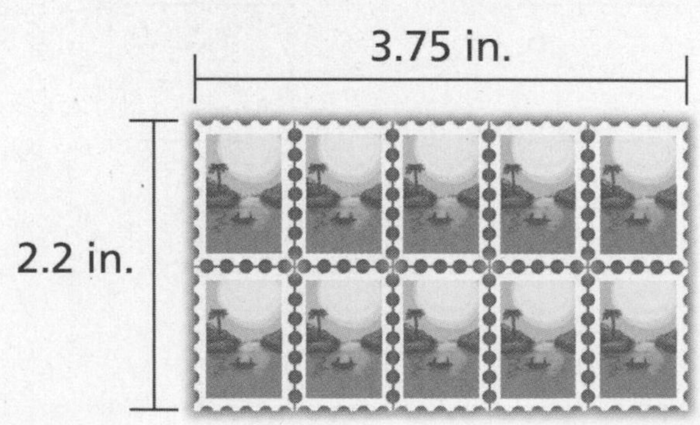

Part A

What is the height of a single stamp? Show your work.

Part B

What is the width of a single stamp? Show your work.

Name ____________________

Homework & Practice 6-4

Divide by a 1-Digit Whole Number

Another Look!

The mass of 6 identical gold bracelets is 75 grams. What is the mass of each bracelet?

Step 1	Step 2	Step 3
Estimate. Since 72 ÷ 6 = 12, start dividing in the tens place. $\begin{array}{r} 1 \\ 6\overline{)75} \\ -6 \\ \hline 1 \end{array}$	Divide the ones. $\begin{array}{r} 12 \\ 6\overline{)75} \\ -6\downarrow \\ \hline 15 \\ -12 \\ \hline 3 \end{array}$ Bring down.	Divide the tenths. $\begin{array}{r} 12.5 \\ 6\overline{)75.0} \\ -6 \\ \hline 15 \\ -12 \\ \hline 30 \\ -30 \\ \hline 0 \end{array}$ Place the decimal point. Annex a zero. Bring down. The mass of each bracelet is 12.5 grams.

Leveled Practice In **1–12**, find each quotient.

1. $\begin{array}{r} \square.\square \\ 5\overline{)32.\square} \\ -\square\square \\ \hline 20 \\ -\square\square \\ \hline \square \end{array}$

2. $\begin{array}{r} \square.\square\square \\ 7\overline{)3.36} \\ -\square\square \\ \hline \square\square \\ -\square\square \\ \hline \square \end{array}$

3. 4)9.76

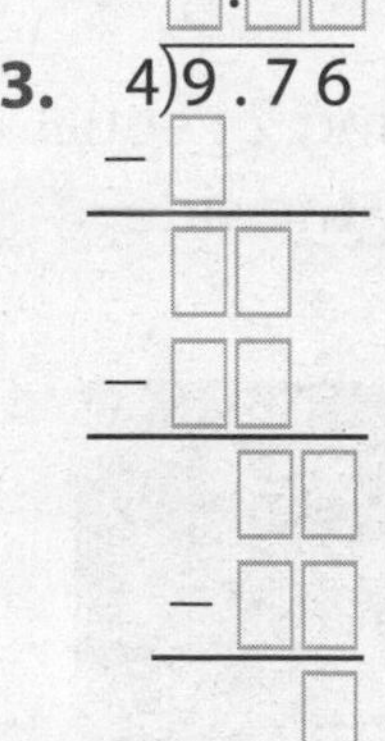

4. 8)92.

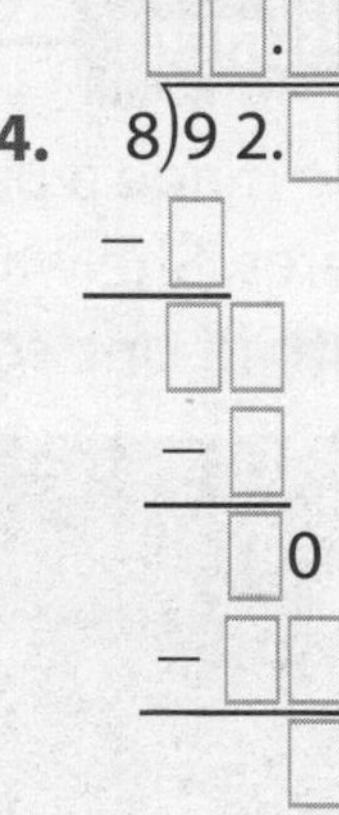

5. 13 ÷ 2

6. 5.58 ÷ 9

7. 27.6 ÷ 8

8. 30.17 ÷ 7

9. 15 ÷ 4

10. 37.8 ÷ 7

11. 4.95 ÷ 9

12. 5.04 ÷ 6

13. Reasoning Ned calculated $17 \div 4 = 4.25$. Use estimation to see if his answer is reasonable. How can you check his exact answer?

14. Nathan drove 275.2 miles on 8 gallons of gas. Divide 275.2 by 8 to find the average number of miles per gallon for Nathan's car.

15. Model with Math Sara is making punch for her party. Her punch bowl holds 600 ounces for 80 servings of punch. Write and solve an equation to find how many ounces of punch are in each serving.

16. Make Sense and Persevere A school auditorium has three sections for seating. One section has 16 rows with 14 seats per row. The other two sections each have 18 rows with 10 seats per row. How many seats are in the three sections in all?

17. Higher Order Thinking Paul and Richard are dividing $36.25 \div 5$. Paul says that the first digit of the quotient is in the ones place. Richard says it is in the tens place. Who is right? How do you know?

Assessment

18. Gayle made a baby quilt using 24 equal squares. She wants to know the side length of one square.

Part A

Describe one way to find the answer.

Part B

What is the side length of one square? Write an equation to show your work.

Name ______________________

Lesson 6-5
Divide by a 2-Digit Whole Number

I can …
divide decimals by a two-digit whole number.

I can also model with math to solve problems.

Solve & Share Stan has a rectangular piece of carpet with an area of 23.4 square meters. The piece of carpet is 13 meters long. What is the width of the piece of carpet? ***Solve this problem any way you choose.***

Model with Math
You can write an equation to model the problem.

Look Back! Reasoning How could you estimate the width of the piece of carpet?

Essential Question: How Do You Divide Decimals by 2-Digit Numbers?

A

Erin's garden has an area of 84.8 square feet. She knows the length is 16 feet. What is the width of Erin's garden? How can you solve $84.8 \div 16 = w$?

B

You can find the width by dividing.

$$\begin{array}{r} 5.3 \\ 16\overline{)84.8} \\ -80 \\ \hline 4\,8 \\ -4\,8 \\ \hline 0 \end{array}$$

The decimal point in the quotient goes right above the decimal point in the dividend.

The width of the garden is 5.3 feet.

C

The model shows that when the garden has an area of 84.8 square feet and a length of 16 feet, the width is 5.3 feet.

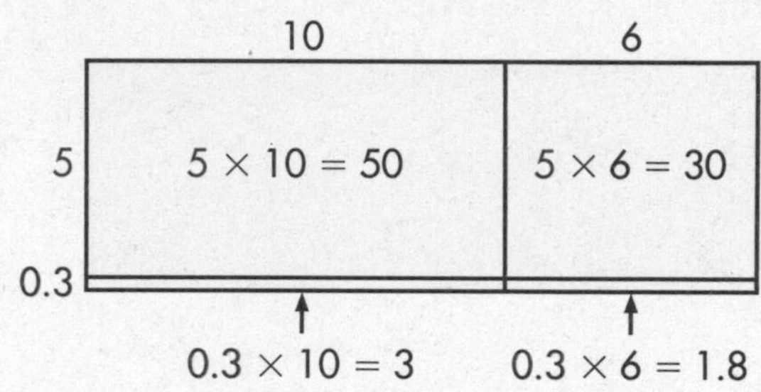

$$50 + 30 + 3 + 1.8 = 84.8$$
$$16 \times 5.3 = 84.8$$
$$84.8 \div 16 = 5.3$$

Convince Me! Reasoning To find the width of the garden above, Amy divided 848 by 16 and got 53. How could she then use estimation to place the decimal point?

Name ____________________

Practice Buddy | Tools | Assessment

Guided Practice*

Do You Understand?

In **1** and **2**, use the example on the previous page.

1. Where is 5.3 shown in the diagram?

2. Use Structure How can you check that the quotient 5.3 is reasonable? Explain.

Do You Know How?

In **3** and **4**, complete the division problem.

3. 49)306.25
Quotient: ☐.2☐
− ☐9☐
1☐☐
− 98
☐☐☐
− 245
☐

4. 15)14.4☐
Quotient: 0.☐☐
− ☐☐☐
9☐
− ☐0
☐

Independent Practice

Leveled Practice In **5–12**, find each quotient.

5. 17)78.2
Quotient: ☐.☐
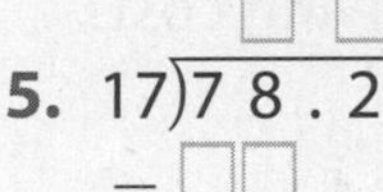
− ☐☐
☐☐☐
− ☐☐☐
0

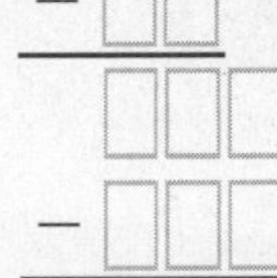

6. 40)232.0
Quotient: ☐.☐
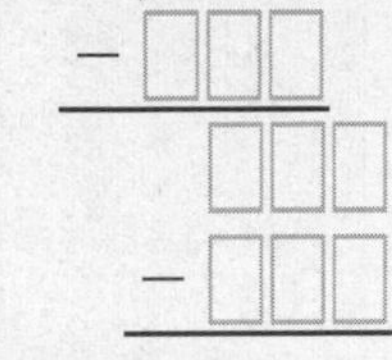
− ☐☐☐
☐☐☐
− ☐☐☐
0

7. 53)304.75
Quotient: ☐.7☐
− ☐6☐
3☐☐
− 371
☐☐☐
− 265
☐

8. 18)15.3☐
Quotient: 0.☐☐
− ☐☐☐
9☐
− ☐0
☐

9. 27)91.8

10. 15)3.9

11. 88)396

12. 50)247.5

*For another example, see Set D on page 358.

Problem Solving

13. Sharon pays $98.75 for twenty-five 14-ounce boxes of Yummy Flakes cereal. How much does one box of cereal cost?

14. Reasoning Javier bought a new TV for $479.76. He will make equal payments each month for 2 years. How can Javier use compatible numbers to estimate each payment?

15. Higher Order Thinking The area of the rectangular flowerbed shown is 20.4 square meters. How many meters of edging are needed to go around the flowerbed? Explain.

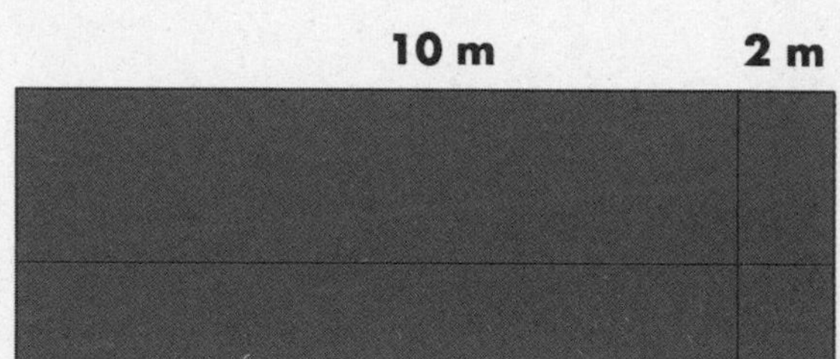

16. Make Sense and Persevere Ms. Wang is shopping for a new refrigerator. Brand A costs $569 and uses 635 kilowatt-hours per year. Brand B costs $647 and uses 582 kilowatt-hours per year. If electricity costs $0.18 per kilowatt-hour, how much would Ms. Wang save on electricity per year by buying Brand B?

17. Pat is driving from Seattle to Los Angeles. The distance is 1,135 miles. For the first 250 miles, it costs Pat $0.29 a mile to drive. After that, her driving cost is $0.16 a mile. What is Pat's total driving cost?

Assessment

18. Which is equal to 27.3 divided by 13?

Ⓐ 0.21
Ⓑ 2.01
Ⓒ 2.1
Ⓓ 21

19. Which is equal to 73.5 divided by 21?

Ⓐ 0.35
Ⓑ 3.05
Ⓒ 3.5
Ⓓ 30.5

Name ______________________

Homework & Practice 6-5

Divide by a 2-Digit Whole Number

Another Look!

The area of a sketch pad is 93.5 square inches. The length of the sketch pad is 11 inches. What is the width of the sketch pad?

First, estimate the width:
$93.5 \div 11$ is about
$90 \div 10 = 9$.

Divide 93.5 by 11.

$$\begin{array}{r} 8.5 \\ 11\overline{)93.5} \\ -88 \\ \hline 55 \\ -55 \\ \hline 0 \end{array}$$

8.5 is close to the estimate of 9, so the answer is reasonable.

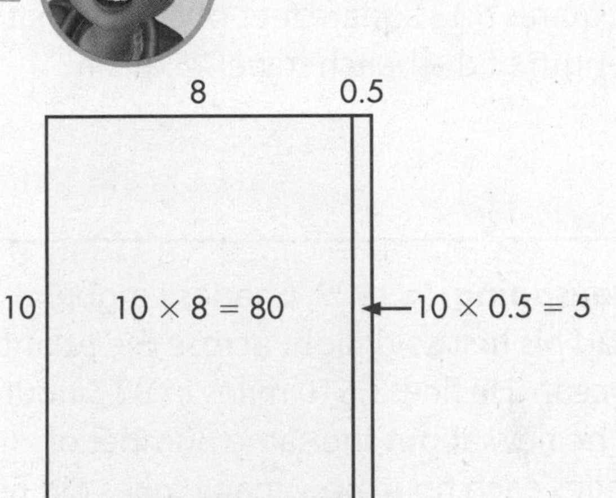

The width of the sketch pad is 8.5 inches.

Leveled Practice In **1–12**, find each quotient.

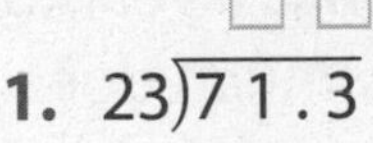

1. $23\overline{)71.3}$

2. $80\overline{)192.0}$

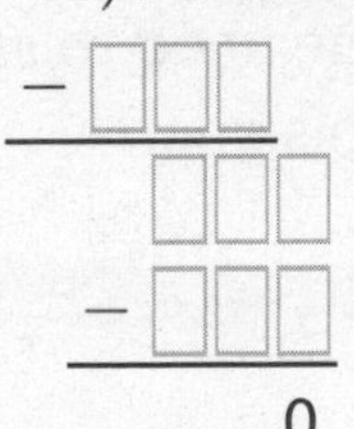

3. $42\overline{)23.94}$

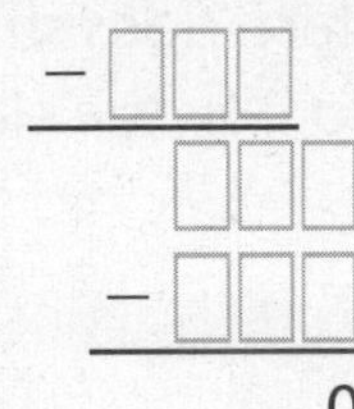

4. $18\overline{)40.50}$

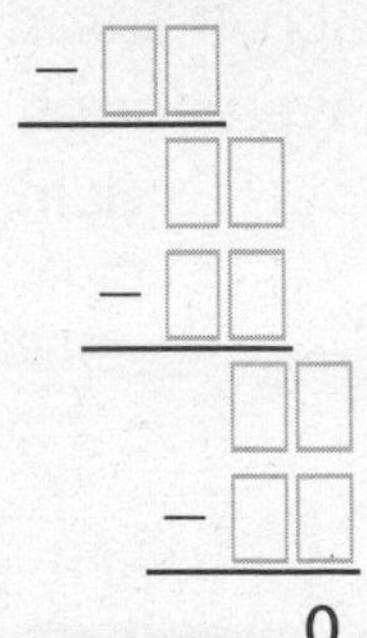

5. $26\overline{)98.8}$

6. $17\overline{)14.62}$

7. $25\overline{)160}$

8. $60\overline{)343.2}$

9. $83.2 \div 26$

10. $25.6 \div 4$

11. $90.54 \div 18$

12. $2.4 \div 16$

13. The longest spin of a basketball on one finger is 255 minutes. About how many hours is that?

14. Kara paid $24.64 to ship 11 packages. Each package was the same size and weight. How much did it cost to ship 1 package?

15. Higher Order Thinking Liza needs a total of 22.23 square feet of terry cloth to make a beach towel and a beach bag. The beach bag requires 5.13 square feet of cloth. What is the length of the beach towel? Explain.

3 feet

16. Reasoning In 1927, Charles Lindbergh had his first solo flight across the Atlantic Ocean. He flew 3,610 miles in 33.5 hours. If he flew about the same number of miles each hour, how many miles did he fly each hour?

17. Tiffany deposited the following amounts in her savings account last month: $6.74, $5.21, $5.53, and $3.52. Divide the sum by 30 to find the average amount she saved per day for the month. Show your work.

18. Make Sense and Persevere Susan bought 3 plants that cost $2.75 each. She wants to buy 3 clay pots that cost $4.15 each. If Susan had $20 to start, does she have enough money to also buy the clay pots? Explain.

19. Todd is saving for a vacation. The cost of his vacation is $1,089. Todd has a year to save the money. About how much does he need to save each month to reach his goal?

✓ Assessment

20. Which is equal to 78.2 divided by 17?

Ⓐ 0.46

Ⓑ 4.06

Ⓒ 4.6

Ⓓ 46

21. Which is equal to 12.74 divided by 13?

Ⓐ 0.09

Ⓑ 0.98

Ⓒ 9.08

Ⓓ 9.8

Name ______________________

Lesson 6-6
Use Number Sense to Divide Decimals

I can ...
use number sense to help solve decimal division problems.

I can also reason about math.

Solve & Share For the equations below, decide where to place the decimal point in each quotient. Explain your reasoning for one of the equations. ***Solve these problems any way you choose.***

16.38 ÷ 0.52 = 3 1 5

35.49 ÷ 1.2 = 2 9 5 7 5

0.4 ÷ 0.32 = 1 2 5

Look Back! **Construct Arguments** Explain how you can use number sense to place the decimal point in the equation below.

163.8 ÷ 5.2 = 315

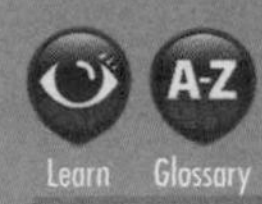
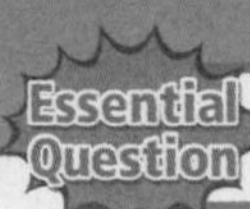
Learn Glossary

Essential Question: How Can You Use Number Sense for Decimal Division?

A

How many quarters are in $15.50? The decimal point is missing in the quotient of the equation below. Use number sense to place the decimal point in the correct position.

$15.50 ÷ $0.25 = 6 2 0

Think about the relative size of the dividend and the divisor.

B

Estimation and number sense are helpful in placing the decimal point in quotients.

You know that $15.50 ÷ 1 = $15.50.

Since 0.25 is less than 1, the quotient $15.50 ÷ $0.25 is greater than $15.50.

Since there are 4 quarters in $1, there are about 4 × 15 = 60 quarters in $15.50.

So, the decimal point is between the 2 and the 0.

$15.50 ÷ $0.25 = 62.0

There are 62 quarters in $15.50.

C

Where should you place the decimal point in the equation below?

1.2 ÷ 2.5 = 4 8 0

You know that 1.2 ÷ 1.2 = 1.

Since the divisor 2.5 is greater than the dividend 1.2, you know that the quotient will be less than 1.

Since 1.2 is about half of 2.5, the quotient will be close to 0.5.

So, the decimal point is before the 4.

1.2 ÷ 2.5 = .480 or 0.48

Convince Me! Critique Reasoning Malcolm says that 3.9 ÷ 0.52 is about 2. Cory says that the quotient is about 8. Who is correct? Explain your reasoning.

Name ______________________________

Practice Buddy | Tools | Assessment

Guided Practice*

Do You Understand?

1. **Reasoning** If the dividend is 2.63 and the divisor is less than 1, what can you say about the quotient?

2. Lena found that 1.44 ÷ 1.2 = 0.12. Did she put the decimal point in the correct place? Explain.

Do You Know How?

In **3–6**, use number sense to decide where the decimal point belongs in the quotient.

3. 7.68 ÷ 1.5 = 5 1 2

4. 256.5 ÷ 2.5 = 1 0 2 6

5. 1127.84 ÷ 3.8 = 2 9 6 8

6. 96.0 ÷ 0.96 = 1 0 0 0 0

Independent Practice

In **7–12**, use number sense to decide where the decimal point belongs in the quotient.

7. 14.73 ÷ 6.96 = 2 1 1 6 3 7 9 3

8. 20.15 ÷ 31.2 = 6 4 5 8 3 3 3

9. 0.98 ÷ 0.50 = 1 9 6

10. 107.22 ÷ 0.99 = 1 0 8 3 0 3 0

11. 16.456 ÷ 2.2 = 7 4 8

12. 1.26 ÷ 0.48 = 2 6 2 5

The decimal point in each of the quotients below may be in the wrong place. In **13–16**, use number sense to decide. If it is incorrect, give the correct quotient.

13. 7.02 ÷ 2.6 = 2.7

14. 49.84 ÷ 0.56 = 8.9

15. 337.5 ÷ 0.75 = 450

16. 0.36 ÷ 0.12 = 30.0

For another example, see Set E on page 359.

Problem Solving

17. Number Sense Jane needs to know how many dimes are in $45.60. After dividing on the calculator, she sees the display read 4 5 6 0. Where should Jane place the decimal point in her answer?

18. Mr. Jones has a new car. The manufacturer says that the car should get about 28 miles per gallon in the city. About how many miles can Mr. Jones drive on 11.5 gallons of gas? At $2.89 per gallon, how much would that cost?

19. Higher Order Thinking Mason and Thomas are working on a decimal division problem. Mason states that $3.96 \div 0.3 = 1.32$. Thomas states that the quotient is 13.2. Who is correct?

Explain your answer.

20. Write two decimals whose quotient is close to 2.3.

____ ÷ ____ is about 2.3

21. Construct Arguments A 26.2 mile marathon has water stops every 0.5 mile. Is it reasonable to say that there are about 40 water stops? Explain your answer.

Assessment

22. Which is the quotient of $0.42 \div 1.4$?

Ⓐ 30

Ⓑ 3

Ⓒ 0.3

Ⓓ 0.03

23. Which is the quotient of $3.36 \div 3.2$?

Ⓐ 105

Ⓑ 10.5

Ⓒ 1.05

Ⓓ 0.105

Name ____________________

Help | Practice Buddy | Tools | Games

Homework & Practice 6-6

Use Number Sense to Divide Decimals

Another Look!

How are the dividend, divisor, and quotient related in decimal division?

Example	Divisor	Quotient
4.41 ÷ 0.3 = 14.7	Less than 1	Greater than the dividend
4.41 ÷ 4.5 = 0.98	Close to dividend	Close to 1
4.41 ÷ 9.8 = 0.45	Greater than the dividend	Less than 1

In the last example, the dividend, 4.41, is about half of the divisor, 9.8, and the quotient, 0.45, is close to 0.5 or $\frac{1}{2}$.

1. Without dividing, consider what you know about the quotient of 4.7 ÷ 15.25. Fill in the blanks.

What is the divisor? ________ What is the dividend? ________

Is the divisor less than 1? ________ Is the divisor greater than the dividend? ________

The quotient of 4.7 ÷ 15.25 is ________ than 1.

In **2–5**, use number sense to decide where the decimal point belongs in the quotient.

2. \$3.75 ÷ \$0.25 = 1 5 0 0

3. 2.28 ÷ 0.95 = 2 4 0

4. 4.08 ÷ 6.4 = 6 3 7 5

5. 730.5 ÷ 1.5 = 4 8 7

The decimal point in each of the quotients below may be in the wrong place. In **6–9**, use number sense to decide. If it is incorrect, give the correct quotient.

6. 0.36 ÷ 0.24 = 1.5

7. 2.6 ÷ 6.4 = 40.625

8. \$3.40 ÷ \$0.05 = \$6.80

9. 191.88 ÷ 23.4 = 8.2

10. **Number Sense** Is the quotient for 63.2 ÷ 0.8 greater than or less than 63.2? Explain.

11. **Critique Reasoning** Kelly says that 5 is a good estimate for 4.8 ÷ 0.9. Is she correct? Why?

12. At a gas station, the price of regular gas was $3.80 per gallon on Monday. The price increased to $3.85 per gallon on Tuesday. Round the price per gallon for each day to the nearest tenth of a dollar.

13. Jillian uses 1.41 pounds of almonds and 3.27 pounds of raisins to make a trail mix. Then she divides the trail mix equally into 6 bags. How much trail mix is in each bag?

14. A-Z **Vocabulary** Write a division equation with decimals. Identify the dividend, divisor, and quotient.

15. Last weekend, 1,270 students participated in the music festival. Write 1,270 in expanded form using exponents.

16. **Higher Order Thinking** The labels for the pictures show how fast a quarter horse can run in miles per hour and how fast a garden snail can move. About how many times as fast as the snail's speed is the quarter horse's speed? Explain.

Assessment

17. Which is the quotient 3.12 ÷ 6.5?

Ⓐ 0.048
Ⓑ 0.48
Ⓒ 4.8
Ⓓ 48

18. Which is the quotient 1.26 ÷ 0.15?

Ⓐ 0.084
Ⓑ 0.84
Ⓒ 8.4
Ⓓ 84

Name ______________________________

Solve

Lesson 6-7
Divide by a Decimal

I can ...
divide a decimal by another decimal.

I can also model with math to solve problems.

Solve & Share

Aaron buys erasers for his pencils. Each eraser costs $0.20. The total cost is $1.20. How many erasers does Aaron buy? ***Solve this problem any way you choose.***

Model with Math
You can model the problem using hundredth grids or other drawings.
Show your work!

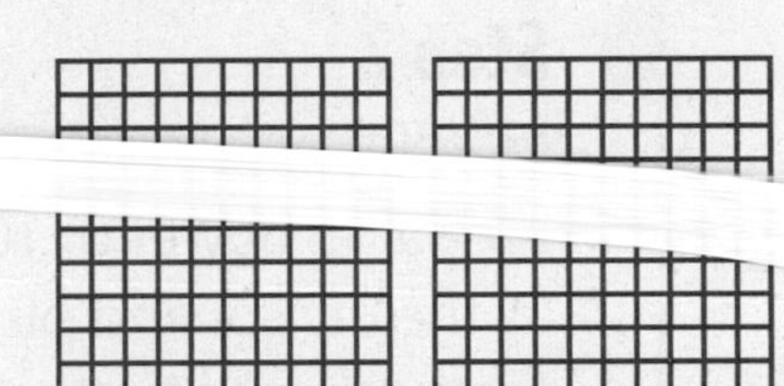

Look Back! Reasoning What power of 10 can you multiply both 1.20 and 0.20 by to get a whole number? What whole numbers do you get?

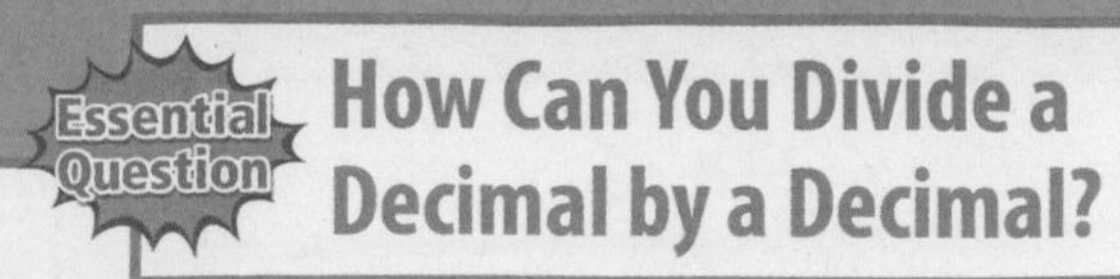

How Can You Divide a Decimal by a Decimal?

A

Michelle purchases several bottles of water. Before tax is added, the total cost is \$3.60 and the cost of each bottle is \$1.20. How many bottles did she buy?

Divide \$3.60 by \$1.20.

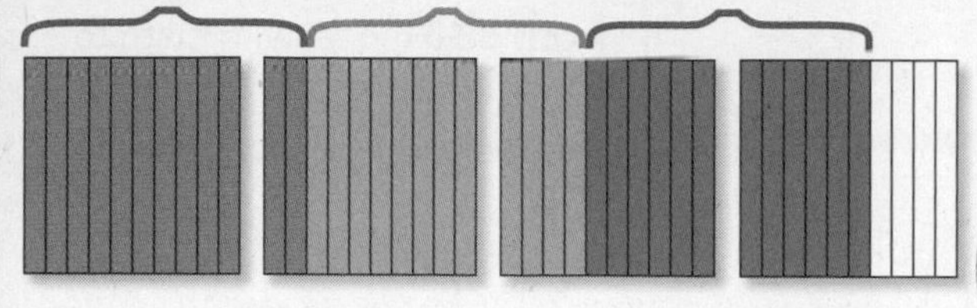

You can use grids to show how many groups of 1.2 are in 3.6. Remember that 1.20 = 1.2 and 3.60 = 3.6.

B

Step 1

Estimate the quotient:
$4 \div 1 = 4$

Multiply the divisor by a power of 10 so the product is a whole number.

$1.2\overline{)3.6}$

Multiply 1.2 by 10^1 or 10.

C

Step 2

Multiply the dividend by the same power of 10 as the divisor and place the decimal point in the quotient.

$1.2\overline{)3.6}$ $\quad 1.2 \times 10 = 12$
$\quad 3.6 \times 10 = 36$

So, find $12\overline{)36.}$

D

Step 3

Divide.

$$\begin{array}{r} 3 \\ 12\overline{)36} \\ -\,36 \\ \hline 0 \end{array}$$

3 is close to the estimate of 4, so the answer is reasonable.

Michelle purchased 3 bottles of water.

Convince Me! **Construct Arguments** Is $3.6 \div 1.2$ equal to, less than, or greater than $36 \div 12$? Explain.

Name ____________________

Guided Practice*

Do You Understand?

1. **Generalize** When dividing by a decimal, why can you multiply the divisor and dividend by the same power of 10?

2. What power of 10 would you multiply the dividend and divisor by to make 2.85 ÷ 0.95 easier to divide?

Do You Know How?

In **3–6**, find each quotient.

3. 2 ÷ 0.5

4. 1.25 ÷ 0.25

5. 2.1 ÷ 0.7

6. 6.6 ÷ 0.3

Think about how the dividend, divisor, and quotient are related.

Independent Practice

In **7–10**, write a power of 10 you would multiply the divisor by to make it a whole number. Then write the equivalent problem.

7. 23.56 ÷ 0.04

8. 73.2 ÷ 0.6

9. 0.3 ÷ 0.5

10. 2.73 ÷ 0.78

In **11–22**, find each quotient.

11. 0.25)0.62

12. 0.04)4.56

13. 0.05)0.02

14. 0.1)182.8

15. 0.03)17.25

16. 0.8)56.8

17. 0.06)6.24

18. 2.5)1.5

19. 5.5)24.2

20. 0.85)0.34

21. 0.09)0.36

22. 0.22)48.62

*For another example, see Set F on page 359.

Problem Solving

23. What number would you multiply the dividend and divisor by to make 5.72 ÷ 0.52 easier to divide?

24. **Be Precise** Carol bought 4 pork chops and 3 steaks. Each pork chop weighed 0.35 pound and each steak weighed 0.8 pound. How many pounds of meat did Carol buy in all?

25. **Construct Arguments** Tim estimates that 60 ÷ 5.7 is about 10. Will the actual quotient be greater than or less than 10? Explain.

26. **Reasoning** Dex estimates that 4,989 ÷ 0.89 is about 500. Is his estimate reasonable? Why or why not?

27. **Higher Order Thinking** Susan solves 1.4 ÷ 0.2 using the diagram at the right. Is her reasoning correct? Explain her thinking.

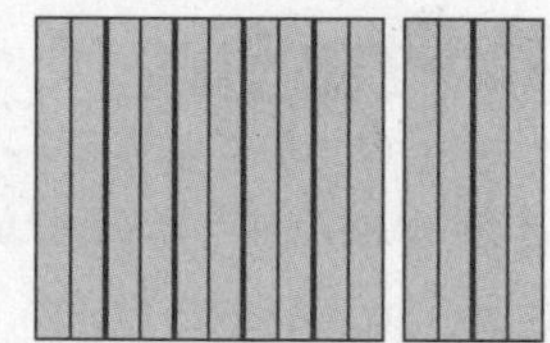

28. **Use Structure** The same dividend is divided by 0.1 and 0.01. How do the quotients compare? Explain your thinking.

29. **Vocabulary** Give three examples of a **power** of 10. Explain why one of your examples is a power of 10.

Assessment

30. Does the expression have a quotient of 4? Choose Yes or No.

2.8 ÷ 0.7	○ Yes	○ No
0.28 ÷ 7	○ Yes	○ No
2.8 ÷ 0.07	○ Yes	○ No
0.28 ÷ 0.07	○ Yes	○ No

31. Does the expression have a quotient of 9? Choose Yes or No.

1.35 ÷ 1.5	○ Yes	○ No
1.35 ÷ 0.15	○ Yes	○ No
13.5 ÷ 1.5	○ Yes	○ No
13.5 ÷ 0.15	○ Yes	○ No

Name ______________________________

Homework & Practice 6-7

Divide by a Decimal

Another Look!

Find $1.47 \div 0.42$.

Remember to multiply the divisor and the dividend by the same power of 10.

Step 1	Step 2	Step 3
Think of a power of 10 to multiply the divisor by so it is a whole number. 0.42 Multiply by 10^2 or 100.	Multiply the dividend by the same power of 10 and place the decimal point in the quotient. $0.42 \times 10^2 = 42$ $1.47 \times 10^2 = 147$ $0.42\overline{)1.47} = 42\overline{)147.}$	Divide. $\begin{array}{r} 3.5 \\ 42\overline{)147.0} \\ -126 \\ \hline 21\,0 \\ -21\,0 \\ \hline 0 \end{array}$ So, $1.47 \div 0.42 = 3.5$.

In **1–4**, write the power of 10 to multiply the divisor by to make it a whole number. Then write the equivalent problem.

1. $80.5 \div 3.5$ **2.** $12.74 \div 0.98$ **3.** $26.4 \div 0.3$ **4.** $1.65 \div 0.05$

In **5–16**, find each quotient.

5. $0.32\overline{)1.92}$ **6.** $3.5\overline{)21.7}$ **7.** $0.01\overline{)8.64}$ **8.** $0.4\overline{)0.3}$

9. $1.6\overline{)8.8}$ **10.** $3.4\overline{)79.9}$ **11.** $0.03\overline{)3.21}$ **12.** $0.75\overline{)5.25}$

13. $2.3\overline{)27.6}$ **14.** $0.07\overline{)1.05}$ **15.** $0.12\overline{)11.16}$ **16.** $0.04\overline{)8.52}$

17. **Model with Math** Three friends paid $26.25 to see a movie. How much did each ticket cost?

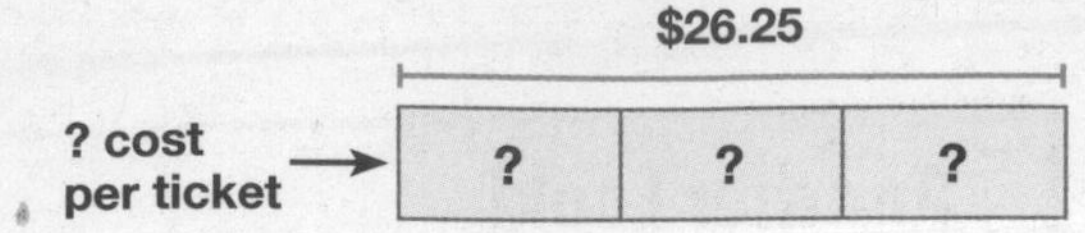

18. In a timed typing test, Lara typed 63 words per minute. Estimate the number of words she should be able to type in half an hour. Show your work.

19. A stack of sheets of tissue paper is about 2.5 inches high. Each sheet is about 0.01 inch thick. How many sheets are in the stack? Show your work.

20. **Reasoning** Is the quotient for $41 \div 0.8$ greater or less than 41? Explain.

21. **Construct Arguments** How does the quotient $10.5 \div 1.5$ compare to the quotient $105 \div 15$? Explain.

22. **Number Sense** The fence next to the creek near Adam's house leans a little more each year because the bank of the creek is eroding. If the fence leans about 3.7 degrees more each year, estimate how many more degrees the fence will lean after 5 years.

23. **Higher Order Thinking** The Clark family must pay $2,820 in property tax on their home this year. Their house payment is $752 per month. What is their payment each month with the tax? Assume that the tax is paid in equal monthly installments.

✔ Assessment

24. Does the expression have a quotient of 8? Choose Yes or No.

$0.56 \div 0.07$	○ Yes	○ No
$0.56 \div 0.7$	○ Yes	○ No
$5.6 \div 0.07$	○ Yes	○ No
$5.6 \div 0.7$	○ Yes	○ No

25. Does the expression have a quotient of 4? Choose Yes or No.

$4.8 \div 0.12$	○ Yes	○ No
$4.8 \div 1.2$	○ Yes	○ No
$0.48 \div 1.2$	○ Yes	○ No
$0.48 \div 0.12$	○ Yes	○ No

Name ______________________________

Solve & Share

Steven feeds his rabbit 2.4 pounds of food each week. How many weeks will a bag of food last?

Lesson 6-8

Continue to Divide with Decimals

I can ...
divide decimals by adding one or more zeros to the dividend if necessary.

I can also generalize from examples.

Look Back! Make Sense and Persevere How can you check that your answer to the problem makes sense?

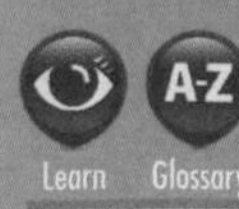

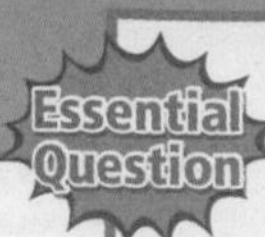

How Does Annexing Zeros to the Dividend Help You Divide Decimals?

A

How much protein is in 1 liter of orange juice?

Divide 9.12 by 1.5.

1.5 liters
9.12 grams protein

Sometimes you need to annex zeros to the dividend so you can keep dividing.

B

Step 1

Estimate the quotient. Use multiplication and number sense.

$\blacksquare \times 1.5 = 9.12$

$1 \times 1.5 = 1.5$

$\leftarrow 9.12$

$10 \times 1.5 = 15$

Since 9.12 is between 1.5 and 15, the quotient is between 1 and 10.

C

Step 2

Multiply the divisor and dividend by the same power of 10 to make the divisor a whole number. Then place the decimal point in the quotient.

$1.5\overline{)9.12} = 15\overline{)91.2}$

D

Step 3

Divide. Annex zeros as needed.

$$\begin{array}{r} 6.08 \\ 15\overline{)91.20} \\ -\underline{90} \\ 1\,2 \\ -\underline{0} \\ 1\,20 \\ -\underline{1\,20} \\ 0 \end{array}$$

6.08 is between 1 and 10, so the answer is reasonable.

1 liter of orange juice contains 6.08 grams of protein.

Convince Me! **Be Precise** Show how to check that the quotient is correct.

Name ____

Practice Buddy Tools Assessment

Guided Practice*

Do You Understand?

1. Janie solved 5.4 ÷ 1.2. Gary solved 4.8 ÷ 1.6. Why did Janie place a zero to the right of the dividend but Gary did not?

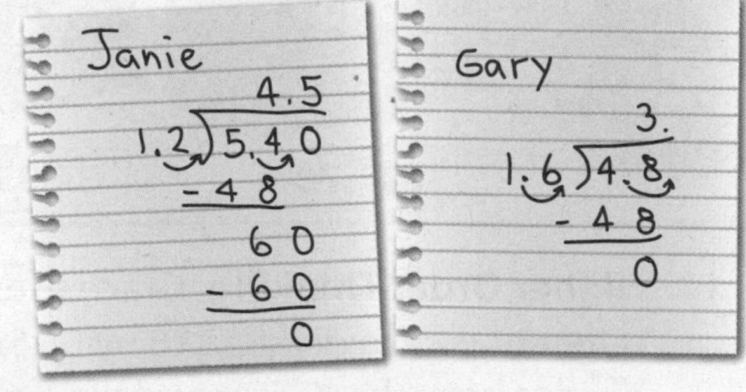

Do You Know How?

In **2–5**, find each quotient. Annex zeros as needed.

2. $1.8\overline{)0.72}$ **3.** $0.45\overline{)4.14}$

4. 5.6 ÷ 0.14 **5.** 0.76 ÷ 0.25

Independent Practice

In **6–14**, find each quotient. Annex zeros as needed.

6. $0.32\overline{)2.08}$ **7.** $0.43\overline{)3.01}$ **8.** $6.2\overline{)6.51}$

9. 35 ÷ 0.5 **10.** 102.3 ÷ 4.4 **11.** 9.3 ÷ 0.31

12. 25.44 ÷ 0.06 **13.** 90 ÷ 0.45 **14.** 3.24 ÷ 0.48

*For another example, see Set F on page 359.

Problem Solving

15. A lawn service is treating grass with weed killer. They mix 2.5 gallons of weed killer with water for each acre of grass. How many acres can they treat with 18.5 gallons of weed killer?

16. Cindy paid $1.74 for 0.25 pound of tuna salad. What was the cost of 1 pound of tuna salad?

17. **Construct Arguments** Which bag of charcoal costs less per pound? Explain.

Divide the price by the number of pounds for each bag to compare each cost.

$11.70 **$4.95**

18. **Make Sense and Persevere** Tickets to a rock concert cost $32.50 each. The school choir bought 54 tickets for the Saturday concert and 33 tickets for the Sunday concert. How much did the choir pay in all for the tickets?

19. **Higher Order Thinking** Grace uses a different way to divide 2.16 by 0.25. She divides both the divisor and dividend by 0.01 to make an equivalent problem with a whole-number divisor. Is her work correct? Explain.

Assessment

20. Which is the quotient 3.57 ÷ 0.84?

Ⓐ 0.0425
Ⓑ 0.425
Ⓒ 4.25
Ⓓ 42.5

21. A 2.5-liter tub of ice cream contains 93.5 grams of saturated fat. How many grams of saturated fat are in one liter of ice cream?

Ⓐ 0.364 gram
Ⓑ 37.4 grams
Ⓒ 36.4 grams
Ⓓ 3.74 grams

Name ____________________

Homework & Practice 6-8

Continue to Divide with Decimals

Another Look!

The cost of a taxi ride to the airport is \$48.06. The cost per mile is \$0.72. How many miles is the taxi ride?

Estimate the quotient by rounding: $48 \div 1 = 48$. The actual answer is greater than 48.06, the dividend, because the divisor is less than 1.

Multiply the divisor and dividend by the same power of 10 to make the divisor a whole number. Place the decimal point in the quotient.

$0.72\overline{)48.06} = 72\overline{)4806.}$

Divide. Annex zeros as needed.

$$\begin{array}{r} 66.75 \\ 72\overline{)4806.00} \\ -432 \\ 486 \\ -432 \\ 540 \\ -504 \\ 360 \\ -360 \\ 0 \end{array}$$

The taxi ride is 66.75 miles long.

The answer is reasonable because it is close to the estimate.

In **1–9**, find each quotient. Annex zeros as needed.

1. $0.64\overline{)5.44}$

2. $0.28\overline{)1.12}$

3. $4.2\overline{)12.81}$

4. $0.5\overline{)65}$

5. $4.8\overline{)85.2}$

6. $0.17\overline{)6.8}$

7. $0.07\overline{)32.34}$

8. $0.75\overline{)60}$

9. $0.35\overline{)2.352}$

10. Show how to check your answer to Exercise 9.

11. Olivia bought a piece of ribbon priced at \$0.56 per yard. The total cost was \$1.54. How many yards did she buy?

12. **Math and Science** A *therm* is a unit of heat. The Hogans pay \$0.38 per therm of natural gas. In September, they paid \$19.57 for natural gas. How many therms did they use?

13. A jewelry designer makes rings with different gemstones. List the gemstones in order from least to greatest mass.

14. How many times as great as the mass of each emerald is the mass of each sapphire?

DATA

Gemstone	Mass (grams)
Diamond	0.145
Ruby	0.206
Sapphire	0.315
Emerald	0.18

15. **Critique Reasoning** Neil has a \$20 gift certificate for an online store. He wants to buy 5 apps priced at \$0.99 each and headphones priced at \$15.49, including shipping and tax. He uses rounding to estimate the total cost: $(5 \times \$1) + \$15 = \$20$. Neil says his gift certificate is worth more than the total cost. Is Neil correct? Explain.

16. **Higher Order Thinking** Use the fact that $4.86 \div 0.45 = 10.8$. Find $4.86 \div 4.5$ without dividing. Explain your work.

✓ Assessment

17. Which is the quotient for $0.9 \div 0.75$?

Ⓐ 102

Ⓑ 12

Ⓒ 0.12

Ⓓ 1.2

18. Julia pays \$4.56 to ship a package that weighs 9.5 ounces. Which is the cost to ship 1 ounce?

Ⓐ \$0.48

Ⓑ \$0.46

Ⓒ 4.8¢

Ⓓ \$4.80

Name ___________________________

Problem Solving

Lesson 6-9

Reasoning

I can ...
make sense of quantities and relationships in problem situations.

I can also solve decimal problems.

Solve & Share

Aaron has three slabs of beeswax. He plans to melt them and use all of the wax to form 36 candles. If all the candles are the same size and weight, how much will each candle weigh? Use reasoning to decide.

BEESWAX 8.2 lb

BEESWAX 8.1 lb

BEESWAX 8.9 lb

Thinking Habits

Be a good thinker! These questions can help you.

- What do the numbers and symbols in the problem mean?
- How are the numbers or quantities related?
- How can I represent a word problem using pictures, numbers, or equations?

Look Back! Reasoning Suppose Aaron wants each candle to weigh 0.5 pound. How many candles could he make with the beeswax?

How Can You Use Reasoning to Solve Problems?

A

Ms. Watson is mixing mint green paint for her art class. She combines full bottles of blue, yellow, and white paint. How many 3.5-fluid ounce jars can she fill? Use reasoning to decide.

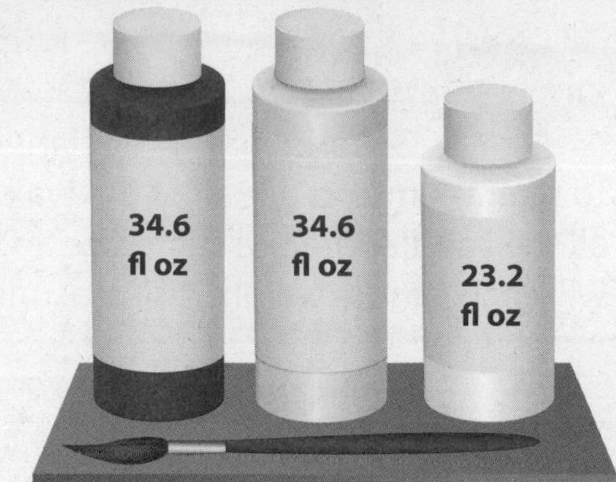

What do I need to do to solve this problem?

I need to add the three quantities of paint. Then I need to divide the sum by the capacity of a jar.

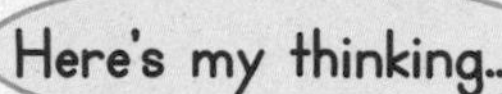

B

How can I use reasoning to solve this problem?

I can

- identify the quantities I know.
- draw a bar diagram to show relationships.
- give the answer using the correct unit.

C

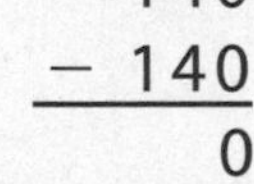

Use bar diagrams to show how the quantities are related.

First, find the sum of the three quantities of paint in the mixture.

? total number of fluid ounces

34.6	34.6	23.2

$$\begin{array}{r} 34.6 \\ 34.6 \\ +\ 23.2 \\ \hline 92.4 \end{array}$$

Then, divide 92.4 by 3.5 to find the number of jars that can be filled. Annex zeros as needed.

92.4

3.5 → ?

$$\begin{array}{r} 26.4 \\ 3.5\overline{)92.40} \\ -\ 70 \\ \hline 224 \\ -\ 210 \\ \hline 140 \\ -\ 140 \\ \hline 0 \end{array}$$

Ms. Watson can fill 26 jars. The 27th jar will be only partially filled.

Convince Me! Reasoning Ms. Watson is mixing 34.6 fluid ounces of red paint and 18.6 fluid ounces of yellow paint to make orange paint. How many 3.5-fluid ounce jars can she fill? Use reasoning to decide.

Name ______________________________

Guided Practice*

Reasoning

Miranda mixed 34.5 fluid ounces of blue paint, 40.5 fluid ounces of red paint, and 2 fluid ounces of black paint to make purple paint. She poured the same amount of the purple paint into each of 14 jars. How much paint did she pour in each jar?

Use reasoning to decide how the quantities in the problem are related.

1. Explain what each of the quantities in the problem means.

2. Describe one way to solve the problem.

3. What is the solution to the problem? Explain.

Independent Practice

Reasoning

Sue made chicken soup by combining the entire can of soup shown with a full can of water. How many 10-fluid ounce bowls can she fill with the soup? How much soup will be left over?

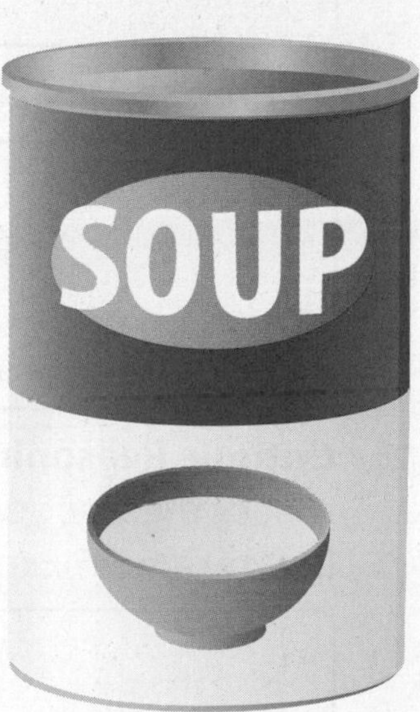

18.6 fl oz

4. Explain what each of the quantities in the problem means.

5. Describe one way to solve the problem.

6. What is the solution to the problem? Explain.

*For another example, see Set G on page 360.

Problem Solving

Performance Assessment

Cooking Competition

Lucas's cooking class is having a cooking competition. There are 6 teams. Each student brought supplies that will be shared equally among the teams. The table shows the supplies Lucas brought. If the supplies are shared equally among the teams, how much of each supply will each team get?

DATA

Competition Supplies	Price
2 sacks of flour, 4.5 pounds per sack	\$2.67 per sack
3 boxes of rice, 3.5 cups per box	\$1.89 per box
15 pounds of ground turkey	\$2.36 per pound

7. Make Sense and Persevere Do you need all of the information given above to solve the problem? Explain.

8. Reasoning Describe how to solve the problem.

9. Model with Math Write equations to represent how much of each supply each team will get.

10. Be Precise What is the solution to the problem? Explain.

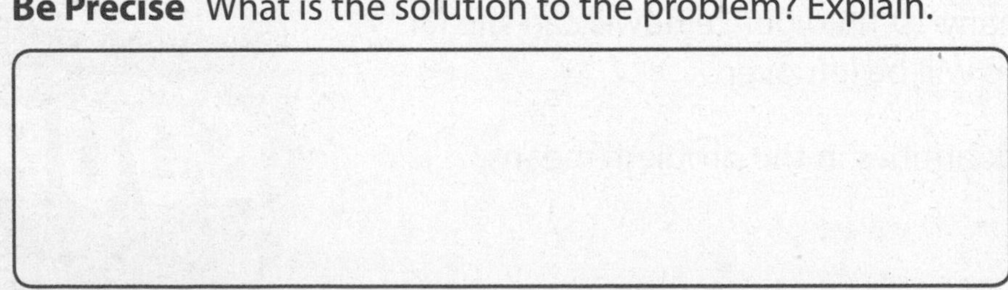

11. Critique Reasoning Lucas says that to find the total cost of the rice, you should multiply 3.5 by \$1.89. Do you agree? Explain.

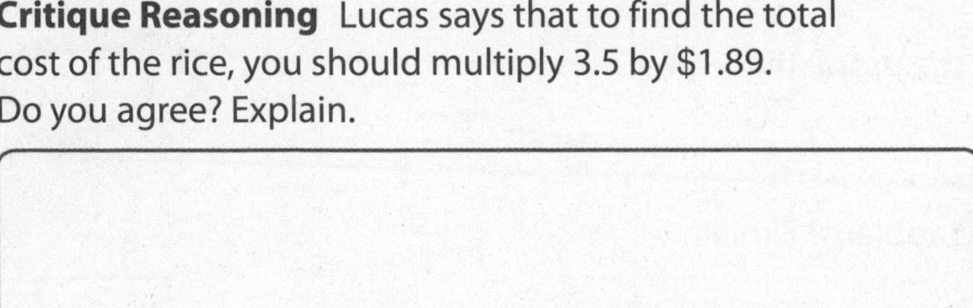

Name ___________________________

Homework & Practice 6-9
Reasoning

Another Look!

Kim bought granola bars for the soccer team. Each granola bar cost \$0.89. She paid \$38.13, including \$0.75 for sales tax. How many granola bars did she buy?

Tell how you can use reasoning to solve the problem.

- I can write an equation to show relationships.
- I can give the answer using the correct unit.

Write an equation to find the total cost of the granola bars before tax.

\$38.13 − \$0.75 = \$37.38

Divide to find the number of granola bars.

```
       42
0.89)37.38
    −356
      178
     −178
        0
```

So, Kim bought 42 granola bars for the soccer team.

Reasoning

Over the summer, Mr. Patel refilled a bird feeder 24 times using 6 cups of seed each time. A bag of seed holds 32 cups. How many bags of seed did Mr. Patel use?

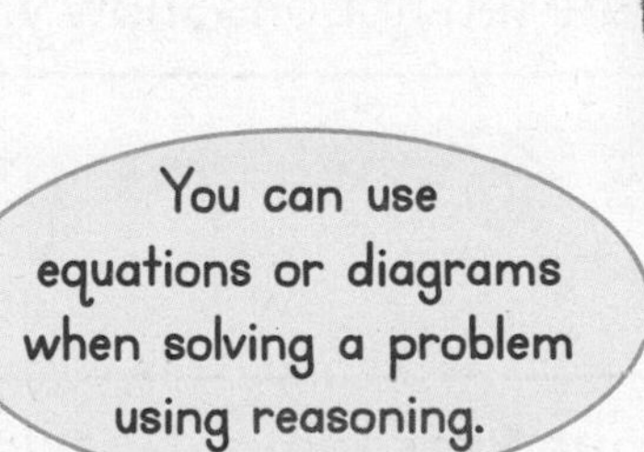

1. Describe one way to solve the problem.

2. Write an equation or draw bar diagrams to represent the problem.

3. What is the solution to the problem? Explain.

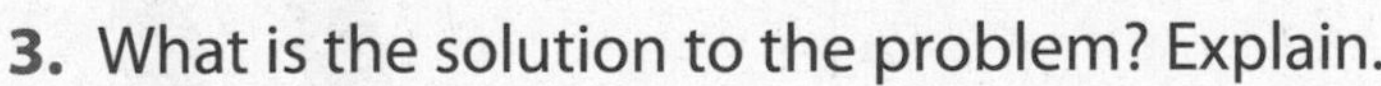

Performance Assessment

Greeting Cards
Jana is making greeting cards that are 4 inches long and 3.5 inches wide to sell at a craft fair. She decorates each card by putting a strip of red ribbon along the border all the way around the card. The table shows the amount of ribbon she has on hand.

DATA

Ribbon	Length (inches)
Gold	144
Red	96
Orange	152

4. Make Sense and Persevere Explain what each of the quantities means. Are all of the quantities given in the same units?

5. Model with Math Draw a diagram of the card and show how it is decorated. Label the width and length of the card.

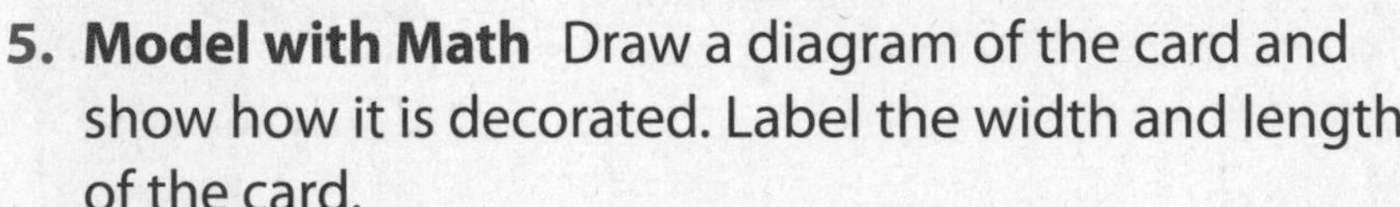

6. Reasoning How could you determine the amount of red ribbon needed for one card?

7. Be Precise How many greeting cards can Jana decorate with the red ribbon? Show your work.

8. Critique Reasoning Jana decides to make some additional cards that are 7.5 inches long and 5 inches wide. She glues a strip of gold ribbon along each of the longer sides. She says that since $144 \div 7.5 = 19.2$, she can decorate 19 cards with gold ribbon. Do you agree? Explain.

Remember, you can use reasoning to find the amount of ribbon needed for each card.

Name ______________________________

Fluency Practice Activity

Follow the Path

Solve each problem. Follow products that are multiples of 20 to shade a path from **START** to **FINISH**. You can only move up, down, right, or left.

I can ...
multiply multi-digit whole numbers.

Start				
120 × 35	745 × 30	123 × 37	350 × 63	241 × 67
312 × 40	300 × 80	486 × 40	860 × 36	523 × 28
526 × 45	101 × 57	670 × 35	606 × 90	647 × 27
105 × 50	273 × 73	475 × 85	464 × 65	173 × 23
710 × 71	157 × 86	243 × 42	660 × 16	12,345 × 76
				Finish

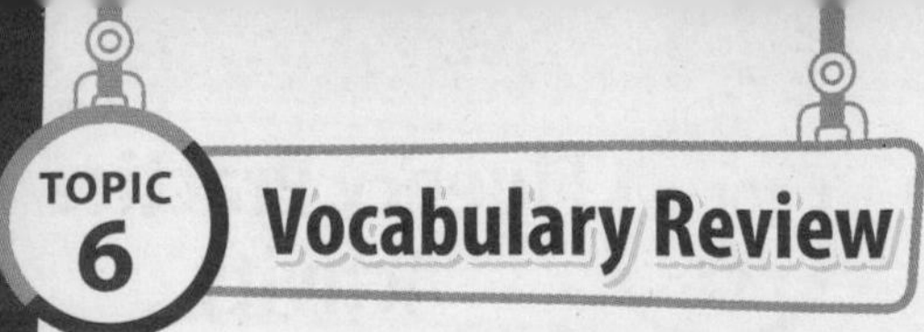

Glossary

Word List

- estimate
- exponent
- hundredths
- power
- quotient
- rounding
- tenths
- thousandths

Understand Vocabulary

Write *always, sometimes,* or *never.*

1. A digit in the hundredths place has $\frac{1}{10}$ the value of the same digit in the tenths place. ______________

2. The answer to a division problem is less than the divisor.
____

3. A whole number divided by a decimal number is a whole number. ______________

4. Dividing by 10^3 moves the decimal point in the dividend three places to the left. ______________

5. Multiplying the dividend and the divisor by the same power of 10 changes the quotient. ______________

6. The answer to a division problem is greater than the divisor.
____

Write T for true or F for false.

______ **7.** $3.65 \div 5.2 < 1$

______ **8.** $48 \div 0.6 = 0.8$

______ **9.** $2.42 \div 2.1 > 1$

______ **10.** $4.9 \div 0.8 < 4.9$

Use Vocabulary in Writing

11. Mary says the digits in the quotient of $381.109 \div 0.86$ are 4 4 3 1 5, but she doesn't know where to place the decimal point. How can Mary use number sense to place the decimal point? Use at least three terms from the Word List in your answer.

Name ______________________________

TOPIC 6

Reteaching

Set A pages 301–306

Find 340.5 ÷ 100.

Dividing by 10, or 10^1, means moving the decimal point one place to the left.

Dividing by 100, or 10^2, means moving the decimal point two places to the left.

Dividing by 1,000, or 10^3, means moving the decimal point three places to the left.

$340.5 \div 10^2 = 3.405 = 3.405$

Remember that when dividing decimals by a power of 10, you may need to use one or more zeros as placeholders.

Use mental math to find each quotient.

1. $34.6 \div 10^1$
2. $6{,}483 \div 10^2$
3. 148.3 ÷ 100
4. $29.9 \div 10^1$
5. 70.7 ÷ 10
6. $5{,}913 \div 10^3$

Set B pages 307–312

Estimate 27.3 ÷ 7.1. Use compatible numbers.

27.3 ÷ 7.1
↓ ↓
28 ÷ 7 = 4

So, 27.3 ÷ 7.1 is about 4.

Estimate 42.5 ÷ 11. Use rounding.

42.5 ÷ 11
↓ ↓
40 ÷ 10 = 4

So, 42.5 ÷ 11 is about 4.

Remember that compatible numbers are numbers that are easy to compute in your head.

Write a number sentence that shows a way to estimate each quotient.

1. 26.2 ÷ 5
2. 49.6 ÷ 7.8
3. 121 ÷ 12.75
4. 32.41 ÷ 10.9
5. 82.4 ÷ 3.7
6. 28.5 ÷ 0.94

Set C pages 313–318, 319–324

Find 1.14 ÷ 3.

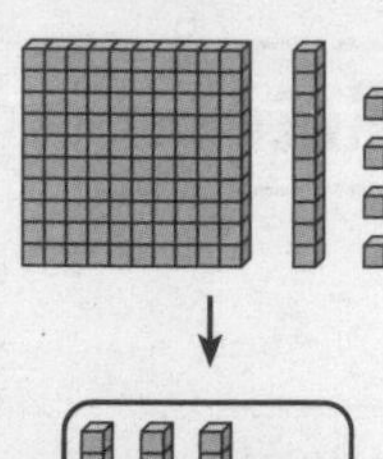

Estimate first.
1.14 ÷ 3 is less than 1, so start dividing in the tenths place.

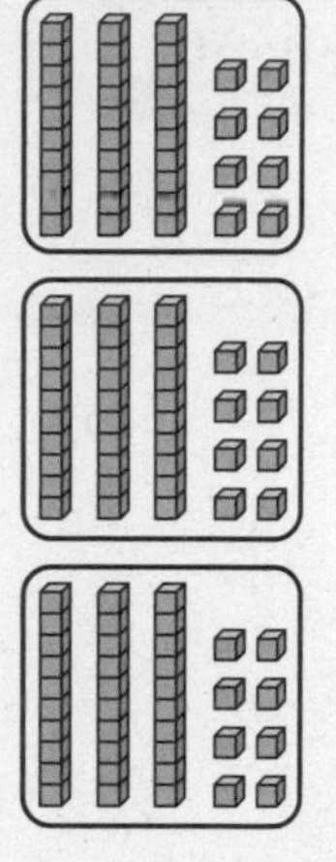

$$\begin{array}{r} 0.38 \\ 3\overline{)1.14} \\ -\ 9 \\ \hline 24 \\ -\ 24 \\ \hline 0 \end{array}$$

Remember to place the decimal point in the quotient above the decimal point in the dividend. Annex zeros as needed.

Divide. Use models to help.

1. 6.58 ÷ 7
2. 156 ÷ 8
3. 34.2 ÷ 3
4. 5.84 ÷ 4
5. Michelle pays $66.85 for a costume pattern and 8 yards of fabric. The costume pattern costs $4.85. How much does each yard of the fabric cost?

Set D pages 325–330

Find 94.5 ÷ 15.

Estimate first.

94.5 ÷ 15 is close to 100 ÷ 20 = 5, so start dividing with the ones place.

$$\begin{array}{r} 6.3 \\ 15\overline{)94.5} \\ -\ 90 \\ \hline 45 \\ -\ 45 \\ \hline 0 \end{array}$$

So, 94.5 ÷ 15 = 6.3.

Remember that you can check your calculation by multiplying the quotient by the divisor.

Find each quotient.

1. 91.2 ÷ 16
2. 361.5 ÷ 15
3. 29.04 ÷ 22
4. 144 ÷ 45
5. A 12-ounce bottle of shampoo costs $4.20. A 16-ounce bottle costs $6.88. Which shampoo costs less per ounce? How do you know?

Name ______________________________

TOPIC 6

Reteaching
Continued

Set E pages 331–336

The decimal point is missing in the quotient below. Use number sense to place the decimal point correctly.

4.35 ÷ 5.8 = 750

The divisor, 5.8, is greater than the dividend, 4.35, so the quotient will be less than 1. The decimal point should be placed before the 7.

So, 4.35 ÷ 5.8 = .750 or 0.75.

Remember that if the divisor is less than the dividend, the quotient will be greater than 1.

Use number sense to correctly place the decimal point.

1. 339.48 ÷ 6.9 = 492

2. 18.72 ÷ 15.6 = 120

3. 7.77 ÷ 21 = 370

4. 4,185.44 ÷ 7.4 = 5656

Set F pages 337–342, 343–348

Find 57.9 ÷ 0.6.

Since 0.6 has one decimal place, move the decimal point one place to the right in both the divisor and the dividend. Then divide.

```
      96.5
0.6)57.90
    54
     39
     36
      30
      30
       0
```

Annex more zeros in the dividend if needed.

So, 57.9 ÷ 0.6 = 96.5.

Remember to place the decimal point in the quotient above the decimal point in the dividend before dividing.

1. 84 ÷ 3.2 **2.** 81 ÷ 3.6

3. 16.4 ÷ 0.8 **4.** 136.5 ÷ 4.2

5. 22.22 ÷ 2.2 **6.** 54.78 ÷ 6.6

7. 71.04 ÷ 7.4 **8.** 40.02 ÷ 8.7

9. 9.6 ÷ 0.03 **10.** 74.48 ÷ 9.8

Set G pages 349–354

Think about these questions to help you **reason abstractly and quantitatively.**

Thinking Habits

- What do the numbers and symbols in the problem mean?
- How are the numbers or quantities related?
- How can I represent a word problem using pictures, numbers, or equations?

Zoey has a goal of saving $750 for a vacation. Her vacation will last 6 days. She wants to save the same amount each week for 12 weeks to reach her goal. How much should she save each week?

Which quantities do you need to solve the problem?

The savings goal is $750; Zoey will save for 12 weeks.

Will Zoey need to save more than or less than $80 each week? Explain your reasoning.

Less than; 12 × $80 = $960, but she only needs to save $750.

How much should she save each week? Write an equation to represent the problem.

$62.50; $750 ÷ 12 = $62.50

Remember to check the reasonableness of a solution by making sure your calculations are correct, and that you answered all of the questions that were asked.

Ian uses 4 feet of ribbon to wrap each package. How many packages can he wrap with 5.6 yards of ribbon?

Remember there are 3 feet in a yard.

1. Describe one way to solve the problem.

2. What is the solution to the problem? Show your work.

A bushel of apples weighs about 42 pounds. There are 4 pecks in a bushel. It takes 2 pounds of apples to make one pie. How many pies can you make with one peck of apples?

3. How are the numbers in the problem related?

4. Describe one way to solve the problem.

5. Solve the problem. Show your work.

Name ______________________________

1. Mr. Dodd filled the gas tank on his lawn mower with 3.8 gallons of gas. He mowed his yard 10 times on the same tank of gas. He used the same amount of gas each time. How much gas did he use each time?

   Ⓐ 0.038 gallon
   Ⓑ 0.38 gallon
   Ⓒ 38 gallons
   Ⓓ 380 gallons

2. Kimberly scored a total of 35.08 points in four events for her gymnastic competition. If she scored the same amount in each event, how many points did she score on each?

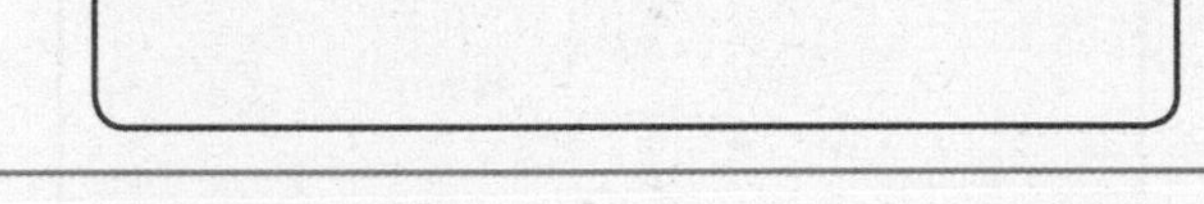

3. Draw lines to match each expression on the left with the correct quotient on the right. Use number sense and estimation to help.

Expression	Quotient
$21.6 \div 1.8$	22.5
$10.23 \div 0.55$	12
$78.75 \div 3.5$	6.45
$29.67 \div 4.6$	18.6

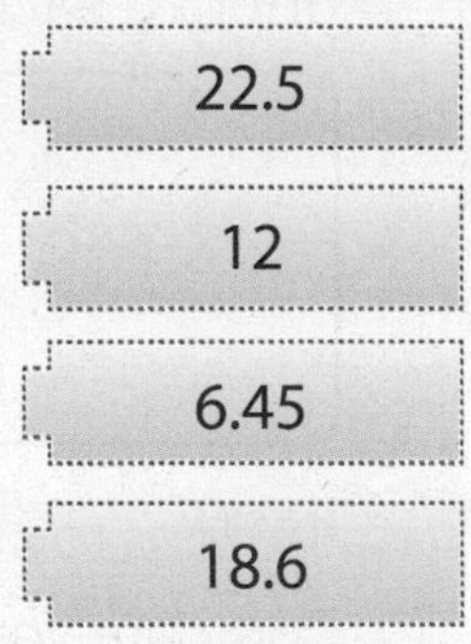

4. For questions 4a–4d, choose Yes or No to tell if the number 10^3 will make each equation true.

   4a. $8.5 \div \square = 0.085$ ○ Yes ○ No
   4b. $850 \div \square = 0.85$ ○ Yes ○ No
   4c. $8{,}500 \div \square = 8.5$ ○ Yes ○ No
   4d. $0.85 \div \square = 850$ ○ Yes ○ No

5. The chef at a restaurant bought 37 pounds of salad for $46.25. How much did she pay for each pound of salad?

   Ⓐ $0.125
   Ⓑ $1.25
   Ⓒ $1.30
   Ⓓ $12.50

6. Kathleen spent $231 on concert tickets for herself and 11 friends. Each ticket cost the same.

   Part A

   Estimate the cost of each ticket. Write an equation to show your work.

   Part B

   Find the exact cost of each ticket. Compare your answer to your estimate to check for reasonableness.

7. Choose all the expressions that are equal to $1.25 \div 10$.

   ☐ $12.5 \div 10^2$
   ☐ $0.125 \div 100$
   ☐ $1{,}250 \div 10^4$
   ☐ $12.5 \div 1$
   ☐ $125 \div 1{,}000$

8. Which division problem does the model Tess made represent?

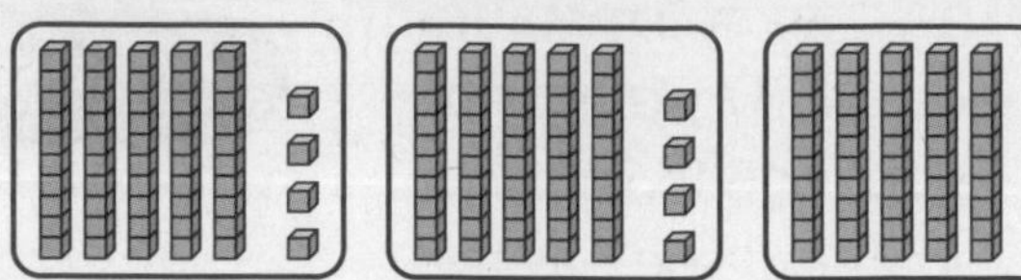

Ⓐ $1.35 \div 3 = 0.45$

Ⓑ $1.35 \div 3 = 0.54$

Ⓒ $1.62 \div 3 = 0.45$

Ⓓ $1.62 \div 3 = 0.54$

9. If 8 ounces of canned pumpkin have 82 calories, how many calories are in one ounce?

Ⓐ 16.25 calories

Ⓑ 12.5 calories

Ⓒ 10.25 calories

Ⓓ 10.025 calories

10. Marisol writes the equation $1.6 \div n = 0.016$.

Part A

What value of n makes the equation true? Write your answer using an exponent.

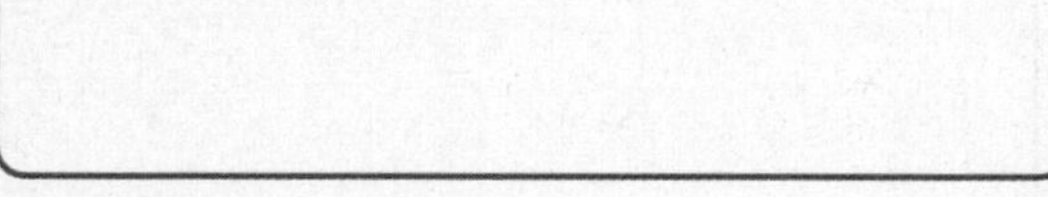

Part B

Explain how you know your answer is correct.

11. Eileen bought 8 roses for \$45.50. Which is the best way to estimate the cost of one rose?

Ⓐ $\$45 \div 5 = \$9.00$

Ⓑ $\$48 \div 8 = \$6.00$

Ⓒ $\$45 \div 10 = \$0.45$

Ⓓ $\$40 \div 8 = \$0.50$

12. Toby's faucet dripped a total of 1.92 liters of water in 24 hours. The faucet dripped the same amount each hour.

Part A

Estimate how many liters his faucet dripped each hour. Write an equation to model your work.

Part B

Find the exact amount of water that dripped each hour.

Part C

Compare your estimate to your answer. Is your answer reasonable? Explain.

Name ______________________________

13. Draw lines to match each expression on the left with the correct quotient on the right.

Expression	Quotient
$0.78 \div 10$	0.708
$708 \div 10^4$	0.078
$70.8 \div 10^2$	0.78
$780 \div 10^3$	0.0708

14. Diego is making a large mural. He draws a hexagon with a perimeter of 10.5 meters. Each side of the hexagon is the same length.

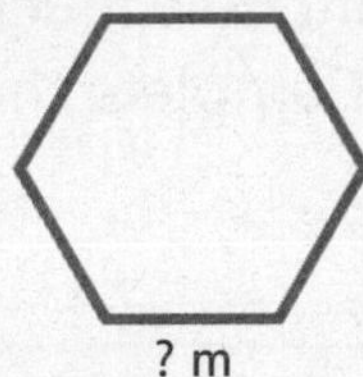

Part A

How many meters long is each side of Diego's hexagon? Write an equation to model your work.

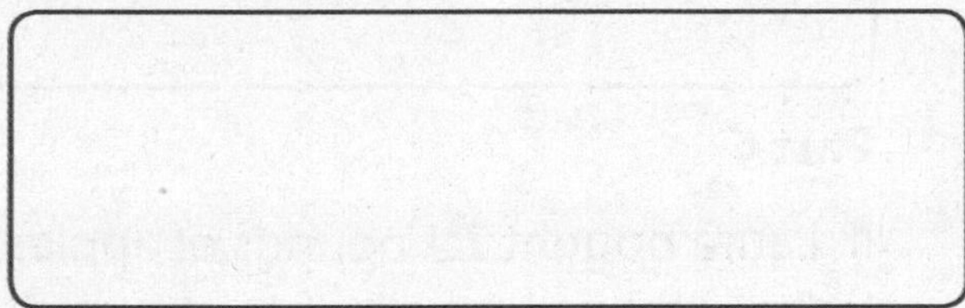

Part B

The total cost of the supplies to paint the mural is $38.70. Diego and 9 friends divide the total cost equally. How much does each person pay?

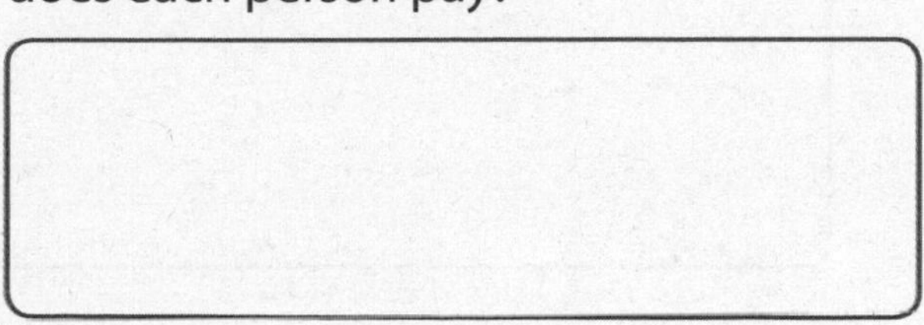

15. For questions 15a-15d, choose Yes or No to tell if the number 40.3 will make each equation true.

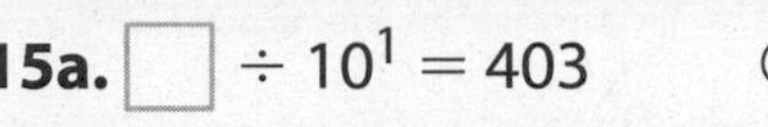

15a. $\square \div 10^1 = 403$ ○ Yes ○ No

15b. $\square \div 10^2 = 0.403$ ○ Yes ○ No

15c. $\square \div 10^0 = 40.3$ ○ Yes ○ No

15d. $\square \div 10^3 = 4.03$ ○ Yes ○ No

16. Lou's Diner spent $12.80 on 8 pounds of potatoes. What was the cost of one pound of potatoes?

17. How many quarters are there in $30? Solve the equation $30 \div 0.25$ to help you.

Ⓐ 12 quarters

Ⓑ 20 quarters

Ⓒ 120 quarters

Ⓓ 200 quarters

18. A group of 5 friends bought a bag of grapes to share equally. If the bag of grapes weighs 10.25 pounds, how much is each person's share? Write an equation to model your work.

19. Choose all the expressions that are equal to $6.1 \div 10^2$.

- ☐ $61 \div 1{,}000$
- ☐ $6.1 \div 10^5$
- ☐ $0.61 \div 10$
- ☐ $6{,}100 \div 10^6$
- ☐ $0.61 \div 10^3$

20. Karen divided 560.9 by 10^3 and got a quotient of 0.5609. Julio thinks the quotient should be 5.609. Who is correct? Explain your answer.

21. June says that there should be a decimal point in the quotient below after the 4. Is she correct? Use number sense to explain your answer.

$43.94 \div 5.2 = 845$

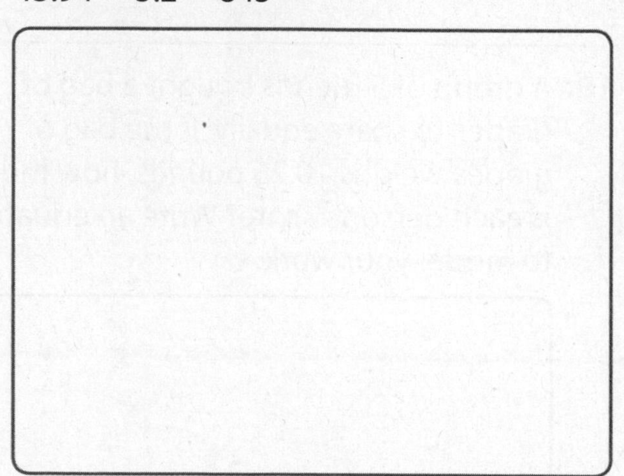

22. Three coworkers decided to buy fruit to share at lunchtime. Antonio spent $1.47 on bananas. Laura spent $2.88 on apples. Suzanne spent $2.85 on oranges.

Part A

Complete the bar diagram to find out how much they spent in all on fruit.

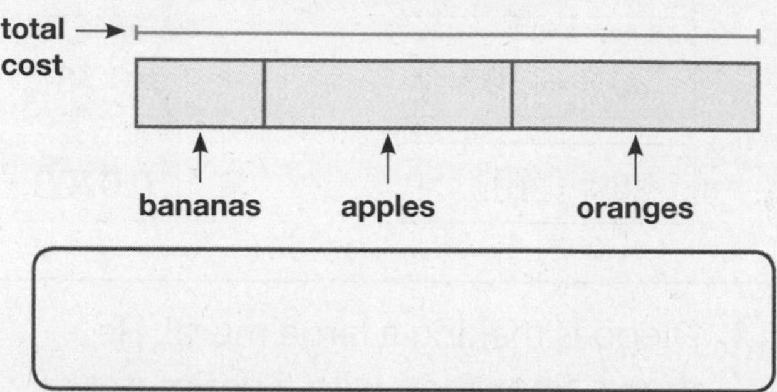

Part B

They evenly divided the cost of the 3 types of fruit. How much did each person pay? Complete the bar diagram to help you.

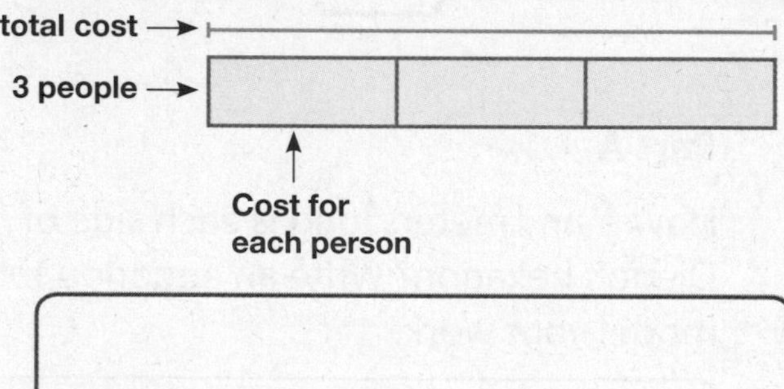

Part C

If Laura bought 2.1 pounds of apples, is the price per pound of apples greater than or less than $1? How can you tell?

Name ___________________________

TOPIC 6

Performance Assessment

Cooking Competition

Lydia is organizing a cooking competition at her school. She ordered some basic supplies to share among the teams that are competing. The teams will be bringing other ingredients as well.

Use the list at the right to answer the questions.

Cooking Supplies
738.4 grams, flour
8.25 liters, milk
5.4 liters, olive oil
87.6 grams, salt
36 eggs

1. If 10 of the teams divide the olive oil equally, how much will each team receive? Write an equation to model your work.

2. Eight teams agree to share the flour equally.

Part A

About how many grams of flour will each team get? Use compatible numbers to estimate. Write an equation to show how you estimated.

Part B

Find the actual amount of flour each team will receive. Show your work.

3. Several teams agree to share the salt equally. Each team will be given 7.3 grams of salt. How many teams agree to share the salt? Write a division equation to model the problem. Then write an equivalent equation using whole numbers.

4. Malcolm calculated how many liters of milk each team would get if 6 teams shared the milk equally. His work is shown at the right, but he forgot to place the decimal point in the quotient. Where should he place the decimal point? Explain.

$8.25 \div 6 = 1375$

5. Lydia decides to provide cheddar cheese for the competition. She buys 4.2 kilograms for $39.90.

Part A

She estimates the cost of 1 kilogram of cheese to be $1. Is her estimate reasonable? Explain.

Part B

To find the actual cost of 1 kilogram of cheese, Lydia needs to divide $39.90 by 4.2. How can she change the division problem to an equivalent problem using whole numbers? Write and solve the equivalent problem.

Part C

If 7 teams share the cheese equally, how much cheese will each team get?

Use Equivalent Fractions to Add and Subtract Fractions

Essential Questions: How can sums and differences of fractions and mixed numbers be estimated? What are standard procedures for adding and subtracting fractions and mixed numbers?

Did you know that the fossil of the oldest known flying mammal – a bat – was found in Wyoming?

Fossil evidence shows that around 50 million years ago, Earth's climate was warm, and land and oceans were filled with life.

Make no bones about it! You can find fossils of ancient animals today! Here's a project about fossils!

Math and Science Project: Fossils Tell Story

Do Research Use the Internet or other sources to find out more about fossils. What are fossils? How and where do we find them? What do they tell us about the past? What can they tell us about the future? Pay particular attention to fossils from the Eocene epoch.

Journal: Write a Report Include what you found. Also in your report:

- Describe a fossil that you have seen or would like to find.
- Tell if there are any fossils where you live.
- Make up and solve addition and subtraction problems with fractions and mixed numbers about fossils.

Name ______________________________

Review What You Know

Vocabulary

Choose the best term from the box. Write it on the blank.

- denominator
- numerator
- fraction
- unit fraction
- mixed number

1. A ______________ has a whole number part and a fraction part.

2. A ______________ represents the number of equal parts in one whole.

3. A ______________ has a numerator of 1.

4. A symbol used to name one or more parts of a whole or a set, or a location on the number line is a ______________.

Compare Fractions

Compare. Write >, <, or = for each ◯.

5. $\frac{1}{5}$ ◯ $\frac{1}{15}$

6. $\frac{17}{10}$ ◯ $\frac{17}{5}$

7. $\frac{5}{25}$ ◯ $\frac{2}{5}$

8. $\frac{12}{27}$ ◯ $\frac{6}{9}$

9. $\frac{11}{16}$ ◯ $\frac{2}{8}$

10. $\frac{2}{7}$ ◯ $\frac{1}{5}$

11. Liam bought $\frac{5}{8}$ pound of cherries. Harrison bought more cherries than Liam. Which could be the amount of cherries that Harrison bought?

Ⓐ $\frac{1}{2}$ pound Ⓑ $\frac{2}{5}$ pound Ⓒ $\frac{2}{3}$ pound Ⓓ $\frac{3}{5}$ pound

12. Jamie has read $\frac{1}{4}$ of a book. Raul has read $\frac{3}{4}$ of the same book. Who is closer to reading the whole book? Explain.

Equivalent Fractions

Write a fraction equivalent to each fraction.

13. $\frac{6}{18}$

14. $\frac{12}{22}$

15. $\frac{15}{25}$

16. $\frac{8}{26}$

17. $\frac{14}{35}$

18. $\frac{4}{18}$

19. $\frac{1}{7}$

20. $\frac{4}{11}$

A-Z Glossary

My Word Cards

Use the examples for each word on the front of the card to help complete the definitions on the back.

$\frac{1}{4}, \frac{1}{3}, \frac{1}{2}, \frac{2}{3}, \frac{3}{4}$

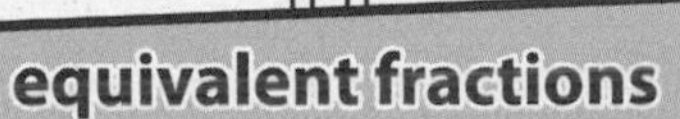

$\frac{1}{4} \times \frac{3}{3} = \frac{3}{12}$

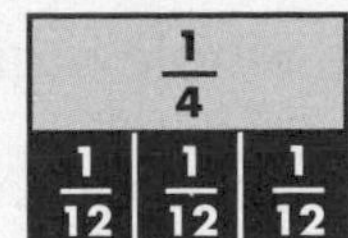

common denominator

$\frac{2 \times 5}{3 \times 5} = \frac{10}{15}$ $\frac{1 \times 3}{5 \times 3} = \frac{3}{15}$

15 is a common denominator for $\frac{2}{3}$ and $\frac{1}{5}$.

mixed number

$1\frac{2}{3}$

My Word Cards

Complete the definition. Extend learning by writing your own definitions.

______________ are fractions that name the same part of a whole region, length, or set.

Common fractions used for estimating, such as $\frac{1}{4}$, $\frac{1}{3}$, $\frac{1}{2}$, $\frac{2}{3}$, and $\frac{3}{4}$, are called ______________.

A number that has a whole-number part and a fractional part is called a ______________.

A ______________ is a number that is the denominator of two or more fractions.

Name ____________________

Solve

Lesson 7-1
Estimate Sums and Differences of Fractions

I can . . .
estimate sums and differences of fractions.

I can also reason about math.

Solve & Share

Jack needs about $1\frac{1}{2}$ yards of string. He has three pieces of string that are different lengths. Without finding the exact amount, which two pieces should he choose to get closest to $1\frac{1}{2}$ yards of string? ***Solve this problem any way you choose.***

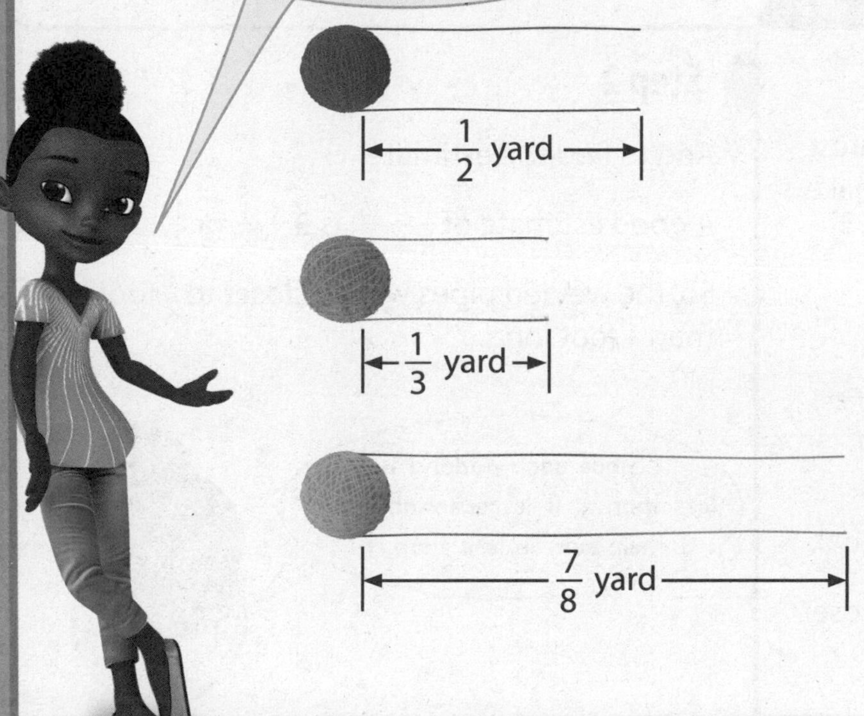

Look Back! Generalize How can a number line help you estimate?

Learn Glossary

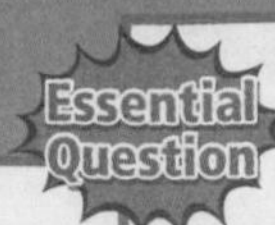

How Can You Estimate the Sum of Two Fractions?

A

Mr. Fish is welding together two copper pipes to repair a leak. He will use the pipes shown. Is the new pipe closer to $\frac{1}{2}$ foot or 1 foot long? Explain.

Estimate the sum $\frac{1}{6} + \frac{5}{12}$ to find about how long the combined pipes will be.

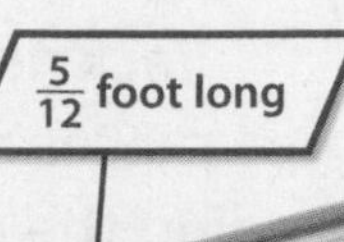

$\frac{5}{12}$ foot long

$\frac{1}{6}$ foot long

You can add to find the sum.

B

Step 1

Replace each fraction with the nearest half or whole. A number line can make it easy to decide if each fraction is closest to 0, $\frac{1}{2}$, or 1.

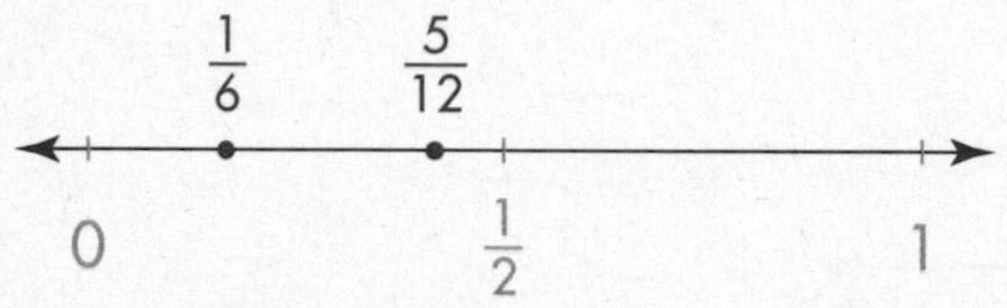

$\frac{1}{6}$ is between 0 and $\frac{1}{2}$, but is closer to 0.

$\frac{5}{12}$ is also between 0 and $\frac{1}{2}$, but is closer to the benchmark fraction $\frac{1}{2}$.

C

Step 2

Add to find the estimate.

A good estimate of $\frac{1}{6} + \frac{5}{12}$ is $0 + \frac{1}{2}$, or $\frac{1}{2}$.

So, the welded pipes will be closer to $\frac{1}{2}$ foot than 1 foot long.

Since each addend is less than $\frac{1}{2}$, it is reasonable that their sum is less than 1.

Convince Me! **Critique Reasoning** Nolini says that if the denominator is more than twice the numerator, the fraction can always be replaced with 0. Is she correct? Give an example in your explanation.

Name ____________________

Practice Buddy Tools Assessment

Guided Practice*

Do You Understand?

1. **Reasoning** In the problem at the top of page 372, would you get the same estimate if Mr. Fish's pipes measured $\frac{2}{6}$ foot and $\frac{7}{12}$ foot?

2. **Number Sense** If a fraction has a 1 in the numerator and a number greater than 2 in the denominator, will the fraction be closer to 0, $\frac{1}{2}$, or 1? Explain.

Do You Know How?

In **3** and **4**, use a number line to tell if each fraction is closest to 0, $\frac{1}{2}$, or 1. Then estimate the sum or difference.

3. 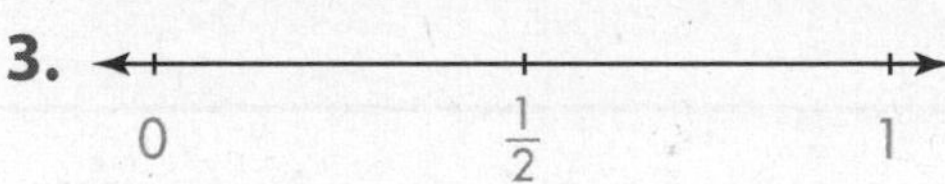

a $\frac{11}{12}$ **Closest to:** ______

b $\frac{1}{6}$ **Closest to:** ______

Estimate the sum $\frac{11}{12} + \frac{1}{6}$.

c 1 + ______ = ______

4. 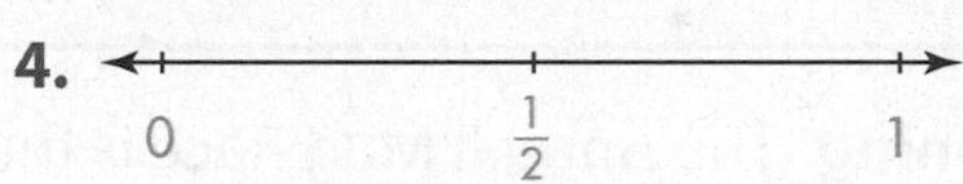

a $\frac{14}{16}$ **Closest to:** ______

b $\frac{5}{8}$ **Closest to:** ______

Estimate the difference $\frac{14}{16} - \frac{5}{8}$.

c ______ − ______ = ______

Independent Practice

Leveled Practice In **5**, use a number line to tell if each fraction is closest to 0, $\frac{1}{2}$, or 1. In **6–11**, estimate the sum or difference by replacing each fraction with 0, $\frac{1}{2}$, or 1.

5. 0 $\frac{1}{2}$ 1

a $\frac{7}{8}$ **Closest to:** ______

b $\frac{5}{12}$ **Closest to:** ______

Estimate the difference $\frac{7}{8} - \frac{5}{12}$.

c ______ − ______ = ______

6. $\frac{9}{10} + \frac{5}{6}$

7. $\frac{11}{18} - \frac{2}{9}$

8. $\frac{1}{16} + \frac{2}{15}$

9. $\frac{24}{25} - \frac{1}{9}$

10. $\frac{3}{36} + \frac{1}{10}$

11. $\frac{37}{40} - \frac{26}{50}$

*For another example, see Set A on page 445.

Problem Solving

12. **Number Sense** Name two fractions that are closer to 1 than to $\frac{1}{2}$. Then, name two fractions that are closer to $\frac{1}{2}$ than to 0 or 1 and two other fractions that are closer to 0 than to $\frac{1}{2}$. Find two of your fractions that have a sum of about $1\frac{1}{2}$.

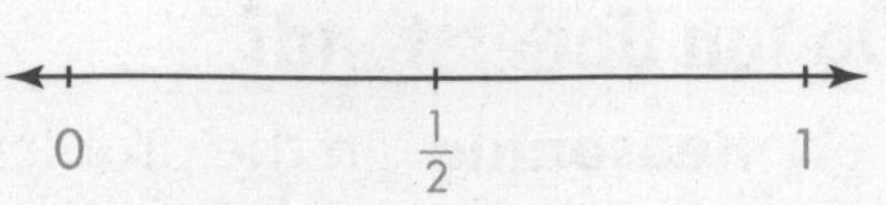

13. **Higher Order Thinking** How would you estimate whether $\frac{27}{50}$ is closer to $\frac{1}{2}$ or 1 without using a number line? Explain.

14. Katie made a bag of trail mix with $\frac{1}{2}$ cup of raisins, $\frac{3}{5}$ cup of banana chips, and $\frac{3}{8}$ cup of peanuts. About how much trail mix did Katie make?

15. **Reasoning** The Annual Mug Race is the longest river sailboat race in the world. The event is run along the St. Johns River, which is 310 miles long. About how many times as long as the race is the river?

Do you need an exact answer or an estimate? How do you know?

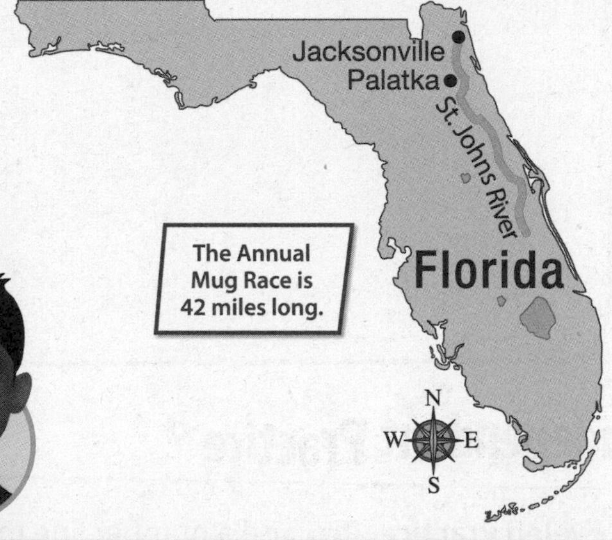

Assessment

16. Draw lines to match each expression on the left to its estimate on the right.

$\frac{11}{12} - \frac{5}{6}$	0
$\frac{5}{9} - \frac{1}{10}$	$\frac{1}{2}$
$\frac{15}{16} - \frac{1}{12}$	1

17. Draw lines to match each expression on the left to its estimate on the right.

$\frac{1}{30} + \frac{4}{6}$	0
$\frac{8}{9} + \frac{1}{5}$	$\frac{1}{2}$
$\frac{2}{20} + \frac{1}{12}$	1

Name ______________________

Help | Practice Buddy | Tools | Games

Homework & Practice 7-1

Estimate Sums and Differences of Fractions

Another Look!

Estimate $\frac{10}{12} - \frac{4}{9}$.

You can use halfway numbers to help decide if each fraction is closest to 0, to $\frac{1}{2}$, or to 1.

Step 1

Is $\frac{10}{12}$ closest to 0, $\frac{1}{2}$, or 1?

Find the halfway number between 0 and the denominator.

6 is halfway between 0 and 12.

Decide if the numerator is about the same as the halfway number, closer to 0, or closer to 12.

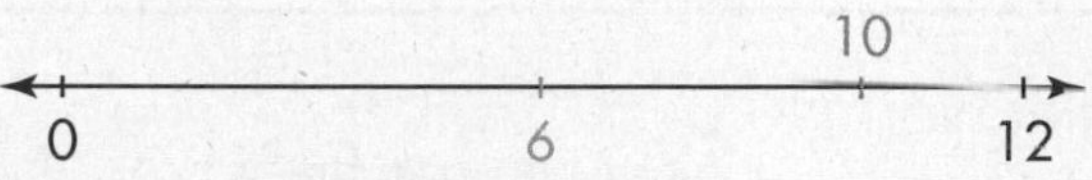

10 is closest to 12.

So, $\frac{10}{12}$ is closest to 1.

Step 2

Is $\frac{4}{9}$ closest to 0, $\frac{1}{2}$, or 1?

If the numerator is closest to the halfway number, the fraction is closest to $\frac{1}{2}$.

$4\frac{1}{2}$ is halfway between 0 and 9.

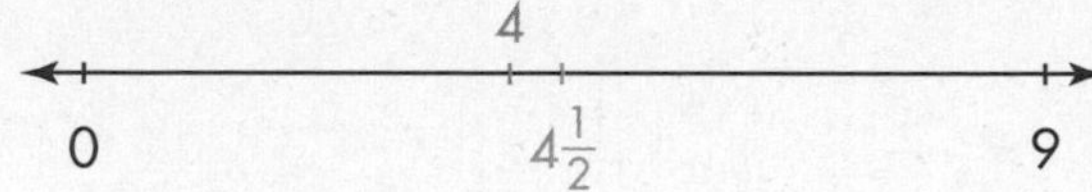

4 is closest to $4\frac{1}{2}$.

So, $\frac{4}{9}$ is closest to $\frac{1}{2}$.

$\frac{10}{12} - \frac{4}{9}$ is about $1 - \frac{1}{2} = \frac{1}{2}$.

Leveled Practice In **1–7**, estimate each sum or difference by replacing each fraction with 0, $\frac{1}{2}$, or 1.

1. 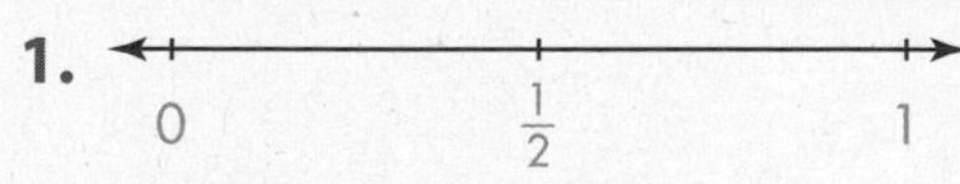

$\frac{4}{18} + \frac{3}{7}$

$\frac{4}{18}$ **Closest to:** ______

$\frac{3}{7}$ **Closest to:** ______

Estimate:

______ + ______ = ______

2. $\frac{8}{15} + \frac{2}{5}$

3. $\frac{17}{21} - \frac{2}{10}$

4. $\frac{8}{10} + \frac{4}{9}$

5. $\frac{12}{15} - \frac{3}{7}$

6. $\frac{15}{20} + \frac{7}{8}$

7. $\frac{8}{14} - \frac{4}{10}$

8. Reasoning Sam and Lou need a total of 1 foot of wire for a science project. Sam's wire measured $\frac{8}{12}$-foot long. Lou's wire measured $\frac{7}{8}$-foot long. Do they have enough wire for the science project? Explain your reasoning.

9. Construct Arguments Katya measured the growth of a plant seedling. The seedling grew $\frac{1}{3}$ inch by the end of the first week and another $\frac{5}{6}$ inch by the end of the second week. About how much did the seedling grow in the first 2 weeks? Explain how you made your estimate.

10. A scientist measured the amount of rain that fell in a town during one month. How much more rainfall was there in Week 4 than in Week 1?

DATA

March Rainfall

Week	Millimeters
1	2.6
2	3.32
3	4.06
4	4.07

11. Higher Order Thinking Jack is growing Red Wiggler worms to help make compost. He measured the lengths of two young worms. The 10-day old worm is $\frac{10}{12}$ inch long. The 20-day old worm is $1\frac{4}{6}$ inches long. About how much longer is the 20-day old worm than the 10-day old worm? Explain how you found your estimate.

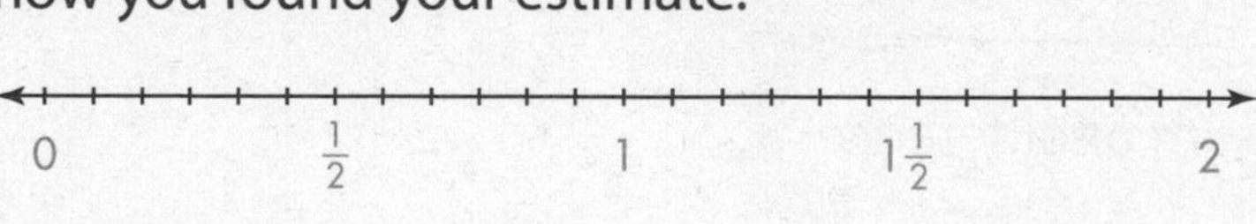

Assessment

12. Draw lines to match each expression on the left to its estimate on the right.

Expression	Estimate
$\frac{1}{6} - \frac{1}{8}$	0
$\frac{10}{12} - \frac{1}{16}$	$\frac{1}{2}$
$\frac{9}{10} - \frac{4}{9}$	1

13. Draw lines to match each expression on the left to its estimate on the right.

Expression	Estimate
$\frac{1}{10} + \frac{1}{3}$	0
$\frac{1}{12} + \frac{1}{9}$	$\frac{1}{2}$
$\frac{4}{7} + \frac{1}{2}$	1

Name ______________________

Lesson 7-2
Find Common Denominators

I can …
find common denominators for fractions with unlike denominators.

I can also model with math to solve problems.

Solve & Share

Sue wants $\frac{1}{2}$ of a rectangular pan of cornbread. Dena wants $\frac{1}{3}$ of the same pan of cornbread. How should you cut the cornbread so that each girl gets the size portion she wants? ***Solve this problem any way you choose.***

Model with Math
You can draw a picture to represent the pan as 1 whole. Then solve. *Show your work!*

Look Back! Construct Arguments Is there more than one way to divide the pan of cornbread into equal-sized parts? Explain how you know.

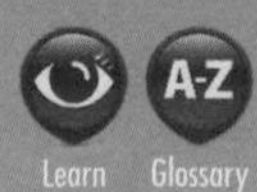

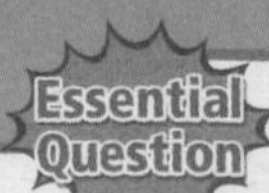

How Can You Find Common Denominators?

A

Tyrone partitioned a rectangle into thirds. Sally partitioned a rectangle of the same size into fourths. How could you partition a rectangle of the same size so that you see both thirds and fourths?

You can partition a rectangle to show thirds or fourths.

Thirds

Fourths

B This rectangle is partitioned into thirds and fourths.

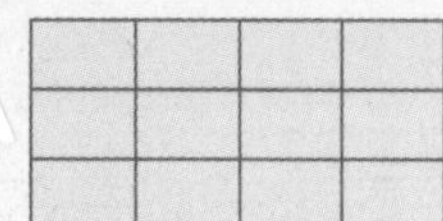

Twelfths

The rectangle is partitioned into 12 equal parts. Each part is $\frac{1}{12}$.

C The fractions $\frac{1}{3}$ and $\frac{1}{4}$ can be renamed with equivalent fractions.

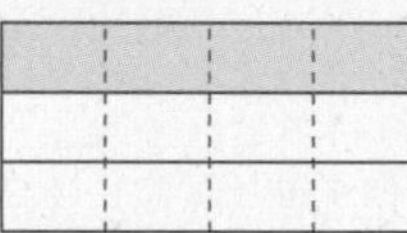

$\frac{1}{3} = \frac{4}{12}$ $\frac{1}{4} = \frac{3}{12}$

Fractions that have the same denominators, such as $\frac{4}{12}$ and $\frac{3}{12}$, are said to have common denominators.

Convince Me! **Model with Math** Draw rectangles such as the ones above to find fractions equivalent to $\frac{2}{5}$ and $\frac{1}{3}$ that have the same denominator.

Name ______________________________

Another Example

Find a common denominator for $\frac{7}{12}$ and $\frac{5}{6}$. Then rename each fraction with an equivalent fraction.

One Way

Multiply the denominators to find a common denominator: $12 \times 6 = 72$.

Write equivalent fractions with denominators of 72.

$$\frac{7}{12} = \frac{7 \times 6}{12 \times 6} = \frac{42}{72} \qquad \frac{5}{6} = \frac{5 \times 12}{6 \times 12} = \frac{60}{72}$$

So, $\frac{42}{72}$ and $\frac{60}{72}$ is one way to name $\frac{7}{12}$ and $\frac{5}{6}$ with a common denominator.

Another Way

Think of a number that is a multiple of the other.

You know that 12 is a multiple of 6.

$$\frac{5}{6} = \frac{5 \times 2}{6 \times 2} = \frac{10}{12}$$

So, $\frac{7}{12}$ and $\frac{10}{12}$ is another way to name $\frac{7}{12}$ and $\frac{5}{6}$ with a common denominator.

Guided Practice*

Do You Understand?

1. In the example on the previous page, how many twelfths are in each $\frac{1}{3}$ section of Tyrone's rectangle? How many twelfths are in each $\frac{1}{4}$ section of Sally's rectangle?

Do You Know How?

In **2** and **3**, find a common denominator for each pair of fractions.

2. $\frac{3}{8}$ and $\frac{2}{3}$ **3.** $\frac{1}{6}$ and $\frac{4}{3}$

Independent Practice

In **4–11**, find a common denominator for each pair of fractions. Then write equivalent fractions with the common denominator.

4. $\frac{2}{5}$ and $\frac{1}{6}$ **5.** $\frac{1}{3}$ and $\frac{4}{5}$ **6.** $\frac{5}{8}$ and $\frac{3}{4}$ **7.** $\frac{3}{10}$ and $\frac{9}{8}$

8. $\frac{3}{7}$ and $\frac{1}{2}$ **9.** $\frac{5}{12}$ and $\frac{3}{5}$ **10.** $\frac{7}{9}$ and $\frac{2}{3}$ **11.** $\frac{3}{8}$ and $\frac{9}{20}$

*For another example, see Set B on page 445.

Problem Solving

12. **Critique Reasoning** Explain any mistakes in the renaming of the fractions below. Show the correct renaming.

$\frac{3}{4} = \frac{9}{12} \qquad \frac{2}{3} = \frac{6}{12}$

13. **Higher Order Thinking** For keeping business records, every three months of a year is called a quarter. How many months are equal to three-quarters of a year? Explain how you found your answer.

14. **Model with Math** Nelda baked two kinds of pasta in pans. Each pan was the same size. She sliced one pan of pasta into 6 equal pieces. She sliced the other pan into 8 equal pieces. How can the pans of pasta now be sliced so that both pans have the same-sized pieces? Draw on the pictures to show your work. If Nelda has served 6 pieces from one pan so far, what fraction of one pan has she served?

15. **Number Sense** What is the price of premium gasoline rounded to the nearest dollar? rounded to the nearest dime? rounded to the nearest penny?

DATA

Gasoline Prices

Grade	Price (per gallon)
Regular	$4.199
Premium	$4.409
Diesel	$5.019

Assessment

16. Choose all the common denominators for $\frac{2}{3}$ and $\frac{3}{4}$.

- ☐ 8
- ☐ 12
- ☐ 16
- ☐ 36
- ☐ 48

17. Choose all the common denominators for $\frac{11}{12}$ and $\frac{4}{5}$.

- ☐ 12
- ☐ 17
- ☐ 30
- ☐ 60
- ☐ 125

Name ______________________

Help | Practice Buddy | Tools | Games

Homework & Practice 7-2

Find Common Denominators

Another Look!

Rename $\frac{4}{10}$ and $\frac{3}{8}$ using a common denominator.

Remember: A multiple is a product of the number and any nonzero whole number.

Step 1

Find a common denominator for $\frac{4}{10}$ and $\frac{3}{8}$.

List multiples of the denominators 10 and 8. Then look for a common multiple.

10: 10, 20, 30, 40
8: 8, 16, 24, 32, 40

The number 40 can be used as the common denominator.

Step 2

Rename $\frac{4}{10}$ and $\frac{3}{8}$ using 40 as the common denominator.

Multiply the numerator and denominator by the same nonzero number.

$\frac{4}{10}$ $\frac{4 \times 4}{10 \times 4} = \frac{16}{40}$ $\frac{3}{8}$ $\frac{3 \times 5}{8 \times 5} = \frac{15}{40}$

So, $\frac{16}{40}$ and $\frac{15}{40}$ is one way to name $\frac{4}{10}$ and $\frac{3}{8}$ using a common denominator.

In **1–9**, find a common denominator for each pair of fractions. Then write equivalent fractions with the common denominator.

1. $\frac{1}{3}$ and $\frac{4}{9}$

$\frac{1}{3}$ **Multiples of the denominator:** ______________ **Rename** $\frac{1}{3}$: ________

$\frac{4}{9}$ **Multiples of the denominator:** ______________ **Rename** $\frac{4}{9}$: ________

Common Denominator: ______ **Rename.** $\frac{1 \times \square}{3 \times \square} = \frac{\square}{\square}$ $\frac{4 \times \square}{9 \times \square} = \frac{\square}{\square}$

2. $\frac{3}{4}$ and $\frac{2}{5}$

3. $\frac{4}{7}$ and $\frac{2}{3}$

4. $\frac{1}{2}$ and $\frac{7}{11}$

5. $\frac{5}{12}$ and $\frac{3}{5}$

6. $\frac{5}{4}$ and $\frac{11}{16}$

7. $\frac{6}{7}$ and $\frac{1}{5}$

8. $\frac{9}{15}$ and $\frac{4}{9}$

9. $\frac{5}{6}$ and $\frac{8}{21}$

10. On the Dell River, a boat will pass the Colby drawbridge and then the Wave drawbridge. Rename each of the two drawbridge opening times. There are 60 minutes in an hour so use 60 as a common denominator. Then rename each opening time using another common denominator. Explain how you found your answers.

DATA

Dell River Drawbridge Openings

Bridge Name	Time of Opening
Asher Cross	On the hour
Colby	On the $\frac{3}{4}$ hour
Rainbow	On the $\frac{2}{3}$ hour
Red Bank	On the $\frac{1}{4}$ hour
Wave	On the $\frac{1}{6}$ hour

11. Higher Order Thinking Phil baked two kinds of pies. Each pie pan was the same size. He served $\frac{1}{2}$ of the blueberry pie. He served $\frac{1}{4}$ of the apple pie. If each pie had 8 pieces to start, what fraction in eighths of the apple pie did he serve? How many more pieces of the blueberry pie than the apple pie did he serve?

12. Look for Relationships Shelly is trying to improve her running time for a track race. She ran the first race in 43.13 seconds. Her time was 43.1 seconds in the second race and 43.07 seconds in the third race. If this pattern continues, what will Shelly's time be in the fourth race?

13. Make Sense and Persevere Alicia measured $\frac{1}{4}$ yard of the Blue Diamonds fabric and $\frac{5}{6}$ yard of the Yellow Bonnets fabric to make a quilt. Rename each length of fabric. Use the number of inches in a yard as a common denominator.
HINT: 1 yard = 3 feet; 1 foot = 12 inches

Assessment

14. Choose all the common denominators for $\frac{2}{3}$ and $\frac{7}{9}$.

- ☐ 6
- ☐ 9
- ☐ 18
- ☐ 27
- ☐ 30

15. Choose all the common denominators for $\frac{1}{9}$ and $\frac{1}{2}$.

- ☐ 11
- ☐ 16
- ☐ 18
- ☐ 36
- ☐ 45

Name ______________________________________  Solve

Solve & Share

Over the weekend, Eleni ate $\frac{1}{4}$ box of cereal, and Freddie ate $\frac{3}{8}$ of the same box. What portion of the box of cereal did they eat in all?

Lesson 7-3
Add Fractions with Unlike Denominators

I can ...
add fractions with unlike denominators.

I can also choose and use a math tool to solve problems.

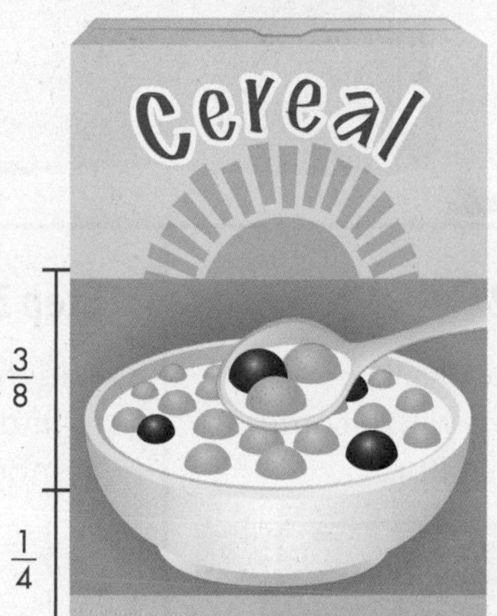

$\frac{3}{8}$

$\frac{1}{4}$

Use Appropriate Tools
You can use fraction strips to represent adding fractions.
Show your work!

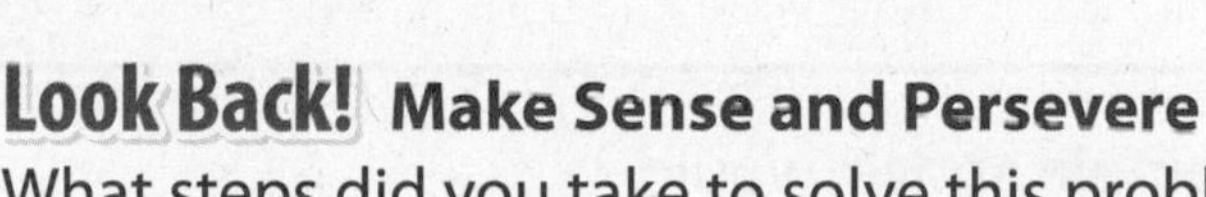

Look Back! Make Sense and Persevere
What steps did you take to solve this problem?

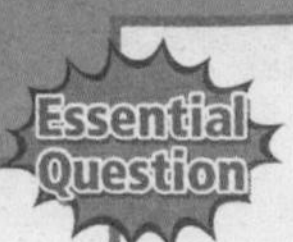

How Can You Add Fractions with Unlike Denominators?

A

Alex rode his scooter from his house to the park. Later, he rode from the park to baseball practice. How far did Alex ride?

You can add to find the total distance that Alex rode his scooter.

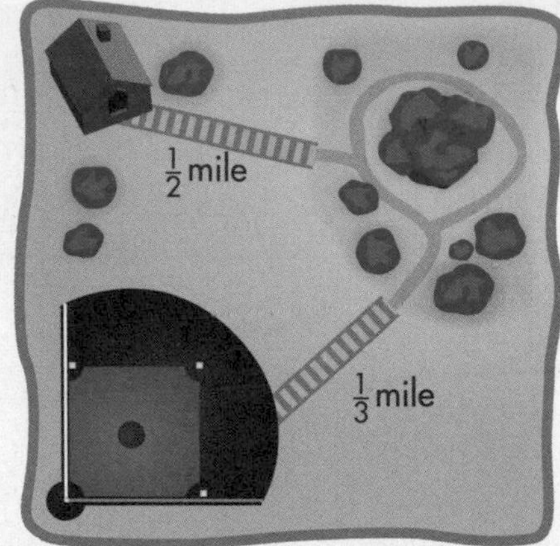

B

Step 1

Change the fractions to equivalent fractions with a common, or like, denominator.

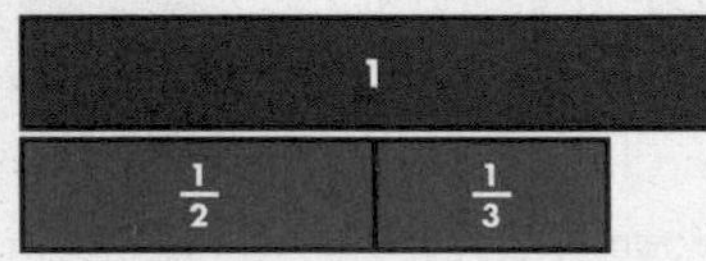

Multiples of 2: 2, 4, 6, 8, 10, 12, . . .

Multiples of 3: 3, 6, 9, 12, . . .

The number 6 is a common multiple of 2 and 3, so $\frac{1}{2}$ and $\frac{1}{3}$ can both be rewritten with a common denominator of 6.

C

Step 2

Write equivalent fractions with a common denominator.

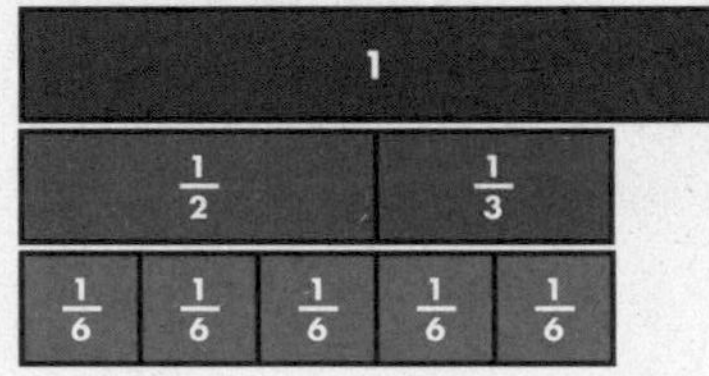

$$\frac{1}{2} \times \frac{3}{3} = \frac{3}{6}$$

$$\frac{1}{3} \times \frac{2}{2} = \frac{2}{6}$$

D

Step 3

Add the fractions to find the total number of sixths.

$$\begin{array}{r} \frac{1}{2} = \frac{3}{6} \\ + \frac{1}{3} = \frac{2}{6} \\ \hline \frac{5}{6} \end{array}$$

Alex rode his scooter $\frac{5}{6}$ mile.

Convince Me! **Construct Arguments** In the example above, would you get the same sum if you used 12 as the common denominator? Explain.

Name ______________________________

Another Example

Find $\frac{5}{12} + \frac{1}{4}$.

$\frac{5}{12} + \frac{1}{4} = \frac{5}{12} + \frac{3}{12}$ Write equivalent fractions with common denominators.

$= \frac{5+3}{12} = \frac{8}{12}$ or $\frac{2}{3}$ Find the total number of twelfths by adding the numerators.

Guided Practice*

Do You Understand?

1. In the example at the top of page 384, if the park was $\frac{1}{8}$ mile from baseball practice instead of $\frac{1}{3}$ mile, how far would Alex ride his scooter in all?

2. **Vocabulary** Rico and Nita solved the same problem. Rico got $\frac{6}{8}$ for an answer, and Nita got $\frac{3}{4}$. Which answer is correct? Use the term *equivalent fraction* in your explanation.

Do You Know How?

Find the sum. Use fraction strips to help.

3. $\frac{1}{2} + \frac{1}{4} = \frac{\square}{\square} + \frac{\square}{\square} = \frac{\square}{\square}$

1			
$\frac{1}{2}$		$\frac{1}{4}$	
$\frac{1}{4}$	$\frac{1}{4}$	$\frac{1}{4}$	

Independent Practice

In **4** and **5**, find each sum. Use fraction strips to help.

Remember that you can use multiples to find a common denominator.

4. $\frac{1}{2} + \frac{2}{5} = \frac{\square}{\square} + \frac{\square}{\square} = \frac{\square}{\square}$

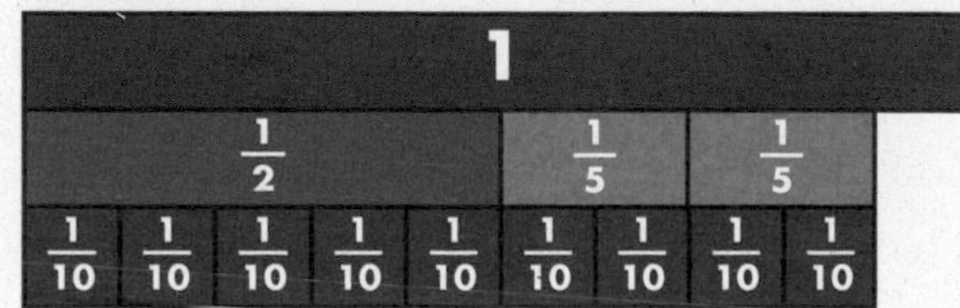

5. $\frac{1}{6} + \frac{1}{3} + \frac{1}{6} =$

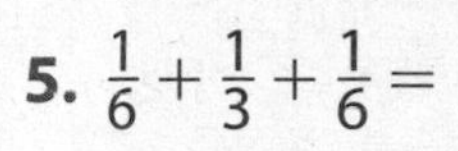

$\frac{\square}{\square} + \frac{\square}{\square} + \frac{\square}{\square} = \frac{\square}{\square} = \frac{\square}{\square}$

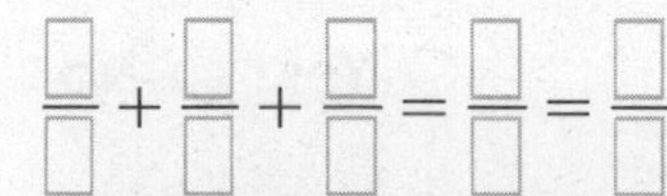

1			
$\frac{1}{6}$	$\frac{1}{3}$		$\frac{1}{6}$
$\frac{1}{6}$	$\frac{1}{6}$	$\frac{1}{6}$	$\frac{1}{6}$

*For another example, see Set C on page 446.

Problem Solving

6. Construct Arguments Explain why the denominator 6 in $\frac{3}{6}$ is not changed when adding the fractions.

$$\begin{array}{r} \frac{3}{6} = \frac{3}{6} \\ + \frac{1}{3} = \frac{2}{6} \\ \hline \frac{5}{6} \end{array}$$

7. Model with Math About $\frac{1}{10}$ of the bones in your body are in your skull. Your hands have about $\frac{1}{4}$ of the bones in your body. Write and solve an equation to find the fraction of the bones in your body that are in your hands or skull.

8. Math and Science Of 36 chemical elements, 2 are named for women scientists and 25 are named for places. What fraction of these 36 elements are named for women or places? Show your work.

9. Higher Order Thinking Roger made a table showing how he spends his time in one day. How many days will go by before Roger has slept the equivalent of one day? Explain how you found your answer.

DATA

Amount of Time Spent on Activities in One Day

Activity	Part of Day
Work	$\frac{1}{3}$ day
Sleep	$\frac{3}{8}$ day
Meals	$\frac{1}{8}$ day
Computer	$\frac{1}{6}$ day

Assessment

10. Choose Yes or No to tell if the fraction $\frac{1}{2}$ will make each equation true.

$\square + \frac{5}{5} = \frac{3}{2}$ ○ Yes ○ No

$\frac{1}{10} + \frac{2}{5} = \square$ ○ Yes ○ No

$\frac{1}{2} + \square = \frac{1}{4}$ ○ Yes ○ No

$\frac{1}{6} + \frac{1}{3} = \square$ ○ Yes ○ No

11. Choose Yes or No to tell if the fraction $\frac{4}{7}$ will make each equation true.

$\frac{1}{14} + \square = \frac{9}{14}$ ○ Yes ○ No

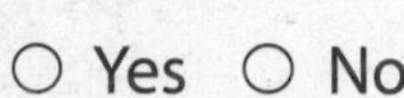

$\frac{2}{4} + \frac{2}{3} = \square$ ○ Yes ○ No

$\square + \frac{2}{7} = \frac{6}{7}$ ○ Yes ○ No

$\frac{1}{10} + \square = \frac{47}{70}$ ○ Yes ○ No

Name ______________________

Help | Practice Buddy | Tools | Games

Homework & Practice 7-3

Add Fractions with Unlike Denominators

Another Look!

Find $\frac{1}{6} + \frac{5}{8}$.

Remember: A multiple is a product of the number and any nonzero whole number.

Step 1	**Step 2**	**Step 3**
List multiples of the denominators. Look for a multiple that is the same in both lists. Choose the least one. 6: 6, 12, 18, 24, 30, 36, 42, 48 8: 8, 16, 24, 32, 40, 48 24 and 48 are common multiples of 6 and 8. 24 is the lesser of the two.	Write equivalent fractions using the common multiple as the denominator. $\frac{1}{6}$ $\frac{1 \times 4}{6 \times 4} = \frac{4}{24}$ $\frac{5}{8}$ $\frac{5 \times 3}{8 \times 3} = \frac{15}{24}$	Add the fractions to find the total number of twenty-fourths. $\frac{4}{24} + \frac{15}{24} =$ $\frac{4 + 15}{24} = \frac{19}{24}$ So, $\frac{1}{6} + \frac{5}{8} = \frac{19}{24}$.

In **1–4**, find each sum.

1. $\frac{1}{2} + \frac{1}{6}$

Least multiple that is the same: ____

Add using renamed fractions:

____ + ____ = ____ or $\frac{\square}{\square}$

2. $\frac{1}{9} + \frac{5}{6}$

Least multiple that is the same: ____

Add using renamed fractions:

____ + ____ = ____

3. $\frac{4}{5} + \frac{1}{15}$

Least multiple that is the same: ____

Add using renamed fractions:

____ + ____ = ____

4. $\frac{2}{8} + \frac{1}{2}$

Least multiple that is the same: ____

Add using renamed fractions:

____ + ____ = ____ or $\frac{\square}{\square}$

5. Model with Math Before school, Janine spends $\frac{1}{10}$ hour making the bed, $\frac{1}{5}$ hour getting dressed, and $\frac{1}{2}$ hour eating breakfast. What fraction of an hour does she spend doing these activities? Complete the drawing of fraction strips to show the solution.

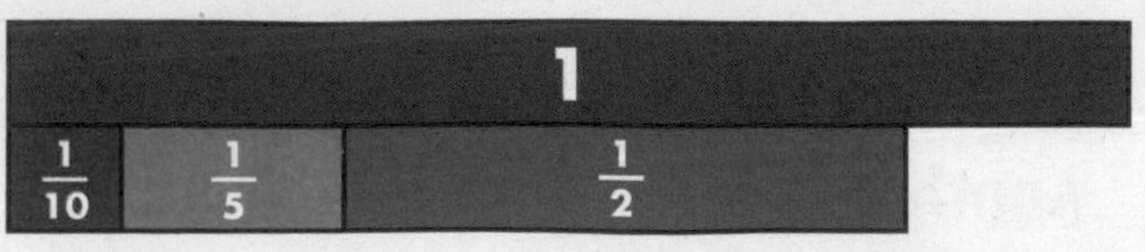

6. Math and Science Hair color is an inherited trait. In Marci's family, her mother has brown hair. Her father has blond hair. The family has 6 children in all. Of the 6 children, $\frac{1}{3}$ of them have blond hair, $\frac{1}{6}$ of them have red hair, and $\frac{1}{2}$ of them have brown hair. What fraction of the children have red or brown hair?

7. Abdul bought a loaf of bread for \$1.59 and a package of cheese for \$2.69. How much did Abdul spend? Complete the diagram below.

?

8. Higher Order Thinking Robert wants to walk one mile for exercise each day. He made a table to show the distance from his home to each of four different places. What is the total distance from home to the store and back home, and from home to the library and back home? If Robert walks this total distance, will he walk one mile? Explain how you found your answer.

DATA

Walking Distances from Home to Each Place

Place	Distance
Bank	$\frac{1}{5}$ mile
Library	$\frac{1}{10}$ mile
Park	$\frac{1}{2}$ mile
Store	$\frac{1}{4}$ mile

Assessment

9. Choose Yes or No to tell if the fraction $\frac{2}{3}$ will make each equation true.

$\frac{1}{3} + \frac{1}{3} = \square$ ○ Yes ○ No

$\frac{1}{6} + \frac{1}{6} = \square$ ○ Yes ○ No

$\square + \frac{6}{9} = \frac{4}{3}$ ○ Yes ○ No

$\frac{2}{5} + \square = \frac{14}{15}$ ○ Yes ○ No

10. Choose Yes or No to tell if the fraction $\frac{4}{5}$ will make each equation true.

$\frac{1}{5} + \square = 1$ ○ Yes ○ No

$\frac{1}{2} + \frac{3}{10} = \square$ ○ Yes ○ No

$\frac{7}{10} + \frac{1}{10} = \square$ ○ Yes ○ No

$\square + \frac{1}{15} = \frac{14}{15}$ ○ Yes ○ No

Name ______________________________

Lesson 7-4
Subtract Fractions with Unlike Denominators

I can ...
subtract fractions with unlike denominators.

I can also look for patterns to solve problems.

Solve & Share

Rose bought the length of copper pipe shown below. She used $\frac{1}{2}$ yard to repair a water line in her house. How much pipe does she have left? ***Solve this problem any way you choose.***

$\frac{4}{6}$ yard

Look Back! Generalize How is subtracting fractions with unlike denominators similar to adding fractions with unlike denominators?

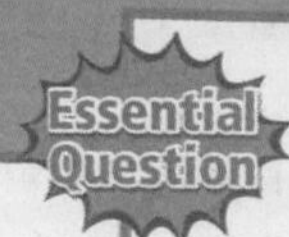

Essential Question

How Can You Subtract Fractions with Unlike Denominators?

A

Linda used $\frac{1}{4}$ yard of the fabric she bought for a sewing project. How much fabric did she have left?

You can use subtraction to find how much fabric was left.

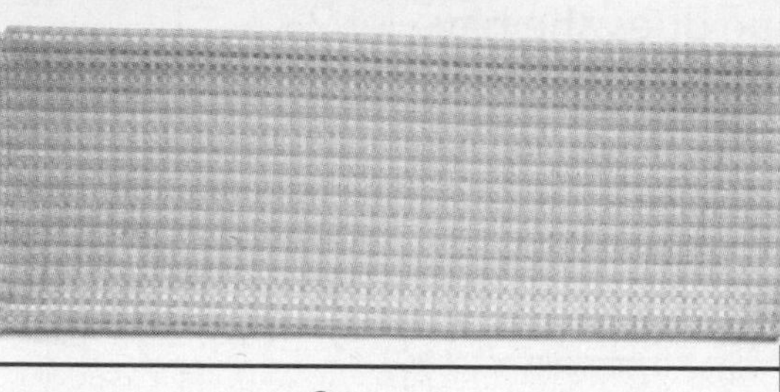

$\frac{2}{3}$ yard

B

Step 1

Find a common multiple of the denominators.

Multiples of 3: 3, 6, 9, 12, . . .

Multiples of 4: 4, 8, 12, . . .

The number 12 is a multiple of 3 and 4. Write equivalent fractions with a denominator of 12 for $\frac{2}{3}$ and $\frac{1}{4}$.

C

Step 2

Use the Identity Property to rename the fractions with a common denominator.

$\frac{2}{3} \times \frac{4}{4} = \frac{8}{12}$

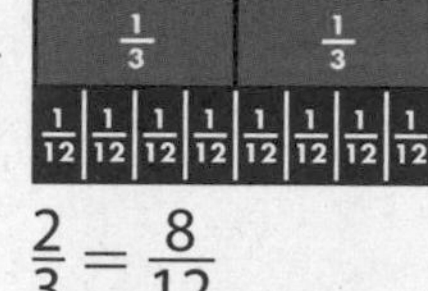

$\frac{2}{3} = \frac{8}{12}$

$\frac{1}{4} \times \frac{3}{3} = \frac{3}{12}$

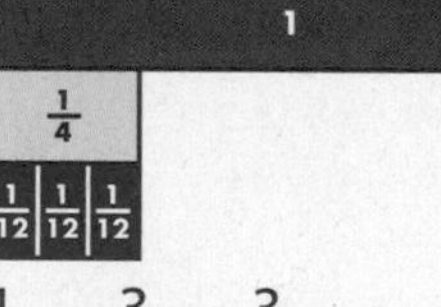

$\frac{1}{4} \times \frac{3}{3} = \frac{3}{12}$

D

Step 3

Subtract the numerators.

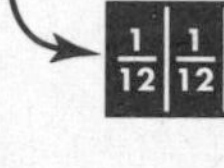

$$\begin{array}{r} \frac{2}{3} = \frac{8}{12} \\ -\frac{1}{4} = \frac{3}{12} \\ \hline \frac{5}{12} \end{array}$$

Linda has $\frac{5}{12}$ yard of fabric left.

Convince Me! **Critique Reasoning** Suppose Linda had $\frac{2}{3}$ of a yard of fabric and told Sandra that she used $\frac{3}{4}$ of a yard. Sandra says this is not possible. Do you agree? Explain your answer.

Name ______________________

Practice Buddy Tools Assessment

Guided Practice*

Do You Understand?

1. **Reasoning** In the example on page 390, is it possible to use a common denominator greater than 12 and get the correct answer? Why or why not?

2. In the example on page 390, if Linda had started with one yard of fabric and used $\frac{5}{8}$ of a yard, how much fabric would be left?

Do You Know How?

For **3–6**, find each difference.

3. $\frac{4}{7} = \frac{12}{21}$
$-\frac{1}{3} = \frac{7}{21}$

4. $\frac{5}{8}$
$-\frac{1}{4}$

5. $\frac{7}{8}$
$-\frac{1}{3}$

6. $\frac{4}{5} = \frac{24}{30}$
$-\frac{1}{6} = \frac{5}{30}$

Independent Practice

Leveled Practice In **7–16**, find each difference.

7. $\frac{1}{4} = \frac{\square}{8}$
$-\frac{1}{8} = \frac{\square}{8}$
$\frac{\square}{\square}$

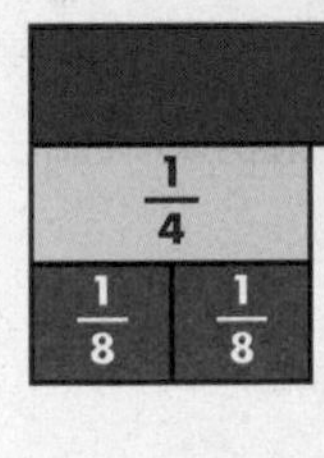

8. $\frac{2}{3} = \frac{\square}{6}$
$-\frac{1}{2} = \frac{\square}{6}$
$\frac{\square}{\square}$

9. $\frac{2}{3} - \frac{5}{9}$

10. $\frac{4}{5} - \frac{1}{4}$

11. $\frac{3}{2} - \frac{7}{12}$

12. $\frac{6}{7} - \frac{1}{2}$

13. $\frac{7}{10} - \frac{2}{5}$

14. $\frac{13}{16} - \frac{1}{4}$

15. $\frac{2}{9} - \frac{1}{6}$

16. $\frac{6}{5} - \frac{3}{8}$

*For another example, see Set C on page 446.

Problem Solving

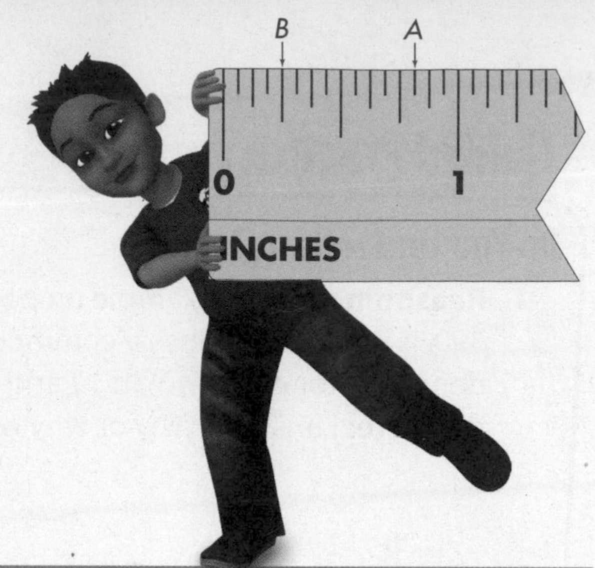

17. **Model with Math** Write and solve an equation to find the difference between the location of Point *A* and Point *B* on the ruler.

18. **Algebra** Write an addition and a subtraction equation for the diagram. Then find the missing value.

x	
$\frac{1}{4}$	$\frac{3}{8}$

19. **Construct Arguments** Why do fractions need to have a common denominator before you add or subtract them?

20. **Number Sense** Without using paper and pencil, how would you find the sum of 9.8 and 2.6?

21. **Higher Order Thinking** Find two fractions with a difference of $\frac{1}{5}$ but with neither denominator equal to 5.

Assessment

22. Choose the correct numbers from the box below to complete the subtraction sentence that follows.

$\frac{9}{10}$ $\frac{2}{3}$ $\frac{1}{30}$ $\frac{6}{7}$ $\frac{17}{30}$

$\square - \frac{1}{3} = \square$

23. Choose the correct numbers from the box below to complete the subtraction sentence that follows.

$\frac{11}{12}$ $\frac{1}{6}$ $\frac{1}{4}$ $\frac{1}{2}$ $\frac{3}{4}$

$\square - \square = \frac{7}{12}$

Name ______________________

Homework & Practice 7-4

Subtract Fractions with Unlike Denominators

Another Look!

Beth wants to exercise for $\frac{4}{5}$ hour. So far, she has exercised for $\frac{2}{3}$ hour. What fraction of an hour does she have left to exercise?

Step 1

Find a common multiple.

Multiples of 5:
5, 10, 15, 20

Multiples of 3:
3, 6, 9, 12, 15

Since 15 is a multiple of both 5 and 3, use 15 as a common denominator.

Step 2

Write equivalent fractions.

$\frac{4}{5} \times \frac{3}{3} = \frac{12}{15}$

$\frac{4}{5} = \frac{12}{15}$

$\frac{2}{3} \times \frac{5}{5} = \frac{10}{15}$

$\frac{2}{3} = \frac{10}{15}$

Step 3

Subtract the numerators.

$\frac{12}{15} - \frac{10}{15} = \frac{2}{15}$

Beth has $\frac{2}{15}$ hour left.

In **1–8**, find each difference.

1. $\frac{1}{3} = \frac{\square}{6}$, $-\frac{1}{6} = \frac{\square}{6}$, $\frac{\square}{\square}$

2. $\frac{2}{3} = \frac{\square}{12}$, $-\frac{5}{12} = \frac{\square}{12}$

3. $\frac{3}{5} = \frac{\square}{15}$, $-\frac{1}{3} = \frac{\square}{15}$

4. $\frac{2}{9} = \frac{\square}{72}$, $-\frac{1}{8} = \frac{\square}{72}$

5. $\frac{3}{4} - \frac{2}{5}$

6. $\frac{4}{3} - \frac{2}{5}$

7. $\frac{8}{8} - \frac{4}{9}$

8. $\frac{17}{18} - \frac{2}{3}$

Use the table for **9** and **10**. The trail around Mirror Lake in Yosemite National Park is 5 miles long.

Hiker	Fraction of Trail Hiked
Andrea	$\frac{2}{5}$
Jon	$\frac{1}{2}$
Callie	$\frac{4}{5}$

9. What fraction describes how much more of the trail Jon hiked than Andrea hiked?

10. What fraction describes how much more of the trail Callie hiked than Jon hiked?

---

11. Critique Reasoning Amy said that the perimeter of the triangle below is less than 10 yards. Do you agree with her? Why or why not?

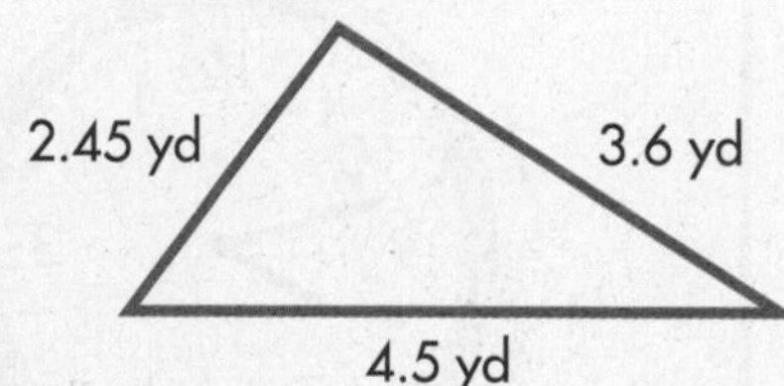

12. Model with Math Eva had $\frac{7}{8}$ gallon of paint. Her brother Ivan used $\frac{1}{4}$ gallon to paint his model boat. Eva needs at least $\frac{1}{2}$ gallon to paint her bookshelf. Did Ivan leave her enough paint? Write an equation and fill in the bar diagram to solve.

?

---

13. Paul's dad made a turkey pot pie for dinner on Wednesday. The family ate $\frac{4}{8}$ of the pie. On Thursday after school, Paul ate $\frac{2}{16}$ of the pie for a snack. What fraction of the pie remained?

14. Higher Order Thinking Write a real-world problem in which you would subtract fractions with unlike denominators. Then solve your problem.

Assessment

15. Choose the correct numbers from the box below to complete the subtraction sentence that follows.

$\frac{1}{2}$ $\frac{5}{14}$ $\frac{3}{7}$ $\frac{1}{7}$ $\frac{1}{14}$

$\square - \frac{3}{7} = \square$

16. Choose the correct numbers from the box below to complete the subtraction sentence that follows.

$\frac{1}{36}$ $\frac{3}{5}$ $\frac{1}{20}$ $\frac{5}{36}$ $\frac{7}{9}$

$\square - \frac{3}{4} = \square$

Name ______________________________

Lesson 7-5
Add and Subtract Fractions

I can ...
write equivalent fractions to add and subtract fractions with unlike denominators.

I can also reason about math.

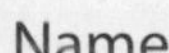

Solve & Share Tyler and Dean ordered pizza. Tyler ate $\frac{1}{2}$ of the pizza and Dean ate $\frac{1}{3}$ of the pizza. How much of the pizza was eaten, and how much is left? ***Solve this problem any way you choose.***

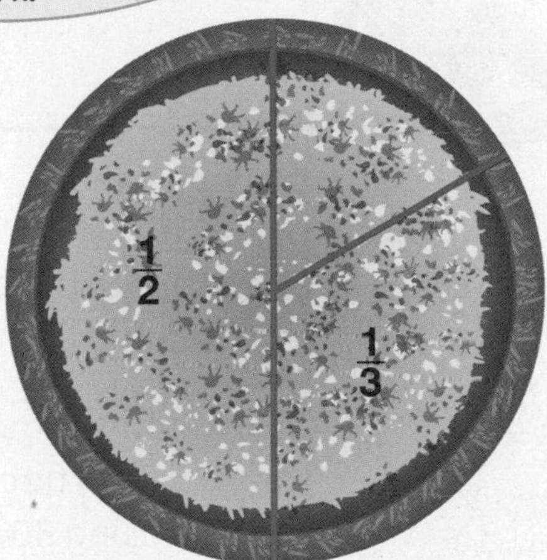

Look Back! Make Sense and Persevere How can you check that your answer makes sense?

How Can Adding and Subtracting Fractions Help You Solve Problems?

A

Kayla had $\frac{9}{10}$ gallon of paint. She painted the ceilings in her bedroom and bathroom. How much paint does she have left after painting the two ceilings?

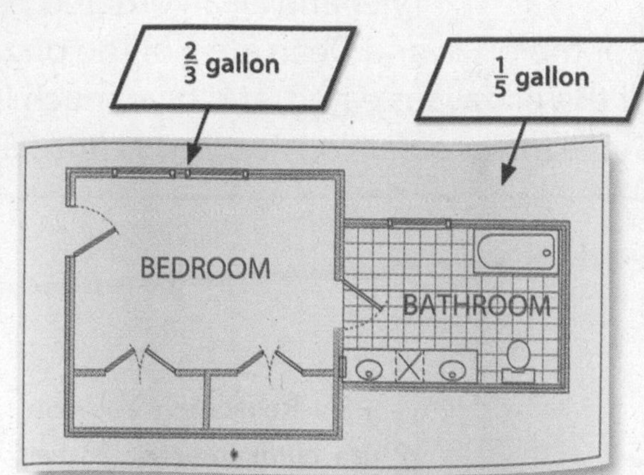

B

Step 1

Add to find out how much paint Kayla used for the two ceilings.

To add, write each fraction using 15 as the denominator.

$$\begin{array}{r} \frac{2}{3} = \frac{10}{15} \\ +\ \frac{1}{5} = \frac{3}{15} \\ \hline \frac{13}{15} \end{array}$$

Kayla used $\frac{13}{15}$ gallon of paint.

C

Step 2

Subtract the amount of paint Kayla used from the amount she started with.

To subtract, write each fraction using 30 as the denominator.

$$\begin{array}{r} \frac{9}{10} = \frac{27}{30} \\ -\ \frac{13}{15} = \frac{26}{30} \\ \hline \frac{1}{30} \end{array}$$

Kayla has $\frac{1}{30}$ gallon of paint left.

Convince Me! **Make Sense and Persevere** For the problem above, how would you use estimation to check that the answer is reasonable?

Name ________________

Guided Practice*

Do You Understand?

1. In the example on page 396, how much more paint did Kayla use to paint the bedroom ceiling than the bathroom ceiling?

2. **Number Sense** Kevin estimated the difference of $\frac{9}{10} - \frac{4}{8}$ to be 0. Is his estimate reasonable? Explain.

Do You Know How?

For **3–6**, find the sum or difference.

3. $\frac{1}{15} + \frac{1}{6}$

4. $\frac{7}{16} - \frac{1}{4}$

5. $\frac{7}{8} - \frac{3}{6}$

6. $\frac{7}{8} + \left(\frac{4}{8} - \frac{2}{4}\right)$

Independent Practice

In **7–22**, find the sum or difference.

7. $\frac{4}{50} + \frac{3}{5}$

8. $\frac{2}{3} - \frac{7}{12}$

9. $\frac{9}{10} + \frac{2}{100}$

10. $\frac{4}{9} + \frac{1}{4}$

11. $\frac{17}{15} - \frac{1}{3}$

12. $\frac{7}{16} + \frac{3}{8}$

13. $\frac{2}{5} + \frac{1}{4}$

14. $\frac{1}{7} + \frac{1}{2}$

15. $\frac{1}{2} - \frac{3}{16}$

16. $\frac{7}{8} - \frac{2}{3}$

17. $\frac{11}{12} - \frac{4}{6}$

18. $\frac{7}{18} + \frac{5}{9}$

19. $\left(\frac{7}{8} + \frac{1}{12}\right) - \frac{1}{2}$

20. $\left(\frac{11}{18} - \frac{4}{9}\right) + \frac{1}{6}$

21. $\frac{13}{14} - \left(\frac{1}{2} + \frac{2}{7}\right)$

22. $\frac{1}{6} + \left(\frac{15}{15} - \frac{7}{10}\right)$

*For another example, see Set C on page 446.

Problem Solving

23. The table shows the amounts of ingredients needed to make a pizza. How much more cheese do you need than pepperoni and mushrooms combined? Show how you solved the problem.

DATA

Ingredient	Amount
Cheese	$\frac{3}{4}$ c
Pepperoni	$\frac{1}{3}$ c
Mushrooms	$\frac{1}{4}$ c

24. Reasoning Charlie's goal is to use less than 50 gallons of water per day. His water bill for the month showed that he used 1,524 gallons of water in 30 days. Did Charlie meet his goal this month? Explain how you decided.

25. Construct Arguments Jereen spent $\frac{1}{4}$ hour on homework before school, another $\frac{1}{2}$ hour after she got home, and a final $\frac{1}{3}$ hour after dinner. Did she spend more or less than 1 hour on homework in all? Explain.

26. Model with Math Carl has three lengths of cable, $\frac{5}{6}$ yard long, $\frac{1}{4}$ yard long, and $\frac{2}{3}$ yard long. If he uses 1 yard of cable, how much cable is left? Explain your work.

1 yard		x
$\frac{1}{4}$	$\frac{5}{6}$	$\frac{2}{3}$

27. Higher Order Thinking Find two fractions with a sum of $\frac{2}{3}$ but with neither denominator equal to 3.

Assessment

28. Joel made some muffins. He gave $\frac{1}{4}$ of the muffins to a neighbor. He took $\frac{3}{8}$ of the muffins to school. What fraction of the muffins is left?

Ⓐ $\frac{4}{12}$

Ⓑ $\frac{3}{8}$

Ⓒ $\frac{5}{12}$

Ⓓ $\frac{8}{8}$

29. If two sides of an isosceles triangle each measure $\frac{1}{4}$ ft, and the third side measures $\frac{3}{8}$ ft, what is the perimeter of the triangle?

Ⓐ $\frac{5}{8}$ ft

Ⓑ $\frac{7}{8}$ ft

Ⓒ $\frac{7}{16}$ ft

Ⓓ $\frac{7}{32}$ ft

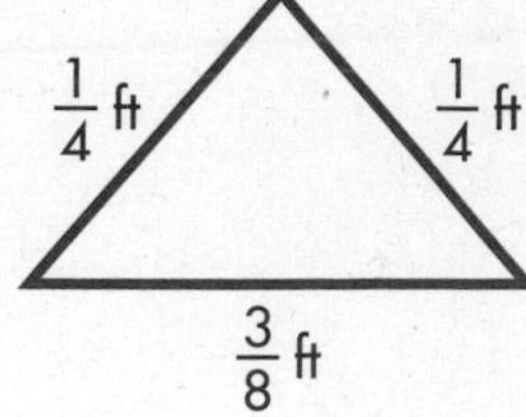

Name ____________________

Homework & Practice 7-5

Add and Subtract Fractions

Another Look!

Carla wants to make a Veggie Toss using eggplant, green peppers, spring onions, and mushrooms. She already has eggplant at home. How many pounds of the other ingredients does she need in all? Use data from the recipe.

Veggie Toss Recipe

Eggplant	$\frac{3}{4}$ pound (lb)
Green peppers	$\frac{1}{3}$ pound (lb)
Spring onions	$\frac{1}{4}$ pound (lb)
Mushrooms	$\frac{3}{8}$ pound (lb)

Step 1

List the amounts of green peppers, spring onions, and mushrooms. Then, find a common denominator and rename each fraction.

$$\left(\frac{1}{3}+\frac{1}{4}\right)+\frac{3}{8}=\left(\frac{8}{24}+\frac{6}{24}\right)+\frac{9}{24}$$

Step 2

Add the renamed fraction amounts.

$$\frac{14}{24}+\frac{9}{24}=\frac{23}{24}$$

Carla needs $\frac{23}{24}$ pound of the other veggies in all.

In **1–12**, find the sum or difference.

1. $\frac{1}{12} + \frac{7}{9}$

2. $\frac{4}{18} + \frac{2}{9}$

3. $\frac{1}{3} + \frac{1}{5}$

4. $\frac{5}{15} + \frac{3}{5}$

5. $\frac{1}{2}-\left(\frac{1}{8}+\frac{1}{8}\right)$

6. $\frac{3}{4}+\left(\frac{1}{4}-\frac{1}{6}\right)$

7. $\left(\frac{1}{2}+\frac{3}{20}\right)-\frac{2}{20}$

8. $\left(\frac{2}{5}+\frac{1}{5}\right)-\frac{3}{10}$

9. $\frac{5}{4}-\frac{5}{8}$

10. $\frac{2}{3}-\frac{2}{7}$

11. $\frac{12}{15}-\frac{1}{6}$

12. $\frac{5}{9}-\frac{3}{8}$

13. The table shows the amounts of two ingredients Tara used to make a snack mix. She ate $\frac{5}{8}$ cup of the snack mix for lunch. How much of the mix is left? Show how you solved.

DATA

Ingredient	Amount
Rice Crackers	$\frac{3}{4}$ c
Pretzels	$\frac{2}{3}$ c

14. Samantha is making soup. To make the broth, she combines $\frac{2}{5}$ cup of vegetable stock and $\frac{2}{3}$ cup of chicken stock. Boiling the broth causes $\frac{1}{4}$ cup of the liquid to evaporate. How much broth is left after it is boiled? Show how you solved.

15. Number Sense Mary has three lengths of cable, $\frac{3}{6}$ yard long, $\frac{1}{4}$ yard long, and $\frac{1}{3}$ yard long. Which two pieces together make a length of $\frac{20}{24}$ yard?

16. Critique Reasoning A kitten's heartbeat can be as fast as 240 beats per minute. To find the number of times a kitten's heart beats in 30 seconds, Aiden says divide 240 by 30. Do you agree with him? Why or why not?

17. Use Structure Explain how you know the quotients $540 \div 90$ and $5{,}400 \div 900$ are equal without doing any computation.

18. Higher Order Thinking Write an addition and subtraction problem and equation for the diagram. Then find the missing value.

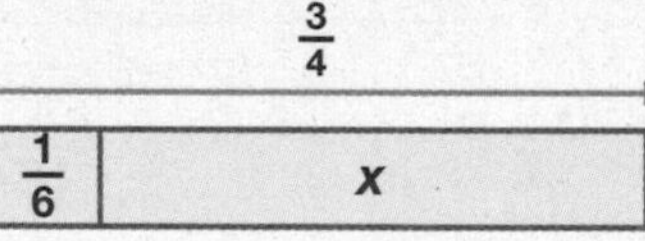

Assessment

19. Mariko's social studies class lasts $\frac{5}{6}$ of an hour. Only $\frac{3}{12}$ of an hour has passed. What fraction of an hour remains for Mariko's social studies class?

Ⓐ $\frac{1}{3}$ hour
Ⓑ $\frac{4}{9}$ hour
Ⓒ $\frac{7}{12}$ hour
Ⓓ $\frac{13}{12}$ hour

20. A plumber is fitting a water pipe that is $\frac{3}{4}$ foot long on to a water pipe that is $\frac{2}{12}$ foot long. How long will the finished pipe be?

Ⓐ $\frac{11}{12}$ foot
Ⓑ $\frac{8}{16}$ foot
Ⓒ $\frac{2}{12}$ foot
Ⓓ 1 foot

Name ______________________

Lesson 7-6

Estimate Sums and Differences of Mixed Numbers

I can ...
estimate sums and differences of fractions and mixed numbers.

I can also generalize from examples.

Solve & Share

Alex has five cups of strawberries. He wants to use $1\frac{3}{4}$ cups of strawberries for a fruit salad and $3\frac{1}{2}$ cups for jam. Does Alex have enough strawberries to make both recipes? ***Solve this problem any way you choose.***

Generalize You can estimate because you just need to know if Alex has enough. *Show your work!*

Look Back! Make Sense and Persevere Does it make sense to use 1 cup and 3 cups to estimate if Alex has enough strawberries? Explain.

Learn Glossary

What Are Some Ways to Estimate?

A

Jamila's mom wants to make a size 10 dress and jacket. About how many yards of fabric does she need?

Estimate the sum $2\frac{1}{4} + 1\frac{5}{8}$ to find how many yards of fabric she needs.

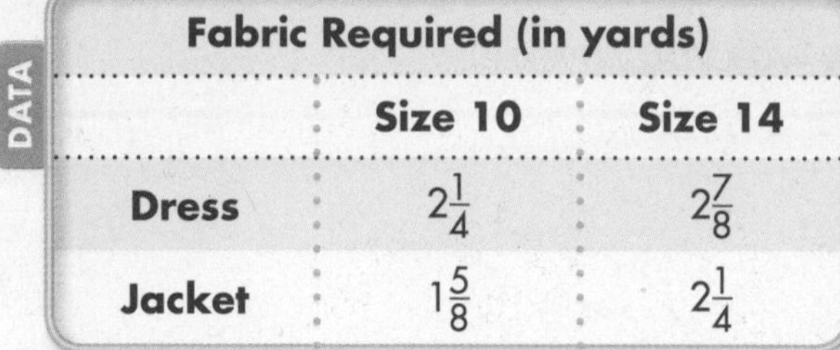

DATA

Fabric Required (in yards)		
	Size 10	Size 14
Dress	$2\frac{1}{4}$	$2\frac{7}{8}$
Jacket	$1\frac{5}{8}$	$2\frac{1}{4}$

B

One Way

Use a number line to round fractions and mixed numbers to the nearest whole number.

$1\frac{5}{8}$ rounds to 2 $2\frac{1}{4}$ rounds to 2

1 $\frac{1}{2}$ $\frac{5}{8}$ 2 $\frac{1}{4}$ $\frac{1}{2}$ 3

So, $2\frac{1}{4} + 1\frac{5}{8} \approx 2 + 2$, or 4.

Jamila's mom needs about 4 yards of fabric.

C

Another Way

Use $\frac{1}{2}$ as a benchmark fraction.

Replace each fraction with the nearest $\frac{1}{2}$ unit.

$1\frac{5}{8}$ is close to $1\frac{1}{2}$.

$2\frac{1}{4}$ is halfway between 2 and $2\frac{1}{2}$.

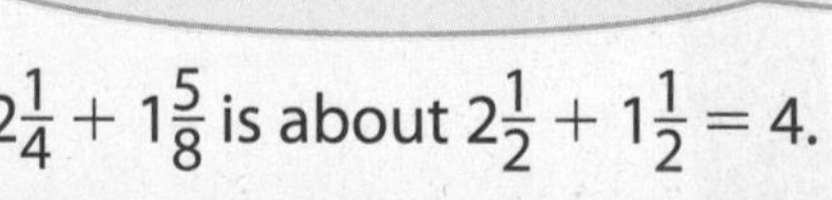

So, $2\frac{1}{4} + 1\frac{5}{8}$ is about $2\frac{1}{2} + 1\frac{1}{2} = 4$.

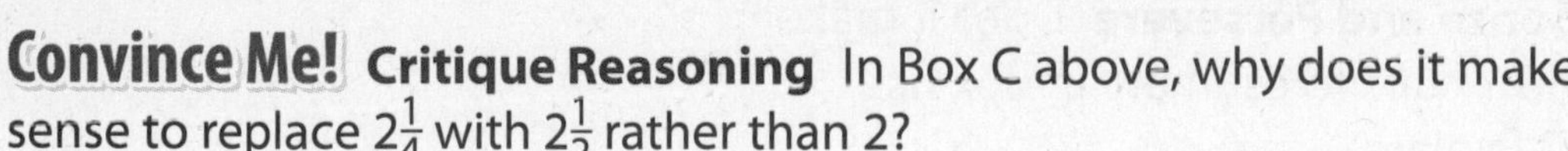

Convince Me! **Critique Reasoning** In Box C above, why does it make sense to replace $2\frac{1}{4}$ with $2\frac{1}{2}$ rather than 2?

Name ______________________________

Practice Buddy Tools Assessment

Guided Practice*

Do You Understand?

1. **Generalize** To estimate with mixed numbers, when should you round to the next greater whole number?

2. When should you estimate a sum or difference?

Do You Know How?

In **3–5**, round to the nearest whole number.

3. $\frac{3}{4}$ **4.** $1\frac{5}{7}$ **5.** $2\frac{3}{10}$

In **6** and **7**, estimate each sum or difference using benchmark fractions.

6. $2\frac{5}{9} - 1\frac{1}{3}$ **7.** $2\frac{4}{10} + 3\frac{5}{8}$

Independent Practice

Leveled Practice In **8–11**, use the number line to round the mixed numbers to the nearest whole numbers.

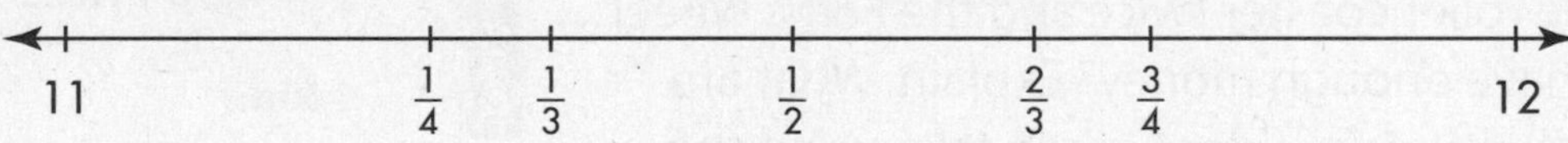

8. $11\frac{4}{6}$ **9.** $11\frac{2}{8}$ **10.** $11\frac{8}{12}$ **11.** $11\frac{4}{10}$

In **12–20**, estimate each sum or difference.

12. $2\frac{1}{8} - \frac{5}{7}$ **13.** $12\frac{1}{3} + 2\frac{1}{4}$ **14.** $2\frac{2}{3} + \frac{7}{8} + 6\frac{7}{12}$

15. $1\frac{10}{15} - \frac{8}{9}$ **16.** $10\frac{5}{6} - 2\frac{3}{8}$ **17.** $12\frac{8}{25} + 13\frac{5}{9}$

18. $48\frac{1}{10} - 2\frac{7}{9}$ **19.** $33\frac{14}{15} + 23\frac{9}{25}$ **20.** $14\frac{4}{9} + 25\frac{1}{6} + 7\frac{11}{18}$

*For another example, see Set D on page 446.

Problem Solving

21. Reasoning Use the recipes to answer the questions.

a Estimate how many cups of Fruit Trail Mix the recipe can make.

b Estimate how many cups of Traditional Trail Mix the recipe can make.

c Estimate how much trail mix you would have if you made both recipes.

Fruit Trail Mix

- $\frac{1}{2}$ cup raisins
- $\frac{3}{8}$ cup sunflower seeds
- 1 cup unsalted peanuts
- $\frac{1}{4}$ cup coconut

Traditional Trail Mix

- $1\frac{1}{3}$ cup raisins
- 1 cup sunflower seeds
- $1\frac{3}{4}$ cup unsalted peanuts
- 1 cup cashews

22. Kim is $3\frac{5}{8}$ inches taller than Colleen. If Kim is $60\frac{3}{4}$ inches tall, what is the best estimate of Colleen's height?

23. Higher Order Thinking Last week Jason walked $3\frac{1}{4}$ miles each day for 3 days and $4\frac{5}{8}$ miles each day for 4 days. About how many miles did Jason walk last week?

24. Make Sense and Persevere Cal has $12.50 to spend. He wants to ride the roller coaster twice and the Ferris wheel once. Does Cal have enough money? Explain. What are 3 possible combinations of rides Cal can take using the money he has?

DATA

Ride Prices

Ride	Cost
Carousel	$3.75
Ferris Wheel	$4.25
Roller Coaster	$5.50

Assessment

25. Which is the best estimate for $2\frac{2}{9} + 9\frac{3}{4}$?

Ⓐ 8
Ⓑ 10
Ⓒ 12
Ⓓ 13

26. Which is the best estimate for $13\frac{1}{12} - 1\frac{9}{10}$?

Ⓐ 11
Ⓑ 12
Ⓒ 14
Ⓓ 15

Name ________________________________

Help | Practice Buddy | Tools | Games

Homework & Practice 7-6

Estimate Sums and Differences of Mixed Numbers

Another Look!

Kyra has $4\frac{1}{8}$ yards of red ribbon and $7\frac{2}{3}$ yards of blue ribbon. About how many yards of ribbon does she have?

Round both numbers to the nearest whole number. Then add or subtract.

Estimate $4\frac{1}{8} + 7\frac{2}{3}$.

$4\frac{1}{8}$ rounds to 4.

$7\frac{2}{3}$ rounds to 8.

$4 + 8 = 12$

So, $4\frac{1}{8} + 7\frac{2}{3}$ is about 12.

Kyra has about 12 yards of ribbon.

If the fractional part of a mixed number is greater than or equal to $\frac{1}{2}$, round to the next greater whole number. If it is less than $\frac{1}{2}$, use only the whole number.

In **1–8**, round to the nearest whole number.

1. $8\frac{5}{6}$ **2.** $13\frac{8}{9}$ **3.** $43\frac{1}{3}$ **4.** $6\frac{6}{7}$

5. $7\frac{40}{81}$ **6.** $29\frac{4}{5}$ **7.** $88\frac{2}{4}$ **8.** $20\frac{3}{10}$

In **9–17**, estimate each sum or difference.

9. $7\frac{1}{9} + 8\frac{2}{5}$ **10.** $14\frac{5}{8} - 3\frac{7}{10}$ **11.** $2\frac{1}{4} + 5\frac{1}{2} + 10\frac{3}{4}$

12. $11\frac{3}{5} - 4\frac{1}{12}$ **13.** $9 + 3\frac{11}{14} + 5\frac{1}{9}$ **14.** $15\frac{6}{7} - 12\frac{2}{10}$

15. $3\frac{2}{5} + 6\frac{5}{7}$ **16.** $20\frac{1}{3} - 9\frac{1}{2}$ **17.** $25\frac{7}{8} + 8\frac{7}{12}$

Use the table for **18–20**.

18. Critique Reasoning Robert says his better long jump was about 1 foot farther than May's better long jump. Is he correct? Explain.

DATA

Participant	Event	Distance
Robert	Long Jump	**1.** $6\frac{1}{12}$ ft **2.** $5\frac{2}{3}$ ft
	Softball Throw	$62\frac{1}{5}$ ft
May	Long Jump	**1.** $4\frac{2}{3}$ ft **2.** $4\frac{3}{4}$ ft
	Softball Throw	$71\frac{7}{8}$ ft

19. If the school record for the softball throw is 78 feet, about how much farther must Robert throw the ball to match the record?

20. About how much farther is May's softball throw than Robert's softball throw?

21. Higher Order Thinking Use the problem $\frac{3}{5} + \frac{3}{4}$. First, round each fraction and estimate the sum. Then, add the two fractions using a common denominator and round the result. Which is closer to the actual sum?

22. Be Precise To make one batch of granola, Linda mixes 1 pound of oat flakes, 6 ounces of walnuts, 5 ounces of raisins, and 4 ounces of sunflower seeds. How many pounds of granola does one batch make?

Assessment

23. Which is the best estimate for $10\frac{1}{9} - \frac{1}{4}$?

Ⓐ 9
Ⓑ 10
Ⓒ 11
Ⓓ 12

24. Which is the best estimate for $1\frac{4}{5} + 12\frac{1}{3}$?

Ⓐ 10
Ⓑ 11
Ⓒ 13
Ⓓ 14

Name ______________________

Lesson 7-7
Use Models to Add Mixed Numbers

I can ...
add mixed numbers using models.

I can also choose and use a math tool to solve problems.

Solve & Share Martina is baking bread. She mixes $1\frac{3}{4}$ cups of flour with other ingredients. Then she adds $4\frac{1}{2}$ cups of flour to the mixture. How many cups of flour does she need? ***Solve this problem any way you choose.***

Use Appropriate Tools
You can use fraction strips to help add mixed numbers.
Show your work!

Look Back! Reasoning Explain how you can estimate the sum above.

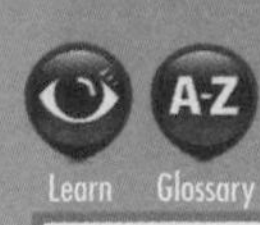

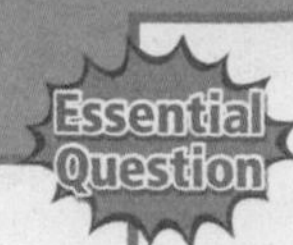

How Can You Model Addition of Mixed Numbers?

A

Bill has 2 boards he will use to make picture frames. What is the total length of the boards Bill has to make picture frames?

You can find a common denominator to add the fractions.

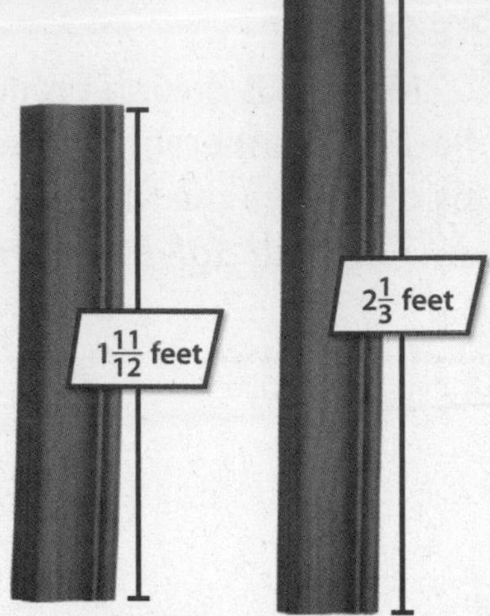

B

Step 1

Rename the fractional parts as equivalent fractions with a like denominator. Add the fractions.

$$\begin{array}{r} 2\frac{4}{12} \\ +\ 1\frac{11}{12} \\ \hline \frac{15}{12} \end{array}$$

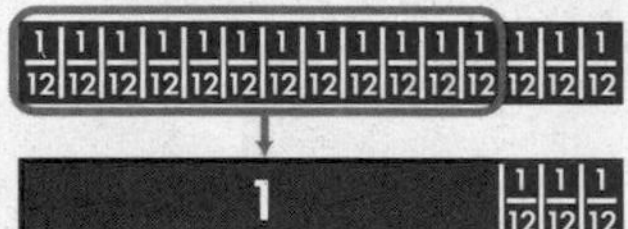

Rename $\frac{15}{12}$ as $1\frac{3}{12}$.

C

Step 2

Add the whole number parts.

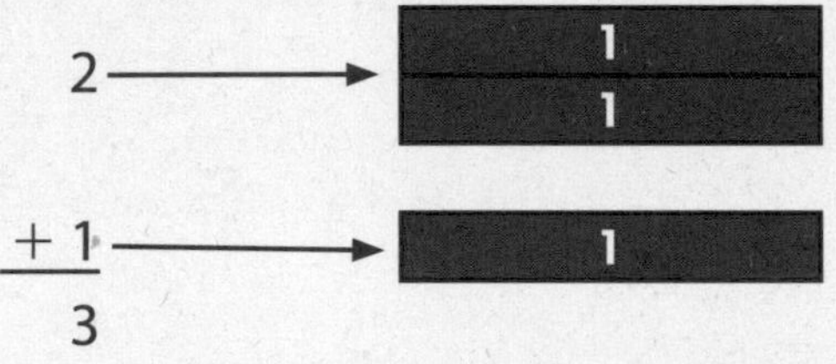

$$\begin{array}{r} 2 \\ +\ 1 \\ \hline 3 \end{array}$$

Then add the sum of the fractional parts.

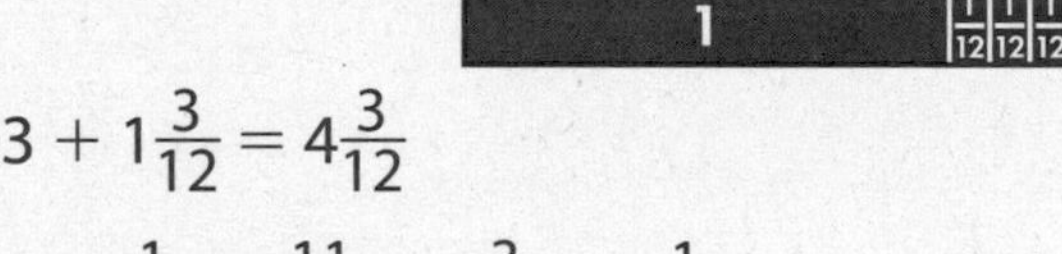

$3 + 1\frac{3}{12} = 4\frac{3}{12}$

So, $2\frac{1}{3} + 1\frac{11}{12} = 4\frac{3}{12}$ or $4\frac{1}{4}$

The total length of the boards is $4\frac{1}{4}$ feet.

Convince Me! **Critique Reasoning** Tom has 2 boards that are the same length as Bill's. He says that he found the total length of the boards by adding 28 twelfths and 23 twelfths. Does his method work? Explain.

Name ________________________________

Guided Practice*

Do You Understand?

1. **Construct Arguments** When adding two mixed numbers, does it ever make sense to rename the fractional sum? Explain.

Do You Know How?

In **2–5**, use fraction strips to find each sum.

2. $1\frac{1}{10} + 2\frac{4}{5}$

3. $1\frac{1}{2} + 2\frac{3}{4}$

4. $3\frac{2}{3} + 1\frac{4}{6}$

5. $3\frac{1}{6} + 2\frac{2}{3}$

Independent Practice

Leveled Practice In **6** and **7**, use each model to find the sum.

6. Charles used $1\frac{2}{3}$ cups of walnuts and $2\frac{1}{6}$ cups of cranberries to make breakfast bread. How many cups of walnuts and cranberries did he use in all?

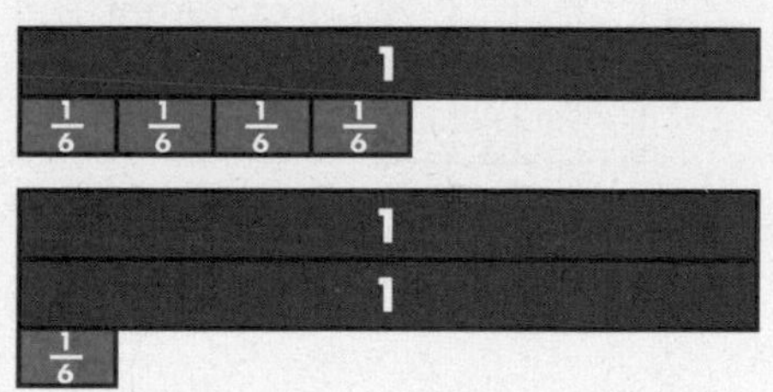

7. Mary worked $2\frac{3}{4}$ hours on Monday and $1\frac{1}{2}$ hours on Tuesday. How many hours did she work in all on Monday and Tuesday?

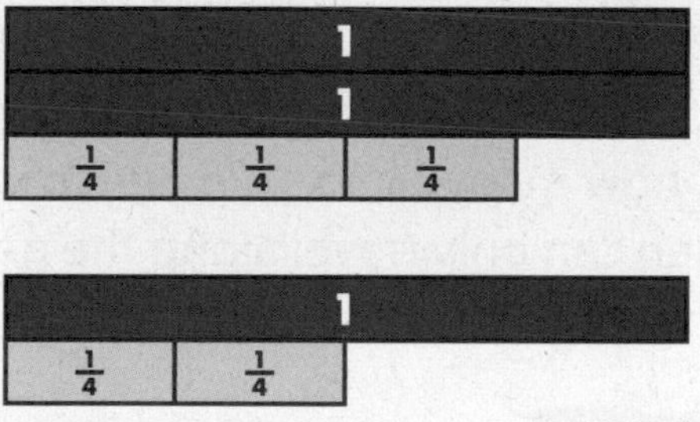

In **8–16**, use fraction strips to find each sum.

8. $2\frac{6}{10} + 1\frac{3}{5}$

9. $4\frac{5}{6} + 1\frac{7}{12}$

10. $4\frac{2}{5} + 3\frac{7}{10}$

11. $3\frac{1}{2} + 1\frac{3}{4}$

12. $1\frac{7}{8} + 5\frac{1}{4}$

13. $2\frac{6}{12} + 1\frac{1}{2}$

14. $3\frac{2}{5} + 1\frac{9}{10}$

15. $2\frac{7}{12} + 1\frac{3}{4}$

16. $2\frac{7}{8} + 5\frac{1}{2}$

*For another example, see Set E on page 447.

Problem Solving

17. Lindsey used $1\frac{1}{4}$ gallons of tan paint for the ceiling and $4\frac{3}{8}$ gallons of green paint for the walls of her kitchen. How much paint did Lindsey use in all? Use fraction strips to help.

18. Paul said, "I walked $2\frac{1}{2}$ miles on Saturday and $2\frac{3}{4}$ miles on Sunday." How many miles is that in all?

19. Higher Order Thinking Tori is making muffins. The recipe calls for $2\frac{5}{6}$ cups of brown sugar for the muffins and $1\frac{1}{3}$ cups of brown sugar for the topping. Tori has 4 cups of brown sugar. Does she have enough brown sugar to make the muffins and the topping? Explain.

You can use fraction strips or a number line to compare amounts.

In **20** and **21**, use the map. Each unit represents one block.

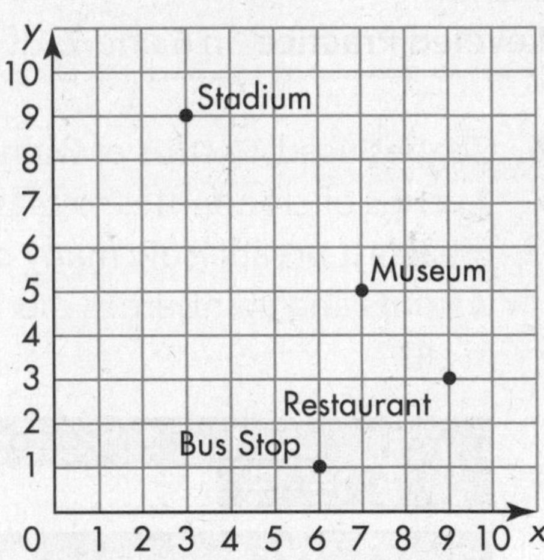

20. Ben left the museum and walked 4 blocks to his next destination. What was Ben's destination?

21. Make Sense and Persevere Ben walked from the restaurant to the bus stop. Then he took the bus to the stadium. If he took the shortest route, how many blocks did Ben travel? Note that Ben can only travel along the grid lines.

Assessment

22. Liam used $2\frac{3}{4}$ cups of milk and $1\frac{1}{2}$ cups of cheese in a recipe. How many cups of cheese and milk did Liam use?

Ⓐ 3 cups

Ⓑ $3\frac{4}{6}$ cups

Ⓒ $4\frac{1}{4}$ cups

Ⓓ $4\frac{3}{4}$ cups

23. Garrett ran $21\frac{1}{2}$ miles last week. He ran $17\frac{7}{8}$ miles this week. How many miles did he run in all?

Ⓐ 38 miles

Ⓑ $38\frac{1}{2}$ miles

Ⓒ $39\frac{3}{8}$ miles

Ⓓ $39\frac{7}{8}$ miles

Name ______________________

Help Practice Buddy Tools Games

Homework & Practice 7-7

Use Models to Add Mixed Numbers

Another Look!

Draw a model to add $1\frac{7}{8} + 2\frac{1}{4}$.

Remember that you can use what you know about adding fractions to help you add mixed numbers.

Step 1

Model each addend using fraction strips.

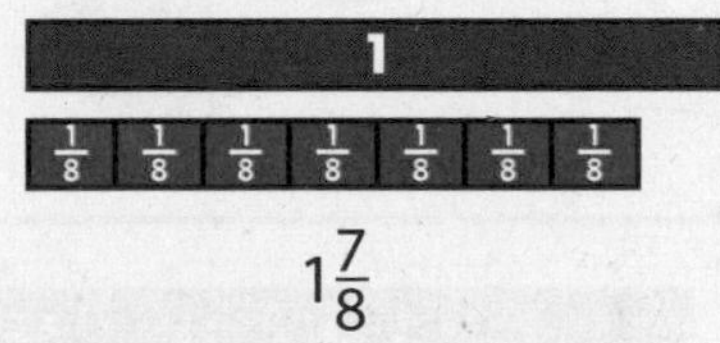

$1\frac{7}{8}$

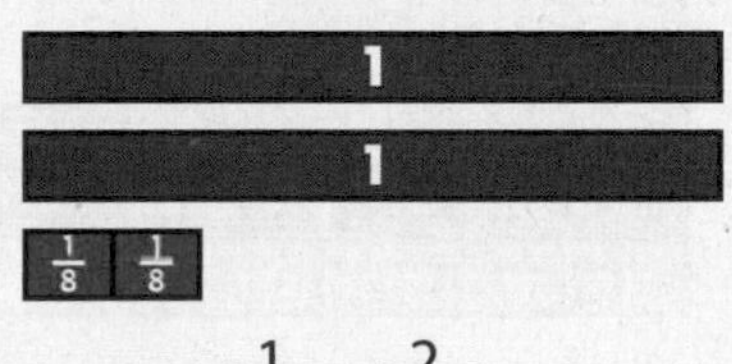

$2\frac{1}{4} = 2\frac{2}{8}$

Step 2

Add the fractions. Regroup if possible.

$$\frac{7}{8} + \frac{2}{8} = \frac{9}{8} = 1\frac{1}{8}$$

$\frac{8}{8} = 1$

$\frac{1}{8}$ left

Step 3

Add the whole numbers to the regrouped fractions. Write the sum.

So, $1\frac{7}{8} + 2\frac{1}{4} = 3\frac{9}{8} = 4\frac{1}{8}$.

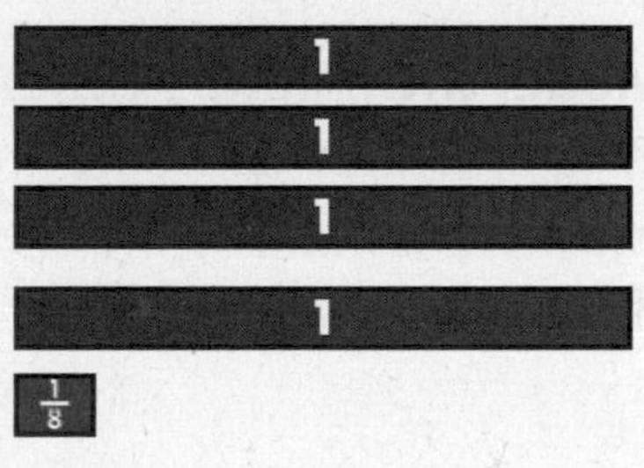

In **1–12**, use fraction strips to find each sum.

1. $3\frac{1}{2} + 1\frac{4}{8}$

2. $2\frac{5}{12} + 4\frac{1}{4}$

3. $3\frac{3}{4} + 3\frac{1}{2}$

4. $2\frac{5}{8} + 4\frac{3}{4}$

5. $5\frac{1}{3} + 3\frac{5}{6}$

6. $2\frac{1}{2} + 6\frac{3}{4}$

7. $3\frac{1}{4} + 4\frac{7}{8}$

8. $4\frac{5}{6} + 5\frac{7}{12}$

9. $2\frac{1}{4} + 4\frac{5}{8}$

10. $6\frac{1}{2} + 7\frac{3}{4}$

11. $4\frac{5}{8} + 6\frac{1}{2}$

12. $2\frac{1}{3} + 4\frac{5}{12}$

13. **Model with Math** Ken used $1\frac{3}{8}$ cups of walnuts and $1\frac{3}{4}$ cups of raisins to make trail mix. How many total cups of trail mix did he make?

14. Ken added $\frac{5}{8}$ cup more walnuts to the trail mix. How many cups of trail mix does he have?

15. **Higher Order Thinking** Kayla walked $1\frac{1}{4}$ miles from home to school. Then she walked $1\frac{3}{4}$ miles from school to the store and $2\frac{1}{2}$ miles from the store to the library. How many miles did Kayla walk from school to the library?

16. A painter mixes $\frac{1}{4}$ gallon of red paint, 3 quarts of yellow paint, and 2 quarts of white paint. How many quarts of paint are in the mixture?

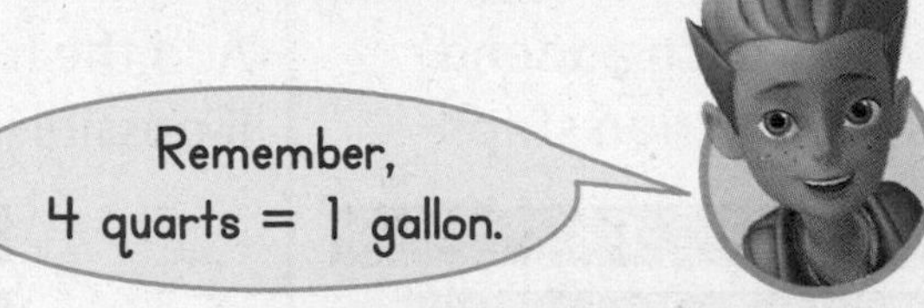

17. **Model with Math** Rachel has a board that is $1\frac{7}{12}$ feet long and another board that is $2\frac{11}{12}$ feet long. Write an expression Rachel can use to find the total length in feet of the two boards.

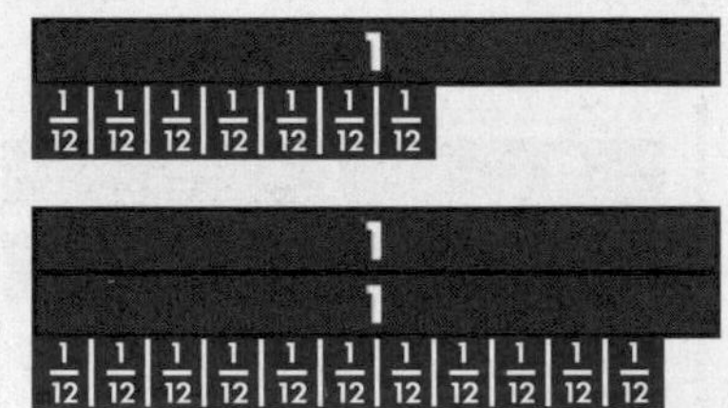

18. Lori went to the movies. She spent \$9.50 for a movie ticket, \$5.50 for a box of popcorn, and \$2.25 for a drink. How much did Lori spend in all? Show your work.

19. **Construct Arguments** Jane is adding $3\frac{1}{4} + 2\frac{7}{8}$ using fraction strips. How can she rename the sum of the fraction parts of the problem? Explain your thinking.

Assessment

20. McKenna spends $1\frac{3}{4}$ hours mopping the floors and $3\frac{3}{8}$ hours mowing and weeding the yard. How many hours does she spend on her chores?

Ⓐ 4 hours
Ⓑ $4\frac{1}{8}$ hours
Ⓒ 5 hours
Ⓓ $5\frac{1}{8}$ hours

21. Jackie's rain gauge showed $12\frac{2}{5}$ centimeters on April 15 and $15\frac{2}{10}$ centimeters on April 30. How many centimeters of rain fell in April?

Ⓐ 27 cm
Ⓑ $27\frac{3}{5}$ cm
Ⓒ $27\frac{4}{5}$ cm
Ⓓ 28 cm

Name ______________________________ 

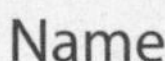

Lesson 7-8
Add Mixed Numbers

I can …
add mixed numbers.

I can also look for patterns to solve problems.

Solve & Share Joaquin used two types of flour in a muffin recipe. How much flour did he use in all? ***Solve any way you choose.***

Use Structure
Use what you know about adding fractions. *Show your work!*

Basic Muffins

$\frac{1}{2}$ c milk

$\frac{1}{3}$ c melted butter

2 eggs

$1\frac{1}{2}$ c whole wheat flour

$1\frac{2}{3}$ c buckwheat flour

1 tsp baking powder

Look Back! Construct Arguments How is adding mixed numbers with unlike denominators the same as adding fractions with unlike denominators? How is it different?

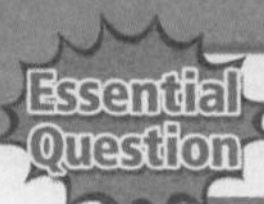

Learn Glossary

Essential Question How Can You Add Mixed Numbers?

A

Rhoda mixes $1\frac{1}{2}$ cups of sand with $2\frac{2}{3}$ cups of potting mixture to prepare soil for her cactus plants. After mixing them together, how many cups of soil does Rhoda have?

B

Step 1

Find $2\frac{2}{3} + 1\frac{1}{2}$.

Write equivalent fractions with a common denominator.

$$\begin{array}{r} 2\frac{2}{3} = 2\frac{4}{6} \\ + 1\frac{1}{2} = 1\frac{3}{6} \\ \hline \end{array}$$

C

Step 2

Add the fractions.

$$\begin{array}{r} 2\frac{2}{3} = 2\frac{4}{6} \\ + 1\frac{1}{2} = 1\frac{3}{6} \\ \hline \frac{7}{6} \end{array}$$

D

Step 3

Add the whole numbers.

$$\begin{array}{r} 2\frac{2}{3} = 2\frac{4}{6} \\ + 1\frac{1}{2} = 1\frac{3}{6} \\ \hline 3\frac{7}{6} \end{array}$$

Rewrite $\frac{7}{6}$ as a mixed number.

$$3\frac{7}{6} = 3 + 1\frac{1}{6} = 4\frac{1}{6}$$

Rhoda has $4\frac{1}{6}$ cups of soil.

Convince Me! Critique Reasoning Kyle used 9 as an estimate for $3\frac{1}{6} + 5\frac{7}{8}$. He got $9\frac{1}{24}$ for the exact sum. Is his calculated answer reasonable? Explain.

Name ____________________

Practice Buddy Tools Assessment

Guided Practice*

Do You Understand?

1. **Reasoning** How is adding mixed numbers like adding fractions and whole numbers?

2. Look at the example on page 414. Why is the denominator 6 used in the equivalent fractions?

Do You Know How?

In **3–6**, estimate and then find each sum.

3. $1\frac{7}{8} = 1\frac{\square}{8}$
$+\ 1\frac{1}{4} = 1\frac{\square}{8}$

4. $2\frac{2}{5} = 2\frac{\square}{30}$
$+\ 5\frac{5}{6} = 5\frac{\square}{30}$

5. $4\frac{1}{9} + 1\frac{1}{3}$

6. $6\frac{5}{12} + 4\frac{5}{8}$

Independent Practice

Leveled Practice In **7–18**, estimate and then find each sum.

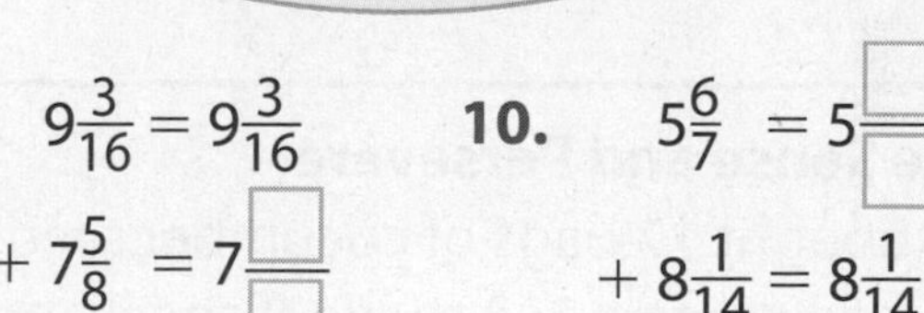

7. $3\frac{1}{6} = 3\frac{\square}{6}$
$+\ 5\frac{2}{3} = 5\frac{\square}{6}$

8. $11\frac{1}{2} = 11\frac{\square}{10}$
$+\ 10\frac{3}{5} = 10\frac{\square}{10}$

9. $9\frac{3}{16} = 9\frac{3}{16}$
$+\ 7\frac{5}{8} = 7\frac{\square}{\square}$

10. $5\frac{6}{7} = 5\frac{\square}{\square}$
$+\ 8\frac{1}{14} = 8\frac{1}{14}$

11. $4\frac{1}{10}$
$+\ 6\frac{1}{2}$

12. $9\frac{7}{12}$
$+\ 4\frac{3}{4}$

13. 5
$+\ 3\frac{1}{8}$

14. $8\frac{3}{4}$
$+\ 7\frac{3}{4}$

15. $2\frac{3}{4} + 7\frac{3}{5}$

16. $3\frac{8}{9} + 8\frac{1}{2}$

17. $1\frac{7}{12} + 2\frac{3}{8}$

18. $3\frac{11}{12} + 9\frac{1}{16}$

*For another example, see Set G on page 448.

Problem Solving

19. Use the map to find the answer.

a What is the distance from the start to the end of the trail?

b Louise walked from the start of the trail to the bird lookout and back. Did she walk a longer or shorter distance than if she had walked from the start of the trail to the end? Explain.

c Another day, Louise walked from the start of the trail to the end. At the end, she realized she forgot her binoculars at the bird lookout. She walked from the end of the trail to the bird lookout and back. What is the total distance she walked?

20. Higher Order Thinking Twice a day Cameron's cat eats 4 ounces of dry cat food and 2 ounces of wet cat food. Dry food comes in 5-pound bags. Wet food comes in 6-ounce cans.

a How many cans of wet food should he buy to feed his cat for a week?

b How many ounces of wet cat food will be left over at the end of the week?

c How many days can he feed his cat from a 5-pound bag of dry food?

21. Make Sense and Persevere Julia bought 12 bags of cucumber seeds. Each bag contains 42 seeds. If she plants one half of the seeds, how many seeds does she have left?

22. Critique Reasoning John added $2\frac{7}{12}$ and $5\frac{2}{3}$ and got $7\frac{1}{4}$ as the sum. Is John's answer reasonable? Explain.

Assessment

23. A male Parson's chameleon can be up to $23\frac{1}{2}$ inches long. It can extend its tongue up to $35\frac{1}{4}$ inches to catch its food. Write an addition sentence to show the total length of a male Parson's chameleon when its tongue is fully extended.

24. Arnie skated $1\frac{3}{4}$ miles from home to the lake. He skated $1\frac{1}{3}$ miles around the lake and then skated back home. Write an addition sentence to show how many miles Arnie skated in all.

Name ________________________

Help Practice Buddy Tools Games

Homework & Practice 7-8

Add Mixed Numbers

Another Look!

Randy did homework for $2\frac{5}{6}$ hours. Then he played soccer for $1\frac{3}{4}$ hours. How many hours did he spend on the two activities?

Before you add, you need to write equivalent fractions.

Step 1

Write equivalent fractions with a common denominator. You can use fraction strips to show the equivalent fractions.

$2\frac{5}{6} = 2\frac{10}{12}$ $\quad$ $1\frac{3}{4} = 1\frac{9}{12}$

Step 2

Add the fraction part of the mixed numbers first. Then add the whole numbers.

$\frac{9}{12} + \frac{10}{12} = \frac{19}{12}$

$1 + 2 = 3$

$\frac{19}{12} + 3 = 3\frac{19}{12}$

Step 3

Regroup $\frac{19}{12}$ as $1\frac{7}{12}$. Find the sum.

$3\frac{19}{12} = 3 + 1\frac{7}{12} = 4\frac{7}{12}$

Randy spent $4\frac{7}{12}$ hours on the two activities.

In **1–12**, find each sum.

Remember to use an estimate to check that your answer is reasonable.

1. $2\frac{5}{6} = 2\frac{\square\square}{12}$
$+\ 3\frac{1}{4} = 3\frac{\square}{12}$

2. $5\frac{2}{5} = 5\frac{\square}{10}$
$+\ 4\frac{1}{2} = 4\frac{\square}{10}$

3. $1\frac{3}{8}$
$+\ 6\frac{3}{4}$

4. $10\frac{1}{3} + \frac{7}{9}$

5. $3\frac{1}{4} + 6\frac{2}{3}$

6. $2\frac{1}{2} + 2\frac{1}{6}$

7. $3\frac{7}{8} + 5\frac{2}{3}$

8. $4\frac{5}{6} + 9\frac{5}{9}$

9. $15\frac{1}{3} + 1\frac{5}{12}$

10. $12\frac{3}{4} + 6\frac{3}{8}$

11. $14\frac{7}{10} + 3\frac{3}{5}$

12. $8\frac{5}{8} + 7\frac{7}{16}$

13. Reasoning Tirzah wants to put a fence around her garden. She has 22 yards of fence material. Does she have enough to go all the way around the garden? Explain why or why not.

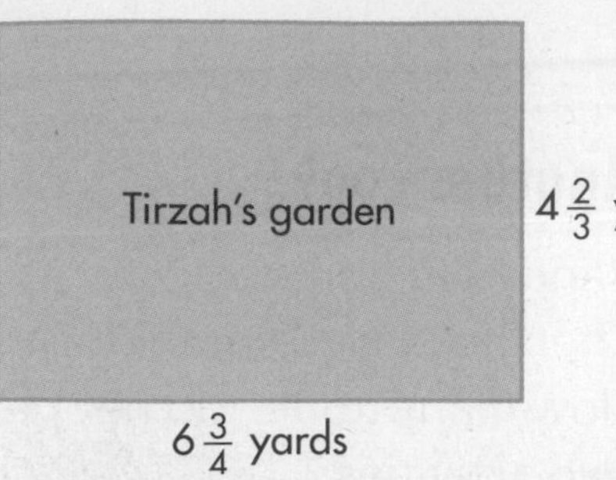

14. Higher Order Thinking Lake Trail is $4\frac{3}{5}$ miles long. Outlook Trail is $5\frac{5}{6}$ miles long. Pinewoods Trail is $1\frac{3}{10}$ miles longer than Lake Trail. Which trail is longer, Pinewoods Trail or Outlook Trail? Explain.

15. Reasoning Can the sum of two mixed numbers be equal to 2? Explain.

Use the data table for **16–18**.

16. Joan reads that the mass of an average elephant's brain is $3\frac{4}{10}$ kilograms greater than an average man's brain. How many kilograms is an average elephant's brain?

DATA

Vital Organ Measures

Average woman's brain	$1\frac{3}{10}$ kg	$2\frac{4}{5}$ lb
Average man's brain	$1\frac{2}{5}$ kg	3 lb
Average human heart	$\frac{3}{10}$ kg	$\frac{7}{10}$ lb

17. What is the total mass of an average man's brain and heart in kilograms (kg)?

18. What is the total weight of an average woman's brain and heart in pounds (lb)?

Assessment

19. Larry studied $2\frac{1}{4}$ hours Monday. He studied $2\frac{5}{6}$ hours Tuesday. Write an addition sentence to show how many hours he spent studying Monday and Tuesday.

20. Trish drove $18\frac{1}{8}$ miles yesterday. She drove $13\frac{2}{3}$ miles today. Write an addition sentence to show how many miles Trish drove in all.

Name ____________________

Lesson 7-9
Use Models to Subtract Mixed Numbers

I can ...
use models to subtract mixed numbers.

I can also generalize from examples.

Solve & Share

Clara and Erin volunteered at an animal shelter a total of $9\frac{5}{6}$ hours. Clara worked for $4\frac{1}{3}$ hours. How many hours did Erin work? ***You can use fraction strips to solve this problem.***

Generalize
How can you use what you know about adding mixed numbers to help you subtract mixed numbers? *Show your work!*

Look Back! Reasoning How can you estimate the difference for the problem above? Explain your thinking.

How Can You Model Subtraction of Mixed Numbers?

A

James needs $1\frac{11}{12}$ inches of pipe to repair a small part of a bicycle frame. He has a pipe that is $2\frac{1}{2}$ inches long. Does he have enough pipe left over to fix a $\frac{3}{4}$-inch piece of frame on another bike?

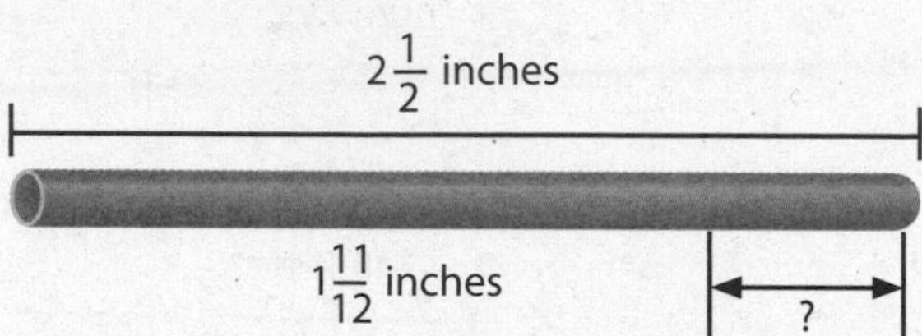

B

Step 1

Model the number you are subtracting from, $2\frac{6}{12}$.

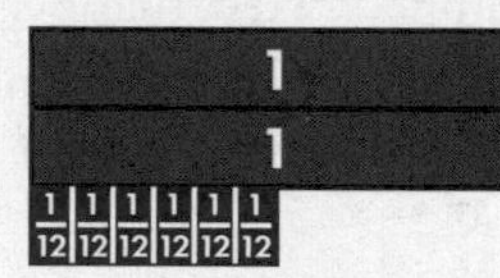

If the fraction you will be subtracting is greater than the fraction part of the number you model, rename 1 whole.

Since $\frac{11}{12} > \frac{6}{12}$, rename 1 whole as $\frac{12}{12}$.

C

Step 2

Use your renamed model to cross out the number that you are subtracting, $1\frac{11}{12}$.

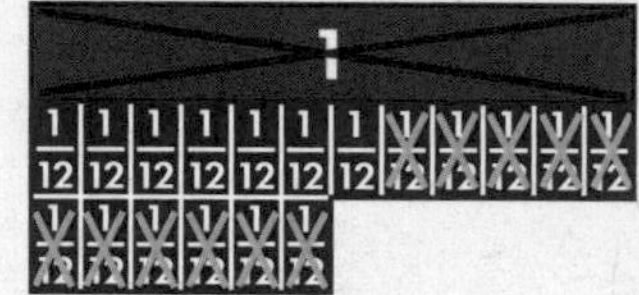

There are $\frac{7}{12}$ left.

So, $2\frac{1}{2} - 1\frac{11}{12} = \frac{7}{12}$.

James will have $\frac{7}{12}$ inch of pipe left. He does not have enough for the other bike.

Convince Me! **Use Appropriate Tools**

Use fraction strips to find $5\frac{1}{2} - 2\frac{3}{4}$.

Name ___________________________________

Practice Buddy Tools Assessment

Guided Practice*

Do You Understand?

1. **Construct Arguments** When subtracting two mixed numbers, is it always necessary to rename one of the wholes? Explain.

Do You Know How?

In **2–5**, use fraction strips to find each difference.

2. $4\frac{5}{6} - 2\frac{1}{3}$

3. $4\frac{1}{8} - 3\frac{3}{4}$

4. $5\frac{1}{2} - 2\frac{5}{6}$

5. $5\frac{4}{10} - 3\frac{4}{5}$

Independent Practice

In **6** and **7**, use each model to find the difference.

6. Terrell lives $2\frac{5}{6}$ blocks away from his best friend. His school is $4\frac{1}{3}$ blocks away in the same direction. If he stops at his best friend's house first, how much farther do they have to walk to school?

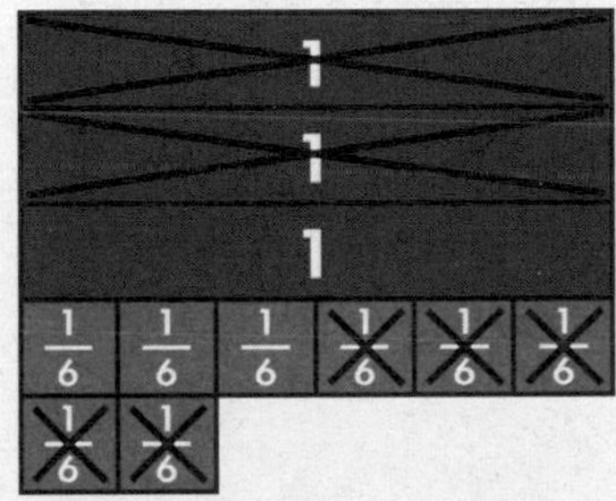

7. Tina bought $3\frac{1}{2}$ pounds of turkey and $2\frac{1}{4}$ pounds of cheese. She used $1\frac{1}{2}$ pounds of cheese to make macaroni and cheese. How much cheese does she have left?

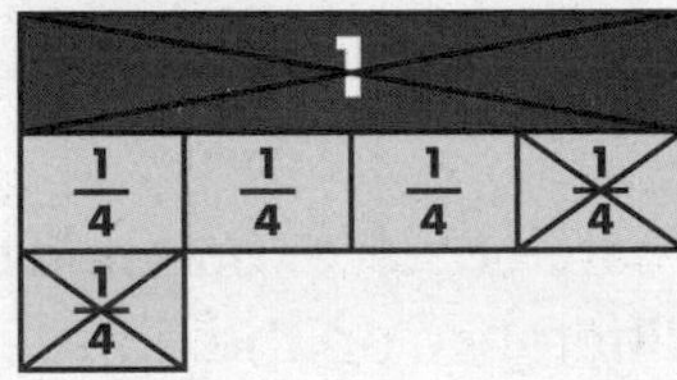

In **8–15**, use fraction strips to find each difference.

8. $12\frac{3}{4} - 9\frac{5}{8}$

9. $8\frac{1}{6} - 7\frac{2}{3}$

10. $13\frac{7}{9} - 10\frac{2}{3}$

11. $3\frac{1}{12} - 2\frac{3}{4}$

12. $6\frac{3}{4} - 3\frac{11}{12}$

13. $4\frac{3}{5} - 1\frac{1}{10}$

14. $6\frac{1}{2} - 3\frac{7}{10}$

15. $6\frac{2}{3} - 4\frac{2}{9}$

*For another example, see Set F on page 447.

Problem Solving

For **16** and **17**, use the table at the right.

16. How much longer is a Red Oak leaf than a Sugar Maple leaf? Write an equation to model your work.

17. How much longer is a Red Oak leaf than a Paper Birch leaf? Write an equation to model your work.

DATA

Tree Leaf Lengths

Tree	Leaf Length (in.)
Sugar Maple	$6\frac{3}{4}$
Red Oak	$8\frac{1}{2}$
Paper Birch	$3\frac{5}{8}$

18. Higher Order Thinking Lemmy walked $3\frac{1}{2}$ miles on Saturday and $4\frac{3}{4}$ miles on Sunday. Ronnie walked $5\frac{3}{8}$ miles on Saturday. Who walked farther? How much farther?

19. Model with Math Jamal is buying lunch for his family. He buys 4 drinks that each cost $1.75 and 4 sandwiches that each cost $7.50. If the prices include tax and he also leaves an $7 tip, how much does he spend in all? Write equations to show your work.

Assessment

20. Draw lines to match each expression on the left to its difference on the right.

Expression	Difference
$12\frac{1}{2} - 10\frac{11}{12}$	$1\frac{3}{4}$
$5\frac{2}{3} - 4\frac{4}{9}$	$1\frac{7}{12}$
$12\frac{3}{4} - 11\frac{1}{2}$	$1\frac{2}{9}$
$6\frac{1}{4} - 4\frac{1}{2}$	$1\frac{1}{4}$

21. Draw lines to match each expression on the left to its difference on the right.

Expression	Difference
$13\frac{5}{6} - 10\frac{1}{3}$	$2\frac{3}{5}$
$4\frac{1}{2} - 1\frac{2}{3}$	$2\frac{5}{6}$
$14\frac{3}{10} - 10\frac{3}{5}$	$3\frac{7}{10}$
$12\frac{4}{10} - 9\frac{4}{5}$	$3\frac{1}{2}$

Name ______________________________

Homework & Practice 7-9

Use Models to Subtract Mixed Numbers

Another Look!

Draw a model to find $2\frac{1}{5} - 1\frac{3}{10}$.

Remember to check that your answer makes sense.

Step 1

Rename the fractions with a common denominator. Use the common denominator to model the number you are subtracting from, $2\frac{1}{5}$ or $2\frac{2}{10}$.

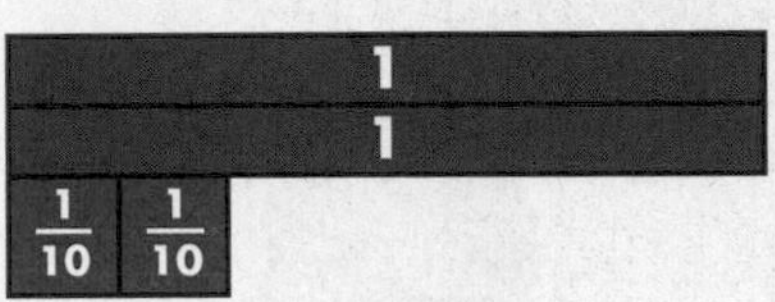

Step 2

Rename $2\frac{2}{10}$ as $1\frac{12}{10}$. Cross out one whole and $\frac{3}{10}$ to show subtracting $1\frac{3}{10}$.

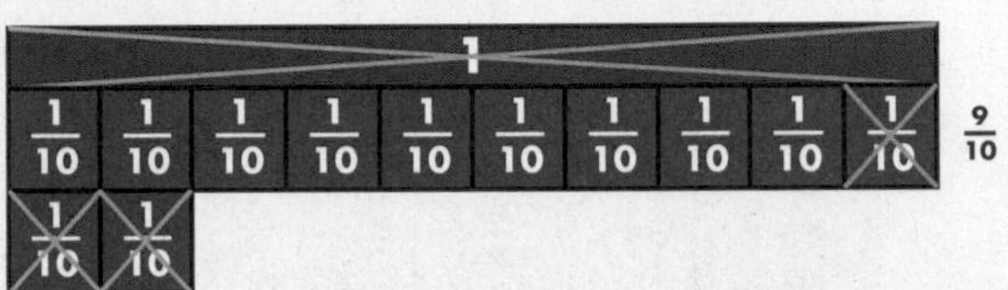

Write the parts of the model that are left as a fraction or mixed number.

So, $2\frac{1}{5} - 1\frac{3}{10} = \frac{9}{10}$.

In **1–12**, find each difference.

Use fraction strips to help.

1. $6\frac{1}{4} - 3\frac{5}{8}$

2. $4 - 1\frac{1}{2}$

3. $5\frac{1}{3} - 3\frac{1}{6}$

4. $7\frac{2}{5} - 4\frac{7}{10}$

5. $12\frac{3}{4} - 11\frac{7}{8}$

6. $9\frac{3}{10} - 2\frac{2}{5}$

7. $8\frac{1}{4} - 2\frac{5}{12}$

8. $12\frac{1}{3} - 5\frac{4}{6}$

9. $9\frac{1}{2} - 6\frac{9}{10}$

10. $3\frac{4}{5} - 1\frac{4}{10}$

11. $7\frac{1}{4} - 3\frac{5}{8}$

12. $10\frac{1}{3} - 7\frac{5}{9}$

13. Model with Math Use the model to find the difference. $3\frac{1}{5} - 1\frac{4}{5}$

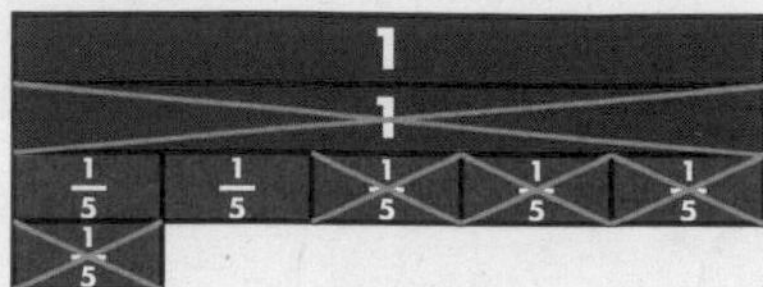

14. Micah's rain gauge showed that $9\frac{1}{2}$ centimeters of rain fell last month. This month, the rain gauge measured $10\frac{3}{10}$ centimeters. How many more centimeters of rain fell this month?

15. Higher Order Thinking Suppose you are finding $8\frac{3}{10} - 6\frac{4}{5}$. Do you need to rename $8\frac{3}{10}$? If so, explain how you rename it to subtract. Then find the difference.

16. Critique Reasoning Danny said 12.309 rounded to the nearest tenth is 12.4. Is Danny correct? Explain.

17. Math and Science Fossils show that insects were much larger around 300 million years ago than they are today. The table at the right shows some of the wing lengths found in fossils. How much longer was the wing length of the dragonfly than the wing length of the fly?

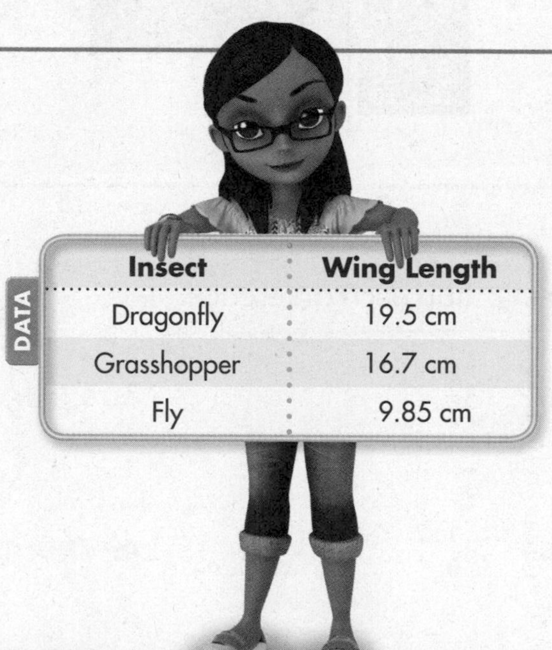

DATA

Insect	Wing Length
Dragonfly	19.5 cm
Grasshopper	16.7 cm
Fly	9.85 cm

Assessment

18. Draw a line to match each expression on the left to its difference on the right.

Expression	Difference
$1\frac{1}{2} - \frac{3}{4}$	$2\frac{1}{3}$
$6\frac{1}{6} - 3\frac{5}{6}$	$1\frac{1}{2}$
$12\frac{5}{6} - 11\frac{1}{3}$	$1\frac{7}{8}$
$14\frac{5}{8} - 12\frac{3}{4}$	$\frac{3}{4}$

19. Draw a line to match each expression on the left to its difference on the right.

Expression	Difference
$12\frac{1}{3} - 10\frac{2}{9}$	$2\frac{1}{9}$
$6\frac{2}{12} - 4\frac{5}{6}$	$1\frac{7}{8}$
$15\frac{3}{4} - 13\frac{7}{8}$	$1\frac{7}{9}$
$3\frac{4}{9} - 1\frac{2}{3}$	$1\frac{1}{3}$

Name ______________________

Solve

Lesson 7-10
Subtract Mixed Numbers

I can ...
subtract mixed numbers.

I can also look for patterns to solve problems.

Solve & Share

Evan walks $2\frac{1}{8}$ miles to his aunt's house. He has already walked $\frac{3}{4}$ mile. How much farther does he have to go? ***Solve this problem any way you choose.***

$2\frac{1}{8}$ miles

$\frac{3}{4}$	x

Look Back! Critique Reasoning Jon said, "Changing $\frac{3}{4}$ to $\frac{6}{8}$ makes this problem easier." What do you think Jon meant?

How Can You Subtract Mixed Numbers?

A

A golf ball measures about $1\frac{2}{3}$ inches across the center. What is the difference between the distance across the center of the hole and the golf ball?

You can use subtraction to find the difference.

B

Step 1

Write equivalent fractions with a common denominator.

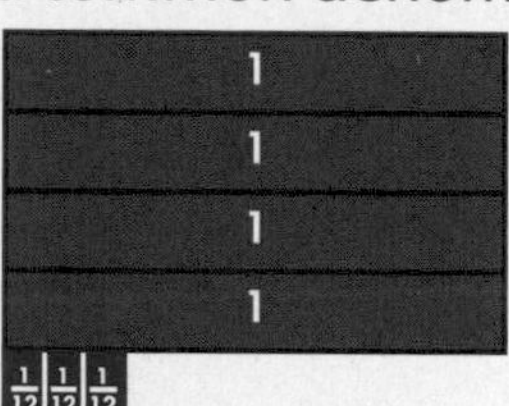

$$\begin{array}{r} 4\frac{1}{4} = 4\frac{3}{12} \\ -\ 1\frac{2}{3} = 1\frac{8}{12} \\ \hline \end{array}$$

Since $\frac{8}{12} > \frac{3}{12}$, you can rename 1 as $\frac{12}{12}$ to subtract.

C

Step 2

Rename $4\frac{3}{12}$ to show more twelfths.

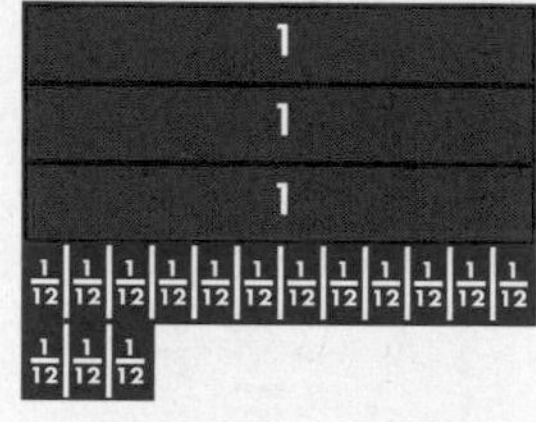

$$\begin{array}{r} 4\frac{3}{12} = 3\frac{15}{12} \\ -\ 1\frac{8}{12} = 1\frac{8}{12} \\ \hline \end{array}$$

D

Step 3

Subtract the fractions. Then subtract the whole numbers.

$$\begin{array}{r} 4\frac{1}{4} = 4\frac{3}{12} = 3\frac{15}{12} \\ -\ 1\frac{2}{3} = 1\frac{8}{12} = 1\frac{8}{12} \\ \hline 2\frac{7}{12} \end{array}$$

The hole is $2\frac{7}{12}$ inches wider.

Convince Me! Critique Reasoning Estimate $8\frac{1}{3} - 3\frac{3}{4}$. Tell how you got your estimate. Susi subtracted and found the actual difference to be $5\frac{7}{12}$. Is her answer reasonable? Explain.

Name ______________________________

Practice Buddy   Tools   Assessment

Another Example

Sometimes you may have to rename a whole number to subtract.
Find the difference of $6 - 2\frac{3}{8}$.

$$\begin{array}{r} 6 \\ -\,2\frac{3}{8} \\ \hline \end{array} \longrightarrow \text{rename} \longrightarrow \begin{array}{r} 5\frac{8}{8} \\ -\,2\frac{3}{8} \\ \hline 3\frac{5}{8} \end{array}$$

Guided Practice*

Do You Understand?

1. In the example above, why do you need to rename the 6?

2. Reasoning In the example on page 426, could two golf balls fall into the hole at the same time? Explain your reasoning.

Do You Know How?

In **3–6**, estimate and then find each difference.

3. $7\frac{2}{3} = 7\frac{\square}{6} = 6\frac{\square}{6}$
$-\,3\frac{5}{6} = 3\frac{\square}{6} = 3\frac{\square}{6}$

4. $5 = \square\frac{\square}{4}$
$-\,2\frac{3}{4} = 2\frac{3}{4}$

5. $6\frac{3}{10} - 1\frac{4}{5}$

6. $9\frac{1}{3} - 4\frac{3}{4}$

Independent Practice

In **7–18**, estimate and then find each difference.

7. $8\frac{1}{4} = 8\frac{\square}{8} = 7\frac{\square}{8}$
$-\,2\frac{7}{8} = 2\frac{\square}{8} = 2\frac{\square}{8}$

8. $3\frac{1}{2} = 3\frac{\square}{6}$
$-\,1\frac{1}{3} = 1\frac{\square}{6}$

9. $4\frac{1}{8}$
$-\,1\frac{1}{2}$

10. 6
$-\,2\frac{4}{5}$

11. $6\frac{1}{3} - 5\frac{2}{3}$

12. $9\frac{1}{2} - 6\frac{3}{4}$

13. $8\frac{3}{16} - 3\frac{5}{8}$

14. $7\frac{1}{2} - \frac{7}{10}$

15. $15\frac{1}{6} - 4\frac{3}{8}$

16. $13\frac{1}{12} - 8\frac{1}{4}$

17. $6\frac{1}{3} - 2\frac{3}{5}$

18. $10\frac{5}{12} - 4\frac{7}{8}$

*For another example, see Set G on page 448.

Problem Solving

19. Model with Math The average weight of a basketball is $21\frac{1}{10}$ ounces. The average weight of a baseball is $5\frac{1}{4}$ ounces. How many more ounces does the basketball weigh? Write the missing numbers in the diagram.

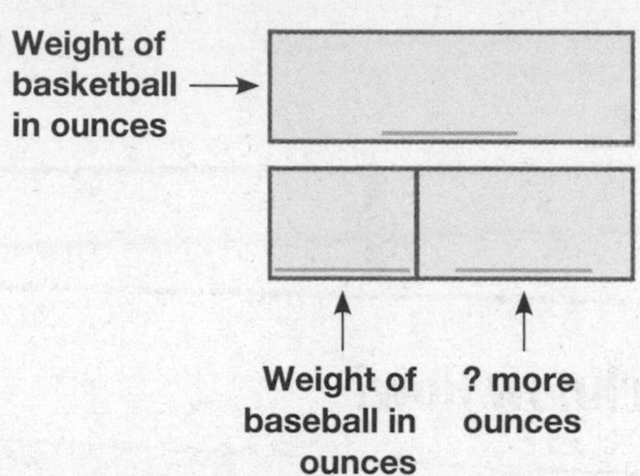

20. Math and Science The smallest mammals on Earth are the bumblebee bat and the Etruscan pygmy shrew. The length of a certain bumblebee bat is $1\frac{9}{50}$ inches. The length of a certain Etruscan pygmy shrew is $1\frac{21}{50}$ inches. How much smaller is the bat than the shrew?

21. Be Precise How are the purple quadrilateral and the green quadrilateral alike? How are they different?

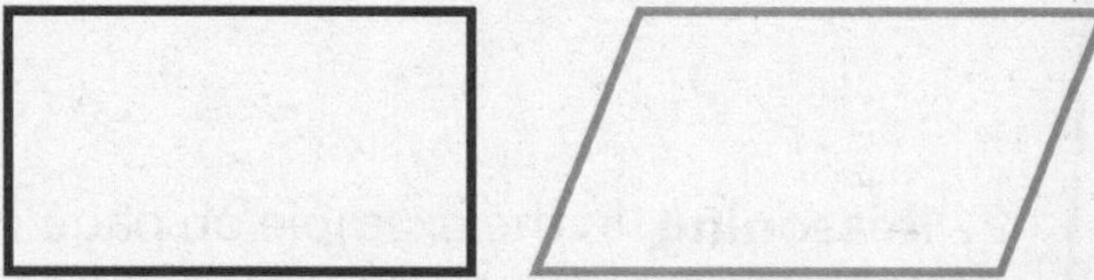

22. Higher Order Thinking Sam used the model to find $2\frac{5}{12} - 1\frac{7}{12}$. Did Sam model the problem correctly? Explain. If not, show how the problem should have been modeled and find the difference.

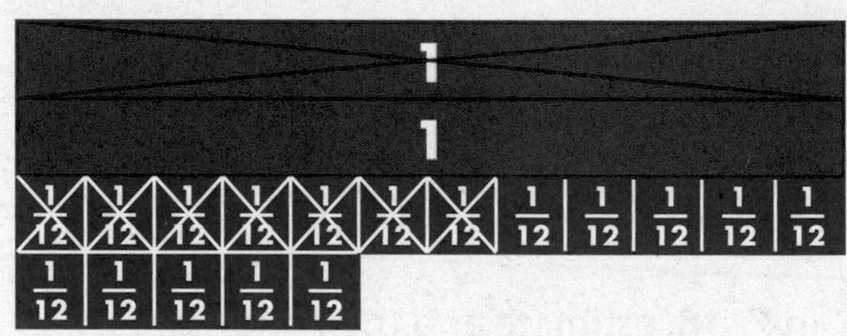

Assessment

23. Choose the correct number from the box below to complete the subtraction sentence that follows.

1	2	3	4	5

$3\frac{5}{8} - 1\frac{\square}{4} = 2\frac{3}{8}$

24. Choose the correct number from the box below to complete the subtraction sentence that follows.

2	4	5	10	15

$14\frac{1}{10} - 3\frac{1}{\square} = 10\frac{3}{5}$

Name ____________________

Help | Practice Buddy | Tools | Games

Homework & Practice 7-10

Subtract Mixed Numbers

Another Look!

The Plainville Zoo has had elephants for $2\frac{2}{3}$ years. The zoo has had zebras for $1\frac{1}{2}$ years. How many more years has the zoo had elephants?

Remember: You need a common denominator to subtract fractions.

Step 1

Write equivalent fractions with a common denominator. You can use fraction strips.

$2\frac{2}{3} = 2\frac{4}{6}$

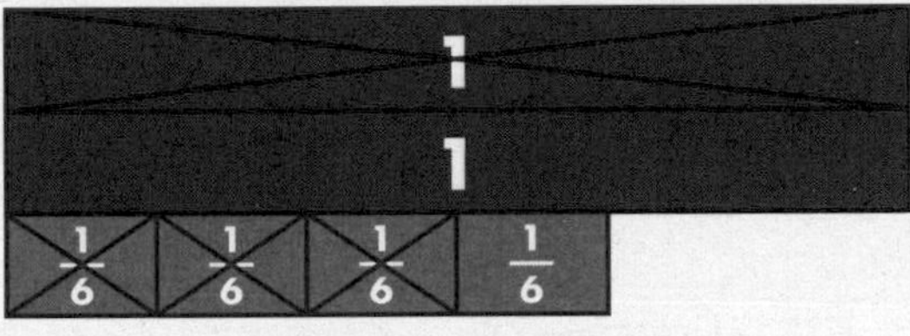

$1\frac{1}{2} = 1\frac{3}{6}$

Step 2

Find the difference $2\frac{4}{6} - 1\frac{3}{6}$. Subtract the fractions. Then subtract the whole numbers.

$\frac{4}{6} - \frac{3}{6} = \frac{1}{6}$ $\quad$ $2 - 1 = 1$

So, $2\frac{2}{3} - 1\frac{1}{2} = 1\frac{1}{6}$.

The zoo has had the elephants $1\frac{1}{6}$ years longer.

In **1–9**, find each difference.

1. $4\frac{3}{5} = 4\frac{\square}{15}$
$-\,2\frac{1}{3} = 2\frac{\square}{15}$

2. 5
$-\,3\frac{5}{6}$

3. $10\frac{5}{8}$
$-\,5\frac{3}{4}$

4. $5\frac{6}{7}$
$-\,1\frac{1}{2}$

5. 3
$-\,1\frac{3}{4}$

6. $6\frac{5}{6}$
$-\,5\frac{1}{2}$

7. $7\frac{3}{10} - 2\frac{1}{5}$

8. $9\frac{2}{3} - 6\frac{1}{2}$

9. $8\frac{1}{4} - \frac{7}{8}$

10. Reasoning To find the difference of $7 - 3\frac{5}{12}$, how do you rename the 7?

11. Higher Order Thinking Is it necessary to rename $4\frac{1}{4}$ to subtract $\frac{3}{4}$? Explain.

Use the table for **12–15**. The table shows the length and width of different bird eggs.

DATA

Egg Sizes in Inches (in.)

Bird	Length	Width
Canada goose	$3\frac{2}{5}$	$2\frac{3}{10}$
Robin	$\frac{3}{4}$	$\frac{3}{5}$
Turtle dove	$1\frac{1}{5}$	$\frac{9}{10}$
Raven	$1\frac{9}{10}$	$1\frac{3}{10}$

12. How much longer is the Canada goose egg than the raven egg?

13. How much wider is the turtle dove egg than the robin egg?

14. Write the birds in order from the shortest egg to the longest egg.

15. Model with Math Write and solve an equation to find the difference between the length and width of a turtle dove egg.

Assessment

16. Choose the correct number from the box below to complete the subtraction sentence that follows.

1	2	6	8	24	48

$1\frac{5}{6} - \frac{3}{8} = 1\frac{11}{\square}$

17. Choose the correct number from the box below to complete the subtraction sentence that follows.

1	2	3	4	5	6

$9\frac{5}{12} - 3\frac{2}{3} = 5\frac{\square}{4}$

Name ___________________________________

Solve

Lesson 7-11
Add and Subtract Mixed Numbers

I can …
add and subtract mixed numbers.

I can also reason about math.

Solve & Share

Tim has 15 feet of wrapping paper. He uses $4\frac{1}{3}$ feet for his daughter's present and $5\frac{3}{8}$ feet for his niece's present. How much wrapping paper does Tim have left? ***Solve this problem any way you choose.***

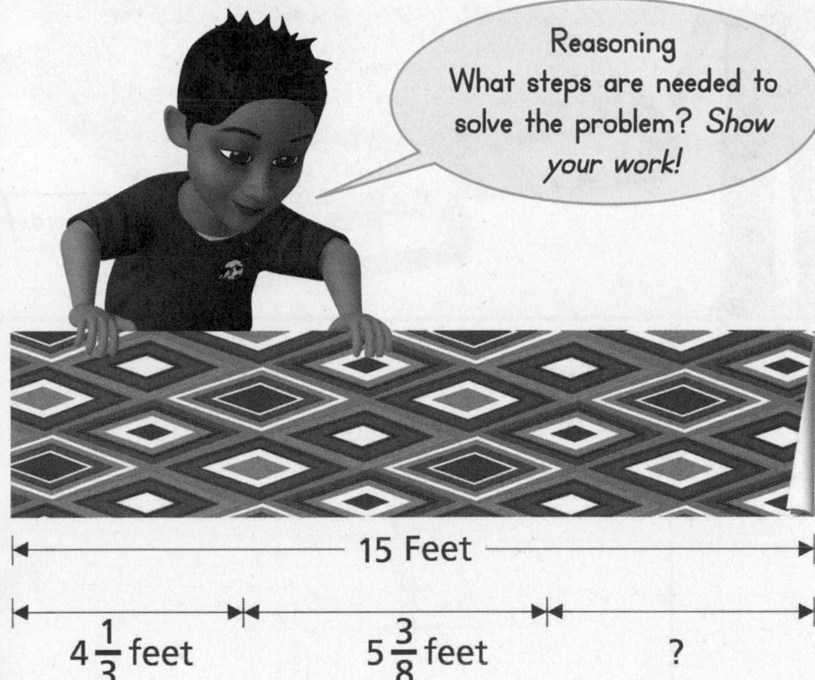

Look Back! Construct Arguments In the problem above, how could you have estimated the amount of wrapping paper that is left?

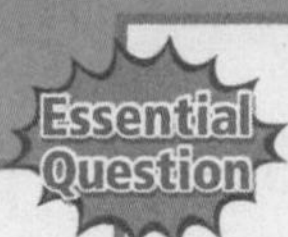

Essential Question

How Can Adding and Subtracting Mixed Numbers Help You Solve Problems?

A

Clarisse has two lengths of fabric to make covers for a sofa and chair. The covers require $9\frac{2}{3}$ yards of fabric. How much fabric will Clarisse have left?

Find a common denominator when adding and subtracting fractions.

B

Step 1

Add to find out how much fabric Clarisse has in all.

$$\begin{array}{r} 5\frac{3}{4} = 5\frac{9}{12} \\ +\ 7\frac{5}{6} = 7\frac{10}{12} \\ \hline 12\frac{19}{12} = 13\frac{7}{12} \end{array}$$

Clarisse has $13\frac{7}{12}$ yards of fabric in all.

C

Step 2

Subtract the amount she will use from the total length of fabric.

$$\begin{array}{r} 13\frac{7}{12} = 12\frac{19}{12} \\ -\ \ 9\frac{2}{3} = \ \ 9\frac{8}{12} \\ \hline 3\frac{11}{12} \end{array}$$

Clarisse will have $3\frac{11}{12}$ yards of fabric left.

Convince Me! **Make Sense and Persevere** Clarisse has $14\frac{3}{4}$ yards of fabric to cover another sofa and chair. The new sofa needs $9\frac{1}{6}$ yards of fabric and the new chair needs $4\frac{1}{3}$ yards of fabric. Estimate to decide if Clarisse has enough fabric. If so, how much fabric will she have left?

Name ___________________

Guided Practice*

Do You Understand?

1. **Reasoning** In the example on page 432, why do you add before you subtract?

2. **Construct Arguments** In the example on page 432, does Clarisse have enough fabric left over to make two cushions that each use $2\frac{1}{3}$ yards of fabric? Explain.

Do You Know How?

In **3–5**, find the sum or difference.

3. $5\frac{1}{9} - 2\frac{2}{3}$

4. $2\frac{1}{4} + 8\frac{2}{3}$

5. $6\frac{7}{25} - 3\frac{9}{50}$

In **6–9**, solve. Do the addition in the parentheses first.

6. $4\frac{3}{5} + 11\frac{2}{15}$

7. $8\frac{2}{3} - 3\frac{3}{4}$

8. $\left(7\frac{2}{3} + 3\frac{4}{5}\right) - 1\frac{4}{15}$

9. $8\frac{2}{5} - \left(3\frac{2}{3} + 2\frac{3}{5}\right)$

Independent Practice

In **10–14**, find each sum or difference.

10. $9\frac{1}{3} - 4\frac{1}{6}$

11. $12\frac{1}{4} - 9\frac{3}{5}$

12. $6\frac{3}{5} + 1\frac{3}{25}$

13. $3\frac{4}{9} + 2\frac{2}{3}$

14. $5\frac{31}{75} - 3\frac{2}{25}$

In **15–20**, solve. Do the operation in the parentheses first.

15. $\left(2\frac{5}{8} + 2\frac{1}{2}\right) - 4\frac{2}{3}$

16. $\left(5\frac{3}{4} + 1\frac{5}{6}\right) - 6\frac{7}{12}$

17. $4\frac{3}{5} + \left(8\frac{1}{5} - 7\frac{3}{10}\right)$

18. $\left(13 - 10\frac{1}{3}\right) + 2\frac{2}{3}$

19. $\left(2\frac{1}{2} + 3\frac{1}{4}\right) - 1\frac{1}{4}$

20. $2\frac{3}{14} + \left(15\frac{4}{7} - 6\frac{3}{4}\right)$

*For another example, see Set G on page 448.

Problem Solving

In **21–23**, use the table below.

DATA

Frog Species	Body Length (cm)	Maximum Jump (cm)
Bullfrog	$20\frac{3}{10}$	$213\frac{1}{2}$
Leopard frog	$12\frac{1}{2}$	$162\frac{1}{2}$
South African sharp-nosed frog	$7\frac{3}{5}$	$334\frac{2}{5}$

21. Be Precise How much longer is the maximum jump of a South African sharp-nosed frog than the maximum jump of a leopard frog?

22. How many centimeters long is a bullfrog? Round to the nearest whole number.

23. Higher Order Thinking Which frog jumps about 10 times its body length? Explain how you found your answer.

24. A-Z **Vocabulary** Write three numbers that are **common denominators** of $\frac{7}{15}$ and $\frac{3}{5}$.

25. Marie plants 12 packages of vegetable seeds in a community garden. Each package costs $1.97 with tax. What is the total cost of the seeds?

Assessment

26. Does the mixed number $5\frac{3}{8}$ make each equation true? Choose Yes or No.

$\square - 4\frac{1}{6} = 1\frac{1}{12}$ ○ Yes ○ No

$10\frac{11}{12} - 5\frac{3}{8} = \square$ ○ Yes ○ No

$\square + 1\frac{1}{4} = 6\frac{5}{8}$ ○ Yes ○ No

$3\frac{1}{8} + 1\frac{3}{4} + \frac{1}{2} = \square$ ○ Yes ○ No

27. Does the mixed number $3\frac{1}{3}$ make each equation true? Choose Yes or No.

$3\frac{1}{3} - \square = 0$ ○ Yes ○ No

$2\frac{2}{5} + \square = 5\frac{3}{8}$ ○ Yes ○ No

$9\frac{1}{12} - 6\frac{3}{4} = \square$ ○ Yes ○ No

$\square - 3\frac{1}{9} = \frac{2}{9}$ ○ Yes ○ No

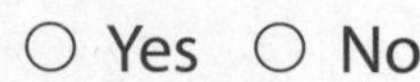

Name ____________________

Homework & Practice 7-11

Add and Subtract Mixed Numbers

Another Look!

A park ranger had $4\frac{1}{8}$ cups of birdseed. He bought $6\frac{1}{4}$ more cups of birdseed. Then he filled the park's bird feeders, using $2\frac{1}{2}$ cups of birdseed. How much birdseed is left?

You can write an expression to help solve the problem: $\left(4\frac{1}{8} + 6\frac{1}{4}\right) - 2\frac{1}{2}$

Always perform operations in parentheses first.

Step 1 Add the mixed numbers in parentheses first. Find a common denominator.

$4\frac{1}{8} + 6\frac{1}{4}$

$4\frac{1}{8} + 6\frac{2}{8} = 10\frac{3}{8}$

Step 2 Subtract $2\frac{1}{2}$ from the sum you found. Find a common denominator.

$10\frac{3}{8} - 2\frac{1}{2}$

$10\frac{3}{8} - 2\frac{4}{8}$ You can't subtract $\frac{4}{8}$ from $\frac{3}{8}$. Regroup $10\frac{3}{8}$ as $9\frac{11}{8}$.

Step 3 Find the difference.

$9\frac{11}{8} - 2\frac{4}{8} = 7\frac{7}{8}$

So, there are $7\frac{7}{8}$ cups of birdseed left.

In **1–9**, solve. Do the operation in parentheses first.

Remember to rename your answer as an equivalent mixed number.

1. $\left(5\frac{1}{2} + 2\frac{3}{4}\right) - 3\frac{1}{2}$

2. $10\frac{5}{16} - \left(5\frac{1}{4} + 2\frac{9}{16}\right)$

3. $5\frac{3}{8} + \left(6\frac{3}{4} - 4\frac{1}{8}\right)$

4. $\frac{6}{9} + \frac{5}{18} + 1\frac{3}{6}$

5. $1\frac{4}{10} + 1\frac{3}{20} + 1\frac{1}{5}$

6. $\left(4\frac{2}{3} + 1\frac{1}{6}\right) - 1\frac{5}{6}$

7. $\left(3\frac{3}{8} - 1\frac{1}{5}\right) + 1\frac{7}{8}$

8. $1\frac{6}{7} + \left(4\frac{13}{14} - 3\frac{1}{2}\right)$

9. $10\frac{5}{8} - \left(4\frac{3}{4} + 2\frac{5}{8}\right)$

10. **Reasoning** Joel is $2\frac{1}{2}$ inches shorter than Carlos. Carlos is $1\frac{1}{4}$ inches taller than Dan. If Dan is $58\frac{1}{4}$ inches tall, how many inches tall is Joel?

11. Suzy spent $6\frac{7}{8}$ days working on her English paper, $3\frac{1}{6}$ days doing her science project, and $1\frac{1}{2}$ days studying for her math test. How many more days did Suzy spend on her English paper and math test combined than on her science project?

12. **Higher Order Thinking** Veronica needs to buy $1\frac{3}{4}$ pounds of cheese. When the clerk places some cheese in a container and weighs it, the scale shows $1\frac{1}{4}$ pounds. The container weighs $\frac{1}{16}$ pound. How many more pounds of cheese should be added to the scale to get the amount that Veronica needs? Explain how you solved the problem.

13. At a museum, Jenny learned about a fossil that was three billion, four hundred million years old. Write the fossil's age in standard form and expanded form.

14. **Model with Math** Four students raised \$264 for a charity by washing cars. The students received \$8 for each car they washed. How many cars did they wash?

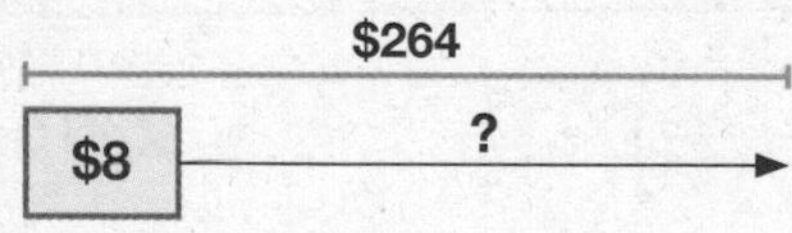

Assessment

15. Does the mixed number $1\frac{3}{4}$ make each equation true? Choose Yes or No.

$2\frac{1}{4} - \frac{6}{7} = \square$ ○ Yes ○ No

$2\frac{5}{12} - \square = \frac{2}{3}$ ○ Yes ○ No

$7\frac{1}{12} - 5\frac{3}{8} = \square$ ○ Yes ○ No

$\square + \frac{7}{10} = 2\frac{9}{20}$ ○ Yes ○ No

16. Does the mixed number $2\frac{1}{2}$ make each equation true? Choose Yes or No.

$9\frac{1}{8} - 6\frac{3}{4} = \square$ ○ Yes ○ No

$\square - 1\frac{1}{2} = 2$ ○ Yes ○ No

$\square + 1\frac{1}{8} = 3\frac{5}{8}$ ○ Yes ○ No

$1\frac{1}{2} + \frac{5}{8} + \frac{4}{7} = \square$ ○ Yes ○ No

Name ____________________

Problem Solving

Lesson 7-12

Model with Math

I can . . .
apply the math I know to solve problems.

I can also add and subtract fractions and mixed numbers.

Solve & Share

Annie found three seashells at the beach. How much shorter is the Scotch Bonnet seashell than the combined lengths of the two Alphabet Cone seashells? ***Solve this problem any way you choose. Use a diagram to help.***

Scotch Bonnet $2\frac{1}{8}$ inches

Alphabet Cone $1\frac{3}{4}$ inches

Thinking Habits

Be a good thinker! These questions can help you.

- How can I use math I know to help solve this problem?
- How can I use pictures, objects, or an equation to represent the problem?
- Can I write an equation to show the problem?

Look Back! Model with Mathematics What is another way to represent this problem?

How Can You Represent a Problem with a Bar Diagram?

A

The first step of a recipe is to mix the flour, white sugar, and brown sugar. Will a bowl that holds 4 cups be large enough?

Cupcakes

- $1\frac{3}{4}$ cups flour
- $\frac{1}{2}$ cup brown sugar
- $1\frac{1}{4}$ cups white sugar
- $2\frac{1}{2}$ teaspoons baking powder
- $\frac{1}{2}$ teaspoon salt
- $\frac{2}{3}$ cup butter
- 2 eggs
- 1 cup milk

What do I need to do to solve the problem?

I need to find the total amount of the first three ingredients and compare that amount to 4 cups.

B **How can I model with math?**

I can

- use math I know to help solve this problem.
- use a diagram to represent and solve this problem.
- write an equation involving fractions or mixed numbers.
- decide if my results make sense.

C I will use a bar diagram and an equation to represent the situation.

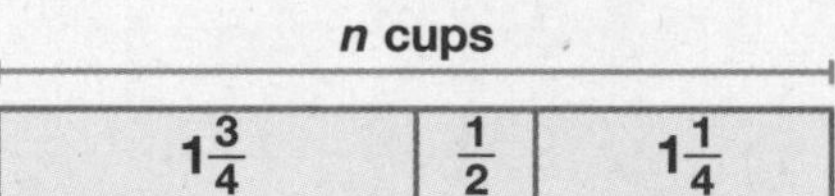

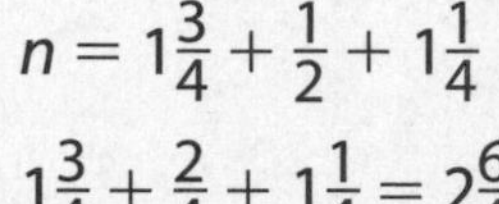

$n = 1\frac{3}{4} + \frac{1}{2} + 1\frac{1}{4}$

$1\frac{3}{4} + \frac{2}{4} + 1\frac{1}{4} = 2\frac{6}{4}$

I can write this answer as a mixed number. $2\frac{6}{4} = 3\frac{2}{4}$ or $3\frac{1}{2}$

There are $3\frac{1}{2}$ cups of ingredients, and $3\frac{1}{2}$ is less than 4. So, the 4-cup bowl is large enough.

Convince Me! **Model with Mathematics** How many more cups of ingredients could still fit in the bowl? Use a bar diagram and an equation to represent the problem.

Name ______________________________

Practice Buddy Tools Assessment

Guided Practice*

Model with Math

Phillip wants to run a total of 3 miles each day. Monday morning, he ran $1\frac{7}{8}$ miles. How many more miles does he still need to run?

1. Draw a diagram to represent the problem.

2. Write and solve an equation for this problem. How did you find the solution?

3. How many more miles does Phillip still need to run?

Independent Practice

Model with Math

A landscaper used $2\frac{1}{2}$ tons of sunburst pebbles, $3\frac{1}{4}$ tons of black polished pebbles, and $\frac{5}{8}$ ton of river pebbles. What was the total weight of the pebbles?

4. Draw a diagram and write an equation to represent the problem.

5. Solve the equation. What fraction computations did you do?

6. How many tons of pebbles did the landscaper use?

*For another example, see Set H on page 448.

Problem Solving

Performance Assessment

Camp Activities
During the 6-hour session at day camp, Roland participated in boating, hiking, and lunch. The rest of the session was free time. How much time did Roland spend on the three activities? How much free time did he have?

DATA

Camp Activities	
Swiming	$\frac{3}{4}$ hour
Boating	$1\frac{1}{2}$ hours
Crafts	$1\frac{3}{4}$ hours
Hiking	$2\frac{1}{2}$ hours
Lunch	$1\frac{1}{4}$ hours

7. **Make Sense and Persevere** What do you know and what do you need to find?

8. **Reasoning** Describe the quantities and operations you will use to find how much time Roland spent on the planned activities. Which quantities and operations will you use to find how much free time Roland had?

9. **Model with Math** Draw a diagram and use an equation to help you find how much time Roland spent on the activities. Then draw a diagram and use an equation to help you find how much free time Roland had.

Name ______________________________

Homework & Practice 7-12
Model with Math

Another Look!

Each Monday in science class, students measure the height of their plants. In week 3, Andrew's plant was $4\frac{3}{4}$ inches tall. In week 4, his plant was $5\frac{3}{8}$ inches tall. How much had the plant grown from week 3 to week 4?

Tell how you can use math to model the problem.

- I can use math I know to help solve the problem.
- I can use bar diagrams and equations to represent and solve this problem.

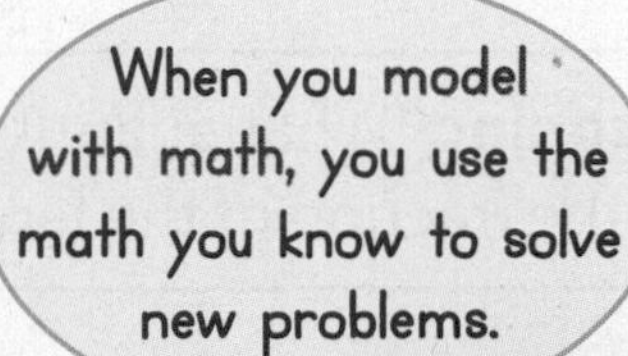

Draw a bar diagram and write an equation to solve.

$5\frac{3}{8}$ inches

$4\frac{3}{4}$	g

$4\frac{3}{4} + g = 5\frac{3}{8}$

$$\begin{array}{r} 5\frac{3}{8} = 4\frac{11}{8} \\ -4\frac{3}{4} = 4\frac{6}{8} \\ \hline \frac{5}{8} \end{array}$$

The plant grew $\frac{5}{8}$ inch.

Model with Math

Mrs. Lohens made curtains for her children's bedrooms. She used $4\frac{3}{4}$ yards of fabric for Nicky's room and $6\frac{5}{8}$ yards for Linda's room. How much fabric did she use in all?

1. Draw a diagram and write an equation to represent the problem.

2. Solve the equation. What fraction computations did you do?

3. How much fabric did Mrs. Lohens use for the curtains?

Performance Assessment

Fans in the Bleachers
In the bleachers at the basketball game, $\frac{1}{4}$ of the fans are adult men, and $\frac{5}{12}$ are adult women. What fraction of the fans are adults? What fraction of the fans are children?

4. **Make Sense and Persevere** What do you know and what do you need to find?

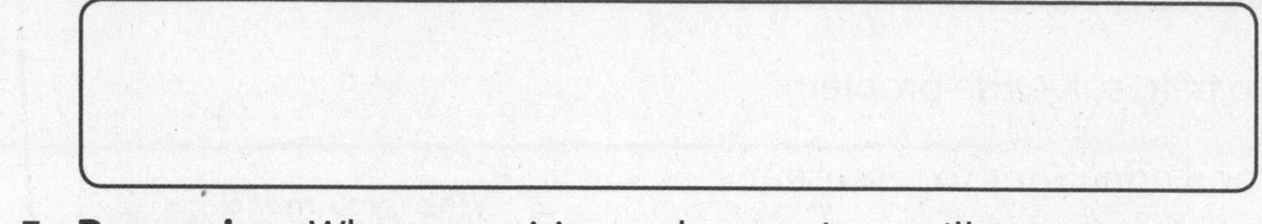

5. **Reasoning** What quantities and operations will you use to find the fraction of the fans that is adults? that is children?

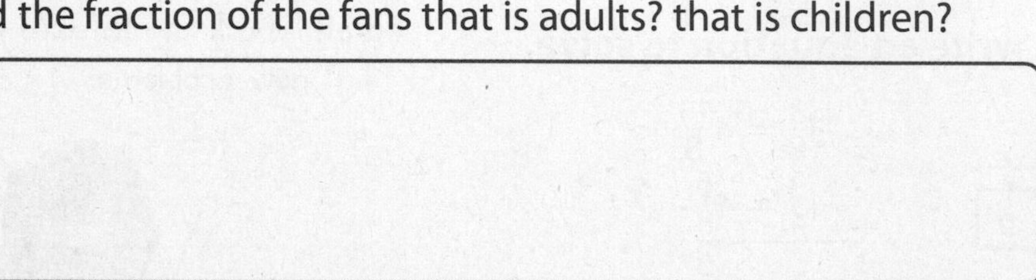

6. **Critique Reasoning** Phyllis says you have to know the number of fans in order to determine the fraction of the fans that are children. Is she right? Explain.

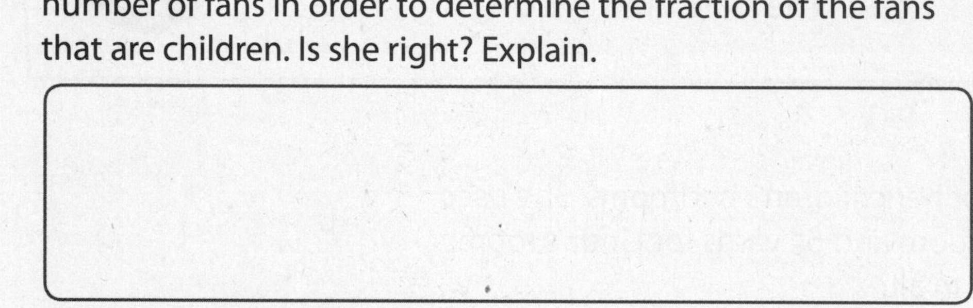

7. **Model with Math** Draw a diagram and use an equation to help you find the fraction of the fans that are adults. Then draw a diagram and use an equation to help you find the fraction of the fans that are children.

Name ___

Fluency Practice Activity

TOPIC 7

I can ...
multiply multi-digit whole numbers.

Find a Match

Work with a partner. Point to a clue.

Read the clue.

Look below the clues to find a match. Write the clue letter in the box next to the match.

Find a match for every clue.

Clues

A The product is exactly 70,500.

B The product is between 65,000 and 70,000.

C The product is exactly 40,000.

D The product is about 40,000.

E The product is between 30,000 and 35,000.

F The product is between 10,000 and 30,000.

G The product is exactly 10,000.

H The product is less than 10,000.

☐ 100×99	☐ 100×100	☐ 705×100	☐ $2,000 \times 12$
☐ $4,500 \times 15$	☐ $3,050 \times 11$	☐ 403×100	☐ 400×100

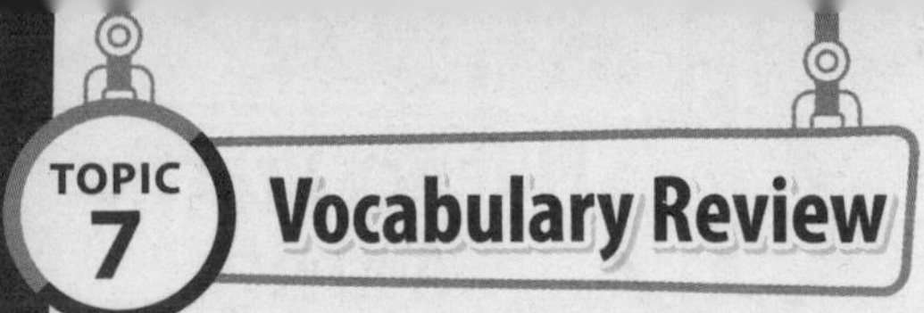

TOPIC 7 Vocabulary Review

Word List

- benchmark fractions
- common denominator
- equivalent fractions
- mixed number

Understand Vocabulary

Write *always, sometimes,* or *never*.

1. A fraction can __________ be renamed as a mixed number.

2. The sum of a mixed number and a whole number is _______ a mixed number.

3. $\frac{1}{5}$ is _____ used as a benchmark fraction.

4. Equivalent fractions _______ have the same value.

For each of these terms, give an example and a non-example.

	Example	Non-example
5. benchmark fraction	____________	____________
6. mixed number	____________	____________
7. equivalent fractions	____________	____________

Draw a line from each number in Column A to the same value in Column B.

Column A	Column B
8. $3\frac{4}{9} + 2\frac{5}{6}$	$5\frac{2}{3}$
9. $7 - 2\frac{2}{3}$	$\frac{3}{5}$
10. $4\frac{1}{2} + 1\frac{1}{6}$	$4\frac{1}{3}$
11. $\frac{7}{12} + \frac{5}{8}$	$\frac{29}{24}$
	$6\frac{5}{18}$

Use Vocabulary in Writing

12. How can you write a fraction equivalent to $\frac{60}{80}$ with a denominator that is less than 80?

Name ___

Reteaching

Set A pages 371–376

Estimate the sum or difference by replacing each fraction with 0, $\frac{1}{2}$, or 1.

Estimate $\frac{4}{5} + \frac{5}{8}$.

Step 1 $\frac{4}{5}$ is close to 1.

Step 2 $\frac{5}{8}$ is close to $\frac{4}{8}$ or $\frac{1}{2}$.

Step 3 $1 + \frac{1}{2} = 1\frac{1}{2}$

So, $\frac{4}{5} + \frac{5}{8}$ is about $1\frac{1}{2}$.

Estimate $\frac{7}{12} - \frac{1}{8}$.

Step 1 $\frac{7}{12}$ is close to $\frac{6}{12}$ or $\frac{1}{2}$.

Step 2 $\frac{1}{8}$ is close to 0.

Step 3 $\frac{1}{2} - 0 = \frac{1}{2}$

So, $\frac{7}{12} - \frac{1}{8}$ is about $\frac{1}{2}$.

Remember that you can use a number line to decide if a fraction is closest to 0, $\frac{1}{2}$, or 1.

Estimate each sum or difference.

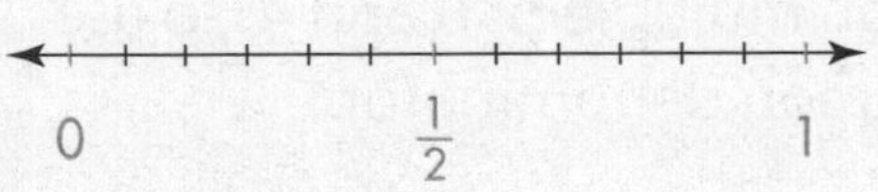

0 $\frac{1}{2}$ 1

1. $\frac{2}{3} + \frac{5}{6}$

2. $\frac{7}{8} - \frac{5}{12}$

3. $\frac{1}{8} + \frac{1}{16}$

4. $\frac{5}{8} - \frac{1}{6}$

5. $\frac{1}{5} + \frac{1}{3}$

6. $\frac{11}{12} - \frac{1}{10}$

7. $\frac{9}{10} + \frac{1}{5}$

8. $\frac{3}{5} - \frac{1}{12}$

Set B pages 377–382

Find a common denominator for $\frac{4}{9}$ and $\frac{1}{3}$. Then rename each fraction as an equivalent fraction with the common denominator.

Step 1 Multiply the denominators: $9 \times 3 = 27$, so 27 is a common denominator.

Step 2 Rename the fractions:

$\frac{4}{9} = \frac{4}{9} \times \frac{3}{3} = \frac{12}{27}$

$\frac{1}{3} = \frac{1}{3} \times \frac{9}{9} = \frac{9}{27}$

So, $\frac{4}{9} = \frac{12}{27}$ and $\frac{1}{3} = \frac{9}{27}$.

Remember you can check to see if one denominator is a multiple of the other. Since 9 is a multiple of 3, another common denominator for the fractions $\frac{4}{9}$ and $\frac{1}{3}$ is 9.

Find a common denominator. Then rename each fraction as an equivalent fraction with the common denominator.

1. $\frac{3}{5}$ and $\frac{7}{10}$

2. $\frac{5}{6}$ and $\frac{7}{18}$

3. $\frac{3}{7}$ and $\frac{1}{4}$

Set C pages 383–388, 389–394, 395–400

Find $\frac{5}{6} - \frac{3}{4}$.

Step 1 Find a common denominator by listing multiples of 6 and 4.

6: 6, 12, 18, 24, 30, 36, 42
4: 4, 8, 12, 16, 20, 24, 28, 32

12 is a common multiple of 6 and 4, so use 12 as the common denominator.

Step 2 Use the Identity Property to write equivalent fractions.

$\frac{5}{6} = \frac{5 \times 2}{6 \times 2} = \frac{10}{12}$ $\frac{3}{4} = \frac{3 \times 3}{4 \times 3} = \frac{9}{12}$

Step 3 Subtract.

$\frac{10}{12} - \frac{9}{12} = \frac{1}{12}$

Remember to multiply the numerator and denominator by the same number when writing an equivalent fraction.

1. $\frac{2}{5} + \frac{3}{10}$
2. $\frac{1}{9} + \frac{5}{6}$
3. $\frac{3}{4} - \frac{5}{12}$
4. $\frac{7}{8} - \frac{2}{3}$
5. $\frac{1}{12} + \frac{3}{8}$
6. $\frac{4}{5} - \frac{2}{15}$
7. Teresa spends $\frac{1}{3}$ of her day at school. She spends $\frac{1}{12}$ of her day eating meals. What fraction of the day does Teresa spend at school or eating meals?

Set D pages 401–406

Estimate $5\frac{1}{3} + 9\frac{9}{11}$.

To round a mixed number to the nearest whole number, compare the fraction part of the mixed number to $\frac{1}{2}$.

If the fraction part is less than $\frac{1}{2}$, round to the nearest lesser whole number.

$5\frac{1}{3}$ rounds to 5.

If the fraction part is greater than or equal to $\frac{1}{2}$, round to the nearest greater whole number.

$9\frac{9}{11}$ rounds to 10.

So, $5\frac{1}{3} + 9\frac{9}{11} \approx 5 + 10 = 15$.

Remember that you can also use benchmark fractions such as $\frac{1}{4}$, $\frac{1}{3}$, $\frac{1}{2}$, $\frac{2}{3}$, and $\frac{3}{4}$ to help you estimate.

Estimate each sum or difference.

1. $3\frac{1}{4} - 1\frac{1}{2}$
2. $5\frac{2}{9} + 4\frac{11}{13}$
3. $2\frac{3}{8} + 5\frac{3}{5}$
4. $9\frac{3}{7} - 6\frac{2}{5}$
5. $8\frac{5}{6} - 2\frac{1}{2}$
6. $7\frac{3}{4} + 5\frac{1}{8}$
7. $11\frac{5}{12} + \frac{7}{8}$
8. $13\frac{4}{5} - 8\frac{1}{6}$
9. A mark on the side of a pier shows the water is $4\frac{7}{8}$ feet deep. At high tide, the water level rises $2\frac{1}{4}$ feet. About how deep is the water at high tide?

Name ____________________

Set E pages 407–412

Find $1\frac{1}{4} + 1\frac{7}{8}$.

Step 1 Rename the fractions with a common denominator. Model the addends and add the fractional parts.

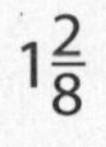

$+ 1\frac{7}{8}$

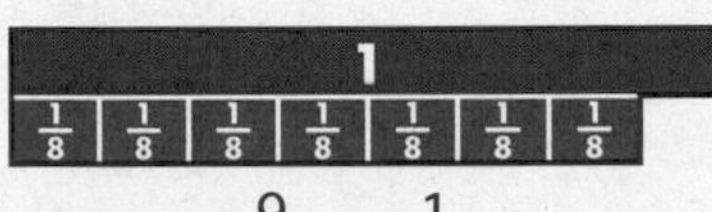

$\frac{9}{8}$ Rename $\frac{9}{8}$ as $1\frac{1}{8}$.

Step 2 Add the whole numbers to the regrouped fractions.

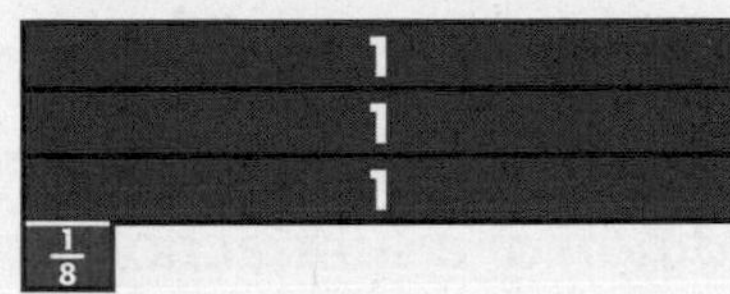

So, $1\frac{1}{4} + 1\frac{7}{8} = 3\frac{1}{8}$.

Remember that you may need to rename a fraction as a mixed number.

Use a model to find each sum.

1. $2\frac{5}{6} + 1\frac{5}{6}$
2. $1\frac{1}{2} + 3\frac{3}{4}$
3. $2\frac{3}{10} + 2\frac{4}{5}$
4. $2\frac{1}{4} + 5\frac{11}{12}$
5. $6\frac{2}{3} + 5\frac{5}{6}$
6. $7\frac{1}{3} + 8\frac{7}{9}$
7. $8\frac{4}{10} + 2\frac{3}{5}$
8. $3\frac{1}{3} + 9\frac{11}{12}$

Set F pages 419–424

Find $2\frac{1}{3} - 1\frac{5}{6}$. Rename $2\frac{1}{3}$ as $2\frac{2}{6}$.

Step 1 Model the number you are subtracting from, $2\frac{1}{3}$ or $2\frac{2}{6}$. Since $\frac{5}{6} > \frac{2}{6}$, rename 1 whole as $\frac{6}{6}$.

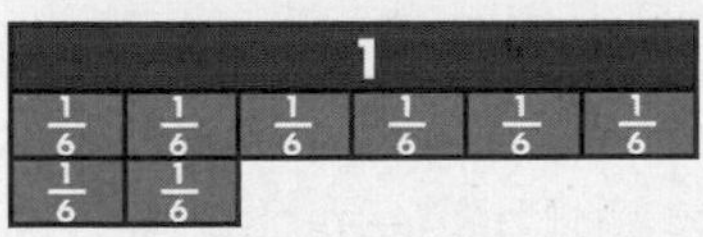

Step 2 Cross out the number you are subtracting, $1\frac{5}{6}$.

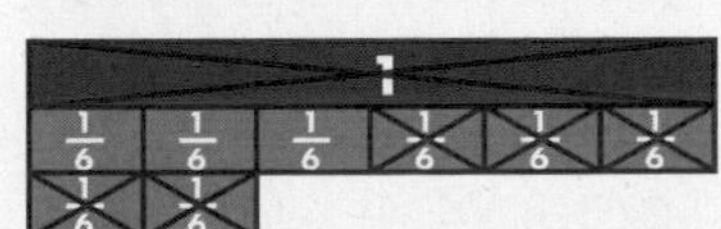

The answer is the amount that is left.

So, $2\frac{1}{3} - 1\frac{5}{6} = \frac{3}{6}$ or $\frac{1}{2}$.

Remember that the difference is the part of the model that is not crossed out.

Use a model to find each difference.

1. $15\frac{6}{10} - 3\frac{4}{5}$
2. $6\frac{3}{4} - 5\frac{1}{2}$
3. $4\frac{1}{6} - 1\frac{2}{3}$
4. $12\frac{1}{4} - 7\frac{1}{2}$
5. $9\frac{7}{10} - 3\frac{4}{5}$
6. $5\frac{5}{8} - 3\frac{1}{4}$

Set G pages 413–418, 425–430, 431–436

Gil has two lengths of wallpaper, $2\frac{3}{4}$ yards and $1\frac{7}{8}$ yards long. He used some and now has $1\frac{5}{6}$ yards left. How many yards of wallpaper did Gil use?

Step 1

Add to find the total amount of wallpaper Gil has.

$$\begin{array}{r} 2\frac{3}{4} = 2\frac{18}{24} \\ +\ 1\frac{7}{8} = 1\frac{21}{24} \\ \hline 3\frac{39}{24} \end{array}$$

Step 2

Subtract to find the amount of wallpaper Gil used.

$$\begin{array}{r} 3\frac{39}{24} = 3\frac{39}{24} \\ -\ 1\frac{5}{6} = 1\frac{20}{24} \\ \hline 2\frac{19}{24} \end{array}$$

Gil used $2\frac{19}{24}$ yards of wallpaper.

Remember when you add or subtract mixed numbers, rename the fractional parts to have a common denominator.

Solve. Do the operation in the parentheses first.

1. $5\frac{1}{2} + 2\frac{1}{8}$
2. $7\frac{5}{6} - 3\frac{2}{3}$
3. $3\frac{1}{4} + 1\frac{5}{6}$
4. $9 - 3\frac{3}{8}$
5. $\left(2\frac{1}{6} + 3\frac{3}{4}\right) - 1\frac{5}{12}$
6. $\left(4\frac{4}{5} + 7\frac{1}{3}\right) - 1\frac{7}{15}$

Set H pages 437–442

Think about these questions to help you **model with math**.

Thinking Habits

- How can I use math I know to help solve this problem?
- How can I use pictures, objects, or an equation to represent the problem?
- How can I use numbers, words, and symbols to solve the problem?

Remember that a bar diagram can help you write an addition or a subtraction equation.

Draw a bar diagram and write an equation to solve.

1. Justin jogs $3\frac{2}{5}$ miles every morning. He jogs $4\frac{6}{10}$ miles every evening. How many miles does he jog every day?

2. Last year Mia planted a tree that was $5\frac{11}{12}$ feet tall. This year the tree is $7\frac{2}{3}$ feet tall. How many feet did the tree grow?

TOPIC 7

Assessment

Name ____________________

1. In questions 1a–1d, choose Yes or No to tell if the number $\frac{1}{2}$ will make each equation true.

1a. $\frac{1}{18} + \square = \frac{10}{18}$ ○ Yes ○ No

1b. $\frac{1}{3} + \square = \frac{1}{5}$ ○ Yes ○ No

1c. $\frac{5}{8} - \square = \frac{1}{8}$ ○ Yes ○ No

1d. $\frac{3}{4} - \square = \frac{1}{4}$ ○ Yes ○ No

2. Choose all the expressions that are equal to $\frac{2}{3}$.

- ☐ $\frac{1}{6} + \frac{1}{2}$
- ☐ $\frac{2}{9} + \frac{7}{18}$
- ☐ $\frac{5}{12} + \frac{1}{4}$
- ☐ $1\frac{1}{6} - \frac{1}{3}$
- ☐ $2 - 1\frac{1}{3}$

3. Tim has $\frac{5}{12}$ of a jar of blackberry jam and $\frac{3}{8}$ of a jar of strawberry jam. Write $\frac{5}{12}$ and $\frac{3}{8}$ using a common denominator.

4. Sandra drove for $\frac{1}{3}$ hour to get to the store. Then she drove $\frac{1}{5}$ hour to get to the library. What fraction of an hour did Sandra drive in all?

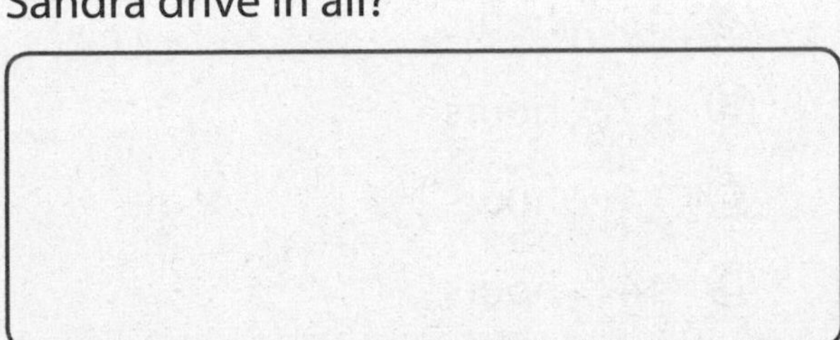

5. The bar diagram below shows the fractional parts of a pizza eaten by Pablo and Jamie.

? pizza eaten

$\frac{1}{3}$	$\frac{1}{4}$

Part A

Rename each fraction using a common denominator.

Part B

Use the renamed fractions to write and solve an equation to find the total amount of pizza eaten.

6. Draw lines to match each expression on the left to its sum on the right.

Expression	Sum
$\frac{1}{4} + \frac{3}{8}$	$\frac{5}{12}$
$\frac{1}{4} + \frac{7}{10}$	$1\frac{1}{6}$
$\frac{1}{4} + \frac{11}{12}$	$\frac{5}{8}$
$\frac{1}{4} + \frac{1}{6}$	$\frac{19}{20}$

7. Benjamin and his sister shared a large sandwich. Benjamin ate $\frac{3}{5}$ of the sandwich and his sister ate $\frac{1}{7}$ of the sandwich.

Part A

Estimate how much more Benjamin ate than his sister. Explain how you found your estimate.

Part B

How much more did Benjamin eat than his sister? Find the exact amount.

8. Which expression is the best estimate for $3\frac{1}{8} - 1\frac{3}{4}$?

Ⓐ $3 - 1$

Ⓑ $3 - 2$

Ⓒ $4 - 1$

Ⓓ $4 - 2$

9. Write the number in the box that makes the statement true.

$2\frac{7}{12} = 1\frac{\square}{12}$

10. Mona bought $3\frac{3}{8}$ pounds of cheddar cheese. She used $2\frac{3}{4}$ pounds to make sandwiches. Which expression shows how much cheese is left?

Ⓐ $3\frac{3}{8} + \frac{3}{4}$

Ⓑ $3\frac{3}{8} + 2\frac{3}{4}$

Ⓒ $3\frac{3}{8} - 2\frac{3}{4}$

Ⓓ $3\frac{3}{8} - \frac{3}{4}$

11. Marie needs $2\frac{1}{4}$ yards of fabric. She already has $1\frac{3}{8}$ yards. How many more yards of fabric does she need?

Ⓐ $\frac{1}{8}$ yard

Ⓑ $\frac{3}{4}$ yard

Ⓒ $\frac{7}{8}$ yard

Ⓓ $1\frac{7}{8}$ yards

12. During a trip, Martha drove $\frac{1}{6}$ of the time, Chris drove $\frac{1}{4}$ of the time, and Juan drove the rest of the time. What fraction of the time did Juan drive?

13. Gilberto worked $3\frac{1}{4}$ hours on Thursday, $4\frac{2}{5}$ hours on Friday, and $6\frac{1}{2}$ hours on Saturday. How many hours did he work in all during the three days?

Ⓐ $13\frac{1}{10}$ hours

Ⓑ $13\frac{3}{20}$ hours

Ⓒ $14\frac{1}{10}$ hours

Ⓓ $14\frac{3}{20}$ hours

Name ____

14. Vita used the model below to find the sum of two mixed numbers. What is the sum? Show your work.

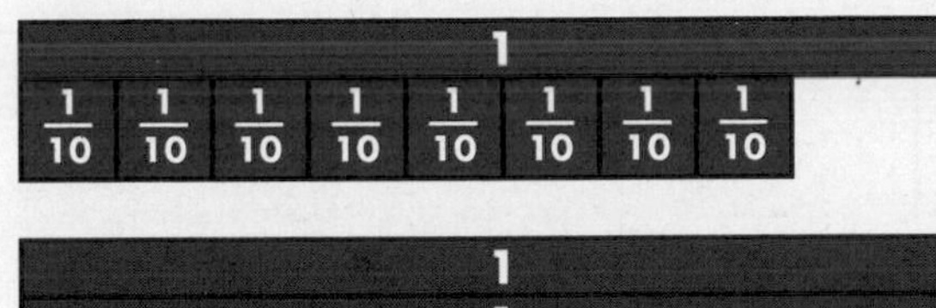

15. Diego wants to find $4\frac{1}{5} - \frac{7}{10}$.

Part A

Explain why he must rename $4\frac{1}{5}$ in order to do the subtraction.

Part B

Explain how to rename $4\frac{1}{5}$ in order to do the subtraction.

16. In questions 16a–16d, does the number $1\frac{3}{8}$ make each equation true? Choose Yes or No.

16a. $\frac{1}{4} + \square = 1\frac{7}{8}$ ○ Yes ○ No

16b. $2\frac{3}{4} + \square = 4\frac{1}{8}$ ○ Yes ○ No

16c. $4 - \square = 2\frac{5}{8}$ ○ Yes ○ No

16d. $3\frac{1}{2} - \square = 2\frac{1}{4}$ ○ Yes ○ No

17. Mica read $\frac{1}{6}$ of a book on Monday and $\frac{3}{8}$ on Tuesday. Susan read $\frac{5}{6}$ of the same book. How much more of the book has Susan read than Mica?

Ⓐ $\frac{14}{24}$

Ⓑ $\frac{8}{24}$

Ⓒ $\frac{7}{12}$

Ⓓ $\frac{7}{24}$

18. A pelican has a wingspan of $8\frac{1}{5}$ feet. An eagle has a wingspan of $6\frac{2}{3}$ feet. How much longer is the wingspan of a pelican?

19. Subtract the sum of $4\frac{3}{4}$ and $5\frac{2}{3}$ from $12\frac{1}{2}$.

20. Draw lines to match each expression on the left to its sum on the right.

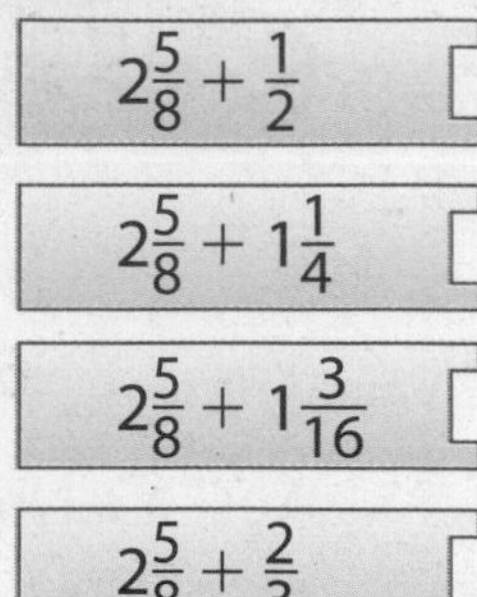

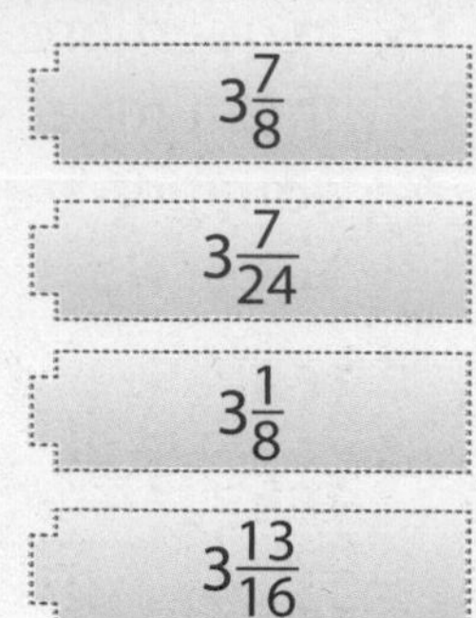

21. To estimate the sum of two mixed numbers, Carla rounds one number to 3 and the other number to 7. Which is the number she rounds to 3?

Ⓐ $2\frac{5}{8}$

Ⓑ $2\frac{11}{30}$

Ⓒ $3\frac{4}{6}$

Ⓓ $3\frac{7}{9}$

22. Mark is making a small frame in the shape of an equilateral triangle with the dimensions shown below. What is the perimeter of the frame?

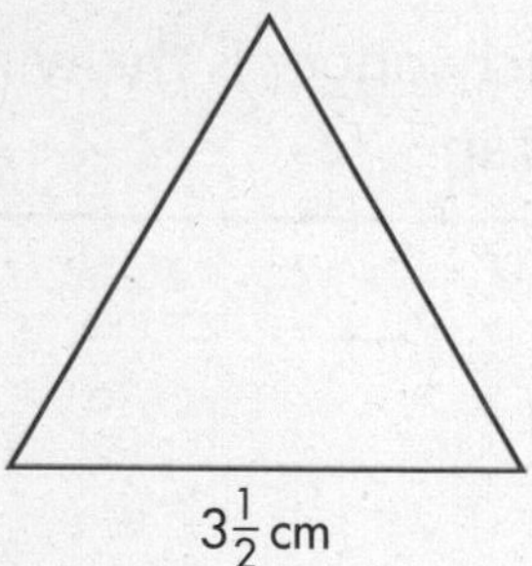

Ⓐ $6\frac{1}{2}$ cm

Ⓑ $9\frac{1}{2}$ cm

Ⓒ $9\frac{1}{6}$ cm

Ⓓ $10\frac{1}{2}$ cm

23. A baker uses food coloring to color cake batter. He needs $4\frac{1}{8}$ ounces of green food coloring. The baker only has $2\frac{1}{2}$ ounces. How much more green food coloring does he need?

24. Models for two mixed numbers are shown below. What is the sum of the numbers? Show your work.

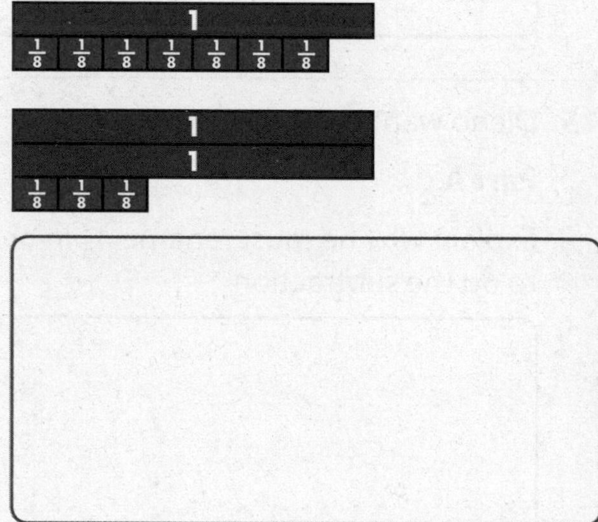

25. Dawson says that the expression $\left(2\frac{4}{10} + 8\frac{4}{5}\right) - 3\frac{1}{5}$ is equal to a whole number. Do you agree? Explain.

Name ____________________

Tying Knots

Liam and Pam each have a length of thick rope. Liam has tied an overhand knot in his rope. The overhand knot is a basic knot often used as a basis for other types of knots.

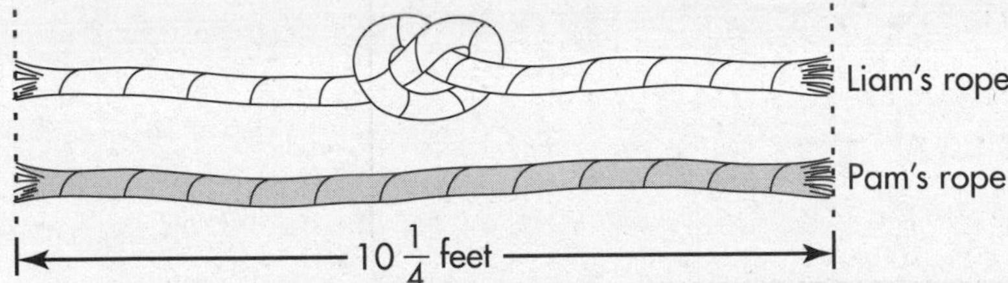

1. Liam untied the overhand knot. The full length of the rope is shown below. How much rope did the knot use?

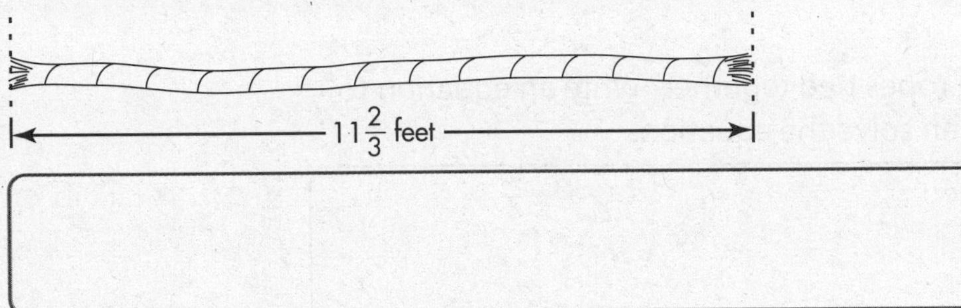

2. Liam laid his untied rope end-to-end with Pam's rope.

Part A

About how long would the two ropes be? Explain how you got your estimate.

Part B

Explain whether the actual length would be greater or less than your estimate.

3. Liam and Pam tied their two ropes together with a square knot. The knot used $1\frac{1}{8}$ feet of rope. How long is their rope? Explain.

4. Marco has a rope that is 16 feet long. He ties his rope to Liam and Pam's rope with a square knot that uses $1\frac{1}{8}$ feet of rope.

Part A

How long are the three ropes tied together? Write an equation to model the problem. Then solve the equation.

Part B

Liam. Pam, and Marco decide to shorten the tied ropes by cutting off $\frac{2}{5}$ foot from one end and $\frac{1}{6}$ foot from the other end. About how much rope is cut off in all? Explain.

Part C

How long are the tied ropes now? Show your work.

Glossary

acute angle An angle whose measure is between 0° and 90°

acute triangle A triangle whose angles are all acute angles

Addition Property of Equality The same number can be added to both sides of an equation and the sides remain equal.

algebraic expression A mathematical phrase involving a variable or variables, numbers, and operations
Example: $x - 3$

angle A figure formed by two rays that have the same endpoint

area The number of square units needed to cover a surface or figure

array A way of displaying objects in rows and columns

Associative Property of Addition Addends can be regrouped and the sum remains the same.
Example: $1 + (3 + 5) = (1 + 3) + 5$

Associative Property of Multiplication Factors can be regrouped and the product remains the same.
Example: $2 \times (4 \times 10) = (2 \times 4) \times 10$

attribute A characteristic of a shape

axis (plural: axes) Either of two lines drawn perpendicular to each other in a graph

bar diagram A tool used to help understand and solve word problems; it is also known as a strip diagram or a tape diagram.

bar graph A display that uses bars to show and compare data

base The number that is used as a factor, when a number is written using exponents

base (of a polygon) The side of a polygon to which the height is perpendicular

base (of a solid) The face of a solid that is used to name the solid

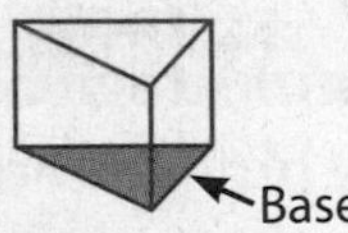

benchmark fraction Common fractions used for estimating, such as $\frac{1}{4}$, $\frac{1}{3}$, $\frac{1}{2}$, $\frac{2}{3}$, and $\frac{3}{4}$

braces Symbols { and } that are used with parentheses and brackets in mathematical expressions and equations to group numbers or variables together

brackets The symbols [and] that are used to group numbers or variables in mathematical expressions.

breaking apart A mental math method used to rewrite a number as the sum of numbers to form an easier problem

capacity The volume of a container measured in liquid units

Celsius A scale for measuring temperature in the metric system

centimeter (cm) A metric unit of length; 100 centimeters is equal to one meter.

circle A closed plane figure made up of all the points that are the same distance from a given point

common denominator A number that is the denominator of two or more fractions

common multiple A number that is a multiple of two or more numbers

Commutative Property of Addition The order of addends can be changed and the sum remains the same. *Example:* $3 + 7 = 7 + 3$

Commutative Property of Multiplication The order of factors can be changed and the product remains the same. *Example:* $3 \times 5 = 5 \times 3$

compatible numbers Numbers that are easy to compute with mentally

compensation Adjusting a number to make a computation easier and balancing the adjustment by changing another number

composite number A whole number greater than one with more than two factors

composite shape A figure made up of two or more shapes

coordinate grid A grid that is used to locate points in a plane using an ordered pair of numbers

coordinates The two numbers in an ordered pair

corresponding Matching terms in a pattern

corresponding terms Terms that match each other in a pair of number sequences

cube A solid figure with six identical squares as its faces

cubic unit The volume of a cube that measures 1 unit on each edge

cup (c) A customary unit of capacity; one cup is equal to eight fluid ounces.

customary units of measure Units of measure that are used in the United States

data Collected information

decimal A number with one or more places to the right of a decimal point

degree (°) A unit of measure for angles; also, a unit of measure for temperature

denominator The number below the fraction bar in a fraction

difference The result of subtracting one number from another

digits The symbols used to show numbers: 0, 1, 2, 3, 4, 5, 6, 7, 8, 9

discrete data Data where only whole numbers are possible

Distributive Property Multiplying a sum (or difference) by a number is the same as multiplying each number in the sum (or difference) by the number and adding (or subtracting) the products.
Example: $3 \times (10 + 4) = (3 \times 10) + (3 \times 4)$

dividend The number to be divided

divisible A number is divisible by another number if there is no remainder after dividing.

Division Property of Equality Both sides of an equation can be divided by the same nonzero number and the sides remain equal.

divisor The number by which another number is divided
Example: In $32 \div 4 = 8$, 4 is the divisor.

dot plot A display of responses along a number line with dots used to indicate the number of times a response occurred
See also: line plot

edge A line segment where two faces meet in a solid figure

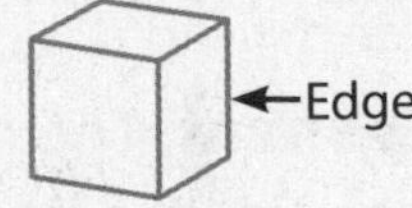

elapsed time The amount of time between the beginning of an event and the end of the event

equation A number sentence that uses an equal sign to show that two expressions have the same value
Example: $9 + 3 = 12$

equilateral triangle A triangle whose sides all have the same length

equivalent decimals Decimals that name the same amount
Example: $0.7 = 0.70$

equivalent fractions Fractions that name the same part of a whole region, length, or set

estimate To give an approximate value rather than an exact answer

evaluate Replace an expression with an equivalent value

expanded form A way to write a number that shows the place value of each digit
Example: $3 \times 1{,}000 + 5 \times 100 + 6 \times 10 + 2 \times 1$ or $3 \times 10^3 + 5 \times 10^2 + 6 \times 10^1 + 2 \times 10^0$

expanded notation A number written as the sum of the values of its digits

exponent The number that tells how many times a base number is used as a factor

face A flat surface of a solid figure

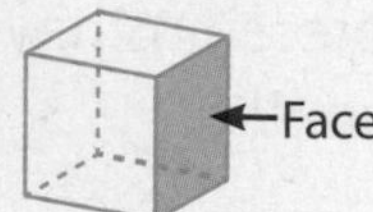

factors Numbers that are multiplied to get a product

Fahrenheit A scale for measuring temperature in the customary system

fluid ounce (fl oz) A customary unit of capacity equal to 2 tablespoons

foot (ft) A customary unit of length equal to 12 inches

formula A rule that uses symbols to relate two or more quantities

fraction A symbol, such as $\frac{2}{3}$, $\frac{5}{1}$, or $\frac{8}{5}$, used to describe one or more parts of a whole that is divided into equal parts. A fraction can name a part of a whole, a part of a set, a location on a number line, or a division of whole numbers.

frequency table A table used to show the number of times each response occurs in a set of data

gallon (gal) A unit for measuring capacity in the customary system; one gallon is equal to four quarts.

gram (g) A metric unit of mass; one gram is equal to 1,000 milligrams.

greater than symbol ($>$) A symbol that points away from a greater number or expression
Example: $450 > 449$

height of a polygon The length of a segment from one vertex of a polygon perpendicular to its base

height of a solid In a prism, the perpendicular distance between the top and bottom bases of the figure

hexagon A polygon with 6 sides

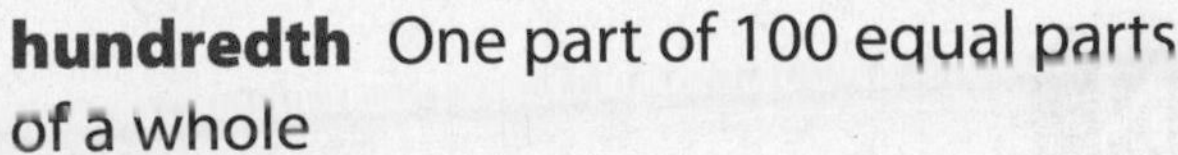

hundredth One part of 100 equal parts of a whole

kilometer (km) A metric unit of length; one kilometer is equal to 1,000 meters.

Identity Property of Addition The sum of any number and zero is that number.

Identity Property of Multiplication The product of any number and one is that number.

inch (in.) A customary unit of length; 12 inches are equal to one foot.

intersecting lines Lines that pass through the same point

interval (on a graph) The difference between consecutive numbers on an axis of a graph

inverse operations Operations that undo each other
Example: Adding 6 and subtracting 6 are inverse operations.

isosceles triangle A triangle with at least two sides of the same length

kilogram (kg) A metric unit of mass; one kilogram is equal to 1,000 grams.

less than symbol ($<$) A symbol that points towards a lesser number or expression
Example: $305 < 320$

line A straight path of points that goes on forever in two directions

line graph A graph that connects points to show how data change over time

line of symmetry The line on which a figure can be folded so that both halves are the same

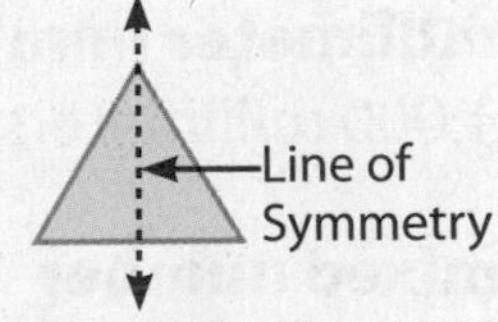

line plot A display of responses along a number line, with dots or Xs recorded above the responses to indicate the number of times a response occurred

line segment Part of a line having two endpoints

liter (L) A metric unit of capacity; one liter is equal to 1,000 milliliters

mass The measure of the quantity of matter in an object

meter (m) A metric unit of length; One meter is equal to 100 centimeters.

metric units of measure Units of measure commonly used by scientists

mile (mi) A customary unit of length equal to 5,280 feet

milligram (mg) A metric unit of mass; 1,000 milligrams is equal to one gram.

milliliter (mL) A metric unit of capacity; 1,000 milliliters is equal to one liter.

millimeter (mm) A metric unit of length; 1,000 millimeters is equal to one meter.

mixed number A number that has a whole-number part and a fraction part

multiple The product of a given whole number and any non-zero whole number

multiple of 10 A number that has 10 as a factor

Multiplication Property of Equality Both sides of an equation can be multiplied by the same nonzero number and the sides remain equal.

multiplicative inverse (reciprocal) Two numbers whose product is one

number name A way to write a number using words

number sequence A set of numbers that follows a rule

numerator The number above the fraction bar in a fraction

numerical data Data involving numbers including measurement data

numerical expression A mathematical phrase that contains numbers and at least one operation
Example: $325 + 50$

obtuse angle An angle whose measure is between 90° and 180°

135°

obtuse triangle A triangle in which one angle is an obtuse angle

octagon A polygon with 8 sides

order of operations The order in which operations are done in calculations. Work inside parentheses, brackets, and braces is done first. Next, terms with exponents are evaluated. Then, multiplication and division are done in order from left to right, and finally addition and subtraction are done in order from left to right.

ordered pair A pair of numbers used to locate a point on a coordinate grid

origin The point where the two axes of a coordinate grid intersect; the origin is represented by the ordered pair (0, 0).

ounce (oz) A customary unit of weight; 16 ounces is equal to one pound.

outlier A value that is much greater or much less than the other values in a data set

overestimate An estimate that is greater than the actual answer

parallel lines In a plane, lines that never cross and stay the same distance apart

parallelogram A quadrilateral with both pairs of opposite sides parallel and equal in length

parentheses The symbols (and) used to group numbers or variables in mathematical expressions
Example: 3(15 − 7)

partial products Products found by breaking one of two factors into ones, tens, hundreds, and so on, and then multiplying each of these by the other factor

pentagon A polygon with 5 sides

perfect square A number that is the product of a counting number multiplied by itself

perimeter The distance around a figure

period In a number, a group of three digits, separated by commas, starting from the right

perpendicular lines Two lines that intersect to form square corners or right angles

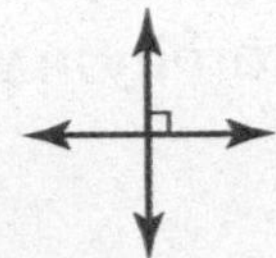

pint (pt) A customary unit of capacity equal to 2 cups

place value The position of a digit in a number that is used to determine the value of the digit
Example: In 5,318, the 3 is in the hundreds place. So, the 3 has a value of 300.

plane An endless flat surface

point An exact location in space

polygon A closed plane figure made up of line segments

pound (lb) A customary unit of weight equal to 16 ounces

power The product that results from multiplying the same number over and over

prime number A whole number greater than 1 that has exactly two factors, itself and 1

prism A solid figure with two identical parallel bases and faces that are parallelograms

product The number that is the result of multiplying two or more factors

protractor A tool used to measure and draw angles

pyramid A solid figure with a base that is a polygon whose faces are triangles with a common vertex

quadrilateral A polygon with 4 sides

quart (qt) A customary unit of capacity equal to 2 pints

quotient The answer to a division problem

ray Part of a line that has one endpoint and extends forever in one direction.

reciprocal A given number is a reciprocal of another number if the product of the numbers is one.
Example: The numbers $\frac{1}{8}$ and $\frac{8}{1}$ are reciprocals because $\frac{1}{8} \times \frac{8}{1} = 1$.

rectangle A parallelogram with four right angles

rectangular prism A solid figure with 6 rectangular faces

regular polygon A polygon that has sides of equal length and angles of equal measure

remainder The amount that is left after dividing a number into equal parts

rhombus A parallelogram with all sides the same length

right angle An angle whose measure is 90°

right triangle A triangle in which one angle is a right angle

rounding A process that determines which multiple of 10, 100, 1,000, and so on, a number is closest to

sample A representative part of a larger group

scale (in a graph) A series of numbers at equal intervals along an axis on a graph

scalene triangle A triangle in which no sides have the same length

sides (of an angle) The two rays that form an angle

sides of a polygon The line segments that form a polygon

solid figure (also: solid) A figure that has three dimensions (length, width, and height)

solution The value of the variable that makes the equation true

square A rectangle with all sides the same length

square unit A square with sides one unit long used to measure area

standard form A common way of writing a number with commas separating groups of three digits starting from the right
Example: 3,458,901

stem-and-leaf plot A way to organize numerical data using place value

straight angle An angle measuring 180°

Subtraction Property of Equality The same number can be subtracted from both sides of an equation and the sides remain equal.

sum The result of adding two or more addends

survey A question or questions used to gather information

symmetric A figure is symmetric if it can be folded on a line to form two halves that fit exactly on top of each other.

T

tablespoon (tbsp) A customary unit of capacity; two tablespoons is equal to one fluid ounce.

tenth One of ten equal parts of a whole

terms Numbers in a sequence or variables, such as x and y, in an algebraic expression

thousandth One of 1,000 equal parts of a whole

three-dimensional shape A solid with three dimensions that has volume, such as a rectangular prism

ton (T) A customary unit of weight equal to 2,000 pounds

trapezoid A quadrilateral that has exactly one pair of parallel sides

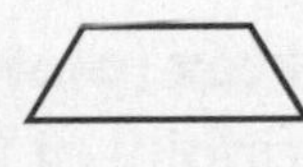

trend A relationship between two sets of data that shows up as a pattern in a graph

triangle A polygon with 3 sides

U

underestimate An estimate that is less than the actual answer

unknown A symbol or letter, such as x, that represents a number in an expression or equation

unit cube A cube that measures one unit on each side

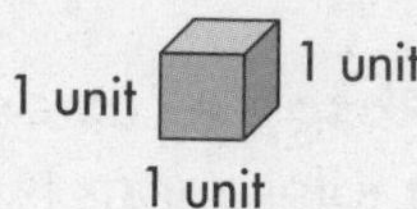

unit fraction A fraction with a numerator of 1

value (of a digit) The number a digit represents, which is determined by the position of the digit; see also *place value*

variable A letter, such as *n*, that represents a number in an expression or an equation

vertex (plural: vertices) **a.** The common endpoint of the two rays in an angle; **b.** A point at which two sides of a polygon meet; **c.** The point at which three or more edges meet in a solid figure

volume The number of cubic units needed to fill a solid figure

weight A measure of how light or how heavy something is

whole numbers The numbers 0, 1, 2, 3, 4, and so on

word form A way to write a number using words; see also *number name*

***x*-axis** A horizontal number line on a coordinate grid

***x*-coordinate** The first number in an ordered pair, which names the distance to the right or left from the origin along the *x*-axis

***y*-axis** A vertical number line on a coordinate grid

***y*-coordinate** The second number in an ordered pair, which names the distance up or down from the origin along the *y*-axis

yard (yd) A customary unit of length equal to 3 feet

Zero Property of Multiplication The product of any number and 0 is 0.

Photographs

Photo locators denoted as follows: Top (T), Center (C), Bottom (B), Left (L), Right (R), Background (Bkgd)

001 Daniel Prudek/Shutterstock; **006** Risteski Goce/Shutterstock; **014** John Foxx/Thinkstock; **024** Vladislav Gajic/Fotolia; **030C** Hemera Technologies/Getty Images; **030L** James Steidl/Fotolia; **030R** Ivelin Radkov/Fotolia; **055** Ilyas Kalimullin/Shutterstock; **060** Pearson Education; **084L** Corbis; **084R** Robert Marien/Corbis; **109** Leungchopan/Shutterstock; **126** Pearson Education; **132** Cphoto/Fotolia; **143** Tatiana Popova/Shutterstock; **163** Smileus/Shutterstock; **166** Pearson Education; **172** Pearson Education; **183** Viacheslav Krylov/Fotolia; **195** Alisonhancock/Fotolia; **237** Tom Wang/Shutterstock; **246** Pearson Education; **258** Pearson Education; **264** Visions of America/Alamy; **299** Lisastrachan/Fotolia; **332BL** Pearson Education; **332BR** Pearson Education; **332TL** Pearson Education; **332TR** Pearson Education; **336L** Getty Images; **336R** Getty Images; **367** Marcio Jose Bastos Silva/Shutterstock; **372** Pearson Education; **390** Pearson Education; **414L** Pearson Education; **414R** Esanbanhao/Fotolia; **426** Image Source/Jupiter images; **437B** by-studio/Fotolia; **437T** Paul Orr/Shutterstock; **455** Simone van den Berg/Fotolia; **462** Bikeriderlondon/Shutterstock; **476** Pearson Education; **523** Zest_Marina/Fotolia; **546** Pearson Education; **558** Bev/Fotolia; **583** Morgan Lane Photography/Shutterstock; **596** Pearson Education; **631** Iktomi/Fotolia; **633L** Pearson Education; **633R** Pavlo Sachek/Fotolia; **635** Pearson Education; **637** Pearson Education; **646C** Pearson Education; **646L** Pearson Education; **646R** Pearson Education; **652** Getty Images; **664** Pearson Education; **666** Pearson Education; **670L** Marianne de Jong/Shutterstock; **670R** Brocreative/Fotolia; **693B** Volff/Fotolia; **693T** Evgeny Karandaev/Shutterstock; **695** Jon Beard/Shutterstock; **731** Natalia Pavlova/Fotolia; **773** Solarseven/Shutterstock; **790** Pearson Education; **809** kalafoto/Fotolia; **843** leekris/Fotolia; **845** Michael J Thompson/ShutterStock; **854** 2010/Photos to Go/Photolibrary; **888** Corbis; **920B** hotshotsworldwide/Fotolia; **920TL** Jupiter Images; **920TR** Jupiter Images.